RUSSIA

LAND OF THE SU...

FINLAND

UKRAINE

HUNGARY

RUMANIA

Belgrade

Bucharest

CRIMEA

BLACK SEA

CASPIAN SEA

CAUCASUS

ARMENIA

YUGOSLAVIA

BULGARIA

MACEDONIA

Salonika

GREECE

Mycenae

Corinth

Athens

Olympia

Sparta

CYCLADES
ISLANDS

Cnossus

CRETE

AEGEAN SEA

Constantinople
(Istanbul)

Troy

LYDIA

IONIA

CARIA

RHODES

ASIA MINOR

LAND of the
HITTITES

Carchemish

Antioch

CYPRUS

Sidon

Tyre

PHOENICIA

Damascus

SYRIA

Euphrates River

Tigris River

ASSYRIA

AKKAD

• Nineveh

• Assur

MEDIA

LURISTAN

MESOPOTAMIA

BABYLONIA

• Baghdad

PERSIA

Babylon •

• Lagash

ELAM

PALESTINE

CANAAN

• Jerusalem

Alexandria

NILE
DELTA

Ur •

SUMERIA

Susa

EGYPT

(See back endpaper)

RED SEA

ARABIA

PERSIAN
GULF

• Medina

Mecca

A NEW
WORLD HISTORY OF ART

OTHER BOOKS BY SHELDON CHENEY

A NEW
WORLD HISTORY
OF ART

THE COLLEGE EDITION

SHELDON CHENEY

HOLT, RINEHART AND WINSTON

A NEW WORLD HISTORY OF ART

APRIL, 1963

A completely revised edition, with additional text, of A *World History of Art,* which was first published in November 1937; the eighth printing was issued in June 1952. Copyright 1937 by Sheldon Cheney.

The author wishes to record thanks to publishers and authors for the use of copyrighted material as follows: he is grateful to the Oxford University Press for permission to quote from T. E. Shaw's translation of the *Odyssey;* to the Marshall Jones Company for a quotation from Ralph Adams Cram's *The Significance of Gothic;* to Charles Scribner's Sons for quotations from Lisle March Phillipps's *Form and Colour;* to the Liveright Publishing Corporation for a quotation from Hendrick Willem van Loon's *R. v. R.;* to Harper & Brothers for a quotation from Rachel Annand Taylor's *Leonardo the Florentine;* to Alfred A. Knopf, Inc., for quotations from Arthur Waley's *The Temple and Other Poems* and Witter Bynner's *The Jade Mountain;* to Dodd Mead & Company for a quotation from *Penguin Island,* by Anatole France, in the translation by A. W. Evans; to the editor and the publishers of the *Encyclopædia Britannica* for a quotation from an article by Laurence Binyon; and to H. G. Wells, the Macmillan Company, and the Garden City Publishing Company for quotations from *The Outline of History.*

21386–0116

PRINTED IN THE UNITED STATES OF AMERICA

LIBRARY OF CONGRESS CATALOG CARD NUMBER: 56–9221

PREFACE

IN WRITING THIS BOOK, which might be termed an appreciative history of art, I have sought to capture certain virtues:

(1) the sense of a single story, integrated for continuity and sustained interest;

(2) a simply explained *modern* interpretation;

(3) a personal enthusiasm that would lead the reader to *experience* works of art rather than merely to learn about a number of masterpieces;

(4) readability.

In the book upon which the present one is based, entitled more simply *A World History of Art,* it required eight pages of preface to explain and support these aims. In this version two pages suffice.

The claims that a mildly revolutionary author made in that book, pointing out especially that there was inconsistency in judging *any* art from other than the modern point of view, need not be pursued further. In this second half of the twentieth century, almost all writers of art history are on one side. We can afford to forget together that So-and-So's paintings were not shown, perhaps not mentioned, through generations of art instruction, although now a half-chapter must be given them in every book. The struggle for a modern attitude toward the past is won—as is the fight for the inclusion of the magnificent art achievements of the Orient.

A fifth aim, concerning illustrations, has been in the author's mind from the beginning. My conviction is that reproductions (even without color in very many cases) can be relied upon to yield up much of the enjoyment that the originals afford—if the reproductions are of sufficient size. In this book I have tried, aided by sympathetic publishers, to keep the plates large enough to be givers of pleasure in themselves.

The change of title to *A New World History of Art* is warranted in these ways: At the start there are added eight pages of illustrations in col-

or, and an eighteen-page Introduction in the form of an essay on "The Approach to Art." The Descriptive Bibliography is wholly new, as is the combined Glossary-Index. Maps are added. There are nearly 100 new illustrations. The entire text has been reset, permitting extensive rewriting—in innumerable small matters, and in larger matters such as added paragraphs to cover recent archaeological finds or new accreditings, or inserted sections (usually about architecture) which did not get written into the older edition.

I hope that some readers of both old and new versions will feel also a difference of spirit in the writing. The older text may well have been argumentative, the tone controversial. I hope that this new volume will carry the reader on to enjoyment more quietly. I wrote in the original preface that "art is joyous, if one can get at it," and expressed mistrust of some "who surround it with a cemetery of dates and data, of whys and wherefores." If I also quarreled a little and scolded a good deal, I hope now to have left quarrels behind, to have cleared more effectively the reader's way to personal response.

The inclusion of the word "New" in our title has an intrinsic advantage in this: It will prevent a confusion that sometimes arose in the minds of potential readers and puzzled booksellers. A decade after *A World History of Art* had found its audience, there came into the field a book entitled *History of World Art*. That history, no doubt, has its merits and its faults—as has mine. But neither volume is served well by the confusing likeness of title. The appearance of *A New World History of Art* will, I hope, restore to us a distinctive and easily remembered identity among the books on art history.

The reviewers, when earlier versions of the book appeared, commented upon the number of quotations from philosophers, artists, and teachers that are woven into the text. If it is Captain Cook

v

who speaks sagely on page 1 and Henry Moore on page 642—and between them a long list from Pliny and Plotinus and Bargagli to Savonarola and Ruskin and Cézanne—it is because I wanted my readers to recognize the impetus, perhaps the wisdom, behind the varied manifestations of art. I have planted these "leads"—any one of which an alert student might follow—intentionally.

Quotations of considerable length are listed on our copyright page, just following the title page. My obligations to writers of earlier art histories, and to authors whose books have been a special inspiration to me, are beyond recording here (the bibliography briefly characterizes their works and implies a debt of gratitude); but I must mention especially Elie Faure, and after him José Pijoan, and after them certain writers in specialized branches of art history, D. Talbot Rice, John Addington Symonds, Clive Bell, Roger Fry, and Laurence Binyon.

Of those who aided in the rewriting of the book I will single out only one for grateful mention: Stanley Burnshaw. It was he who suggested the plan for enlargement by addition of a section of color plates and an introductory essay on the enjoyment of art—this by way of carrying the volume still further into the field of appreciation, not merely history; he also, in a genial report on the book's shortcomings, led to considerable rewriting. My friends the publishers have been helpful and patient beyond the call of professional relations between publisher and writer. To them all I am grateful.

Obviously the great museums have contributed to any success the book may have. If only for a sort of amazement after counting up debts for illustrative material, I must thank the staff of the Metropolitan Museum of Art. They not only sanctioned reproduction of fifty-three pictures and other objects from their own collections but permitted use of photographs taken by their explor-

ing staff members (notably in Egypt), and lent numerous prints from their photograph-loan collection. The Metropolitan Museum of Art and the Museum of Modern Art in New York are the two museums I visit oftenest. It is a pleasure to say that I have found friendship and courtesy and help in each, besides a wealth of enjoyment in their galleries.

Oscar Wilde once wrote: "You may have noticed how, for some time, Nature has set herself to resemble the landscapes of Corot." Today there is detected less of humor and more of serious significance in that famous quip.

An artist divines in nature something not revealed to other eyes, and he puts the resultant impression into art terms. The observer at first calls it untruth, then somehow (if he is openminded) widens his vision and finds the enhanced image within his appreciation. Finally when he returns to nature he meets the apparent miracle of a landscape alive with the artist's particular created beauty.

Perhaps even the historian, if he has seen more than others in the diorite statue of Khafre or in a *Venus* by Cranach, may by some juggling of records, ideas, and graphic illustration afford his reader new eyes to direct toward that picture or statue. I can ask nothing better for my history of art than that it thus, in some small measure, increase perception. If one could lead his readers to see the pictures of Titian as El Greco saw them, or El Greco's pictures as Cézanne saw them, or Cézanne's pictures as a considerable number of today's moderns are seeing them—touched apparently with a mystical beauty—a train of enjoyment might be started that would mean fresh enjoyment of works of art from the Lascaux cave paintings to the productions of the latest schools of abstraction. To know with the mind what events and works lie between should be merely a device for stimulating that sort of perception.

CONTENTS

NOTE ON ILLUSTRATIONS

Because a serial list would be useless for reference where so many titles are included —in this case 519 separate pictures—the list of illustrations sometimes placed at this point is omitted. Instead, the titles and artists are listed in the Index at the end of the book. Italic figures, preceded by the letters *ill.*, are employed for illustrations (e.g., *ill., 497*) to distinguish them from text entries, which are in Roman figures (e.g., 497).

The illustration facing the title page is
Holbein: *Double Portrait, Sir Thomas Godsalve and His Son John. State Gallery, Dresden.*

The illustration at the top of the title page is
Assyrian Winged Figure, stone relief, detail. *Walters Gallery, Baltimore.*

The lower illustration on the title page is reproduced and identified on page 653.

I. Portrait head of Nofretete, a queen of Egypt, c. 1370 B.C.; painted limestone. The monumental style of Egyptian sculpture (see illustrations on pages 43, 47-60) is here relaxed in the interest of vivaciousness and subtle revelation of character. Seemingly realistic, the method is yet one of intensification of feeling, even of distortion, as in the impossibly thin neck, the overlong thin nose. The coloring comes to many as a shock in the present era when art-lovers have been conditioned to stone sculpture invariably the color of stone. The truth is that the Egyptians painted their stone statues. A more shocking fact is that the Greeks also painted *their* stone sculptures. Remembrance of this exquisite portrait may, beyond memory's pleasure, lead many to widen their tolerance, even their appreciation, of a type of art unfamiliar in the modern world. (In the Egyptian Museum, Berlin. Color plate by courtesy of J. Greenwald, New York.)

II. Head from Sandro Botticelli's *The Birth of Venus*. (For the complete picture, see page 361.) Here one sees an epitome of the forces that made the Italian Renaissance. Something remains of the glow of Byzantine mosaic and fresco, something of the freshness of spirit of the Sienese school and Giotto and Fra Angelico, along with the fullness of classic beauty and the magic of draftsmanship and color that are essentially Florentine. Nevertheless Botticelli is an individualist. The glowing, golden quality of the picture comes partly, no doubt, from the model, but also from the artist's own vision, and out of his conception of what painting might have been in the classic period of ancient Greece. His means are simple, linear; the result an appealing grace. (In the Uffizi Gallery, Florence. Color plate by courtesy of Simon and Schuster, Inc.)

III. *The Creation of Adam*, a fresco on the ceiling of the Sistine Chapel, Rome. This painting is typical of the powerful compositions by Michelangelo, genius of the high Renaissance. Believing himself sculptor rather than painter, he went over to the picturing art by command, and the figures of the Sistine ceiling took on something of the monumentality, the amplitude, and the grandeur of his stone sculptures. Nevertheless as painter he composed gracefully, pictorially, and without violating the flat. This *Creation of Adam*, so simple and direct in statement, is a masterpiece of movement, as rhythmically conceived, as cunningly adjusted in space, as any modern could ask. God and the first man, set out in elemental grandeur. (In the Sistine Chapel, the Vatican Palace, Rome. Color plate by courtesy of Simon and Schuster, Inc.)

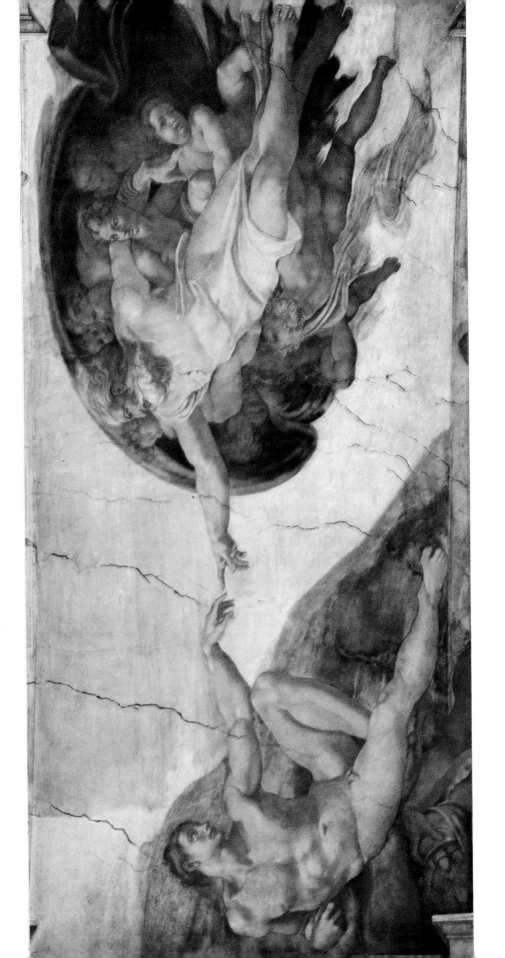

IV. *View of Toledo,* by El Greco, one of the earliest great landscapes in the history of Western painting. The artist, not born or trained in Spain, yet seems to give us the very feeling of a Spanish scene, somber, stormy, brooding. One of the greatest of all masters of plastic vitality, of form organization, he affords the observer here an experience of agreeable rhythms and counter-rhythms, of main theme and counterpoint. Paths for the eye are stressed and disappear and are stressed again. The natural elements of the scene are contrived, distorted, their aesthetic appeal intensified. The sky (so often merely a backdrop in painting) contributes actively, almost wildly, to the symphonic play of movement-elements, to an integrated, arbitrary design. This is landscape by an individualist, a mystic. (By courtesy of the Metropolitan Museum of Art.)

V. *The Wedding Dance*, by Brueghel the Elder, the first example here of the picturing of homely life, in a glorified genre study full of human interest. The greater wonder of the painting, however, is in the sinuous movement of the composition and the fitting-in of the many minor rhythms. The observer should note (or feel) how each dancer's figure is rounded, how each dancing couple forms a rhythmic unit, how all the dancers together are in a circling group that starts the main plastic movement. This carries the eye to the high horizon line, then safely returns it from the peasants at the back to the middle and the dancers again. Beyond all this are the homely touches, the occasional humorous interpolations, the inexhaustible human interest. The painter, a Fleming, had gained breadth from contact with the Italians, without forfeiting the intimate virtues of Northern art. (In the Detroit Institute of Arts. Color plate by courtesy of Simon and Schuster, Inc.)

VI. Head, detail, by Rembrandt—sheer masterly painting, based on impeccable draftsmanship, rendered dramatic by the artist's way of placing his figures in bursts of light amid darkest shadow. As portraitist Rembrandt is among the leaders: the outward representation is superbly done, and at the same time inward character is magically revealed. In each of Rembrandt's portraits there is, too, a sense of the dignity of man—one feels it in this detail — and communication of an individual's soul-experience. The print here possesses a patina-like richness resulting partly from time's mellowing (the reproduction was made, as it happens, just before the picture was thoroughly cleaned). Here there is something of grandeur and something of tenderness—and superb use of paint. For some Rembrandt is the master of all masters. (Part of the painting *The Man with a Magnifying Glass*. By courtesy of the Metropolitan Museum of Art.)

VII. *Portrait of a Young Woman,* by Degas. This is portraiture as it developed after 1850, of the avowedly realistic school. Indeed, here realistic portrayal is seen at its very best. We perceive the woman, her femininity, her pretty coloring, her quiet self-assurance. We note, too, the appropriate velvety feel of Degas' painting method, and the marvelous truth of his drawing. Yet in these pages he is under a disadvantage, in that his picture comes just after the Rembrandt with its dignity, revelation of character, striking chiaroscuro, and exceptionally dramatic way of using paint. Degas' young woman is appealing, charming. The loss of more profound values is to be measured as nineteenth-century art's sacrifice to realism. In Degas' time the camera had come in; it was thought that the painter's art must compete with photography. (In the Louvre, Paris. Color plate by courtesy of Harry N. Abrams, New York.)

VIII. *Lower Manhattan,* by Marin. This cityscape, a water-color of 1920, indicates how revolutionary was the break between the nineteenth-century realists and the twentieth-century expressionists. Fidelity to outward nature and the painstaking method of smoothed-down painting have been abandoned. Instead here is a stab toward expression of the city's meaning. John Marin was a gentle genius with an explosive technique. He captured by means of a few quickly realized elements the spirit of New York at that time. No observer will fail to feel the drive of the city's forces, the thrust upward of its skyscrapers, the push forward of its pounding "el," the energetic, half-subterranean rushing about of its people. All this is expressed within an improvisation intuitively conceived, yet perfectly based on plastic order. The form-organization in itself is the larger giver of aesthetic pleasure. The Marin of 1920 stands at about mid-point between Cézanne's radical but quiet innovations and the practice of the abstract expressionists of the 1950s. Painting is, in Marin's hands, again profoundly creative, conditioned by what is felt rather than by what is seen. In John Marin traits of Oriental and of Western art are merged. (Collection of Philip L. Goodwin, New York.)

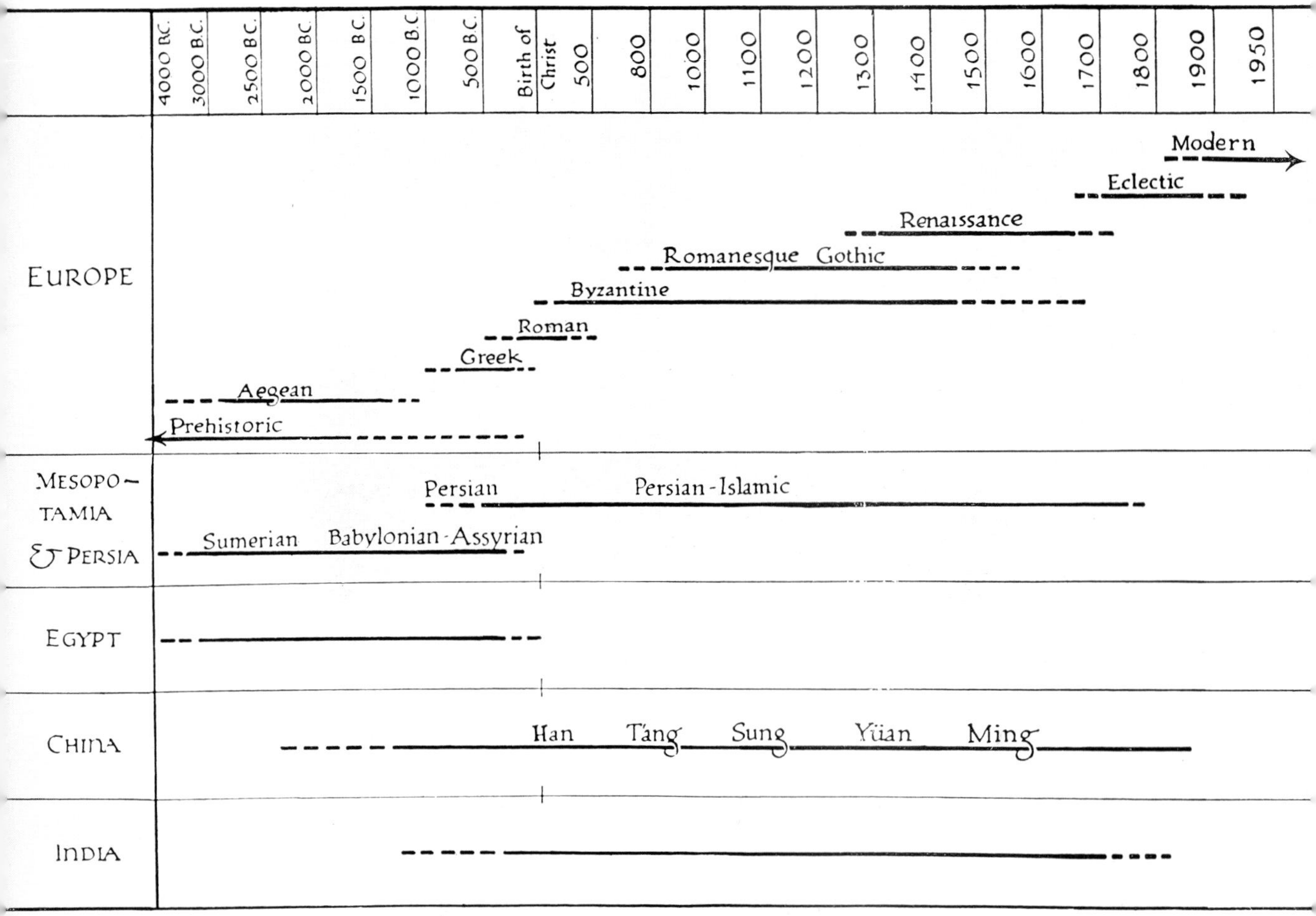

	4000 B.C.	3000 B.C.	2500 B.C.	2000 B.C.	1500 B.C.	1000 B.C.	500 B.C.	Birth of Christ	500	800	1000	1100	1200	1300	1400	1500	1600	1700	1800	1900	1950

EUROPE

Modern

Eclectic

Renaissance

Romanesque   Gothic

Byzantine

Roman

Greek

Aegean

Prehistoric

MESOPOTAMIA & PERSIA

Persian   Persian-Islamic

Sumerian   Babylonian-Assyrian

EGYPT

CHINA

Han   Tang   Sung   Yüan   Ming

INDIA

Chart of the time periods of art in Europe, with indications of concurrent developments in the principal Oriental countries and Egypt, 4000 B.C. — A.D. 1950. (Time periods not drawn to scale.)

INTRODUCTION: THE APPROACH TO ART

THERE IS in language no equivalent for art, the thing itself. The formal and emotive essence of the visual art work escapes words. The living part is intangible, and cannot be talked or reasoned out into the open. Whether the writer's intention involves a circuit of the realm of art by means of history or a push toward understanding by means of analysis, all he can fairly hope to do is to indicate approaches, roughly mapping the paths from the known margins toward the center, where lie, mysterious still, the creation and the enjoyment, the artistic expression and the aesthetic response.

"What is art?" used to be the standard opening question at the beginning of every book of history or criticism. Now, in the second half of the twentieth century, it is seldom seriously asked. The vast territory newly opened to the arts and the falling of barriers that once kept out enjoyers and investigators (art is found universally, in every place where man has been) and the swift and continuous rewriting of what is called "art opinion"—all these discourage, among those who deal with actual works, the attempt to define what is art.

It is wiser to agree here at the beginning that we all know what art is. Then we can go on to scan the ways in which certain qualities of art mystify the inquiring observer (the seasoned gallery-goer as well as the beginning student), and so on to enjoyment, which is our main concern.

Art, stripped of its mysteries for the moment, is, as all can see, a body of "works." Let us remind ourselves how far this body is borne in upon the consciousness of each one of us daily, hourly. Regard the accumulation of buildings, pictures, statues, furniture, textiles, containers, to name

Daumier: *The Towman*

only a few principal categories in the visual-arts field. Pausing over only the most unpretentious of these divisions, containers, one is forced to exclaim: What a feeble word to suggest the wonders we have known, in the painted pottery of so-called savages, in the beautifully proportioned vases of the Greeks, in the joyously colored bowls of the Persians, in the exquisite creations in jug and jar and vase of the Chinese! And beyond these precious things, which mostly are spending their final years in museums, are the containers produced in our own recent times, the handmade or machine-made glasses and canisters and bottles and pans, often multiplied in the millions. Each object is a part of the body of art, by reason of some man's designing.

The body of world art thus is enormous. It is by this heritage, more than by any other, that later men judge the achievements of past nations and civilizations. The products of such an artist as Execias or El Greco or Rembrandt outlast the fame and often the names of kings. These works profoundly move other men centuries afterward. And so ubiquitous is art (and so efficient are modern archaeologists) that our knowledge and our enjoyment extend to all the continents and reach back to the Old Stone Age, over a time-spread of possibly fifty thousand years. The body of art, it may be added, includes some parts that you may have failed to visualize along with the larger categories—say, weapons (beginning only with *shaped* ones, not just natural stones or jawbones or casual limbs of wood), tattooing, pins, gardens, and motor-cars.

Quality Is the One Criterion

It is the hope of every person facing the accumulation of inherited art to establish some sort of criterion of judgment. Especially he will hope to exercise this judgment when approaching those more intensely expressive works which are objects of pilgrimage, in museums or ancient caves, in gallery or palace, or, in the case of the building art, temples and cathedrals and skyscrapers.

The first rule of progress amid so great an accumulation is that the observer recognize *quality*—through learning at first, then by feeling spontaneously, when familiarity with art has grown. "Has it quality?" we are likely to ask. Or "Has it style?" Has it the special excellence that is imparted to the work because the artist put in a measure of his imagination, a little bit of his own soul? Style in this sense has but a relative connection with *the* styles, classic, Gothic, modern, etc. These you will learn from history as convenient aids to sorting out in your mind the characteristics of a dozen streams within the one world flow of art.

But long before that, the observer should feel style of the sort that connotes a certain excellence, that marks the work as belonging to the top-quality segment in any field of art. Quality or style is, indeed, your basic clue to understanding. It may be recognized in an arrowhead or ax-head of the American Indians, in a tiny sculpture of the Scythians, in a huge sculpture of Michelangelo, in a portrait by Titian or in a scene under the glaze of a Persian Rhages bowl. It is bound up at once in a boldness, a spiritedness, a personal originality, and in formal subtleties that are of so delicate an order that they all but elude description.

It is here that personal discrimination begins. As the sense of quality, of style, grows, the student will be enabled to separate (roughly) the things that are characterful art from the vast mass of flat and stale art that accumulates alongside the real or experience-giving sort. In every age (and generally continuing into the next one) there are innumerable men toiling to produce works that are spirited and reflective of the civilization of the time; but the majority of them are parroters, in the auditory arts, and copyists, dully reproducing the authentic thing, in the visual arts. The body is there, but the soul-quality comes through but faintly.

Art Is Friendly

The wise men of the world have from time immemorial grouped the arts with the noblest and profoundest activities of the human mind. Art, like religion, may demand of you, even at the adult level (unless you had a *very* careful bringing-up) a sort of initiation, even sustained application, before it yields up all its riches of experience. But this initiation involves a maximum of friendly and pleasurable activity.

Art is friendly and spontaneous. The profoundest experience of art is radiant, soul-warming, infinitely deep and personal. It is a sort of secret, thoughtless delight. At its candescent moment it is ravishing—and then it concerns the intellect not at all.

In the enjoyment of art, however, as in so many phases of living, it is difficult to sustain experience on the luminous level. There is inevitably a falling back. On the lower planes and slopes there is a wide range of experiences, joyous still; but these are likely to be intellectual or emotional rather than profoundly aesthetic. Writers on art have a bad habit of isolating the top aesthetic thrill, and then choosing for illustration the masterpieces of creation that afford that thrill, thus making it seem that enjoyment of art is the possession of a chosen few. The implication is that seasoned enjoyers are an exclusive club, to which the beginner or the average enjoyer on the intellectual plane can hardly aspire.

On the contrary, the wise man trains himself by "absorbing" art on all the levels open to him. Even in collections as rich as those of the Metropolitan Museum or of any of the great national galleries, he will find that many of the pictures appeal as emotional ticklers or as examples of admirable technique or as reasonable, rational transcriptions. The point is that, with feeding on these lesser things, the appetite for the highest art grows. You have only to keep your whole mind open. Even if you are enjoying pictures that some of your associates or guides consider oversimple or dull or "merely illustrational," you may be sure that your appreciation increases with continued contact. Persist, and you will begin to see or feel subtleties not at first patent to you. Indeed, your own preferences will so change that the very pictures that you at first admired will some years later appear obvious and negligible. Many great collectors of paintings and sculp-

tures have testified to this change in their understanding and their taste—and in the nature of their enjoyment. As if out of affection for an old friend whose interests are no longer his, a collector may retain in an inconspicuous place among his later purchases a picture by Bouguereau or a statuette by Barye, which appeals to the intellect by a marvelous fidelity to nature and a caressing technique, though inspiration and formal creativeness are largely lacking. In similar manner the beginner in the field of appreciation, taking up his first history book of art, will inevitably like the familiar things illustrated, the realistic things, the sentimental things—which fulfill his notion of art, by reason of his too exclusive diet of magazine-cover pictures, Christmas cards, and the like. But he should know that the absorption in sentimental illustration is but a beginning phase. He need only persist and he will move on easily to better types of illustrational art, and beyond.

The role of one's intellect in the appreciation of art is of varied sorts, and the typical person of intellectual bent finds many pleasures in living with the small arts, and in visiting museums. But his immediate pleasure subsists largely in recognition of the familiar subject, recognition of the reasonable and the ideal, and recognition of expert technique or craftsmanship. His mind is given to analysis and to the pigeonholing of facts and comparative virtues. These pleasures are natural and commendable. But they should not be accepted as the whole or the main part of the art of enjoyment. There is that other response that discounts or sidetracks the intellect, that comes with an approach by way of the intuition, that ends with a more profound and lasting experience.

Because the modern or contemporary movement, which has revolutionized painting, sculpture, and architecture to an almost incredible extent, has stressed the deep-down formal element, and has encouraged the intuitional approach, it is sometimes hard for the respectable advocates of intellectual pleasure to be heard. Teachers and writers of art history, who are the average man's chosen guide in a vast and sometimes baffling field, quickly placed themselves on the side of spontaneous response. They discounted knowing about art, plumped for direct experience of art. Asserting that preparation for enjoyment is less a matter of definitions, factual knowledge, and analysis than it is a self-conditioning in the way of contemplation and self-giving, they well-nigh revolutionized art education.

In summary of this matter of the profounder pleasures afforded by the highest art as contrasted with the commoner enjoyment experienced by us all in the more familiar and generally realistic range, let me proffer two admonitions:

1. Like what you like. Keep an open mind toward what you cannot yet like. Do not be frightened by teachers or guides who talk about a mysterious deeper feeling or aesthetic mood that you haven't yet experienced. Take refuge, if you wish, with the man who says, "Art is what I like; for me it is not art if I don't enjoy it." My business in this book is to pick up your interest where you are.

2. Never forget, however, that the mass of opinion in this second half of the twentieth century is that the better part of enjoyment of art is to be found in qualities not at first obvious. That is, profoundest aesthetic enjoyment comes when the deeper part of the mind leaps to recognition of formal, emotional, and mystic values. These are not often resident in a picture with easily understood sentimental appeal, in the most elementary illustration.

I ask you, then, not to give up any art that you enjoy; only that you expose yourself to a wide range of works in the arts. They are the true teachers, the sure improvers of your taste and capacity. Meantime respect the sincerity of those of us who speak confidently of a higher appeal, a profounder response.

On the heights, where the most serious art prevails, nothing, I believe, is truer than this: Art at its best is a renewal of something deep in ourselves. The spirit appropriates, as something already of itself, the formal or mystical element, which we call order or rhythm or form. It is something the artist puts in, which the observer's innermost faculties recognize as their own. Plotinus said, "The soul includes a faculty peculiarly open to beauty, a faculty incomparably sure in appreciation of its own."

Now, to get back to the subject with which this section of the Introduction opened—the accessibility and easy companionability of art—let me remind you that not all the friendliness should be on one side, in the picture or statue. On his part the observer should be friendly, open-minded, relaxed in approach, utterly responsive. Sooner or later he will find, in the presence of great works, that there is a progression toward spontaneous response and the experience of aesthetic mood. He will more easily give himself unselfconsciously to the pictures. Sweeter then will be the enjoyment.

Artists

The artist sees differently from other people. Each artist sees differently from all other artists. His way of seeing and realizing gives individuality and a special kind of life to his picture. (We are speaking of painters here, the creative ones.)

Confronted by a flower, or by an inspiring sweep of mountain country, or by a "situation," he puts his faculties to it in a way not common to other mortals. His designing sensibility gets busy with it. He goes off into a daze. You may think that this puts him into line with the daft and the unhinged, and you are right. The difference is that he detaches his mind not to enter a region of irresponsible action but to give rein to his composing, his creative sense. He lives with his subject, loves it, forms his inner vision of it, and somehow gets this down in a design, a picture, open to our searching minds. This explanation may sound like a considerable rigmarole. It probably is true only of those artists capable of the most serious creation—of Fra Angelico, whose eyes streamed tears as he painted a *Crucifixion;* of Cézanne, who when he died bore the reputation of a misanthrope, so withdrawn and touchy was he while he sought to fix in his canvas what he called "realization."

Actually there are as many ways of seeing outwardly and imagining inwardly as there are creative artists. The transformation from concrete to creative image may be swift, even instantaneous, or it may involve a slow succession of processes from vague feeling to final realization. What we call temperament enters in strongly here. There are moody, contemplative artists. There are others who are nervously temperamental, quickly sensitive, and excitable. One way or another each arrives at an original image or vision peculiar to himself.

The artist's seeing at the moment of vision may have got very far from the shape and size and color, from the "normally seen" components, of the object or the situation. The object has suggested the picture, has been contributory to it; but the painter's intuition for formal design, his mood, perhaps his life-philosophy, have been central to the created thing.

There are artists who call themselves illustrators. They necessarily stay closer to the object or the situation. They fall considerably short of the sort of creation and transformation about which we were talking when we called to mind Fra Angelico and Cézanne a few paragraphs back. They are aligned with the realistic (even naturalistic) painters who aim no higher than a faithful transcription from the surface of nature —a pretty interpretation of an incident or a view or a picturesque character.

At the other extreme, at the opposite pole from the artists who "merely" illustrate or reproduce, are the painters and sculptors who in our time call themselves modern. They are generally careless of the outward view; they believe that they are expressing the spirit or feeling of the thing, within an aesthetically valid order, born out of their special way of imaging.

Aligned with the work of the Western moderns is the vast body of Oriental art, especially that of the painters in the historic Chinese tradition. For splendor, vitality, and delicacy no Western display of landscape painting can compare with the Far Eastern achievement. Let me recall to your mind the way in which the Chinese painter has always worked. He never, I believe, went out to depict a certain landscape or bit of nature. He might go to the mountains and live for two or three weeks or months. He absorbed the spirit of nature, attuned his soul to it. When he returned he painted a landscape, but it followed the topographical features of no one place. Rather it was the fruit of his total feeling for nature, a distillation of all that he had felt during his sojourn. His picture existed to evoke, by some subtle achievement of form-movement, the spirit of the place, or the spirit of the artist's contemplation. As he had come to intuitive awareness of the form of universality in the mountains, he sought to express the everlasting rhythms of the universe in his picture.

A great deal of confusion exists in the writing about the approach to art—really our subject in this Introduction—confusion arising from failure to realize the differences in intention among artists, and failure to differentiate the artist's approach from the observer's. From now on we shall be talking about the observer. Since "seeing" is a word continually used of the artist's activity, and equally important in the observer's lexicon, let us consider how far it may be an absolute, how far bound up with the observer's experience and training.

On Seeing

Of three men visiting the Sistine Chapel in Rome, one may stand lost in an ecstasy spiritual and other-worldly, his mind stilled, Michelangelo's forms moving through his consciousness with an unaccustomed grandeur of rhythm, with a powerful, pulsing vitality outside nature. He has leaped the barriers of time and place, and the hindrances of analysis and memory. A second man gazes delightedly at this or that ceiling group, recognizing classical allusion and Biblical incidents of the Creation, the Expulsion, and the Flood, or loses himself in tracing out the intricate stories woven into *The Last Judgment*; and he is not unaware of pleasing geometrical composition and a pervading sense of flowing power, or again of a surging emotional response coloring his intellectual pleasure. The third man, having counted over as many features of the illustrated Bible stories as have remained in his mind from childhood—his only entry being by way of familiar subject-matter—goes away earlier, unmoved, and he much more than the others is aware of the crick in his neck induced by looking up at the immortal ceiling.

We can agree, perhaps, that any of us would prefer to be in the shoes of the first observer. He experienced fully. All these art-tourists probably had what is called perfect eyesight. Yet, in a very true sense, one saw, one half-saw, one failed to see.

Similarly, among visitors to the Sainte Chapelle in Paris, one stands utterly oblivious, his senses drowned in the surge of color, his whole existence become a mood, a feeling, a participation. But a neighbor tourist remarks, "Pretty glass, isn't it?"—and starts down the little winding stairway, sane and cool, his mind convinced that he has "seen" and pigeonholed one more masterpiece of art.

Every creative work of art has its varied effect upon any group of beholders. If you and I came face to face with the *Madonna of the Chair* (page 370) by Raphael, or Whistler's *Battersea Bridge* (page 611), we should in either case be seeing different pictures. What is in a creative picture is inexhaustible; it is inexhaustible to you and to me; it is inexhaustible until all the world has beheld it and responded.

Contrary to the immediate, seeming evidence of the eye, which may report an obvious "view," a plain counterfeit of nature, the picture or sculpture likely has a hundred facets, a thousand hidden aspects and implied meanings. Even you, as your moods change, will perceive a certain picture tonight, and, on the same canvas, a different one in the morning.

The idea that any one of us sees "normally" is preposterous. The eye is the precious instrument through which visual impressions reach us. But it is the mind that sees. Each one of us has been trained, not to see in the artist's sense, but to observe as much as may be useful in life as we have lived it. In these days of crowded impressions and hit-and-run seeing, it is a wonder if we get down to the picture's core or essence at all.

We see, almost mechanically, the familiar and the expected. We normally avoid seeing in depth. Our eyes are trained to exclude what is not traditionally expressive. We see inventorily. We see by categories.

Seeing is thus a double or a multiple process. There is an inner, or adduced, seeing in addition to that of the physical eye. When the observer's intuitive sense of design or rhythm is strong, he sees *through* the eye. The Chinese put it this way: the outer eye merely sees; for understanding and enjoyment one must employ the inner eye.

The inner eye can be trained. The best teachers are the art works themselves. If you associate with great paintings, if you approach them in a mood of serenity, of receptiveness, and spend unhurried hours with them, they will speak to you, helping to awake your understanding, adding to your deep-down experience.

The English poet-artist William Blake put down in many versions his indictment of both artists and observers who too fully trusted to their outward eyes. Only "if the doors of perception were cleansed," he wrote, could the true or infinite world be perceived. And: "I question not my corporeal or vegetative eye any more than I question a window concerning a sight. I look through it and not with it." Another English poet who was no stranger to inner seeing, Rupert Brooke, spoke of the time when we are "no longer blinded by our eyes."

It was William Blake who provided one of the most straightforward and most sensible statements about reproductive art, a statement quoted again and again by the moderns during the first half of the twentieth century, during their fight for a foothold in the galleries then dominated by the painters of literary realism and naturalism. "No man of sense can think that an imitation of an object of nature is the art of painting, or that such imitation, which anyone may easily perform, is worthy of notice, much less that such an art should be the glory and pride of a nation. . . . A man sets himself down with colors and with all the articles of painting; he puts a model before him and he copies that so neat as to make it a deception: now let any man of sense ask himself one question: is this art? can it be worthy of admiration to anybody of understanding? . . . Or is it glorious to a nation to produce such contemptible copies?"

As to ways of seeing, I should like to add one more observation. (This observation, out of researches of my own, I would not want you to accept as truth before you conduct a personal test.) The eye—the corporeal eye, that is—never stays still in looking at a picture. You cannot, to save you, look at one portion of a canvas and hold your eye to that spot. The eye is naturally a roving member. In contemplation of a picture, it moves.

Part of the secret of the pleasure afforded by Giotto's *Deposition from the Cross* (page 325) or Giorgione's *Soldier and Gypsy* (page 394) or Marin's *Wind on Land and Sea* (page 634) is that an ordered relationship amounting to a movement path has been invented by the artist in his use of the spatial and plastic elements. A great deal of the harmony, rhythm, or order in creative painting is thus put in intuitively or knowingly by the artist, as a movement element. We here touch upon that mysterious thing, form, which the moderns talk about ceaselessly, sometimes not relating it directly to movement.

At any rate, the observer's eye moves. In a secret way its movement is guided. The inner being thus is pleasured. There is a detectable movement path in the successful modern picture, and in El Greco's *Christ in the Garden* (page 411) and in Ma Yüan's *Sage in Meditation* (page 191). The picture thus has a life of its own, in a sense unknown in merely illustrational or facsimile painting. (Another warning: Do not search for the path of movement as a line. Rather it is a moseying-along of the inner eye, induced, no doubt, partly by line, which has directional force—as in Daumier's *The Uprising* [page 605]— but, in any complex picture, also by arrangement of planes, which can step the eye backward or pull it forward by overlapping edges or tipping, by the balancing of volumes in space, by utilizing colors and textures which have inward pull or outward push, and so forth. It is, for the inner eye, not movement on the surface, but movement in space.)

Sensibility to form and some slight knowledge about movement in the picture are assuredly a part of the modern observer's equipment for seeing art. Most books about contemporary painting and sculpture are based upon someone's theory of form-movement or formal organization. This Introduction, no less than any other attempted explication, must come to grips with the subject of form—as it does a few pages farther on— if only because awareness of a fundamental formal element is a special knowledge belonging to our time.

We all can learn by sensing the drift of art appreciation during the period of thirty or forty years that have just passed. To this end, we can profitably go back and check certain traditional guideposts. These are negative in character, warning us off areas once considered the brightest in art, but areas less luminous in today's prospect.

Guideposts

1. First is the signpost that warns us all off the territory of naturalism (a word I use to denominate the extreme type of detailed, imitative realism). The thin pleasures of naturalism are all right as one of the lesser enjoyments in the field of the graphic arts, after the observer has learned to take in the values that are more profound. We need not linger over this particular guidepost, since already we have seen William Blake's statement about "contemptible copies." There is all about us evidence that critics, writers, and teachers have got the naturalism of the nineteenth century into perspective, knowing that allegiance to it is not modern. But it is well for the reader to reflect that a half-century ago the "revolutionaries" of art had to meet an almost solid front of belief that documentary fidelity was a top virtue in visual art. (In architecture the building was then judged for the success achieved by the designer in "adapting" the Greek style or the Gothic style or the Renaissance style to the façade—another sort of "contemptible copying.")

"Art is art because it is not nature," said the German poet Goethe. So let the guidepost that points to the area of naturalism and to that of the closely allied selective but literal realism act as a caution rather than as an invitation. For the benefit of those observers who still incline to a substantially naturalistic art, let us be reminded again that any mind that is normally alert must respond, and not without pleasure, to a marvelously photographic rendering in paint of a characterful face or a picaresque figure or a pretty pasture with cattle; the response to such reproductive fidelity and to the obvious human interest is put in question by modern artists and critics only because it falls short of the full aesthetic response.

2. The second guidepost or warning-post is inscribed "storytelling" or "literary art." The amount of literary art you will meet in the mid-twentieth-century galleries will be but a fraction of that which was to be seen in 1850 or in 1900 or even in 1930. It used to be said of the Royal Academy exhibitions in London, "Every picture a story"—a virtue then, a warning now.

The test is whether the picture exists rather as a sentimental diversion than as an aesthetic entity with a life of its own. A picture entitled *Baby's First Steps, The Empty Sleeve, Her Man Is on the Sea,* or *The Mortgage* will of course divert your mind. But the chances are that a bookish or poetic sentiment, or, oftener than not, a trumped-up sentimentality, has been interposed between you and the strictly pictorial values. In its lowest form it is at the level of the "corn" so often mentioned by vaudevilleans or the artists of radio when someone descends just too far into the obvious, the timeworn, or the bathetic.

No one wishes to bar the picture that is an intensified expression of the artist's feeling over circumstance and event. One warns only against a primarily literary and mental approach. A special fondness for anecdotal pictures, for story pictures, for the composition that tugs at the heartstrings or evokes sentimental recollections, is nowadays considered a danger signal if you wish to penetrate to the heart of the visual arts.

Let the storytellers hold by words, which are their natural medium (though sensuous and rhythmic values enter in too)—words which are intellectual symbols or signals. In enjoying painting it is better if the intellect is not immediately

signaled to—or the memory. In this respect the visual arts are more like music.

The Doctor by Luke Fildes is a perfect example of realistic storytelling art. Our response is conditioned by memory because no one of us has escaped experience of some similar sickbed scene. Realists among critics have heaped endless praise on the picture—"One of the noblest and most dramatic works of art of the nineteenth century." And they have underlined the emotional values the observer should not miss: "The beautiful child of the farmer is sick—so sick that the mother, seeing the perplexity on the face of the great-hearted doctor, realizes that her beloved darling is in imminent danger . . . and seeks surcease in tears. The strong, fine farmer affectionately puts his hand on her shoulder with a reassuring touch . . . " And so the description goes on in a book dealing with art appreciation, dated 1925. But how much, asks the modern, has this to do with aesthetic response or downright painting excellence? It is worth while to ponder a statement by W. Martin Conway, penned early in the twentieth century: "The fact is that a picture one can describe is not likely to be a good picture. If the actual description of a picture makes interesting reading, the picture itself is not likely to please." There is something of overstatement here, but a basic truth too.

A postscript might be added to point out that *propaganda* art is equally a danger, alerting the intellect and destroying the opportunity for feeling one's way into the picture, for contemplative enjoyment. Now, when it has been discovered that visual instruction affords a directness, vividness, and speed not possible to other mediums, propaganda art flourishes. But we should know its limitations and its purposes. Argument, like anecdote, is properly developed by the spoken or written word. When introduced into painting it reduces that medium to illustration or worse.

There is an element of danger here. The great body of Christian mural painting might be termed (by unbelievers) propagandist. This is hardly in any substantial sense true, as regards most lovers of art. These depictions of the life of Jesus, or of the Virgin Mary, or of, say, Saint Francis, permit reliving, on the part of the observer, of a truth already accepted, the resurgence of a feeling of spiritual tenderness, of religious compassion—all sympathetic to aesthetic response. There is, moreover, some purely pictorial excellence, an analogue to inspired religious feeling, that lifts a Christian picture by such a man as Duccio, Giotto, or Raphael into the estate of universal art, eloquent to the nonbeliever, whether skeptic of our Western world or a traveler from Asiatic lands who may be Buddhist or Taoist or Hindu.

An example is the reverent and joyous appreciation of Hindus for the Christian art of, say, the Vatican collection, or Giotto's murals in the Arena Chapel at Padua. A reverse example is that of the dedicated Christian who gives himself up to the riches of the Buddhist murals in the Ajanta Caves of India. His enjoyment of the decorative splendor, the superb draftsmanship, and the opulent Indian imagery is mixed, probably, with associative pleasures out of his understanding of the salient episodes of the Buddha's life and of the reverence of the Indian mind (which admits no antagonism between an austere idealism and appreciation of sensuous loveliness).

Buddhist art survives even more magnificently in sculpture than in painting. What nonbeliever who has rested gratefully in the quiet Oriental rooms of our museums can help brightening at the thought of the Indian or Siamese or, it may be, Chinese relics of Buddhism enshrined there? The sculptor of the *Head of Buddha* illustrated on page 219 succeeded in setting up some universal aesthetic appeal while perpetuating in stone an indescribable sweetness of character, an inner repose attainable by human beings and central in Buddhist teaching. Here the reposeful, monumental sculptural art has been utilized with absolute fitness. Doubtless some religious art is heavily propagandist, but only the overselfconscious skeptic or sectarian should find a bar between his enjoyment and this stone from the studio of an unknown Cambodian sculptor. No less should Fra Angelico's work or El Greco's— the one artist never painted other than a reli-

gious scene, the other seldom—appeal universally.

3. The third warning-post is pretty far from the main approaches to art, though but a generation or two ago it was central. This is the guidepost to art that serves morality. Of course art in decent circles of living *is* moral, but that it should commonly *point up* a moral is outside everyone's expectation in today's studios and galleries. Moral lesson, like story and argument, belongs to the realm of words, where logic can be developed and the conscience be addressed.

4. The last guidepost is inscribed "Romantic or Escape Art." It stands at the approach to an area seldom entered by the contemporary artist; yet academy exhibitions and most museums still offer examples which, in their colorful and exciting way, are a temptation to us all. But the moderns seem to have proved their point: the observer should not look at art as affording escape or consolation.

Life is hard, no doubt. The unaccustomed and the exotic, when pictured, provide appealing and convenient channels to forgetfulness. The heroic adventurer and the sympathetic lover afford consolation for drab existence, a shelter from life as it routinely is. Certainly the art of painting comforts the soul, and at its best it intensifies living; but the avowed romantics have too often falsified life, or conducted us to areas where melodrama is rife, to be fully trusted.

Ever since Delacroix (the French painter, who died in 1863) there have been minor schools of painting and sculpture called romantic, dealing with the long ago and far away, culling theatrical scenes from war and legend, affording the observer tantalizing peeks into harem or desert camp. Castles and attractively decayed ruins, Oriental lion hunts and shipwrecks and heroic rescues—these were staples of romantic painting. They were all set down with an appropriate technique of tumultuous movement and heightened color. The technical means, the sense of movement in the canvas (with formal order taking the place of the tumultuous) and the reveling in color, were destined to go on into the main stream of modern painting, to Cézanne and Gauguin, to van Gogh and Matisse and Rouault, to Kandinski and Marin.

Greuze: *The Broken Pitcher. Louvre*

Perhaps it is only false romance that should be warned against, only the forcedly picturesque and the glamorously strange, or the love scenes sometimes heatedly explicit or again poetically fogged over. For there is a valid romantic strain in every human life. The unexplainable love of man for woman, the love of the Christian for God, the devotion of the Buddhist to every least bit of life—all these involve romance.

The development of psychoanalysis helped unseat the romantics; it became clear how certain forms of art were being used as wish-fulfillment and vicarious compensation. The escape in art was seen as hardly more lasting or important than that afforded by drink.

Here, just before the discussion of form, are pictures illustrating the sentimental-realistic approach and the creative rhythmic one. *The Broken Pitcher* by Jean-Baptiste Greuze is an example of popular, widely approved art. A pretty girl, an appealing incident, and a naturalistic presentation combine in a picture that is "liked" by everyone. Titian's *Frederick of Saxony* creates a contrasting art-climate. Subject really

Titian: *Frederick of Saxony. Kunsthistorisches Museum, Vienna*

does not count. We intuitively recognize this as great painting. We know we shall return to it repeatedly, not for sentiment or likeness but for aesthetic experience.

The Key to Enjoyment

In glancing back over the four guideposts, the observer comes up with one safe generalization about changes in the approach to art during, say, the past seventy-five years: there has been a marked retreat from interest in subject-matter as such. Descriptive art and literary art and instructional art are less evident in the studio, the home, and the museum than at any time in the recent past. We have to find out only what is in the picture or statue that more or less takes the place of subject elements—or adds inestimably to their importance. Here we come to the difficult question of what *form* is, in the modern meaning. For the formal values in the canvas are what afford a deeper response—form in its sense of rhythmic pictorial movement, in its way of signaling a difference from the model, in its over-tones of soul-satisfaction.

Thus far are we from the people "only yesterday" who thought of painting as a transcription of nature's beauty, as in a landscape, a flower, a body, a face; or a clever teller of a story. In the second half of the twentieth century almost all critics and teachers agree that to believe that a picture or statue is good because the original in nature was beautiful is to confuse oneself in the pursuit of aesthetic satisfaction. They are likely to agree too that the main effort of latter-day artists, in whatever country, has been to capture and fix the quality that we call form. The Chinese, centuries ago, called it rhythmic vitality or the life-energy in the picture.

Form may be difficult to pin down as an idea precisely because it is the sum of all the intangible, nameless attributes in the work of art. We are dealing with phenomena not explained by any dictionary definition of the word. And yet the observer must *feel* form, in the extra-dictionary sense, to attain the best of the enjoyment to be got from El Greco's *Christ in the Garden* (page 411) or Michelangelo's *Pietà* (page 379).

Again, like what you enjoy. You may begin as an extrovert, even hostile to the idea of the inner eye, and to the idea that a mysterious bundle of components has been put into the art work to pleasure that inner eye. But spread your appreciation gradually, patiently, and at least a glimmering of what is meant by "form" will come to you—and of what is meant by contemplative seeing. If you frequent galleries and "talk art" even in the most casual way, you cannot help being conquered. You are a modern living among moderns. Practically everybody, by trusting intuition before knowledge, by living—without conscious hostility—with art works richly form-endowed, can come to friendly, quiet, profound enjoyment of such masterly examples as Rembrandt's *Portrait of a Man* (page 483) or the twentieth-century Lehmbruck's *Kneeling Figure* (page 645).

Paradoxically a little knowledge of the course of the modern revolution, of the way in which form-consciousness came to be at the heart of the subject, is essential.

Form, Sensibility, and a Little History

Roughly a half-century ago Clive Bell wrote an essay entitled "The Aesthetic Hypothesis" that started the still vigorous discussion of formal organization. Bell argued that all creative works of art are endowed by their producers with a quality capable of evoking an aesthetic response, and he proposed that this quality be named "significant form." The most precious faculty for an individual approaching a work of art, he added, is aesthetic sensibility, that is, sensibility to form. Other traits in the painting or sculpture, its informative, descriptive, or literary values, he marked down as secondary and unimportant.

During the following thirty years all the realists in the world gibed at Clive Bell. The critics who bolstered the prevailing opinion, whether in museum or in marketplace, made rich fun of aesthetes who talked of some precious, unseeable formal significance. But as post-realistic painters and sculptors multiplied, as gallery-goers tried to explain what it was that affected them so deeply in the paintings of Cézanne and Rouault and Kokoschka, or the sculptures of Lehmbruck and Brancusi and Moore, it became evident that Bell had stumbled upon the one truth that best explains the Modern, that is, the post-realistic development in art. Nothing is more certain today than this: the interest of the creative painter or sculptor has been transferred to art that is endowed with an intangible quality which most people call form.

Conviction has steadily grown, too, that in providing an understanding of the modern or form-seeking schools, Clive Bell also laid the most solid footing for excursions into art's past. Sensibility to the significance of form provided a new yardstick and test, and most art histories from 1935 on were written or rewritten with the primary aim of opening readers' faculties to the experience of form. Some of the rewritten works, of course, failed of being modern. But the change in approach to the subject had been admirably accomplished by the early nineteen-fifties, as the shelf of art histories in any bookstore testified. The book you are reading, as it initially appeared in 1937, was perhaps the first to lay out the whole condensed story of Oriental as well as Occidental art, with emphasis upon the reader's *experience* of the art work as all-important. The aim was explicitly set forth: that the reader's aesthetic sensibility be sharpened, that he be led to feel with his author-companion the expressive form values, whether in a Scythian bronze, a medieval cathedral, or a Cézanne landscape. Later rewritings of the book have been undertaken partly to remove the repeated arguments against the realists and nature-servers in art—arguments necessary in the pioneering book that it was, but superfluous and tiresome when practically everybody has gone over to the modern side.

Before Clive Bell's epoch-marking pronouncement there had been the statement of Walter Pater that "all the arts tend toward the condition of music," which may be put down now as a singularly incisive and prophetic declaration. The remark contained the implications of a general turn toward other than objective values, toward rhythmic and deeply emotional art. Many years earlier Goethe had spoken of architecture as "frozen music."

Clive Bell wrote his memorable essay at about the time when the cubist painters of Paris came to international notice, a point worth noting because the cubists were the first group, before the avowed abstractionists, to attempt the isolated expression of form. They helped clarify the theory of formal organization within the canvas.

Of course it was soon seen that Bell's statement about form was an oversimplification; but the talk about and writings upon the problem of spatial or plastic form continued, and such critics and collectors as Roger Fry, Albert C. Barnes, and Herbert Read went on to establish the "form theory" as the norm of judgment as regards modern art. There were the differences of approach and the contrary vocabularies, the personal name-calling and the bickering, that are the rule where theories of art are discussed. The one point that needs making here is that a revolution occurred in both art practice and theorizing about art; and somehow the word "form,"

and the thought of form as giving life to the work apart from nature, lay at the heart of it all.

(One should repeat, perhaps, that form has got very far from meaning mere "shape," and that it is not technique. Masters of technical means—among whom might be counted Bouguereau at one extreme of polished, "accurate" execution and John Singer Sargent at the other extreme, of a dashing, self-proclaiming technique —may fail utterly in the realm of formal invention.)

Abstraction

Although in the mid-twentieth century abstract art is the most noticeable thing in the international galleries, and "abstract expressionism" widely named as the representative art, or perhaps the representative experimental art, of the age of machines and atomic progress, nevertheless in visual art the picture-subject does overwhelmingly survive. Your book of history need hardly add any account at all of wholly abstract or nonrepresentational painting and sculpture, so meager is the bulk of this sort of thing in the total perspective of the ages. Certainly the main body of new painting will not become abstract in your lifetime or mine. Nevertheless, if you close your mind to abstraction you may be cutting yourself off from the chance to understand, or enjoy, recent art fully. The reason is that the form values we have been speaking of are abstract.

Recently I was in Washington, and as usual I went to spend a quiet hour in the restful Phillips Gallery. In one of the rooms there was a painting labeled *Abstraction*, by Georges Braque. Two little girls came into the gallery. They paused, and one asked the other, "Abstraction— what is that?" Immediately the other girl answered, "Abstraction—that's something you don't know what it is."

I believe that there is no better definition, whether in dictionary or book on art. Perhaps you will prefer to emphasize the end—". . . don't know what it is." I prefer to remember that this child recognized the "something." In music assuredly there is something, in a symphony or a fugue, though anyone might be hard put to it to explain what it is. The arts of painting and sculpture are claiming the privilege of composing abstractly, as one might compose music, without likeness to outward nature.

What has been established is that in the visual arts, as in music, it is possible for the artist to express elements of life and nature not to be detected by the eye or ear. He invents or "sees" and implants in the canvas rhythms or forms or what you will, and the beholder (or listener) detects some echo of the cosmic architecture and cosmic movement. In the art of painting it is not necessary for the artist to sacrifice natural appearances entirely to do this; but what may be called the form-organization of the partly objective picture *is* an abstract element. The abstractionist painters are merely the most logical and most ruthless of those pushing modernism in the direction away from subject-interest in the old representational sense, and toward an effective rhythmic order.

One who has knocked about studios, museums, and galleries for the better part of a lifetime comes naturally by an understanding of such terms as post-impressionism, expressionism, and abstract art, and then sometimes writes as if every beginner knows their significance. Despite an effort to put everything in the simplest terms, these recently coined names of schools or types of art may have been too casually introduced in these pages. Really they are very simple; their meaning derives from commonly circulated words. It should not take anyone more than five minutes to master them.

Impressionism was the final phase of the march toward realism that had begun way back in the days of the Renaissance. Impressionism, a revolutionary movement in the 1870s because it challenged all the sorts of academic realism then popular, itself became a popular type of art by 1890 and has persisted up to our own time. Especially it was a sort of painting based upon catching the immediate aspect of the scene—the impression. Details were forgotten, the subject was fogged over, almost lost in a shimmering veil of color.

Post-impressionism means, of course, merely the art that came after impressionism. All the sorts of revolt against realism, the differing experiments of Cézanne, van Gogh, Seurat, Matisse, Picasso, and the many other pioneers of what is now generally termed modern art, were lumped together for discussion under the name post-impressionism. It came into currency internationally in the years just after 1910. Nevertheless, the word lacked precision of definition because any term suggesting merely "afterness," or any other time-relation, is historically weak.

In the search for another name suggesting the basic character of contemporary revolutionary art, one, *expressionism,* has seemed the most acceptable. It will probably denominate in future history the art of the period between impressionism and whatever turns out to be the next great revolutionary movement—the modernism of tomorrow. Not only is the word *expressionism* an admirable foil to *impressionism,* but it points up the contrast of the latest art, expressive of hidden values, to the outwardly realistic or representational sort, whether derived from close study of nature or from a quick impression.

As a part of *expressionism,* abstract art is separated out by reason of the dictionary meaning of "abstract." Roughly it means art that is apart from any particular object. This may mean that the art is wholly nonrepresentational or that any recognizable object in it is incidental, contributory to the design only in the slightest way. Another dictionary definition suggests a differing sort of abstract art: a sort that fixes in the picture or sculpture an epitome or summary of a class of objects. Such are the "bird stones" of the American Indians. There are, too, pictures in which the futurists or other moderns treated an abstract subject such as "speed" by summarizing the movement-lines of automobiles. Thus there is an immense amount of semi-abstract art in the exhibition halls, marking every stage of nonrepresentational picture or "statue" up to absolute abstraction. Those who purified painting of all objects, even of suggestions of objects, tried to run away with the title "abstractionists," and, failing in the face of the numerous semi-abstractionists, hit on the title, "non-objectivists."

In any case, the three terms in contemporary usage that will be useful to you in developing a modern approach are "post-impressionism," "expressionism," and "abstract art"—simple words. I have tried to speak simply of them, and to illustrate them in a way that explains them. For the rest—fauvism, cubism, surrealism, and the like—it is for the final chapters of the book to give each its definition and place.

What Is Expressed in Expressionism

Sometimes the point is made, and it seems to light up the approach to recent art, that three sorts of revelation are easily marked in expressionist painting and sculpture. First is the deeper or hidden aspect in the subject, a sensed world order not visible to the superficial observer—an inner character, an essential organism, a pulsing vitality.

Second is the element that the artist puts in by reason of being different from all other artists: *his* way of seeing, his sensibility, his image, his method of transforming the world. (This was the origin of "expressionism" as a name. It was first coined in Germany about 1911 because the German moderns in particular stressed the artist's inner and peculiar conception, *his* vision and *his* emotion.)

Third, there is an expressive element out of the materials and the tools of the art, an intenser expression of the values resident in the medium. In painting this appears most obviously as a heightened colorfulness (or "paintiness") in pictures. The artist nowadays is likely to "declare his medium" by piling his pigments in knobby ridges and patches and by leaving a record of the swing of the brush; whereas at the end of the nineteenth century the academic ideal was to temper the color and to smooth down the brushwork until there resulted a perfectly smooth finish, as uniform and expressionless as the paint on the hood of your car. The impressionists were then coming to a limited popularity, and Cézanne, van Gogh, and a few other isolated painters were being shown at obscure galleries in Paris; but the academy exhibitions in Paris, in London, practically everywhere, were dominated by the followers of Bouguereau and Meissonier and others in the museum-painters tradition. Modern galleries and modern rooms in historical museums have an increased air of color and life because the typical painter has capitalized upon his brush and colors for a more intense "painty" effect.

The most characteristic modern sculpture, the sort that the artist carves directly from stone, likewise declares the feeling of its material, its heaviness and blockiness and reposefulness. The massive and the lithic look are treasured. This implies, of course, a creative feeling for the stone on the part of the artist, leading him to visualize his subject within a transformation that will retain the feeling of the monumental block, its weightiness and amplitude.

The revolutionary drift of modern architecture similarly is bound up with creative use of materials; though here one has a second and equally potent concept, truth to use. At first modern architects (except a few who were imaginative geniuses, most notably Frank Lloyd Wright) contented themselves with capitalizing upon the new materials and tools, so that a so-called "International Style" emerged, in which the beholder became conscious chiefly of the bare bones of building, honestly declared. Later one remembered that showing the bones was not enough, and a certain monotony became apparent. The idioms of machine-age building could be learned by any architectural apprentice, but imagination and originality could not. This is the reason why the modern architecture in New York City, impressive and breathtaking as it is in its soaring lines and bright, clean surfaces, soon seemed like routine variations upon a not deeply felt theme. But when you encounter Frank Lloyd Wright's house built at Bear Run, Pennsylvania, (page 651) you know that here is a profound artist's creation in terms of modern materials and methods of building—as much a product of this age and its vision as the Parthenon at Athens (page 121) was a product of fifth-century B.C. Greece.

The three elements which the modern artist thus puts into his work in a new way, the three elements I have mentioned here, are but a small part of the total form-expression which great art embraces. But in becoming conscious of these things in works of art—that is, in learning to feel the soul of the subject, the individual contribution out of the artist's imagination and emotional expression, and the good solid sense of the materials nobly used—you may enrich your whole journey through art history. To be conscious of these values inevitably opens the way to appreciation of others involved in the mysteries of form and expression.

To most of us it must be a perpetual wonder how a painting gets done. Before us is a square of canvas (or an oblong of silk or paper), perfectly ordinary material. The next time we see it we enter into a painting which is a new creation in the world, possibly affording an experience unforgettable, to which we may return at intervals throughout our lives.

Strictly speaking, the materials of painting are a flat surface and some pigments. This does not take us very far toward a picture from the hand of Leonardo or Goya. But it is well to remember the flat surface, because the flatness conditions all painting as an art. A frame around the canvas emphasizes that the artist is giving you, on the flat but apparently beyond it, a composition with movement, depth, and a path for the eye. An artist cannot draw a line or paint an object on the surface without developing the illusion of depth. A picture becomes really a manipulated, hollowed-out space behind the surface of the canvas, filled with things the painter wants to put in. If he puts them in negligently, the observer's eye may seem to see a figure falling forward through the picture frame onto the floor, or his eye may be carelessly led through the backdrop of the hollowed-out space or jumped across the frame and out of the picture altogether.

In short, the materials of painting are not merely a canvas square and a handful of pigments, but the means by which the artist develops, in a seemingly bounded, hollowed-out space, an irresistible movement-composition, a sort of traffic-guide for the observer's eye. He does this by knowing the directional effect (up and down and across the canvas, but most importantly

inward and outward in space) of another category of the materials of his art. These, as mentioned on page xv, are line, color, texture, volumes suspended or balanced in space, light and dark (chiaroscuro), and plane arrangement.

This mention of a second sort of material in painting is added because you may find your pleasure in a van Gogh painting or a Matisse increased if subconsciously your mind is trained to count over the ways in which certain colors —the yellow-red range—push forward, and others —the pale blues, for instance—recede; or to notice when heavy texturing bulges forward, in contrast with untextured parts that pale away. This is like knowing, though vaguely, when certain groups of instruments take over in a symphony.

Of none of these things should you be taking stock at your first meeting with a work of art. You should read a painting as spontaneously as you read a poem, without thinking how you learned to read, without seeking out the poet's special method of statement. But later, as an adept, you will find yourself deriving a different sort of pleasure—intellectual, if you like—in study of the means.

Of Contemplative Seeing

Finally, in trying to draw together the basic ideas recorded in this Introduction, I cannot but return to a phrase used casually here and there: contemplative seeing. In sections dealing with the body of art—and we should visualize it as one body, one unity, throughout the ages—and with art's friendliness, and with varying ways of seeing (though we must avoid some of these ways), the main drift of idea has been that the beholder can train himself to be not merely a spectator of a building, a picture, or a statue, but possessor of it in the profoundest sense, experiencing its richness and pith and essence. It is natural that each one of us should be a *mere* beholder at first, or after a literal schooling; but the road is open and easily traveled to this other, prized attainment.

Indeed, there is a modern and a better way of approaching art, a way that defers knowledge *about* pictures until creative seeing has been achieved, until the observer has established, or re-established, a faculty of losing himself in the tide of formal and emotional communication. At first one need only approach in friendliness, the intellect in repose, the mind washed free of prejudice or expectation. The living work of art will do the rest. Gradually the beholder finds the habit happily fixed upon him, the habit of a silent, non-reasoning, contemplative receptiveness.

This habit, which I call visual contemplation, means that some inner faculty—the soul, if you like—leaps to recognition of the order, mood, or truth of a picture before the message or realism of the subject-matter awakens the mind or memory. In other words, one should *feel* the order, the movement, the formal vitality in the work, become one with its rhythm, before recognition of what is stated or delineated. The ability to transcend or postpone the intellect's reaction thus opens a way of direct communication through the eyes to the deeper self.

This is a high ideal. Such a method of enjoyment is not inspired by all types of art, perhaps only by the most moving. Nor can one claim that it is *the* method for all types of observer. Men strangely differ in their temperaments and in their capacities. It would be arrogant to suggest exclusion of anyone whose own present method of seeing brings him joy of, say, a less contemplative sort. What can be said is that seeing reposefully, receptively, is the method of response that most fitly matches today's way of artistic creation. It belongs especially to what we all know to be the modern or contemporary movement in the visual arts. Without intending to exclude any happy observer, I am commending as the highest ideal of our time the theory of contemplative seeing.

In the nonvisual arts there is a perfect parallel. Practically all listeners to serious music prize that receptiveness, that response, not asking for reports from the memory, knowing that the listener must make the intellectual part of his mind a blank for fullest enjoyment emotionally and spiritually. Contemplative hearing is standard; the way of contemplative seeing in the enjoyment

of architecture, painting, and sculpture should hardly seem strange or difficult to the modern generation.

Art is now seen as a key and model for all balanced education. The emphasis has returned from material ends to inner apprehension and spiritual perception. On every side, not only in the visual arts but in all the realms of living, it is recognized how plodding is the intellect alone, how necessary it is that science and intellectual knowledge be measured from some higher ground of intuitional understanding and philosophical illumination. Basic are the reposeful sensibility, the spontaneous experience, the emotional immersion, a flame kindled within. It is not easy for the thinking, scheming man to make room in his life and in education for this sort of training, of response to the world and to art; but in the other direction there seems only disaster.

Art is a special gift to children, savages, and spiritual seers. (This is a fact made clear by writers only in the present era.) Children and savages have it as their own, being intuitive; the seer has it by a native deeper seeing. Indeed, what is the original meaning of "seer" if not a man endowed with the gift of deep seeing, of a special sort of "clairvoyance"? Contemplation is the seer's way into participation, possession, and finally self-loss in the art work.

Monumental and Minuscule

Writers of books tend to sift their materials until only the larger monuments survive. To know the monumental and the exalted is good. We are on the highest ground of enjoyment, perhaps, when we are in the presence of works "of a certain magnitude." But just as poetic tragedy, of which Aristotle used the phrase, is but one type of drama, and, however exalted, affords but one type of experience in a wide range possible in enjoyment of the theater art, so the grander types of painting, sculpture, and architecture need not dwarf unduly the more familiar water-color picture or the print, the statuette or the coin, the chapel or the cottage. The test is whether quality or style is in the work, whether it has its own formal excellence in its own class.

Certainly we are more immediately impressed, or overwhelmed, as we step into Chartres Cathedral or into the Rembrandt rooms at the National Gallery in Washington. Contemplative vision, and the silence necessary to it, are more spontaneously evoked in the presence of grandeur, a dignified stature, and the exalted simplicity which Rembrandt, for instance, seems to have painted into every one of his canvases. Grandeur (unless it be false, as in the case of overdecorated architecture) is naturally conducive to a mood of quietude, exaltation, and surrender of self.

Nevertheless, there is formal beauty too in the statuette that may be on your desk or mantel, though it be no more than three inches high—perhaps one of the indescribably spirited animal figures of the Lurs, or a Greek archaic miniature bronze. For the matter of that, you will find the familiar buffalo nickel well worthy of your contemplative gaze, though the scope is very small. There are miracles of expressiveness in linear art —in drawings and woodcuts and engravings. Don't cut off your appreciation from these little things—between journeys to the cathedrals and museum rooms. They are your more familiar way into friendly intercourse with art, into enjoyment and communion.

There are moods and kinds and phases of art, all accessible and all rewarding. My hope is that the contemplative approach will *in the end* bring you to participation in them all. Theoretically your appreciative faculties should function in some such sequence as this: perception of and response to the formal and mystic elements; then the emotional impact; finally the intellectual stimulus, whether recollective or literary or satiric.

To see art spiritually and to write persuasively is the aim of the historian. No other road is open to the writer who would assume the role of guide to the present generation, a generation that will, properly, combine an understanding of the excellencies of past art with the *way* of understanding which belongs especially to this age. It seemed to this writer that the modern way is to know art as joyous, to approach it without traditional mental hindrance, to experience it in the deepest part of the self. One develops thus a habit of aesthetic awareness, and one possesses each work as peculiarly one's own.

A NEW

WORLD HISTORY OF ART

I: WHEN ART WAS YOUNG:
PREHISTORIC AND PRIMITIVE ARTS

IT WAS Captain Cook, writing in the eighteenth century about the savages of Tierra del Fuego, who recorded a truth that explains the art of primitive people everywhere: "They are content to be naked, but ambitious to be fine." It seemed to the great explorer, as to all his generation, a strange thing, arguing a childish disproportion in moral and cultural values, that men and women not civilized enough to clothe their bodies should care to decorate them. Charles Darwin, too, visited the Fuegians in the eighteen-thirties and observed with surprise that when they were given a bolt of red cloth they entirely overlooked its utility as covering for their nakedness. Instead they tore it into strips and wore them in the

wrong places, for show, without regard to warmth or modesty.

Apparently it is a trait universal among the "lowest" people known today that they are "ambitious to be fine." And as far back as the roots of human culture have been traced, in history and prehistory, the instinct to decorate is evident. There may be no clothing, no alphabet, and no logical thinking, but rudimentary adornment is ever-present: art *is*.

It was long after Captain Cook's voyages, and almost a century after Darwin's observation, that specialists in art began to take from the hands of archaeologists and ethnologists the examples of early man's intuitive skill in ornamentation and,

Horse. Wall painting. Cave of Lascaux, France. Paleolithic

more rarely, in representation. Today the art museums are retrieving from the "natural history" collections the weapons of the South Sea Islander, the pottery of the Pueblo and the Mayan, and the sculpture, formerly considered crude, of the Easter Islander and the prehistoric caveman. Of all the art once scorned and discarded, and now brought back for aesthetic enjoyment, the primitive has most notably come alive in the twentieth century. Not even the rediscovery of El Greco—classic example of revolutionary reappraisal—is more striking than the elevation of products of uncivilized peoples to an honored place in the galleries of approved art.

The "Beginnings" of Art

The works called "primitive" are widely distributed over both space and time. The cave paintings of the hunting peoples of the Pyrenees are dated by some archaeologists at 10,000 B.C., by others at 30,000 or 50,000 B.C.; whereas the collected carvings of the Maoris and the Tlingits, the baskets of the Pomos, and the latest rock drawings of the Bushmen are, in the main, products almost contemporaneous with our own generation. Geographically the display of primitive arts is drawn from territories as separated as Central Africa, Alaska, the South Sea Islands, France, and Ecuador.

From this a lesson is clear: it is useless to seek the origin of art in one place, or to attempt to date it at one moment in time. There is, indeed, no authority for speaking of the beginnings of art; we may do so merely as a convenience. The great number of objects known as "early" are products of ancient and recent peoples scattered over the several continents. The true beginnings elude the searcher because they lie beyond any frontiers explored or explorable. There are, in a true sense, beginnings being made today.

And indeed in this matter the would-be historian is confounded by paradox on every side. The paintings on the walls of Altamira in Spain, made by cavemen while the great ice sheet of the glacial age still covered most of Europe, millenniums before the beginnings of Asian, Egyptian,

and Aegean civilizations, are now judged to be "modern" in the truest creative sense. On the other hand the present-day cult images of obscure Negro tribes still considered less than civilized are perfectly in character beside early Egyptian god-kings and the Han animals of China. The houses and utensils of the Maoris—those native New Zealanders whose culture was all but exterminated in the nineteenth century by the ruthless march of the European white—are now recognized as more distinctively beautiful and subtly stylized than the prevailing decorative modes of the conquering English. The Maoris could not read or write, and their art was different from the academic European nineteenth-century product. Hence their culture was tagged "barbaric" by the invaders. But today the barbaric product is regarded as more richly decorative, more sensitively expressive, than the run-out classic European. Such are the confusing currents, or changes of current, set up by intensive study of the arts that the Victorians termed savage and crude, or merely "primitive."

Despite the confusion, however, there can be detected an elusive likeness among most of the works of early art recently brought to light. Remembering that some of the wider cultures have been described as primitive merely because their modes of ornament and representation lack the high polish and refined naturalism of European traditional practice, and that these will ultimately be judged as different, but not elementary, cultures—such as, for instance, the Mayan and the West African Benin—one may note a distinctive first aspect, a recognizable character, in most of the works called primitive. It arises, perhaps, from a preserved simplicity, an uninvolved directness of statement, and an intuitive grasp of decorative unity. The link is one of feeling, of approach, of unidentifiable nuances of formal expression, rather than a material or a stylistic likeness. There is a stamp of special vividness or direct vigor in art not yet civilized, which marks it off as a product of unlettered, not yet mature men.

This art is typically unstudied, not too deeply considered, spontaneous in origin, generally free from exact imitational intent. It may thus appear

Giraffes. Cave painting, Southern Rhodesia. Facsimile. *Frobenius Collection, Research Institute for the Morphology of Civilization, Frankfort-on-Main*

naïve or crude to the logic-trained adult European or American; for, if thinking has been part of the creative process, it is comparable to the thoughts of children, who are unlogical, disconcertingly direct, with an instinctive feeling for composition and order but without prepossession about "art as imitation" or about moral intention or narrative interest.

In the childhood of art the creator feels near to God, expressing himself with clairvoyant directness and inspired vividness. Primitive art, in the right sense, is of that golden time when the soul feels near the Great Source, when a harmonious order is divined in nature, when the shaping hands obey an inner feeling of rhythmic progression and cosmic symmetry.

The study of primitive art may be undertaken first in either of two vast fields. Today the approach is oftener by way of the arts and crafts of living savages—peoples who exist still, or have existed until very recently, in an elementary hunting life, untouched by the march of major Occidental or Oriental cultures. This is the field

surest to yield examples truly primitive. It is then possible to cross over into the other field, that of prehistoric archaeology, of relics recovered from the silt of the ages and from caves reopened.

Ernst Grosse, a famous German scientist, observed in 1897 that the word "primitive" was being applied to such a mixed collection of products that no true deduction or conclusion was possible. He made the point that the best approach to the beginnings would be through the study of peoples still at the lowest stage of culture—that is, peoples without writing or agriculture or use of metals—and he proposed a start among the surviving tribes still in the hunting stage. He laid out for systematic comparison the arts of the African Bushmen, the Australians, the Eskimos, and such remnant tribes as the Fuegians of South America and the Andaman Islanders of the Bay of Bengal.

If Grosse put his finger on the real, material origin of art, it did not greatly help those who are interested from the point of view of aesthetic

Figure. Easter Island. *British Museum*

ions are barbaric, the design is often compositionally sound, the decorative effect pleasing. In the "applied art" that is supposed to have developed next—in the ornamentation and shaping of weapons, weapon-handles, baskets, pottery, probably in that order—there is a wealth of visually engaging, not to say impressive, design. After the early crafts products came sculpture and painting, perhaps by way of ritual mask and totem. Architecture was a late addition to the consciously matured arts.

A scientific study of the evidence, then, leaves little doubt that human tribes, no matter how isolated, independently developed ornamentation and, usually, graphic representation. A generalization seems justified: that the instinct for art is universal. But only a little way along the road of artistic creation there are wide divergencies. An earlier generation's favorite theories on the origin of art seem completely set aside. It no longer seems proved that art grew out of religious ritual and devotional exercise. Nor can the theory of a purely utilitarian origin any longer be seriously defended. The widely advertised generalization that all primitive ornament is symbolic has likewise collapsed. Against all these theories the advocate of the belief that art arose as intuitive expression, simply because creating it and seeing it "pleased" creator and beholder, seems to have as good a case as any, although his contention too is unprovable.

The fact is that at a certain stage in man's ascent from animal-like dependence upon nature art appears, and its roots are inextricably tangled with those of dawning religious thought and activity, with economic conditions and utilitarian customs, and—beyond explaining—with impulses and pleasures not understood, with play and love and spiritual intimations. But no one of these may confidently be said to be the mother of art.

Why should we greatly care about the nature of the origin, if the object speaks to us visually, emotionally, aesthetically? Again and again the rhythm holds us; a new revelation of order, of design, is apparent. The moment our eyes catch sight of a cave painting, a Negro king's scepter, or a Maori carved oar, the light of enjoyment leaps up within us. Even among those "lowest"

experience and enjoyment. For he concluded that the "ambition to be fine" led first to body-marking —that art began with painting, scarifying, and tattooing the skin for adornment. This practice is common to all the primitive hunting tribes still existing except the Eskimos (whose skin, because of the climate, is never displayed, and therefore is not a good place for decoration). The art that is technically first, then, however intricate, colorful, and "stylish" in execution, is by its nature hardly open to our enjoyment.

But a little farther along in time, when hairdress had evolved into removable headdress, and when necklaces and girdles or loincloths had developed into something approaching clothes, the evidences of artistic achievement were such as may be seen in our museums—and, if the fash-

Amerindian basket design: gambling tray of the Tulare tribe, California.
University Museum, Philadelphia

peoples—despite the limitations imposed by the scarcity of materials, by the comparative rudeness of the tools of art, by the paucity of techniques and motives—we find examples that stir us no less certainly than do the works of the artists of our own European-American culture.

Typical Primitive Art

A basket of the Tulare Indians, an ivory carving by the Eskimos, an ancestral figure from Central Africa, a decorated wooden bowl from Melanesia—these are fair examples of the arts among the least civilized, the least intellectual of

the world's people; all have an authentic plastic completeness, are rich in emotional appeal. All, moreover, are in accord with one another, and again with the latest manifestations of Western art—with the new "stripped" architecture, with expressionist sculpture and machine-age crafts. They are separated only from the products of the great ages of realism.

As primitive works they are direct-speaking and vigorous, and generally naïve. They are far from nature as seen. But they are plastically alive. ("Plastic" is a word used by most twentieth-century writers on art, not merely to describe three-dimensional or moldable material but to define the thing in sculpture or picture or utensil

Amerindian baskets, California tribes. *American Museum of Natural History, New York*

less limited by the conventions of ornamentation. Ornament may be defined as design within a predetermined space, for decorative effect. It leans heavily upon the elementary principles of symmetry, contrast, and repetition; whereas the arts of free delineation are more usually asymmetrical, without repetition, and of a dynamic unity. The Eskimos incised drawings on ivory or bone; their independent figures show a notable skill in the use of rudimentary graver or knife, and there is primitive devotion to the purely sculptural values.

Geographically midway between these two peoples almost innocent of the commonest cultural accomplishments, there is a district in which the outstanding art is again different. Among the Indians of Puget Sound, British Columbia, and lower Alaska, more "advanced" than either the Eskimos or the Pomos, woodcarving is the supreme art. Vessels are of wood, canoes are of wood; there is wood sculpture, as in the widely known masks and totem poles, and there are even wooden huts and wooden hats. Other arts are practiced, including weaving, bone-carving, basketry, and decorative painting. But the Northwest Indians—again the men—are most accomplished as skilled carpenters and sculptors in wood.

The very different development of the arts and crafts in these three independent North American cultures suggests some of the formative factors. Obviously the plentifulness of certain sorts of material, together with the influence of rigorous or friendly climate, helped to shape the first channels and courses of artistic development. Also the virtual monopoly of art by the women in one case, and its restriction to the men in the other two, suggest a plural rather than a single origin and path of early art.

The true primitive artists of Africa are the Bushmen. Their achievement is most pronounced in rock paintings, a sort of outdoor mural art. And the points that have particularly interested both the art student and the ethnologist are these: The Bushmen have observed and recorded the movements of animals with a degree of accuracy very seldom, if ever, attained in the course of civilized art. Although figures of men

that makes it a complete aesthetic entity, a creation with an indescribable extra dimension. The word implies at once movement and spiritedness and hidden life.)

The Pomo Indians of California, so little advanced in the cultural scale that they had no agriculture, are said to have excelled all the rest of the world, ancient and modern, in basket-making. The basket shapes are sometimes as beautifully proportioned as Chinese bowls or Greek vases; the weaves are technically of an extraordinary fineness and textural grace; the ornamental designs are fitted both to the materials of the art and to the use of the receptacle—and they speak, beyond this, of that extra sense which endows an object with an orderly rightness and imparts to it a contagious rhythm. Basket-making was the outstanding art of the Pomos; it was exclusively the work of the women.

The Eskimos, on the other hand, are best represented by carvings and engravings on the ivory of walrus tusks. Here the artists are the men, and their gift is more in the field of representation, is

Mural. Mtoko Cave, Southern Rhodesia. *Reproduction, Frobenius staff*

appear in their scenes of war and hunting, very seldom are flower or tree forms found. That is, the Bushmen saw more sharply than other peoples the things that interested them in their hunting existence. Furthermore, they occasionally depict the animals in other than the simple profile view common to most elementary peoples; and they display more understanding of the technique of perspective than does any other artist group untrained in scientific optics. By a convention of diminishing size they achieve the sense of space and the effect of remote figures.

At the time that the works of the Bushmen were first studied, the canon of natural imitation was central in the judgment of art, and the discoverers were thrilled by the realistic accuracy of observation and delineation, and by the perspectives. Perhaps it is more to the point today to consider that this still savage people so masterfully pulled free from casual surrounding circumstances the figures that interested them, and composed with not a little strictly mural intuition. The drawings have an additional claim on our attention as representing, of all known works, the nearest approach in method to the masterpieces of the cavemen of the Reindeer Age. There are scientists who, on this evidence, believe that the Bushmen are racially linked to the European cavemen of Paleolithic times.

Negro sculpture, best known of the arts commonly grouped as "primitive," ranges from the products of tribes only a little above the estate of Bushmen and Eskimos to those of peoples quite obviously civilized. There are even cultures that have gone through a cycle from vigorous beginning to decadence. Certainly among the famous Benin bronzes there are evidences of a strong early flowering of the aesthetic instinct, along with later examples that are overdecorated and aesthetically run out. And yet among the ancestral figures of West African and Central African tribes the world has recovered some of the finest things in the entire range of recognizably primitive sculpture. Here is manifest the distinctive formal expression, the intensification of the sculptural life of the piece rather than the life of the model, the lover-like regard for materials, the concentration of feeling.

If some primitive tribes have expressed their artistic impulses best in carving, and others in basketry, still others, not far removed from the beginnings of man in a hunting life, have left their most eloquent record in pottery. Pottery-making was not among the earliest crafts, but it flourished everywhere in the New Stone Age, so that most of the major lines of civilized artistic development, such as the Babylonian, Egyptian, Aegean, or Chinese, can be traced back to the end of a Stone Age period distinguished by rudely or skillfully decorated pottery. Among those peoples who were out of the direct line of civilization and persisted through classical and

Early American pottery. *American Museum of Natural History, New York, and University Museum, Philadelphia*

Christian times as unlettered barbarians, pottery, invented perhaps independently, became a foremost means of artistic expression. Today Pueblo pottery, for instance, has been rediscovered as primitively beautiful, in both ancient and recent examples.

It is fitting that mention of this art, so accessible but still so eloquent of humankind near to nature, of artists with an intuitive rather than a studied devotion to creative expression, should close a brief review of the arts of "contemporaneous primitive peoples." For aside from polished stone implements, seldom decorated, the relics of prehistoric cultures most commonly unearthed for our delight are potsherds and jugs and plates. No less has the potter's art survived today in its every phase, from the continuing strong ornamental jars and bowls of the American Southwest, of Mexico, and of some "peasant" regions of Europe, to the exquisitely refined vases and bowls of the Orient.

The motives are more elaborate at the end of this art's development, the means more refined, but the feeling, the artist's way of approach, and the observer's delight are little changed. And in-

deed in that generic likeness is the key to the enjoyment of primitive phases of art. As soon as one unlocks the appreciative faculty, seeing the "savage" as a phase of oneself, the childhood of art as a part of all art, one recognizes that the unintellectual but eagerly expressive shaper of a Tulare or Pomo basket or a Pueblo decorated bowl has poured into his work a measure of authentic plastic value, a timeless formal loveliness.

Not too much effort, please, to reason it out. Let us say: Here is art, enjoyable to us; by way of collateral interest, here is what we know—or deduce—of the life and thought of the human beings who created it. It is not necessary to discover just what power set a man to work to ornament his pots, paint pictures on the walls of his cave or on the face of his shield.

He was a man very much like you and me, a body born into a disordered and not too sympathetic world, a pent-up, limited individual in a varied society, beginning to use his brain consciously to overcome natural handicaps; beyond that, he was a bundle of unaccountable perceptions, instincts, emotions. He saw the marvelous, sometimes terrifying world about him, guessing at larger secrets and forces behind it. He fought the (other) animals, protected his young, reproduced his kind. Why did he become an artist, recording images, fixing sensations, expressing feelings? Who can know? Did *he*? Was it to set up a contrast to the disordered surrounding world —an echo of a felt harmonious order beyond common seeing? Was it an attempt at explanation? Or supplication? Or merely emotional overflow?

In one way or another all plastic art is an expression of how a man feels in the universe, set down in images visually affective to other men, who feel and enjoy that something too—expression on the one side, pleasure on the other. A bit of order in a disordered world; a bit of unity in a disjointed environment; a hint of controlled rhythm among the endless casual motions and vibrations and shocks that make up life—and the savage grasped the heart of it before our elaborate processes of criticism and explanation had begun. That is, he got down in comprehensible equivalents, in a form that in itself has vitality, movement, rhythm, the thing that essentially is life in art. Let us enjoy as spontaneously as we can the Pomo basket, the carved Haida totem of British Columbia, the cavemen's "Venus."

Theories of Art's Genesis

No one would deny the gains made in the name of intellectual civilization. If spontaneous art suffered in the more arid periods of reasoned philosophies and material inventiveness—and it is a commonplace that it did—perhaps the world nevertheless benefited because more people were thereby released for aesthetic enjoyment. The mistake would be to consider material and intellectual advance the whole of progress, or even its major phase and aim. Every prophet of the day counts up the corresponding losses in the realm of the spirit.

Art, no less, returns to pick up the lost threads of intuitional, abstract, and emotional expression, asks once more for the direct aesthetic response. Scientific, highly documented art is discounted;

the wisdom of the childhood of art is prized; the unstudied pots, baskets, and idols are set up on stages for our enjoyment in a hundred museums, in a thousand homes. But let us not deny that *knowledge* of art *after* seeing may increase or echo the pleasure. Even a glance at the several theories advanced as to the way of art's first coming may multiply enjoyment.

Without subscribing to one theory above the others—for the perplexities are many, and our position as enjoyers demands no final conclusion or allegiance—we may gain something by considering some of the most widely publicized theories as to art's genesis, as to how the near-savage peoples came to have art at all.

The first of these ascribes earliest art to an inborn urge to ornamentation. Artistic expression, being universal to Homo sapiens, may fairly be attributed to an innate impulse to be fine, to improve the "looks" of oneself and one's surroundings. The lowest form, painting and tattooing of the body, was undertaken, the ornamentalists believe, merely for pleasure in adornment and in being admired for that adornment. This simple theory of "art for the eye's sake" has been subjected to some modifications, however, in which are taken into consideration the impulses to create sexual attractiveness and to stand out from one's fellows.

In any case, even the most elementary striping and spotting of the body would develop pattern and composition. By the time the urge was carried over to the enrichment of baskets and clay pots there might already be "motives" developed: repeated thin and thick stripes, or fields of dots or zigzag lines, even geometrical figures such as circles and diamonds. Ornament might first appear on seams, margins, joints, and so become bands of repeated figures, or running borders, dividing the total area into "fields" of decoration.

It is just here that the utilitarian influence strongly enters in. There are, of course, elaborate theories to the effect that art arises only out of use. But it seems fairer to say that use *conditions* art, rather than that it gives rise to art. One of the patent truths about primitive "applied art" is that it rarely runs counter to utilitarian values. It accents structure, enriches texture, adds variety

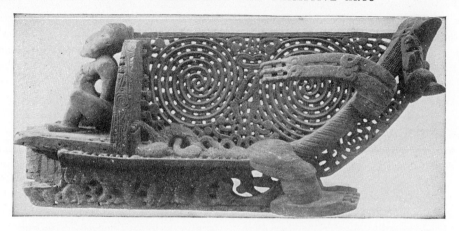

Carved wooden prow of a canoe. Maori. *American Museum of Natural History*

of effect; but it seldom becomes so concerned with show that structure is distorted or use values are impaired.

The weakness of the ornamentation theory is that it fails to cover those types of art that have sometimes been esteemed the most important of all: the arts of free delineation. From the elementary impulse toward decoration men were somehow led to the composition of pictures and statues that took their subject-matter from nature. Ornamentation was then no longer the main object. There was a different sort of pleasure and meaning involved.

It was from this distinction between decoration and delineation that a group of theorists drew their evidence and their arguments for a religious origin of art, and they enjoyed for a time a remarkable vogue. Art, they said, had indubitably grown up as an adjunct of magic and religion. Because most of the early figures discovered were—or might have been—idols, totems, and fetishes, it was inferred that all were invented as offerings to the gods. Even the cave paintings dealt almost unfailingly with animals, and they were doubtless a symbolic offering to the gods to the end that the hunter might be favored in the chase of the pictured beasts. To these interpretations of representational art there was appended a theory that music, dramatic art, and poetry had grown out of the dance, and that the dance had originated as religious ritual. Even

every form of ornament was found to be symbolic. *All* art had grown out of superstition, belief in magic, devotion, ritual.

It is true that evidences of religious beliefs and activities have been found wherever investigation of early man has been made. Religion seems to have existed "in the beginning"—like art. And it is easy to see, throughout civilized history, how intimately and nobly the arts have served ritual and devotion. But the general theory is no longer put forward so dogmatically as it used to be.

Is it not probable that, if men thought of art works as being pleasing to the gods, it was because at an earlier stage art had already pleased people? The best must be dedicated to the tribal deities. But how did the dance, the image, the decorated vessel come to be considered good? Did not the *pleasure* of art come before the devotional *utilization* of art?

Indeed some extreme critics of the religious theory suggest that activity in art preceded religion and led men into conscious pursuit of the latter, rather than the other way round. Sensitivity to a sort of mystic beauty, to the expression of something beyond visible nature, might prepare the way for the creation of gods and for idolatry. Even the so-called "Venuses" of Neolithic times pose the question: are the ideas primarily associated with a Venus-like figure—beauty, pleasure, desire—to be so confidently tagged "religious"? May we not say rather that the desire and the feeling for beauty existed first, then crystallized into a cherished god-symbol?

It may be added that the application of the religious-symbol theory to every particle of ornament—the zigzag meaning lightning, the circle a sun, the arc a rainbow, the triangle a mountain —is by no means as acceptable as it once was. It has been found that where the symbolic significance was supposed to have been long fixed there is not uniformity of interpretation, and a member of one primitive tribe, pressed for an explanation of the motives on the pottery or baskets of another, will "read in" new meanings.

It seems as likely that ornament began in markings without symbolic intent, pure inventions, or copies from butterfly wings or shells or snakes or flowers; and that later generations, seeing a likeness to an animal or rain or a mountain in the design—as you or I might see a face in the clouds—developed a tradition of spirits and devils symbolized by it. And doubtless *thereafter* the motives were repeated with devotional intent. Thus the Hopi or Navajo or Arapaho symbolism. Thus an almost abstract ornamental language, often with double meanings: a mere series of parallel strokes signifying running water and also life unending; two crosses, the morning star, guiding men. Without in any way belittling the importance of these symbolic languages, these formalized equivalents of natural surroundings and ideas, one may still question whether they are not of secondary value in understanding the Hopi pot or the Navajo blanket; and particularly whether the development of so complex a language did not come after a simple birth of art in the impulse to please or to express one's joy in living.

A fourth major theory expounds the view that man creates out of an innate necessity, that to express something intuitively felt within but not evident in the outer sense-world is the primary aim of existence. This overflow of the emotions, this creation of an object bearing a special sort of artistic life, is considered a phenomenon important enough to stand on its own feet, so to speak. It needs no explanation as being an aid to the use of things or as being called out by

Small totem. Stone, Haida Indians.
American Museum of Natural History

religious piety or fear. It is a reality of its own sort. And indeed this "sheer creation" theory seems as defensible today as any.

The realists, of course, see art's origin in an instinct to imitate, to reproduce the objects and actions observed in nature. But this seems now a narrow view, adopted during the age of materialism, and it has lost authority since the challenge of expressionism to Victorian naturalism. It would seem to be sufficiently answered, as far as primitive art is concerned, by the fact that, while ornamental art is universal, reproductive art is not. Everywhere one finds body-painting and scarification, or ornamental design in pottery and weaving, or pleasingly shaped arrows and axes. But not even among all surviving tribes are drawing and representational sculpture found. In short, there was art before imitation.

We need pause no more than a moment over the myths invented by the imitationalists to account for the birth of art. Perhaps the best-known is the one recounted by a writer of ancient Rome: that a girl grasped from the hearth a half-burned stick and traced the outline of her lover's shadow as cast by the flames on the rock wall of the cave. From that beginning is supposed to have grown the whole body of civilized art. But certainly the myth is too facile and sentimental to explain the vast complex of tools and vessels, of ornaments and idols, of picturing and dressing and building, that constitutes early art. The evidence seems to lead back to only one possible generalization: it is an innate impulse in man to create in visually affective terms, in living image and ornament; it is natural in him to delight in formal creations.

Out of impulse and instinct, along with early thought, crystallizing social custom, and emerging religious feeling, arises this duality of formal expression and aesthetic appreciation. It is early complicated by practical purposes—use, devotion, sexual attraction, and symbolism—but it is art as soon as living, expressive form is produced, and that seems to happen as soon as man can be said to be man.

The Cave Paintings

The "masterpieces" of prehistoric art are, all agree, the paintings of the Reindeer Age on the walls and ceilings of caves in Europe and Africa. If we had been pursuing the course of art chronologically (instead of picking up the thread in the products of still-existing primitive peoples) we should have begun with the cavemen's pictures. When you read of Cro-Magnon art or the art of the Troglodytes, the pictures made by the cave-dwellers of the Paleolithic or Old Stone Age are meant.

Had we met these amazing works first, we might have been misled into assuming that the ancient artist sprang, fully equipped and a master of his craft, from the brain of some Cro-Magnon

Zeus. It is more likely that the painters of the bison and reindeer and mammoth on the rock walls in Spain and France represent the culmination of a long apprenticeship, the ripe fruit at the end of age-long development. For these earliest pictures have features considered typical of the true masterpiece: plastic completeness, intense life, monumental proportions. They also often have that incidental virtue which was for the Victorians a basic excellence—extraordinary truth to observation.

Before the era of the cave paintings there were ages in which sculpture was the outstanding art. We need not go into the methods by which the archaeologists arrived at this conclusion; they concern the layers of debris left by successive cultures on the floors of the caves, the order in which are found the relics of hunting man—and sculptor-man and painter-man. Historians will have new facts about the earliest skills, and perhaps a revision of the more or less guessed-at dates of the first incidence of the several arts, when scientists carry further the "carbon-testing" process which they widely developed in the nineteen-fifties. This is a method of measuring the age of an object by testing the radioactivity of a certain type of carbon; the loss of radioactivity in a "sample" from a site indicates the date of objects found at that level.

The chronological sequence of early enduring products is this (there is no way, of course, in which the perishable arts such as tattooing and basketry can be correlated): first of all there were rudely chipped flint weapons, and stone clubs and tools hardly altered from the useful shapes nature had provided, although the technique improved gradually over very great periods of time; then the rudest sculptures, mostly obese "Venuses," and, with them or preceding them, designs scratched on reindeer horns, and occasionally horn designs in the round; then wall scratchings; and finally wall paintings. All these arts developed in the Paleolithic or Old Stone Age, which may have been thirty thousand or a mere fifteen thousand or twelve thousand years ago.

The arts of the following Neolithic period, the New Stone Age—the stone weapons and pottery of the Swiss lake-dwellers, of early man in Brit-

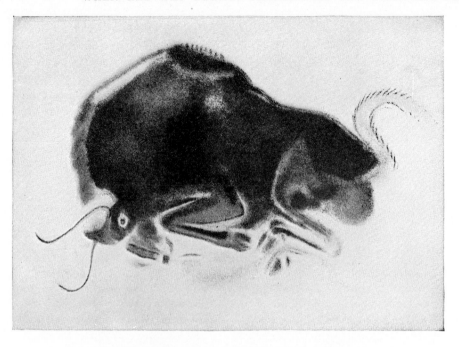

Bison Charging. Cave painting. Altamira, Spain.
Facsimile by Abbé Henri Breuil

ain, and of savages in a hundred other localities
—have little traceable connection with the Paleolithic. The stone axes are often polished, the
flints beautifully shaped and refined, and pottery
is a common industrial product. But curiously
enough there is no art of the New Stone Age
that rivals in originality, plastic effectiveness, and
sheer artistry the murals of the caveman of so
many centuries earlier.

The cave paintings at Altamira in Spain and
in the Dordogne cliffs of France are hardly to be
classed as polychrome works. Color is utilized
beautifully, but there are seldom more than two
hues in one composition. A single color, however
—red, ocher, or brown—may be used with extraordinary variation of intensity. Many of the
animals assume, by virtue of the drawing and
color gradations, a remarkable largeness and
roundness, and a sort of sculptural fullness in
space. Within the limits natural to the isolated
figure (without compositional relationship to
background, frame, or depicted environment)
they achieve a sense of plastic completeness.

This is accomplished with a fine economy of
line, with extraordinary concentration upon essentials. The caveman has a masterly understanding of what to leave out. His pictures represent,
indeed, a graphic art that is mature, certain, economical, intensified. The more is the wonder,
since the artists must have worked with the
rudest tools, on imperfect wall surfaces, by fire-
light and torchlight.

The outlines are rhythmic, flowing, variable,
the lines vigorous and crisp, or on occasion melting and sensitive. The modeled forms undulate,
move. They are vibrant with a life of their own.

These are the works of true savages, of men
existing by the hunt, still far from agriculture
and alphabet and metal-crafts, living close to the
animals, sheltered only by the caves provided by
mother earth. They have fire, they practice rude
stone tool-making, they have invented sewing-
needles of bone; yet they are eons from the dawn
of architecture, law, and writing. But already art
has swung in a great circle from barest ornament
and roughly shaped stone weapon to sculpture
and bas-relief and finally to two-dimensional
drawing and painting. Man has achieved a sum-

Mammoth. Cave painting. Les Eyzies, Dordogne, France.
Facsimile in Frobenius Collection

mit of pictorial art; he has traveled a course that will be traversed again only by struggle through from ten thousand to thirty thousand years. He has developed a mature painting technique and a lasting pictorial achievement.

The most likely explanation of this art is that it represents the work of the artist as priest, that depiction of animals has now become part of a ritual preparatory to the all-important hunt. The animals depicted are generally those fitted for food, particularly the bison and the reindeer. Lions, jackals, snakes, and other "useless" species are noticeably infrequent in the Cro-Magnon gallery of art. Many of the paintings, too, are placed in the most remote and inaccessible inner caves and grottos. They were obviously not intended merely for adornment. It is suggestive of the religious or magical theory, moreover, that there are savages of today whose magic-makers scratch or paint the quarry-animal on rocks as part of ceremonies preceding the hunt.

The German scientist Leo Frobenius, reasoning from this apparent survival, and refusing to believe that a culture so vital as that of the Cro-Magnons could simply die out (as practically all authorities once inferred had been the case), organized between 1904 and 1935 a series of explorations among the caves and cliffs of Europe and Africa, and traced a line of probable descent for the cave-wall artists. It now seems proved that during the late Ice Age they moved down into Africa. Frobenius and his associates discovered rock engravings and paintings at sites scattered from the northern Sahara to the Transvaal. These are dated variously from 10,000 B.C. to the nineteenth century A.D. The two styles existing in European cave art, termed by scientists Francocantabrian and Levant, are recognizable in the African examples: the one concerned with animal "portraits," generally monumental in size; the other with action pictures of men and their enterprises. A great deal that was learned of leg-

Fragments of "temple."
Stonehenge, England

end and of surviving custom, in relation to the works of art, supported the idea of their ceremonial purpose.

Here apparently is an example of the work of art—sometimes consummately artistic—as an adjunct of religious or magical ceremony. It throws little light on the controversy over the origin of aesthetic expression and appreciation, for this painting is at a culmination, far from whatever may have been its first source, accompanying perhaps a highly developed religious consciousness. It affords a fair parallel to the later art of temple and cathedral, of Egyptian murals, Buddhist sculptures, and Christian stained glass. We have not the slightest idea, of course, of the emotions of the priest-artists as they "painted," or of the hunter-community as it used these pictures magically. Trained enjoyment of art in our sense—in the era of museums and art education and unlimited ownership of minor works of art—was then unknown.

Nevertheless, today any pilgrim visiting the cave of Lascaux in the southwest of France will feel the thrill and the joy that come when one allows all one's senses and being to be immersed in a transcending experience of art. Modern man, conditioned by the early twentieth-century acceptance of the art of Altamira and of Les Eyzies as both authentic and splendid, should have been prepared to accept the cathedral-like display of the paintings of Lascaux man without cavil. Discovered in 1940 by two small boys in search of a dog, this new and most magnificent cave at first came under suspicion. Only in 1949 did full appreciation and the first books arrive; only in 1955 was there published forth a full—and monumental—photographic record, in color, of the paintings. They seem more mature and more richly disposed than any earlier find. There even seems to be a progression—as on a pilgrimage—from the lesser exhibits to the crowning experience, the revelation of the largest of the figures, a bison topping sixteen feet. One may go to France now with "Lascaux" written in at almost the top of the list that enumerates Chartres and Amiens and the Louvre as affording rich and almost unique aesthetic experiences.

For years after the discovery of the first cave murals archaeologists and critics refused to accept them as works left by prehistoric savages. Emi-

Primitive "Venus," ascribed to Old Stone Age,
from cave at Willendorf, Austria

examples of outdoor painting or drawing on rocks or cliffs in the Americas, but there has been no major discovery of prehistoric cave art.

While the accuracy of delineation and the amazing fidelity to observed movement still seem a virtue, the greater wonder is that the Dordogne and Altamira and African murals have an artistic aliveness of their own, that in the achievement of expressive form (in addition to the transcription of interesting natural forms) they rank with the sensitive and impressive graphic work of the Chinese and Japanese, and in vigor with the animal art of the Scythians.

Sculpture in the Stone Ages

If the cave paintings are relics of magic-working rites, there is on the other hand evidence of mere decorative impulse in the contemporaneous and earlier carved-horn dart throwers and weapon handles of the men of the Old Stone Age. These are often incised with drawings of the animals that appear on the rock walls, and sometimes the draftsman is superbly economical and expressive. At other times the shaping and ornamentation are abstract.

The Cro-Magnon sculptures in the round are interesting and crudely expressive, but in general they lack the skillful touch and the vitality of the paintings. The commonest type-figure is a so-called "Venus," very fat and flabby according to modern notions of womanly beauty, but sculpturally sound in conception, and the individual figures are sometimes plastically alive and effective. The Willendorf and Mentone Venuses (found at Willendorf, Austria, and Mentone, France) are typical. These may be votive figures, having to do with rites designed to conserve or increase the fruitfulness of women. There are also fully rounded and half-relief animal figures in some of the caves of the Pyrenees. They are characterized by the lifelikeness that is so notable, not to say startling, in the painted bison and reindeer.

After the Old Stone Age came a pause for change of climate and scene. When the curtain lifts again the caveman is gone from Europe and

nent authorities insisted that the pictures had been "planted" by some recent eccentric or joker. The fact that seemed conclusive proof of a recent origin was the lifelikeness of the figures, their anatomical correctness, and their perfectly observed attitudes. No artist before the invention of the camera, critics insisted, could have been endowed with such understanding of instantaneous pose and fleeting movement. For years a controversy raged over the authenticity of the first discovered murals, at Altamira in Spain, and it was only after further exploration had brought to light scores of widely separated examples in Spain and in France that skepticism was stilled. Today this prehistoric art can be seen *in situ* in a dozen localities in southwestern Europe, the Sahara Atlas Mountains, the Libyan Desert, South Africa, and Scandinavia. There are minor

graphic art has immeasurably retrogressed. But the weapons of the Neolithic or New Stone Age, as has been already noted, are refined in technique and—if one may be permitted the word—in feeling. The stone is shaped more sensitively than were the Paleolithic weapons, and the surface is brought to a pleasing polish. New arts that depend upon proportioning and ornament have been ushered in, most notably pottery. Pottery especially will be a link to the emerging civilizations of Sumeria and Egypt and Mycenae. In the New Stone Age savage man is beginning to abandon a life of wandering and establishes communal centers. He is domesticating certain animals and is rudely initiating agriculture. He also weaves cloth. The end of the New Stone Age is the beginning of the Bronze Age, when metal weapons begin to take the place of stone. Metal jewelry becomes common, and metal vessels occasionally stand beside the decorated pottery. The relics indicate an advance in ornamentation and in sureness of the human hand in craftsmanship. With the Age of Bronze and the Age of Iron, civilization is reached, and written history.

It is worth noting that the two stages of culture known as the Old and the New Stone Ages were lived through in widely separated parts of the earth, and that relics of the Neolithic Age have been discovered beneath the foundations of civilized society on five continents. But the dates are variable, and Europe was to remain in the prehistoric "ages" long after historic cultures, intellectually and artistically advanced, had developed in the valleys of the Nile and the Euphrates, in Persia and India and China.

It was in the New Stone Age that Western Europe and England saw the erection of menhir, dolmen, and cromlech—huge stone pillars or slabs raised up as isolated monuments or in logical architectural order. A few fragmentary "temples," such as that at Stonehenge in England and the "table rocks" of Brittany, are evidence of prehistoric beginnings of conscious architecture, but they have little structural significance; the contemporaneous structures of wood and reed and hide have of course disappeared. The menhirs and occasional slabs in the dolmens are sometimes enriched with engraved or sculptured orna-

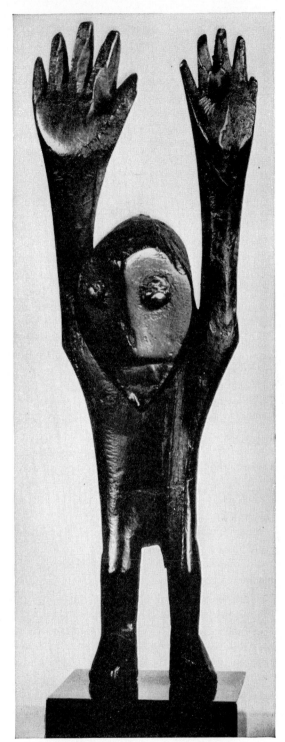

Ritual figure. Wood. Belgian Congo.
Collection of John P. Anderson

ment. But the true beginnings of architectural design may more profitably be studied in the tombs on the Nile and in the earliest ruins in Mesopotamia. What is left at Stonehenge impresses the observer rather as a magnificent sculptural fragment than as a constructed building, and the dolmens—each consisting of a flat rock resting on a group of stone posts—are scarcely more than curiosities.

The Continuing Youth of Art

The rather sparse relics of the New Stone Age, and of the Bronze Age, insofar as they belong to prehistory, are marked by that simplicity and that plastic sensibility which are characteristic of the true, recurring childhood of art. The Old Stone Age at its most mature and superb point of mastery, in the cave paintings, and the Neolithic stage as exemplified in the products of nineteenth-century Amerindian or Polynesian cultures, partake of the same informing "primitive spirit." And it is this strong, youthful spirit of art, this unrealistic statement, and this intuitive plastic expression, that the French and German moderns of 1905-25 self-consciously tried to recapture. In their avid search for the essential rhythmic quality, for the formal synthesis, they turned the world's attention to many a lost or obscured culture.

"Primitive" became a blanket term of approval —and in the general excitement it was made to cover some cultures not now to be denied the label "civilized." Searchers for the true primitive example will do well to note that a great deal of the art that was brought out of "uncivilized" Africa and out of South, Central, and North America, as well as the Maori art and large sections of the Melanesian, is really eloquent of cultures aesthetically well advanced, the product of inventive and—up to a point—thinking peoples. There is reason to call the Maoris spiritually

mature, and to call the natives of New Guinea civilized in their own special way; and the African nations are found to have sometimes had agriculture, urban organization, foreign diplomacy, and medicine. The Mayans of Mexico are known to have excelled in such abstruse subjects as astronomy and engineering.

These are not, in short, to be classed with the cultures in which man is still close to the purely animal life, where he is hunter and fisher, without agriculture or constructed shelter or skilled manufactures. They are not rightly called primitive nations, and theirs has not remained a primitive art. And yet something of primitive directness, simplicity, and formal vigor has persisted. Their artists seem never to have lost the early vividness of statement in an over-refinement of means, never to have substituted imitational representation for formal creation. They avoided the pitfalls spread for the European artist by over-intellectualized culture, by academic rule-making, by the camera-mind.

Those non-European civilizations, whether African or American or of the South Seas, find places later, in the main story of "historic" art. But because the spirit of the childhood of art lingered on—and in limited African and American areas persists even today—there are added among the illustrations here a primitively plain Negro sculpture and a Maori woodcarving, of the intermediate time or continuing youth of art. These are for the reader's enjoyment and to remind him that from the first appearance of conscious art among men certain timeless excellences were achieved, certain fundamental values grasped, and that these were handed down traditionally in some simple civilizations.

Almost at the source a basic plastic aliveness distinguished men's efforts to express themselves in visual ornament and image. The same aliveness underlies some art that never "grew up." The differences are rather in the elaboration of subject-matter, the refinements of finish, and the intricacy of surface pattern.

II: THE EARLIEST KNOWN WORLDS:
ASIATIC CENTERS OF ART

OUT OF the excavated ruins of Lagash, a city-state that flourished nearly fifty centuries ago in Sumeria (a kingdom in Southwest Asia, later part of Babylonia), explorers have recovered fragments of a stone tablet, sculptured in low relief, which had been set up as a war memorial by King Eannatum. On one side the monument recounts in picture and text the military exploits of the all-conquering king. He is depicted oversize, leading his compact and orderly phalanx of soldiers into battle, the while they trample underfoot the bodies of the slain. Nearby are heaps of their dead enemies,

while above are vultures carrying away dismembered parts of the slaughtered. On the other side of the tablet a god is shown upholding the heraldic device of the city-state of Lagash and neatly destroying its enemies.

This one tablet, which is labeled by historians the earliest known instance of a story told in pictures, of sustained visual art, may be offered as an example of the spirit that most often dominates Sumerian, then Babylonian, then Assyrian art. From 2800 B.C., the date of the tablet or "stele," to the fall of the Chaldeans before the Persians in the sixth century B.C., war itself was

Bull. Sheet copper over wood. Sumeria, c. 3100 B.C. *University Museum, Philadelphia*

to be first among the arts; the standard subject-matter of pictorial artists was to be kings, gods, military conquest, and hunting. The gods bulk less and less as time goes on, and animals, particularly bulls and lions, bulk larger; but throughout, war is the supreme interest, and the conquering king is the dominant figure. King Eannatum ushers in an art that is imperialistic, illustrative, useful for frightening enemies and thrilling patriots. The psychology is almost startlingly up-to-date. Eannatum's stele clearly warns that God is on his side, that his soldiers are invincible in battle, and that might makes right. The first narrative art, depicting the union of dictator and God, blood and divine destiny, is an adjunct of imperialism.

To round out the first impression of Babylonian-Assyrian art, one should read a stele commemorating the exploits of an Assyrian king who ruled 1500 years later. It bears a relief showing King Esarhaddon, so large that his figure almost overflows the panel, with small gods in attendance. In his grasp are ropes ringed through the noses of two subjected kings, who kneel, very shrunken and abject, in supplication. The inscription identifies the conquered ones as the kings of Egypt and Tyre. The lesson is clear. The towering Monarch of Monarchs has subdued the outstanding rulers of the world—only, historians now say, Esarhaddon never did succeed in subduing the king of Egypt, and in this stele he is prematurely boasting. From this the student may add one more item to the catalogue of psychological modernisms to be credited to those ancient kings: they had already developed a custom not unknown to imperialistic command in our own time—celebrate the victories, obscure the defeats, claim everything. Nothing succeeds like a show of success.

Babylonian-Assyrian sculpture is the first artistic fruit of this spirit—typically realistic, propagandist, and showy; a little empty, unspiritual, repetitive. The art of the world is like that down through history wherever the imperialistic philosophy prevails, whether the empire be Alexandrian, Roman, or Napoleonic. But of all the art developed under the psychology of the militaristic, conquering spirit, the Babylonian-Assyrian is the most engaging, best able to afford a distinctive pleasure by its mitigation of the violent event with a naïve frankness and a provocative realism.

It is well that the story of civilized art may begin chronologically with these practical, purposeful works of the peoples who settled on the banks of the Tigris and the Euphrates, for they are more easily understandable than the contemporary Egyptian work, which is tinged with the mysteries of the spirit, and rich in abstract and formal qualities. Great art has both values, of course—an inner one that grows out of imagination, vision, and inspirational handling of stone or paints or metal or clay, and an outer one gained from keen observation of nature and life. Egyptian art is supremely of the brooding, inward, creative man; Mesopotamian art is, in general, of the outward, observing, practical man. Thus the latter has close affinity with such European cultures as the Greek and the Renaissance. And the narrative reliefs that form so predominant a part of it, dealing with exploits of war and the hunt, with kings and captives, with wounded or fleeing animals, with slaughter and revenge and plunder, afford a beginning point nearer to the emergence of the human race from savagery.

The purposeful art of Babylonia and Assyria is the healthy product of the ruler by brute power. In it one recognizes a driving force very common in Western art: the successful adventurer and conqueror seeking self-glorification, setting up a record of his exploits, a warning to the weak and the envious, an advertisement of his physical prowess. There is no mystery here, no effort spent on the subtle expression of vague mystic stirrings in the artist's soul.

There is no doubt from the evidence that the Assyrian or Babylonian artist goes into battle and the hunt at the king's side, that he observes victor and vanquished, hunter and hunted, and takes orders as to how he shall interpret, select, record. There is little time to invite the soul, little freedom for expanding the creative urge. He sets the happening down realistically and in a way that will glorify the king's name and ornament the king's walls.

He does not forget his birthright entirely. After all, at bottom he is still an artist, something more than *mere* recorder. He adds a modicum of composition, style, craftsmanship, finish—else his work would not speak to us of today with a certain eloquence. To observed truth he adds a little expressive truth out of himself. But, unlike Egyptian art, which lives strongly, with an inward vitality brought up out of the depths of stone and the artist's sense of image, Assyrian-Babylonian sculpture has this inward vitality at almost its lowest vibration, while muscular life is shown at its most intense. It is literally the muscular man who is celebrated. The arms and legs swell with power, the shoulders are broad and strong. The gods, too, are athletic, bull-necked, with bulging biceps and virile beards.

Later the king-figure becomes stereotyped, invariably appears monumental among his pygmy followers, always wears the same fixed expression. Even the gods are more individualized. So are the little votive figures—though the religious subjects gradually disappear during the twenty-three hundred years of Mesopotamian domination of the Near East. In the end the animals are the most human part of Assyrian art.

Along with monumental expression there develops a more intimate body of works, graceful and delicate, and cut free from the necessity to illustrate and instruct. In the minor and useful arts and in miniature sculptures, especially seals, the design is often finely decorative, the craftsmanship expert, and the object lastingly appealing. This is particularly true of the early or Sumerian period, when the sense of design is firm and the motive fresh, before the artist's intention and integrity have been disciplined and therefore weakened.

The Eastern Mediterranean Cultures

The pageant of earliest civilized art unfolds against the geographical backdrop of a single restricted part of the world in a small measure of time. The scene is the land touching upon the Eastern end of the Mediterranean Sea; the time the centuries on either side of 3000 B.C.

The development of the cave art of the Reindeer Age is unexplained and perhaps always

will be, and there is an unbridged gap between the widespread Neolithic art (of the Polished-Stone Age) and the first art products of civically organized peoples; but we do know that the latter appeared earliest in Mesopotamia and Egypt, two fertile valleys separated by less than a thousand miles, with only the lands of Syria and Palestine between them. Taking them together as a single Mediterranean region—and perhaps adding to them Persia and the adjoining Asiatic steppes—we have here the cradle of historic art. We can trace from these beginnings the motives, techniques, and styles that reached their maturity in the buildings and sculpture and minor arts of Babylonia, Assyria, Persia, and Egypt, and were diffused through bordering cultures to Greece and Rome and thus to all the West on the one hand, and to India and, less influentially, to the Far East on the other.

The relationship between the art of Mesopotamia and that of Egypt is indicated again and again in the unfolding of three thousand years of their known history. Whether it was the people of the Nile or of the Euphrates who "invented" conscious expression through art as a part of maturing civilization and taught the other, is still debated. The weight of the evidence is a little in favor of Sumeria.

The findings in both regions, if they are of a period before 3200 B.C., can be only tentatively dated, and enthusiastic archaeologists, loyal to one or the other valley, make conflicting claims. Egypt achieved a first-rate art much sooner than Mesopotamia, and its art as a whole was destined to surpass that of the other; but both emerged almost at the same time, and the Mesopotamian contribution is perhaps the more illuminating for the student, a better introduction to the "world stream."

At this time, when the peoples of North Africa and western Asia were thus jointly giving the first impulse to the current of art, Europe still lay in Stone Age savagery and obscurity. Our forefathers there were "prehistoric," without written language, without metals, without communal organization or organized warfare. Waves of cultural enlightenment and artistic invention were to circle from the two fertile valleys, and

Worshiper. Stone.
Sumeria.
*Oriental Institute,
University of Chicago*

from the lands between, until first the Aegean isles and shores, then the body of Greece, and finally all of Europe, were "civilized." This process we shall see graphically demonstrated with the spread of art. The question, why did conscious art and civilization first emerge where they did? cannot be answered in terms of a single racial achievement. The pioneer civilized artists appeared among peoples who cannot be proved to have been racially pure. Prehistoric Egypt was probably a melting-pot with ingredients from the Negro south and the Semite east as well as from the Berber peoples of the Libyan coast; while in early Babylonian history the

Sumerians and Semites are almost equally evident, with problematic Indo-Iranian ("Aryan") elements pushing in from the north and the Aryan-speaking Persians from the east.

But if we accept the evidence that civilization began in this eastern Mediterranean area, it is fairly easy to see why, of all the possible inhabited lands, the two river valleys fostered invention and continuous aesthetic consciousness, and why the chain of recorded human history began there. Settled life and the impulse to the arts came where men had lightened the heavy burden of working and fighting. The two fertile valleys—the Fertile Crescent of Mesopotamia and the Fertile Ribbon that is Egypt—invited men to permanent occupation, won them away from nomadism and the insecurities of the hunting life, and led them to cooperative effort in irrigation and communal ordering of everyday existence. The face of the land, its rich soils, abundant waters, and nurturing sunshine, facilitated pastoral and agricultural development, encouraged group thinking and social organization, and afforded a margin of leisure above work which is essential to artistic creation.

Babylonia was the "garden eastward in Eden" planted by "the Lord God," blessed with abundant water and "every tree that is pleasant to the sight and good for food." Here men found that life could be made rich and easy. By group organization they could repel invaders. By the invention of a system of irrigation they actually did increase fertility until the grain yielded a two hundredfold and three hundredfold return to the sower, as Herodotus tells us.

Perhaps it was this marvelous fruitfulness, bringing men an unparalleled margin of leisure, that fostered the development of two epochal inventions, craftswork in metal and a written language. Or perhaps it was because they had had the intelligence to work metals and invent a pictorial language that the dwellers in Eden had also the initiative to plan control of their river waters by canals and dikes. One way or the other, the first civilized culture developed on the lower Euphrates. Here was the beginning of the chain of known art that reaches unbrokenly down to the Europe and Asia and Americas of five millenniums later.

It is well to hold clearly in mind the geographical features of the land that cradled the culture of both East and West, to picture the Fertile Crescent as it arches over the Arabian Peninsula—one end dipping southward down through Syria and Palestine toward Egypt; the other southeastward, its tip enclosing the silt-plains where the Tigris and the Euphrates mingle their waters at the edge of the Persian Gulf; and the center embracing the main Assyrian valley between the two rivers as they flow south and east from the mountains of Armenia to the Gulf. Of the three rough divisions within

the Crescent, the western portion enters only incidentally into early settled history, though the Syrians and Phoenicians were later to take on civilization from their neighbors, both east and west, and become carriers of the crafts and skills. The central division, roughly Assyria, also was slow to catch up with the civilization of the more advanced Babylonians to the southward, and these in turn traced their finest institutions and arts back to the small section known, before its incorporation into the later Babylonian kingdom, as Sumeria. It is in the southeast tip of the Crescent that history first appears.

Sumeria and Its Art

Sumeria was an aggregate of city-states, on the Euphrates close to the Persian Gulf. The Sumerians are no longer supposed to have been the earliest inhabitants of the region, but rather "invaders," though it is still undecided whence they came and just whom they displaced. At the dawn of known history they were dominant, giving their name to the section; contributing the earliest and most lasting of the written languages of the region (the Sumerian pictograph writing was father to the cuneiform characters that were to spread over so much of the Near East); developing skills in the metals before their neighbors; using the wheel; and taking epochal steps forward in civil organization, warfare, law, and the arts. It is possible that they came from the Iranian Plateau to the east, bringing these accomplishments with them from some still undiscovered Persian or Scythian birthplace of culture.

Professor C. Leonard Woolley, who has done more than any other, as archaeologist and writer, to dig the Sumerians out of obscurity and place them prominently in the first episode of the pageant of human civilization, is willing to give them precedence over the once vaunted Akkadians, or true Babylonians, as founders of Asiatic civilization. He then goes further, placing them before the Egyptians, as pioneer lawgivers, as inventors, and as artists. He points out that in the period when the communities of Sumeria were flourishing—say, from 3500 B.C.—Egypt still

Two friezes from Sumerian building, c. 3100 B.C. The one below is a milking scene.
University Museum, Philadelphia

had no metals, had not invented or discovered the potter's wheel, and owned no written language.

As to the legendary origins of the Sumerian arts, Professor Woolley quotes a Babylonian named Berossus, of about 300 B.C., who stated that the towns of Sumeria were founded by a race of half-men, half-fish, who came out of the Persian Gulf under the leadership of Oannes; and "all things that make for the amelioration of life were bequeathed to men by Oannes, and since that time no further inventions have been made." And Berossus, in fact, mentions just those accomplishments which modern historians count most critical in the rise of man: agriculture, use of metals, and writing. It is likely that these advances developed together, in one push forward of the human intelligence; and the earliest datable evidences of them are found in Sumeria.

Excavations at Tepe Gawra in Iraq in 1936-37 brought to light the foundation walls of a "pre-Sumerian" acropolis, dated before 4000 B.C., and relics indicating that the "Painted Pottery Peoples," long considered primitive except in their mastery of ceramic art, "enjoyed an advanced and balanced civilization." The evidence is offered of planned community building, even of monumental architecture, with interior piers and pilasters; of religious activities centered in temples; of seals; of the first datable gold beads, these

representing also the first metal work; of musical instruments; of an earthen jar bearing "the first landscape painting"—all ascribed to a time five hundred years or more before the date previously accepted as marking the dawn of history and civilized art. In other words, Mesopotamian peoples who had been identified vaguely as of the late Stone Age cultural level are now known to have had many of the cultural attainments commonly accepted as pertaining to civilization. The excavators at Tepe Gawra, sent out by the University of Pennsylvania in collaboration with the American School of Oriental Research, had already, over a period of years, uncovered several "world's oldest" cities. They have expressed the *hope* of finding evidences of first settled or recognizably civilized man at levels to be dated 7000 or 7500 B.C.

The Stele of the Vultures mentioned at this chapter's opening, choked with narrative action and devoted to a patriotic lesson, is an example of late Sumerian art, but is less representative of the spirit of that art as a whole than of a strain that was to survive, by the chances of unfolding history, and to be expanded in the succeeding Babylonian and Assyrian developments. The rather sophisticated little animal figures, in the round and in low relief, the shell plaques and the seals, are more in character as products of the *early* city-states' studios. The spirit is in general more human and more ingratiating than anything in the later and larger cultures into which the Sumerian was to be absorbed. There is more of frankly decorative art here, and less of boastful and violent narrative, more ornament, more love of miniature refinement, and there are more animals—all typically Persian and Scythian rather than true Mesopotamian traits. And, curiously enough, there is in one phase of art in early Sumeria a degree of unforced realism, of fidelity to surface nature, not to be surpassed until Greek times. That is, in the centuries before 3000 B.C. men were making statuettes and reliefs so characteristically "lifelike" that not for twenty-five centuries would imitative skill go higher.

The art works that survive have to do mostly with gods and kings and upper-class personages. They are votive figures, reliefs commemorative of honors paid to the gods, and articles of luxury and show. Architecture yields up only ruins too fragmentary to warrant detailed speculation regarding the "looks" of monumental or domestic buildings, though it is a fact technically of great significance that the Sumerians were using rudimentary arches and vaults several centuries before 3000 B.C. The common building material was the clay brick, since the country lacks both stone and wood in any abundance, and the architectural forms were doubtless plain and block-like, as befits brick construction. The earliest feature of monumental building seems to have been the temple tower, perhaps an artificial substitute for the hilltop from which the gods had been worshiped, and this may have been ancestor equally of Assyrian ziggurat, Moslem dome and minaret, and Christian campanile and steeple. The ziggurat at Ur, as well as later ones in Babylon and Assyria, was constructed in successively smaller stories, the one at the top bearing an altar. Access from the ground (or platform) below was usually by ramps. The "building" was really a shaped hill, without rooms—except for the temple on top—a sort of stepped pyramid.

Low relief sculpture was freely used on building walls and, in materials less heavy than stone, as ornament on luxurious furniture; and the independent tablet-monuments, or stelae, gradu-

Head. Stone. Sumeria, c. 2500 B.C.
Fogg Museum of Art

ally became common. It is likely that the world's treasure of sculptured works from Sumeria will be greatly increased, since only a few sites have up to now been excavated—the most important at Ur, Lagash, Eridu, Kish, and Nippur—but from the examples that have come to light one can already form a picture of societies that delighted in refined workmanship in metals and stone and shell, and in colorful decoration and intricate pattern; and there are a few works that indicate a considerable sense of sheer plastic invention.

The reliefs commonly known as early Sumerian—such as the Tablet of Ur-Nina—and made well before 3000 B.C. are generally marked by crudities not to be described as mere archaisms or as naïve distortions for direct sculptural effect. They are, rather, downright inept and uncraftsmanlike. But the frieze of figures of men and animals once affixed to a wall of a temple at al'Ubaid near Ur, made of limestone reliefs set into darker stone panels, is uniquely effective and engagingly decorative. The façade seems to have been extraordinarily enriched with various types of sculpture in addition to mosaic inlays. Remains have been found of several of the limestone friezes, and there were extensive copper reliefs, including a large hammered panel over the door, depicting a lion-headed eagle and two stags, and a pictorial frieze in copper. Around a

Donkey. Mascot on Sumerian rein-guide.
From Queen Shub-ad's chariot, 3100 B.C.

ledge below these several relief features was a row of oxen in the round, made of beaten sheet copper over wood. The building is of the middle of the thirty-first century B.C.

While monumental works of an earlier date are lacking, there is some indication that this art had been preceded by a long development of mature drawing and carving. The shell-plaques attached to gameboards, musical instruments, and furniture afford evidence of exceptionally spirited patterning, with figures at once characteristic and cunningly conventionalized for heraldic effect. Sometimes these are in carved low relief against a contrasting background. There are also patterns made up of squares of shell with spirited linear designs engraved or incised. The lines were filled with a red or sometimes black paste to make the drawing stand out clear and crisp, by a process paralleled forty centuries later in European *niello* work.

There are statues in the round, of the true Sumerian period, which give evidence of an aptitude for the full-sculptural medium, although

there is nothing that approaches the nobility and the subtle aesthetic expressiveness of the Egyptian statues of the Old Kingdom period. A priest in the attitude of adoration is one of the true sculptural votive figures, with real "feeling for the stone," and without the later stiff formalization. But from the time of this unique statue of the thirty-first century, down to the time of King Gudea, about the twenty-fifth century, there seems very little change in the conventions of the art, and certainly no great gain in mastery. Some of the later full-length statues of King Gudea are massive, effectively simplified and reposeful. But there is little of the inner sculptural life, of the plastic expressiveness, that so distinguishes contemporary rock-cutting along the Nile.

It is rather in the field of figurines, and particularly when animals are dealt with, that a distinctive excellence is achieved. There is, for example, the figure of a donkey which Queen Shub-ad had attached as a mascot to the rein-guide on the yoke of her chariot asses. It is a pretty bit of realistic sculpture, showing canny observation, but with due regard to the figure's use and placing too. Sculpturally appealing also are certain bulls' heads in silver and copper. Some of these were ornaments on lyres and perhaps should not be judged independently. But the values are of the sort that render the fragments effective even when wrenched from the original context. They are massively true to the original model, but also compositionally felt and sculpturally realized.

Incidentally, the modern world owes its knowledge of Queen Shub-ad's donkey and these bulls' heads, and the shell-plaques from gameboards, to one rich find of excavators at Ur, and their preservation to a custom common during early human civilization. According to the etiquette of the First Dynasty, about 3100 B.C., when the queen died a goodly number of her ladies-in-waiting were entombed in her burial chamber in the royal cemetery, to give her what aid and comfort they could in the after-life. With them were walled in such earthly treasures as the queen's chariot and harps and chaplets and toilet articles.

The art in general, of headdresses, jewelry,

Mosaicked harp
with bull's head in gold,
from Queen Shub-ad's grave.
*University Museum,
Philadelphia*

gold vessels, and statues, runs to excessive ornamentation and lack of taste in adapting observed natural detail to decorative or plastic purposes. It is, in fact, already a decadent standard of art that we have here, of a time when the ability to formalize beautifully, common to so many primitive peoples, had passed into florid overabundance and into a striving after exact representation for its own sake. Some of the discovered chaplets are like flowered wreaths copied directly from nature into gold and other precious stuffs. Each leaf is true to its botanical model; every vein is shown. Art is no longer creation nor selective adaptation, but imitation of natural beauty.

A miniature art originated by the Sumerians, and to be perpetuated through the Babylonian-Assyrian supremacy, was the sculpturing of cylindrical seals in low relief. Writing in Mesopotamia was done on wet clay slabs, which later hardened into permanent tablets. It is owing to the indestructible character of these tablet documents and "books" that the twentieth-century world knows so much of the details of Sumerian and later Mesopotamian literature and life. To sign the clay, or mark it with his device, the important personage carried a personal seal, and this commonly was ornamental and pictorial. "Every Babylonian," wrote Herodotus, "carries a seal, and a staff carved at the top into the form of an apple, a rose, a lily, an eagle, or a like device."

A small cylinder of hard stone, such as obsidian, agate, or quartz, or of the softer alabaster, was carved as a "negative," in intaglio, so that the impression of it in the clay came out in relief.

Seals. *Oriental Institute, Chicago, and University Museum, Philadelphia*

It usually showed a composition with figures, and very often was a token of the owner's devotion to a certain god. Literally thousands of cylinder seals (not to mention flat, ring, and cone varieties) have been recovered, as well as innumerable clay documents bearing their impressions.

The early examples may show roughly geometrical designs or solar images, and there are also primitive pictographic inscriptions. Certainly soon after 3500 B.C. the figured seals begin to reflect a considerable skill in relief picturing and a high sense of stylization. There is a sharpness, a crisp delineation of separated figures against uninvolved backgrounds, which perfectly belongs to this exquisite lapidary art.

Babylon

When the Sumerian culture as such disappeared, a Semitic people known as the Akkadians, who had long been resident in the north, and indeed in Sumeria itself, prevailed for a time. They are supposed to have possessed a ruder art, and it may well be that they had taken the rudiments of their culture from the Sumerians, merely adapting in grosser form the refinements developed in the city-states of the south.

At any rate, after a period during which the Akkadian-Babylonian and the Sumerian elements were very mixed—there was even a group of Sumerian kings with Akkadian names—there came a union of all the inhabitants from the Gulf of Persia to the city of Babylon, and extensions of domain northward over the Assyrians. Here begins the art more properly known as Babylonian.

Even earlier there had been halting attempts to consolidate the communities of the lower plains, and some temporary empires had been patched together. Sargon of Akkad had brought the Semitic element into power over the Sumerian about 2600 B.C., but there had been no great change in art. King Naram-Sin, third after Sargon, is memorialized in a stele which shows a great advance of realistic figure-delineation and modeling, in stone-cutting with many figures; and there are crumbled evidences of magnificent buildings during the Third Dynasty of Ur. But the differences are by no means epochal in significance, and the examples from this larger Sumerian culture seem less important than those of the early dynasties.

When the Semite King Hammurabi finally hammered one Babylonian empire out of the confusion of quarreling racial groups, out of jealous city-states, each with its own rulers and gods, it was again Sumerian art, rather than anything distinctively Babylonian, that lived on. The city of Babylon now became the capital, giving a new name to the empire, and it was, according to existing records, adorned with palaces and temples magnificently conceived and decorated. Unfortunately later invasions, and the decay of Babylonian power before Hittite, Kassite, and finally Assyrian assaults, completely destroyed the architectural monuments. In 689 B.C., boasts King Sennacherib of Assyria, he razed the city and inundated the ruins. Even the sculpture and minor relics of this period are scarce, and not very important.

The stele containing the Code of Hammurabi, preserved because it was carried away by a Persian conqueror, is one of the most famous archaeological finds of modern times, but its value is primarily sociological. A rounded diorite shaft nearly eight feet in height is inscribed with

3600 lines of cuneiform text, setting forth the laws newly codified by Hammurabi for the just conduct of the people of his kingdom. Above the inscription the stele is adorned with a carved relief, showing the sun-god handing the code down to the king. The workmanship is good and the picturing uninvolved, and somehow the very simplicity of conception makes the work memorable. The standard of official art was thus good, but not distinguished. The stele, hardly more than a routine official work, shows no advance over average Sumerian sculpture; yet it is competent and attractive, considering the date—about 2100 B.C.

It is rather in some of the seals that the best evidence of continuing artistic sensibility exists. In summary it may be said that the two great periods of Mesopotamian art came before and after the Babylonian political supremacy, and that only the minor arts continued in richly expressive phases as a link between them.

The Art of Assyria

Striking work does not reappear until leadership has passed to the Assyrians of the upper Mesopotamian Valley. The Semitic peoples there —origins unknown—had coalesced into something loosely national several centuries earlier, and had maintained their own character, and, to an extent, their own institutions, under Babylonian domination, while doubtless assimilating Babylonian-Sumerian cultural traits. Shortly after 1300 B.C. they were making a bid for the rule of the entire Mesopotamian Empire. It was, however, only after four more centuries of changing fortunes that, in 885 B.C., there came the dawn of the era of Assyrian imperial magnificence and expansion, inaugurated by the king-god Ashurnatsirpal.

The magnificence and the glory were very militaristic, and in this period we see a wholehearted devotion to art concerned with conqueror-kings and wars and hunts. The heavenly deities, always a shifting galaxy in the ancient Near East, are rearranged to bring a war-god to supreme position. Campaign follows campaign

Stone figure in attitude of adoration. Sumerian. *Louvre*

under successive great monarchs—Sargon II, Sennacherib, Esarhaddon, and finally Ashurbanipal —until even Egypt is conquered; and the exploits of each campaign must be recorded by court artists and scribes. More blood flows in this pictorial art than in any other in world history.

The era is summed up in the architectural splendors and sculptural adornments of the palaces of Sennacherib and Ashurbanipal at Nineveh. There are other works, to be sure: statues and vases and seals. Even the sculptured reliefs of the palace walls are more than a depiction of violent exploits. We can read in them of gardens and plants, of fishing, excursions, and feasts, of gods and love, of luxurious carpets and richly embroidered garments, and of women and children. There is here a mine of interest, not only for the student of manners and customs but for the botanist and ethnologist. In a depicted

King Ashurnatsirpal and Attendant. Stone relief from wall of the king's palace,
Nimrud, 9th century B.C. *Louvre*

group of tribute-bearers the characteristics of each
physical type can be recognized: the Jews, for instance, show those striking facial traits that can
be seen in some Jewish people to this day. (The
time of Sennacherib is the age of the prophecies
of Isaiah.) But in the subject-matter of the reliefs
war is first, hunting a good second, and the rest of
life an incidental third.

Sennacherib transformed the hamlet of Nineveh into the capital of an empire, possibly to
avoid developed cities and elaborate palaces associated with earlier kings. There he set out to
build distinctively and gloriously in his own
name. There he erected for himself "the palace
that has no rival," which was actually its official
name.

The palaces of the Assyrian kings were more
than places of royal residence and imperial business. Long before, the rulers had claimed divine

sanction if not divine heritage: the king was part
god and directly related by function or birth to
the supreme national deity. So the temple was a
wing of the palace, or perhaps its very heart. But
a wise and practical king did not leave too much
of the business of foresight and protection to the
gods. The temple-palace was a fortress as well.

There must have been a striking difference in
visual effect between the outside fortified walls
and towers, plain and grim, and the pomp and
magnificence of decoration and life within. A
whole cityful of favored people dwelt there:
nobles, defenders, favorites, politicians. For the
king's quarters and those of his wives, the gods,
and their priests, the appointments were sumptuous, but the utilitarian outside brick walls were
comparatively sheer and blank—a combination to
be noted often in later history, in Byzantine
church, medieval keep, Florentine palace, and

Hunting Scene. King Ashurnatsirpal's palace, Nimrud.
Stone relief, 9th century B.C. *British Museum*

Spanish castle. A ceremonial doorway brought the color and enrichment of the interior to the façade in flanking sculpture and inset copper reliefs, and in narrow bands of glazed brick that continued out along the fortress walls. The traditional architectural features were, in most particulars, from the Sumerian by way of the Babylonian, and the ritual ziggurat or tower dominated; but the sentinel figures at the main entry are said to be of Hittite origin. And of course there were luxurious embellishments from farther east. Already, too, there had been for long an exchange of art products with Egypt. All this the Assyrian monarchs brought into one focus, one show of art. It is likely that the designers and craftsmen were largely imported from other countries—Phoenicia and Syria and Egypt—each doing his part without a clear idea of the whole. But the result was grand.

King Sennacherib himself tells of his palace at Nineveh, in a tablet dictated to one of his scribes and translated in our own time at the British Museum: "Cedar, cypress, and pine, timbers from Sinai and thick bars of bronze, did I set in the doorways, and in the dwelling-rooms did I leave openings like lofty windows. Great statues of alabaster wearing crowns with thorns did I set on either side of the doorways . . . great winged bulls of white stone did I carve in the City of Tastriate beyond the Tigris for the great gates, and great trees did I cut from the neighboring forests to build rafts on which to transport them. . . . With much effort and amid many difficulties were they brought to the gates of my palace." The temple portion of the building was especially sumptuous, and was described by the king as "rooms of gold and silver, of crystal, alabaster, and ivory, built for the dwelling of my God."

There is here, in the monarch's planning of dazzling outlays of architectural and decorative works, and in his arrogating to himself as imperial master the products of creative artists, a prototype of Hadrian and of Louis XIV. But if the "I" of his account is to be taken literally, Sennacherib did indeed have the born constructor's sense of sound engineering and inventive building; for he speaks familiarly of problems of lighting successfully met, in ways that dispelled "the darkness of the old palaces," and of hydraulic inventions that brought running water into the buildings.

Whether he had taste or artistic vision to weld this effort into a unity or a sustained and vigorous style is more open to question. Certainly the winged bulls that he had such trouble with before he got them installed at his front gate were dull and lifeless enough. (Two similar ones, from the palace of Ashurnatsirpal, now repose in the entry hall of the Metropolitan Museum in New York.) And one suspects a very mixed effect in the interiors. They were colorful and showy, no doubt, with sculptured alabaster panels,

Hunting Scene. Ashurbanipal's palace, Nineveh. *British Museum*

glazed-tile insets, painted stucco murals, and lots of furnishings set around. But the restorations of the archaeologists and the recovered fragments themselves will not convince the modern observer of a subtly designed ensemble or a distinctively beautiful style.

The obsession with pain, torture, and conquest is illustrated particularly in the alabaster reliefs with which the brick walls were lined inside the main rooms. Some are of Sennacherib's time. The ones better known to the public are of Ashurbanipal's era, two reigns later. (An extensive and fascinating series has long been exhibited in the British Museum.)

There is no reason to read sadism into these records of violence and suffering; they demonstrate rather the candid realism of rulers who lived by a philosophy of "might makes right." The king has spread out a picture-book of his career as he would like his subjects to think of it. His predecessors were depicted trampling their dead enemies or holding nets filled with severed heads. His artists must show more heads in his net and greater heaps of the slaughtered and trampled. It is a point of honor that they outdo all earlier chroniclers in setting forth the magnitude of his conquests. They conveniently forget any defeats and reverses—what patriotic artist does not?—and they exaggerate the numbers of the enemies slain or of the lions killed.

They convey the grisly lessons of war effec-tively and in detail. But it is when they come to the depiction of animals in the hunt that they display deep emotional feeling, as well as a more sensitive hand in delineation. The human figure is almost without exception stiffly conventional, even wooden. But the animals are observed with a sort of cold sympathy and are superbly drawn. They are living, nobly strong, lithe. Most lifelike of all are the hunted lions when they are wounded. The artist has observed these dying beasts with a camera eye and has got down the salient and telltale facts, the drag of paralyzed legs, the snarling jaws, the fury of the final leap. Today we cannot remember the prowess of the king without also remembering his cruelty, his disposition to boast of bloody slaughter. The lions run a straighter course to our admiration and pity.

The merit here is, of course, one of realism. The reliefs touch a high spot in pictorial sculpture, but one perhaps not so high as the Victorian discoverers of the Nineveh treasures judged. The stone murals constitute a remarkable achievement; they tell stirring stories in an idiom ornamentally formalized, if a bit heavy, with thrusts into compelling realism at intervals; but in general they lack the architectural unity of superlatively great sculpture.

Within a traditional formalization there is disturbing reversion to naturalistic imitation for its own sake. Every rosette on a costume is worked out minutely, every nail on a hand, all the reins

Wounded Lioness. Detail from Ashurbanipal's palace. *British Museum*

from charioteer to horses, and every feather in a wing. Seldom does the placing of the figures on the background, or the grouping, approach the intuitive compositional sense long before displayed by Egyptian sculptors. We are aware of the achievement of records as colossal and audacious as the kingly dictators could have desired. But we are seldom aware of the artist's vision transcending his mission and his materials.

But perhaps it is enough of distinction that the great Assyrian imperialists thus generously subsidized artists, let them live, at the price of turning their art to the service of king and state; that thus early in the rise of human civilization those few men who existed for the expression of an inner vision and urge—sculptors, decorators, and poets—were permitted to continue at their work, no matter on what terms, beside priests, merchants, and soldiers. The point we have reached in history is still before the childhood of Greek art, which used to be counted the very cradle of serious aesthetic activity. And though

we may feel disturbed at the thought of an art bound to dynastic purpose and a king's personal publicity, we know that it was as much a victim of established Babylonian-Assyrian tradition as of Ashurbanipal's selfishness. As a matter of fact, there is other evidence of Ashurbanipal's genuine interest in the things of the mind. He took an epochal step forward when he gathered documents and books and established one of the earliest known libraries. The 22,000 inscribed tablets, collected at his order to preserve accumulated knowledge in fields of religious tradition, scientific discovery, history, and general literature, and systematically catalogued, have been found in the ruins of the palace at Nineveh. Ashurbanipal himself made a special point of the fact that, as a prince, he had learned reading and writing, in addition to the more noble arts of riding and hunting and ruling.

After the fall of Assyria, which came about, the historians say, because too many men were taken from the farms and impressed into the

Lion. Glazed terra-cotta relief from the Street of Parades, Babylon, c. 570 B.C.
Metropolitan Museum of Art, New York

army, the ruling power passed southward again, to Babylon, now resurgent under another invading people, the Chaldeans. These were destined to rebuild the Mesopotamian empire, to dominate the Near East briefly, then to see their state collapse because the ruling class overreached the limits of safe exploitation. This downfall marked the end of Babylonian-Assyrian independence, the last stand of the local Semites against a succession of foreign overlords; foreign domination began in 538 B.C. with the Persians, and continued into the twentieth century, when Iraq was under a British mandate. In the records the Chaldean Empire is sometimes known as the Neo-Babylonian Empire.

The Chaldeans

Here art is again summed up in the magnificent court of a ruler. In rebuilding Babylon, Nebuchadnezzar erected new temples to the ancient gods and constructed a palace of surpassing splendor. All the essential features of Assyrian monumental architecture seem to have been retained; it was the further push into luxuriousness and grandeur that gave Nebuchadnezzar's achievement distinction—and world fame. The richly gardened terraces of the palace were the celebrated "hanging gardens" which the Greeks counted among the Seven Wonders of the World.

And probably the temple tower, or an earlier one on its site, was the Biblical Tower of Babel. (It was Nebuchadnezzar who first destroyed Jerusalem and carried the Hebrews into captivity in Babylonia.)

Today the art lover and the student of archaeology have uncovered far more than legend to testify to the magnificence of the city constructed by Nebuchadnezzar. For the ruins have been searched, detailed drawings have been made of palace and temple, and the famous Ishtar Gate, which stood at the end of the Street of Parades, was transferred and rebuilt in a museum in Berlin. On the brick towers one may see the polychrome design, with animals carefully depicted in high coloring. The effect is gay, the drawing admirable, the craftsmanship impeccably expert.

But sculpture has lost its structural relationship to architecture. Each figure is independent, and the items are merely added up in symmetrical rows. Plastic initiative has run out long before this. True formal creation has ceased. And as one looks back to the early Sumerian art that had developed a few miles to the south nearly thirty centuries earlier, one feels that the mighty empires that succeeded those tiny city-states added not a great deal to the progress of expression in art. Just as, in the realm of civil organization, the ideas of bigness, expansion, wealth, and power carried state after state into swollen empires certain to collapse—though indubitably advancing

The Ishtar Gate.
Babylon, c. 570 B.C.
*Near-Asiatic Museum,
Berlin*

the quantitative sum of civilization—so the ideas of bigness, show, and luxury carried the arts into disunity and floridity. In comparison with anything found on the site of the new Babylon, the sculpture of Ur and Lagash is fresh and strong and adventurous, though 3000 years nearer primitive art.

The imperial art of both Assyria and Neo-Babylon, then, is at the sophisticated terminus of the long road, where men no longer see the work as a creative entity, as a single self-sufficient formal achievement; they lose the importance of the architectural whole, the plastic synthesis. They are diverted by marvelously imitated detail, by flourish and ostentation. This is the art of luxury, of refined divertissement, of royal advertising, the typical example of art as a record of a run-out civilization.

The Hebrews, a people puritanical and—in ancient history—insensitive to the suavities of the visual arts, loathed the spuriousness of the show put on by this last Babylon. Saint John the Divine, in the apocalyptic vision of the end of the world, makes the city of Babylon a symbol of all that is abandoned and iniquitous, and incidentally affords a glimpse of the luxurious abominations—including some innocent arts—spawned under the last of her kings:

And after these things I saw another angel come down from heaven . . .
And he cried mightily with a strong voice, saying, Babylon the great is fallen, is fallen, and is become the habitation of devils, and the hold of every foul spirit. . . .
And the kings of earth, who have . . . lived deliciously with her, shall bewail her, and lament

Bull Capital. Palace of Artaxerxes, Susa. Persian, 4th century B.C. *Louvre*

for her, when they see the smoke of her burning,

Standing afar off for the fear of her torment, saying, Alas, alas, that great city Babylon, that mighty city! For in one hour is thy judgment come.

And the merchants of the earth shall weep and mourn over her; for no man buyeth their merchandise any more:

The merchandise of gold, and silver, and precious stones, and of pearls, and fine linen, and purple, and silk, and scarlet, and all thyine wood, and all manner vessels of ivory, and all manner vessels of most precious wood, and of brass, and iron, and marble,

And cinnamon, and odours, and ointments, and frankincense, and wine, and oil, and fine flour, and wheat, and beasts, and sheep, and horses, and chariots, and slaves, and souls of men.

And the fruits that thy soul lusted after are departed from thee, and all things which were dainty and goodly are departed from thee, and thou shalt find them no more at all.

The end, according to Daniel, came like this: One night in the year 539 B.C. Belshazzar, last king of Babylonia, "made a great feast to a thousand of his lords, and drank wine before the thousand. Belshazzar, whiles he tasted the wine, commanded to bring the golden and silver vessels which his father Nebuchadnezzar had taken out of the temple which was in Jerusalem; that the

Tribute Bearers. Stairway relief in ruins of the palace of Darius, Persepolis. Persian

king and his princes, his wives, and his concubines, might drink therein."

But the royal guests drank not to the God whose temple had been despoiled. Instead they "praised the gods of gold, and of silver, of brass, of iron, of wood, and of stone." In the same hour there appeared a hand, writing on the wall, and Daniel read out the meaning to King Belshazzar: "Thou art weighed in the balances and art found wanting. . . . Thy kingdom is divided, and given to the Medes and Persians." That night "was Belshazzar the king of the Chaldeans slain. And Darius the Median took the kingdom."

The Persians

Where did these alien conquerors come from? The Persian Cyrus, who should be substituted for Darius in Daniel's account (and Nabonidus

for Belshazzar), was the ruler over a small country and a comparative handful of people, whose ideal, said Herodotus, was "to ride and to shoot and to tell the truth." He conquered the Medes, blood relatives of the Persians, the rich Lydians under King Croesus, and finally Babylonia, before he died. His son Cambyses pushed out the bounds of the Empire until even Egypt was a vassal. Under the later Darius the Great, the Persian Empire was to become the broadest of pre-Roman dominions.

Up to this time the Persians had had but meager art of their own, compared with the Chaldean display. They now saw the gorgeous palaces and temples of their subject peoples, at Babylon and Nineveh and Thebes, and doubtless their hearts began to yearn for grandeur, for luxurious embellishment, for extravagant and impressive art.

There is an ancient record which tells how the

Ibex. Part of bronze horse-bit, Luristan, Persia. *University Museum, Philadelphia*

materials of, and the artisans for, the palace at Susa were brought from a great many places: from nearby Babylonia and Assyria, from Lydia and Caria, from Egypt in Africa, and from Bactria up toward the Siberian steppes. The various stylistic features to be expected from the many collaborators can be found in the structures at Persepolis and Susa, the first expressions of monumental art in Persia. The palaces are on the Babylonian scale and follow closely the terrace or platform plan. There is something of the Egyptian hypostyle hall (a hall whose roof rests on columns) in the audience chambers. The sculptured murals point directly back to Assyria, both in their conception and in their shallow-relief technique; they are unmistakably in the line of descent from Ashurnatsirpal's galleries of documentation.

And yet there is something new, a different atmosphere. The relief figures are better disposed, more expertly patterned on the backgrounds. Certainly there is less interest in naturalistic detail. Observed characteristics and familiar peculiarities are less insisted upon. There is a hint of an elegant formalism. The Assyrian-Babylonian descent into realism is stayed; the direction is reversed toward formal and decorative ordering. All this is graphically shown in the panel from the frieze of the *Tribute-Bearers,* which is a feature of the stairway leading to the audience hall of the palace at Persepolis. Especially evident is the new sense of elegance, of compositional unity.

The columns of the audience hall of the palace at Susa were topped by capitals, each one carrying two kneeling oxen. Again the sculptured composition has values not seen in Mesopotamian work. Obviously a fresh spirit has come into sculpture. The animals are vigorous, graceful, alert, stylized. In the light of later work, this must be marked as typically Persian.

Just so did a new spirited vitality enter into the sentinel figures in the gateway of the palace of Xerxes at Persepolis. Studied as they obviously were from the standard Babylonian winged fig-

Lions. Stone column-base, excavated near Antioch. C. 1000 B.C. Hittite

ures, they signalize a feeling for animal sculpture that had been lost, perhaps, when the Assyrians took over the archetype from the Hittites. The Persians brought back something of the northern spirited manipulation of decorative elements.

A basic distinction in art methods is here made apparent. The Assyrians and Babylonians, in spite of an occasional wooden sort of conventionalization, leaned toward a realistic art that is akin to the Cretan and Mycenaean, the prototypes of the Graeco-Roman or classic development. Persia, after sifting out the ingredients gathered up from captive peoples, turned in the opposite direction, toward an art decorative in intention, formalized in aspect, and rich in color and incidental patterning. Whether the impulse may not have entered farther back, in a Scythian or Indo-Iranian reservoir of Aryan cultural beginnings, is a question to be considered in later chapters, and especially in Chapter XII, where the main story of Persian art is told. Pertinent here is a mention (with an illustration) of the vigorous, formalized sculpture of Luristan, long since

achieved by a once nomadic people settled in a part of Persia. The Lurs had been inventors of a distinctive and spirited animal art related, on stylistic grounds, to the unrealistic and rhythmic art of the Scythians.

Unlike the large sculptured gate-monsters, and the architectural capitals, the polychromed glazed reliefs on the Susa palace walls are wholly Babylonian in feeling and aspect. The animals and the bowmen might have been drawn on the clay by the same hand that did the bulls and lions of the Ishtar Gate.

In another direction, notably in the tomb of Cyrus at Pasagardae, there is a foreign sobriety and restraint, due no doubt to the Persian king's admiration for Greek culture. The building seems to indicate that Grecian architects had been imported. But this Western influence was destined, like the Babylonian realism, to disappear under what was soon to become a typical Oriental way of art.

If Persian culture at this time—that of the Achaemenids, the dynasty founded by Cyrus—

Stag Hunt. Stone, Malatya (ancient Milid), c. 12th century B.C. Hittite. *Louvre*

was partly derivative, a foundation was quickly laid for one of the great distinctive art-styles of the future. Persia was to have a long and noble history in the creative fields, from the time of the next revival, the Sassanian (c. 226-641 A.D.), to the seventeenth century. Persian art, more than any other, was to determine the style-marks of Byzantine and Moslem art.

The Hittites

The art of the Hittites, though influenced by work from several far places, was most closely related to that of the Mesopotamians. The Hittite seals were patently reflective of Assyrian models. But the main body of the art uncovered in Hittite cities is of independent and prior origin. It consists especially of bas-relief sculptures cut in stone—these were to be copied and refined by the Assyrians until they became the marvelous mile-long murals of the palaces at Nineveh—and free-standing sphinxes that likewise were to be adopted, as gateway guardians, by the Mesopo-

tamians and, after them, the Persians. For a great people, highly skilled in war and diplomacy, Hittite expression in art, while strong, simple, and forthright, is undistinguished in technique and limited in imagination. Its character, however, is unmistakable.

The Hittites, at least partly an Indo-European migrant group, made their civilization in the "land of Hatti," the high, mountainous area of Anatolia in Asia Minor, where they became the first people to mine and use iron. They were the "sons of Heth" of the Bible. About 2000 B.C. they began organizing widely scattered city-states, and eventually forged an "empire" that spread throughout Northern Syria and well down toward Palestine. In the 1600s B.C. they were strong enough to overthrow a Babylonian dynasty. Several centuries later they were instrumental in the downfall of the Egyptian empire. Through wars, treaties, alliances, and dynastic marriages, they came more than once, before their empire collapsed, near to a first place in world power.

The state religion—let us say, about 1500 B.C.—

Figured silver dish. Phoenician. *Walters Art Gallery, Baltimore*

was one of nature-worship. The weather-god and the sun-goddess appeared at the top of an amazingly long list of minor gods representing the elements or natural objects. Each of the federated city-states might have its local god; and indeed "the thousand gods of Hatti" are invoked in state documents and treaties. A great deal of the sculptural art is concerned with these gods, and with religious festivals when the king made official visits of worship to them. In one case a procession of all the gods is presented.

The Hittite artists were specialists in cutting sculpture in natural rock formations. They were many centuries ahead of the Persians who carved out the famous tombs and sculptures at Naksh-I-Rustum (shown on page 254). Although remains of this rock-cut art have been reported from many parts of the old Hittite country, the best known monument is at Yazilikaya, close to Boghazkeui, capital of the Kingdom of Hatti. It is here that a procession of the "thousand gods" was attempted. It is really two processions, on two cliffs that converge upon a central sanctuary.

The bas-reliefs on the open cliffs, possibly because they have been damaged by the weathering of more than three millennia, seem artistically on the simple, heavy side. Better examples of the Hittite genius, perhaps, are to be seen in the bas-reliefs from inside walls, such as those excavated at Carchemish, or the fragment in the Louvre illustrating a stag hunt. These are from a later period of Hittite history, perhaps from the ninth or eighth century B.C. As can be seen from the *Stag Hunt*, the formalization is firmer than in the Mesopotamian murals. There is a tendency to square the figures, and each one is kept uniformly flat against a featureless flat background. Altogether the Hittite "style" shows a better sense of filling space compositionally; but it does, of course, fall far short of the vividness and naturalness of depiction in the latest Assyrian reliefs.

At this time, when the Hittite nation was disappearing from history (though various combinations of Hittite-dominated city-states are heard of down to early Christian times), the countries to the south became known especially for the manufacture of bronze figurines. Syria and Palestine, as also Phoenicia, were on the highroads of commerce and culture, and subject to cross-currents of influence. It is no surprise to find their arts at one time reminiscent of Babylonian work, at another of Mycenaean, with occasional reminders of the distinctive expressiveness of Egypt.

In the twentieth century archaeologists have been systematically digging out the evidences of those borderland civilizations. Phoenicia has left —as far as has been discovered—no art legacy so

valuable as the intellectual one embodied in the alphabet handed down to Western nations, none so distinctive as the tradition of maritime invention and commercial exploration which made famous Sidon and Tyre. Lydia is remembered for the introduction of designed coinage. The fixing of a value relationship between gold and silver coins was appropriately an innovation of the gold-obsessed King Croesus of Lydia. Syria was to enter into art history later as a cradle of Eastern Christian art, and again as a prime center of Moslem rule and culture; but it has left only secondary evidences from the time of the Babylonian and Hittite domination of the Near East. A few statuettes in museum collections are noteworthy for a special reason: they are votive offerings in copper, and perhaps among them are the world's earliest specimens of the human figure represented in metal. The isle of Cyprus was to become a fusing bowl into which the Mycenaean, Ionian, and Babylonian streams poured, and it was to have a more or less distinctive sculptural art, and be in turn a source of influence on the Greeks.

But all these threads are still tangled. It is necessary to go back to the history of Egypt and of the Aegean civilizations before any lucid account is possible.

III: PYRAMID, STATUE, AND
PICTURE IN EGYPT

WHAT IS most characteristic about Egypt is its enduringness. Here the continuous record of man spans three times the age of the Christian civilization—but in nature nothing has changed, neither the ageless Nile, the unfailing flood and recession, the ever-present sun, nor the flanking deserts. Here Mother Earth broods, sustains, continues, and allows no interruption.

Twenty-six known dynasties of native kings had come and gone before Plato visited Egypt. Alexander and the Romans were episodes in a following lesser age, still before Christ was born in nearby Palestine. The Cross came, and centuries later gave way to the Crescent; but the Nile endured, and the ancient Egyptian art endured, for the river and the desert, obscuring men and institutions, find their counterpart only in Egyptian art. In it too the rhythm is slow, ponderous, enduring. Where Western art is brilliant, nervous, staccato, Egyptian art is massive, silent, certain. The rock-cut tombs, the pyramids and the basalt statues, outlast empires. The sun still shines on pyramid, temple, domed mosque, and minaret, and the opened tombs reveal art that is as living, as compelling, as it was forty-five centuries ago.

On the map the fertile ribbon that is Egypt hangs like a pennant shaken from the lower corner of the fertile crescent of Mesopotamia and

Seated figure of King Khafre, detail. *Cairo Museum*

43

Syria. Of all the world, art came earliest to these two valley regions. The reason in each case is the same. Civilization and culture develop where physical living has been made secure, where nature has succored man but has left just enough obstacles to challenge his wits, to enforce cooperation and self-discipline.

It all begins in the fertility of the soil. Before the arts can be conceived and born, men must be able to live without too great hardship, be freed from too exhausting labor. The easy culture of the plow and the permanence of the hearth are indispensable preliminaries, and these the land of Egypt assured.

Egypt is an elongated oasis, a narrow strip of fields marvelously productive when watered, stretching for seven hundred miles between the parched Arabian and Libyan deserts. The strange circumstance of a thread of productive land between unproductive wastes not only eased the work of living but acted as a warranty of security in another way. There was no constant danger of attack from either flank; only the Mediterranean and Equatorial Africa at the two distant ends of the ribbon afforded approach. Between wars the Egyptians enjoyed peace for centuries on end, a case almost unique in the history of man.

Isolation afforded institutions and art a stability and persistence never known in Chaldea and Assyria, or, later, in Persia, Greece, or Rome. Between the first dated kingdom and the Assyrian invasion, twenty-seven centuries later, the succession of native Egyptian kings was broken by only one interregnum of foreign domination. There was time for the slow gestation and development of a typically Egyptian art. Between the amazingly beautiful diorite statue of Khafre and the celebrated portraits of Ikhnaton and his queen, fifteen centuries rolled away. Within a shorter period the art of Greece was born, flowered, withered, was reborn in the show of Rome, and again died.

The Egyptian People

When the people known as Egyptian are discovered in dated history, there is already a body of civilized customs and institutions, of skills and crafts. The Neolithic advance here has been one with that of Asia and Europe, and archaeologists exhibit undated weapons and pottery with all the characteristic Stone Age proportioning, and ornamentation without refinement. When the curtain is really lifted—no one knows how many centuries later, yet forty centuries before Christ—there is already an advanced culture, with agricultural skills, picture writing, manufacture, navigation, and building in brick.

It is usual in dating events in Egyptian history to begin with 4241 B.C. A native historian of the third century B.C. left chronological tables figured to that year. It was then, perhaps, that the first calendar of 365 days was introduced; for the first time the counting of years began.

The First Dynasty, which means merely the first *identified* house of rulers, reigned from about 3400 years before Christ. Then came what is termed the Old Kingdom, established about 2980 B.C. The latter was destined to last through the fall of six ruling houses and eight centuries, and to include one of the world's most fruitful periods of creative art, that in which the great pyramids and the most noble statues were produced.

Egyptologists find it convenient to refer to the Old Kingdom as the golden age of art, and to note roughly two other near-golden ages: in the Middle Kingdom, from about 2000 B.C.; and in the New Kingdom, about 1370 B.C. During the long decline thereafter are found minor renaissances before the typical Egyptian virtues are dissipated under Greek, then Roman, then Islamic domination.

Who were the Egyptian people? What was the racial make-up, what the character of this nation destined to create the first very great body of potent and immortal art? As we first come to know them, the Egyptians are described by ethnologists vaguely as part of a crystallizing Eastern Mediterranean civilization, with fused elements probably from lower (Negro) Africa, from the Semitic lands, and from the African Mediterranean coast (a Berber strain). The evidence is fragmentary and mixed: a Hamitic language, at least one typically Central African deity (a hippopotamus god), and the absence of physical characteristics clearly Semitic or Negro. The chances are that this nation was more than usually the result of the draining of diverse racial groups into a favored land, and of their long intermingling.

The possibility of alien antecedents of Egyptian art is even more in the realm of misty speculation. Certainly the architecture is native, out of the soil and the local trees and stone. Elie Faure has offered with reserve the suggestion that the sculpture of Egypt is a true descendant of the prehistoric Negro idol; that thus, through the later diffusion of the arts of the Nile into Aegean, Greek, and Near Eastern lands, and so over all Europe and across Asia to China, the European and Asiatic artists derived some of the rhythmic sensitivity of the Negro.

Far too much has been written about death, fear, and morbid introspection as determining factors in Egyptian life and art. It is necessary, by way of correction, to emphasize the normal cheerfulness and love of gaiety in the native character. The thought of death did not lie like a pall over the comings and goings, the work and the play, of this essentially sunny people. It is true that gods, god-kings, and their priests, ruled and demanded implicit obedience; that everyone believed that the more important part of existence came after death. The wise man made provision for a carrying over of the normal pleasures of life into that infinitely longer term; and the building that was constructed to last, to outwit accident and time, was the tomb, not the house or palace. But even the sculptured reliefs and painted murals in the tombs often turn from religious and somber subject-matter to record the lighter joys of living; and when tomb offerings were sealed up with the body they were intended not for propitiation of the gods but as an assurance that the deceased might be eternally surrounded with the good foods, the flowers, the arts to which he had been happily accustomed on this earth.

The evidence of the ancient Egyptian cheerfulness, even lightheartedness, came to light with the reading of thousands of routine and literary documents, and with fuller study of sculptured reliefs and mural paintings. Can anyone sur-

round with an atmosphere of gloom or obsessive piety the girl poet who wrote for her lover "the beautiful and gladsome songs of thy sister, whom thy heart loves, as she walks in the fields"? Her daily work is the snaring of wild ducks in the marshes, but in love she forgets to set snares and awkwardly frightens the birds.

> The wild duck scatter far, and now
> Again they light upon the bough
>   And cry to their kind;
> Soon they gather in the sea—
> But unharmed I let them be,
> For love has filled my mind.

Once, "remembering the love-light in thine eyes," she opens the trap to let a bird escape. "What will my angry mother say?" But she sings nevertheless.

The late Arthur Weigall, most human of Egyptologists, particularly stressed the lightheartedness of the dwellers, early and late, in the valley of the Nile. He quoted the love songs that are so like modern lyrics (the one above is paraphrased from his pages), and he insisted upon the sunshine, laughter, and feasting, the pleasure pavilions and gardens and excursion boats. He noted that asceticism was unknown in Egypt before Christian times; forty centuries passed without its corrective or deterring influence. Hathor and Bast, goddesses of pleasure—not in the spiritual sense of the word, the records indicate—were in the normal hierarchy of deities.

The mummies, the rock-cut tombs, and the Book of the Dead misled the earlier investigators. For the tombs and heaviest statues were the first to be dug up, and they survived in greater number because they had been fashioned to endure through eternity. So the Western world deduced that the Nile-dwellers were a somber, funereal-minded, and puritanical people. Only later did the bright jewelry, the decorated beds, the down cushions, the love poems, the lip rouge, and the eye tint come to notice, and the colorful murals picturing hunters and musicians and dancers, flowers and fruits. Doubtless any list of the major and profound works of Egyptian art must begin with the pyramids, the granite and diorite statues, and the sculptured tomb walls. But there are too the everyday arts of insinuating decoration, a range of lovingly shaped wine jars and perfume boxes, and felicitous and colorful pictures of daily life.

There is reason to believe that, if the collective Egyptian mind dwelt on the long sleep of death, it came to a familiar conclusion: that one does well to spend the waking hours of today in the more attainable groves of happiness, with a reasonable regard to the pleasures of the senses. There seems to have been about the usual proportion between innocent heart-freeing diversion and excessive indulgence in drunkenness and sensuality, while the priests assumed the main burden of philosophic thinking.

"Tombs" is not the word for the structures in which so much of Egyptian art has been brought to light. Within the protecting pyramid or mastaba (a flat-topped tomb-house), which may appear forbidding because it is lacking in exterior color or ornamentation, there is likely to be a series of rooms more like a livable villa in furnishings and decorations. Within this the mummy may best be thought of as a man nicely wrapped up for his long journey and sweetened with gums, spices, and perfumes. When you dig him up, thirty centuries later, you will likely still find the flowers around him, and bowls of fruit, and jewelry, and reminders of dancing girls and jaunts up the river.

Religious faith has always been a powerful determinant of artistic expression, and loyalty to kings is only second in influence. Temple, cathedral, palace, and tomb, idol and royal portrait, the picturing of religious legends and of courtly pageantry and diversion—take these from the body of world art, and only a fragment of the treasure of the past remains. Egypt had its fair share of likenesses of god and priest, of king and noble, and its quota of temples and crypts. The priest caste ruled—with the pharaoh or king as chief priest, or king-god. In general the priests made the rules for artists. Serious art was within a religious tradition.

The gods were many in Egypt, and not so very awe-inspiring if one obeyed implicitly and did not forget the priests in harvest month or on payday. There was, indeed, a nice balance of the aloof and the familiar, of a mystery commanding respect with human and animal attributes that are understandable and likable. For worship the sun-god was supreme, and this might be the Nile-god too. The sun and the Nile were the two obvious, familiar, and never-changing facts of the geographical environment. To them, personified, must be addressed the respect, the propitiation, the thanks, that are bound up in religious sentiment. No less the well-known animals; once tribal totems or personal fetishes, perhaps, they became associated with specific god-ideas. The cow and the jackal, the serpent and the hawk, the lion and the goat—the deity was imagined in the guise of one of these.

This animal idolatry is notable particularly for those who believe that art is a continually changing venture into formalized expression, continually renewed out of love and understanding of nature. Even if the artist were forced by a priesthood to serve gods alone, here would be a treasure house of familiar and beloved models ready to his hand. If his aptitude for reproducing the characteristic appearance of lion or bull were reinforced by a burning faith in the hidden god-aspect of the animal, by a desire to form it in a larger significance, as symbolizing the order and rhythm at the heart of the world, might he not the better transcend mere reproduction, mere portraiture, and rise to art as creation, as revelation? Might he not thus come to express the insinuating intimate reality of the animal as seen, as known in daily life, and add the divine implication, the artist's subjective contribution?

It is thus that Egyptian art is to be viewed and enjoyed: it is so amazingly true to model and attitude, with selectiveness, and yet so true to inner vision.

The Pyramids

The temples of the Old Kingdom period have lapsed into ruin. Of architecture there is practically nothing left from the golden age except the pyramids. These are monuments enough to any civilization, perhaps, but it is significant that the tombs of kings, rather than the houses of the

Portrait statue. Wood, 6th Dynasty, Gizeh. *Museum of Fine Arts, Boston*

gods, should have claimed men's most enduring expression in the building art. Certain temple sites and ruins have been excavated, particularly in the pyramid and other burial-ground areas, and considerable information has been amassed as to how the early Egyptians built; but there is little to engage the eye as surviving architectural composition.

The temples of the Fourth and Fifth Dynasties, the very height of the Old Kingdom's flowering and the period of surpassingly great sculpture, seem to have been severely geometrical, heavy, scarcely ornamented at all. Toward the end of this period the squared granite pillars became less severe columns, with palm-like forms or added lotus-bud capitals. Most of the conventional language of the building art—ornament, overhang, slight inward slope of exterior walls—can be traced back to primitive building with mud over tied-together palm sticks or papyrus reeds, or to the first brick construction along the Nile. The arch was early known and occasionally used. But of all the early activity we have only fragmentary evidence.

The pyramids, monuments unique and unforgettable, constitute the outstanding architectural achievement of the age. They rise from the desert like clusters of man-shaped mountains, mathematically severe, geometrically serene, looming up impressively. Their purpose was twofold. Each pyramid encloses far down in the mountainous solidity of the structure a tomb-chamber and connected rooms designed as the owner's home in the after-life. The second purpose, naturally more evident in the pyramids of the kings, was to impress the living, to rear an inescapably imposing memorial.

The architectural virtues of the pyramids are all on the side of simplicity, largeness, and regularity. There is no ornament, no ranging of decorative columns, no elaboration of doorways, no enrichment of edges; only the naked, four-sided erection, rising to take the sun, announcing to all beholders the uncompromising majesty of the god-king. There was nonetheless subtle planning and adjustment: the slope carefully studied, the mass calculated, to determine the exact angle against the sky. Or so at least we must believe, since so many generations of wanderers in Egypt have been impressed. The pyramids speak, it may be, remotely, impersonally, overwhelmingly, but they live architecturally; they are alive with their own unique architectural vitality. Men are moved by them, vibrate to their elemental rhythm.

For those who are moved but ask if it is not a natural rather than an artistic effect that moves them, there can be only one answer: art is what

man contrives, and no one is competent to say that what is contrived intricately, with the refinements of late sculptural decoration and ornamentation, is superior, as art, to that which remains close to basic forms, nakedly impressive. The pyramids may move men primarily as mass, as weight, as unbroken upward thrust, and as much might be said of Mont Blanc or Mount Rainier; but the precision and the calculated proportioning and balance are notable too, and mark the pile as artificial, as a new creation, as outside nature, with definite artistic intent—by which the observer fifty centuries later is thrilled just as were the subjects of Khufu or of Khafre, the kings who reared the monuments.

A school of thought has arisen which ascribes mystical significance to the form of the great pyramids. Throughout art, the argument goes, the aesthetic response is partly to a calculated *order* within the painting, statue, or building. The artist is inspired, beyond all matters of subject and use, to fix in each of his works an echo of the rhythm or continuing order of the universe, a revelation of the ultimate balance and repose of the cosmos. As creator he works in the stuff of the spinning spheres, the heavenly axes and tensions and orbital paths. He intuitively designs a new world reflecting cosmic principles.

Well, the pyramids, the mystics say, exhibit the most amazing correspondences and relationships in the measurements of line and area, of weight and mass. No one, to be sure, has been able to unravel the mystery of just how certain mathematical visual relationships, certain geometrical hidden figures, call forth a pleasurable or ecstatic response in the human soul, in the deep region beyond sense and brain, affording satisfaction, a consciousness of unity with the source of creation. There is no formula for plastic creation. Suffice it to say that the pyramids have this deep-cutting rightness. They are geometric, musical; for music, the least literal and least intellectually explainable of the arts, the most elusive and most unaccountably moving, is also the most exactly mathematical.

Behind the sheer aesthetic and monumental effect comes trailing the intellectual curiosity, the inevitable question of how. By what method

The Sphinx and Pyramid. Gizeh, about 2800 B.C.

was this stupendous engineering feat accomplished? The great pyramid, that of Khufu, in the group at Gizeh which was one of the Seven Wonders of the World in Greek times, covers an area of thirteen acres. Each side is about 755 feet long at the base-line. The stone in the practically solid structure totals more than three million cubic yards. This colossal structure, in which the average single stone block weighs two and one-half tons, was erected without modern lifting machinery. But engineers have shown how with equipment of ramps, wedges, and other elementary devices, the task could be accomplished, granted armies of human workmen. The Greek historian Herodotus recorded the legend that one hundred thousand men were occupied twenty years in the erection of the Great Pyramid. These were, of course, slaves.

Today the exterior of the Great Pyramid is comparatively rough and unfinished, but once it was resplendent in a perfectly fitted and polished shell of limestone. This coating was removed in the course of the ages as builders in nearby Cairo needed and helped themselves to the nicely polished blocks of stone for use in such alien structures as mosques and monasteries and tourist hotels.

The pyramids are logical outgrowths of the primitive Egyptian's common tomb-under-a-heap-of-sand. The sandpile was enlarged and the top flattened. Then more enduring materials were utilized, and the tomb-house became a raised terrace, still with sloping sides and flat top—a *mastaba,* as the Arabic has it, from a word meaning "bench." Finally a king had mastabas piled on top of one another, in diminishing size, thus arriving at the step pyramid. And so, from its general form, the "perfect" pyramid.

But the interior chambers were not enlarged to match. The great pyramids are almost solid rock; the space given to rooms and passages constitutes a very small fraction of the total volume.

Sculpture in the Old Kingdom Period

Sculpture was the art pre-eminent among those immortalized in this cradle of the monumental arts, during the Egyptian Old Kingdom Period. It was, remember, three thousand years

Seated figure of King Khafre. Diorite, c. 2800 B.C. *Cairo Museum*

before the Greeks who only yesterday were accounted the supreme sculptors of the "ancient"
world.

The celebrated Sphinx of Gizeh is significant
in that a Pharaoh and his architects could con-
ceive and execute a statue of such colossal scale,
and in artistic relationship to nearby pyramid
and temple. With it architectural invention escapes the limitations of a single building and
deals with the plan and appearance of a considerable area—a reach forward to a super-archi-
tecture that has hardly yet matured in our West-

ern milieu, and then in an almost exclusively theoretical way, in city planning and "idealistic" community planning.

The Sphinx could not have moved so many observers to exclamations of wonder and delight if it did not possess genuine sculptural merits in addition to its imposing size and the novel use of a natural stone outcropping for its material mass. It dominates its desert and fits perfectly with the magnitude of the pyramids.

The much-remarked enigmatic expression is partly, no doubt, an accident of time, and the use of the Sphinx as a symbol of inscrutability is a matter of secondary importance in any case, a literary or intellectual addition. But it is likely that the original unravaged monument partook generously of that true sculptural proportioning, that calculated massing of volumes, which is the key virtue of the art. Something of this essential sculptural effectiveness remains even today, after "restorers" have added their mutilations to those of time.

The Sphinx also expresses kingly aloofness and imperiousness. He is the watcher, looking over common men's heads, the king-god who drew his power and his distinction from divine communion beyond the earthly world. The visitor today *feels* this sense of kingliness. The portrait head on the lion body was a convention of the time, one of many conventions by which the artist might impress the popular mind with the divinity and majesty of the ruler.

Fortunately there are lesser monuments of the same reign that have survived intact. Not of the same exceptional physical dimensions, they yet breathe the sense of largeness, massive order, and noble proportioning which is of the very essence of stone sculpture. Of this sort is the diorite statue of Khafre, who was also the king who ordered the building of the Sphinx. Diorite is one of the most intractable of stones, and modern sculptors have expressed amazement that so finished a monument could have been chiseled and ground out of so flintlike a material. But there is no faintest lack of mastery here. The *Khafre* is supremely craftsmanlike, even while supremely living.

What is it in this work that moves us, that yields, five thousand years after its making, the warming pleasure of the sculptural experience? Even as we respond, we know not how or why, to the abstract order and measured rhythm of the stone, we delight in the truth and depth and feeling of the portraiture. Here is a king of ancient Egypt. The man is before us in every feature, every telling lineament—not the individual man unsupported, but the individual inspired, become superman. The god-king idea is fused with the individual identity, determines attitude and expression, gives largeness and a true grandeur to frame and bulk and stature. The god in this case is also symbolically in attendance, is visually bound up in the headdress, a part of the physical synthesis. This is the man-king-god in one representation, one breathing entity.

The sense of nobility conveyed is but half of the king; the other half is of the lithic medium nobly used. Stone lends itself, in a master's hand, to the expression of organic order, characterful solidity, immobile calm. Half of what we feel intuitively in our enjoyment of Egyptian sculpture is the quality of the stone, multiplied, concentrated, revealed. The integrity of the block of granite remains; strong movement is confined; *its* power is revealed.

By no means are all the multitudinous statues of the Old Kingdom equally alive and potent. The conventions of sculptured portraiture had been fixed long before: a few hardly changing attitudes, an arrangement only slightly asymmetrical, a standardized body with only the face subject to true portrait treatment. This setting of rules and types resulted in a great amount of inferior, routine statue-making, with artistic potency as a secondary consideration. Often the sculptural formalization has degenerated to meaningless rigidity and empty rhetoric. The kingliness has become a formula, unvaried from good Pharaoh to bad, from one family of routine sculptors to another.

The statue of this early period, to be sure, never degenerates into overelaboration or labored delineation of natural detail. It is in general large and broad; but in its inferior forms it lacks the sensitive adjustment, the plastic aliveness, the inner vision. There are, however, figures that

Village Magistrate. Wood. *Cairo Museum*

approach the *Khafre* in nobility and subtlety. Some are in stone, some in wood; and, still within the golden age, the first metal statues appear.

Perhaps the most stirring sculptural conception in wood preserved from the pre-Buddhist civilizations is the statue known as the *Shekh El-Beled* or the *Village Magistrate*. It is impossible to tell how far the wood may have gained, in grain and finish, in the fifty centuries during which it kept its vigil in a tomb. During that period it lost —mercifully, it must seem to us now—a coat of paint. In any case, the "effect" seems absolutely right. The solidity, the architectonic structure, and the reposeful and powerful bearing seem perfectly calculated, masterfully achieved.

Again the lifelikeness is twofold: true to individual character and station, and intensely *of the medium*. The man lives again in essence, and then doubly so because of the formal vitality of the sculpture as such. As a matter of fact the portrait is so true to type—a self-satisfied "official" type persisting still today—that the native workers who dug up the piece under the direction of archaeologists exclaimed immediately, "The village magistrate!" and so it has been known ever since by the name of the local Shekh, El-Beled. Thus is great art, often, particularized expression in language universally recognizable. The literal mind sees in the artistic generalization a particular known appearance or identity. The observer trained to aesthetic enjoyment finds the particular a bridge to the regions of a profound order, of spiritual satisfaction.

It would be possible, doubtless, to trace a tendency to individual freedom of expression through the course of the Fourth and Fifth Dynasties, which mark the summit of the Old Kingdom's artistic achievement. But it is of the essence of the matter, if one is to *enjoy* Egyptian sculpture, that one recognize first the combination of virtues: truth to individual model, psychological understanding of what the subject stands for, and masterly sculptural expressiveness.

It would be easy to note, and find a slightly different pleasure in, the increased natural lifelikeness and alertness of the best-known of the early metal statues, the *King Pepi I and His Son* in the Cairo Museum, or the father-and-son group in the Louvre. In the common family group of man and wife, or man, wife, and children, there is a drift toward sentiment, despite the maintenance of the traditional rigid frontal attitude.

There is something touching about the wifely hand that commonly reaches across to rest upon the stiffened arm of the spouse and master.

Despite the rigidity of the body and the enforced convention of a few set attitudes, the faces in early Egyptian sculpture are widely varied. If the conventions were ordained and enforced, as we must believe, by the ruling powers, priestly and kingly, no less was the individualism of portraiture a result of belief and custom. When the statue was not intended to impress the populace, it was designed to stand in a tomb as the double of a man; some say to take his place when the mummy decayed, others that the statue represented the double that walked with him in life, his personality. The Egyptians had noticed, no doubt, that the mummified figure shrank, changed in looks, was no longer, after the wear of years, the true man in aspect. And if the gods should mistake the identity of the tomb occupant, all the delicacies and furnishings intended for his use in the long after-life might be diverted to the delectation of another. No amount of labeling would serve so well as a statue, an exact image of the individual man as he appeared in life, a crystallization of his personal characteristics.

In any case, here, almost at the birth of monumental sculpture, portraiture came to a noble blending of individualism and idealization seldom approached in later ages. The likeness may be curbed for greater plastic expressiveness, the features summarized, the head mitered or swathed to give mass. But the face can be accepted only as the very essence of the man who sat to the sculptor. Comparisons of statues of the same king or noble permit no other deduction. Khafre is always recognizable as Khafre once you have met one of his likenesses. As a matter of fact, there were twenty-three statues of King Khafre in the tomb from which the one shown on page 50 was taken, though only nine survive.

Old Kingdom Murals

To the solid, rocklike statues the wall-reliefs afford a striking and pleasing contrast, but within

Head of Thutmose III. *Cairo Museum*

the limits of great sculpture. The inside stone walls of the rooms in the mastabas of kings and nobles were worked over with shallow sculptured relief pictures and fitted-in hieroglyphics. The reliefs were tinted after the cutting. The effect is rich and engaging and charming beyond any other display of large-surface low-relief in history.

Ti was head builder of the royal pyramids under King Khafre, and therefore something of a figure in the art affairs and social life of his time. Today we know his every physical characteristic and not a little of his inner character from the portrait statue found in his tomb at

Relief. Wood, 3rd Dynasty. *Cairo Museum*

are so masterly, so uniformly excellent, that they rank with the great murals of all ages. At the same time the natural truth, the observed detail, is so exact that scientists can name every bird, every flower, and can even point out the slave with adenoids and the tribute-bearer who came from Ethiopia.

Since the Egyptian believed that what was on the wall of his tomb would be enjoyed forever in the after-life, there was reason to crowd in every pleasurable activity experienced on earth—in his household, his recreations, his arts, his travels, his profession, and particularly in his observation of the birds and beasts and flowers around him. Ti's farm slaves are shown plowing, sowing, harvesting, threshing. The fish are caught for dinner, or the cattle slaughtered and quartered. The boats of the Nile are seen, the bird-trappers are at work in the marshes, the hunters dispatch their quarry, the milking and herding, the keeping of accounts, the exploits of war are shown. Musicians play and slender slave-girls dance while the master's wives are bathed and powdered. But it is perhaps animals that most of all live with a lifelikeness that betokens long and loving observation and fellowship: suave cats and waddling ducks, geese, ibises, donkeys, and antelopes.

To have disengaged these subjects so simply from the casual profusion of nature and life, to have rendered them so freshly, rhythmically, strongly, to have brought appearance-validity so docilely within the confines of stone-picturing, of cut line, shallow relief, and simple flat-area coloring, is a miracle—one more indication that here sculpture leaped almost at once to a world peak.

A sort of childlike, poetic attitude toward life is indelibly fixed here, beginning with the naïve faith that the companions, pursuits, and pleasures of the tomb's occupant will be with him forever because the pictures are with him, and again in the fresh simplicity of observation, feeling, and recreation. Notable are the linear harmonies, the toylike profile figures, the illusion of a complete scene, a complete world, given without detail, without light and shade, but with joy at once of living and of picturing. Here is exceptional con-

Sakkara. But the more extraordinary and likable art linked with his name is in the series of tinted reliefs on the walls of his home-for-the-ages, a tomb very untomblike in the color, freshness, and range of subject-matter of the sculpture, and in the lightness of touch of the unknown artists.

Without ever departing from the conventions of low-relief sculpture, from the technique of almost flattened volume, linear rhythm, and sweetly undulating planes, the sculptor fixes in continuous panels an amazing range of scenes from contemporary luxurious life. The workmanship and aesthetic potency of the relief pictures

Hippopotamus. Blue faïence, 12th Dynasty. *Metropolitan Museum of Art*

tagious vitality, without insistent naturalism or thought-out documentation. The development marks a summit of "light" art: the felicitous expression of a world delighted in, fixed easily, with the transparent formalism of that eternal child-time of man which sees incompletely perhaps, but intuitively gets down the facts in which the observer will find himself participating.

The naïve conventions of Old Kingdom relief-cutting distress some observers. They want the artists of the Nile to have known "scientific" truth—that is, the conventions of the camera-eye. They find the lack of background vistas, particularly of perspective, a denial of their own scientifically bolstered image of nature. Especially they are annoyed because, while the cat or the duck is perfectly and "truthfully" suggested, the man nearby is drawn with face and feet in profile and shoulders full front.

From the start the wall-sculptors and painters had perpetuated certain primitive conventions. Before logic ruled, artists depicted the features of nature as commonly known, not as seen in one moment of time in a particularized attitude. For the most part men and animals were reproduced in profile. This was what most vividly impressed the retina and became stored in the memory. But

an eye was shown full front—an oval with a round pupil. When an eye was put into a profile head it was not the profile eye but the remembered full-front eye. And when figures began to be drawn *en face* (and shoulders were always so shown) the feet were left in profile. This is the most sharply registered view of legs and feet.

As the realists of later ages began to ask if the picture was logically true, the European critics fell upon these conventions and marked them as *gaucheries*. Today, as the freeing winds of expressionism blow over the Western world, some of the primitive "distortions" are seen as artistically right—or perhaps as merely unimportant. Certainly a few out-of-place eyes and turned-around feet no longer divert the contemplative eye from the fine total decorative effect of the Egyptian murals. It has been discovered that from the absolute photographic point of view all art is a convention. How far the artist strays from camera truth is inconsequential as long as a vital artistic organism, a new aesthetic entity, is created and made to live in its own plastic and decorative completeness.

Another convention is common to wall-reliefs and many free-standing groups of statues. The king is very much larger than his subjects, and

Relief from a tomb. Sakkara, 6th Dynasty. *Cairo Museum*

the master of the house (or of the tomb) is depicted as a giant among his associates—slaves, wives, pets, and other household paraphernalia. The wife bulks larger than the servants, but is a mere circumstance to the man.

The painting of the Old Kingdom is not of the importance of the sculpture and the architecture. It is, indeed, not often to be dissociated from sculptured reliefs. After the decline of the Old Kingdom there is a long period of darkened history and not much notable art of any sort.

The Arts of the Middle Kingdom

Such vast stretches of time are included in Egyptian history that, in order to make clear any sort of unity, and to avoid confusing reservations and wanderings, one must skim over periods of many centuries, which under any other civilization would perhaps be considered as celebrated "ages." Thus almost a millennium is allowed to elapse after the decline of art in the Old Kingdom, before the curtain is again rung up, on what is in effect a renaissance. It is now the time known to historians as the Middle Kingdom, which began about the twenty-second century B.C. The Egyptian capital has been moved up the Nile to Thebes. An attempt is being made to

recapture the glories of the Old Kingdom's artistry. In sculpture the artists never quite arrive at the miraculous synthesis, though their statues would stand out as impressive in many another age. On the other hand, architecture becomes more important and more broadly expressive; the Old Kingdom had left nothing more than the pyramids.

The temples of the Theban builders rose to larger importance than their tombs, though often the temple was still an adjunct of the sepulcher cut in a rock cliff. West of the city of Thebes, on the desert's edge, there were constructed so many royal sepulchers that the area is known as the Valley of the Royal Tombs. This is the famous "Necropolis" or city of the dead at Abydos. The one-time pyramid-chapel was commonly built near the Nile banks, below the cliffs and adjoining the town, so that the builder might have convenient access to his patron-god during his lifetime, and his survivors might conveniently bring offerings in his honor, and perhaps replenish his supplies, after his death.

Among the royal tombs excavated in the valley, the best-known date back to the New rather than the Middle Kingdom. Outstanding in popular interest is that of Tutenkhamon. But foremost among the cliff-edge temples is that of Queen Hatshepsut, of which the remains are sufficiently

Queen Hatshepsut. Limestone, 18th Dynasty. *Metropolitan Museum of Art*

intact to impress visitors to the site today. Despite its New Kingdom date it is probably a reversion to Middle Kingdom types, and it is the archaeologists' chief evidence of forms in that time.

The architecture is more serene, more restrained, and, many will say, more beautiful than that of the contemporary and later temples which are more often paraded as typically Egyptian.

Wall relief, Temple of Amon, Karnak

There is an aspect nearer to early Greek sober building, with no exuberance in flowered capitals and columns traced all over. There is refinement in the simple polygonal pillars, and restraint in the simple terraced repetition of court and colonnade, as there is also a thoughtful fitness of temple to towering and protecting arc-cliff behind.

If the outward effect seems somewhat cold and overformal today, it is to be remembered that sculpture and trees may once have added a grace now lacking. The temple was approached by an avenue lined with sphinxes and doubtless innumerable incidental statues. The queen herself had it recorded on the inner walls, in both words and picture reliefs, that the gardens were luxuriant and exotic. She sent an expedition to distant Punt on the Gulf of Aden, "the land of incense," and to this day we can see a graphic representation of slaves loading the boats there with trees and bundles of spices and other valu-

able cargo, even cows and monkeys. The royal lady had her artist-scribes set down full descriptions in the captions. An oracle of Amon had commanded her "to establish Punt for him in his house, to plant the trees of God's land beside his temple in his garden." And so, the muralist recorded, "It was done."

The temples of Amon at Karnak and Luxor, both situated in the Theban area, are the showpieces of middle and late building, and indeed of all Egyptian architecture aside from the pyramids—enormous erections built progressively through many dynasties. The fat, closely spaced columns, profusely decorated, with capitals elaborated out of the early lotus-bud and papyrus motives; the massive pylon gates; the incredibly rich tracing-over of every plane surface with reliefs and inscriptions; and above all the colossal size of the monuments—these characteristics have made a powerful impression upon visitors from the outside world through all recorded ages.

Columns, Temple of Amon, Karnak

The size of the Karnak temple is so great that the central ceremonial hall alone could be fitted down neatly over Notre Dame Cathedral in Paris. Never again did the building art dare to rear such structures, until the coming of steel-cage construction had made possible the erection of the now familiar American skyscraper.

The ceremonial or hypostyle hall is the heart of the typical temple. Behind it is a sanctuary, and before it a public forecourt, and these too are enormous and lavishly decorated. Outside, an avenue of sphinxes formed an appropriate ap-

A god, detail. Granite, Karnak, 18th Dynasty

proach. The whole, at Luxor and at Karnak, was dedicated to the worship of Amon. The architects of the Middle and the New Kingdoms seem to have exhausted themselves in the achievement of this one type of building. Temples and tombs tell almost the whole story of permanent Egyptian architecture.

Sculpture under the Middle Kingdom flowered in some monuments not greatly inferior to the Old Kingdom standards. There are free-standing statues and reliefs that carry on enjoyably the tradition of Memphis and Sakkara. But the seeds of dilettantism have been sown, and that other degenerating influence, mass production, enters in. There are numberless mediocre and lifeless sphinxes, and neat imitations of the old king-figures, and repetitions of this and that god-fetish. But the inspiration has been dulled; the old magic synthesis of nature and sculptural form is lacking. The conventions that could once be varied into individually living images are rigidly stereotyped. The effects are repetitious and dull.

There are exceptions, approaching the plastic and moving nobility of the seated *Khafre* in diorite and the wooden *Village Magistrate*. But the best things of the period, as left to us, are detached heads. The probable explanation is that the conventions of body representation had crystallized, had become academic—the life is gone from the figures, of which the crouching, skirt-enveloped priest or scribe is a common type—and all the artist's love and invention center in the face. At any rate, there are heads that rank high in combined sensitivity and massiveness, and there is no reason why we should not take our joy of these fragments, forgetting the rest.

Relief sculpture of the Middle Kingdom is in a better way. It has a fresh note. The naïve conventions found in the reliefs of the Sakkara tombs are less noticeable, and the fresh childhood vision has measurably passed. The artists know more, possibly feel less. But the reliefs of Queen Hatshepsut's temple are engaging and decorative. Color counts for more, though the artist does not insist upon his work as painting rather than sculptural drawing. It should be added that the mural art was extended to the inner and outer walls of stone sarcophagi, and to chair panels and other utilitarian surfaces.

The queen's temple walls tell long stories of the building and furnishing of the shrine, with excursions, like the one to Punt, in search of plants and precious woods; and there are gods, ceremonies, painted offerings, and innumerable souvenirs of the queen's life and reign. Hatshepsut was involved in intrigue and controversy, and made such bitter enemies that after her death every representation of her on the walls was erased, usually to make way for the image of her successor.

It might be claimed that Egyptian builders went to extremes in their devotion to relief decoration, pictorial and descriptive. The great temples yield up not only their flat walls, but every inch of column-surface and architrave and door-jamb to the picture-artists. Structural members are overridden, joints obscured, and architecture is in general sacrificed for a relief-decorator's holiday. The result should be downright bad—destructive of building unity, unarchitectonic, cheapening. All the rules of structure are against the working-over of the weight-carrying members. But perhaps this is all compensated for in the richness of the coating. The audacious scale of the sculptural job fits in with the daring of the enormous temple piles. Probably these Egyptian temples never had the architectural purity of the Greek Doric temples, or of the pyramids, in any case. The fat columns—perhaps over-all tracery is right for them! And the reliefs yield so much enjoyment when studied separately that even an architectural purist would hesitate to condemn them.

There are equally appealing things in the jewelry, the pottery, and the minor crafts of the time. The bracelets, necklaces, and armlets are endlessly satisfying. Color is gorgeously used in vase and brooch. Human and animal forms are beautifully simplified and stylized in relief for jewel-box or comb. There is mastery of form and technique in a thousand miniature use-objects and fetishes to be found in representative museum collections.

The New Kingdom: Renaissance, Then Revolution

Between the Middle and the New Kingdoms there was a break in tradition. Egypt was under a foreign yoke. When the country had been freed and reintegrated, the arts again knew a renaissance. Sculpture, above all, found new nourishment. The kings who delivered the country and went on to imperial grandeur and renewed display were those of the Eighteenth Dynasty, established in 1580 B.C. The outstanding figure in this succession was Thutmose III, whose portrait statues sometimes match the dignity of the Old Kingdom sculpture, as in the example on page

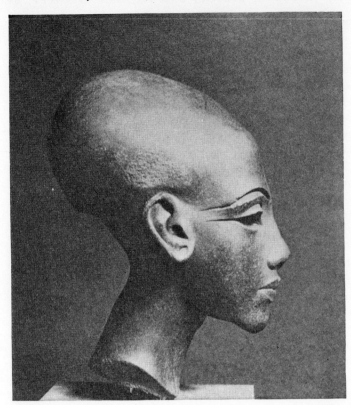

Ikhnaton's Daughter.
Sandstone, El Amarna.
Egyptian Museum,
Berlin

53. His exploits in extending the bounds of the Egyptian empire in Syria, the Aegean Isles, and Nubia mainly supplied the motives for the reliefs on the walls at Karnak. But it was four reigns later that the greater development, or revolution, in art occurred.

Ikhnaton, known to the conservative archaeologists, and to the priests of his own time, as "the heretic king," but today widely lauded as an admirable iconoclast and prophet, introduced a new sort of portraiture. The traditional conventions were dropped; the artist was given full latitude in depicting and sharpening the peculiar characteristics of his sitter, and a psychologically interesting portrait resulted. The purely sculptural values are not lost, though there is less of the mountainous repose and less of the powerful enclosed sculptural movement. In general, vitality gives way before vivacity, and solidity yields to natural appearance.

Portrait heads of Ikhnaton himself, and of his queen, Nofretete, are among the most amazing and enjoyable things in the whole range of individual portraiture. The truth is more than surface realism. It is a revelation of inner character, and it gives away the man more certainly than the camera ever could. A whole school of twentieth-century modernism is anticipated in this New Kingdom achievement. The psychological sculpture of Epstein is no more penetrating, hardly more Freudian.

It is, however, just as well to be cautious in accepting the belief of realistic-minded archaeologists (supported by doctors) that the portraits with elongated heads are exact images of the royal family far along in macrocephalous degeneration. We moderns have heard the distortions and malformations in El Greco's paintings and in Cambodian sculpture explained by learned scientists as naturalistic portrayals of abnormalities, only to find later a more satisfying, artist's reason for them. There are too many elongated heads in the Egyptian reliefs of the time to permit explanation on grounds other than that they are a convention with compositional purpose.

But the utter lifelikeness of facial aspect remains. There remains too the subtle psychic revelation, the report on the man's soul. The sculptor has gone deeper into the make-up of the sitter's personality than ever before. Perhaps earlier kings had forbidden the too personal probing, had wanted individual variance cloaked under a generalization of nobility and kingliness. There is no doubt that Ikhnaton, in contrast, asked that the soul be brought up into the light, the inner man expressed with the outer, all bars let down. Even the queen is done without idealization, without enlargement or suppression. In the famous colored limestone in Berlin, to be sure, she wears her jeweled collar and her high decorated headdress. But the thin neck and angular jaw are not even glossed over. Perhaps the very thinness adds a spiritual impression. In any case, here is the alert, eager inner being brought forth intimately to the observer. One should not miss the perfect lilt of the head, the poise of all faculties in readiness, the vivacious repose. (Color Plate I, following page viii, is an illustration of this.)

Just what is the connection between the aesthetic revolution in Ikhnaton's time and the religious overturn he accomplished? No one has been able to say. This king, born Amenhotep IV, and brought up to worship the most exacting and powerful of competing gods, became the world's first outstanding monotheist. He turned from foreign conquests and elaborate political-ecclesiastic intrigue to attempt the reorganization of national life on a unified spiritual basis. Eventually his empire went to pieces, and the priests of the many traditional gods regained the ruling power; but only after he had officially banished all other deities in favor of Aton, the sun-god, god of light, and the one Truth. Amenhotep changed his own name to Ikhnaton—"the living spirit of Aton."

Besides being the first outstanding monotheist in history, Ikhnaton claims our attention as one of the rare rulers deeply actuated by the artistic spirit. To the fact that he encouraged his sculptors to cultivate absolute freedom of observation and portrayal there is to be added that he was a poet strangely suggesting the Hebrew psalmists, and that he undertook building projects with a vision and a wholemindedness seldom paralleled

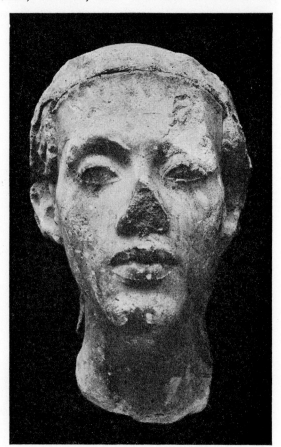

Ikhnaton. Plaster, 18th Dynasty, *Egyptian Museum, Berlin*

in history. He planned no structure so grandiose as the temples at Luxor and Karnak. Indeed he pulled free of all those imposing and showy projects to which successive kings before him had been content to add their bits—trying to outshine in decorative augmentation and fulsome inscription all earlier kings.

He entirely abandoned the Theban center with its many gods and temples, and built a new capital city at el-Amarna, farther down the Nile. In the ruins of his palace were found the "psychologic" portrait heads that have so amazed and delighted modern eyes. In these ruins too were discovered the tablet letters, the king's correspondence with colonial governors and tributary but restive rulers, which throw so clear a light

Rameses II, detail. Quartzite, 19th Dynasty. *Metropolitan Museum of Art*

on world affairs of the time—pointing up the truth, incidentally, that a peace-loving, art-loving monarch, with revolutionary vision and spiritual insight, is no match for politicians and priests who are intent upon conserving or restoring the old established order of privilege and prosperity.

The wall-reliefs at el-Amarna, like the busts, are instinct with a new spirit. They bring in questionable as well as admirable freedoms. The rhythms are more melodious. But the figures

Whip handle. Tinted ivory, 18th Dynasty. *Metropolitan Museum of Art*

often turn bulbous and exaggerated, escaping from the flat-relief idiom, and the panels are overcrowded. Observation slips into caricature. But let us not make a mistake: at their best these still are great examples of the low-relief art. Among the perhaps less successful large compositions are bits of relief that stand out in startling beauty. It was the fortune of archaeologists to break into the studio of one of Ikhnaton's sculptors, and the models and trial pieces found there are extraordinarily engaging.

Return to Tradition:
Nineteenth Dynasty Sculpture

After the interlude of Ikhnaton, Egypt returned to the old gods, to the old imperialism, and to the old arts. The only possible inference is that the priests, when they restored Amon and the animal cults and the old superstitions, took over control of the artists and deliberately snuffed out the spirit of freedom that the heretic king had introduced. A little of the freshness of observation was carried on. But most of the celebrated art associated with the name of Ikhnaton's son-in-law, Tutenkhamon, is routine "furniture," ostentatiously embellished but by no means achieving a summit of Egyptian art. A recent historian, connecting the "Tutenkhamon treasure" with the idea of the restored wealth and

luxuriousness of the Egyptian court at the time, unwittingly characterized this sort of art perfectly when he wrote: "Fancy articles are known in richer abundance than at any other period." The evidence of sound craftsmanship is clear, but originality, virility, and simplicity have disappeared in the face of the demand for extravagant decoration and virtuosity.

There were to be revivals and renaissances of other sorts, but far from the spirit and form of Ikhnaton's artists. During the following dynasty, the Nineteenth, there were splendors under Seti I and Rameses II. The latter, incidentally, added temporarily to his laurels by inscribing his name on any building or statue out of the past that appealed to his fancy; though he did also restore half-ruined temples and build new ones, and kept schools—if not factories—of sculptors busy. In exceptional busts and sphinxes and colossi the old stone massiveness returns; the sculptural form asserts itself strongly and compellingly. One is reminded that, outside the sudden flame of the Aton revolution, art burned steadily, as a single Egyptian expression, from the thirty-fourth century B.C. to the thirteenth century of Rameses II —fully two thousand years of development and variation and persisting Egyptian character. Today the most superficial student of sculpture would name the diorite *Khafre* and the quartzite *Rameses II* as unmistakably Egyptian works, as akin in spirit and intent and craftsmanship. Both

Relief: fragment of sculptor's model. Limestone, late period. *Metropolitan Museum*

bear the marks of great and essential sculpture; the latter less packed with power and movement and mountainous repose, no doubt, but in a sculptural language distinguished and capable of the impression of magnitude.

Later Egyptian Sculpture

Once more, even after the sensationalism and coarseness of the later things in the reign of Rameses II, there was to be a brief revival of this monumental, essentially Egyptian art, under the Saite kings, whose line began about 950 B.C., far down in Hebrew Biblical times, and continued through the period of Persian domination. The Saite monuments sometimes add an elegance, a smooth stylization unknown before, but the best pieces are marked by the old direct "thinking in stone," by the integrity of the block, the pristine sculptural honesty. In the finish there is more refinement. The hieratic control of subject-matter was evidently relaxed, for there are fewer gods, sphinx-kings, and fetishes. The sweetness of nature's outlines and forms is oftener transferred into the statue. There are even female nudes,

Amenhotep III in His Chariot, detail. Relief on a stele. *Cairo Museum*

studied with evident relish and modeled with comparative fidelity to observation.

The reliefs remained to the end distinctive, characterful, and recognizably Egyptian. In Ikhnaton's time there had been a drift toward a rather flabby naturalism, not to mention an unpleasant caricaturist element, along with the better artists' capture of a new freedom. The later things—and there are critics who account the reliefs of the period of the Ramessid kings the supreme masterpieces of low-sculptural art—returned to a stricter formalism and a more understanding regard for the crisp stone-cut line. There is a softer quality, a tender sensibility, but the conventions remain. From the unbelievably great number of relief pictures extant, the modern student can choose panels, friezes, and bits, particularly of the later periods of the Saite kings and even Greek-Ptolemaic times, that seduce the eye and engage the senses. The figures have a melodious fluency; garments cling to bodies caressingly (when there are garments); harmonious little waves flow into one another; the forms are rhythmic and lyric. It is, of course, sculpture now near a decline. For robust tastes it is already too smooth, suave, and evasive of the heavy mass and the hard-cut line. Beyond the outstanding ingratiating things there is a vast decadent output.

Thirty Centuries of Painting

Painting as a separate art was by this time immemorially old. Twenty-five hundred years before, it had notably separated itself from the bas-relief picturing. During the Old Kingdom it had touched heights of naturalistic, yet poster-like, depiction that thrilled the discoverers and critics of our own nineteenth century. But the most frequently illustrated exhibit from those olden times, the frieze known as *The Geese of Medum,* is notable for its exactitude of rendering, along with a stencil-like sharpness, rather than for plastic sensibility. The panel, from a tomb-chapel at Medum, is in the Cairo Museum.

It was rather in the New Kingdom that painting took its place beside, and independently of, sculptural relief. The wall-compositions seem stiffly conventional and attitudinized when compared with the "free" painting of Europe or the wash pictures of China and Japan. It is true certainly that the art in Egypt missed something of the development that might have been expected from the very facility of the brush as contrasted with the sculptor's chisel. Traditional method and perhaps priestly control determined a rocklike

Harvest Scenes. Mural. Thebes, 15th century B.C.

conventionalism that persisted until Greek times.

Nevertheless, there are fine virtues, even stirring achievements, within the narrow limits allowed by custom. The tomb murals of the Theban area are particularly rich, sensitive, and vital. There are eye-filling fragments, and whole walls beautifully spaced and colored.

A word should be said, perhaps, about the mixing of lettering and pictures. The inevitable combination of illustration and inscription adds to the formalism and introduces a difficulty for the Western mind trained to take a picture alone, as expression in one sort of language, and not properly to be mixed with another. The Westerner's long acceptance of the selective drawing (or photograph) as the norm of pictorial art has something to do with this; perhaps too the fact that his own writing and lettering have long ago ceased to be pictorial or richly decorative. In any case, the individual will do well, in approaching art in Egypt or Persia or the Far East, to cultivate a single eye for picture and incidental text. The tomb mural, like the later Persian "illumi-

nated manuscript," is to be regarded as one plastic organization, as a single decorative composition. As such, New Kingdom wall-scenes are a never-ending pleasure.

The subjects are as widely varied as those of the sculptured reliefs, ranging from devotional exercises and funerary scenes to domestic and recreational episodes and the depiction of familiar flowers and trees and pets. There is extraordinary truth of observation, within the controlling convention. Birds and animals are shown in exact characteristic outline, marking, and pose; men are fixed in the particular revealing attitude of the moment. The whole is an almost encyclopedic treatise on men's occupations, customs, recreation, and tastes.

But there are, too, the grouping, the composition, the particular Egyptian stylization, to lift the achievement above the attractiveness of routine documentation. The method is linear, with flat and rather monotonous coloring added, as might be expected where painting practically grew out of colored relief-art. But the rhythms

Portrait. Encaustic, from a mummy-case, Fâyum. Graeco-Egyptian. *Louvre*

are decorative, and the whole effect vivacious and colorful.

Thus, although monumental sculpture remains the typical art, the unsurpassed achievement of Egypt, contemporary painting has its claims to world attention and appreciation. Within rather tight conventions it grew and flowered and de-

clined as engaging design-with-color, as pleasing wall decoration. In another direction too it developed a distinctive and beautiful technique: in the illustrated manuscripts known as Books of the Dead. These papyrus rolls were designed for tomb burial with a king or rich man, and served as guides for the deceased or his double on the devotional side of the after-life. They are books of the mysteries of the gods, and in general they seem to have commanded the talents of artists as masterly as those who decorated the walls.

Seldom has a nation maintained its own methods and traditions of an art over such extended periods. Only after thirty-five centuries of characteristic production, only after many generations of rule by foreign overlords, did the Egyptians set aside their own ways and produce work obviously based upon alien principles. Shortly after the opening of the Christian era, painting in Egypt developed, under Roman (or Greek) in-fluence, a special type of fairly realistic portraiture, for use on mummy cases. The portrait heads are life-size, in encaustic on wood or linen. They are forthright and vigorous, and somehow decorative—not too unlike a type developed by the modernist painters in Paris soon after 1900. But this is, in the light of true Egyptian achievement, merely a postscript to the story. It is sculpture, the art of enduring stone, that expresses Egypt, that speaks, three thousand or five thousand years later, of a mastery of the stone surpassed only, perhaps, in the sculpture of Central and Far Asia.

Eagle. Faïence ornament from a wooden box, c. 400 B.C. *Metropolitan Museum of Art*

IV: ART IN PRE-HOMERIC EUROPE:
THE AEGEAN CULTURE

At Vaphio, near Sparta, in the year 1889, Greek archaeologists lifted the stone slabs covering an ancient warrior's grave. There was disclosed a cache of weapons, jewels, and vases, exactly as loving hands had placed them at head, foot, and either hand of the brave departed some thirty-five hundred years earlier. The treasure was particularly rich not only by reason of the number of golden vessels and gems included but also for the light it cast upon the pre-Homeric world. It afforded a sort of cross-section view of the decorative art of the early Aegean civilization.

The warrior's bronze sword and dagger, and his silver earpick, and the bronze sheath of his scepter, lay beside the beads of his necklace and the engraved gems of his bracelets. But most notable, and indeed the highlight among all the discovered relics of the heroic age, were two cups of gold boldly wrought with story scenes: one depicting a hunting episode with trapped wild bulls fighting their captors; the other, bulls tamed and led to sacrifice.

These are the celebrated Vaphio Cups, familiar to every student of art from replicas in countless museums, and described as masterpieces in numberless essays and books. They are a symbol that popularly stands for the Aegean or pre-Greek civilization. They represent the extraordinary skill of Aegean craftsmen. They also reveal, let it be added, the questionable taste of those ancient peoples—their rather florid full-blown luxurious-

Horse and Rider. Clay, Attica. Archaic Greek. *Museum of Fine Arts, Boston* ness and their love of realistic depiction. These drinking cups, indeed, afford a key to art as it was in the only civilized regions of Europe fifteen centuries before Christ, a millennium before the childhood of Greek culture.

The Aegean Culture

The uncovering of the Vaphio tomb formed a chapter in an archaeological adventure of the nineteenth century, a serial exploration of forgotten lands that was in itself romantic, exciting, and almost incredible. A poor boy in Germany, one Heinrich Schliemann, had read the stirring Homeric poems, and he had dreamed of going to Greece and Troy to prove the existence of the described heroes and cities as actual, not mythical, people and places. Schliemann in middle life, having lived his Alger-story, in which he made a fortune from international trade and mastered seven languages, betook himself to Greece in 1868. Defying all scholarly opinion, he dug for the remains of Homer's (and Helen's) Troy at Hissarlik on the coast of Asia Minor near the Dardanelles, and for the tombs of Agamemnon and Clytemnestra at Mycenae in Argolis. He not only found the legendary city of the *Iliad*, and the graves and belongings of his heroes—or of other heroic-age personages very like them—but dug up fabulous treasures of gold and silver, including a queen's diadem and golden masks and pectorals and handfuls of gems. At Troy and in the Mycenaean citadel and at Tiryns he uncovered the outlines of the life and the art of the peoples about whom Homer had written.

Out of Schliemann's work and books, and those of his follower Dorpfeld, and of Tsountas, who found the Vaphio Cups, has been constructed the picture of a long-forgotten pre-Greek culture, now known as Aegean, which takes its place as one of the major manifestations of human enterprise and advance. It is seen, too, as the first European crystallization of art-consciousness, the very cradle of Greek custom, thought, and craftsmanship.

In the end the uncovered Aegean civilization is found to embrace vastly more than the legendary Homeric people and events. Homer was a late and very sketchy historian, writing seven centuries after the most notable exploits of the Cretan sea-kings, and four centuries after the fall of Troy. The *Iliad* and the *Odyssey* formed a sort of cumulative catch-all of popular legend, theology, and remembered history. Through centuries the facts of the Trojan War and Odysseus' wanderings had mixed with myth and popular fiction. Nevertheless, a comparison of descriptions in the two epics with lately discovered examples of Aegean art leaves no doubt that Homer— whether single or "collective" bard—fixed as accurately as a poet is supposed to the features of architecture and decoration and fine-wrought weapon.

The arrival of Odysseus at the palace of Alcinous—that would be about 1180 B.C.—is thus vividly described (in the translation of T. E. Shaw):

Odysseus stood there, not crossing its copper threshold . . . the brilliance within the high-ceiled rooms of noble Alcinous was like the sheen of sun or moon: for the inner walls were copper-plated in sections, from the entering-in to the furthest recesses of the house; and the cornice which ran around them was glazed in blue. Gates of gold closed the great house: the doorposts which stood up from the brazen threshold were of silver, and silver, too, was the lintel overhead: while the handle of the door was gold. Each side of the porch stood figures of dogs ingeniously contrived by Hephaestus the craftsman out of gold and silver, to be ageless, undying watchdogs for this house of the great-hearted Alcinous. Here and there along the walls were thrones, spaced from the inmost part to the outer door. . . . The feasters in the great hall after dark were lighted by the flaring torches which golden figures of youths, standing on well-made pedestals, held in their hands. Of the fifty women servants who maintain this house . . . some weave at the looms, while others sit carding wool upon distaffs which flutter like the leaves of a tall poplar: and so close is the texture of their linen that even fine oil will not pass through it. . . . Athene gave them this genius to make beautiful things.

This praise of the palace of Alcinous seems

fulsome in the reading today, and one cannot wonder that the Victorians and the Greeks alike put it down to fable. Nevertheless, the details have been verified again and again by Schliemann and his followers. The ruined palaces have been uncovered, and evidences found of the high-ceiled rooms, the metal adornments, the glazed friezes, the thrones, and the luxurious furnishings. And the craftsmanship might indeed be a gift of the gods, so accomplished were the workers in gold, bronze, clay, and precious stone.

A second detailed description, even more filled with wonder at a work of art, is found in that passage of the *Iliad* describing the shield of Achilles. Homer credits the design and making of it to the god-artificer Hephaestus, in a passage reading (in the Lang, Leaf, and Myers translation):

First fashioned he a shield great and strong, adorning it all over. . . . There wrought he the earth, and the heavens, and the sea, and the unwearying sun, and the moon waxing to the full, and the signs every one wherewith the heavens are crowned, Pleiads and Hyads and Orion's might, and the Bear. . . . Also he fashioned thereon two fair cities of mortal men. In the one were espousals and marriage feasts, and beneath the blaze of torches they were leading the brides from their chambers through the city. . . . But around the other city were two armies in siege with glittering arms. . . . Furthermore he set in the shield a soft fresh-ploughed field, rich tilth and wide, the third time ploughed; and many ploughers therein drave their yokes to and fro as they wheeled about. . . . Boys gathering corn and bearing it in their arms gave it constantly to the binders; and among them the king in silence was standing at the swathe with his staff, rejoicing in his heart. . . . Also he set therein a vineyard teeming plenteously with clusters, wrought fair in gold; black were the grapes, but the vines hung throughout on silver poles. . . . Also did the glorious lame god devise a dancing-place. . . . Also he set therein the great might of the River of Ocean around the uttermost rim of the cunningly-fashioned shield.

One can no longer wave aside this seemingly impossible list of constellations, cities, feasts, battles, dancing throngs, the earth itself, the ocean, as the product of poetic license—or as impossible of representation in metal. For if one examines the picturing in the outstanding goldsmiths' and bronze-workers' art from Mycenaean or Minoan times, one finds that there are metal objects in every way as ambitious as this within their smaller compass. It is not impossible that some day a fortunate archaeologist will turn up with his spade Achilles' shield or its peer, and find the account accurate. Homer's description gives a perfect picture of Aegean art at its height: the amazing skill and the crowded content, the athletic vigor and the intricacy and the lifelikeness. That it might be termed florid and therefore mediocre art, in all but the technical mastery and the realism, is not of great importance here.

What does signify is that out of the uncovered remains of the pre-Homeric world has been woven a stirring picture of a mighty civilization, a close-knit culture extending from Crete to Greece proper to Asia Minor, and to outposts in Sicily and Cyprus and Sardinia. This was a pre-Greek integration that held together for nearly two thousand years, a vigorous if scattered polity that dominated a great part of the territory first wrested by mankind from primal wilderness.

If the ruins of Troy and Cnossus and Tiryns, and the relics from Mycenae and Vaphio and Dendra, were of scattered "styles" and dissimilar types there would be no historical warrant for setting up Aegean civilization and its art beside the Babylonian and the Egyptian products. But Aegean art is almost as distinctive as the one, and, to the Western world, more significant, more formative, than the other, if only in its heritage to the Greeks.

The whole cycle of Aegean artistic culture can be charted as a thing separate from the parallel developments on the Nile and the Euphrates, can be traced from Neolithic crudity through rise, climax, and fall. It is no singly centered manifestation; it is rather the shifting, fluctuating activity of groups of like-living and intermingling communities within the bowl of the Aegean Sea. But its monuments and mementos are, stylistically, of a piece.

Without the relics of Aegean art the archaeologists would be unable to say that this was a unit, a cultural entity, from the evidence of racial origin or political organization. But through the rise, triumph, and fall of Cretan sea-kings, through a subsequent Mycenaean period, through a decadent era of dispersed peoples and foreign invasions, a single tide of art flows recognizably.

Here are the weapons and the pots, the tombs and the palaces, the fine-wrought gold vessels, and the distinctively engraved gems to prove that the first civilized culture on European soil was not derived as a whole from the Orient, was not merely a mixture of crossing elements from Egypt, Babylonia, and Syria. We can visualize the admirals and mariners of the island kings pushing their vessels to the mouth of the Nile and to Asiatic shores, doubtless absorbing much from their frequent and many-sided commercial contacts with older cultures. But this remained nonetheless a creative national entity, itself shaping and feeding the fire that was to flame again in Athens, then in Rome, and so to light Europe in many ages after.

The period and the place of Aegean art have a storied air, a romantic aura. Homer and the Greek dramatists and poets so mingled myth with fact, so wove for us all a fabric wherein real kings and maids and heroes and shepherds walked with Olympian gods and field-deities and divinely favored nymphs, that it is difficult to remember that the Aegeans were actual men and women, of common flesh and blood. Yet they must have had to make a living, to perform the daily round of work and play and devotion.

The localities from which the Aegean relics have come are blessed with names that themselves cast a golden haze over the subject; for the graven cups and inlaid swords and ivory statuettes are found in Troy and Argolis, in Samos and Rhodes, in Cnossus and Lesbos, among the Cyclades and in Arcady.

The Cretans seem to have been less serious about their gods than were the Egyptians, with whom they had occasional intercourse, sometimes commercial and political, sometimes piratical. They built no separate temples; they were content with shrines in palaces, and perhaps in humbler dwellings; though religious symbols are

frequent in their decorative art, and small images of goddesses or priestesses are found. Nor was the divinity or priestly character of the king insisted upon. He cultivated no air of remoteness, did not isolate himself. Indeed the caste system is here far less evident than elsewhere in the ancient world. Among the higher virtues was reckoned hospitality, as Homer so often testified.

That the Cretans were not predominantly a fighting people is argued by some extensive palaces without fortifications and by the comparative infrequency of the warrior figure in pictorial art —in striking contrast to the Babylonian relics. They were commercial and seafaring pioneers, and by that reason examples of their arts are occasionally found in tombs on the Nile, in Palestine, in Sicily, Italy, and Sardinia. Egypt in turn particularly influenced their craft techniques and their ideas of art.

Some historians, escaping the romantic view, have realistically called them the sea-pirates of Crete; and it is probable that the line between commerce and brigandage was not then nicely drawn. At home the daring and realism of the seafaring way of life were matched by a largeness and naturalism and color in decoration, dress, and sports. The Aegeans—the leaders, at least—were markedly given to splendor in adornment and in pleasures. Racially, all authorities agree, the pre-Homeric peoples of Greece and the Aegean basin were not of the stock that later became, as invaders, the Greeks of classic history; but they mingled with those who are said to have "driven them out."

The Spirit of Aegean Art

What is the spirit of this art that marks it off so decisively from the Babylonian or Persian expression? Why is it said that here begins, not only geographically but aesthetically, the true art of Europe, the classic heritage, the Western manner?

Looking forward to mature Greek art—say of a thousand years after the fall of Cnossus—one may characterize it as having a believable reality, a sweet reasonableness, a logic of truth to nature, that is foreign to Oriental manifestations. It is the art of intellectually mature peoples. The mystic element, the naïve and delicate sensuousness have gone out of it.

Aegean art early came to this logical clarity, this reasonable delineation of the world. Typically it is realistic rather than imaginative or formalistic. Its subject-matter is drawn from familiar life, from local events. The testimony of the eye is respected more than the urge to formal creation. It is thus more intimately human. It registers easily, taxes no one's imagination, pleases by reminders of known things. By the same token it is nearly always somewhat thin, obvious, intellectually engaging rather than aesthetically compelling. It reproduces the movement of outward life, speaks little of the stillness and the calm imagery of the inward spirit.

For a time, of course, it had its early strength, its naïve conventions, its direct leap to formal expressiveness. Remnants of the childhood phase of its designing lingered on in local pockets (or islands) until almost the day when the Dorian Greeks whipped all the other elements into the Greek nation. A highly prized example may be seen in the Cycladic marbles, small fetish-figures that range—as here illustrated—from charmingly stylized approximations of the womanly form to almost abstract versions of the body, like miniature fiddles or spatulas. But sooner than elsewhere the primitive virtues gave way before the sophisticated desire for realism and luxurious ornamentation. Perhaps ideas of foreign luxury-art were imported and misinterpreted. The Vaphio Cups, the golden jewelry, the painted vases, the Homeric descriptions, the women's costumes as depicted in the murals, all indicate an early transition into the naturalistic and the superficially decorative, even the capricious. From this phase art passed on to stylization, but of a sort neither deeply original nor inventive. Here is a fashion of art rather than one of the world styles. And yet of its sort it is masterly and intriguing; and its artists were the forefathers of the Greeks, of the Romans, and of the intellectual West.

It was due to the accidents of time and exploration that what is today called Aegean art was first

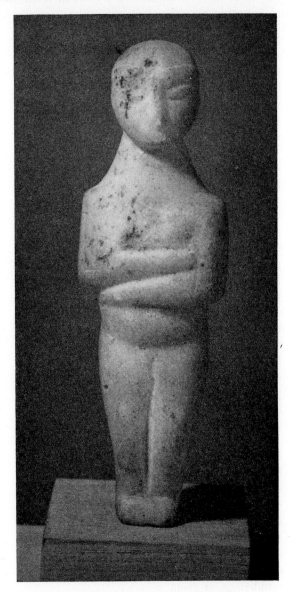

Figure. Marble, this size. Cycladic, Melos

studied as Mycenaean, then as Cretan or Minoan. The unity of the whole has been discerned only after comparison of these two main manifestations, which had been uncovered in the wrong order, and the fitting in of evidence from literally hundreds of other centers.

The student does well to fix in mind the two main recognized divisions of Aegean art: the

Minoan, so named for King Minos, from whose palace at Cnossus in Crete the outstanding evidence has been recovered; and the Mycenaean, as exemplified in the palace and tombs and trinkets uncovered by Schliemann at Mycenae in Argolis, on the Greek mainland. All other manifestations, whether Trojan, Cypriote, Cycladic, or whatever other local variation, can be related to these two.

Although Neolithic pottery exhibits differences as between the Peloponnesus and Crete, it is supposed that in general the earliest art of the Aegean basin pertained to a single racial and cultural growth. There was likeness through the opening of the Bronze Age, and there is ample evidence of intercommunication later over the great area from Thessaly to Crete, from Troy to Rhodes, and even as far as Cyprus. The primitive pottery is interestingly decorative, the stone bowls are well formed, the first metal weapons are functionally pleasing, and the jewelry is fairly agreeable. There are, too, the usual crude terra-cotta figurines. Some of the polished stone bowls are exceptionally proportioned, with decorative exploitation of the natural striations; but this may indicate an early link with Egypt rather than native invention.

From the twilight of the Neolithic era to the noon of the Bronze Age, the story is best told first in terms of the findings at Cnossus and elsewhere in Crete. The kings of a few Cretan cities were, so far as is now known, politically the leading characters of the entire Aegean drama to 1450 B.C., and the representative history of the art of the region may be said to begin with their emergence from the darkness of Neolithic tribal wanderings, at about 3000 B.C.

The Sea-Kings of Crete, and Minoan Art

When Schliemann scratched over parts of Crete in search of Homeric relics he was less fortunate than at Troy and Mycenae. It was Sir Arthur Evans instead who uncovered, about the year 1900, the ruins of the palace and city of Cnossus. This had been for considerable ages the very heart and center of the Aegean world; it was known to Homer as chief of the hundred Cretan

cities. In honor of King Minos, Evans called the culture disclosed by his explorations the "Minoan," and he constructed an elaborate chronology by which all later archaeologists have classified their finds, whether in Crete or Greece or the minor islands, as Early, or Middle, or Late Minoan. There was of course the usual scholarly controversy over the matter; it was contended, for instance, that the wrong king was being honored, since Minos was at the end of the Cnossian dynasties and since he probably ruled at the time of the destruction of this culture rather than during its development and flowering. This was the King Minos whose wife was alleged, in myth, to have given birth to the Minotaur, the bull-headed human monster that fed, in the Labyrinth, on the maidens and youths periodically levied as tribute from Athens, till Theseus, with the help of Minos's daughter Ariadne, dispatched the monster.

But Evans' terminology and chronology have proved so useful that all Aegean art down to the fall of Troy is likely to be identified by his categories. The terms First, Second, and Third Mycenaean Periods are useful for reference too, since Cretan and mainland art do not exactly correspond.

Evans, by using scientific archaeological methods, measuring deposits from bedrock to topmost ruins (generally the remains of several cities or palaces are superimposed on each site), and by ascertaining dates of isolated Egyptian relics found at Cnossus, and of Cretan objects found in Egyptian tombs, constructed a standard table covering cultural and artistic development from the first emergence to the final destruction of Cnossus. Roughly his Early Minoan Period extended from 3000 B.C. to about 2100 B.C. The Middle Minoan Period extended to 1580 B.C. or thereabouts, and the Late Minoan, covering the outstanding architectural and mural works, from 1580 to about 1400 B.C., or, including the entire process of decadence, to 1100 B.C.

Pottery is the art in which the evidence of the growth of the culture is most complete, and the Aegean vases and bowls are doubly important historically because they were also to lead on to that vase-painting which is Greece's greatest

Mycenaean Vase. *Metropolitan Museum of Art*

achievement in graphic art. In shape the pots and bowls and vases show the usual satisfying proportioning from a very early period, with incised ornamentation or elementary painting. It is rather in the variety of shapes, refinement of technique, and abundance of ornament that gradual advance is witnessed. Particularly in the Middle Minoan Period, rich polychrome designs appear, and the delicacy of the pieces is marked; the glazes take on a porcelain-like subtlety. Toward the end, in the Late Period, there is the tendency toward stylization and geometrization which may be a link with the Greek development of a millennium later.

In general, however, the ornament on Cretan pottery may be said to run to a sort of florid naturalism. It is seldom sensitive and is frequently capricious. The design is almost invariably asymmetrical. The flower-sprays and animals and fish are often so directly copied from nature that it is less correct to speak of the "motives" than to call them depictions. Particularly common are the seaweeds, shells, octopuses, and fish of the surrounding seas, as befits the work of craftsmen in a maritime civilization. The human body is not an important element.

Perhaps the high mark of Aegean ceramic achievement was reached in the eggshell ware of the Middle Minoan Period, as seen especially in examples found in the Royal Pottery Stores of the palace at Cnossus. The late so-called "palace style" vases are more elaborate and showy, but delicacy and ceramic propriety have been lost.

Sculpture was, strangely enough, a minor art in Crete. The comparatively small amount found

Cow and Calf. Faïence relief, Cnossus, reproduction. *Metropolitan Museum of Art*

is bound up with the potter's craft rather than with stone or metal working, though there are stone figures from the nearby islands. The outstanding pieces are faïence, glazed clay, or mere terra cotta. Among them are the so-called snake-goddesses, or priestesses of the snake cult. These partly undressed but otherwise elaborately costumed female figures, with snakes entwining upper body and arms or held at arm's length, are terra-cotta statuettes finished in colored glaze. An example at the Boston Museum is by exception ivory, with gold bands. It is perhaps more important artistically than those actually found in the Cnossus palace. In its present restored state it has sculptural unity to a degree apparently unusual at the time, as well as notable truth to the model.

But the snake-goddess type and all known examples are really more of interest for what they tell of religious custom than for plastic values. As so often in Aegean work, the broader sculptural virtues and the sensitive rhythmic adjustments are commonly obscured by the artist's desire to dwell upon every detail of natural form and every bit of ornament on a ceremonial dress.

More satisfying for rhythmic linear grace and simplification of form—due in part perhaps to their fragmentary condition—are the two faïence reliefs which were once parts of a series on the walls of a shrine in the Cnossian palace.[1] The plaques, one showing a she-goat suckling a kid, with another kid closing the group, and the other a cow suckling her calf, have no doubt a religious significance. But what is exceptional is the compositional completeness of each piece. There is approach to the play of main mass and minor, and there are binding linear melodies. In subject-matter both reliefs are notably true to observed significant detail and movement.

---

[1] Although restorations and replicas are in general excluded from the illustrations appearing in this book, exceptions have been made here. The available photographs of original Aegean antiquities are so far inferior to those of reproductions that five of the latter are shown. These include the cow-and-calf plaque, the *Boxer Vase,* the Vaphio Cups, the Mycenaean daggers, and a mural painting. All are from reproductions in the Metropolitan Museum of Art, New York, and the photographs are used by courtesy of the Extension Division of the Museum.

Snake-Goddess. Ivory and gold. *Museum of Fine Arts, Boston*

Large sculpture is almost nonexistent at the excavated sites of the Cretan and Mycenaean civilizations. The famous Lion Gate at Mycenae is an exception, but there is little to enjoy in its two cramped and battered lions. There is no trace of monumental metal statues like the golden

The so-called *Harvester's Vase* is extraordinarily alive with depicted movement, and explains its episode with graphic vitality and documentary accuracy. The crowd of merrymakers sweeps along in some sort of ceremonial procession all the way round the jug. The singers, with wide-open mouths, and the harvesters, with flails over their shoulders, are caught up in a lilting, rhythmic movement. This is far too elaborate a scene for such a small bit of stonework. It cannot do other than breed confusion for the eye. But it is marvelously detailed and vivacious. Stone vases were probably painted or covered with gold leaf, thus—the purist notes—adding another factor disturbing to sculptural calm and stonelike simplicity.

The *Boxer Vase* suffers less from confusion of figures. But it is so long and slender, being in the form of a horn, that the relief figures, in four bands around the vessel, are only fragmentarily in sight from any one point of view. The modeling here is not far from masterly, at least in the matter of the bulls.

In metal work, too, it is relief rather than free figure that is significant. Some bronze figurines and ceremonial ax-heads in bronze and gold, vigorous and broad, represent a craft that finds fuller expression in figured cups and jewelry. Supremacy in this art lies less in the Cretan cities than on the Mycenaean mainland, and descriptions are better left to a later section, not primarily Minoan.

The Boxer Vase. Steatite rhyton, Hagia Triada, reproduction. *Original, Candia Museum*

youths with torches mentioned by Homer. Religion did not call for god-images and conspicuous idols.

In stone the reliefs on steatite vessels alone are outstanding. The most interesting are three vases found not at Cnossus but at Hagia Triada on the lower coast of Crete. The workmanship is none too expert, but the action indicated in two of the works is vigorous, and the forms are bold. Considered merely as illustrational art, the compositions are spirited and arresting.

Minoan Painting and Architecture

Cretan life and Aegean ways of design are more justly illustrated in the mural paintings uncovered in the palace of Minos, though one must add the precautionary note that these have been restored, probably with too much enthusiasm and conjecture, by Sir Arthur Evans' staff. It needs to be said at once, too, that most of the so-called copies in museums and in books are replicas of Victorian restorations, and that frequently only a slight fragment or two formed the basis of the composition.

But there is authentic evidence that the murals

Leaping Bull Scene. Painted mural, partly reconstructed. *Candia Museum*

were bright in color, highly stylized in manner, and generally florid in decorative accessory such as frieze or incidental pattern. The illustrational scenes indicate little of the Egyptian sense of well-spaced composition. But the figures lie flat in true mural conventionalization.

The subjects of Minoan mural paintings range from stylized animals, gardens, and plants to single ceremonial figures, bullfighting episodes, and complex court scenes. The medium is lime-plaster fresco, and the colors are separately blocked on, usually without gradation or merging, over an outline drawing. A few simple bright colors suffice. The wall-paintings at Cnossus are all from the latest Minoan period, about 1500 B.C., though there have been found fragments of the mural art of the ruined palaces underneath the one of that date now partially restored. A few smaller paintings exist, chiefly on the side of a sarcophagus recovered at Hagia Triada. These are in flat mural technique and standard fresh colors. Occasionally fresco was superimposed on a mural design modeled in slight relief.

Adding the evidence of the wall-paintings to that of the statuettes, one comes to a conclusion not without interest in relating this era to that of the later Greeks. The figures in the Aegean wall-paintings, as in the statuette of the snake-goddess, are beautifully set up, straight, the men high-chested, the women with breasts full and firm. In the murals and in the minor sculpture and on seals there is a convention of the shoulders held

back and the waist pinched in, heightening the impression. Goddess, bullfighter, court lady, and field worker alike are distinguished by this idiom. All seem nobly strong, athletic, and poised. This perhaps signalized a native physique of slender, lithe strength that was a characteristic of the sea-kings' peoples. The pinched-waist convention is seen in certain figures in Egyptian tomb murals, characterizing what are now supposed to be tribute-bearers from the Aegean cities. In any case, in addition to the general realism of pre-Homeric art, the glorification of the human physique seems also to indicate a direct line of descent from Aegean to Greek.

A second convention of Cretan painting is that the man's flesh is indicated by a dark tone, the woman's by a light tone. This is useful in identifying male and female toreadors in the bull-fighting or bull-leaping scenes, for it seems that girls entered into the sport dressed as boys. Here, perhaps, in the forced entry of slaves into the bull ring, is the basis in fact for the legend that Athenian maidens and youths were fed to the bull-headed Minotaur.

The palace in which the murals at Cnossus exist might well be used to test the truth of Homer's architectural descriptions. There is a complex of courts, halls, and rooms magnificent in extent. Now that some of the decorations have been restored it is possible to visualize too the color and luxurious splendor that once surrounded the sea-kings and their courtiers. There were neighboring crowded towns of unpretentious houses, some of them two-storied. Evans estimated that Cnossus at the time of this restored palace, the last of several on the site, had a population of one hundred thousand. But only the art of the palace and the nobles remains.

Conjectural restorations suggest what may have been the visual aspects of the exterior architecture, but the remaining foundations and fragments, the column bases, and the few depictions in murals offer little to the student's aesthetic enjoyment. Aegean architecture is lost beyond recovery. Moreover, the great palaces were probably built a piece at a time, more to live in than to look at. They had good baths and drains, and a wealth of interior furnishings, but they were not monumental or unified.

The palace at Cnossus is nonetheless interesting for its indications of a way of life generously sprinkled through with the arts. The throne-room is large and well paved and has at one end what seems to be a sumptuous bathing pool. The walls were gaily figured, and the high-backed throne is still in place, though its decorations have been shorn off.

Other features are the many storerooms, in some of which huge jars were found. The storage chambers are so numerous and so large that archaeologists have inferred the existence of a great commercial trade in oils and metals and other precious commodities, centered in the royal palace. Someday the world will know more about these matters, for written records exist in great numbers. They are still largely undeciphered. But in 1954 an amateur archaeologist came forward with translations of a few key words, and made certain that scholars will unravel the several mysteries surrounding the "Minoan" script —which had already been marked as related to the Greek and as belonging to the Indo-European language group. When the script has been fully mastered, and the "documents" have been painstakingly translated, the world will gain in knowledge of the customs, history, and arts in the Aegean lands. J. L. Myres in *The Dawn of History* has ventured the opinion that the clay tablets found in the palace at Cnossus include "inventories of treasure and stores, and receipts for chariots, armour, metal vessels, ingots of copper . . . and smaller quantities of unworked gold by weight. Other tablets contain lists of persons, male and female; perhaps tribute paid in slaves, or in person, as in the Greek legend of the Minotaur."

That the Minotaur may well have been the legendary representation of a sacred bull actually kept in the Cnossian palace by King Minos seems doubly likely when the ground-plan of the edifice is studied. For here are parts that form a veritable maze or labyrinth, with long corridors, false entrances to lead one down blind halls, and rooms to be reached only after many tortuous turnings. Haphazard planning may explain part of it: there is no symmetry in Aegean architecture, no axial planning. Nevertheless, the Labyrinth of the legend is demonstrably there in Minos's palace, where also are frescoes of bull-leaping. Greek legend has it that the designer of the Labyrinth was the famous artificer Daedalus, first of mortals to invent a way of flying. Since the essential truth of so much similar lore has been confirmed, further discoveries may yet reveal the facts behind the triumph and tragedy of the Daedalus-Icarus legend.

The word "labyrinth" came into the Greek language and so down to us from this remembered feature of the Cnossian palace. The palace in turn got the name from a sacred emblem, the double ax, which is found in decorations on its walls and represented in golden votive emblems found in the sanctuary. The building is sometimes called the "Palace of the Double Ax"—that is, of the *labrys*.

The ruins of other palaces unearthed in Cretan cities confirm the impression of Aegean architecture as massive, diffuse, and structurally simple, on an uncentered plan and disunified in effect. So far as can be judged, the actual architectural refinements were slight; the columns lacked elaborately shaped capitals and organic moldings; but the applied surface ornament was colorful and sumptuous.

Small engraved seals have been found at Cnossus that show more skill and taste than went into larger objects and monuments. And the craftsmanship in a game-board found in Minos's palace is amazingly clever in its inlays and decoration, in its use of precious metals, ivory, and enamel. But it is in that other part of the Aegean story, the Mycenaean, that the smaller crafts are illustrated at their best.

Of Cnossus it remains only to say that the imperialism of the Cretan kings ran the usual course. After a period of great prosperity and power—for the court class, at least—the culture apparently collapsed and all but disappeared. Cnossus was finally burned, and no further palaces were built on the ruins.

Cretan art was not important after 1400 B.C. Thereafter the Mycenaeans were leaders of the Aegean civilization—or perhaps chief among a circle of prosperous cooperating communities. The final snuffing out of Cnossus may not have occurred until 1100 B.C., but, three centuries before, leadership had passed to the mainland cities. Some authorities believe that these cities had been founded by Cretan colonists.

The Mycenaean Culture

The Greeks in their time knew of the ruins of Mycenae and Tiryns, and counted them as relics of a civilization of vague "original peoples" of Hellas, though ascribing some of their marvelous works to gods and god-men. The walls, made of huge blocks of stone, in particular seemed to be proof of a vanished race of supermen. The traveler Pausanias, writing in the second century A.D., noted that "there are visible remains of the walls and of the gate that has lions over it. These were erected, they say, by the Cyclopes."

The Lion Gate at Mycenae, famous then as now, is almost the sole surviving example of monumental Aegean sculpture, in or out of buildings. A triangular stone over a lintel is carved with two confronted lions flanking an engaged pillar, the whole forming a sort of heraldic shield celebrating the pillar-emblem (which had religious significance in Crete as well). The extraordinarily large blocks of stone around the lonely sculptural composition gave rise to the legend of a Cyclopean origin. To modern archaeologists they signify rather that the people of Argolis, unlike the Cretans, felt the need to fortify heavily their palace-homes and their treasuries.

In the "Grave Circle" at Mycenae there were discovered some commemorative stones carved in low relief which indicate, with the Lion Gate, that sculpture was more advanced here in the golden period than it had ever been at Cnossus. The figure compositions and the geometric patterning fill the panel-areas with a surer sense of plastic ordering, with greater satisfaction to the eye, than any of the stone fragments uncovered at Crete—though falling far short of Egyptian mastery. There is little of note in terra-cotta modeling, but two fragments of a box suggest that sculpture in wood may have been well advanced. There is, in metal sculpture, a large bull's head of silver with horns of sheet gold, the whole very naturalistically treated.

But it is where the arts of sculpture and jewel-working meet that the Mycenaeans and their neighbors of the Peloponnesus were supreme. There are gold buckles and pins and dress accessories with geometric ornamentation either abstract or flower-derived; elaborately decorative crowns and diadems and necklaces; gold and silver cups, sometimes patterned over, or with story scenes in relief. Even the vessels and utensils which elsewhere would be of pottery are here worked in sheet copper or bronze. Perhaps most beautiful, as a series, are the swords and daggers, bronze blades inlaid with more precious metals, in designs ranging from reticent abstract patterning to crowded pictorial schemes.

In these weapons is touched a high mark of ancient craftsmanship. The method of inlay, later known as damascening, is not difficult. On the shaped blade, and perhaps hilt, outlines of the design are scratched, and the metal within the outlined figures is removed to a slight depth, with space hollowed out under each edge—technically an "undercut." The gold and silver inlays are pressed in and hammered, and the whole is polished. The resulting contrasts in color and texture heighten the interest of the linear and rhythmic design and lend it richness.

The art as the Aegeans practiced it is seen in many variations, most often with gold and silver

Mycenaean daggers, damascened, reproductions. *National Museum, Athens*

floriation or figure as inlay and incrustation, though there are also designs of simple, direct engraving. Among the finest recovered examples are the blades with hunting scenes. The fitting of the elements of the design to the long narrow space shows a rare feeling for compositional order. There is here that which is so generally lacking in Aegean murals and stone vases: elaborate picturing without loss to functional integrity. The formal relationship of representation to available space and frame is duly observed.

The golden crowns and diadems tend to be florid and heavy-handed, and the masks in thin sheet gold—placed apparently over the faces of warriors at burial—are sculpturally unimportant. But many of the buckles, buttons, and minor dress ornaments have a delicacy within richness that puts to shame much of the jewelry of modern times. The engraved designs are geometrical —circles and spirals—and conventionalized flower and insect forms. One series of disks in almost uniform size, probably used as dress ornaments, runs to formalized butterflies, blossoms, and octopuses. Animals enter into the more freely designed individual buckles and pendants. They are sufficient to mark the Mycenaean craftsmen as master sculptors in miniature.

The golden cups found at Mycenae are as a group extraordinarily beautiful in proportioning and in workmanship. If they have been overshadowed in popular and critical interest by the Vaphio Cups, which belong to the same mainland phase of Aegean art, it is because the latter are more excitingly figured, with elaborate story-scenes of bull-hunting and sacrifice. There is a superior quality of art in the simpler, reticently ornamented vessels, both those which are mug-shaped and flat-bottomed and the suavely curved pedestaled forms. The rounding of some of the goblets, with an indescribable delicacy of line, reminds one of a legend recounted by Greek writers, that Helen of Troy molded golden cups to the form of her own breasts.

The Vaphio Cups, to be sure, represent better the spirit of Aegean art as a whole. They are luxuriously ornamental, and there is a journalistic exactness in their pictured episodes. They might, in fact, stand for the artistic expression of periods overintellectualized and sophisticated in taste. Products comparable in character, showing decoration pushed to extremes of profuseness and labored to a minute natural exactitude, might be cited from the same period in Babylon, from the period of Greece's deterioration, or Rome's, or from the High Renaissance—to recall but a few parallels in history.

For all the praise that has been heaped by savants and craftsmen on the Vaphio Cups, their

Figured gold cups, Vaphio, reproductions. *National Museum, Athens*

virtues are primarily in a perfect technique. That an artist should have shown so much on a small golden surface is marvelous; marvelous too the joining of outer figured shell and inner smooth vessel. But this is scarcely organic art. The design protrudes. The bulging figures are inconsistent with the uses of the utensil. The whole is showy. It is only when they are accepted as specimens of illustration that one marvels at them, noting with wonder the vigor and lifelikeness of the bulls and men, and the sharp detail of rope and foliage, and the whole air of swift observation and careless mastery. Here indeed, as some Victorian authority remarked, is the work of a pre-Homeric Cellini. Here is exactly the sixteenth-century cleverness, realism, and extravagance; also the blunted sense of organic form.

The late Greeks, of course, were appreciative of the realism and the marvelous craftsmanship. Hesiod, who, like Homer, wrote of the heroic age, summed up better than any subsequent writer the wonders of this early artisanship. In the *Theogony* (as translated by Elton) occur these lines, in a passage describing a golden diadem devised by Hephaestus for Athena:

Full many works of curious craft, to sight
Wondrous, he grav'd thereon; full many beasts
Of earth, and fishes of the rolling main;
Of these innumerable he there had wrought
And elegance of art there shown profuse,
And admirable—e'en as though they moved
In very life, and uttered animal sounds.

It is illuminating that, alike in Mycenaean times, in the era of the dawn of Greek literature, and in the period of the Greek culmination, the life-likeness of the object depicted was considered supremely important.

One other art, also miniature, flourished in Mycenae, and perhaps throughout the Aegean world. It was that of gem-engraving, as exemplified in seals. There are gold seal rings with picture designs, and also unnumbered thousands of emblems cut on precious or semi-precious stones. A seal of this sort appears on the wrist of a cup-bearer shown on a Cnossian mural, though the signet seems to have been oftener worn on a necklace. It may be inferred that every person of standing in Aegean society had his own device and the means for impressing it in clay.

The subjects are sometimes pictographic or hieroglyphic—in the Mycenaean-Cretan writing that is "partly syllabic, partly ideographic"—or heraldic, or freely pictorial. Animal motives are favorites, and there is often the muscular vigor and lively action already noted in the modeling of the Vaphio Cups, and here perfectly appropriate. Hunting scenes are common, and the human figure is used both decoratively and for realistic purposes. Combats of warriors are not uncommon. At the other extreme are agricultural and nautical symbols and conventionalized natural forms. The craftsmanship and the sense of design are in general very high. Scores of examples are pleasing in composition, decoratively striking, and in a fitting crisp and bold style.

The story told in terms of Mycenae and Cnossus might be recounted in part as pertaining to Tiryns or Dendra. The many centers were interdependent; their separate cultures overlapped, influenced one another, formed together the integral but varied civilization that is called Aegean. Sometimes one branch of art was more advanced at one city than in the others; but in general the arts as described are typical of the scattered communities, whether in Argolis and Laconia or in the Cyclades or in Crete. Only Troy, on the distant Asian shore, and Cyprus, down in the eastern Mediterranean, demand separate notations—and Troy less for intrinsically valuable work than for the confirmation offered there of the outlines of the total Aegean development.

Troy

From about 3000 B.C., at the beginning of the Bronze Age, the history of Troy has been traced by explorations on the site at Hissarlik and on the Trojan Plain. Because the settlement was strategically placed not only on the seaway from Aegean ports to the Black Sea but also in relation to a mainland route from Asia to Europe, it was affected by many cultural cross-currents. Its arts are therefore less purely Aegean than are the Cretan and Peloponnesian manifestations. Up to the time of the Mycenaean zenith, when Troy—at the time of the "Sixth City"—turned definitely Aegean, there is evidence of independent origin and development, and in some of the arts a strong influence from Cyprus and the Orient. The Trojans, moreover, were traders into Europe by way of the Danube Valley, and doubtless took as well as gave in that direction.

The early pottery was very little decorated; but some polished greenstone or jade axes are outstanding, and the goldsmith's art, especially as applied to articles of personal adornment, was advanced. After this independent, or Oriental, phase of prosperity and importance, lasting perhaps to 2000 B.C., the city seems to have lapsed into obscurity; the traces of two flimsy villages now lie over the remains of more pretentious urban building.

But in the sixteenth century B.C. the Minoan-Mycenaean wave of cultural and political advancement spread this far. The architecture of that time is on a par with the dressed stone palaces and houses of contemporary Crete and Mycenae, and Mycenaean pottery exists beside an improved local sort. Troy then became the city and citadel known to Homer by song and legend. And the arts became interdependent with those of Mycenae and Cnossus. Some historians believe that Troy, perhaps through Asiatic influence, had at this time temples—a distinguishing circumstance, since the other Aegean communities yield few traces of separate buildings commemorating the gods.

Shortly after the Trojan War came the further Dorian invasions which plunged the Aegean communities into their dark ages. There followed in Crete and Hellas and Troy alike the near-extinction of the arts.

Cyprus

The story of Cyprus is quite another matter. Independent at first, and of composite racial make-up later, the island peoples exhibit cultural lines crossing at many points with those of Babylonia, Syria, and Egypt, yet most entangled with the Aegean. The fact that the word "copper" comes from "Cyprus" indicates a special importance held by this metal-producing community along the highways of civilization in the Bronze Age.

From the evidence of the period from 3000 B.C. to about 1600 B.C. it is possible to infer an independent origin and growth for the island crafts. But the early pottery is not unusually fine, nor are the metal weapons and utensils, at first of copper, then of bronze. The true artistic advance came in a following period, when Mycenaean influences—perhaps even in the form of an invasion—were dominant. There was then a vigorous push forward in the several arts, including pottery-design and metalsmithing.

It was then that Cyprus became a part of the extensive give-and-take of art manufacture and art trade in the Aegean basin. There are relics from a time before the Trojan War, but perhaps the main service of the Cyprian people was to

Head. Terra cotta, Cypriote. *Metropolitan Museum of Art*

carry on civilization after the decline of Western Aegean culture. The more favorably situated cities of Cyprus escaped the destructive deluge of tribesmen from the north. It may well be that the islanders were the latest to continue the Minoan-Mycenaean impulse.

In any case, there came in Cyprus, after the collapse of Aegean civilization and before classic Greece, a development of sculpture that is unique. It must have been Cypriote first, for neither Crete nor Mycenae had comparable sculptured works, and the entry of Oriental influence and motives can be marked only *after* the submission of seven kings of the cities of Cyprus to Sargon of Assyria in 709 B.C. Moreover, there

is not the wooden lifelessness of Assyrian sculpture. At another time it was Egypt that afforded models and exercised sway over the island craftsmen and artists. They evidently were not above copying any popular article "for the trade"—but within a local freedom of interpretation. And for a time Cypriote sculpture in both stone and clay was distinctive and important. It was more truly sculptural and individualized than any other development in the Aegean area before the Greek.

Most of the Cypriote statues had a votive purpose. They are found largely in sanctuaries. It seems that the citizens, wanting to pay due personal respect to their gods without neglect of more pressing affairs, developed a custom of supplying an effigy to do devotion at the shrine for them. It did not much matter whether the image was a likeness or not; a sensible god would know whose the impulse and the gift. Thus there grew up the convention of a few type figures, in standardized worshipful or respectful attitudes. A man or woman could buy one of these ready-mades, dedicate it once for all, and be quit of personal attendance. A rich man might go to the extent of commissioning an individual portrait. There are, too, images of the gods themselves, of priests, and of a specially common sort of attendant known as the Temple Boy.

As illustrated in recovered examples (the Metropolitan Museum in New York has hundreds) about ninety-nine per cent of them are as routine and mediocre as might be expected where such factory methods pertained. But there are many agreeably competent heads, and an occasional piece characterized by both human interest and sculptural beauty. The full-length *Bearded Aphrodite* in the Metropolitan Museum's collection is one of the suavest and most mature sculptural works of its century, the sixth B.C. An alien influence is evident in the Assyrian helmet, but the graceful conventionalization of draperies, hair braids, and beard constitute something new in Eastern Mediterranean art. Greek sculpture of the mainland had not progressed so far at this time.

There are historians who refuse to recognize any strings of descent from the earlier Aegeans to the sculptors of Cyprus. They term these statues Graeco-Phoenician, meaning that the archaic Greeks—who may be described as the conquered Aegeans now assimilated to the Dorian invaders, forming the one race out of which classic Greece was presently to rise—mixed with the Phoenicians to create a special island culture, not very different from that shaping slowly in Greece, yet not too different from marginal developments on the Asiatic mainland. The historian Carotti is even willing to merge Cypriote art with Phoenician, treating it wholly under a section entitled "The Phoenicians."

Phoenicia, the country that took over control of the Aegean and Mediterranean sea routes after the decline of Mycenaean power, never matched its commercial supremacy with mastery in the fields of art. The Phoenicians are known to have been clever craftsmen and copyists, hardly more. They could take hints from Egypt, Assyria, or Cyprus itself, pound out an object somewhat like an imported original, and perhaps multiply a likely trade piece in a hundred copies. These went out in their ships along all the commercial routes to the westward, and thus "Phoenician art" is encountered in many a tomb thousands of miles from Tyre and Sidon. Carthage, the colonial city founded by Tyrian traders on the North African coast opposite Sicily, before 800 B.C., doubtless became a second center for scattering this trade-art, along with such leading commodities as copper and ivory and slaves.

To the art student it is illuminating to see the Phoenician and Punic galleys thus carrying artwares throughout the length of the known European and African worlds; even though the examples in general are mediocre copies or approximations of creative products. But it is hardly fair to tag Cypriote art as merely a phase of the unoriginal Phoenician contribution, considering the well-proved Mycenaean heritage, genetic and linguistic as well as artistic, and the existence of a body of Cypriote sculpture superior to anything Phoenician. The lines of nationality, of domination, of transmittance, become very confused here, for Cyprus became vassal in turn of Assyria, of Egypt, of Persia, only to return to a later alliance with the newly amalgamated Greece, to which certain predominantly Greek communities on the island had long been loyal.

If one turns to neighboring Palestine, the influences are no less mixed. The Israelites seem not to have been born craftsmen, however great their literature. Biblical accounts are filled with references to artificers imported by the Israelites. When King Solomon bought from Hiram, King of Tyre, cedar and fir trees needed for the Temple at Jerusalem, and later sent an army of his own men to Lebanon to hew and haul timbers, the work was carried forward by "Solomon's builders and Hiram's builders." Later when Solomon planned his own palace, and one for Pharaoh's daughter, whom he had taken to wife,

Bearded Aphrodite. Limestone. Cypriote, wears Assyrian helmet.
Metropolitan Museum of Art

he obtained a craftsman from Phoenicia: "His father was a man of Tyre, a worker in brass: and he was filled with wisdom, and understanding, and cunning to work all works in brass. And he came to King Solomon, and wrought all his work."

This sort of work, in temple and palace, turned out to be everything from colossal brass pillars with wonderful "chapiters" bearing pomegranates, and a molten sea (or sacrificial basin) on the backs of twelve oxen—"and the sea was set above upon them, and all their hinder parts were inward"—to highly intricate wheeled receptacles with sculptural adornments, and commoner shovels and "lavers." There are enumerated too the additional works that "Solomon made," the vessels and candlesticks and censers and altar, all of gold, to which he added in the Temple the historic treasures of David.

Such were the wonders of Solomon's palace that so impressed the Queen of Sheba. No one can doubt that this Israelite capital, religious and royal, designed largely by Phoenicians, was one of the showiest architectural works of pre-Roman times. It was probably stylistically very mixed. The structural features were mostly out of Egypt. The cherubim abounding were from Assyria. But the rooms were finished in "sheets of gold."

The chroniclers go on to tell how "King Solomon loved many strange women" and strayed away after their gods, Ashtoreth (or Ishtar), and "Milcom the abomination of the Ammonites."

And so the true Lord was angry with him, and it was not long before King Solomon's group of magnificent buildings was "rent." The Babylonians were the immediate instruments of destruction. Later, when another temple had been built, and rebuilt, the Romans obliterated it. Worse, the Christians were to erect churches on the site, only to be followed by the Mohammedans, who have a mosque there to this day. Thus did a work of art celebrated in its era, perhaps the most pretentious and certainly the most overloaded up to that time, perish. And students see in it now only an interesting example of the vicissitudes of art, and a strange example of the crossing of nationalistic or racial creative currents.

The Aegean basin and the eastern Mediterranean lands, indeed, afford a prime illustration of the scientific truth that neither a "pure" culture nor a pure race exists. And yet the next development in this area was so distinctive, so shaped by ways of doing and thinking new in man's cultural advance, that it became a norm to which Europe returned at intervals through twenty-four centuries: the Greek.

V: GREECE AND
THE NORM OF WESTERN ART

Iт was Greece," wrote Lechat, "that inaugurated art properly so-called: universal art, not created for the eyes and intelligence of the Greeks alone. Egypt had had Egyptian art. With the art of Greece, human art really begins."

Lechat had taken as text for his book *La Sculpture Grecque* a saying of the French painter Ingres, last of the Western masters to dedicate his life to the search for "Greek purity": "There was once on the earth a little corner of land where, under the most beautiful skies, . . . the arts and letters bathed nature in a second light, for all the earth's people and for all generations to come."

Even after the dawn of the twentieth century there was, for a decade or two, this common acceptance of Greek art as the beginning—and almost the end—of mature, civilized art.

All of us who were students in those days were taught to accept "the Greek miracle" and "Athenian perfection" as ideas beyond challenge or comparison. We were expected to believe uncritically in the legend of a people gifted and inspired above all others. We were accustomed and content to see the Parthenon, the *Venus of Milo,* and the figured vases with a glamorous light upon them, as of an eminence unquestioned and unquestionable. Classical education bathed

Horse and Rider. Archaic Greek. *Acropolis Museum, Athens*

Hellas and the Grecian isles in a golden haze.

In the larger view there is no question that the Greeks more than any others had shaped our Western cultural inheritance. European practice and ideals of art had been based upon a study of Greek works. Shelley's exclamation still rings down the corridors of our universities and our art schools: "We are all Greeks. Our laws, our literature, our religion, our arts, have their root in Greece."

In the weaving of the design of European learning and grace and art the Greek-Roman-Renaissance thread is predominant and determining. The word "classic" means, by dictionary definition, "of the first class, of allowed excellence." Greek art ran off with the label "classic." It has been used, by common consent, to identify first of all the products of Hellas from the fifth century on, and then the whole train of imitative and reflecting achievements: Roman, Renaissance, and, until recently, "modern" works of art in the logically clear Greek tradition. Greek classic art has been the norm for Europe and America.

In spite of growing and persistent challenges to the pre-eminence of Greek classicism, most observers, it is certain, do not so much doubt the superiority of the Greek heritage and achievement as gaze wistfully at a retreating but longed-for excellence. Modern psychology has made clear the reason for this indecision, which begins in a paradox: although we talk of ancient times and of ancient Greek art, we of today are the real ancients of world history. In the nature of time, ours is the oldest of civilizations. Greece was born and lived when the world was new and shining, when art was an adventure, and logical thinking and philosophy a youthful game played with exuberance and zest. Our sighing and our affection are for a time when life was uncomplicated, free, spontaneous, when art works were shaped in a certain clarity, with the sweet impress of a fresh joy in life and a pagan trustfulness. To whatever extent in our latest maturity we ancients may become disillusioned about the depth and formal intensity of Greek visual art, we cannot shake the fact of its clear morning-light appeal, its dawn-brightness.

There has been, nevertheless, in the decades since the opening of the twentieth century, an inevasible challenge to the classicists, and a turn, among foremost creative artists, directly away from Greek aims and ideals. Strange forces have been borne in from a rediscovered Orient, and out of the West's own machine-conditioned way of life. The whole trend of thought and practice is away from the classic outlines and the classic spirit. It begins to come clear that what Western Europe accomplished in its imitation of Greece was not classic but neoclassic—or, to be more cruelly precise, *pseudo-classic*—and it is perhaps one of the marks of our maturity that the pendulum now definitely swings in the opposite direction.

And yet, with all the reservations and rerankings and markings-down accounted for, the Greek culture stands out as an almost unparalleled single national advance. It holds the essence of one of the two outstanding world ways of art. To get at the heart of its quality and its methods more critically than did our fathers, while keeping our conviction of a distinctive and determining achievement, may serve to open our eyes wider to the excellences and variations of all world art.

Greek artists, free of limitations imposed by priest or by king, shaped their ideas to a prevailing philosophy of rationalism and humanism. Their art is distinctively clear, intellectual, and true to the seen object. Mystery is abhorred, the meaning of nature overlooked, the divinity of the gods minimized. All interest centers in man, his doings, his pleasures, his feats, the idealization of his outward aspects. If he still has spiritual vision, if he experiences intimations of a life more profound than can be explained by reason alone, they are forgotten. For the first time in the history of art, the *thinking* man controls.

The key to the understanding of Greek civilization, as well as of Greek art, is in this matter of a thinking approach. It is difficult for the man of today, to whom cultivation means primarily training of the intellect, to realize how unanalytically and childishly most peoples before the Greeks had accepted the world. Life then was commonly considered objectively, without

Apollo. From pediment group, Temple of Zeus, Olympia. *Olympia Museum*

questioning about causes, without the labor of "thinking things out." Gods sufficed to account for the phenomenal world. A special caste of priests looked after the relationship of community and individual to the unknown. A wise man accepted and believed what he was told. It is to the glory of the Greeks that for the first time a considerable body of men developed an intellectual curiosity, asked questions about causes, found it exciting to meet and discuss the nature of things, to conjecture about the objectives of life and the methods of bettering human conditions.

That they perpetuated many illogical ideas and conditions out of earlier existence, that they fostered slavery and warlike pursuits, and evolved a materialistic philosophy, and thus went down to national ruin, need not diminish admiration for that one advance. It was the first mass challenge to "blind" nature, and the first wide use of logical thought to solve human problems.

Except for a very few leaders, men had been as children before. Now, on one side of human capabilities, they had grown up. The scientific spirit was born. Thought became a prime instrument of advance. Analysis preceded action. Anaxagoras said: "All things were in chaos until Mind arose and made order."

The effect upon art was both releasing and confining. Intelligence was able to isolate beauty, to rationalize about its desirability, to encourage multiplication and production. But the intellect soon confined practice to aspects seen and copied, to emotions usual and rational, to the idealization of physical attributes. The clear, steady, light-of-day quality of Greek sculpture and the logically arrived at refinements of Greek architecture have much to tell us of one of humanity's epochal evolutionary moves forward. But of those enrichments of color, pattern, and melodious rhythm in which the senses delight without asking why, there is no more than an occasional hint in the entire range of Greek production, from late archaic statue and vase to shallow Hellenistic counterfeit of nature. Of those overtones that arise from giving rein to the soul, leading the artist to depart from the normal seen aspect, the Greeks knew little. They capitalized upon the intelligence and philosophy of their age; but in doing so they lost sight entirely of what some primitive peoples had known, and what we today begin to accept, as a test of art's permanent worth: its content of a quality of truth from regions beyond and above rational analysis. Greek art is above all explainable, reasoned, sight-bound.

Of the two ways, then, in which the spectator's consciousness can be reached, by intelligence or by intuition, the Greek artist chose the former exclusively; and he carried intellectually studied art to its apogee. The Romans, following unimaginatively, were content to play at imitating the Greek achievement in its decline. The Renaissance scholars who picked up the classic impetus, during a second historic release of the human mind into intellectual freedom, perpetuated both the rationalism and for a time the confining thought-bound approach.

The *Apollo Belvedere*, the *Hermes* of Praxiteles, and the *Venus of Milo*, three works praised beyond stint in the older books, may be taken as typical of the classical tradition and method. In them the idealized realism of the Greeks is perfectly exemplified: man, physically perfect, presented as a god; nature copied truthfully and prettily; art transmitting a rational ideal, with a minimum of sensuous enrichment or spiritual implication. Today, to most eyes, they begin to look obvious. But we may believe that appreciation has been shifting back to earlier, stronger, less prettified works, rather than diverted wholly from the Greek accomplishment. These are, nevertheless, nearer the Greek typical product, symbolizing as they do realism and humanism carried to their logical extreme of expression, with masterly intelligence and noble clarity.

The Ancient Greek Culture

Ancient Greece was peculiarly one nation, despite geographical conditions that broke the country into semi-independent city-states, and political custom that bred inter-city jealousies and frequent civil wars. The binding elements were a common, if loosely defined, religion, a common language and literature, and like ways of life strengthened by commercial intercourse. Even more striking in its human and aesthetic influence was the national interest in the Olympic Games. To this festival, held every fourth year, traveled distinguished delegates, and especially the honored athletes, from all the cities of the Greek mainland, from the Aegean islands, and even from the distant colonies in Asia Minor, Sicily, and Italy.

From this unity arose in part the distinctive likeness that runs through the relics of Greek art. It is not only the subjects of graphic art that are endlessly repeated: first the chariot races, then the idealized athletic figures; the gods and goddesses (very human) and the exploits of half-divine heroes, Heracles, Achilles, and Odysseus; the sportive satyrs, the joyous nymphs; the centaurs and Amazons and Winged Victories; and later the genre bits. There is also a likeness of method, of approach, of a certain kind of grace, of sober but athletic thinking. It is as implicit in the sculptor's figures as in the finely proportioned, mathematically calculated temples and vases.

Even when there were "schools," and in spite of influences assimilated from Egypt and the East, there is the sense of oneness, of a body

Vase-painting. Red-figured, 5th century B.C. *Metropolitan Museum of Art*

of art with a single direction. It is not unified by priestly constraint, as was Egyptian art through most of its development, or by imperial direction, as art was in Babylonia-Assyria; but no less is the mark of a caste upon it—of the free nobles who generally ruled the Greek city-states. It is a reflection of their tastes and beliefs. The Hellenes lived in a time when religion was a part of everyday social life. Acquiescence, if not active devotional exercise, was a foregone conclusion, a badge of citizenship. Spiritual awareness and mystic communion were not encouraged except among the members of the secret mystery cults. The official Greek religion was matter-of-fact and human, at one with living.

Art celebrated those qualities good in man, marked them out as pertaining to godhead. The athlete was religious, the god was athletic. Both were intellectual. Here, indeed, body and mind are one, and the spirit, so far as it is understood, completes the harmony.

The unity, the distinctive likeness, almost throughout the story of Greek art, is thus an expression of man, of his way of living, of the faith he held. This is communal art in the sense that it is not controlled by priests and kings. It is, finally, the first fixation of a typical Western standard of living and of art, as against the Eastern; and so it is momentous for Europe.

The Dorians who pressed down in successive waves out of the north about eleven centuries before Christ, to conquer earlier inhabitants of Hellas and the Cycladic Isles and Troy, were not, according to tradition, "artistic." They were known to later historians as barbarians who destroyed the Aegean culture of Mycenae and Tiryns and Dendra, just as similar tribes, probably closely related to them, had overwhelmed Cnossus. There was a long period of darkness between the time of the great invasions from the north and the beginnings of Greek art proper. These dark ages of Hellas may be indicated roughly as extending from the eleventh to the seventh century B.C.

The fire kindled by the Cretans and the Mycenaeans was probably never wholly extinguished. The savage Dorian invaders smothered a civilization, lived without its radiance, but kept alive some sparks of it, found the warmth good, and gradually relighted the flame. What happened in the four centuries of near-darkness is largely matter for conjecture. Certainly ships were still sailing the Aegean and the Mediterranean. Phoenicia then took over mastery of the sea routes, but there were doubtless trading vessels of many other seafaring peoples, including the Dorian-Aegeans, on the Mediterranean waters. The arts of Mesopotamia, of

Egypt, and of Cyprus (itself half Greek) must have filtered in. But the twin root of Greek art, along with the Dorian, is supposed to be Ionic.

The Ionians were a people of western Asia Minor and certain of the Aegean Islands who developed their own culture earlier than did any of the other communities that were to merge in the Greek civilization. Tradition has it that Ionia was settled about the time of the Dorian invasion of the Peloponnesus; and it may have been the fleeing bands of Mycenaeans who crossed the sea to form a new settlement, or it may have been Dorians and the fleeing ones mixed. The long cessation here, as in Greece proper, would seem to argue Dorian preponderance. In any case, there was independent growth when once the cultural advance began. And indeed, because Ionia was on the Asiatic side of the Aegean Sea, such influences as came from outside were less from the old homeland than from Babylonia-Assyria, Persia, and Egypt. Ionian architecture may be marked as Eastern in feeling, the volute capital having prototypes in both Persia and Egypt; and Ionian sculpture is Egyptian-simple rather than of the naturalistic Mycenaean stamp. Early Greek art, then, may be considered to be the result of many racial influences. But it is notable that the central fact of Minoan and Mycenaean graphic art, its realism, was soon to be firmly re-established, despite invasion, interruption, and confusing cross-current.

Vase-Painting

The life and spirit of the early Greeks, their abundant mythology and varied activities, their institutions and pleasures and beliefs, are copiously published forth in one only of the visual arts. Not sculpture, heralded often as the typical, the supreme Hellenic achievement, but vase-painting gives us the Greeks as they were, affording illustration of the fullness of their interests, the occasional exuberance of their emotion, their worship of heroes rather than gods, their drinking and racing and lovemaking.

In this painted pottery, as in dramatic poetry, there is the combination of nobility and intimate expression. In the picturing on vases remains the one rich record of faith and happening, of elevated thought and the lower passions, of custom and episode. Here is marked, too, the highest point touched by the Greek formal sensibility in visual art. The vase proportions are as exquisitely calculated as those of the Parthenon and the Temple of the Wingless Victory. On the early vessels there is a decorative stylization more appealing than anything else in the entire range of relics left by the Hellenes. The vases constitute at once their heraldry, their book of devotions, and their comic supplement. As illustration this is endlessly engaging, even exciting; as design it is satisfying, eye-filling, exquisite.

At first the objective pageant is less of the Greeks, of their ways, their loves, their immediate personal living, than of their legendary heroes and inherited minor gods. The pictured exploits are those of Homeric and Olympian demi-gods and half-mythological kings and warriors. The obscenities are those of satyrs and maenads, not of real men and women. Occasionally, particularly as archaisms pass, as formalism weakens in the face of increasing realism, the intimate occasion and the familiar scene are recorded. There are bits from the athletic games, or a funeral, two comic actors, or women in the shower-bath. But more usually there are goddesses and heroes, the satyrs pursuing reluctant (or willing) maenads; the legends of the Trojan War, the Argonauts, and the Amazons; or rushing chariots, combats with mythological monsters, and Olympian romances.

Reserved and remote from personal emotional documentation as it thus is at most points, illustrating life according to a literary-allegorical convention, with men's feelings shown only through legendary anecdote and heroic analogy, the vase-record is still a revealing indication of Greek character. It fixes graphically the heroes and the great affairs recorded by Homer, Aeschylus, and Sophocles, but it equally parallels the coarseness and humor of Aristophanes.

It is partly the existence of the occasional exuberance and the "unclassic" joyousness that

Horses and Warriors. Black-figured drawing. *State Museum, Berlin*

has at times served to obscure the richness of the pottery paintings as an artistic achievement. But there are many other reasons why scholar, critic, and student sometimes overlooked or discounted so rich a store of formal art. The vase-shapes were symmetrical, "pure," chartable, and were therefore praised, dryly but extensively. The paintings or drawings, on the other hand, were formalized and stylized, and in that they were unlike the bulk of recognized (and approved) art.

The vases were discovered in large numbers, moreover, only in the nineteenth century. The serious visual arts, the "fine" arts, were considered to be architecture, sculpture, and painting in the large. Greek pottery was classed as an industrial product and so "necessarily among the lower forms of art," as one authority puts it. It is only as men return to enjoying and judging the quality of the thing itself, not in relation to size, that the living values emerge and establish themselves. Only within the present generation has it been respectable to enjoy vase-paintings for what they are as formalized art.

Technically, as decorative pottery, the Greek vases do not constitute the world's finest display. Considered as an exercise in a mode of design, as clay vessels, shaped, finished, ornamented, to afford a single formal appeal, a sensuous impression, they are less notable than the Persian or the Chinese products. Except for examples from the very early periods, they exhibit less than perfect unity of design, scant coordination of physical form and pictorial or ornamental embellishment. Their peculiar virtues lie in qualities that must in a sense be detached by the eye from the not too congruous whole.

But in two directions the achievement is so exceptional, so beautiful, that one finds it worth while to override the common rule that the detail cannot fairly be taken without relation to the whole, that only an excellence within a unity can be taken as valid. One of the supreme achievements is in the architecture of the vase. The other is in the decorative picture taken as such, at first as highly stylized, semi-pictorial space-composition, later as spirited and eye-filling illustration.

The enjoyment of the shapes of the amphoras and cups and pitchers is a pleasure allowed by classicists and dissenters alike. The drinking cups are made shallow and wide, and are suavely curved for visual appeal. The storage jars are built up strongly, architecturally, for noble solidity, in reposeful proportion. Even the squat little cosmetic jars have their purity of outline, their exquisite adjustment of profile and mass.

There is a specialized literature on the subject of Greek proportioning of forms. The specialists find it very exciting that the Parthenon and innumerable vases conform to statable geometrical rules of space division. And for the casual appreciator too it is worth noting that the testimony of the eye, which detects a certain logic of structure, a purity of expression, in the amphora or the cup, is confirmed by actual measurement. The width is likely to bear a certain relationship to the height, in one of the simpler ratios (as determined not arithmetically but in terms of areas); and this relationship is repeated in the minor relationships of parts. The formulas for proportioning have been worked out diagrammatically, most notably by Jay Hambidge in his theory of "dynamic symmetry," and by less-known investigators of "the golden mean" and "the divine proportion."

That the Greek vases, as measured in outstandingly beautiful examples, can thus be diagrammed geometrically may well be considered significant. Certainly they appeal as extraordinarily "right," with a sweetly exquisite harmony of parts; and it may increase the enjoyment to know that a secret mathematical rhythm lies behind the effect. They are thus brought into line, too, with the hidden principles that distinguish the proportioning of the Pyramids, certain Greek temples, and the surface composition of Giorgione and Poussin. But it may be true that the mechanical explanation of the visual rightness is the reason for the very strict and narrow limitation of the Greek potters to a few stereotyped varieties of vase. The specifica-

tions are mathematical and intellectual. The potter both gains by his knowledge and lets it bind him.

In any case, there is seldom a more delicate pleasure to the eye than in the run of cylices, or shallow drinking cups, in a representative collection. The purposeful attenuation of the lines, the fragile silhouette, the structural grace—these leap straight to our trained understanding. The cylix is an example of intellectually controlled art at its best.

To that other resource of sensuous delight, color, the Greeks seem to have been near-blind. Their pottery as a whole is agreeable enough in what coloring there is: almost exclusively the shades of clay-red and black. But the potters show no interest in carrying the art beyond these elementary color limits. The Egyptians, the Persians, and the Far Eastern peoples show incomparably more invention, more taste; even the American Indians and the Mayans were in this detail the superiors of the Greeks.

But in turning to the pictorial designs, as drawing (or painting) fitted to pottery surface, one finds the Greeks again masters. Particularly in the period known as Archaic, the drawing is appropriately formalized, the black elements are put on in a pattern that is a perfect adjustment of light-dark, and the pictures are friezelike rather than independently illustrative. Pictorial scheme accentuates structure.

The earliest Greek vessels are of a sort that might well argue a fairly direct, if sometimes tenuous, line of descent from the ancient Aegean pottery. As the new Greek nation—of, say, the eighth or early seventh century B.C.—represented an amalgamation of several long-separated groups, orginally of like stocks but variously acted upon, so one may visualize many influences other than those of ancient Hellas and Crete flowing in to affect the art-consciousness of native craftsmen. The first marked "style," that known to the scholars as "geometric," is near enough to the late Minoan or Mycenaean to suggest blood-relationship. There was then a convention of banding; and other abstract formalizations led some distance from the typical Aegean naturalism. In the Greek geometric period the whole

Cylix. Black-figured, 6th century B.C. *Metropolitan Museum of Art*

vessel might be traced over with a series of friezes: bands of circles, zigzags, continuous frets, meanders, etc. The whole was, in late examples, varied with zones in which bird or animal figures, heraldically simple, were repeated as decorative items. Then gradually the geometric elements became less important, men's figures were added to those of animals, and the potters were on the way to the more typical Greek picture-vase.

The geometric-style vessels, despite colorlessness and a rather elementary command of ornament, have a pleasing unity that was to be lost later; and this period and the one immediately following—commonly called the "Orientalized"—afford the richest pleasure to be found in Greek pottery considered as pure ceramic expression, without regard to pictorial interest. The geometric pottery is most amply represented in the "Dipylon" ware, so called from the name of the Athenian cemetery where many examples were found; though some authorities count this a late, separate, or transitional variety, belonging down toward 700 B.C., rather than up toward the beginnings in the heroic age. The mere enjoyer of these things is here in the midst of archaeological controversies. He may have to face the charge that he is favoring styles that are essentially "un-Greek." The local potters must have encountered both the gorgeous fabrics prized in Persia, Babylonia, and Syria, and actual imported vases with the rich Eastern decorative fullness. There are "motives" too that can be traced only to Asiatic metal-chasing. In any case, Greek artisans then began to produce elaborate jars and pitchers less intricately mechanical—profusely strewn, rather, with stylized animals, with rosettes and palmettos stopping up the spaces between.

Most significant is the Corinthian pottery of the mainland, and with it the Rhodian ware—explainable in its alien beauty because Rhodes is an island near Asia Minor. These two varieties mark the one Greek approach to a complete ceramic style, fully developed on all sides, not only in the shaping and architecture and in the imposing drawing. There is in them a sensuous unity, and a carpet-like all-over ornamentalism that was not to be seen again in Europe until the Moors created the Hispano-Moresque pottery.

During the seventh and sixth centuries the fullness gave way to those virtues of "purity" and restraint which are considered more typically Hellenic. Some experiments in color left little permanent trace; the black figure on red ground became standard. The shapes were improved, became graceful and stereotyped. Athens took over leadership in manufacture and export; though the Corinthian artists continued active, and Chalcis was notable among many smaller centers of production.

Amphoras. Geometric style, Dipylon, Athens. *Metropolitan Museum of Art*

Vase-making at this time may be thought of as not so much an isolated studio activity as an organized industry, carried on under pressure of competition for both domestic and foreign markets, in a wide variety of wares ranging from kitchen-plain to fancy. The volume of vessels, painted and unpainted, must have been enormous, for they were used not only for every purpose for which people today manufacture their like—as kitchenware, useful china, ornamental bowls, and vases—but also in place of our glassware and metal containers. Huge storage-jars, common dishes, and tiny receptacles for precious ointments were all in the range of glazed or unglazed pottery; and there were special "lines" such as funeral offerings, appropriately decorated, and elaborate prize-vases to be given (full of olive oil) to winners at the Panathenaic games.

Not fewer than fifty thousand decorated vases of Greek and derivative manufacture are in museums and private collections today. Although the practice of signing vases, as maker or decorator, lasted through only a comparatively brief period, nearly a hundred artists are known by name. Schools of painters flourished, known by the name of the celebrated leader-master.

The Golden Age of Vase-Painting

It is in the early and middle sixth century B.C. that the golden age of Greek pottery should be placed. The picturing had not then forsaken its purpose of decorating appropriately the surface

Execias: *Dionysus Sailing the Sea.* Cylix. *Alte Pinakothek, Munich*

of the globular vessel. Encircling bands still confirm the roundness; the center of gravity of the figures is nicely related to the architecture of the vase. And particularly the drawing is still crisply decorative, light-handed, beautifully unreal.

Execias was an outstanding draftsman with an extraordinary gift for filling space decoratively by means of a few almost fragile pictorial elements. His design of Dionysus in a boat with grapevine and dolphins has been, with good reason, as widely published as any ancient composition. It is notable how the forms of dolphins, leaves, and grape-bunches are transformed into effective decorative items without unreasonable distortion of natural character. But it is the exquisite formal adjustment, the beautifully controlled organization, that gives distinctive character to the design. The artist adds, in the sail, a bit of white ground to the standard black-on-red scheme—an exception to rule which is not rare in Execias' time.

Of an entirely different sort, and slightly earlier date, is the achievement of Clitias in utilizing the non-realist technique to picture a whole series of legendary episodes on one vessel, that known as the *François Vase,* from the name of its nineteenth-century discoverer. There are, in all, ten processional scenes in five lightly marked-off bands running round the jar, with some two hundred and fifty figures. It is in a sense a *tour de force*—and vase-structure *is* obscured—but the all-over effect, the black-and-white distribution (more accurately speaking, black-and-red), is beautifully managed. The pattern is of a piece, the effect of vibration uniform. The individual scenes and figures, moreover, reward with intense pleasure the study given to them. The observer here must accept a convention paralleled in the Chinese scroll-paintings: the entire composition is at no time presented to his eyes. The test of excellence is in two things, that from any view a certain rightness is evident, and that details or coherent areas satisfy when freed from the context.

The amount of movement depicted or implied, and the vigor and precise elegance of the drawing, are extraordinary. How far the vase-artist still departs from realistic intention is indicated by the placing of vases and tripods beneath the bodies of the running horses, where the space would otherwise be too empty for the good of the design. The artist is still decorator rather than illustrator.

In the highly formalized style of Execias and Clitias there are unmarked masterpieces in all the large museums. The little processions of figures around the brims of cylices—they may be of satyrs and maenads, or of mounted horsemen or stags—are particularly rewarding. The horse is a special favorite, has seldom appeared in art with happier decorative effect. Of those who signed highly stylized Archaic work, Amasis and Epictetus are typical—one a contemporary of Execias, the other belonging to the transitional period when red-figured ware was coming in, just before 500 B.C.

At this time "archaisms" still persisted: most front-view bodies have profile heads; the eyes too are the typical memory-image, not the representational thing; figures are "impossibly" slenderized; and horses have too many legs. But the result is gorgeous.

For convenience of reference Greek vase-painting is commonly described as being of two main sorts: designs in black figure and designs in red figure. Until near the end of the sixth century B.C. all pottery was in the simple technique common from primitive times: a natural red-clay ground with picture and ornament standing out in black silhouette or black line, or other dark varnish. Just before the year 500 B.C. a reversal of this order took place. As before, the draftsman outlined his intended figures on the red ground, it may be with some incising instrument or with brush. But then he painted in black *not* the figures themselves but the ground *around* the figures; thenceforward people and objects stood out in red against black, and history speaks of the red-figured vases. In some periods white and purple were sparingly added, but the main classification holds good.

The technical revolution by which the color scheme was reversed was evidently fought over in the profession. But the proponents of the new style soon drove the opposition into line. Black-figured ware practically disappeared. With it went some of the virtues of Greek decorative drawing at its best. The vases were showier, with their larger expanses of black luster. There also was opportunity to do more documentary drawing on the red figures than had been possible on the black. Details within a figure in dark tone against light can be drawn only with a point. The black can be enriched only with a few simple lines to indicate drop of garment, or meeting of two forms or materials; or be brightened with patches of all-over pattern. The method invites the sharp incised line and creates a flat, two-dimensional effect. But a figure in lighter color against dark offers opportunity for multiplication of detail and a generally looser technique, with the brush as instrument. Immediately the art begins on its path toward accurate delineation and elaboration and toward a casual sketchiness. In the end vase forms and picturing both degenerate. The shapes become heavy, the designs florid.

Even before the red-figured ware came in, there was a marked tendency toward elaboration of the picture as such. Storytelling became more important; or perhaps merely more figures were crowded in. Indeed, the archaic virtue of imaginative stylization gave way but slowly. Between the time of the geometrized men and horses on the eighth-century vases and the late sixth-century black-figure scenes, there was every shade of conventionalization. Some of the transitional artists reverted to archaisms. Others, like the sculptors of the time, were learning more about anatomy and weakening their decorative mastery in a dis-

Clitias: *The François Vase. Archaeological Museum, Florence*

play of scientific knowledge. There were even faint essays toward the perspective scene. Pliny recorded wonderingly of Cimon of Cleonae that "he introduced oblique images, and represented the features as seen from varied angles, from behind, above, or below. He marked the limb joints, showed the veins, and reproduced the folds in drapery."

The great period of red-figured vases was just before and during the Periclean age. The painter most praised is Euphronius, who continued to a degree the formalism of Execias, but in compositions fuller-blown and more heavily weighted.

There is still a fine elegance in the drawing—one can imagine Flaxman tracing over the outlines with relish—and a hint of a return toward Oriental richness of texture. But we have no design by Euphronius so delicately adjusted, so sensitive, so fitted to its place on clay, as the *Dionysus* of Execias. Already, in coming to the greatest master of the red-figure period, the student is on the downward slope of the art as stylized design, as decorative art fitted to ceramics.

Illustration becomes more exact. It is often spirited and gay, even dramatic. Individual psychology enters, in facial expression and revealing

Attic red-figured hydria, redrawn design

gesture. But the method is exhibitional, showy, tending toward a sort of drafty virtuosity.

With Euphronius should be mentioned Duris, Euthymides, and Pamphaeus as celebrated masters. (Euthymides inscribed one of his vases with the line, "This outdoes Euphronius," which indicates that Euphronius *was* the real master.) Sosias and Brygus did more to develop expressiveness through gesture and facial play. Brygus is known particularly for specializing in subjects considered today unpermissible. And indeed the satyrs and maenads do, on some of the most beautifully engaging vases, indulge in revels less than conventional.

These are all artists of the period termed by some authorities the very apogee of the art, about 500-460 B.C. F. A. Wright speaks of the red-figured vases as "the crown and triumph of Athenian pottery," and adds that with Brygus "all traces of archaism have disappeared and we see

the full maturity of the art." It seems to this observer, however, that vase-painting had then already entered upon its period of decadence: design had weakened, ornament was on the downgrade toward the florid, representation toward the sentimental, the theatrical, and the grandiloquent. The early unity, the focus, the crisp stylization were gone.

For a time, parallel to the red-figured ware there flourished in a minor way a type of vase with line-drawings on a white "slip," as the all-over coating of white paint is called. These are less successful decoratively but are of exceptional interest as an indication of the methods and ability of easel-painters of the time. The pictures —and one assumes that the white was introduced for more facile drawing—vary from a few examples in the early formalized technique to a late realism. In examples of the latter, Greek draftsmen proved their ability to achieve in outline a

Ludovisi Throne. Relief, marble. *National Museum, Rome*

marvelous accuracy combined with a beautiful economy. Here the "classically pure" outlines of Euphronius are freed from the red-black complex, to stand out naked on the white vessel. As a matter of fact, there was wider experiment with colors, though in restricted amount, both in touches of line and in occasional washes of tone—red, purple, green, or blue.

Vase-painting persisted literally for centuries after the period of the known masters, in Greece and in her colonies, and down into Roman times. There was a period in which the pottery of Greek communities in southern Italy—Tarentum and Paestum—was more popular and more famous than the products of Hellas itself. But the urge toward grandeur and the taste for realistic and literary picturing had degraded the art. Integrity and creativeness alike had fled. The story of a distinctive and once vividly expressive art closes in a record of protracted degeneration and careless representation. The best was past by 500 B.C. The great proportion of acceptable work was completed before 400 B.C.

A postscript paragraph may be added, in order to round out here the story of the classic vase. The Etruscans not only imitated the Greek styles but invented one of their own, manifested espe-

cially in the *bucchero* or *bucchero nero* ware. These are black vases, and upon many of them the painting or drawing is competent and attractive. In Greece and in Italy there had grown up beside vase-painting an art of relief-picturing. This culminated in the Arretine pottery of the Romans, named from the Tuscan city Arretium or Arezzo. Arretine pottery, its only color the red of the clay, and its ornament in abstract or pictorial low relief, became standard for Romans from about 100 B.C. on.

Archaic Greek Sculpture

Greek sculpture has usually been described in two categories. The first, termed Archaic, covers the time from the beginnings to the crisis of the Persian Wars. It includes, roughly, the sculptors from the unnamed primitives to the immediate predecessors of Phidias. The second covers "the period of perfection," 460-320 B.C., including the achievements of Phidias and the other fifth-century practitioners and their fourth-century successors. After these two divisions, of course, there was a minor one, the decadence in the Hellenistic era. In this almost universally accepted classifica-

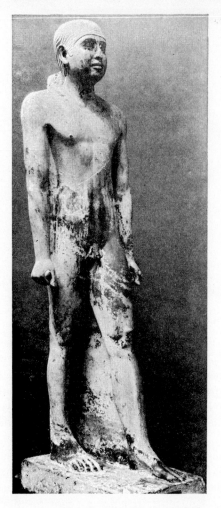

Egyptian. Old Kingdom. Supposed prototype of the Greek "Apollos"

tion, the implication used to be that Archaic Greek works were immature, inept, and inferior, by reason of the sculptors' inability to render counterfeits of the human body accurately, to compass sentiment and character and episode. Beginning with Phidias, Greek mastery was considered complete.

Today, after some decades of re-evaluation, the two categories are as useful as ever, but with this difference: what has been termed Archaic is now understood to include much of the best of the Greek achievement. It is believed that when the masters of the age of Phidias "freed themselves of the feel of the block" they left behind one of the truest assets of the glyptic artist. They then initiated sculptural illustration in place of sculptural creation. Remembering that some of the greatest work was carried over into the transitional period of 480-450 B.C., one may say that Archaic Greek sculpture marks the strong, valid youth and early maturity of the art, the Phidian era the high achievement of the Parthenon figures and the beginning of the decline.

In that early Greece of growing communal consciousness, of expanding commerce, of union in religion and games, when already a national style was forming in ceramic art, when the literature of Homer and Hesiod and Pindar was being diffused, in that formative seventh century there was very little sculpture—or little that lived importantly. The old Aegean peoples had never excelled in the art. There is hardly a thread of influence that comes down from the lonely lions of the Mycenaean gate. A few isolated manifestations afford a keen if slight aesthetic pleasure: the Cycladean marble votive figures (from abstract to angularly real), and the clay or more rarely bronze geometric horses, sometimes with riders—as fascinatingly stylized as the horses on the early vases.

The true origins, besides the national genius that was to make Greek art distinctive, are to be found in Hellenic colonies—if they may be considered such before Greece itself was really formed—toward the Orient, and in Egypt.

Wilenski states categorically that "for three hundred years, and from about 750 B.C., the forms of Greek art were derived from the art of the Egyptians." Hellenists of the old school deny any outside influence. A cautious middle course seems likely to bring one nearer the truth. The Archaic Apollos inevitably suggest Egyptian prototypes, as is graphically illustrated by the photographs of two statues set side by side here. Nevertheless Greece was already marking out distinctive excellencies of a sculpture of her own.

Cyprus, partly Hellenic through the old Mycenaean line, partly Orientalized, has a place in the story of the emerging Greek consciousness. Ionia too, closer to the motherland in spirit, though actually on the Asiatic coast, was doubtless a bridge from the East. Local Greek sculp-

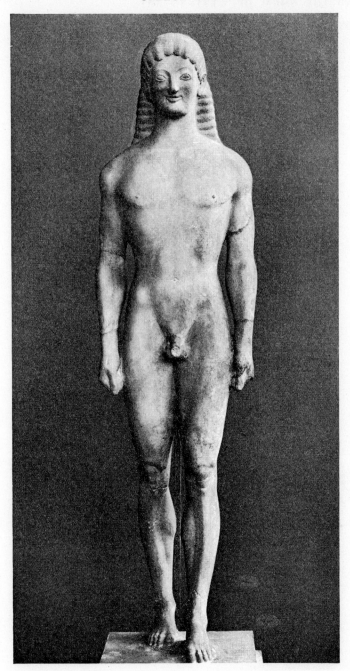

Apollo of Tenea. Glyptothek, Munich

tors, manufacturing rude votive figures, even idols, for obscure temples, must have had in the seventh century an increasing number of models from countries where monumental sculpture al-ready was familiar and suave modeling common.

In any case, the history of the art as Greek in any important sense begins with the early sixth century B.C. The so-called *Hera of Samos* in the

Hera of Samos. Louvre

Louvre, colonial-Ionian in provenance, is an exceptional thing with a fine architectural unity and an exquisite grace. The loss of swellings of the body in the column-like sheathed figure is more than compensated for in an architectonic lift and suavity. There is, no doubt, an Egyptian rigidity or solidity, and an Oriental touch in the formalization, but the grace and the atmosphere

Archaic statue of type known as "Kores." *Acropolis Museum*

are Greek. Native also is the separate treatment of the toes, which is obviously a push toward realism. It may be remarked that Athens was probably little more than a collection of villages, inartistic and unprogressive, at the time this was made in a "colony."

The free-standing Apollos, however, are the typical exhibit of sixth-century achievement. The

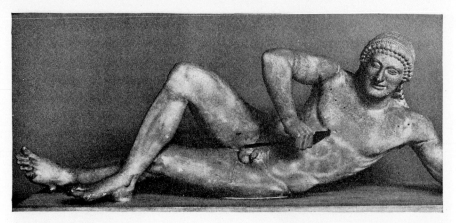

Wounded Warrior. From pediment group, Temple of Aegina. *Glyptothek, Munich*

figure is known in a score of variations, with the same frontal rigidity, hands at sides, left foot forward, reminiscent of the Old Kingdom tomb statues on the Nile. The formalized hair and fixed smile and accented muscles show only slight variations; though of course the quality of the many statues as sheer plastic expression differs widely. The example known as the *Apollo of Tenea* (on page 107) is one of the most impressive. Already the Greek sculptor had advanced over his Egyptian mentors in anatomical truth. There is, too, a new sort of linear rhythm in the repeated arcs of shoulders, breasts, and arbitrarily accented abdominal muscles. For a brief hour in Greek time this playing with rhythmic line will hint of a charming new sort of formalization in sculpture.

The slimness and fleetness of many of the Archaic Apollos lend color to the theory that these are not representations of the sun-god but statues commemorating victories of athletes in the national games. The cult of physical perfection had already grown and was bound to have its effect upon artists who traditionally dealt with the human body as their basic concern. The immaturity of the art may be taken to explain the long delay in showing the youths actually at their running and quoit-throwing. The new idea of glorifying the body and its victory took the turn first in the direction of transferring to the marble the fine physique, the alert poise, and the sweetly molded limb. Idealism was helped rather than

hindered by sticking to a traditional regularity. There is special reason for confounding the athletic figures with Apollo, for he was traditionally the young man's god, and himself manliest of the Olympians. To celebrate him in images was to honor the best in physical youth.

The naked athletes were glorified long before feminine nudity (even in art) was allowed by Greek custom, and there are no Archaic Aphrodites to match the sixth-century Apollos. There are, however, some standardized female figures, known as Kores. In them the true Archaic conventions are the more pronounced, for drapery lends itself to surface formalization; and long hair, whether in braids or *en masse*, affords patterned contrast. There is here an enrichment and a formal grandeur (as overleaf) that are to be too soon lost from Greek work, too quickly given up in favor of a growing naturalism. They reappear in Etruscan art, beautifully, in an achievement that might have been paralleled in Greece if the sculptors there had not been led away in the direction of anatomical realism.

Perhaps those beautiful bodies, witnessed in every attitude of rest and action at the games, had most to do with this realism. Or perhaps it was the rationalism of Greek thought, the impatient waving aside of the illogical, the mystical, the sensuous. Or perhaps the humanism that demanded nothing more of art than an obvious glorification of physical, triumphant man.

In any case, the next step in sculpture was

Demeter, Persephone, and Triptolemus. Eleusis. *National Museum, Athens*

marked by a further approach to exact bodily representation. The figures of the pediment of the Temple at Aegina are still formalized as com-pared with the posed-and-copied gods and heroes of a century later. But already these warriors in the pediment groups have individuality and

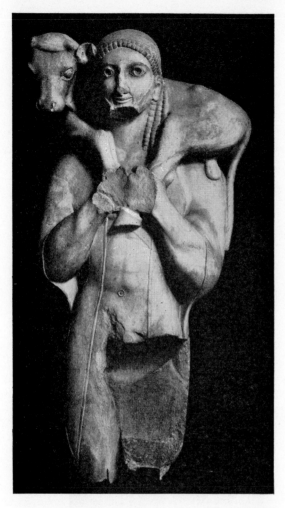

Moschophorus or *Calf-Bearer*. Marble, Athens,
6th century B.C. *Acropolis Museum, Athens*

natural muscle and free movement; if a bit summary, the approximation to nature is still convincing to the observing realist. In the other
direction, they retain a typical sculptural blockiness, an admirable plastic coherence. Particularly
important is this architectonic solidity when, as
here, the individual figure is integral to a group
associated with architectural design. Significantly,
the bodies are more thoroughly studied, and
more naturally treated, than the faces.

From the similar and somewhat later pediment
of the Temple of Zeus in the national sanctuary
of Olympia, there are fragments that touch close

to the high-water mark of all Greek sculpture.
The single well-preserved figure, an Apollo, that
formed the visual center and main axis of the
west pediment group is one of the most admired
of ancient marbles (page 93). There is largeness
here, almost a dignity of the stone, that will be
lost, if not immediately with the passing of the
Olympian sculptor (who may have been Alca-
menes), then soon after the Parthenon groups
have been chiseled. Certainly this Apollo figure
is in itself monumental, firm, almost majestic.
The sculpture is alive and strong; it breathes a
rhythmic vitality not from the model, and it is
not fussed up with detail. Some of the other figures from the Olympian temple, free-standing or
carved in high relief, are similarly sculptural and
formal, yet are indicative of coming change.

One of the greatest modern critics of world art,
Meier-Graefe, ventured the unorthodox thought
that the Greeks never really mastered sculpture
in the full round as it was mastered, for instance,
in Egypt. He implied that their genius was rather
for relief. From the last decades of the Archaic
period dates a series of reliefs that would be
notable in any time or place: the so-called Ludovisi Throne marbles. They are among the most
ingratiating and charming things in Greek art,
though lacking the early strength and largeness.

The relief method, holding together in panels
the complex design of grouped figures, gives
scope to the Greek illustrational impulse without
compositional loss (page 105). The grace of
these Ludovisi figures, the holding to the panel
effect, the adjusted symmetry, the lightly patterned chiseling, seem exceptionally right. Here
is formalization, sparingly but beautifully utilized. The bodies are nonetheless solid, finely
sculptural. The strong uninvolved torso of the
central figure is fully realized. But the frank
patterning of the falling draperies, the lightening
effect of parallel folds traced over the bodies, is
decorative and lyric. The subject is probably the
rise of Persephone after her half-year in the
Underworld, to bring spring to earth.

More fully composed but still holding to certain archaisms—and one of the rare sculptures
appertaining to the "mystery religions" of the

Horse. Bronze. *Metropolitan Museum of Art*

Greeks—is the panel from Eleusis showing Demeter, Persephone, and the youth Triptolemus. It is almost the last flower of the formal method, with already a good deal of softening and rounding of profiles and channels. There are other temple friezes and panels which, even in a half-ruined condition, indicate a noble ancestry for the later relief figures. The fragments, indeed, return one to the thought that much of the best of Greek sculptural achievement came well before 500 B.C.

After our long training in the orthodoxy of classicism, we of today are shocked by the truth that the Greeks painted their marble statues. The conception of a white purity, an innocent colorlessness, was so inbred in us by education, and by the sight of the intellectual *Ledas* and *Ariadnes* of the nineteenth-century neoclassic sculptors, that the thought of highly colored statues revolted

us. But almost universally the ancients added this last unsculptural distraction to the stone surface. In the case of Greece, where color as an artistic asset was never really understood, the paint coating was, by all the evidence, just plain bad—a few elementary hues, not too carefully assorted, perhaps garishly inharmonious. It is a mercy that the weather of twenty-four hundred years has worn them off.

There is something to be said for the painting of monumental pieces designed to be seen in relation to architecture, incidental to such a highly colored building as, for instance, the Parthenon. But a study of world sculpture can lead only to the conclusion that the commoner materials of the art, wood and stone, can be capitalized for their own virtues, that there are inherent plastic values in the woodiness or stoniness of the statue—and that, in general, applied color is calculated to nullify and obscure them.

That a considerable amount of sculpture in wood existed in Greece is certain, although surviving traces are rare. Marbles were commonest. But the Greeks were early masters of the metal processes, and diverting bronze statuettes of the Archaic period are found in every representative collection. Most important are a few larger monuments, such as the *Charioteer of Delphi*, a figure preserved out of a lost group, but sculpturally interesting in its own right, with a column-like lift of body and a general organic simplification, and a beautifully stylized bronze head, wherein there is little sacrifice of sculptural compactness for natural effect.

Less severe, and indeed a very fine example of a plausible truth to appearance modified by artistic conventions, is a solid bronze statuette of a horse now in the Metropolitan Museum, New York. There is here a parallel to the stylized illustrations of the black-figured vases. The animal is spirited, noble, living. The sculpture is controlled, masterly, and exceptionally elegant.

If the chapter breaks off just short of the Parthenon marbles, without quite completing the story of the strong early sculpture of Greece, and without as yet mentioning Greek architecture, it is because there is a segment of background history to be inserted which may make clearer the place of those things in the stream of world art, and afford a new start toward the understanding of "the Greek miracle." The galvanizing of the national consciousness through victories in the Persian Wars, and the culmination of civic idealism in the Periclean plans for rebuilding Athens, had an epochal effect upon the course of the arts. Up to that time the history of graphic and glyptic arts, matured in many loosely federated centers, had been somewhat disunified, as any account must inevitably be. But from about 480 B.C. there was a new focus. For ill or good, Athens and the Athenian philosophy of art were to set Greek sculpture and architecture firmly on the reasonable, intellectual, realistic road.

VI: GREECE: CULMINATION AND DECLINE

THE VICTORY at Marathon was crucial. This was the event determining that the West should remain Western. On that battlefield, by so narrow a margin, the tide of the East was turned back, the spirit of Greece was given reprieve, the way was opened to a new freedom.

The issue did not then seem final. The Persians were to return ten years later, to ravage all of Attica and to sack and destroy Athens twice, in 480 and 479 B.C. But at Marathon the Athenians had shown the mettle of conquerors, and had gained inestimably in confidence and belief. Despite the following disaster at Thermopylae and the evacuation of their city, with the loss even of their temples and sacred citadel, they had discovered the force and power that made inevitable the Athenian successes at Salamis and Plataea. By 478 the new city was being built. This was eighteen years before Pericles came to power.

Athens had never before claimed leadership in the confused and treacherous alliances of Greek city-states and colonies. Sparta had been incom-parably stronger. Culturally the islands and Ionia on the Asiatic shore had been more advanced. Lesbos a century before had touched an unapproached height in lyric poetry—Lesbos, where Alcaeus and Sappho were twin immortals. In philosophy and science, Ephesus and Miletus had been the earlier centers of experiment and development.

In the far west too, particularly in the Sicilian cities, there were then luxurious Greek courts that outshone Athens in all cultural attainments. Sybaris so lolled in the soft refinements and attenuations of art that "Sybarite" is still our most eloquent designation of the over-cushioned sophisticate. Syracuse had attracted Pindar and Anacreon. Selinus had seven noble temples famous for sculptural adornment. Agrigentum in Sicily and Paestum in Italy were noted for their imposing monuments. Nearer home the arts of architecture and sculpture had been beautifully developed, most notably at Olympia and Delphi, at Aegina too, and at Corinth.

It was destined, nevertheless, that soon there would be no rival to Athens in political and

Ilissos. From the east pediment, Parthenon. *British Museum*

moral power, in commercial enterprise, in the arts. No one can say what conjunction of circumstances brought these creative and heroic powers to focus. Was it that seafaring men, broadened and made daring by their contacts with all the known world, were now admitted to the councils? Was it that Athens had changed from an agricultural to an industrial and commercial center? Or was it that the state was ruled by freemen to a greater extent than any yet known to the world?

Whatever the cause, here, in 479 B.C., was the beginning of a release of the artistic impulse hardly paralleled in world history before or after. The art of the theater was to flower with a noble beauty matched but once in all later time; the philosophy of the intellectual West was to emerge full-grown; and the plastic arts were to develop, in one direction, to a perfection of statement not to be surpassed—all within a half-century. This is the home and the hour of Aeschylus and Socrates, of Sophocles and Euripides and Herodotus, of Phidias and Callicrates and Aristophanes.

No one can know how much the patriotic passion and executive genius of Pericles, who came to power in 460 B.C., had to do with the Athenian flowering. Contemporary historians and estimates are necessarily conflicting. Certainly Pericles was generously and understandingly a patron of the arts. To call this the "Age of Pericles" is perhaps to transfer too much praise from Aeschylus and Socrates and Ictinus to an organizing overlord. But without Pericles and without the salon conducted by his beautiful mistress, Aspasia, the artistic life of the city would have been less focused and the appropriations less princely. Even in his patriotic speeches he did not forget the glory brought to Athens by her artists. It was when paying tribute to the soldier dead that he said, with true Greek moderation: "We love beauty without being extravagant, and we love wisdom without being soft."

The beautification of Athens was undertaken in a comprehensive way. It was not a matter of statues to be set up here and there, or of a single temple to be erected. The city was to be made worthy of her destiny. She was to shine out unmistakably as the capital of the confederation of Greek city-states, of all the non-barbarian world. That the leadership was never wholly acknowledged, that the member states were taken aback when Athens decided to beautify herself with funds out of the federation's war-chest, was a mere political circumstance. Artists were given unprecedented opportunity, with results to be seen most remarkably in the Acropolis and its crowning building, the Parthenon. Here is Greek architecture come to its most perfect expression, and Greek sculpture finding its supreme setting.

Time was when men regarded the Acropolis, and with it the whole Periclean achievement in art, as a miraculous outflowering of the creative spirit due to the artists' first escape from enslavement under kings and priests. These critics glorified Greek freedom in contrast with Egyptian thralldom, Western rationalism as against Eastern mysticism, Hellenic clarity and humanism as against Nilotic heaviness and Nilotic forebodings of the hereafter. It now begins to appear that they may have been celebrating doubtful superiorities. In the light of history restudied, and of a fresh appraisal of all artistic values, critics have reversed the judgment that would accord Egyptian sculpture of the Old Kingdom a place aesthetically inferior to the Athenian achievement. Nevertheless, we may still see today, in the Acropolis, a culmination of one way of expression, a climax in the art of the ancient world, the representative expression of the Greek spirit.

The Glories of Greek Architecture

Greek architecture, surviving almost solely in temples, is perhaps the most distinctive in history. A single type of construction is utilized within a single logic of planning, and the ornamental conventions are few and unmistakable.

The origins are to be sought less in the earlier Aegean building of the same lands than in the Oriental cultures that poured their influences into the Greek settlements along the shore of Asia and thence to Hellas itself. The Aegean world had known elaborate and imposing pal-

Doric columns, part of the Parthenon

aces, but these lacked every fundamental that entered into Greek planning. They were asymmetrical, without unity; their decorative features were applied superficially. It is futile to search in them for hints of the Greek integration that was to be seen a millennium later on the same soil.

Logic and order are at the heart of Greek expression. The Hellenes planned their temples according to a coded schema of parts, based first on function, then on a reasoned system of decorative enrichment. Mathematics determined the symmetry, the harmony, the eye's pleasure.

There had never been an architecture in just this sense. The pyramids had been an early, un-adorned fruit of the same spirit. But in matured, thought-out building art, this is the first clear, strong expression, almost unvarying, of a rational, national architectural creed. It is the supreme example of the intellect working logically to create a unified aesthetic effect. There is never a concession to impulse or imagination or caprice. The very mathematics of it established narrow limits beyond which it could not go. Within those limits it is one of the most pleasing, even magnificent expressions of man's urge to build.

Based on elemental pillar-and-beam construc-tion, with never an arch or vault or dome, the system lent itself to explicit statement. Its struc-tural truth was self-evident. The proportioning made the horizontal the longer dimension, and this is known as horizontal-accent architecture— as against Europe's second basic type, the vertical-accent Gothic. The upright pillars, however, normally repeated in ranges of four to twenty, became the primary decorative unit; and Greek building is distinguished for nothing else quite so much as the carefully standardized columns— known later, with their accessories, as the "orders of architecture." For long periods of time West-ern Europe and America accepted the belief that artistic practice, even in the machine age, must be based upon study of the classic "orders." This was part of the neo-Hellenism which was a reli-gion in Europe within our own memory, so that even in the nineteen-twenties Sir Banister Fletcher could write: "Greek architecture stands alone in being accepted as above criticism, and therefore as the standard by which all periods of architecture may be tested."

The two early orders, the Doric and the Ionic, have parallels, if not antecedents, in earlier Egypt, Assyria, and Persia. The stronger of the two, the Doric, retains primitive heaviness and the effect of powerful stability. It was a favorite with the Greek builders through the Archaic period; it was standard in the Greek settlements in Sicily and Italy, and was chosen for the Par-thenon; but it gave way to the more ornamental types in the fourth century. The Doric column and capital are not unlike those to be observed in the Egyptian tombs at Beni-Hasan, though it is not necessary to infer direct copying from that model.

The more graceful and lighter Ionic order, however, has too many parallels in Eastern build-ing not to be marked as an importation from the Orient. Probably the Egyptian lotus-capital had had echoes in Assyria (though there are proto-types in the Sumerian discoveries too); and Ionian culture had developed in advance of that of the Greek mainland, partly by reason of As-syrian influences. When the Ionians refined the feature into something distinctively their own, they carried it back to the Athenians, who were their blood brothers. (The Ionic column is illus-trated on page 123.)

Because many of the finest fragments of an-cient architecture survive in the form of single columns or bits of colonnade, it is not unreason-able to expect the trained eye to know the char-acteristics of the "orders." Even though we no longer accept the dictum of their unmatchable perfection, the Doric and Ionic columns have character and even grandeur, and not seldom an abstract sculptural beauty. The Doric usually stands without a base and is fluted or channeled. Oftenest there are twenty flutings, but examples with twelve, sixteen, eighteen, or twenty-four channels exist; and there is a simple, unadorned capital between column and entablature. The column's height is four to six and a half times its diameter at the base. The column departs from the straight, with a slight swelling at the center known to architects as the "entasis." The Doric column is simple, strong, compelling. It lends itself little to variation. Its exact values may have come down from the time of archaic pillar-worship.

The Ionic, on the other hand, modifies power with grace and appears in many pleasing varia-tions. It is slenderer, it stands on a ringed base, and it carries a capital with a delicately carved volute or scroll-shaped decoration. The height of the whole is about nine times the diameter of the column at the base. The shaft oftenest has twenty-four channels.

The Greek temple as we know it is obviously an achievement at the end of a long development,

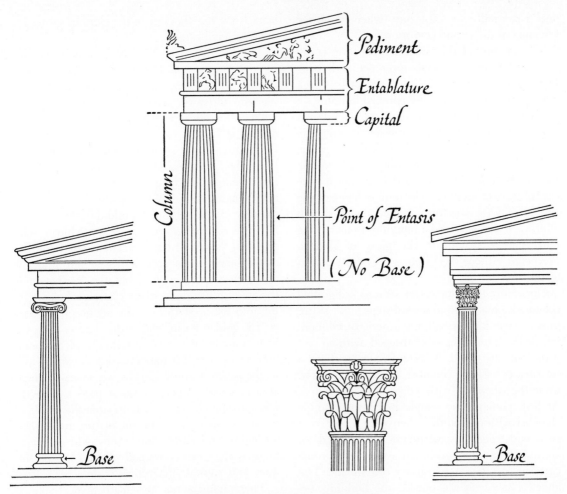

The classic "orders" of architecture.
Above, the Doric order, with explication of parts. At left below, the Ionic order.
At right below, the Corinthian order, with enlarged capital.

the matured expression after centuries of trial and of crystallizing tradition. But its ancestry is no longer traceable in actual examples. There are no existing forerunners of the Greek stone temples. It is now possible, however, to trace their style back, by evidence of construction methods and vestigial remnants, to similar buildings in the more perishable and more primitive materials. The belief that Greek stone architecture is perfectly logical is not a little shaken, indeed, by the discovery that its ornamental idiom grew out of an earlier functional treatment of the wooden members. Most notably, the Doric en-

tablature regularly includes, above the architrave (or first cross-beam), a frieze which is broken by slight projections called "triglyphs," representing ornamental approximations of the old wooden roof-beam ends. There are other ornamental bits suggesting the earlier wooden peg-ends. Indeed, the whole roof structure seems logically designed for timber construction.

There is, moreover, historians' evidence of a change from one material to the other. The columns of the Temple of Hera at Olympia had originally been of wood. As they decayed, stone ones were substituted. Pausanias recorded that one of oak still was doing duty when he visited Olympia in the second century B.C.

The ancestry of the Greek temple form is uncertain. The most plausible inference is that the Doric temple developed out of the early Greek house form. At any rate, the porched building on a rectangular platform is standard. Greek religion did not demand that the temple be a congregating place. Worship was ritualistic and celebrative, and involved no indoor meetings and sermons; the priests were hardly more than guides to successful ways of sacrifice. The temple home of the god or goddess was for glorification, a superb offering to the deity and a reminder to man. The Parthenon was built to the glory of Athena *Parthenos,* Athena the Virgin, the goddess-patron of the city.

Outwardly the temple was seen as a dignified colonnade on a platform several steps high. Within was a windowless hall, the sanctuary, containing the sculptured image of the god, with an end door from the porch. A second room, perhaps a treasury or offering-chamber, commonly backed up to the sanctuary, with a door to the far porch. At first, perhaps, the temple had been a single chamber with one portico; then with a portico at each end; then the colonnade was carried all around. From this, evolution went on in some cases to continuous two-aisled colonnades. The altar for sacrifices was outside the building, before the sanctuary porch, in an open-air sacred enclosure.

Grandeur still resides in the remains of Doric temples at Agrigentum, Paestum, Corinth, Sunium, and Segesta; but the Parthenon is the supreme example of mature Doric architecture. The Acropolis, the hilltop on which the Parthenon stands, gains, by its lift above the plain and the common city, a dignity, a noble remoteness. The group of buildings there, all of a certain magnitude, undomestic and impersonal, affords one of the earliest examples of city-planning comprehensiveness. As a matter of fact, the living quarters of the city below were probably of the meanest, and certainly were unsanitary, haphazard, and far from designed by artists. But the combined shrine and citadel on the hilltop, and the public buildings at the edge of the steep slope, were together one of the glorious spectacles of Greek civilization.

The Parthenon rises above its fellow temples by right of—what? There is only one answer: more art. The Doric columns, incomparably simple and effective, have become slenderer, but without loss of reposeful strength. The proportioning of façades and of parts is exquisite. How far from casual is such an effect one may learn from the Theseum, the comparatively lifeless Doric temple in the plain below—a second-rate achievement, but notable as the best-preserved example of ancient Greek building.

It was a Greek sculptor, not an architect, who said that "successful attainment in art is the result of meticulous accuracy in a multitude of arithmetical proportions"; but the Parthenon is the aptest illustration. Every esoteric scholar delving into the mysteries of "the divine proportion" or "the golden mean" claims the Parthenon as his first example: it has so unfailingly pleased millions of eyes, and it measures out so exactly to a mathematical formula. In the whole aspect there are calculated proportionings of parts and rhythmic correspondences. Then on from the whole to the parts: the areas of the entablature are divided on logical and harmonious ratios; and of course there is the equally refined relationship of column and capital. Perfection within perfection!

These refinements and mathematical adjustments add up to one of the most moving manifestations in the realm of building. Experience confirms the expectation of the mind, the mind that knows that everything reasonable has been done to make the building "perfect." After all, one concludes, intellectualism has its place in art. The mental calculations have contributed to magnificent "building form." The relationships of breadth to height, of part to whole, of unbroken shaft or smooth architrave to decorated members, are within a unity, clear, logical.

Note, too, how naturally the rhythm is initiated and held. The long low steps cover the transition from ground to building, giving stability but making the clean break between nature and structure; then the powerful unimpeded lift of the rhythmic shafts; the first cross-member clear and strong, doubly emphasized; and above

The Parthenon

that, all the frankly decorative elements gathered, disposed in geometrically bounded areas. There is here, despite the survival of wood-age thinking, a sufficient expression of function and structural method and material. The elements of support in relation to down-pressing weight, and the methods of engineering, are externalized without disguise or excessive tracing over.

An age fond of symbolism found in the Greek temple a concrete illustration of moral and spiritual truth, and an expression of the Greek character. The solid foundation platform; the down-pressing mass of architrave, frieze, and roof-structure, counteracting the otherwise too powerful sense of lift; the serenity of the colonnade, modified by the exuberance of sculptured frieze and pediment—all this may be seen as an analogue of the Greek combination of freedom and restraint, of perfectly poised aspiration and reason, of invention and discipline. The columns, some say, mark the rise toward truth or perfection; but the downbearing weight restores balance, caps the too aspiring lift. Thus Fate stops the too presumptuous human reach. Here is the architectural emblem of the Greek philosophy of poise, thoughtful discipline, and restraint.

It is doubtful whether the artist busy with building ever thinks so directly in terms of symbolism, illustration, or allegory, but subconscious forces are probably at work to render any inspired work of art an externalization or a revelation of racial temperament and national thought. For those who find their pleasure heightened by discoveries of symbolism, these speculations may be useful and welcome. Seldom have they had so clear a demonstration in architecture.

The Greek builders, in their search for "perfect" expressiveness, went on to optical refinements unparalleled elsewhere. The entasis, or slight swelling and recession of the profile of the column, is but one of the mathematical tricks to ensure in the beholder's eye the illusion of perfect straightness or exact regularity. Another is that the tops of the columns lean slightly toward the center at each side of the colonnade, the inclination increasing in proportion as they are farther toward each end, because a row of columns which are actually parallel seems more widely spaced at the top corners. (The Parthenon columns of the outer colonnade are inclined, curiously enough, at such angles that all their axes would meet, if continued, at a point one mile up in the air.) Another concession to the eye is the slight curve upward at the center of the main horizontal lines, made because straight steps or straight-set series of columns seem to sag slightly at the center.

These are, of course, intellectually argued refinements, all premised on the idea of mechanical exactitude as ideal. In nineteenth-century intellectualized or scientific estimates of art, they were held up as the ultimate example of creative subtlety; and indeed they constitute an extraordinary, an almost unique instance of refinement in technique. But a generation less committed to the rational approach is less convinced that the eye craves the illusion of mechanical exactitude. There may be little more reason to correct the seeming curve in a colonnade than to straighten the free-hand lines in a painting by use of a ruler. Mechanically justifiable rules may limit a work while endowing it with a certain sort of perfection. Nevertheless, the very existence of such visual refinements affords one of those teasing questions which, in the pondering, increase the observer's understanding of architecture.

Whether or not the sloping columns have essentially to do with it, the Greek temples have a sense of stability with vitality. The Parthenon breathes a deep nobility. It is the final flower of a simple, clearly understandable building development. The abuse of the ages has not destroyed its larger dignity and inbuilt grandeur.

The ornamental features, too, are in general enriching without denial or obscuration of structural truth. The fluting of the columns affords grace and vibration to the otherwise stolid shafts; but the channels reinforce rather than cut across support lines. The frieze is lifted above an architrave kept unadorned, preserving crossbar strength. The transitional members, capitals and moldings, agreeably soften the profile angles without loss of firmness. Supports are cushioned, but without undue softening. Just how great and

distinctive are these achievements may be seen by contrast when the insensitive Romans pick up the Greek elements and use them grandiosely and thoughtlessly, vulgarizing the ornamental features. Nevertheless, Greek ornament as a style of adornment in the minor arts was to be an overwhelming favorite in later ages, even down to the twentieth century. In the Western world the "classic" motives "set the style" for figuring on the stone façades of buildings, on textiles for hanging or for wearing, on mirror frames, and on salt cellars and bookplates and chairs and lampshades. Literally for ages, handbooks of ornament and books on the language of art gave maximum space to the descendant motives of a few clearly marked idioms known first on Greek buildings.

Before turning to the sculpture of the Periclean age—most beautifully represented in the Parthenon—it is well to glance very briefly at the other architecture of the era. While the Doric mode of building seems the typical Greek expression, on account of its greater strength and restraint, the Ionic was hardly less cultivated at this time, and its more appealing gracefulness contributed to the gradual passing of the Doric idiom.

The Ionic expression had already taken form in systematic practice in an exactitude almost as rule-bound as that of the Doric. But the builders of the Erechtheum on the Athenian Acropolis, just after Pericles' time, found occasion to modify the standard plan, and to refine upon the decorative features. There had been pretentious and beautiful temples in the Ionian homeland. In the Asiatic cities of Miletus, Ephesus, and Priene there are examples dating from the fourth century. At Olympia in Greece proper there was a celebrated Ionic temple. On the Acropolis itself the little shrine of Athena Nike, or Temple of the Wingless Victory, utilized Ionic elements. But the Erechtheum, though a variation of the usual arrangement of parts due to the necessity of covering certain bits of ground already sacred and to the requirements of several divinities, is representative of the special features of the mode at its best. The almost fragilely graceful columns are there, the less severe massing, the breaking up of the entablature into more delicate units,

Ionic Temple of Athena Nike, the Acropolis, Athens

and the general lightening of effect and greater enrichment by applied ornamentation. The East Porch (now more or less restored) is, like the Parthenon, Greek architecture at its purest. The doorway within the North Portico has served a thousand architects as classic model in later ages and assorted climes.

The South Porch of the Erechtheum followed an innovation already seen at Delphi. Six statues of maidens, known as caryatids, took the place of the conventional columns. The experiment leaves the building somewhere between architecture and sculpture, and the result is interesting as a novelty rather than for any defensible daring or good purpose in the building art. The statues very likely serve their purpose as supports today with more architectural plausibility than they could have done in the days when their arms, noses, and other members had not been shorn off. Even so, they are a bit ludicrously natural and unmathematical. As the Greeks failed here, so

they often enough failed elsewhere. The monuments they left are not always the matchless and perfect compositions we have been led to believe by other generations.

It is perhaps a limitation of present generations that we are made uneasy by the fact that the Greeks regularly painted their marble temples in polychrome. The whole truth is that they seem not only to have painted them, but to have used gaudy colors for the purpose, indulging generously in red, blue, and gilt. There must have been some endeavor to correlate color and structure, with the structural members kept clear and outstanding, the lower parts little colored, and the upper parts alone flowering in hue as they did in sculptural adornment. But every credible attempt at reconstruction of the half-ruined buildings has resulted in models overheavy and disturbingly unarchitectonic, or excessively traced over and florid; and we can only conclude from evidence at hand that in these later centuries the temples have gained in dignity and repose as they have lost color and some of the profusion of their ornament. The over-ornateness may have existed only in the age of decadence, but that means that the decline had appreciably started before the golden age of Pericles, Phidias, and Ictinus.

The third Greek "order" is obviously a fruit of the decorative spirit. It has no ancestry in engineering or logical calculation. The Corinthian style is hardly more than the Ionic with a showy capital. Within widely different variations there is retained some echo of the volute form in combination with acanthus-leaf foliation. It is related that Callimachus, a sculptor, saw a basket embowered in an acanthus plant and straightway was inspired to create this third order, exactly as nature had designed it. It is the realist's substitute for calculated and formally conceived art.

The Corinthian mode, to the credit of the Greeks, made little headway in Greek times, except as incidental innovation, where a second order was needed for variety within a Doric or Ionic temple or gateway. The Temple of Zeus Olympus (never finished) was an exception in Athens. The Roman architects, filled with the spirit of imperialistic aggrandizement, took the Corinthian mode for their own; in this book illustrations of it are to be seen in the Roman chapter (page 152 and following).

When one has seen the temples, one pretty much has seen Greek architecture. The famous Propylaea on the Acropolis was a monumental temple-like gateway, with a main passage between colonnades, flanked by minor porticoes, in Doric style, as befitted the approach to the Parthenon. The Monument of Lysicrates, of the fourth century B.C., is a graceful, useless composition, in round temple form with engaged Corinthian columns. It has been extravagantly praised by eclectic architects, but it is hardly to be placed beside the earlier strong and characteristic expressions of the Greek spirit. The theaters in the fifth century were unadorned, with great simple bowls of concentric terraces and an unpretentious, perhaps temple-like, stage building.

In the centuries following 400 B.C. architecture rapidly lost both its strength and its purity. The next major step was Rome's adoption of the Greek decorative elements, and her adaptation of them to all sorts of functionless and inappropriate ornamental purposes, on buildings constructed with the un-Greek arch and vault.

The Parthenon Sculptures

Sculpture was in the Periclean age a premier art among the Greeks, partly, no doubt, because it the more perfectly echoed human physical perfection, because it was understandable within the cult of the athlete. In an age when this art predominated—Phidias, a sculptor, was general superintendent of the planning and building of the Parthenon, over Ictinus and Callicrates, the supposed architects—it is to the credit of the reasoning Greek artists that the principles of building were so little obscured behind sculptural decoration or illustration. In general the bases of the structure, the weight-bearing members, and the first horizontals, were kept clear of elaboration or figuring. In the Parthenon and earlier calculated structures, it was deemed that the proper place for exterior sculptures was in the spaces between the triglyphs, or surviving beam-ends, and in the pediment. On the roof, single figures might be set in silhouette against the sky, at gable top and especially gable ends. Within the colonnade in some late Doric temples a continuous frieze ran like a band around the cella's exterior wall, and was seen in bits from the outside, between columns.

The Parthenon sculptures originally appeared on the building in two series, the continuous frieze within the colonnade and the separated panels between the triglyphs; and the two triangular compositions in the pediments. The best preserved of the figures were taken to England early in the nineteenth century, and are universally known, from the name of the man who carried them away in battered remnant form, as the "Elgin marbles."

There is grandeur in the pediment figures. To be judged now only as, literally, individual

The Fates. From east pediment of the Parthenon. *British Museum*

pieces, they are among the major world examples of monumental sculpture. As in the case of the architectural monument of which they were decorative details, they doubtless have gained in sheer aesthetic value by the accidents of time. The sculptors of the Periclean age, judged by other evidence, may be marked as masters at a stage just after the culminating moment. The largeness, the truly sculptural feeling for mass, remains; but the artist is already losing the sense of this in his preoccupation with detail and elaboration. In any case, weather, war, and vandalism, when they have not erased sculptural quality with the rest, have mercifully pared down the heroic pediment figures to a noble simplicity. The eye delights in the sense of contained movement. The tensions between volumes, the powerful plastic aliveness, the sweep and force and might, are inescapable. Keats has suggested the effect, better than any of the critics, in his sonnet "On Seeing the Elgin Marbles." The opening lines are given to the far-ranging but nebulous thoughts inspired by the sight; then:

Such dim-conceivèd glories of the brain
　Bring round the heart an indescribable feud;
So do these wonders a most dizzy pain,
　That mingles Grecian wonder with the rude
Wasting of old Time—with a billowy main—
　A sun—a shadow of a magnitude.

The grand votive statues, such as the outdoor *Athena* on the Acropolis and the colossal image of the same goddess in the cella of the Parthenon, were big enough, by all report, but they seem to have been distressingly and distractingly overdressed, and their largeness and sculptural nobility were lost in excessive detail. The magnitude of the pediment figures is the magnitude of the powerful in repose, of strength kept simple.

It is a matter concerning scholarship rather than art appreciation that the pediment groupings should be reconstructed on paper and their literary significance explained. The best is in the fragmentary figures, which never have lost their living sculptural force. They still breathe plastic vitality. But a different sort of rhythm doubtless resided in the total triangular compositions, confined in their architectural frames, and read by the Athenians as story and allegory. The east pediment group represented the contest of Athena and Poseidon over the site of Athens. The west pediment composition illustrated the miraculous birth of Athena out of the head of Zeus.

The technical problem of fitting elaborate sculptural representations within the confined triangular space of a low pediment was one traditionally challenging to the inventiveness and logic of sculptors collaborating on temple projects. At Aegina, Olympia, and Athens the solutions seem to have been fittingly balanced, decorative, and of one design-idea with the architecture. There was a related flow of movement

Figure from east pediment of the Parthenon. *British Museum*

within the triangle, which was lost in later examples and certainly in every attempted modern imitation.

The panels between the triglyphs under the Parthenon cornice, known as the "metopes," originally ninety-two in number, have been even more disastrously defaced or destroyed than have the pediment groups during their twenty-three centuries of neglect. Each panel, almost square, bore two figures in combat. Sometimes the subjects were taken from mythology, while others are read today as symbolic of moral conflict. Necessarily the standard of sculptural excellence varied. The problem was an eminently difficult one. That some of the many sculptors employed achieved results approaching the triumphs of the pediment figures is indicated in fragments now in the British Museum or still in place on the building.

The low-relief frieze which runs like a decorative band around the outside of the cella wall, within the colonnaded porch, is of another range of excellence. The subject is the ceremonial procession which was an event of the Panathenaic festival held every fourth year. The figures in the sculptural field, which is a little over four feet high and no less than 524 feet long, are mainly those of everyday Athenian life. Even the gods, shown receiving the procession, are intimately real and folk-like, though oversize. To them goes all the world of Athens: priests and elders and sacrifice-bearers, musicians and soldiers, noble youths and patrician maidens.

There is a casualness about the sculptured procession, an informality that would hardly have served within the severe triangles of the pediments. Everything is flowing and lightly accented. Particularly graceful and fluent are the portions depicting horsemen. The animals and riders move forward rhythmically, their bodies crisply raised from the flat and undetailed background. The sense of rhythmic movement, of plastic animation within shallow depth limits, is in parts of the procession superbly accomplished.

There are panels on other buildings of the period which serve to support the unconventional suggestion of Meier-Graefe, to the effect that the genius of the Greeks was less for sculpture

Maiden Fastening Her Sandal. Relief, Temple of Athena Nike. *Acropolis Museum*

in the round than for relief. One of the figures from the procession carved on the platform of the little temple of Athena Nike on the Acropolis goes to prove an almost unique talent for grace-ful, near-realistic low relief. The *Maiden Fastening Her Sandal* lacks, to be sure, the strict for-malization that makes the best of Egyptian relief sculpture appealing, a quality found in some-

The Venus of Milo. Louvre

A few, a very few of the Greek grave monuments so common in museums have a hint of the same grace and fluency. Oftener than not, however, they are wooden and overdetailed; and not infrequently they drip with sentimentality and literary allusion.

Later Greek Sculpture

There is nothing in the range of world art so overpraised as Greek sculpture in the round as achieved after the Periclean culmination. If Phidias was nearly so bad a sculptor as is indicated in our two sources of information about his work—that is, Roman copies and descriptions by ancient observers—the best had passed before Pericles died. From these sources it would also follow that Phidias had as associates among his anonymous helpers on the Parthenon sculptors far greater than himself. Not that the Greek historians and reporters failed to praise him as a master beyond all rivalry; but they gave all the wrong reasons: the marvelous lifelikeness of his work, his meticulous attention to natural detail, his tricks of building up effect.

Formal organization is generally lacking; the plastic rhythm is weak. Art history may yet be rewritten to show that Phidias was the typical figure of the political sculptor, not inventive, never himself creating an aesthetically valid composition, but figuring rather as a great executive able to hold together a large group of architects, builders, and sculptors until the collective glories of the Parthenon emerged. The thirty-nine-foot ivory-and-gold *Athena Parthenos* must have been a horror, as certainly was the colossal *Zeus* at Olympia. Witness the description by J. C. Stobart: [1]

"The flesh parts were of ivory, the clothing of solid gold on a core of wood or stone. Zeus was of colossal size, forty feet high. On his head was

what lesser intensity and rigidity in certain archaic Greek works. But where has a figure stood out from its involved swirls of garment with so sweet a flow of line, so graceful a harmony of linear rhythms? Where in the long history of art is a figure more delightful?

---

[1] In his *The Glory That Was Greece: A Survey of Hellenic Civilization and Culture,* a work readable beyond most histories, and generally excellent, but not escaping, in art judgments, the limitations of that generation which counted the accurate counterfeit the most eminent sculpture.

The Victory of Samothrace. Louvre

a green garland of branched olive; in his right hand he bore a Victory of ivory and gold, in his left a sceptre inlaid with every kind of metal. On the golden robe figures and lilies were chased. The throne was adorned with gold and precious stones and ebony and ivory, with figures painted and sculptured upon it. Even the legs and bars of the throne were adorned with reliefs. Round it were low screens, blue enamel in front, and paintings by the sculptor's brother, Panainos, at the back and sides. The stool on which the god's feet were resting was adorned with figures in gold; the base on which the throne rested, likewise."

Every copy and reconstruction of these popular masterpieces indicates that the description is all too true. This was Greek sculpture already naturalistic, literary, and florid. It is said that about a score of works have been identified as indubitably by Phidias. Hardly one is above a competent standard of realism.

One of the first of the realistic school of sculptors was Myron. His *Discus-Thrower* is superior to any work safely to be ascribed to his contemporary, Phidias, if only in the linear composition and the enclosed movement. Myron carried on the typically Greek tradition of athlete-glorification. The *Discus-Thrower* is known today only from a Roman copy, but is probably a fair illustration of the artist's style, because we know that he was praised in his own time for his exact and unprecedented representations of moving figures of athletes and animals. Where repose of the body had been earlier thought of as the sculptural thing, there was now initiated a cult of action.

The anatomical truth and idealized athleticism of Myron's figures are perhaps truer to the Greek mind than were the archaic Apollos and the heroic pediment figures of the Parthenon. Certainly they were truer to any theory of art formulated in Grecian times. The characteristic attitudes of the racer, the boxer, the discus-thrower, were fixed, it might be at the instant of strain. Sculpture is far from formalization here. It is already well on the road that will end in genre and in melodrama. And Myron was the contemporary of Sophocles, dramatic poet in whom grandeur and an impersonal elevation evoked the profound aesthetic response, who rose above every irrelevancy of time and place.

Polyclitus was the third celebrated sculptor of the fifth century. His interest in anatomical truth and athletic idealization went so far that he wrote a treatise on the subject. By way of illustration he made a statue of the ideal (male) figure, and this "model" became a bone of contention in the Athenian art world. But Polyclitus is reputed to have avoided the attitudinized and strained poses of Myron's work. And indeed there is, comparatively, a welcome calm in the *Maiden* at Munich which is ascribed to him or to his school.

The story of free-standing sculpture from the opening of the fourth century into the Hellenistic times of Alexander and down to the coming of the Romans is a record of the narrowing of the never very broad aesthetic into the most cramping of all conventions, the convention of naturalism. Concerned almost solely with the human figure as such, the sculptor followed a course toward greater and greater circumstantial actuality. He lost the virtue inherent in his marble and his tool and gained the appeal of the illustrator in his clever transfers from life and his forced sentiment. His approach, always intellec-tual, was in the end by way of little things, such as please little minds: trivialities of everyday existence, the sentimental, the anecdotal, the picturesque. He specialized also in naturalistic reminders of abstractions such as Love and Virtue and Abundance.

This was the time marking the full emergence of the scientific spirit. Men were obsessed with the reality of immediate things. Greece had triumphed with the reasoning faculties. She had pushed the aptitudes of her innate intellectual genius to their furthest expression. The Orient, with its mysticism and its non-realistic arts, was alien and barbarian to her.

One of the trends to be observed in fourth-century sculpture is the softening of the gods. The pretty mantelpiece art of Praxiteles offers typical examples. Sculptors' images that had become progressively more youthful, and then effeminate, became, in such examples as his famous *Hermes with the Infant Dionysus*, unmanly and pretty in the extreme. In none but a decadent age would an artist try to put so unsculptural a composition into stone. The separation of parts, the inappropriate light draperies in heavy stone, the painstaking accuracy of delineation in every minor detail, all these deny sculptural perception. Vigor and vision and the feeling for the material have been lost (as seen in the illustration opposite).

The same limitations and the same tame virtues of prettiness and diverting charm are in a host of fourth-century statues. Praxiteles was the recognized master of the period. His *Cnidian Aphrodite*—one of the first female nudes, typically posed beside an urn overhung with stone draperies—is said to have drawn innumerable ancient sightseers to the little island of Cnidus. (This is the Venus that so long wore a tin skirt in the Vatican Gallery.) The *Young Satyr*, known also as the *Marble Faun*, is a perfect reproduction in marble of a languorous body, with hair, scarf, and support in wooden contrast. This was traditionally the second of Praxiteles' masterpieces. There was a famous *Eros*, too, or Cupid, owned by Phryne, the sculptor's mistress, who had posed for the *Cnidian Aphrodite*.

Another outstanding sculptor was Lysippus,

Praxiteles: *Hermes with the Infant Dionysus*. Marble. *Olympia Museum*

who introduced the trick of placing a small refined head upon a large muscular body. He is said to have produced fifteen hundred statues, "each sufficient to have made him famous." Scopas also was of the school producing athletic and naturalistic figures, but his work was marked at times by a drift into the theatric. The anatomical mastery shown in the works of these typical masters is unquestionable, as we might expect. Their "daring" is sometimes praised because they were willing to attempt in marble and bronze the scattered compositional effects more natural to painting. Lysippus, a generation later than Scopas, was official sculptor to Alexander the Great.

The gods are, then, still being idealized, in a facile way. They are shown as more human, in more intimate pose. Portraiture, never before very important in Greece, develops rapidly, with a new accuracy. The face is no longer a type but an individual likeness. Though there have been three centuries of nude males in sculpture, the female figure now for the first time commonly appears unclothed; Aphrodite becomes a favorite.

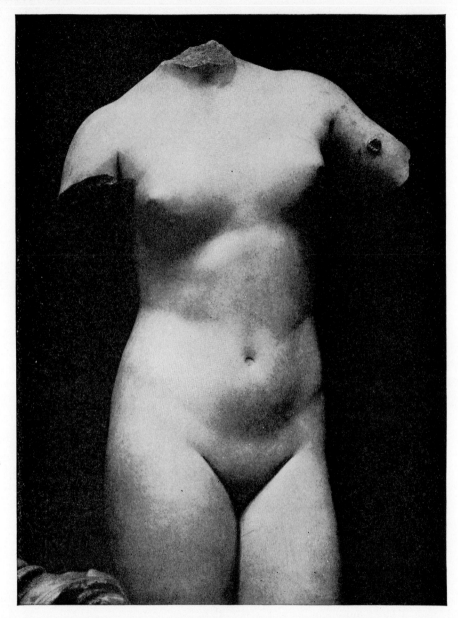

Cyrenean Venus, detail. *Museum of the Thermae, Rome*

Eros comes in for popularity, and is accounted an amusing addition to the sculptural repertory— is, in fact, quite in line with an emergent playful conception.

A few statues by unnamed Hellenistic artists have entered too largely into art history to be overlooked. Two have been greatly aided to their

fame by events outside the sculptors' calculations, by accidents of time. The *Victory of Samothrace* or *Winged Victory* achieves a sense of movement long admired. And indeed the fragment as it stands has, in the massing, more than depicted action. There is an inescapable drive, a pleasing fullness. But it is obviously part of a typical late

Greek work, without plastic cohesion. If the missing parts could be restored, they would in all likelihood result in a whole impossibly scattered in effect, with lamps or wreaths to add symbolism to the composition (page 129).

The *Venus of Milo* (dated about two centuries after Praxiteles) likewise is the gainer through loss of projecting parts. There are virtues in the statue as it is: in linear rhythms, especially accented in the garment folds, and in the transcribed woman's loveliness of the body (see page 128).

And indeed the best things in the sculpture of this late Greek period must be found by a closing of the eyes to formal values and by seeking enjoyment *in the model*. The beauty is most often the transferred desired beauty of the female body. There is nothing of the pinched or slender nymph about these Hellenistic Aphrodites or Phrynes. A full-rounded, solidly cushioned woman is the ideal. But the softness of the flesh and the enchanting nuances of plane and curve are nonetheless intimated. Abounding health with caressability! With some such subconscious surrender we forget the marble, remember the woman. In this range are the irresistible *Cyrenean Venus* at Rome, the *Niobid* at Milan, and the *Syracusan Venus*.

The famous Pergamene sculptures are illustrations of that other road of change, into theatricality. The Acropolis at Pergamon, a Greek city on the Asiatic coast, independent after the break-up of Alexander's empire, had been constructed by a community long known for cultural interests; and when, in 18 B.C., a ruler decided to celebrate a victory by constructing there a magnificent altar to Zeus, the local sculptors had their supreme opportunity. The architectural features were deliberately dwarfed, and place was made for a gigantic sculptured frieze. Scores of figures in high relief, above life-size, were crowded into the panels. The effect is restless and unarchitectural, though decoratively rich as seen from a distance. But the notable thing is the melodramatic forcing of incident and expression. Gods are battling giants—a perfect theme for this disordered, uneasy sort of art—and violence, agony, and stress are depicted with verve and

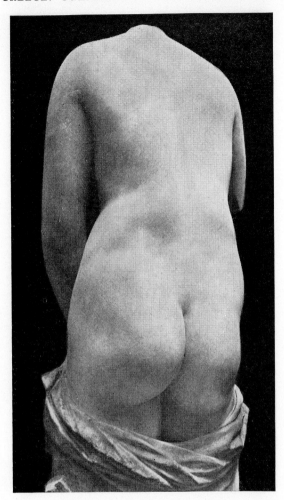

Syracusan Venus. Syracuse Museum

expert sketchiness. It is a summit of vigorous romantic art.

The Rhodian school of sculpture, another extension of the Greek, came to the same end. What was long considered its masterpiece, and indeed a masterpiece of world art, the *Laocoön* group, became a *casus belli* among world critics. This ultra-realistic statue, telling the terrible story of the strangulation of the Trojan priest and his two sons by huge snakes, with all the terror, strain, and contortion faithfully rendered, is now recognized on all sides as extravagant and almost absurdly overwrought. Its technique is as forced as its pathos. Even more involved is the *Farnese Bull* group, a celebrated composition of

Niobid.
Figure from lost group.
Banca Commerciale, Milan

the Rhodian school, now at Naples. Every detail of nature and every exaggerated gesture of life are shown in a riot of forms. The *Bust of Homer* shows this turbulence carried into portraiture.

The Lesser Sculpture of Greece

In one other direction the Greek current trailed off into sterile eddies. The taste for literary and genre bits had asserted itself as early as the period of Praxiteles. In the following three centuries there was time for it to call forth many varieties of intimate sculpture: studies of household living, prettified sentimental incidents, romantic reminders, even satirical comment pushed to the point of caricature. Among the immense number of statues in this field there are some that rise above sentimental or illustrational appeal. The best-known museum pieces, of which casts exist in a great many galleries, are likely to be sculpturally the worst: the *Boy with a Goose*, the *Runner Extracting a Thorn from His Foot*, the Capitoline *Cupid and Psyche*. Most famous in that series is the Pergamene piece, the *Dying Gaul*. But among the smaller Hellenistic bronzes there are also figures from which the plastic sensibility has not wholly fled, to which a breath of order and formalization has miraculously returned.

The Tanagra figurines are a special and appealing group of genre sculptures. The miniature statue was no innovation in Greek art; there had been small votive figures before the emergence of the archaic Apollos or youths. One might even go back to Cretan, Mycenaean, and Cypriote prototypes. Nor had terra cotta, as a material, been overlooked by the great sculptors of earlier periods. But Greek statuettes in terra cotta usually mean to us the genre bits of which the products of Tanagra are most characteristic. There are thousands of these extant. They depict the intimate life and everyday interests of the later Greeks with a fidelity and an appeal found in no other medium. Mostly the pieces are of importance as documentary evidence or amusing records of customs, costumes, games, and foibles of Greek women, though there are gods and the Virtues and the like, too.

The statuettes have been found chiefly in tombs, which some commentators consider sufficient reason for terming them "religious." It is more likely that lay custom (at least in the comparatively late time of the Tanagra industry) decreed that these conventional relics be retained in one's own tomb or offered at the funeral of a friend, without thought of votive service to the gods. There are toys too.

In any case, the modern observer is drawn to the crowded shelves of Tanagra and related statuettes because they are diverting illustrations of the Greek *comédie humaine*. Woman is seen in literally thousands of standing and sitting poses, dressing, promenading, playing games, conversing with friends, nursing children, dancing, lounging, flirting with Cupid, playing with birds. But there are also the allegorical figures and gods and goddesses, and, later, nudes. The commonest Tanagra type, however, is the standing woman with ample garments drawn close to the body. The variations of this single mantled figure are innumerable. The grace and charm were enhanced by rich, but now generally subdued, coloring.

The impulse to reproduce everything, for diversion or offering, gave rise to widespread manufacture of representations of actors, dwarfs, and dancing girls; even fruits, vegetables and nuts. Of course Eros came in for increased vogue, in interpretations from the playful and sweet to the lewd. Sculptors not only in Tanagra but all over Magna Graecia (then no longer a political

Bust of Homer. National Museum, Naples

unit) seem, in the two centuries before Christ, to have catered to this market.

One of the strangest results of the spread of Greek culture in other lands was the crossing of this current with Egyptian run-out formalism, after the foundation and decline of Alexandria.[1] This led eventually to cult images of Hellenized Egyptian gods, as well as to the usual run of genre illustrations and decorative utilitarian ob-

---

[1] When Alexander, the great Macedonian conqueror of Hellas, Asia Minor, Persia, and Egypt, founded the world capital at Alexandria, it became a center of intellectual and scientific advance rather than of art. The world-famous library, the museum that became the equivalent of a university, the laboratories of mathematicians and anatomists and astronomers—all these magnificently served knowledge. But creative art could not be given new life or revived, not even recent Greek creative art. The best that can be said for Alexandria as fosterer of the arts is that it may have served as a link between declining Greece and growing Rome—and an industrial center for the multiplication of standard "goods."

Tanagra figurines. *National Museum, Athens*

jects. At Myrina in Asia Minor the output ran more to divinities, especially those concerned with love. The grotesques, including comedy actors, were there generously represented too. From the Near East and Egypt to Italy and North Africa, the Greek terra-cotta statuette was familiar. The development merged ultimately with the Roman traffic in household trifles and ornaments.

The coins and gems of Greece afford a pleasureland of miniature sculptural beauty. As in the seals of Babylonia and the gems and seals of the Aegean states, one finds delight in the formalized heads, animals, chariots, and emblems fitted so sensitively and compactly into small confines.

Coinage developed both east and west of Lydia (in western Asia Minor) soon after its invention there, supposedly in the seventh century B.C. The designs on the money of the Greek Sicilian cities took on artistic values somewhat before the Athenian sculptors awoke to the opportunity offered in the numismatic medium. The quadriga designs of Syracuse, of the fifth century B.C., are justly celebrated. In general the Archaic coins of the sixth and early fifth centuries are superior to those of the Periclean age and the following Hellenistic and post-Alexandrian periods. The realism of the late portraiture

detracts from the formal and properly mathematical design (conditioned by the circular area), and the vigor and dignity gradually fade out. Grace, delicacy, and a flat exactitude are substituted.

The best gold and silver coins have something of the stylization, the sustained rigid mastery of a few volumes ranged in space, which was typical of Execias' vase designs. The secret lies in the adjustment of volumes to voids, in concentration (since the object is so small), and in an appropriate crisp and vigorous technique. In general the subjects tend to be the portraits of rulers, heraldic emblems, and gods, or important historic characters and events. Each Greek city, in the homeland or Asia Minor or far Sicily, had its own coinage, and the types and individual pieces are therefore almost infinitely varied. In any routine museum collection one can turn up little masterpieces that are plastically alive and rewarding.

The gems and seals are hardly less varied, though enjoyment of them is made more difficult because the object left to us is usually the incised negative. When this is in translucent stone—as is often the case—the effect can be had by placing the gem against bright light. But usually the values of subject, composition, and workmanship

Athenian and colonial coins. *Metropolitan Museum of Art*

are to be studied only in the positives, taken recently and almost uniformly in plaster of Paris. Again the early or Archaic examples are preferable to the later, more detailed compositions. Eventually these developed into the florid and insensitive Graeco-Roman products, though it is certain that exceptional gems were being made by Greek artists for the brisk Roman trade well into Christian times.

Cameo-cutting was an outgrowth of Greek seal-sculpture—which had, of course, an ancestry traceable back to Cretan art, or, through Ionia and the islands, back to Sumeria. The cameo comes to notice only in the Hellenistic era. Worked in two layers of contrasting colors of stone, it often tends to over-showy results. From its miniature forms, it went to larger triumphs in such questionable achievements as the Portland Vase. This celebrated object is not a true cameo product, in that the material is not stone but two layers of glass. The white outer layer is partially cut away, is treated as relief sculpture. The scene depicted is apparently mythological, though the figures have not been identified. The craftsmanship is marvelous, and the vase as a whole is gaudily pretty. But formal sensitivity is at a very low ebb. With mention of this sometime famous curiosity, we have arrived in Roman times.

The Art of Painting

Greek painting was wonderfully "artistic" and more advanced than sculpture, if we may trust the testimony of ancient writers. But as they were, in general, historians primarily interested in battles, custom, and anecdote, or in intellectual philosophies, there is ground for questioning their aesthetic judgment. The reasons they give for the eminence of the Greek painters are generally unrelated (as are their accounts of sculpture) to the formal values that may have been inherent in the murals and easel pictures.

The elder Pliny, of the first century A.D., gathered within his storehouse of knowledge, the *Historia Naturalis*, innumerable records and anecdotes of early artists. To him painting and

Cantharus with painting
ascribed to Brygus.
Museum of Fine Arts, Boston

sculpture were among "the twenty thousand matters worthy of attention." His text is replete with items of this sort (in the translations by K. Jex-Blake):

Polygnotus made a first serious contribution to the development of painting by opening the mouth, showing the teeth, and varying the stiff archaic set of the features. He painted the picture now in the gallery of Pompeius and formerly in front of his Council Chamber, representing a warrior armed with a shield, about whom people argue as to whether he is ascending or descending. . . . The story runs that Parrhasios and Zeuxis entered into competition, Zeuxis exhibiting a picture of some grapes, so true to nature that the birds flew up to the wall of the stage. Parrhasios then displayed a picture of a linen curtain, realistic to such a degree that Zeuxis, elated by the verdict of the birds, cried out that now at last his rival must draw the curtain and show his picture. . . . Apelles' portraits were such perfect likenesses that, incredible as it may sound, Apion the grammarian has left it on record that a physiognomist . . . was able to tell from the portraits alone just how long the sitter had to live or had already lived. . . . He [Peiraïkos] painted barbers' shops, cobblers' stalls, asses, eatables and similar subjects, earning for himself the name of "painter of odds and ends." In these subjects he could give consummate pleasure, selling them for more than other artists received for their large pictures.

Practically every shred of direct evidence regarding the art of painting has disappeared, except post-Alexandrian work—preserved mostly on the mummy-casings from Egypt—and a few Roman copies. Nevertheless, the books ancient and recent are full of the praises of Cimon, Polygnotus, Zeuxis, Apelles, and a host of others. The modern observer who interests himself in art for what it can afford of aesthetic pleasure does well to skim over the subject. As he does so, he will doubtless find himself conjecturing thus:

Since vase-painting is likely to have developed parallel with the larger mural art, if not in a sense reflecting the latter's more pronounced characteristics, there was, by the fifth century, a flourishing school of painters. The art had then developed from crude beginnings, through a strong Archaic mastery, and was taking on the mellower, softer virtues (and limitations) of Phidian realism. In that case it is a major catas-

Roman copy in mosaic of a Greek painting possibly by Philoxenus, detail. Pompeii.
National Museum, Naples

trophe that the larger things corresponding to the vase designs of Execias and Epictetus and Euphronius have been lost. But we can read only too well, in the descriptions and praises of Pausanias, Pliny, and other commentators, the Hellenistic painters' correspondence to effeminate and "touching" Praxitelean sculpture, with the nuances of the model played up to an extreme, probably in combination with some such conventions as the Alexandrians' wooden treatment of the hair and draperies of their statues. There would be, too, the later swing into vigorous forced emotional expression—overwrought technique matching the straining after pathos.

On the other hand, Pliny recorded that in ancient *painting* "the scheme and coloring are simple, without variety or tone, but the lines are rendered with exquisite perfection, thus lending to early works a singular grace. This purity of draftsmanship was gradually lost, and its place taken by a learned technique, by differentiation of light and shade, and by the full resources of rich coloring to which the works of later artists owe their strength." If the Roman reporter had added that the gain meant loss not only of grace and simplicity but of a different sort of strength—formal and plastic—we could credit him with a nice discrimination between beautifully stylized archaism and later illustrationalism.

Certain gorgeously decorative vase-paintings, in both the late black-figured mode and the early red-figured, indicate what the virtues of pre-Periclean mural art may have been. Here are the exquisite perfection of line and the singular grace reported by Pliny, within a lingering stylization but built up into eye-filling decorative compositions. The earlier things, before 500 B.C., would be characterized by a stricter formalization, even an elegance, and a flatter technique—which today would seem more suitable for mural painting. The colors would be less natural, more frankly used for heightening the total effect, though never as a very important element, if the vases are to be considered fair evidence. Perhaps the Corinthians, who are supposed to have founded one of the earliest schools of painting, and to have developed a tapestry-like mural-frieze art before illustrational painting came in, retained for a time the subdued rich color and the sensuous patterning of their seventh-century "Orientalized" vases. But the influence was alien and doubtless soon went out of painting, as it disappeared from vase-drawing.

It is known that many treatises were written on coloring and other phases of the painting art, from the fifth century on. But these, so far as they survive, throw little light on the *quality* of the actual works. We can only surmise the gradual descent into sentimentalism, similar to that instanced in fourth- to first-century sculpture. By the time of the examples now available for study, mostly Egyptian or Italian in provenance, although certainly Greek in execution and spirit, nature and the intellect have triumphed over formal sensibility. Genre and portraiture are most important.

Nor did painting, by its nature so fitted for fluency and the depiction of physical movement, escape the pitfalls of forced action and melodramatic extravagance which were so characteristic of post-Alexandrian sculpture. In Pompeii was found a large mosaic battle-scene which is reputed to be a copy of a famous fourth-century Greek painting, perhaps by Philoxenus. The transfer from one medium to the other may be considered grounds for withholding judgment on its color, drawing, or technical proficiency; but the confused composition, nervous movement, and overfidelity to nonessentials suggest the perfect mural analogue to Pergamene and Rhodian sculpture. Actual Pompeian paintings, when not obviously the work of routine decorators and hack artists, seem in general to reflect this popular overdynamic and overemotional style.

The rest of the surviving evidence is in the portraiture known chiefly from examples attributable to the first and second centuries A.D. Several hundred paintings of heads, approximately life-size, have been recovered from Graeco-Roman tombs in Egypt. Usually on wood, sometimes on linen, they are notably accurate, competent, and uninspired. Occasionally one rises to psychological insight. A certain freshness and directness prevail. Very rarely there is a flash of rhythmic design or a hint of formal excellence. The exhibit as a whole interests modern students as an indication of the point in technical mastery —in this case in encaustic painting—reached by the late Greeks. The conclusion is inescapable: if *great* Greek painting existed, it is likely to have flowered before Salamis.

Greek Theories about Art

Theorizing usually begins when creative energy has run thin. Critics arrive after the creative culmination. Greek theorizing about art began, in a serious way, during the so-called golden age, which was really when the decadence had started. It was, in general, academic, intellectualistic, based on an analysis of contemporary works, and blind to the abiding formal values—but illuminating. The keynote of Greek aesthetics was set in Aristotle's celebrated summary, "Art is imitation." Greek art after the Periclean period might be epitomized as nature marvelously imitated and nature idealized.

Even Socrates seems to have been caught in the limitations of Greek realistic theory. His reasoning is: the artist is to copy what he sees; through knowing many models, he may combine the excellencies of all, and thus arrive at a body nearer ideal; it is better to copy what is beautiful than what is ugly. Plato looked at the art of his time, considered it mimetic in intention and effect, and judged the plastic artist unworthy of a place in the ideal state. (There is a suggestion elsewhere that Plato unwarrantedly appreciated the "barbaric" art of the Egyptians, even as we

Venus Genetrix.
Museum of the Thermae, Rome

do today. This was a real sorrow to the old-school Hellenists. It may however indicate that one Greek philosopher rose above the limitations of his time and his race, to guess a depth of formal value in art not evident in the works of his contemporaries but glimpsed in alien works.)

Aristotle is the typical intellectual critic, the most Greek of theorists, and the one whose opinion has been felt through all after-ages. What damage was done to Western art by parrotings of his facile summary is incalculable.

Art is primarily mimetic, said Aristotle. It must imitate appearances. But the artist's eye must be able to construct nature's ideal out of many observed aspects and details. The work of art is at once a copy and a *correction* of nature. There is, in all Aristotle's words, hardly a suggestion of those values in art which make it a thing separate from nature, or of the experience of order or rhythm which the Chinese ancients, for instance, placed at the heart of aesthetics, and which European critics, at long last, begin to restore to that place. Aristotle would have Greek youths study art, but only that they might the better judge the perfections of the actual human form.

It is well to keep in mind this aspect of Greek thinking about art. It helps explain why classic art is what it is, why it never rose to the color and the decorative richness of Oriental manifestations, and why it seldom approaches the formal excellence of Persian, Chinese, or Javanese art. "Art is perfect when it seems to be nature," wrote Longinus in the third century A.D. The thought

echoes up and down the corridors of Greek philosophy and learning, like a refrain.

When Solon traveled in Egypt, a priest there
said to him, "You Greeks are children." The
later Hellenes could afford to laugh at that,
good-naturedly and with self-satisfaction. With
their intellects they knew they had carried the
arts to a new stage of reasoned perfection.

Today the Egyptian priest's estimate is believed to have truth in it too. The Greeks are
seen to have been blind to many of those forces
that cannot be identified by the senses and
weighed by the mind—the mystic, the spiritual,

the supersensuous elements that go far toward
making art the mysterious thing it is, escaping
intellectual planning and eluding explanation.
The Greeks knew little indeed of that wider and
more mature world. They were precocious children in the realm they had mastered. They did
magnificent things within the clear, light-of-day
idioms of realism. They were the world's first
great science-bound artists. Later generations owe
them a very great debt. But "the Greek miracle"
is at last seen as only one of the many in the long
history of art, and not, perhaps, the transcendent,
the most admirable.

Impression from a Greek engraved gem. *Museum of Fine Arts, Boston*

VII: ROMAN ART AND ENGINEERING; ETRUSCAN ART

And so we come to mighty Rome, conqueror of Gaul and Carthage, of Greece and Egypt, mistress of the Western world through six centuries, capital of the mighty Caesars, unchallenged home of grandeur, spectacle, and magnificence, splendid with the art plundered from a hundred enslaved peoples, giver of laws and morals and military science to all the West. And yet this "Eternal City" was artistically inconsequential. Except in one direction, that of monumental architecture and structural engineering, Rome produced very little distinctive creative art. The Romans cut off rather than absorbed the one significant development on Italian soil, the Etruscan, and turned to import decadent Greek sculptors, decorators, and painters to give a Hellenistic surfacing to their culture. In the aesthetic scales the contribution of mighty Rome weighs more lightly than that of tiny states such as Sumeria and Siena.

Grandeur was Rome's goal, grandeur her one achievement, and perhaps also the secret of the shallowness of her art. The desire to impress by bigness led to magnificent works of engineering and building. But the desire to impress by profusion and pomp led, oftener than not, to adornment of those same works with misused scraps and veneers of Greek architecture and weak imitations of Greek ornamental sculpture. Hellenic moderation and reasonableness became Roman practicality and Roman swagger.

As soon as Rome takes on importance politi-

Wolf of Rome. Bronze, Etruscan. *Museo dei Conservatori, Rome*

cally and culturally—that is, as soon as adjoining Etruria has been subjugated and Carthage successfully challenged—the spirit that dominates the arts is that of the conqueror and the reveler. Architecture is first, but temples no longer enter importantly into the display. The Forum or trading place, the basilica or public meeting-hall, the baths, the sports arenas, the theaters and circuses, are constructed in colossal size, and over them is lavished a wealth of ornamentation. Later there are the palaces, triumphal arches, and ceremonial gateways. Sculpture runs to portraiture on the one hand, to satisfying the desire for personal glorification and commemoration, and on the other to a sketchy ornamentalism, to surface enrichment of architecture.

The plastic arts are not the only ones thus degraded. The great Greek dramas are occasionally produced through centuries of Roman history; but there is no rival, no successor to Aeschylus, Sophocles, and Euripides. Seneca turns their noble vehicle to melodramatic rant. Indeed, the theater sees little straight drama. The bloody spectacles of the gladiatorial arena and the fights of slaves against wild beasts are closer to the Roman taste. In poetry alone there is a cherished legacy to the later world—Vergil, Horace, Ovid—and in the works of the anonymous architect-engineers. Over all else the militarist, lawyer, and trader rule.

There is a story of a Roman general who, while overseeing the transport of some Greek statues from a sacked Eastern city, shouted to his soldiers and slaves a warning that if they broke these works of art he would keep them at work till they produced others as good. Such was the obtuseness of those who took art to Rome. By the surviving evidence it seems certain that the general's mentality and his attitude toward art were typical of the mass of cultivated Romans. Except for the engineers, the story is one of seizing, borrowing, or buying art, of forcing the artist into imitative service, of parading spoils.

Rome's own leaders, cultural and political, proclaimed that her genius was for other sorts of mastery. Vergil wrote in the *Aeneid* (in Theodore C. Williams' translation):

Let others melt and mould the breathing bronze
To forms more fair, aye, out of marble bring
Features that live; let them plead causes well;
Or trace with pointed wand the cycled heaven,
And hail the constellations as they rise;
But thou, O Roman, learn with sovereign sway
To rule the nations. . . .

But having gained sovereign sway over innumerable nations, Rome looked on the bronze or stone faces their artists had made and coveted them; felt, without understanding, the need for art.

The good old Puritan realist Cato, a Roman soldier, moralist, and politician of the third century B.C., complained, in his campaign against women's rights, luxury, and art, of the noxious effect of some Greek sculptures imported from Syracuse. Speaking as consul, he said to the Roman Senate: "Believe me, those statues from Syracuse were brought into this city with injurious effect. I already hear too many commending and admiring the decorations of Athens and Corinth, and ridiculing the earthen images of our Roman gods standing on the fronts of their temples. For my part I prefer these gods." He went on to identify the foreign arts, by implication, with "female luxury." Castigating the women who objected to plain dresses (varicolored costumes, personal ornamentation, and horse-drawn carriages had been forbidden by law, "except on occasion of some public religious solemnity"), he shrewdly foresaw and described the excessive luxury and show that would follow repeal of the blue laws.

"If, Romans," he said, "every individual among us had made it a rule to maintain the prerogative and authority of a husband with respect to his own wife, we should have less trouble with the whole sex. . . . What motive that even common decency will allow to be mentioned is pretended for this female insurrection? Why, say they, that we may shine in gold and purple, that we may ride through the city in our chariots. . . . Luxury if it had never been meddled with would be more tolerable than it will be now, like a wild beast irritated by having been chained, and let loose the more dangerous."

Livy, the historian who reported the event three centuries later, goes on to say that "next day the women poured out in public in much greater numbers, and in a body beset the doors of the tribunes . . . nor did they retire until the prohibitions were withdrawn." Thus the dikes against the luxuries, including the arts of the Greeks, were demolished. Thus was illustrated a phenomenon not uncommon in human history: the streams of art and the impulse toward art can be dammed temporarily by Puritans and hard-headed materialists. The dam will break in due time, and when it breaks there will be a flood not of creative art but of second-hand and showy things—for new creative genius has not been fostered nor invention encouraged.

If Cato was wrong in his basic thinking, there was this much of right in his warning: having eschewed the artistic impulse in her early days, when all energies were being bent to military (and commercial) domination, Rome was certain, once there was a place for the arts, to take up the trivial if not the specious sorts. From no art at all she slid into an art luxurious, extravagant, and decorative. It is the supreme historic example of materialism decking itself in the garments it borrows, without discrimination because without understanding. There is something insensitive and orgiastic, from the outside, in the way in which the conquering Roman spread art around.

There is room for another view, perhaps. Macaulay, writing many centuries later, could express himself with true Catonian contempt: "Leave to the Greek his marble nymphs!" But the modern reader is the more likely to remember the utter degradation of the Roman theater; to recall that philosophers were repeatedly banished, officially, from Rome and Italy; and to conclude that the Roman character, brutal, sensual, and practical, had little use for the arts except as diversion or social show.

What, then, was the place of the artists in the Roman so-called "republican" civilization? It is likely that they were little better than slaves. They were assigned the cultural tasks in Roman homes not because they had been known in Athens or Alexandria as leading practitioners of the arts, but because they had been bought or captured in countries celebrated for learning and craftsmanship. Minor personages—musicians, philosophers, procurers, tutors, cooks, schoolmasters, concubines, and the like—are reported to have been slaves or near-slaves, and the Roman patrician was not likely to class painter or sculptor higher. In imperial times, however, there was to come a rush of culture, with due honor to foreign artists, who would then take their place among the swaggerers, or at least in the respected merchant class.

Rome as a civic entity comes into the light of history in the mid-eighth century B.C., as a trading settlement near the mouth of the Tiber on the western coast of central Italy. Growth and integration are slow in the three centuries following. There are leagues of districts, of the cities of Latium. There is friction with the Etruscans, who occupy adjoining lands, who are already secure in a culture of their own. At times Etruscan teachers, even Etruscan rulers, are imported to Rome, or perhaps force their way in. They are learned from, then discarded or expelled.

Steadily Rome grows. The city's power expands. The practical genius of its people triumphs. Even the sacking of the capital itself by Gauls from the far north, in 390 B.C., is hardly more than an incident, is no real interruption to the nation's march to world power.

Etruria gives in, is completely vassal to Rome, by 290 B.C. A century of cruel wars breaks the power of Carthage, and that city is finally burned by the Romans in 146 B.C. In the same year Corinth is savagely destroyed. Greece is already under the Roman yoke, as are territories from Spain to Asia Minor. The march of conquest will continue until Egypt and Mesopotamia in one direction and Gaul and Britain in the other are added to the empire.

At home, the barbarian Latins have long since been disciplined, trained into typical Roman civilized ways. Classes of patricians and plebeians after a while forget their quarreling, as prosperity and foreign expansion bring them common benefits. They unite to administer the world's

Warrior. Bronze, archaic Etruscan.
Metropolitan Museum of Art

art by displaying the spoils of Syracuse, down to that crowning day of a triple triumph when Caesar Augustus celebrated his victory over the last of the Hellenic powers, statues and other works of art had come to be as much a part of the pageantry of triumphs as captives or military booty. The solemn dedication of these objects in some public building was the natural sequel of the triumphal procession. The great generals of the Republic, and after them the Emperors, had shown themselves zealous for the preservation and arrangement of these collections. Only a short while before Pliny compiled his history of the artists, his patron Vespasian had opened the great Temple of Peace, destined with its surrounding Forum to receive, alongside the treasures of the Temple of Jerusalem, those Greek masterpieces which the greed of Nero had gathered within the Golden House."

This civilization of the fighter, the conqueror, lasted five centuries before Rome was swamped under the invading waves of northern "barbarians"; though early in the fourth century A.D. a new spirit of Christian art had matured under persecution. Christianity had been officially accepted, spelling a better destiny for Europe—bringing in, too, a faith around which an art, and new uses for art, could grow.

The Etruscans: Their Genius for Sculpture

Before Rome emerged politically, and centuries before any art to be termed Roman appeared, the Italian people known as Etruscans had their own culture. Originally they had come over to Italy from the Aegean basin, probably from the Asiatic side. This was at a time when Greece was hardly yet formed as a state, perhaps in the eighth century B.C.; and the Etruscans' art, in so far as it is derivative, seems less Greek than Asiatic, Cypriote, and Ionic. Their sculpture was important and distinctive; they introduced the arch as a structural element into Europe; and in painting and the minor crafts they were expert and inventive. The best of what is called early Roman art is in the contribution of these

first great republic. The rich rule, plunder, exploit; it is an oligarchic republic. When selfishness and indulgence threaten actually to destroy the state unless a single firm hand is given power, republic slips over into empire, a few years before Christ is born. Just then, in the Augustan age, Rome is nearest to an art of her own.

Even then Rome gains a vast amount of art from the treasuries of the Greek world. E. Sellers, in his introduction to *The Elder Pliny's Chapters on the History of Art*, excellently summarizes the matter: "From the day when Marcellus had first induced the Romans to admiration of Greek

Pantheress. Bronze, Roman. *Dumbarton Oaks Collection, Washington, D.C.*

people of another stock who were to be absorbed into the rising Roman state.

Etruria is that portion of Italy sloping from the Apennines to the Mediterranean Sea, north and west of Rome and the Tiber. The Aegean invaders had pushed their predecessors in the region to northward and southward, and came to rule a great territory, with many towns, between the Tiber and the Po. They became the ruling caste with, doubtless, some of the conquered Latins living under their sway, and intermarrying to form a people different from the Greeks who were then setting into their own national mold in Ionia and Hellas. That the Etruscans remained Aegean culturally is indicated by their Greek-like written language, their expert technique in metalwork, and the architectural mode that is primarily Asiatic. As time went on, while the true Romans to the south were still barbaric, Etruria kept its cultural contacts with Athens and Corinth, and with the Greek cities of Sicily and southern Italy.

Many authorities are convinced that the best in Etruscan art was hardly more than an offshoot of the Greek development; and they point to the recorded exile of certain Greek craftsmen from the homeland cities to Etruria as proof of imported art. But this was a comparatively late incident, and as appreciation swings back to so-called archaic work it appears that the Etruscans excelled in a very distinctive way, especially in sculpture. Moreover, the common use of the arch in building indicates a branching or link farther back in the Aegean chain.

Some of the early Etruscan sculptures exhibit a consistent formalization, even a stylization, seldom matched elsewhere—perhaps never paralleled in European practice of the art. The rhythms are more of the surface—linear and ornamental—and less of the basic sculptural ordering of masses than a purist might wish; but there is a charm arresting and unique. The slender forms, the careful formalization of such elements as hair and draperies, and the counter-

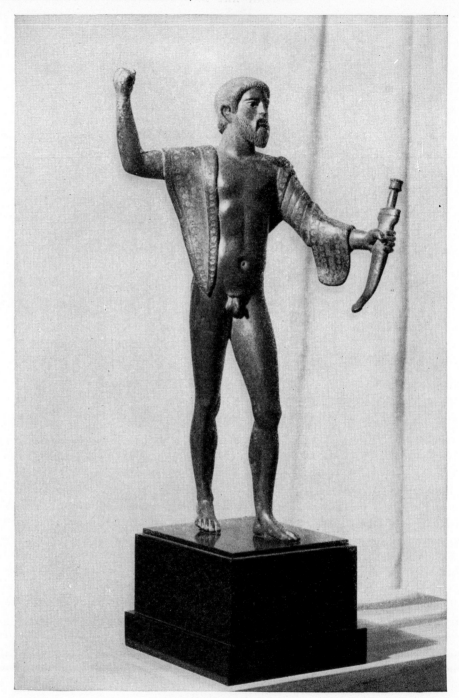

Warrior. Bronze, Etruscan. *William Rockhill Nelson Gallery of Art, Kansas City*

play of smooth and decorated surfaces are well illustrated in the figure of a warrior in the William Rockhill Nelson Gallery in Kansas City, in the smaller bronzes at the Metropolitan Museum in New York, and in a long series of figures in the Archaeological Museum, Florence.

Chimera of Arezzo. Bronze, Etruscan, 5th century B.C.; probably restored by
Benvenuto Cellini. *Archaeological Museum, Florence*

All these are bronzes ascribed to approximately 500 B.C. Even more spiritedly decorative are some of the animals: the *Chimera of Arezzo* and the *Lion of Perugia.* The best of the minor animal reliefs and silhouettes suggest a probable Scythian connection, so simple and powerful is the design, so rich the formal rhythm.

Before the refinement of this formal style, definitely Oriental in its affinities, there was a more primitive type of conventionalized sculpture, especially in terra cotta. It bridged a series of works from small objects to monuments such as the grand but prosy *Warrior* in the Metropolitan Museum, eight feet high. Some of the figures on the lids of sarcophagi are filled with sculptural vitality. From the direct and summary treatment of the two-figure group on the Villa Giulio sarcophagus, plastically strong and finely restrained, there is a gradual decline to the over-detailed, woodenly naturalistic portrait figures on the coffins produced in Etruscan-Roman times.

One documentary feature in these sculptures has a bearing on the estimate of the Etruscans as an art-loving people: the wealth of jewelry and dress accessories portrayed. From this and other evidence we can infer a life (for the aristocracy) both refined and luxurious. There have also been discovered within the tombs the actual jewelry, metal vessels, and figurines. In the entire range of metalcrafts from golden brooch and necklace to bronze engraved cists and even bronze beds, the Etruscan was a master worker. The metal plates of a decorated chariot retain archaic strength; mirrors are incised with linear designs suggesting a masterly sense of composition on the flat; furniture parts range from elaborated abstract or architectural members to vigorous animal-body supports. One of the commonest miniature type-statues was designed for use as handles on large bronze vessels.

The Etruscans indulged their taste for Greek decorated pottery to such an extent that for some decades in the nineteenth century the painted vase was considered an Italianate art. Because the tombs of Etruria yielded up vast numbers of them, it was taken for granted that

Villa Giulio Sarcophagus. Clay, Etruscan, 6th century B.C., Cerveteri

they were a native product. There were local types of pottery, most notably the *bucchero nero* or black ware, but the finer things are now believed to have come from Athens and Chalcis and Corinth.

Painting as an art is commonly thought to have been highly developed by the Etruscans. And indeed the greatest body of pre-Christian mural painting surviving to our times in Europe is to be found in the tombs at Corneto, Chiusi, Vulci, and Cerveteri. But the exhibit is more interesting for the light it throws on methods, conceptions, and the degree of naturalism attained at times than for its intrinsic merit as art. The compositions are uninvolved and posteresque, and the colors fairly harmonious. But there is little subtlety in the space-filling adjustment, and little sense of formal organization. If the painting is a reflection of Greek work, as is generally supposed, it echoes murals or vase-painting of the less creative eras; and may be, indeed, a derivative of the lost Greek murals of the time. At best there is an occasional bit of almost elegant stylization. In any case the display is of most interest to the archaeologist—it is a marvel that examples of so fragile an art should be preserved intact after twenty-three centuries—and as illustration of the life of the pre-Roman era. The

Etruscan nobles are shown as hedonists, in their cups and at their luxurious entertainments. Banqueters, musicians, and dancers are favorite subjects.

The architecture of the Etruscans seems not to have followed the arc of their sculpture. It was structurally rather plain, or even rude, but at the same time likely to be overdecorated, with a lavish Oriental hand, when ornamented at all. The arch they handed on to Roman engineers. A second distinctive feature, terra-cotta members and terra-cotta sculptural decorations, even to colossal figures, gradually fell out of use.

It seems incredible that the Etruscan development, so advanced at the time of the rise of the Romans, should have disappeared to so great an extent in the later Roman fusion. Etruria became part of the Roman realm. As early as the fourth century B.C. Etruscan artists had been called upon to adorn Roman cities. The *Wolf of Rome,* or *Capitoline Wolf,* is Etruscan in workmanship. (Later sculptors, at the time of the Italian Renaissance, added the out-of-scale figures of Romulus and Remus taking suck, to illustrate an ancient legend.) But the Greek influence, coming from Greek colonial cities to the southward, and from the Greek world of the eastern Mediterranean, now in line for subjugation to Rome, all too soon became dominant.

Unfortunately, maturing Rome thus began to draw its models and teachers from regions where Greek art was already decadent and distorted. The Etruscan culture, adding an Italian element to the heritage of strong archaic art, would seem to have offered a better foundation. But at the best it was Hellenistic art, at the worst post-Alexandrian, that fascinated Roman travelers and plunderers. Rome turned away from what virtues Etruscan art had, to become the imitator of the Eastern imitators of true Hellenism. Some authorities, however, argue that, since the Greeks taught the Etruscans, the Etruscans, in teaching the Romans, merely prepared them for a natural return to Greece. This obviously allows too little credit for independent values in Etruria. The beautiful head here, with strength and elegance, is typically Etruscan.

Roman Architecture and Engineering

In architecture a determining impulse and a fundamental principle were developed by the Romans and Etruscans before Greek influence was decisively felt. Etruria gave to Rome the arch and the vault, which were destined to carry Roman engineering into a development directly away from the Greek. Thus was laid the foundation of the art in which the Italic peoples were to surpass the Hellenes: structural engineering. The later official Hellenization of the Western world, particularly under the Emperor Augustus, while it ended in obscuration of much good engineering under second-rate architectural and sculptural decoration, could not hide the glorious feats accomplished by Roman creative engineers.

The daring that went into bridges and aqueducts, baths and arenas, is directly related to a building logic and an inventive grasp of materials and methods. The first problem of monumental architecture is, in a sense, to bridge space. Roofing a great area means carrying heavy materials across spaces impossible to span with the Greeks' simple post-and-lintel system. In the arch, and the vault that grew out of it, the Romans had a

Bust of Caio Norbano Sorice. Bronze, Etruscan. *National Museum, Naples*

means of thrusting the massive Colosseum walls story above story, and of covering a luxurious bathing hall that could accommodate three thousand persons.

These problems were, in the first place, practical and scientific matters, and well within the province of a people expert in law, trade, and administration. It may be added that, whereas the names of sculptors and painters mentioned by later Latin writers are Greek, the names of architects are largely Roman or Etruscan. These native architects probably solved the engineering or construction problems involved with skill and daring, and then turned over to imported artists the comparatively superficial matters of "decoration." Very little integrated architectural art grew out of such a divided arrangement. But when the hand of time stripped the ornamental casing from the Caracalla Baths or the theater at Orange, the walls and arches stood out with a mighty lift and a compelling grandeur. And a "plain" engineering work like the Pont du Gard

Temple of the Sibyl, Tivoli

stirs the blood and lifts the eye with its mathematical vigor.

There were temples in Rome, and throughout her far-flung colonies and provinces. But they were less distinctive and inventive; rather they represented the Greek idea adapted and elaborated. The columns usually carried florid Corinthian capitals—the Doric style in particular seemed over-plain to Latin eyes. Decoration was added elsewhere too, so that in the end no bit of bare wall was tolerated. Even the architrave, kept clean by the Greeks to emphasize the feeling of cross-bar strength, was soon being traced over with Roman ornament.

The so-called Maison Carrée. Roman temple, Nîmes, France

The earlier round structures of the sort, illustrated fragmentarily in the Temple of Vesta at Rome and the Temple of the Sibyl at Tivoli, provided an appealing grace and a pleasing ornamental fullness not known to the architecture of the Hellenes. The more usual adaptation of the Greek rectangular temple is to be seen today in the example at Nîmes in France, known as the Maison Carrée. It illustrates both the survival of the essential Greek form, and the typical Roman (originally Etruscan) changes, such as the podium or raised platform with a flight of steps in front, and the substitution of engaged columns or pilasters along the side walls of the cella, in place of the original continuous colonnade. It is not, however, in arched construction. Even today the building has dignity and a quiet effectiveness.

More important in the history of religious architecture, and more essentially Roman, is the basilica. Originally secular in purpose, it was destined to become an early model for the Christian church, and thus to affect monumental archi-

tecture down to the twentieth century. The basilica was commonly situated in the Forum of a Roman city, and was a place of general assembly for trade, banking, and administration of the law: in simplest words, a meeting hall. The plan that became standard was contrived with a central nave between side aisles; and it was here that clerestory lighting and construction came importantly into European building. Some Roman basilicas had semicircular halls or bays at the end opposite the entrance, corresponding to the later church apse or altar area.

Most existing basilicas are examples built on the general plan of the old combined market, court house, and assembly hall but adapted to the uses of Christian worship. The famous Church of St. Paul Outside the Walls at Rome, though rebuilt in the nineteenth century (on the fourth-century plan), illustrates the impressive simplicity and grandeur of the constructive system, combined with late Roman sumptuous decoration. Where arched construction here sur-

St. Paul Outside the Walls, Rome. Rebuilt in the 19th century on the 4th-century plan

mounts the interior columns, the earlier form had been a continuous architrave, sometimes with gallery above, just under the clerestory windows.

The Pantheon at Rome, technically a temple, was an exceptional type of building, but a superb instance of Roman constructive daring. Today it has lost its interior embellishments, though it is the best preserved of major Roman monuments; but it takes the breath by the vast dimensions, the simplicity of its forms, and the audacity of the structural design. A temple-like forepart or porch lies against an immense circular hall or rotunda, under a low dome. The engineering is elementary: the rotunda walls form the drum from which the dome springs direct; there are no windows. Light is admitted to the building solely through a great circular hole left open to the sky at the top. To sustain the thrust of the dome, the walls are twenty feet thick, and there are eight apse-like niches hollowed in them—one opened to form the main portal, the others designed for statues of gods and later transformed by the Christians into side-chapels. In its time the inside of the dome, richly coffered, and the marble trim of walls and apses, must have been impressively sumptuous; but today it is the grand simplicity of the engineering and the great spaciousness that thrill the visitor. The Pantheon is truly one of the world's most impressive buildings.

The spirit of luxurious grandeur in Roman architecture best expressed itself in palaces, baths, and theaters. The baths in particular became social meeting places of the upper classes, and on them were lavished the most stupendous engineering ingenuity and the most vulgarly ornate architectural decoration. Not only was an incredible number of pools, gymnasia, anointing rooms, and lounging halls to be roofed over, but lecture and studio rooms had to be included in the interior, and a stadium was to adjoin it. It is said that one thousand bath buildings existed in imperial Rome, ranging from the simplest to the immense establishments known by the names of the emperors who built them, Nero, Trajan, Diocletian, etc.

There are sufficient remains of the Baths of

The Pantheon. Second century A.D.

Caracalla to impress the observer today with the daring of Roman engineers in roofing the necessary spaces and buttressing the supporting arches. There are traces of the marble pavements and mosaics, and contemporary descriptions that aid in building up a picture of magnificent decorations and furnishings.

The theaters of Rome itself were usually temporary erections, but often were adorned with almost incredibly rich displays of sculpture and architectural accessory, if one may believe eye-witness reports. Some surviving provincial examples indicate, indeed, that the architecture was thought of as part of the spectacle. One Latin description mentions a stage wall with 360 columns, 3000 statues, and other "special" adornments.

The amphitheaters or arenas have withstood the ravages of time better; and there is enough left of the Colosseum to indicate the type form and to impress the eye—though the complete interior sheathing of colored marbles has disappeared. The structure, built in the first century A.D. and reconstructed in the third, is of concrete with a facing of Travertine marble. The essential building is a marvelous constructive feat: a bowl more than 600 feet long, with 50,000 or 60,000 seats resting on a honeycomb structure of arcades and vaults, with passageways for spectators, rooms for the gladiators, and cells for the wild beasts. To that extent the architecture is functional and honest. But the marble facing to a certain degree weakens the mass effect, denies the engineering, and contrasts badly with the necessarily heavy materials. The columns carry no weight.

Incidentally it may be noted that the Emperor Augustus, of the golden age of Rome, who is said to have boasted that he transformed Rome from a city of brick to a city of marble, was speaking in terms of a veneer. Greek monumental buildings had been of solid marble, and the Egyptian pyramids are mountains of laid-up stone, but the Romans seem not to have had the time or the thoroughness to deal in difficult materials even when they had the materials at hand.

The Pont du Gard. Roman aqueduct in Southern France

Countless monumental-looking walls have turned out to be hardly more than rubble-filled shells. Nevertheless, the Romans are to be credited with developing concrete or aggregate as a major building element.

The commemorative arches, or arches of triumph, were a sort of architecture invented by the Romans in their passion for the show of power, for the display of patriotic service in "works of national honor." They merit hardly more attention than any other frankly ornamental and advertising monument, though there are thought-out symmetry and academic competence in the compositions. They have served as models to fifty generations of triumphant militarists home from their conquests. They may be cited as perfectly symbolizing the side of the Roman character that is brilliantly spectacular.

But in bridges and aqueducts one finds fully asserted again the spirit that is admirable and splendid. These constructions are functional, authentic, mathematical. Waterways strike out across country, daunted by neither hills nor valleys. Gorges are bridged with those honest spans, repeated, unvarying, everlasting. This is the supreme memorial of the Roman as builder. In the thick, heavy, power-breathing Roman wall, and in the regimented arches and vaults, one has artistic Rome, has her engineer-architects in their most honest and typical achievement. When she turned to ornamentation, employed other architects to split the functional Greek columns and paste them uselessly beside the arches, in row over row against the walls, the engineer was eclipsed, a curtain of make-believe was dropped before the true drama of Roman building art. The Pont du Gard has come free of those embellishments; it moves boldly, implacably, nakedly on its business of carrying an aqueduct over hill and valley.

The Forum might be taken as epitome: old temples, increasingly complex and graceful and

Above: Relief on Etruscan sarcophagus, *Museum of Fine Arts, Boston*
Below: *Warrior's Dance*. Relief, stone. *Vatican Museum*

adorned, but with something of Greek simplicity and harmony persisting, set among palaces, basilicas, memorial columns, and arcades; on every side magnificent arched construction, grand vistas, and banks of columns crowned by rich Corinthian capitals; on every side a profusion of vulgarized Greek ornament, interspersed with the new sketchy Roman relief picture-panels—grandeur, exhibitionism, display of wealth.

Roman Sculpture

The sculptors of Rome engaged in the mass production of statue-bodies, and when an order for a full-length portrait-figure came in, the only delay was over the making of a head in actual likeness of the client. It was then screwed onto a stock body and the job was complete. A baker in Rome had a tomb sculptured in the form of his favorite baking oven, with even the flues sticking up realistically. A late Roman Emperor had himself copied oversize in bronze, naked, with every wrinkle, rib, and whisker reproduced, on the premise, possibly, that an imperial Roman blemish would interest populace and posterity more than remote Hellenic idealizations;

and he stands thus today in the Metropolitan Museum in New York. Sculpture was never so popular, so plentiful, and so true to nature unimproved as in the heyday of the Roman Empire.

Nineteenth-century Europe and America could understand that sort of art, and Rome then became model and mentor for the Western world. The term "classic," never very exactly defined, came to cover Roman realism and Roman ornamentalism, as well as Greek lucidity and idealism. French churches, German parliamentary halls, British banks, and American railway terminals took Roman form. Expositions breathed Augustan magnificence. Triumphal arches sprang up in towns and cities here, there, and everywhere, for Washington and for Admiral Dewey and for the homecoming of soldiers from this or that conflict. And our best sculptors went to school to Rome and put Constantinian bas-relief panels on our libraries, stations, and banks alike. They even came, for a while, to rival the Graeco-Romans themselves in that sort of hard, utterly realistic portraiture generally associated with the title "A Roman Senator."

It was in lifelike portraiture that the Roman excelled all other artists. His busts are exact, uncompromising, remorselessly literal transcriptions.

Head of an unknown Roman. Terra cotta. *Museum of Fine Arts, Boston*

We do at first mistake them all for politicians, so ruthless, disillusioned, cruelly sensual are the faces commonly duplicated. These "masters of the world" are fighters and materialists, overfed and misshapen. The sculptor misses no slightest record of character written by experience and indulgence upon the countenances. The lines that betray the shrewd tight mind of the financier, the brutal strength of the militarist, the sour stomach and the disappointed hope of the sensualist—all these are placed in pitiless evidence. It is an amazing record of character, and more explanatory of Roman history than a hundred written volumes.

There are, of course, revelations less brutal, less indicative of corruption, cruelty, and disillusionment. There are even portraits in which a certain nobility of character is implied. The heads of women are at times treated with a tender consideration of feminine grace and gentle character, though uniformly without Greek idealization. The double portrait, usually for grave monuments, tends toward a touching sentimentalism.

From first to last, after Roman art has been Hellenized, the draperies, whether of bust or full-length figure, are wooden and overconspicuous, and dress accessories are overdetailed. The best Roman sculpture is in the characterful faces, and the prime virtue is faithfulness to life. Per-

Roman portrait. Marble. *Metropolitan Museum of Art*

haps this exactitude of rendering was the sculptor's answer—his way of meeting competition—when the practice grew up of making death masks, by wax impression from the face of the deceased.

A strict chronology would show that Etruscan influence had lasted down through the sculpture of the early Republic. There are transitional statues from which the graceful formalization has not wholly disappeared; and middle examples exhibit a vigor and a simplicity of conception not to be credited to Hellenistic importation. The late Republic has left very little notable work. It was rather in the beginnings of imperial

aggrandizement that the art was reborn, floridly and with popular appeal.

When Augustus set out to give Rome the effect of marble, the Greek artists came in droves. They had no need to create. They merely copied old models, repeated Greek successes, gave the *parvenu* public what it wanted. Cicero, for instance, wanted Muses rather than Bacchantes, as Pliny noted; but they would be copies or versions of the Greek originals in any case. And perhaps this was perfectly right, for Cicero's style of oratory and writing had been formed only after the most assiduous study of Attic models; and, leader that he was in Rome, he would feel culturally at

Earth, Air, and Water. Relief in stone from the Ara Pacis, Rome, 1st century A.D.
Uffizi Gallery, Florence

home only when basking in the light of Greece.

The second distinctive sculptural achievement of the Romans was in bas-relief panels. They utterly negate the formalism of the Etruscans; rather they carry on the ornamental and episodic tendencies of Alexandrian and Pergamene work. More and more figures are crowded in. Gradually allegorical and traditional subject-matter give way before representation of contemporary event and episode. Repose is forgotten; movement becomes the new objective. Action scenes afford most scope to the artist—and what so full of action as battles and triumphal processions?

The ideals of stone sculpture are soon forgotten. Modeling suitable to the clay sketch is laboriously transferred to the unsuitable stone. Landscapes and buildings in perspective are attempted in the backgrounds.

There is no questioning the values of the better Roman panels, whether on triumphal arch or altar or sarcophagus, *as illustration*. They tell the action-story or the anecdote clearly and with animation. They remind one of the stirring event; and they instruct the patriot and warn the skeptic. If the intellectual or narrative intention, the physical animation, and the sketchy treatment are all inimical to architectural unity, the answer is that the Roman was not interested in architecture as such. The subject-matter of the panel was the important thing. Above that, the showy effect of multiplied figures and broken surface was rich, impressive. The episode is garlanded amid vines and wreaths and lacery. Among the figures are the symbols of power: *fasces* and trophies and swords. But the story comes first, the literary message; then the eye-filling profusion—not to say confusion—of chiseled captives and soldiers and revelers.

The triumphal arches appropriately bore bas-relief stories of military and political achievement. The heavy building had no use other than to frame a series of sculptural illustrations and commemorative inscriptions, and to advertise, by its own magnificence, the name of a historic character. The Arch of Titus is one of the best known of the simpler arches, and two high-relief panels inside the archway are esteemed as spirited military sculpture. Of the showier examples the Arch of Constantine, near the Colosseum, is first, and scarcely an inch of its surface has escaped the sculptors' hands. Some of the panels are transferred from arches erected in honor of earlier emperors, and the whole therefore affords a sort of progressive review of late Roman relief picturing.

To this day there rises out of the ruins of Trajan's Forum a shaft 110 feet high, traced over with a continuous spiral bas-relief narrative of the Emperor Trajan's exploits. It is an astonishing *tour de force,* hardly equaled even in opulent Asiatic sculpture. Its interest is, of course, chiefly historical, as a record of military campaigns against the barbarians of the North. But it is a major sculptural curiosity too, a series of book-illustrations laboriously translated into stone and spread on a continuous ribbon—most of it up where it cannot, and never could, be seen.

At an earlier date, when the narrative current ran less strong and the crowding of figures was less insisted upon, there had been monuments with a better relationship of sculpture and architecture. A high point in flowing pictorial bas-relief was touched in certain panels of the Ara Pacis, the peace shrine erected by Augustus in A.D. 13. The virtues are largely those of wash drawing; but for observers who are undisturbed by the transposition of the values of one art into another, these have proved harmoniously pleasing. They were endlessly imitated by the best Western sculptors until the present wave of modernism opened the way back to "the feel for the stone" with consequent depreciation of fluent paint values.

In ornament as such—seen chiefly in sculpture, but as a component of decorative painting, too— the Romans brought in fresh motives and methods. They failed to invent architectural accessories so right, for example, as the Greek egg-and-dart molding, or so rich as the Persian arabesques and Moslem paneling. But within the limits of thin naturalistic patterning they introduced unhackneyed materials and composed them pleasingly. The grapevine circles gracefully and is faultlessly natural. Even the rose and the fig are transferred delicately to marble panel or made to entwine mock columns. Gradually the flat backgrounds against which the design once stood out are themselves filled with tracery until high and low relief merge in one play of light and shade. But the observer never loses the identity of grape or acanthus or rose in formalized approximations; the natural shapes and directions and textures are faithfully copied. This is the Roman's achievement and his weakness. Some believe that, in observing nature afresh and escaping traditional stereotypes, he brought art to a new release of invention and composition; but vision and formal creation are relatively absent.

Among the minor genre pieces and the trivia of the Roman household and market place are many statuettes and novelties appealing as sentimental mementos or caricatures or photographic records. Particularly the occasional grotesques, whether of dwarfs or comic actors or peasants, are amusing and revealing. The countless Cupids are too sweet for anything—dancing, playing on lyres, holding up useful lamps or useless pillars, or adorning mirror or jug. Roman coins are not very important as compared with those of the cities incorporated into the Empire, of Syracuse and Tarentum, of the Ionian cities, of Athens and Corinth. Cameo-cutting is considered a typical Roman art. Occasionally the contrast of light and dark striations is delicately manipulated for a striking and rich effect. More often the result is posteresque, even garish. This duo-tone contrast was carried into glass-making, with results to be studied in the Portland Vase, which is as famous as it is artistically suspect.

Roman silverware, greatly prized today by collectors and museums, and praised for the masterly treatment of figures in high relief, is, in the pieces generally exhibited, unfunctional and overelaborate. Plates have their bottoms pushed up in figure-compositions as high as the brim. Silver cups lose their roundness in a confusion of applied figure-sculpturing and entwining parasitic ornamentation. Cup-quality is lost in the overzealousness of the picturer and the opulent decorator. It is the same fault that blemished the main story of Roman plastic art: the obscuring of basic design and the simple virtues of plastic organization under showy surface manipulation. It could be illustrated again in the late pottery of the Italianate peoples. Simple forms degenerate into elaborate ones. The fine proportions are lost. What vase-painting there is lacks relationship to the vessel's architecture. Finally the sides and base and brim must be given over to the sculptor; not only low but high relief destroys the integrity of the vase. From tiny clay pot to colossal marble urn there is an instructive exhibit of the functional designer (who is merely another sort of engineer) thwarted by the enthusiastic decorator.

Roman Painting

The volcano Vesuvius once acted to preserve a cross-section of Roman art as it existed in the homes of representative patrician citizens. At Pompeii one may see the house walls decorated with paintings in the several styles in vogue in A.D. 79. In what would today be called "interior decoration" there was a widespread taste for walls completely painted over with architectural designs, sometimes contrived with illusionistic intention, to make the room seem more spacious or to afford a false vista; sometimes partly or wholly conventionalized, for the decorative effect of a profuse delineation of porticoes, panels, platforms, and vistas, replete with fanciful columns, friezes, and garlands. Into the *mélange* would be admitted occasional pictorial panels, each painted in the manner of an easel picture. These panels, removed for museum preservation, are usually exhibited to us as Roman painting-art.

Pliny's account of painting and painters is concerned largely with records and legends of Greek artists, rather than Roman. He prefaces his section on bronze statuary with a sweeping complaint about the decadence of the arts in his own time, the first century A.D. He writes: "It is extraordinary that when the price given for works of art has risen so enormously, art itself should have lost its claim to our respect. The truth is that the aim of the artist, as of everyone else in our times, is to gain money, not fame as in the old days, when the noblest of their nation thought art one of the paths to glory, and ascribed it even to the gods."

Pliny describes a Rome in which temples, baths, and other public buildings are extensively adorned with pictures, including some of the most famous works of Apelles, Polygnotus, Zeuxis, and others of the Greek realists; and there is frequent mention of the private galleries and collections of the emperors and aristocrats. But the painters with Roman names claim comparatively little space. Pliny writes of them with some reserve:

Nor must I neglect Studius, a painter of the days of Augustus, who introduced a delightful style of decorating walls with representations of villas, harbours, landscape gardens, sacred groves, woods, hills, fishponds, straits, streams and shores, any scene in short that took the fancy. In these he introduced figures of people, on foot, or in boats. . . . Not long before the time of the god Augustus, Arellius had earned distinction at Rome, save for the sacrilege by which he notoriously degraded his art. Always desirous of flattering some woman or other with whom he chanced to be in love, he painted goddesses in the person of his mistresses, of whom his paintings are a mere catalogue. The painter Famulus also lived not long ago; he was grave and severe in his person, while his painting was rich and vivid. He painted an Athena whose eyes are turned to the spectator from whatever side he may be looking.

As might be expected even in the case of a more creative people, most of the preserved pictures, being incidental to the routine ornamentation of the houses of the rich, are dull hack work, interesting chiefly for their age, the almost miraculous manner of their survival, and the light they cast upon Roman customs and beliefs: many are revealing in regard to those excesses, cultish and erotic, which were a part of the life of a disillusioned and self-indulgent class. As formal art, only a hundredth of the painting may be said to have even a trace of character or of lasting value.

What is the explanation of this national betrayal, this negation of art, in field after field— painting, sculpture, metalwork, pottery? What useful lesson can the student of world art take away from this display, in which the highest achievements (except the superb engineering) are in the hard realism of the sculpture and a general florid decorativeness?

A Roman Tragic Actor, with Mask Removed. Roman painting.
National Museum, Naples

The Roman philosophy of life was, speaking very generally, pragmatic and realistic. Cruel and ruthless on one side, it was conducive to self-indulgence on the other. Rome knew little of the triumphs of the spirit. The Romans thought art could be produced by subjugation, borrowing, and compulsion. Roman life never came to a balance; it was propelled by force, motivated by personal ambition. Art is an expression of fine living. The Romans seem never to have come to that sort of living which overflows into inspired expression. In the most practical phase, or foundation, of the most practical art, in engineering, they excelled, and left monuments that still command respect and evoke admiration. The rest bespeaks luxury and display rather than character, conviction, and formal sensibility.

Toward the end the bands of Christian worshipers were taking first indecisive steps in the direction of a very different art. Discountenanced by the true Romans, persecuted, without position, they yet possessed one quality which their persecutors had lacked—and needed before art could be characterful and distinctive: *faith*. It was to be many centuries before that faith was reflected in a great body of art. There were diverse developments of Oriental Christian art, known as Byzantine, before Italy and the peoples of the old Roman colonies to the north, French and German, made their contribution. Rome itself was to create no significant works for a millennium after Constantine. Yet, in the sixteenth century, this was the city of Michelangelo, one of the supreme creative figures of all time.

The final exhibit of Roman art is in the long series of sarcophagi that have become familiar in the great museums of the world. The stone box-sides form an extension of the high-relief sculptural art, in panels that are often dynamic and eye-filling. There is no dividing mark between the pagan and Christian examples. The one shown here may well be of a transitional time. The vintage scene is typically Roman. The introduced figures of the shepherd would, however, signify to the Christian owner the religion of Christ—though the motive had not been uncommon centuries before.

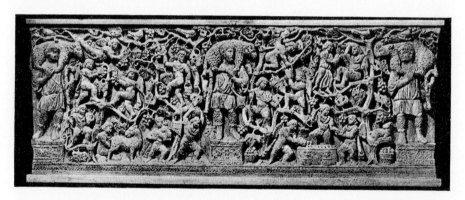

The Good Shepherd. Relief on a Roman sarcophagus. *Lateran Museum*

VIII: FAR EASTERN ART AND
THE INNER EYE

THE Greeks had a saying which, fully understood, affords a key to the secret of Oriental philosophy and Oriental art: "The tree of Knowledge is not the tree of Life." The Hellenes themselves discounted the saying, built their culture on knowledge, on the intellectually knowable. But the Eastern nations from Persia to China were at the same time developing civilizations distinguished by arts suffused with the qualities of the spirit—mystic, colorful, formal. To them the knowable was but the prose of external living. They considered the life of the West pedantically material, superficial, and unillumined. They recognized the tree of Knowledge as a lesser guide to living and to art practice.

The Greek way and the Oriental way—therein is a contrast instructive and decisive: the way of the mind and the way of the spirit. The Greek way was to spurn the unknowable, to distrust what could not be identified by the brain, to advance by intellectualization, to fix in art works the naturally beautiful, the rational, the deduced ideal. Greek art rises out of sensitive observation, and it results in clear, realistic representations—or, in architecture, in logical, functional structure, sparsely ornamented.

Chimera. Bronze statuette. *William Rockhill Nelson Gallery of Art*

The Oriental way is to discount the observed natural phenomenon, to seek the essence of life in intuitively apprehended values, in spiritual intimations, and in the abstract elements of color and creative formal organization. Oriental art, less obviously humanistic, natural, and intellectual, feeds the spirit. Its glories are achieved in the realms of the near-abstract, the contemplatively mystical, and the richly sensuous.

Possibly the best in Western art has arisen when waves of influence have surged in from the East. Just as the most profound of Europe's religions came from Asia, so Europe's visual art has been richest and most warming and satisfying when the rather bare classicism and intellectualism of the West have been quickened by the mysticism, the color (in the widest sense), and the refined aesthetic sensibility borne in by invaders from the Middle and Far East. There can be no doubt that today the West is disillusioned over the art of its post-Renaissance period, and is at last aware that the Greek achievement, for all its perfection of forms, was limited to a narrow segment of the field open to the artist; that the larger body of profound and masterly art belongs to China and Persia, and, in only a slightly lesser degree, to India, Indonesia, and Japan.

The Hindu philosopher, in an effort to express the inexpressible, offers a figure which is helpful to the Western observer dismayed by the surface strangeness of Oriental art. The soul, he says, is an interior eye. It looks not out upon the external world but toward eternal realities. It sees the universe in essence, in spiritual significance. The Oriental addresses his art to this inner eye instead of trying to please the outer eye by familiarity or clever imitation, or the intellect by reasoned expression. The abstract elements in art —color, rhythm, formal vitality—are a language intelligible to the soul and welcome to the inner vision.

This eye in the center of consciousness, atrophied in most Western men through neglect, or deliberately blinded in favor of the reasoning intellect, can be opened, grows sensitive with use. It alone detects the most joyous and profound pleasures possible to art. It is concerned with those values associated with feeling rather than with statement, asks no translation through senses and brain, transports the beholder at once to the source at which the artist found his inspiration and conceived his image.

When the modern theorist speaks of formal excellence, plastic orchestration, and universal rhythms, he is trying to define qualities in art unexplainable in words and not to be reasoned into acceptance; but he is treating of values real and appealing to the inner eye—and sought after and achieved far more in Eastern than in Western art.

The Western eye, one might truly say, has been fact-seeking, nervous, eager for objective report, contemptuous of the unfamiliar. It has been form-blind and imagination-shy. But now for the first time since the Renaissance great numbers of Occidental people are trying to understand the implications of the symbol of the inner eye. They recognize that without stilling the mind and developing an inner contemplative vision they cannot hope to apprehend the message and to relish the formal beauty of a Sung landscape painting or a Chou bronze ritual vessel.

Chinese painting is strange because it is an expression of the soul's quietude, of spiritual contemplation. Its language is more of abstract and universal movement and mood than of observed effect and concrete natural detail. It speaks best to those who meet its quiet with quiet, who come to it innocent of realistic expectation. A spirited monster carved by a Han sculptor is more a product of the feeling evoked by the monster idea, and by masses of stone, than a representation.

The observer who sincerely desires to experience the Oriental work of art—no less than the artist who wishes to break through the restraints put by intellect upon creation—does well to ponder over the symbol of the eye at the center of being. Pondering and understanding, he may find new quietude in living; new insight, even ecstasy, in contemplation; and a new world of formal enjoyment opened before him in the realm of Oriental art. At the best he may experience the glow of the soul, the suffusing illumination of the inner being, which comes with surrender

Ma Yüan: *Landscape with Bridge and Willows*. Sung Dynasty.
Museum of Fine Arts, Boston

to the spirit and its participation in the rhythmic creative ordering of existence.

As a last word about the spirit and intent of Asiatic art one may say that it does not hold up a landscape as an exhibit. It aims rather to enable the beholder to feel his oneness with the creative order, the harmonious oneness at the source of all life. Similarly Asiatic religious painting and sculpture exist, not to instruct and impress and glorify, as does Western religious art, but to afford a feeling of utter peace, of rightness, of suffusing joy. This art is at once direct, gratifying visual experience, the means to a cosmic self-identification, and a conveyor of the feeling of order as the foundation of the spiritual-material world.

Whatever one's personal response, it is no longer possible to refuse to place the body of Asiatic art above that of any other continent. In the great number of masterpieces of painting and sculpture bequeathed to later ages, in the splendor and sensitivity of the art-life of cultured people in era after era, and most of all in the plastic and sensuous richness of the so-called minor arts, in pottery and porcelain, in textile and costuming, and in metalwork and jade and lacquer, the East is superior.

It generally comes as a surprise to the Westerner, in his assumption of superiority—well founded in the fields of science, invention, and warfare—that Orientals look down upon the arts of the West. They have examined realism and have found it an inferior type of expression. They miss the accent of cosmic calm, the abstract signs of spiritual penetration, the serenity that comes after contemplation.

In the world stream of art no current, except possibly the Egyptian, ever flowed through so many millenniums with a single distinctive accent as has the Chinese. The Persian has flowered at intervals through a period as long, but with interruptions. Beside these two the Japanese culture seems comparatively new and immature; yet it has an unbroken history of fourteen hundred years, and its arts were flourishing centuries before the English language was born.

It is time that we of the New World, of Europe and America, recognized this elder Asiatic culture, that we accepted it as in the main stream of the world's significant art. In relating our Western accomplishment to it we shall need to acknowledge not only the surpassing beauty of its manifestations but the enriching influence it has had upon our own visual arts, not only at Byzantium and Ravenna, but in Moorish Spain, in Venice, in nineteenth-century Europe; perhaps, too, in some untraced circuit from Asia across the Bering bridge, or down through Polynesia, across the Pacific Ocean to Peru and Mexico, and so by a back road into the European-derived American culture.

The Magnificence of Early Art

The Stone Age of prehistory yields up in China the usual potteries, stone weapons, and bone implements of beginning craftsmanship. The clay vessels are somewhat more intricately and sensitively ornamented than is pottery in many other Neolithic cultures. One important bit of information prised out of the finds and conclusions of archaeologists is that the Chinese of historic times are descended from Stone Age ancestors resident on the same soil. This had been challenged: for long it was believed by Occidental scholars that the Chinese culture had been imported at an advanced stage from some region to the westward. Now, from the evidence of graves not later than 3000 B.C. and of remains from the Bronze Age, a continuity is proved. This does not preclude the probability, even the

certainty, that influences from the outside were felt again and again.

The historical sequence of certain characteristics is first established in some bronze vessels dated vaguely "after the fourteenth century B.C.," but the magnificent decoration and expert craftsmanship indicate a long antecedent period of experiment and maturation. The ceremonial character of the caldrons, wine-vessels, and bells, often engraved with commemorative inscriptions, leaves no doubt that here the Bronze Age was already a time of sumptuous court custom and refined luxury. Possibly the feudal aristocrats or war lords enjoyed their culture amid conditions of exceptionally savage exploitation and mass murder and against a background of crude superstition; but the relics of art and ritual are nonetheless splendid and everlastingly eloquent of an advanced, if barbaric, civilization.

Although Chinese history is chronicled from about 1000 B.C., it is not until the third century B.C. that scholars describe the forms of life in detail. The priest-kings and feudal lords then gave way to the first Universal Emperor—he officially took that name—who united the country into one empire, built the Great Wall, and carried on the established magnificence of court custom and art. His dynasty gave place to that with which the first great flowering of the sculptural art is associated, the Han Dynasty, which lasted from 206 B.C. to A.D. 220. This is one of the periods of truly outstanding sculpture in all world history. In the same period the aim and methods of painting became fixed; the works are almost wholly lost, however. Pottery also was carried to new refinements.

Since art in China is so closely attuned to the spiritual life, it is well to remind ourselves that in the sixth century B.C. there had lived in that country two of the greatest religious prophets of all time, Lao-tse and Confucius. It was the century of the coming of Buddha to India, and the one preceding the rise of profane philosophy and intellectual inquiry in Greece (these largely took the place of religion in the classic world thereafter). The connection between Chinese painting and the Taoist philosophy, serene, spirit-centered, is not to be missed. Buddhism, when

Stags. Jade ornament. *Metropolitan Museum*

the field of painting, although agreeing that sculpture then declined. This period is represented today by many more actual works, including the first great surviving body of landscape painting—often directly associated with the Taoist emphasis upon inner and abstract values.

There is one further notable, not to say surpassingly lovely, phase of Chinese art in the Ming period. But that corresponds to the Renaissance era in the Western world, from the fourteenth century, and belongs to a later group of chapters. Here the art works of the Han, T'ang, and Sung Dynasties demand attention, for they are related in time to the ancient and medieval art of the Western peoples—and in sculpture we must also consider the bronzes from preceding dynasties. The list of historical periods, that is, dynasties, after a long semi-legendary period, runs thus:

Shang or Yin	1766–1122 B.C.
Chou	1122–255 B.C.
Ch'in	255–206 B.C.
Han	206 B.C.–A.D. 220
Wei	A.D. 220–265
Six Dynasties	265–618
T'ang	618–907
Five Dynasties	907–960
Sung	960–1279
Yüan (Mongol)	1279–1368
Ming	1368–1644
Ch'ing (Manchu)	1644–1912

After 1912, the Republic.

effectively introduced into China in the troubled centuries of the Han Dynasty, brought its own methods and its own emblems, and these were absorbed, not without a lingering influence of Indian-Buddhist art, in the Chinese practice of sculpture and painting during the Wei Dynasty, toward the end of the four-hundred-year period lying between the Han and the T'ang flowerings.

It was with the T'ang Dynasty that Asiatic art recorded its greatest triumphs. In this dynasty's three-century rein (from A.D. 618) the arts extended into annexed lands—and determined the direction of development in independent Korea and Japan, too. Chinese Buddhism fixed its course, somewhat away from the asceticism of India. A more humanistic note suggests the surviving influence of Lao-tse, foreshadowing the later Taoism in which the two religions found harmonious accord. In painting and in sculpture, in porcelain and in small clay figure, in textile and jade, this was one of the most prolific and exciting periods in world history. The life of the nobles was luxurious and gay, and poets, painters, and scholars were invited to the court and encouraged to carry on their work under generous imperial patronage.

Most authorities count the achievement of the Sung Dynasty (960-1279) the more masterly in

Ceremonial Bronzes, Jades, and Pottery

That the artist-craftsman was an important personage in cultured Chinese society from as early as the end of the second millennium B.C. is to be inferred from the ceremonial bronzes produced then and through the following fifteen centuries. It is so usual to designate only free-standing sculpture and painting by the term "fine arts" that decorated vessels are sometimes overlooked as examples of masterly design. But there is a magnificent, even monumental quality

Bronze ritual vessel.
Shang Dynasty,
12th-13th century B.C.
Fogg Museum of Art,
Harvard University

about the great bronze vases, sacrificial urns, and caldrons of the pre-Han period.

In them the Chinese combined a creative handling of large forms with extraordinary richness of decoration. The coordination of functional expressiveness and ornamentation is as nearly perfect as it is in the output of utilitarian or ceremonial metalwork objects of any civilization. The celebrated high-relief silverware of Rome seems in this company to lack integrity and restraint. The point to be observed is that, despite the wealth of ornament, even its profusion, the average vessel is strongly outlined, and the structural and utilitarian values are accentuated rather than obscured.

The motives of the decoration differ with the succeeding periods and changes in national life, and the types of ornamentation vary from the most delicate and intricate all-over pattern to the most pronounced high-relief conventionalizations of animal forms or geometrical figures. The earlier recognizable motives are like formalizations, almost abstract, of fanciful animals, such as dragons and ogres, and the source is probably to be sought in ancient animistic religions. In the example illustrated on page 171 the conven-

tional shape holds, so that one has, at first view, a vessel (on a squared base) richly and abstractly ornamental. But a closer reading of the reliefs would result in discovery of a wealth of symbolism and intimated subject-matter. The illustration on this page shows instead a tiger-headed beast, which at some indeterminate point leaves off; a bird form is then suggested. There is also the intimation that the whole may be a coiled dragon. And from part to part the incidental relief-designs harbor symbol after symbol.

The massiveness so characteristic of early times persists in the Han bronzes. But the decoration is then curbed. There is sometimes rich surface patterning, but it is lighter, often engraved—the earlier custom of casting the entire vessel, with its ornament, in one piece, had resulted in deeper-cut and more strongly dynamic relief. That the Han artists should have refined ornament without impairing the larger vitality and the plastic life of the object, retaining the purity and strength of the outlines, is testimony to exceptional creative sensibility. The simple, admirably functional vessels of that era would be judged elsewhere to be from the early, most virile period of an art development, rather than representa-

Bronze ritual vessel. *Collection of the Chinese Government*

tive of a phase that came after fifteen hundred years of expert production in the field.

In the later manifestations—for bronze manufacture continued, although partially replaced by porcelain, through the T'ang and Sung Dynasties —the strength and the formal inventiveness seeped out. The usual expedients of decadence—

lifeless copying, the use of stock patterns, and the overelaboration of ornament—finally closed the history of a unique craft. It is probable that the religious customs which gave rise both to the uses of many types of vessel and to the ornamental motives had then disappeared. They had afforded inspiration to the artist and encouraged

Plaque with dragons.
Jade ornament.
William Rockhill Nelson
Gallery of Art

the patron; but when ceremony changed, the art declined. What is known definitely of the bronzes is bound up in grave-lore (important always to the ancestor-worshiping Chinese) and literary references to sacrifice and commemorative ritual. The T'ang bronze mirrors are often finely decorative in a rather profuse way, but the earlier ones, in this case too, are more intriguing and more alive.

The manner of ornament of the bronze vessels and bells is repeated in miniature on jade talismans or signets of the pre-Han period. There is, incidentally, in these as in the ornamental bronzes, a striking likeness to decorative compositions of the Mayan civilization in Mexico and Central America, one which gives rise to the interesting hypothesis of a probable cultural link between Asia and America, though this is not historically proved.

The Chinese jades are an outstanding and celebrated contribution to the world's art in little. They range from undecorated amulets in disk, ring, or tablet form, shaped to enhance the native loveliness of the translucent stones—suf-

ficiently beautiful in themselves as "crystallized bits of moonlight"—through abstract, ornamental emblems, to miniature figure pieces. In the latter the formalization is usually rigid, the animals being but summarily indicated in geometric approximations.

While the ancient examples appeal to us today by their firm yet jewel-like sculptural beauty, they had for the artists and users in early times an additional symbolic value. Not only are they found in graves but they were commonly used as charms or fetishes, if we may judge by the placing of them on dead men's mouths and eyes. The elaborate structure of precise symbolism erected in later days by Chinese scholars, who ascribed a specific meaning to each color, pattern, or ornamental motive, is perhaps to be suspected; but one may believe that ideas out of the very old but gradually changing worship of nature and ancestors gave larger significance to these charms. Thus green, red, white, and blue jade, each in a traditional shape, may have signified North, South, East, and West, while there were the proper "signs" for heaven and earth, for fertility,

Mythical Horse.
Bronze statuette,
probably T'ang or Sung.
Cleveland Museum of Art

and for peace; and two natural forms side by side may have stood for wedded bliss. All this is bound up with the intricate network of ritual, sacrifice, and funeral custom that underlay religious observance before the introduction of Buddhism. But today all that counts is that the carved jades are compellingly endowed with the nobility and formal life which we sometimes call beauty.

Pottery is a third instance of surpassing mastery in those early times before sculpture and painting had emerged in what is now considered "characteristic Chinese form." From almost immemorial times the clay vessels had taken on exceptional refinement. Superiority in this craft was to continue through later ages until "china" became the name for the world's most finished pottery, no matter where made. The Persians and the Chinese were supreme masters in this field.

Incomparable and Impossible Animals

Oversize stone monsters, monumentally impressive, incomparably spirited, gorgeously decorative; tiny bronze or gold plaques, fibulas and charms, virilely rhythmic in silhouette and massing, strongly formalized; matchlessly graceful figures in clay and porcelain, polo-players and camels and court ladies, with indescribable sculptural fullness and suavity—these are images that leap to mind at mention of Chinese sculpture: three utterly different branches of the art of carving, each mastered within a single culture. Even then one has not mentioned the Buddhist

Bear. Gilt bronze statuette, Han Dynasty. *City Art Museum, St. Louis*

cave statues that are second only to the Hindu figures, and a very special sort of low-relief mural art, and the medieval full-round figures of Bodhisattvas that constitute one of the noblest and serenest types of religious sculpture in history. No other land exhibits so great a range of excellence in a single art, from miniature plaque to monumental statue, from simplest austere statement to gorgeously elaborated decoration, from calm to exuberance and spirited elegance.

But to begin the description of these exciting monuments and figures and jewel-like emblems with a semblance of order, let us go back to the shadowy era before the Han accession in 206 B.C. There then existed, says legend, or history, colossal bronze statues, but they seem mostly to have been melted up for money under later regimes. There is, indeed, surprisingly little sculpture in the round, considering the mastery long since at-

tained in the design and casting of the bronze dishes, vases, and bells, and in the carving of miniature jade charms. The art exists rather in figures accessory to the utilitarian bronzes. Not uncommonly, vigorous little animals stand up like sentinels at corners of the ceremonial vessel, or lie snugly against the lid; while others, more formalized, constitute handles or spouts or simply lend compositional accents. Often they all but disappear in geometric abstractions.

In the Han Dynasty, however, we see them come down, so to speak, into the open. Soon there are bronze animals, stone animals, and clay animals. The little bronze bears are especially well known; there is in them a tendency toward realism, but they are very simple and broadly proportioned for formal effect. A wide range of favorite pets appears in clay, in miniature, as figures for deposit in tombs, so that the deceased

Lion. Stone

may have beside him the companions he valued in life. In this connection there are also figurines of fine ladies, indicating a gratifying change in etiquette. A wife had formerly been buried alive with her dead husband, but now a clay effigy was entombed as substitute. Along with the wives and servants are the charming little pigs, hens, and ducks. Almost none of these, human figure or animal, is to be compared with the truly surpassing statuettes of the T'ang era, a few centuries later; but there are many arresting and rewarding examples, and a rare demure girl or a spirited horse from one of those ancient Chinese burying places still stirs our deepest admiration.

The monumental statue of a horse beside the tomb of General Ho Ch'ü-ping, who had traveled as far west as the Persian border, is dated by archaeologists at about 117 B.C. and is one of the oldest surviving examples of a type of commemorative art that flourished in China through many centuries. But it is better to skip over this and the other large sculpture of the Han period, and most of the Wei and Six Dynasties period, to the truly grand stone animals of the fifth and sixth centuries A.D. These may be divided into two sorts: lions more or less plain, and lions with

Water Buffalo. Covered vessel, bronze, pre-Han period.
Fogg Museum of Art, Harvard University

additions that make them into unearthly monsters—chimeras and such. In practically all, the sculptural conception and the treatment are so direct, simple, and creative that the figures are lifted to a plane of formal nobility. They are filled with the spirit of the animal *and* with the spirit of creative sculpture. In their massing, proportioning, and rhythmic organization they are impressive, virile, even dramatic. Here, in the large, is the same sculptural vitality or energy of movement, combined with suave, rhythmic conventionalization, which is found at the supreme level in the small animal bronzes. There is in both fields the linear enrichment of surface, the stylization by means of silhouettes echoed in incised lines, of minor rounded forms repeated in juxtaposition. There are few sculptural exhibits in all history so stirring, few monumental sculptures so essentially right.

The larger ones still lie where their creators placed them, often covered completely or partially by the dirt of the ages. Today examples rise up, half uncovered, in farmyard or field, reminders of the glories of Chinese life fourteen centuries ago. Or should one say instead, "the glories of Chinese death"? For these were funerary figures, markers pointing the way to the tomb of a celebrated man, or perhaps indicating the way of the spirit *from* the tomb. There is no record elsewhere on an equally colossal scale of man's age-long preoccupation with life beyond death, except in Egypt. The funerary and commemorative arts of these two ancient civilizations offer a fruitful field of comparative art study.

The art of the Han era had reacted from a certain fullness and ornamentalism of the preceding periods and was direct and vigorous. Despite the linear tracing, not to say patterning, added on the surface of the mountainous masses of the lions and chimeras, no less than on the small bronzes, the general feeling of simplification and of unified rhythm had persisted into post-Han sculp-

Lion. Stone,
monumental sculpture.
*Metropolitan Museum
of Art*

ture. In seeking the source of this lasting influence in works both large and small, and predominantly in animal figures, one is carried back to one of the most fascinating theories in the history of art.

Scythia, Ordos, China

This theory has it that centuries earlier, in far-away northern or western Asia, there had originated a distinctive and instantly recognizable type of sculpture in metals, known until recently as "the Scythian animal art"; and that in the course of time, through repeated migrations of the barbarians of the Eurasian steppes, southward and eastward at first, then westward, the style had been carried to Persia and to the upper valleys of China, where it took hold and became a main root of pre-Buddhist sculpture, and, in the west, to scattered areas of "barbarian culture" from Finland and the land of the Vikings to Visigothic Spain and Lombardy. It was essentially the art of the nomad tribes of the north—pouring out of that Asiatic reservoir which had held from time immemorial shifting and mixing tribes, Aryan and Mongolian, known to later history in a shadowy way as Scythians, Sarmatians, and Huns.

The evidence seen in survivals of the art itself is strongly in favor of a common origin for the Luristan animal figures of Persia, the early animal sculpture of China, and the Scythian originals found in lower Russia. The rare North European examples are so akin in both motives and sculptural feeling or method that an assumed relationship is at least defensible; and there is even reason to wonder whether the Etruscan formalization (so soon snuffed out after the classicized Romans laid hands on it) may not have arisen out of contact of the immigrants to Etruria with the Scythians, or with their neighbors along the Anatolian coast, possibly through the Hittites. Lately the tendency among archae-

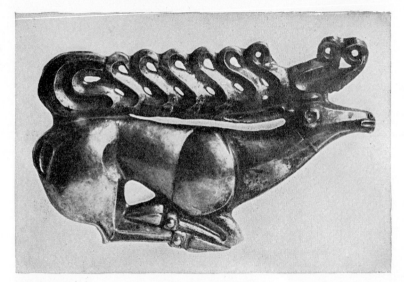

Reindeer.
Scythian gold plaque
from a shield,
7th century B.C.
The Hermitage, Leningrad

ologists has been to drop the name "Scythian art," to speak of "the Eurasian animal art" or "the art of the steppes." Some authorities, attempting to reconcile art terminology to one or another racial classification, speak of this development as Indo-Germanic art, or as the Iranian-European style. At least one broadens the idea and tags it "Amerasiatic."

The single certainty is that one of the great manifestations of the sculptural art exists in a widely scattered yet recognizably related display of animals in metal, found in the tombs of Scythian chiefs in southern Russia and Siberia, in the graves of warriors in Luristan in western Persia, and in the graves on the borders of western China. The many examples discovered in these three chief caches are matched by odd pieces discovered along the European trails of Bronze Age culture.

The Scythian style, if we may still term it that, died out in its own land—unless perchance it had something to do with the vigor of Russo-Byzantine art. In Persia it flowered once, in a restricted district, was lost to sight, but affected manifestations in the other visual arts. In China alone it was absorbed, or rather it triumphed, and found continuous life over a period of many centuries; its spirit spread from the miniature bronze bears and boars and deer to the monumental stone chimeras.

The hallmarks of the style are three: strict decorative formalization, extraordinary plastic vitality, and strong simplification of main motives along with rich counterplay of minor forms. The strength, the unity within richness, may be said to constitute a cardinal virtue of all art in which formal excellence and sensuous adornment are expertly combined; but the effect of concentrated energy, of spirited movement, within a profusely decorative composition is here surpassingly mastered in many of the brooches, talismans, and plaques. Whether in a gold buckle from Scythia itself, or in a Luristan harness-ring, or in an ornamental stag in bronze from the Ordos Desert, there is the vital movement, the dominating, compelling single animal-rhythm, cushioned in decorative outline and patterned accessory.

There is an impression of largeness even in small pieces. Practically always there is distortion of the object as it would be seen by the camera: there is no breath here of the realism of Sumeria and of Crete, of Greece and of Rome. It is decoration, not depiction, that the artist has intended, conventionalization for sculptural vigor, forthright ornamentalism—something added frankly for the sake of richness—and always the extraordinary boldness and virility. There is almost always, too, an avoidance of symmetry, an avoidance inevitable in any art so dynamic and so individualized.

Most of the miniature examples of the style (by far the larger proportion of the whole range)

Harness ornament.
Bronze, Crimea,
6th or 5th century B.C.
The Hermitage, Leningrad

are in low relief. Even when technically "in the round," the figure is considerably flattened. Animals, single or in groups, free figures geometrized until their outlines form their own frames in almost mathematical regularity, ornamental plaques pierced through to give additional sharpness to the silhouette, vigorously carved dagger-handles—these are typical. There is, too, that other nonrealistic touch, the increase of formal elegance by surface patterning—sometimes by traced lines; oftener, as befits sculpture, by repetitions of minor swelling forms, as in the horns of a stag or mountain goat, or in the mane of a horse or lion. This particular sort of sculptural counterpoint is nowhere else manipulated with such telling effect.

Just when the "animal style" entered China is still uncertain. It may have come as a gradual infusion, as wave after wave of invaders from the vague "West" bore in. There is a possibility that the pre-Han bronze vessels had gained their animal masks and claws and occasional full animal figures from contact with the West, if not through invasion from that quarter. Certainly a wide range of decorative motives on earlier examples indicates as much. When independent sculpture appeared, the subject-matter was such that one can only assume the foreign origin; the animals are so often those important to a hunting people, not to an agricultural people like the Chinese.

The actual examples closest to the Scythian and Luristan prototypes are found on the western borders of Old China—mainly in the Ordos Desert, whence their common designation as the Ordos bronzes. From the same direction came the hosts and leaders who again and again conquered the static but lasting Chinese nation.

Chinese and Scythian animal art. *Metropolitan Museum and Eumorfopoulos Collection*

Until archaeologists and anthropologists piece together more of the puzzle of cultural inter-penetration and tribal shifts, it is bootless to do more than accept the fact of a common Eurasian heritage, and to note that in China the animal-art vitality, slowly modified in its miniature forms, passed over into larger sculpture—the result being those outstandingly decorative monumental lions which served as the point of departure for this disgression. But the world is likely to hear more rather than less of a mother art of the Asian steppes.

Bodhisattva on a Double Lotus Petal. Stone, T'ang Dynasty.
Freer Gallery of Art, Washington, D.C.

The entire Scythian or Eurasian art may be a by-product of religion, the visual evidence of a cult of the animal. There is no proof for this, however, and another interpretation may be as valid: that when the development had spread over two continents the cult significance or sym-

Bodhisattva. Dried lacquer, T'ang Dynasty.
Metropolitan Museum of Art

bolism had been pretty well diluted, and the art lived on primarily because of its attractiveness as decoration. But a strictly religious art, definitely limited by tradition and creed, did come full-grown into China, there to undergo modification in accordance with the settled and human-

Seated Bodhisattva. Sung Dynasty. *Museum of Fine Arts, Boston*

istic Chinese spirit, but to maintain at the same time some of its native Indian characteristics.

Buddhist Religious Art

Buddhism followed the trade routes into the China of the middle Han emperors in the centuries just before and after Christ's birth. Already the Greek influence had been felt in India, and this brought about the first representation of Buddha as a man; but the East could not give up its formalism for Hellenistic realism, and the sculptural treatment became conventional and decorative. In India certain attitudes and accessories had become stereotyped; and in another direction (carrying on a pre-Buddhist Brahmanic expression) there was a profuse, exuberant sculptural art of multiplied forms and repeated areas of high and low relief.

All this was carried over into China—bodily, perhaps, in certain examples of the smaller things,

Lao-tse on a Water Buffalo. Bronze statuette, Sung. *Worcester Art Museum*

when in the mid-first century A.D. an emperor, having dreamed of a saint in the West, dispatched emissaries to Central Asia and received back news and tokens of Buddha and his religion. Certainly it was not much later that China became dotted with shrines and monasteries of the Buddhist faith.

Because the new religion celebrated the human body as the temple of the spirit, man became for the first time a main motive in Chinese art. Serenity and compassion entered into the expressiveness; into attitude and facial expression on the one hand, and into the sculptural handling on the other. There came a new kind of plastic rhythm, aided by a melodious and graceful linear counterplay.

From the typical figures of Buddha and of Bodhisattva—a figure midway between human and divine—taken bodily from India, there was to develop a long line of religious effigies. This culminated in the sumptuously enriched yet calm and uninvolved Bodhisattvas of the T'ang era. The best of them seem to breathe a spirit of peace and harmony and repose, to suffuse the temple or shrine with spiritual light. The sculptural method is perfectly fitted to the supra-mundane intention: it reinforces the religious symbolism by its dignity and its felicitously established and delicately echoed play of volume and plane. The figures constitute an impressive reminder of the age-old truth that the spirit of an era and a people may express itself most vitally in art forms.

In the other direction, that of profuse decorative adornment of shrines and temples, Buddhist sculpture in China followed equally the tradition of India, with similar native modification. The iconography was, as we have seen, fixed, not only in certain attitudes of the figure—all in seated or standing positions of relaxation and repose—but in symbolic accessories such as the nimbus or halo, and the draperies. In multiplying carved figures in the cave shrines and sanc-

Buddhist stele, detail.
Limestone, 6th century.
Museum of Fine Arts, Boston

tuaries, the Chinese artists set these larger effigies in appropriate niches, and, as was done in India, surrounded them with countless smaller images carved in relief directly on the flanking rock walls, sometimes multiplying the figures till the entire cave had the effect of being abundantly peopled with gods and supernatural attendants.

The atmosphere of the cave shrines is incomparably rich, and yet austere and mysterious. Considering the wholesale nature of the sculptors' task, the artistic standard is singularly high. Detached areas of the bas-reliefs, no less than single Bodhisattvas or now removed heads, repay study. If the excellence is very like that of the earlier Brahmanic and Buddhist cave-ensembles of India, the point to remember is that there is a like high achievement marked in the two phases. In general, the Chinese is a little more restrained. It rules out the sinuosity and the lighter sensuous decorativeness of the Hindu tradition, and gains thereby a new distinction. Not infrequently the Far Eastern artists introduced remnants of their vigorous animal art, as in the Yün K'ang caves at Shansi, in compositions not unlike the greatest sculptural achievements of Europe as exemplified in the cathedral tympanums in France.

In the Yün K'ang caves it is possible to see in the ensemble—completed after a century and a

Woman. Terra Cotta.
Royal Ontario Museum of Archaeology, Toronto

persed. The spirit of the brooding Compassionate One is not magnified easily, even by the master sculptors, as had been, for instance, the rhythmic vitality, the proud boldness, of the Ordos animals when they were metamorphosed into the oversize stone lions and chimeras.

Often the Chinese sculptors carved stone stelae that are like sections cut from the cave walls (page 185). Buddha sits serene in a central niche, while the surrounding face of the flattened shaft is incised with low-relief Bodhisattvas and attendants, with incidental birds, abstract patternings, and so forth. Sometimes, again, the elements obviously imported with Buddhism are mixed with survivals of the ever-energetic animal art.

A Comédie Humaine in Clay

Finally, there is still another type of Chinese sculpture which has widely and surely captured the Western fancy. (The Chinese, by the way, consider sculpture one of their lesser arts, as compared with painting, calligraphy, and poetry.) The clay statuettes of the T'ang era comprise at once a *comédie humaine* of the cultured life of the period and a diversified and endlessly appealing exhibition of sculptural suavity, elegance, and sheer virtuosity. This is not, like the Buddhist sculpture, a result of artistic impulse carried over into religious and spiritual reverence or reverie. It is an expression, rather, of lighter mood, of love of the graceful, even the playful.

The very subjects are eloquent of a devotion to the recreational sides of life: horseback-riders, polo-players, animal pets, dancing girls, musicians; though there are also more serious pieces—beasts of burden, warriors, and officials. But fascinating as is the documentary picture of living thus fixed for the delight and amusement of later generations, the most notable fact is the unrivaled plastic aliveness, the sculptural verve and vividness, here exhibited. Comparable to the Greek Tanagra figurines in size, method, and range of intimate and genre subject-matter, the Chinese statuettes are superior as pure sculptural art.

The dancing figure or poloist or camel or horse

half of effort, from about A.D. 450 on—the effect of successive minor changes in style and treatment, as new waves of influence bore in from the West, or a revived breath of local tradition swayed the sculptural thought. In general, throughout the caves, the colossal Buddhas are least appealing—the formalization there becomes wooden, and the concentrated feeling is dis-

Camel. Height 6¾ inches,
Six Dynasties.
Seattle Art Museum

immortalizes the spirit or feeling of the subject, even while pushing the boundaries of miniature art into new regions of expressiveness. The object as viewed in nature is penetratingly realized, but the actual visual impression is thrust back, modified, transformed, till an organized equivalent, creatively shaped in the most expressive and concentrated values possible to the materials and methods of clay sculpture, takes its place. Seldom have sculptors combined, in a long series of works, such essential truth to model or character with so eloquent a rhythmic movement; seldom such an aspect of freedom and spontaneity with sound and delightful sculptural orchestration.

The statuettes are usually colored. Commonly they are glazed, although the glaze may have been left off certain portions of the clay where directly applied pigment gives the better effect. As glazed pieces, the statuettes are sometimes omitted from histories of sculptural art and are relegated to the books on pottery instead—as if they were not among the very masterpieces of free sculpture! In any case, their fresh liveliness, brilliant vigor, and full formal beauty are unfor-

gettable, a source of purest aesthetic enjoyment. Fortunately the pieces are finding their way into all the larger Western museums, and even masterly examples are common enough to permit modest private collectors to own them. Probably thousands of figures will yet be dug from ancient graves. Incidentally the subjects prove, as did many of the reliefs in Egyptian tombs, that a people accustomed to make grave-offerings need not by that token be considered inordinately sad or obsessed by grim thoughts of the after-life. The T'ang statuettes are joyous in theme, in every sculptured syllable.

In China there grew up an exceptional sort of shallow-relief art in which an elaborate story composition was outlined on the stone, and the space around the figures and objects cut away to a slight depth. Flat slabs so treated might be used in series around the tomb-room; and the method often was combined with high-relief figures on the Buddhist stelae. This sort of sculpture puts an exceptional burden on silhouette, and the virtues are linear rather than three-dimensional. Indeed, many examples are nearer to engraved than to sculptured stone.

In some examples of the second century A.D., with figures done by scratch-drawing, and backgrounds then chiseled out, there is the usual Chinese vigor, not without a virility reminiscent of the steppe tradition. There is, too, a diverting series of stories and incidents told in the idiom—myth and historical legend, barbarian custom and homeland festival—all pictorially described, to which may be added homilies of filial piety, patriotic sacrifice, and conjugal fidelity. The totality of such works forms a sort of stone picture book of Chinese mythology, folklore, history, and etiquette. Although these early moralistic stone sculptures are the most memorable things in the mode, the shallow-relief art was practiced importantly through many centuries. Some of the T'ang stelae have panels distinguished by fullness and elegance, in the tradition.

Adding together relief and round statue, miniature and colossal figure, stone and bronze and clay, all represented by exceptionally good work, even when judged by world standards—to which may be added a high achievement in wood sculpture, incomparable jade-carving, and a unique sort of portrait sculpture in built-up lacquer—one has in the Chinese manifestations mankind's supreme demonstration of the possibilities and the glories of the sculptural art.

Terra-cotta statuettes from graves, northern Wei.
Royal Ontario Museum of Archaeology, Toronto

IX: CHINESE PAINTING IN
THE GREAT PERIODS

PAINTING is the most characteristic art of China. The sculpture is matched, part for part, in regions of the outside world; never the whole in one place, but one part in Luristan, another in India, still another in medieval France. Even the colossal ogres owe something to the Eurasian stylization that centered elsewhere. Only the grave-figurines are wholly Chinese, without a suspicion of foreign parentage, and universally recognizable as Chinese. But the painting is unique, shaped by the wisdom and love and brooding of this one people, and unrivaled in its sort through all the world.

It is here that the spirit of the national art is most intensely expressed. The Chinese aesthetic canon which fixes the excellence of a painting in a vitality that is of the painting itself rather than of the life or object depicted, which is concerned more to open the way to the soul than to report to the mind—this canon is most implicit in the body of scroll and album paintings. The Oriental painter is a philosopher, a seer, an artist in living. He prepares himself for creative expression by spiritual absorption and by rigorous discipline of the active mind. Having stilled his assertive personal self, in apprehension of mystic meanings and cosmic harmonies, he comes to his brush and ink and field of silk with a supra-sensual aim.

There is more than a sympathetic link between painter and poet. The two are often combined in one person—partly to be explained by the fact that the artist's brush is the only writing medium

Snowy Mountains, detail. Attributed to Kuo Hsi. Sung scroll. *Toledo Museum of Art*

in China, and that calligraphy itself is practiced with an artist's care. For the shading of the writer's lines supports his meaning; the very strokes convey his feeling toward, and the character of, the object. The purposes of the two groups of artists are alike, with a similarity not known in Western painting and poetry.

In much of Western painting there is a strain of assertive ambition—an exhibitionistic spirit, a show of personal emotion, a parade of virtuosity. There is, too, for extraordinarily extended periods, the effort to rival nature, to be scientifically right. The Eastern artist is humble. A great impersonality spreads over his pictures and statues and rugs. The copying of natural aspects, the capping of nature's effects, is the least of his undertakings. He studies nature in the large, concentrating his faculties upon understanding the greatest and the smallest of her phenomena, brooding with her. But his pictures are less a report of something seen than a distillation of a mood or a spirit felt. His most potent language is not the detail or outlines of the composition observed, but the intimation that came to him in contemplation. This he dresses in abstraction of color, line, plane, and volume in space, and by means of it he conveys the inexpressible. Sketches are no part of Oriental composition.

There can be, says the Chinese, no creation of art without peace of soul. The faculty of stilling the reporting senses and the thinking mind, the faculty of expanding the soul, of gazing out silently, even ecstatically, from the center of all being—this faculty is more to be prized than anatomical knowledge and light-and-shade exactitude. To which one may add, also out of the wisdom of the Orient, that there can be no profound *enjoyment* of art without inner peace.

This is not to say that Oriental art lacks magnificence or intense this-world vitality. It is full, vigorous, and rich. At times it runs off into extravagances of color, ornament, or meaninglessly repeated forms. But even in its excesses, the impersonality is likely to remain. The melodramatic sentiment and forced action of Pergamene sculpture, for instance, would be incomprehensible in the Far East, for its emphasis upon story and personal emotion, no less than its realistic intention and the lack of formal organization, marks the development as utterly alien to Eastern intention and spirit.

Some commentators explain Oriental art as primarily symbolic. Even Japanese writers have emphasized this explanation as a bridge between Eastern achievement and Western enjoyment; and indeed Japanese painting and sculpture are far more marked with symbolism than are the Chinese. But those who have fully savored and enjoyed a Sung mountain scene or a Han "unnatural" beast are likely to cry danger at the intrusion of symbol-seekers. A symbolic work, in the general understanding, is that which sets up one intellectual concept to suggest another. Symbolism is a matter of the thinking mind—and intellectualization is very far from the heart of Oriental art.

It is rather expressionism that is characteristically illustrated in the great body of Asiatic art. Even as that term is used, somewhat narrowly, by the current modernists, it fits Eastern art better than it does any large development of Western art before the post-impressionists. Expressionism's three notable traits or qualities may be marked as essentials of Chinese art: utmost exploitation of the peculiar materials and methods of the art, resulting in logical form-organization and rich sensuous values; exceptional reliance upon abstract means and universal rhythms; and expression in terms of the inner understanding or essential "structure" of the subject, rather than by outward or accidental aspects. The intention is to fix the feeling of the thing rather than to reproduce its dimensions and outlines and material details. It is significant that the Chinese, in the first of their canons of painting, speak of rhythmic life or formal movement, whereas the Japanese speak oftener of decorative and symbolic qualities.

In general the symbols in Oriental art are an added rather than an essential interest, lying beyond the values of the created, aesthetically moving complex of formal elements. If the word "symbol" is used more loosely, not in the sense of one idea standing for another but in the sense, for instance, of a landscape suggesting perceptions larger than itself—evoking a sense of peace,

Ma Yüan: *Sage in Meditation*. Sung Dynasty. *Museum of Fine Arts, Boston*

and by further extension occasioning a feeling of release from the turmoil and dust of city-bound existence—then Oriental painting may also be said to be richly symbolic. But it is only in religious painting, chiefly Buddhistic, that a set of symbols, as objects or attitudes or emblems standing for intellectual concepts, is common.

The reliance upon symbolism as an explanation seems to be due to the Western historian's necessity for finding some reason for the hold of Oriental art upon great numbers of people. An appreciation of formal excellence as such has not in the past been a common attainment of the educated "art lover" of Europe and America. The more learned he was, the less feeling he had for abstract, plastic, and deeply rhythmic values. Everybody had been busy pointing out how cleverly the painter had mastered anatomy and scientific perspective and a marvelous fidelity of representation, and adding instruction about the significance of the subject-matter. Naturally the observer missed these "cardinal virtues" in the gallery of Chinese or Japanese art. The perspective is nonexistent; the fidelity is to aspects of nature never brought to his attention; and if there is a story element it is from an alien mythology or a little-understood way of life. He was baffled on all the counts academically discussed and praised: content, technique, truth, moral purpose. He simply was not prepared to recognize

Tung Yüan: *Landscape,* detail of scroll. Sung Dynasty. *Museum of Fine Arts, Boston*

this other virtue in which, he was told, Oriental art excels—this abstract, vital, and expressive form-value. Yet every initiate, every graduate from the intellectualized art of the West to the formalized art of the East, repeats that here are pleasures unexampled, here are harmonies unguessed in the Western modes of art; here is *experience* of art at its purest and most satisfying levels.

The final answer to the one who wishes to enter this field of delights is that he must put himself into the way of continual contact with the actual paintings and sculptures. There is no substitute for experience. That he will come to appreciate them is certain, if only he will make sure of open-mindedness and communion. Meanwhile he can aid his own progress toward understanding by remembering these few basic differences:

Oriental art is not realistic or reproductive. It is considered by its practitioners to be a way of creation, concerned with life-values not to be observed or illustrated in terms of the casual and ephemeral aspects of outward nature. It depends first upon distillation of feeling and then upon expression in nearly abstract elements. On the appreciation side also, art is considered a spiritual concern. Like all spiritual activities, it presupposes calm in the mind and heart, and quietude in the soul. In turn it brings peace, permits blissful comprehension. If one insists upon living life with the brain ever active, scheming, demanding; if one continues to distrust all that is beyond logic and sight; in short, if one refuses to be to some extent a mystic, one might as well give over the arts of the East—except for their gorgeous sensuous color and formal pattern. But for him who makes the effort and achieves re-education and a new receptivity there are undreamed-of glories in those rolled-up scrolls.

Types of Chinese Painting

When Indian Buddhist sculpture was introduced, fully matured, into China, an equally idiomatic art of mural painting came with it. The examples still existing fragmentarily in cave shrines, as modified by Chinese ideas and methods, are by no means negligible or uninteresting, and they led on to a recognizably Chinese Buddhist art; but they are, by reason of the foreign element, out of the main line of development of a characteristic native art.

Mu Ch'i:
Tiger and Waterfall.
Sung Dynasty. *British Museum*

There had already been, long before, expert and original practice. If one is inclined to suspect the literary records which ascribe activities in portraiture, illustration of legend and history, and purely decorative painting to the centuries before Christ, there are nevertheless great painted building tiles produced not later than the second century B.C., in which the future direction of drawing and painting seems already fixed. The floating of the figures in living space, the delicate brush-touch, the calligraphic sensitiveness of the lines, the expressionistic con-

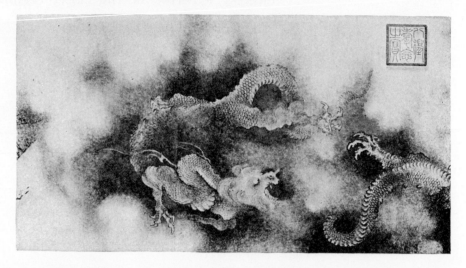

Dragon in Water, detail from *The Nine Dragons Scroll.* Sung Dynasty.
Museum of Fine Arts, Boston

centration on essentials—all these seem to have been learned by the artists long before. There is here, indeed, the directness and nature-distortion not of primitivism but of maturely considered plastic expression, felt for along a path leading directly away from realism. Greek painting had at this time arrived at the other end of the path, at naturalism, after a long progression from the exquisite formalism of Execias and Euphronius. In the subject-matter—or rather subject-approach—too, the main road of Chinese painting was already indicated—not through the eyes but through some deeper sensibility.

Practically every painted work of the following eight hundred years has been lost. But if one puts T'ang or Sung scrolls beside these early tiles it becomes clear that in the intervening centuries, eight or ten or twelve in number, a straight course had been run, the art being gradually refined and perfected rather than changed. The tempered vigor, poetic concentration of statement, and light-sensitive method are racial characteristics.

Written records of certain lost works of that millennium survive. They leave no doubt that the art was almost continuously fostered.

Arthur Waley, British translator of Chinese works, includes in *The Temple and Other Poems*

a translation of Wang Yen-shou's "Description of the Ling-Kuan Palace," written in the second century A.D. The palace that so impressed the poet was a provincial one, constructed by a brother of the famous Emperor Wu. The opening lines describe the sculptural adornments and the later lines the painted murals:

Birds of the air, beasts of the earth
Sprout from the timber; to swift-slanting beams
The coursing tiger clings, or perilously leaping
In a wild onrush rears his shocky mane.
A young dragon wreathes his coils,
And as he prances seems to nod his slithery
 head. . . .
And here all Heaven and Earth is painted, all
 living things
After their tribes, and all wild marryings
Of sort with sort; strange Spirits of the Sea,
Gods of the Hills. To all their thousand guises
Had the painter formed
His reds and blues . . .

One is reminded that in the eighth century a military leader had eighteen painters decorate a temple and considered their work so incomparably fine that he straightway had all eighteen put to death so that the success should never be repeated for his rivals.

There are even a few rare examples attributed

Snowy Mountains, detail. Attributed to Kuo Hsi. Sung scroll. *Toledo Museum of Art*

to known artists of the period. Ku K'ai-chih of the fourth century, reputed to have been an unsurpassed master, accomplished alike in Buddhist symbolic painting and in genre subjects, is represented by a serial scroll-painting now in the British Museum, known as *The Admonitions of the Instructress in the Palace,* and by a roll in the Freer Collection in Washington. Both show an extraordinary subtlety, characteristic mastery of expressive line, and compositional surety. They may be copies by later masters or by hacks—and so either better or worse than the originals. Copying was an honorable and useful activity through all later eras, with a reasonable if not spiritual justification in the Chinese belief that the work of art is a living, life-giving entity in its own right. One of its ways of giving life may be in inspiring later artists to duplication of the original creation, or to slightly varied expression on the same theme.

To the writer it seems profitless to outline for Western readers the periods, schools, and personalities of Chinese painting. Our knowledge of the background of Oriental history is so vague that no correlation can thereby be established between art works and changes in political and social framework. It would seem more useful, therefore, in an introduction and interpretation, to indicate the intention of the Chinese painter, and to convey, if possible, something of the spirit of his work and to afford only the slightest factual guide of chronological succession.

Mountain-and-Water Pictures

It is better to vault over those many centuries during which painting flourished only to leave criticism and legend rather than example, and to arrive in the T'ang era, when the arts flourished under Augustan encouragement, and fortunately under a more than Augustan discrimination and taste. China was never more open to foreign influences; she had commerce then with western Asia and Europe; but Chinese art was never again to be so distinctively itself. Even the invited Indian artists were soon absorbed. Buddhism was by this time a thoroughly Chinese

Waterfall, Tree, and Two Eagles. Sung Dynasty. *Freer Gallery of Art*

institution; and at first the efflorescence of painting took form in Buddhist symbolic works.

Wu Tao-tzǔ, considered by the Chinese their greatest master, is credited with having added new body and importance to painting in the eighth century. The deliberate slightness and delicate understatement carried into his early work out of tradition gave way to a fuller, more powerful style; the historians speak of astonishing power and majestic largeness. The actual murals and silk paintings are known in description only. Wu Tao-tzǔ made hundreds of frescoed murals and was celebrated for other Buddhist works as well. From his period the surviving works—not his own, but others that afford information about methods, stylistic changes, changes of standards—are chiefly Buddhist votive pictures, of Bodhisattvas and other near-celestial beings and Paradise, or portraits. In the more complex paintings, done in a hieratic spirit, in the Indian idiom only slightly modified, there are occasional marginal bits—perhaps portraits of donors—which indicate a different, more strictly Chinese style.

Hsü Shih-ch'ang:
Landscape.
Sung Dynasty
Freer Gallery of Art

But it was landscape painting which came to be, in the T'ang era, the most typical form of expression. By the eighth century there were established traditions of landscape treatment. All carried considerably beyond the intention of the "nature-painting" of the Occident, which of course was not invented until eight centuries later. The Chinese term that corresponds to the word "landscape" signifies literally "mountain and water." Through all after-ages the artist tried to distill the essence of these freest of natural elements, mountains and still or flowing water. As the Taoist sages sought the secret of repose and divine identification in the fastnesses farthest from cities, war, and dust, so the painters sought to fix the feeling of cosmic penetration and absolute spirituality in mountain-and-water pictures.

Already in the eighth century there were different methods and schools. An especially quiet, miniature-like style is ascribed to the first masters. There were, too, poet-painters, who fixed in drawings on silk the emotional inwardness of a word-picture. To say that these pictorial analogues to literary compositions are themselves literary would be to overstate the case: there is no story-interest, no narrative, no transfer of described elements. Rather they are attempts to crystallize, in terms of the other medium, the subjective mood or perception that evoked the poem. It should hardly be necessary to stress a like reticence, even slightness of body, in the two arts, even within the fullest formal and sensuous expressiveness.

The literary association is further recalled in the often-remarked calligraphic character of the linear parts of the design. In Chinese writing the signs are from pictographic origins; that is, the word is a shorthand depiction of the object named, now nearly abstract, though with some faint likeness. There is additional meaning in the way in which the symbol is inscribed, in the flow of the line, its crispness or softness, its delicacy or vigor.

It is hardly an exaggeration to say that writing, under these conditions, becomes a fine art in itself. For instance, the single character for "man" may be shaded and "composed" to signify weak man or strong man, coward or hero, partly by the weakness or virility and verve of the brush strokes. This is the element that cannot be translated when Chinese poems are brought over into the non-pictographic languages, and we are usually left with denatured intellectual equivalents.

Written poems, then, assumed an artistic character due partly to the sensitiveness and creative shading of the calligraphy and to the total visual effect of the manuscript. Handling of the brush became expert and expressive to an extent undreamed of in the Western world. And naturally,

with the poet and painter in the Orient so close together in intention, both finding their material in subjective emotion and intuition, and their method in suggestion, there resulted a strong calligraphic character in the painting, as may be seen in outlines almost unbelievably revealing and in a play of fluent and broken line like inwoven counterpoint.

As an indication of the extent to which the Chinese prized, and still prize, the beauty in writing, one may quote Han Yü, a poet who lived from A.D. 768 to 824. He wrote of the inscriptions on some historic stone drums:

Time has not yet vanquished the beauty of these
    letters—
Looking like sharp daggers that pierce live croco-
    diles,
Like phoenix-mates dancing, like angels hovering
    down,
Like trees of jade and coral with interlocking
    branches,
Like golden cord and iron chain tied together
    tight,
Like incense-tripods flung in the sea, like dragons
    mounting heaven. . . .[1]

Laurence Binyon, twentieth-century British art historian, went to the length of claiming that "painting, for the Chinese, is a branch of handwriting." The primary materials, brush and Chinese ink—an ink with almost magical tonal possibilities—are the same in the two arts. The method of direct application upon silk or soft paper excludes all possibility of "working over" or correcting; and so the paintings have, as a group, a freshness and vitality seldom approached elsewhere.

Binyon, most sensitive among the pioneer interpreters of Oriental art to the West, explained illuminatingly how the calligraphic method and the poet's approach result in the effect of important space, of aliveness in those parts of the field where line and color and object are not. He wrote: "The artist closely observes and stores his observations in his memory. He conceives the

---

[1] Witter Bynner's translation, in *The Jade Mountain: A Chinese Anthology*, quoted by courtesy of the publisher, Alfred A. Knopf.

design, and having completed the mental image of what he intends to paint, he transfers it swiftly and with sure strokes to the silk. . . . The qualities prized by the Chinese in a small ink-painting of bamboos, a favorite subject alike with beginners and masters, are those prized in a piece of fine handwriting, only there is added a keen appreciation of the simultaneous seizure of life and natural character in the subject. . . . It is said that in a master's work 'the idea is present even where the brush has not passed.' And this emphasis on the value of suggestion, of reserves and silences, is important to notice, because no other art has understood like the Chinese how to make empty space a potent factor in the design."

Simplicity with Grandeur

The landscape paintings, of course, shaded off into other types: landscapes with figures, for instance, which led over into genre. In the other direction there were masters devoted particularly to flower studies, and to bird and animal paintings. To all this there was the parallel development of religious painting, revealing and beautiful in its own way, and of portraiture. There were, too, in the T'ang period and in the following era of the Five Dynasties (in the tenth century) many fluctuations of style and method.

Nevertheless, painting, unlike sculpture, came to its culminating excellence only in the Sung era (960-1279). There was a painter-emperor, Hui Tsung, who set out to make his court a center of the arts and to transform his realm by official promotion of cultural activities. He collected five thousand paintings in one of the earliest of the "national galleries" and formed an academy. Perhaps, like Ikhnaton in Egypt, he gave too much attention to matters spiritual and artistic and neglected the army. At any rate the Tatars overran his empire and sent him into exile, where he died. During the century or so that it took for the nation to absorb its new conquerors, the painters are said to have indulged the already developed taste for retreat from the active and troubled world. The art was then most eloquent of the regions propitious for spiritual serenity and repose: the inward world of the soul, and mountain fastnesses, and dreamy mist-covered fields. Thus a slight influence toward realism, felt during Hui Tsung's reign, was turned back.

As typical of the diversity in any one period, it may be noted that in the late Sung era Li T'ang and his pupils, Hsia Kuei and Ma Yüan, developed—according to Binyon—"landscape at its finest; synthetic in conception, impassioned in execution, it unites simplicity with grandeur"; even while Li Sung-nien was carrying on older currents of historical painting and transcribing contemporary living; and while others were transforming Buddhist votive art into gorgeously decorative hangings, and still others were delighting in naturalistic accuracy. There are eight hundred names of painters recorded from the Sung era. All of these currents carried on into the Ming era—but that was in the period of the European Renaissance, and thus belongs to a later chapter. An example is *Deer* by Chou Yüan, page 581.

What is it that so greatly signifies in a Sung landscape? It is, of course, the total aesthetic effect or evocation—a thing indefinable and elusive. There is no other type of art in which the excellence so withdraws in the face of analysis. But because of the strangeness of the Eastern painting to average Western eyes it would seem, for once, useful to trace down the various component elements, actually to pick to pieces one of these fragile works.

On page 200 is a mountain-and-water landscape of the twelfth century. It is entitled *The Emperor Wên Meets the Sage Tzü-ya;* but obviously the subject-interest is not of primary significance to the beholder. To the informed Chinese the knowledge of circumstance, legend, and correlative literary treatment doubtless adds overtones of meaning, pointing up the rightness of this particular setting and of the artist's blending of calm and magnificence. But one needs no literary or historic key to recognize that the work is a formal masterpiece. There is subject-matter in the other sense, apart from figures and legend—a transcript or distillation of natural scene, constituting a typically fine instance of "simplicity with gran-

The Emperor Wên Meets the Sage Tzŭ-ya. Sung Dynasty. *Freer Gallery of Art*

deur." Specifically one may note the essential tree character, the rock structure, and the peacefulness of water, all cushioned in the atmosphere of mountainous grandeur.

All that seems secondary, however, to the symphonic orchestration of formal elements. The sense of movement is extraordinary; yet the picture is poised, reposeful. Every element of design in one-half of the picture field—beginning with tumbled volumes, aggressive line, and clashing planes—is in contrast with the melodious, melt-ing, lyric planes, lines, and volumes of the other half. Nor is the vigor of the main plastic rhythm destructive of that flatness which is a first law of decorative painting. Both the absence of natural shadow and the Oriental method of "laying up" the picture instead of employing scientific perspective contribute to this shallow effect of the field.

This is a composition, incidentally, which, after the observer has noted the striking division into a sumptuously filled and "forward" left half

Chi-en Hsüan: *Winter Landscape.* 13th century. *Fogg Museum, Harvard University*

and a spacious, light, and distant right half, rewards the roaming eye with charming minor bits: the area with the two figures; the little tree to the lower right, characterful as tree but serving as a richly textured bit in the formal ensemble; and the hidden inlet way over at the middle left. But the focus of interest, compositionally and psychologically—the point at which the vision comes to rest, to which the eye returns gratefully after each further circuit of the field—is that misty, harmonious, living space at upper center.

And that brings one to the truth that ultimately the painter's intention and achievement center in something that can be neither depicted nor described. The final thing posed in this picture is intangible—a mood, an evocation.

Objectively this is achieved by understatement. The deeper communication is by abstract means, by a peculiarly full synthesis of formal elements, a sparing use of objective means. The result, the beholder's response, is, like the artist's approach, nearer to contemplation than to observation. One knows that nature has been penetrated, profoundly understood, reflected upon; then harmonized, lifted toward the transcendental. To the

mystic, nature is no external thing to be brought forward as an exhibit for enjoyment. The deeper service is to carry the awareness of man to that center of oneness at which all men and all natural phenomena exist.

Just as one might dwell on those bits where the "treatment" seems especially felicitous—on minor charming passages—so one might pause to enjoy, separately, so to speak, the virtuosity of single formal elements such as line or color. The sensitive calligraphic line might be studied better, perhaps, in the economical depictions of bird or flower or animal, which breed despair in the Western draftsman, so incomparably sensitive and expressive is the delineation. What exquisite balance of form and character there is, too, in the drawing of Ma Yüan's *Landscape with Bridge and Willows* (shown on page 167) and of Ch'en Jung's *Nine Dragons* scroll!

Color is seldom a stressed element in Chinese landscape painting. The lightest touch or faintest wash may be added to the monochrome picture, or as often omitted. But monotone in Chinese ink is not monotone in the Western sense. The range of effects is enormous.

Color rises to a dominating position, however,

in the Sung and Yüan paintings. The rich play of hue and texture in some of the Buddhist hanging pictures is effective beyond description. We see the barbaric opulence oftener in embroidery and woven silk—particularly in the mandarin robes—for these have been preserved and brought to the West in greater number; but there are rare paintings with the quality. The full-colored, full-bodied painting is found in magnificent variation in Tibet and even more notably in Korea.

The frescoes touched a level not surpassed for decorative richness in any other manifestation in the world. The rhythmic adjustment of figures, the vigorous linear interplay, the incomparable Chinese patterning with sensuously seductive color—all these are to be seen as vitally achieved even in fragmentary compositions. Such is *A Vision of Kuan-Yin,* a Ming fresco of 1551 in the Boston Museum.

The roll paintings of the Chinese and Japanese are of a type unknown to the West. The artist begins his picture at one end of a band of silk and works his episodic legend or landscape continuously to the other end. The work is ordinarily kept rolled. It may be displayed, as in our museums, open at a particularly delectable passage; or, in the Oriental fashion, unrolled progressively at a sitting, and enjoyed bit by bit through the whole sequence. The unusual continuous form demands a special fluent technique: the picture must go forward rhythmically, so to speak, yet present a unified pictorial entity in each segment.

The pleasure of unrolling the landscape of a master painter, pausing as one pleases, losing one's outward self in the slowly changing visual experience, is a form of aesthetic enjoyment different from any known to Western peoples. The mechanics of unrolling and rerolling the silk field is as natural as turning to see the changing landscape as one walks through woods and meadows, as automatic as the turning of the leaves of an absorbing book.

Again, and finally, it is the mood that counts when one wanders in a gallery of Chinese mountain-and-water pictures. If one comes with peace in one's heart, with the inner eye open, there is the balm of soul-absorption. This is not passivity, absence of experience, a mere withdrawal; there is dynamic movement in these things, a positive formal experience. But the experience is transmitted by a method which prepares the observer for reposeful consideration, an enjoyment within stillness.

Chinese Art Theory

Hsieh Ho, a painter and writer of the sixth century, set down a word-summary of Chinese aesthetics which has become famous and familiar wherever art students gather. In the first of his "canons" he expressed, better than any modern artist, the heart of the present-day modernist belief. He said that first of all the painting should have "rhythmic vitality and a life-movement of its own." Other translations are: "operation of the spirit of life-movement"; "rhythmic vitality, or spiritual rhythm expressed in the movement of life"; and "the life-movement of the spirit through the rhythm of things."

It is notable that this summary fits both Oriental art as an entity at the opposite pole from Western classic art, and modern expressionist art. The emphasis upon a certain sort of movement, upon rhythmic vitality, and upon the spiritual element parallels a great deal that has been written recently upon movement within the canvas ("plastic orchestration" is the modern term), upon formal expressiveness, and upon the abstract element that is a sort of language of the soul. But most remarkable from the "advanced" point of view is the stress upon a life *in the painting.* For it is fundamental to all thinking about the arts that one recognize two intentions in two vast bodies of works: one the mirroring of the life around us; the other the creation of a new thing that has animation—that is, a life-movement—of its own.

The Chinese consider the mirroring or imitation of natural phenomena secondary. The primary aim is to endow the work with the elements of life—movement, inspiration, the power to communicate—rather than to mirror or interpret. What else, they ask, does *creation* mean?

In other words, the artist, by identifying himself with the spirit, enters into the rhythm out of which all life is created. Out of the cosmic well of creation he carries the breath of the spirit into the material work of art, endows it with independent life, with potential energy, with ordered movement in line, volume, and color. If he has great vigor, sensitiveness, serenity, nobility in his own soul, the painting will breathe forth something of those qualities. Its way of life will be an extension of his way of life. But the first requirement is that it shall itself be rhythmically and spiritually living.

And "when the rhythm is found, we feel that we are put into touch with life, not only our own life, but the life of the whole world." [1]

It will not escape the Western student that Hsieh Ho begins at the very opposite end of the aesthetic field from that which seemed of first importance to Aristotle and to most orthodox Western theorists down to the early twentieth century. To him it would have been inexplicable that the artist should be bound by the canon "Art is imitation."

There are five more canons in Hsieh Ho's "principles." They have to do, roughly, with structure, harmony with the forms of nature, color, composition or space division "according to hierarchic order," and transmission of what the masters have already gained. Other Chinese artists and sages have penned rules almost as pithy and suggestive.

The Chinese, with their passion for ordering and explaining the elements of art, did not, of course, escape the narrowing effect of codifying the acceptable "rules" of composition. The stultifying effects of formula-making were to be observed over long periods, and after the Ming era the history of the arts was one long record of repetition and academic exercise. If one considers the essential creativeness of the traditional models, it is no wonder that even the copies were at times endowed with extraordinary formal

Lin Lingkuei: *Arahat Entering into Nirvana.* Sung Dynasty. *Museum of Fine Arts, Boston*

values. There came to be an art, too, frankly competitive within very restricted limits—painters attempting, for instance, to fix on the silk the most intensely concentrated feeling of bamboo or mice or water-grass. The results are often formally lovely, though they range off into dryly intellectual effects which rest, for full enjoyment, upon

---

[1] Laurence Binyon, in *The Flight of the Dragon.* The quotations from Binyon earlier in the chapter are from his essay on "Chinese Painting" in the *Encyclopaedia Britannica.* I owe a debt also to his book, *The Spirit of Man in Asian Art,* and to the volumes of Waley, Giles, Petrucci, Carter, and Silcock. See the bibliography for annotations about these.

knowledge of tradition and of the previous achievement.

It is easy to see that when all subject-materials have been reduced to formulas, so that it is accepted that there are sixteen ways to draw mountains, and exact laws govern the representation of pines or waterfalls or figures, something of life has been excluded from painting. But the history of the art of painting in China embraces so many periods of surpassing loveliness that the lifeless or imitative interludes may well be forgotten.

If there is no mention of Chinese architecture as an art related to the unexcelled sculpture and painting, it is not because the building art was less esteemed or that it was only negligibly practiced. Rather it is that the monuments—sufficiently described in the ancient books—have almost totally disappeared. What notable buildings survive from the past are of the Ming and later dynasties; and what little is worth recounting of earlier architectural history is better appended to the chapter that treats of post-Renaissance Oriental art. Japanese architecture, too, as known in surviving examples, is of that time. For convenience, and because Japan's *distinctive* achievement came late, that nation's painting and sculpture also are excluded here. It is time to go back to the beginnings of another Oriental story: the Hindu.

X: INDIA AND MAN'S SOUL;
CAMBODIA, SIAM, JAVA

A LITTLE GIRL was taken to see the Oriental art in a great museum and was shown a bronze statue of a Hindu deity. Then she asked shyly, "Why has he six arms?"

That was the Western mind speaking: a departure from natural truth noted and questioned. It was Western education on guard. The mind thus roused and eager for "reasons" would, the Oriental believes, stand in the way of aesthetic response and the enjoyment of form. And indeed it is Western education that makes necessary an explanation of a different approach to art before appreciation is attempted.

The distinctiveness of Indian art begins in an attitude toward the soul. For a few centuries Buddhism modified the spiritual preoccupation of the Hindu artist, introducing a more humanistic interest and intention. But at other times the Brahmanic abstract attitude prevailed. A very great deal of early Indian art, even up to the time of the Islamic invasions, has to do with religion; the great mass of it is shaped in accordance with a racial philosophy and a certain psychological intention.

The soul, says the Hindu sage, is the only reality. Its satisfaction is the only real happiness. The individual man, in permitting himself to slip into a life of materialistic activities and sense-

Relief panels, Borobudur. *Victoria and Albert Museum photograph*

Standing Buddha.
Bronze, Gupta period.
Museum of Fine Arts, Boston

pleasures, is obscuring the true reality and preventing the illumination that comes with the submergence of self in the universal soul. By giving his allegiance to the world and its diversions he is delaying the return of his own spirit to the source, to the fountain of existence, the realm of

light and tranquillity and bliss from which it has been separated. The things that seem so real in outward life are a sort of deception. Turn within. Shun the visible. Happiness, knowledge, immortality are only in the soul conscious of itself.

Out of such statements—in so far as words can

Dancing Siva.
Bronze, 16th century.
William Rockhill Nelson
Gallery of Art

be substituted for the inaudible language of the soul—can be pieced a suggestion of the philosophy of the ancient Hindus.

In so far as art is visible, concrete, it partakes of the nature of the phenomenal world. It cannot be wholly of the Absolute. Strict Brahmanism leads to asceticism and to denial of the pleasures and facts of sense. Art, in that it enters the beholder's or listener's consciousness through a sense channel, and, moreover, is commonly folded within an added sensuousness of its own, is suspect.

But an abstract philosophy must have its prophets and teachers to make a bridge of ideas to the people. Art has a way of carrying a message, of thus serving the prophet and the seer.

Art has, moreover, hidden in itself a portion of the Absolute. It holds in solution something of the inner light; at its best and most abstract, it crystallizes the universal plan. Above all, the image may be an instrument for release from casual living, may serve as agent for identifying the individual consciousness with deity. Therefore the activities of the artist are promoted and valued even in a Brahman-guided civilization.

The monotheism that is basic to the world's great faiths was first conceived by the Hindus: the conception of the One as all-inventing, allcomprehending. The wise man's part was marked as a continual effort to return to identity with the One, the source, through interior initiation and contemplation. Even to this day India's holy

Buddha. Gupta, Mathura, 5th century.
Mathura Museum

the qualities in the native art that distinguish it from the manifestations of all other peoples must be understood in the light of an intention to rise above the senses, and an overwhelming desire to make a non-material advance—apparently away from man and his this-world artistry.

Nevertheless, the conception of monotheism did not prevent the Brahmans from creating a secondary hierarchy to which innumerable lesser gods were admitted, to satisfy popular demand for seeable idols. The way to art was thus opened long before the Buddha brought a second great religion to the country. Within Hindu religious art there is amazing variety, from magnificent and monumental works down to simplifications and trivialities unbelievably widespread.

Indian art thus is not, by token of being religious, unduly austere or gloomy or remote. As compared with the Chinese art, it is man-centered, sense-delighting, and often artificially graceful. It is exuberantly rhythmical, and at times feverishly, deliriously glowing and luxuriant. Yet, in the large, it belongs characteristically to the body of Oriental culture. Like Persian art, it is related to the Chinese by its non-imitational intention and its conventional method, and by the way of life of the shaping artists. Like the art of those other Eastern peoples, it outwardly leans toward a frank formalism and away from realism. It partakes of the Oriental fullness and richness. What may be termed its philosophic texture is unmistakably Asiatic.

Of all Eastern countries India is strangest to the Western mind. The religion that is spiritual rather than theocratic; the knowledge that is sought as a means to release from material reality, instead of as a means to practical mastery over it; and the art that exists less to depict and recreate external living than to lead into a fresh sort of experience—these are both alien and baffling to the pragmatic European mind.

Sculpture is the leading art, and the human figure is overwhelmingly the subject; but anatomical accuracy and individual portraiture are hardly known. Genre is absent. The single figure is almost uniformly that of a man touched with divinity, a legendary character abstractly considered. The beholder's interest is not in per-

men are accorded a prestige and an authority hardly known elsewhere; and among the masses other-worldly interests (it seems to Western visitors) have an extraordinary hold. In the essentials of material progress India has lagged behind other major civilizations. Because the culture of India has been at heart Hindu and Brahmanistic

Miracle
of the Mad Elephant.
Amaravati,
c. 3rd century.
Madras Museum

sonality or in verisimilitude; it is in the image as a bridge to contemplation. The figure is of Buddha or Bodhisattva in order that the beholder may achieve the release and the participation the soul desires. Or it is of Vishnu or Siva as the embodiment of a religious concept. The art is instinctive, increated, not dwelt upon. The appeal is to a region of the mind lying beyond familiar fact and apart from interest in a model.

Appropriately there grew up parallel to Buddhist sculptural art a type of abstract design in line, hardly more than mathematical diagraming, which served the same purpose: through intense contemplation it led to identification of the beholder with the source of all diagraming and all that is universal in life and art. In true sculpture the subject-matter was necessarily suggestive, and the surface treatment may be noted as rhythmic and musical and thus calculated to still the mind and evoke a mood of detachment. But under all

there is the abstract structure, the cosmic diagram.

There are, of course, minor arts, a steady production of decorative utensils and accessories, and branchings of sculpture into seductive ornamental trappings. But seldom has the body of serious art in a great country remained so steadfastly within religious and undocumentary limits. Within those limits it is rich, pervasive, and eye-filling. Incidentally, sculpture and architecture form part of the common background in India, of the environment of the masses. It is part of the story, too, that the whole rich pageant unfolds with hardly a record of an artist's name.

When the Aryan-speaking invaders from the northwest, from Persia or Afghanistan, drove the Dravidian peoples southward from the Indus Valley to the lower peninsula, art already had a history in India. There are prehistoric cave paintings in the Vindhya Mountains strangely like the Paleolithic murals in France and Spain. The relics of the prehistoric ages are commonly like those of Europe and of other parts of Asia. The remains of the Neolithic and first metal cultures include stone weapons, pottery, sculptured fetishes, and dolmens.

There is mystery still about a civilization of which remains have been found in the Indus Valley, in a series of excavations started in 1931 at Mohenjo-Daro, and continued at Harappa, Chandu-Daro, and elsewhere. It seems likely that the Indus civilization may yet be proved to be contemporaneous with the world's "first" civilizations in Sumeria and in Egypt. That is, a third fertile valley may have given opportunity for previously nomadic peoples to settle down, to promote community projects for betterment, to cultivate the land and to domesticate useful animals (including here the elephant), and to initiate the art of writing. All this came about in the Indus Valley at least as early as 3000 B.C.

The Indus Valley culture, called also the Mohenjo-Daro culture, yielded in excavation a whole cityful of houses in brick construction, on a previously thought-out gridiron plan; each house had sanitary facilities that drained into covered community sewers. At Mohenjo-Daro only a great number of seals suggested an advanced sculptural art, the little statues in the round being the usual crude talismanic or offering figures. (It was through the seals that the Indus culture was so readily dated. The people here had contact with the Sumerians, and seals with unmistakable Indian animals were found by archaeologists in Mesopotamian caches, at datable levels.) Larger sculptural work is represented by finds at Harappa. One stone torso might well be stylistically a forerunner of what came to be mature Indian art.

It was many centuries later, according to what we know, that the nation had become truly Indian, with the Iranian or Aryan element absorbed but dominating. No fair estimate is possible of the comparative influence of persisting cultures of the Dravidian or other tribes. But the emergent Vedic religion was that of the Iranian conquerors, and there are other evidences that the national culture substantially came with the invaders or was developed by them. The rigid caste system was in part a device to perpetuate the "superior" racial element in its purity. And indeed the eventual rule of the country was to lie with the Brahmans, once they established themselves as the only priests and teachers. Even though Buddhism, which was destined to prevail as the religion of a large part of the Orient, was born in India and challenged the Hinduism of the Brahmans for ten centuries, it ultimately failed to replace the religion of the Brahmans or to shake the caste system which they decreed.

Sculpture

What may be termed typical Indian sculpture —as the world sees it today—is first found at the time of Asoka, an emperor of the Maurya Dynasty who in the mid-third century B.C. declared Buddhism the official religion of the country. The nation had long been divided into a large number of independent states, and these in turn were rooted in a widespread family or clan organization. It is said that Asoka imported sculptors and that their "court" art is different from that of the native tradition. But it is a puzzle whence could have come artists so masterly. Greek sculpture had declined. It was at this time realistic and sensational. Alexander the Great had invaded northern India a century earlier and had established a chain of Asiatic-Greek colonies or cities, and it may be that some fortunate intermarriage of Greek with Oriental impulse had bred a vision beyond the Hellenistic.

A more likely conjecture, on stylistic evidence, is that the source is Persian. At Persepolis in Persia the Achaemenid development had left monuments not without affinity to the best-known Asokan works, and sculptors borrowed from the contemporary civilization of Persia would carry on a tradition fittingly Oriental. In any case, "court style" and native tradition soon flowed into one characteristic way of art, and for sixteen hundred years there was an unmistakably Indian accomplishment.

The so-called "primitive" convention of frontality long persists, and there is an air of formalism throughout. In the single religious figure a

Sculpture on the Sanchi Gate

certain repose, a silent quality in the stone, is faithfully preserved, as might be expected where the purpose of the image is primarily to assist meditation and to promote the mood in which union with the divine is possible.

When the Western mind considers the adherence to conventions, the impersonal purpose of the statue, and the abstract core, it appears strange that these Hindu figures are endowed with so great a measure of rhythmic excellence, and particularly that the sculptural quality lies in the direction of sensuous and melodic loveliness. The volume is full. The rhythms are fluent and caressing. The actual bodies are physically superb, on the fruitful side. Seldom has sculpture in stone so capitalized on a certain soft loveliness of the human figure. These are not, we are compelled to remind ourselves, nudes for the sake of the nude, or for the sake of the art that can use

the body as medium for romantic imaginings. The quality we enjoy as art, the aesthetic compulsion, is a formal by-product of religious purpose.

The strictly religious image soon developed into a more decorative sort of composition, particularly into stories of the life of the Buddha composed in panels, medallions, and friezes. The figures were then multiplied and became intertwined with ornamental motives. Finally the melodic rhythms were built up into lush patternings of swelling forms and flowing lines. The sensuous curves were forced into seductively sinuous arabesques.

There are critics who, failing to recognize the deeper significance of the single Buddha figure—knowing in themselves, perhaps, nothing of the expressed inner life of the spirit—mark the profuse and luxuriant decorative sculpture as the

Kali with Cymbals.
Bronze, 14th century.
*William Rockhill Nelson
Gallery of Art*

typically Indian thing. Thus Elie Faure, the French art historian, speaks again and again of the *sensual* quality of Indian art, of its intoxicated luxuriance and its riotous liberty. Faure usefully points out a connection of sculpture and architectural ornament with the fecundity of the Indian land, the pantheism of its early peoples, and the easy pleasures of living. When the Iranian invaders came down into the valley lands they had no choice but to indulge the intoxication of the senses. Faure stresses that religion had become only a pretext, and links the Indian development with the medieval European in "its drunken and fecund plunge into the fields of sensation."

This overstressing of Indian sensualism—the Frenchman uses the word again and again—is useful in reminding the Western observer of a truth too often overlooked. The "feel" of the land and of nature always influences the artist. The subtropical fruitfulness of India is mirrored in its art. Nevertheless, the profounder achievement is to be found in the more reticent expression, where the luxuriance is less physical, where the profusion is disciplined to the abstract intention. Gorgeous as the best panels and friezes are, with their swarming figures and insinuating movement, the best, it seems to this observer, is in a quieter, more removed product, less packed with movement and lush forms. The truest art of India is that typified in the religious figure.

Indeed the fragments of sculpture that exist from the age before Asoka, the full flower of Buddhistic expression, and the statues of the

Uma.
Bronze, South India,
12th-14th century.
*Museum of Fine Arts,
Boston*

time of the so-called Hindu Rebirth—all these add up to one body of quiet spiritual art that is the most characteristic Indian product. It is at all times vigorous and brisk—witness the *Kali with Cymbals* on page 212—but the movement is contained and the total effect one of repose. The supreme expression is in the figure of Buddha or Bodhisattva, in which all the subjective and symbolic as well as the sculptural values combine to evoke the meditative, compassionate, otherworldly mood.

Buddhism was the flower of a seed of human-

Avalokitesvara.
Bronze.
Ceylon, 8th century.
Museum of Fine Arts,
Boston

istic mysticism that already lay in the womb of Brahmanic Hinduism. The gentleness, the love, the universality of Buddhism inform the art, and lend to it an accent of stillness, of calm. It was the greater triumph that the sculptors could, even while ministering to the spirit, recall unobtrusively the loveliness of outward life, utilize the swelling volume of the body and the melodic line of the garment in shaping the rhythmic image that would bridge the chasm between worldly life and the state of illumination.

From the accession of Asoka on—from the third century B.C.—there was growing, nevertheless, that other background, growing luxuriantly, spreading over the walls of subterranean temples in marvelous pageants of historical and allegorical relief-picturing, over the pillars and walls and roofs and towers of architecture, filling railing-panels and pillar-fronts with incredibly rich compositions of figures and floral forms and repeated geometrical abstractions. A very great deal of this art is extravagant, illogically destructive of both sculptural unity and architectural form. It ends in a senseless, tasteless piling up of excrescent forms.

It is this that led Lisle March Phillipps to ask, in a book entitled *Form and Colour:* "What are these extraordinary shapes, these complex indeterminate arches, these weird bulbous columns of no fixed shape or outline, these hobgoblin roofs and monstrous protuberances and excrescences, these surfaces that rot with ornament, this indeterminate sculpture that ramifies and spawns in every corner, eating the stone, mothlike, to rags and tatters—what is the explanation of it all, or why do such words as fantastic, whimsical and capricious, and the like spring to our lips to describe it? The answer is simple. All these portents are rendered possible by the abolition of the law of function."

But at the other end, and still within the decorated, "loaded" art, there are rich but controlled architectural panels, and the extraordinary animal sculpture in relief, silhouette, and full-rounded figure of the Sanchi gates. In short, the unnamed Indian sculptors raised bas-relief and high-relief art to an eye-filling richness never surpassed elsewhere; but carried on from masterpieces of luxuriant modeling to riotous confusion and an almost frenzied lavishness. Outside this rather fevered and obtrusive display is that other body of calm, exquisite figuring. It holds to the essential dignity of the human soul without denying sensuous appeal.

In India the historical landmarks, dynasties, conquests, and wars, are comparatively unimportant, as are the divisions by centuries. The basic fact is the Iranian invasion leading to the Vedic religion and philosophy, which in turn fixed the never-shaken caste system. The Buddha Gautama came in the sixth century B.C. and profoundly affected rather than overcame Hinduism as perpetuated by the Brahman caste. Asoka was the one pivotal political figure uniting India, officially recognizing Buddhism. Then after eight centuries the Brahmans ruled again; Buddhism was tolerated and even continuously practiced— though it was in India far less determining as religion and philosophy than it was in China and Japan and Tibet.

The cycle of art history after Asoka is marked by a culmination during the first century B.C., to which the famous sculptured gates at Sanchi have been assigned; by a further rise of Buddhist art, leading into the transitional second century A.D., and so to the "Golden Age" of the third and fourth centuries. Then the emphasis gradually changes back from Buddhist to Brahmanic ideology; the seventh century marks the beginnings of the period known as the Hindu Rebirth.

The specialist in Indian art history divides this stream into almost innumerable currents and schools—which, as a series, can only bewilder the

Head of Bodhisattva. Gandhara. *Victoria and Albert Museum*

art lover coming in search of enjoyment. The Andhra development of the second century, distinguished notably by the reliefs at Amaravati (page 209), should be mentioned by name even in the briefest review, since some authorities mention it as a point of final mastery. It is characterized by a special concession to realism and a sophistication not again attained.

The following "Golden Age" is known as the Gupta, and there is in it a partial return toward restraint, formalism, and tranquillity. Of the following "early medieval" period the famous cliff sculptures at Mamallapuram are the most notable. They are in direct descent from the Gupta style, although a product of a provincial or collateral school, and they deal with Vedic

Head of Buddha. Stone, Borobudur

On the northwest borderland of India, near Afghanistan, there grew up a hybrid art which had influence upon the sculpture of all the Far East, especially in China, Korea, and Japan. At Gandhara the Greeks established an outpost after Alexander's push into northern India. When the tide of Buddhist faith flowed into this borderland and met the cultural stream from the West, there arose a sculptural art in which the Indian elements were modified by Hellenistic clarity. The head shown on page 215 is different from anything in the earlier Hindu repertory of rather full-blown expression. An old Greek spirit of idealism, "purity," and even prettiness has lingered on, has been transformed but not lost in the encounter with Indian opulence. Many of the heads found in the Gandhara region are thus attractive in the classic manner.

On the other hand, the larger relics, mostly reliefs with crowded figures, are generally mediocre or even crude. In them the meeting of East and West results in a blending of late Greek, or Pergamene, ideals of vigorous movement with routine Hindu iconography. Nevertheless, the figures of Buddha had by this time taken on some of the idioms of classic expression—so perfectly fitting with Buddhist serenity and peace—and this modified style was to be carried on into a dozen other lands. It is sometimes said that the now classic Hindu Buddha image shows the great religious teacher modified by the likeness of the Greek Apollo.

rather than Buddhist legendry. From the ninth century on, the Hindu spirit prevailed; sculpture gradually became hard and linear, and finally stereotyped.

Up to the second century A.D. the figure of Buddha had not been permitted in representation. A symbol had always served, for there is a prohibition against images implied in the impersonality of Gautama Buddha's philosophy. But once the image had been accepted, as deity or guide to the seeker, the two main currents of sculptural practice—producing on the one hand the single or dominating reposeful figure, on the other the profuse many-figured decorative reliefs—existed side by side. In the latter, Vedic subjects yielded to Buddhist; then the story elements were mixed. Finally Hinduism again absorbed Buddhism, and the Buddhist legendry merely illustrated as well as others the Brahmanic principles. The single-figure iconography, however, then tended to consist of representations of Siva, Vishnu, Parvati, and others of the non-Buddhist gallery of gods.

Architecture and Painting

The architecture of early India has so generally disappeared that little more than conjecture about it is possible. The oldest surviving monuments are—except for the numerous but featureless houses excavated at Mohenjo-Daro—the Buddhist *stupas* or reliquaries. They are admirably simple in general form—a circular mound with flattened or domed top, set on a terraced base. The decorative effectiveness lies chiefly in the carved balustrades set up around the whole solid "building." At Sanchi, where there is one of the best examples, four richly ornamented gateways are spaced at equal intervals outside the foundation terrace.

After the stupas came those bewilderingly decorated cave-buildings, illogical as architecture, but eloquent of painstaking devotion. Although the "structure" was chiseled out of solid stone, not built up piece by piece, the unimaginative builders copied traditional masonry architecture. Columns are carved with bases, capitals, and architraves just as if all these had been assembled from separately shaped blocks of stone. Beyond the masonry elements, in turn, are members and idioms of a still earlier type of construction in wood. The instance may remind one that the aesthetic mind of India has been controlled by tradition more than that of any other surviving nation.

What the free-standing temples of the earlier periods may have been is conjectured from the remote evidence of the cave-temple copies and from representations in early mural sculptures. The oldest surviving temples in the open are of a type so overloaded that they evoke from the Western observer the sort of surprise and usually distaste voiced by Phillipps.

The illogic of the building and the obscuration of structure under the writhing garment of sculpture seem to remove early Hindu architecture from consideration with significant developments elsewhere. This changed when the Moslems invaded the country, bringing in the rich but controlled Islamic decorativeness; but up to the time of the conquest in the ninth century there were no monuments even remotely approaching in beauty and restraint the Indian-Moslem Taj Mahal.

In India painting has not been one of the supreme arts. At no time apparently did it assume the comparative importance it had in China in the T'ang and Sung periods, or in Western European countries from the time of the early Renaissance. The surviving Indian works are of two sorts mainly: the mural art of the golden era of Buddhism, and the independent painting, miniature in its dimensions and in its delicate virtues, which came to this land with the Moslem conquerors, known as Indo-Persian painting. The frescoes alone call for mention beside Indian

Relief, detail. Borobudur

sculpture—which is, essentially, *the* Hindu art.

In the caves of Ajanta exists the most famous surviving body of Indian painted murals. References in literature indicate that the art had roots reaching back as far as three or four centuries before Christ. There are even fragmentary frescoes attributed to artists of the second or at latest the first century B.C. At Ajanta the series of wall-pictures, found in sixteen of twenty-nine contiguous cave-buildings which had been used as monastic quarters and chapels, give evidence of having been painted at intervals over a period of six centuries from about A.D. 50. The oldest have affinity with the sculptures of the time of the Sanchi gates, and there are middle-period figures which suggest a Hellenic influence of the sort felt in the Gandhara statues; but the greater proportion are assigned to the sixth and seventh centuries.

In these the typical Indian method is found— a method less tonal than linear, of a sort to be placed midway between drawing and painting. The artists, working on a damp plaster ground, relied very much upon outlines, filled the broader

Borobudur relief,
detail.
*Victoria and Albert Museum
photograph*

areas with color washes, and finished off with draftsman's detail. Light and shade were used arbitrarily. The chief virtues are those already noted in connection with Indian sculpture: vigorous design, a highly rhythmical compositional sense, and rich decorative patterning. The subjects are almost uniformly from Buddhist legendry. The figures are voluminous, the "canvases" crowded; the color is gay, and an air of magnificence lies over what is, in intention, religious painting. The compositions range from easel-size to wall pictures twenty feet in width.

There are on the walls of the cave galleries at Sigiriya in Ceylon frescoes not dissimilar in technique and method. They too illustrate how the distinctive Indian fullness and grace spread over from the typical art of sculpture to the less practiced art of painting. That the methods and subject-matter of Indian Buddhist mural art were carried with the religion of Buddha into China has already been noted.

Java, Cambodia, Siam

The Indian civilization of the Golden Age pushed out until it embraced extensive lands to the southeast. In Ceylon the development of art so closely parallels that on the mainland that it may be considered a part of the Indian achievement. And indeed some of the best-known sculpture in the Indian Buddhist tradition, and of the Hindu Rebirth, is in the contribution of this island. But in the less directly affected regions of Siam, Indo-China, and Indonesia, and particularly in Java, the Indian religions, language, and arts penetrated cultures of peoples of another racial origin and resulted in distinctive and important art developments.

The civilizations that thus took over the Sanskrit language and the Hindu-Buddhist sculpture and architecture flourished in general from the ninth to the thirteenth century. One of the main influences was the tide of Buddhism, which long before had swept over Tibet and China, and then into Korea and Japan. But the independent nature of the Malayan and Indonesian manifestation is indicated in the parallel growth of Brahmanic *and* Buddhist cultures. To this day both faiths exist in Bali. In short, the Javan and Cambodian and Siamese cultures—to name the three artistically most important—took on the general form of Hindu civilization but modified the outlines and emphasis in accordance with national character. At Borobudur in Central Java is an eighth-century temple or sanctuary which might be put down by the inexpert eye as an unalloyed masterpiece of Indian architecture. Here are the monumental spread, the terraced masses, the intricately indented and carved forms, the profusion of ornamentation. There are no fewer than four hundred and thirty-six niches for larger statues (as counted by Grousset, the great French Orientalist), and the stupa-form that crowns the structure is echoed in seventy-two smaller reliquary-mounds on one of the several terraces. And yet the composition is, on close study, comparatively simplified, the logic of building less obscured than in Indian architecture. From this it may be inferred that the colonial Indian states yielded little to the mother country in the matters of architectural profusion and magnificence; yet there is that native note of logic and restraint.

The sculpture at Borobudur is highly distinctive; it deserves to be known as one of the world's shrines of the art. The massive Buddha figures are distinguished by the grave, tranquil impressiveness that lies at the heart of one great division of Oriental sculpture; they have an admirable plastic simplicity and largeness, and a spacious impersonality of meaning. The relief panels, in contrast, are warmly human, profusely embroidered, and seductively graceful. At times the artists descend to what would be in other hands dryly literal content. They surround the dominant figure-groups with trees and flowers, houses and ships, pots and umbrellas, in a docu-

Head of Buddha. Stone; Khmer. Siam.
Reginald LeMay Collection

mented narrative which should result in prosaic illustration. But the natural objects are, in general, so conventionalized and so subordinated that they become ornamental accompaniment and enriching display.

The single heads and single figures, when detached from the rhythmic context, are likely to have extraordinary plastic aliveness and fullness. The bodies are in the voluptuous Hindu tradition. The treatment is caressing, rounded, tender. The figure-groups—and these are the heart of the panel-compositions—are handled with consummate decorative artistry. As pattern they have just the right regularity with just the needed variation. The volumes swell and return and

Head of Buddha. Cambodia

this as a special sort, a limited kind of sculpture. Within its limits it is gorgeous and unsurpassed.

Twice again the mature sculpture of the Gupta period was to flower in the eastern Indianized lands: in Cambodia and in Siam, and only a little less luxuriantly in Champa—all parts of the Indo-Chinese Peninsula. The Khmer civilization of Cambodia has left two architectural monuments to testify to the magnificence of its culture, the temple of Angkor Vat and the palace of Angkor Thom, both of a size to memorialize what was, from the ninth to the twelfth century, a mighty empire. The building at Angkor Vat, indeed, is the largest in the world.

The Khmers and the Siamese alike had taken their court language and their religions from India, and the derivation of their art from that of the motherland is evident. But, like the Javanese, they modified the way of statement, the sculptural language, so that their works survive in their own right, as something separate. Someone has summed up the content of their art by saying that they immortalized their own land along with the Hindu heaven.

The great Cambodian wall-reliefs, for instance, could generically belong to no other major development than the Indian. Yet the native taste and inheritance have laid a restraining hand on the swelling forms and the luxuriant patterning. Wall sense is better preserved; an almost curtain-like effect is achieved. The figures are no less profusely multiplied than in India and Java, but they are kept flatter to the stone. The decorative background is more evenly traced over with trees, architectural motives, or geometric floriation. Nonetheless the sense of movement is exceptional; the main narrative drive is kept clear. The miles of such murals include an astonishingly varied pageant of legendary and local life, of religion and history, of battles and hunting and luxurious indulgences, of kings and deities and elephants and snakes, of marriages and funerals and picnics.

There are later, deeper-cut works, more showily elaborated. They are a return to that Indian style that might almost be termed Oriental baroque, bordering on the flamboyant and grotesque. At Angkor Vat there are also high-relief bits that

swell again. The linear melodies weave in and out and then repeat. The panel as a whole vibrates with movement—yet seldom loses its poise. The abstract unity embracing this rich contrapuntal interplay is complete, confined, sustained.

There survive at Borobudur sixteen hundred of these sculptured murals. They are story-scenes of the life of Buddha. It is typical of Indian and of Buddhist art that the sculptors permitted themselves to delight in dancing girls and musicians and lovers no less than in Bodhisattvas and pious pilgrims; in fruits and flowers no less than in symbols of withdrawal and godliness.

If there is a lush sensuousness, a voluptuous grace, over all—so that the luxuriant fullness in the feminine forms is seen in horses and elephants as well as in dancing girls and temptresses, and the swelling soft curve of breast and hip is caught equally in lotus petal and fruit—it is part of the sustained loveliness, at once youthful and mature, of Indian stylization. It marks

Frieze of the Dancers,
detail. Angkor Vat

are endlessly engaging even while amusingly light in spirit. Such is the extraordinary frieze of dancing girls which has been so often reproduced in Western travel-books—and merits an illustration here, as in all inclusive histories of art.

The most profound Khmer achievement is in a distinctive type of head, particularly in representations of the Buddha. There is native as well as Hindu foreshadowing of this iconographic art. There is even a well-recognized "pre-Angkorian style," characterized by a simplicity and summariness of sculptural statement that have more affinity with China than with India. But by the beginning of the tenth century the Hindu tide was running strong—there are legends of the marriage of local princesses or local goddesses to the Brahmans from the north—and thenceforward what is known as the Cambodian type-figure was established. The sculptural culmination came three centuries later, coincident with the building of Angkor Vat.

Seldom has a type-statue been so often repeated in stone with the essential virtue held intact. Every Western museum now has its Cambodian Buddha head, and generally the fragment ranks high even among selected world masterpieces.

Facial expression and plastic means seldom are so beautifully coordinated; the spiritual implications and abstract harmony seldom so happily fused. The face is gentle, relaxed, eloquent of inner tranquillity. Compassion, understanding, release, are implicit. The purely sculptural elements are perfectly shaped to support and confirm the gentle power, the spiritual calm. The massiveness of the volume is retained, but is qualified by the formal tracery of the hair, is tenderly varied in the reticent modeling of the features. This majesty and dignity of the stone, this quiet mastery of plastic orchestration, perfectly externalizes the Buddhist mystic identification with the divine, and diffuses in its own way the inner light.

We may believe, as Grousset suggests, that sculpture in India never quite arrived at such quiet dignity, such comprehending humanism, because there Buddhism insufficiently overcame the Brahmanic impersonality and intellectualism. In any case, Khmer art here touches a summit. In a sense it is more Hindu than the Hindu achievement. At least by lifting the achievement to more humanly comprehensible terms, it may stand to the world as a supreme revelation of the art that is designed to minister to the soul. It is

Head of Buddha. Bronze, Siam, 13th-14th century. *Reginald LeMay Collection*

mystic-human art at its best. It evokes, reveals, tranquilizes, illumines, even while affording the plastic experience purely and intensely.

As much might be said for the Buddhist sculpture that developed in Siam or Thailand; though the figures, and particularly the heads, run through a series of types, and some of these fail to reveal to quite so extraordinary a degree the sweetness and compassion of the Buddha's character. Nevertheless the Siamese exhibit as a whole is, for sheer sculptural excellence, one of the major national expressions in all the "far Indian" territories.

The Siamese story begins in relics brought from India, through Burma, or carved by Indian artists in Siam. These may date from the third century B.C., the time of Asoka in India; though most of the evidence points back to the Gupta, or Golden Age in the mother country, of the fifth century. There were extensive Hindu or Brahman invasions, though Buddhism soon outran Brahmanism in appeal to the native populations of Siam and the other Southeast Asian states. These peoples were already very much mixed racially. About the year 1000 A.D. the Khmers from the south pushed up over most of Siam, and there is a well-marked Khmer school in the sequence of Siamese sculptural styles. But the Thais then pushed down from the north and broke the Cambodian power—a gradual process, lasting from the twelfth to the mid-fifteenth century. They became the true Siamese of later history. That they brought certain artistic idioms with them from their old home in China is witnessed in the like forms of the temple roofs in Siam and China.

In sculpture there is a difference that clearly suggests influences from China. The facial aspect changed, especially in transition of the squared Cambodian face to an insistently oval type. The eyebrows became arched; the nose was narrower. The mouth, too, was less wide, the lips more delicate. Eventually the nose became long and thin, and the whole head took on ovoid form. These mutations, which cover a magnificent range, are suggested in the three Siamese heads illustrated here. A pre-Khmer or "Mon" style —which might be called "Mon-Indian"—had been followed by the invading Cambodian style from the south. It, in turn, was followed by heads with oval faces. The Mon style is suggested in the two illustrations on the page opposite, obviously closer to Indian prototypes; while the Siamese-Cambodian style is beautifully exemplified on page

Head of Buddha. Terra cotta; Mon, Siam;
6th-7th century. *National Museum, Bangkok*

Mask of Buddha. Stucco. Siam.
Reginald LeMay Collection

219. Finally, on page 222 is seen a head in the late ovoid idiom—and in a different medium, bronze. It is worth noticing that among the four illustrations there are examples in four mediums —stone, stucco, terra cotta, and bronze. Mastery such as is shown in any one of these varied pieces might be considered notable. To find so many sorts of mastery is but one more miracle of sculpture as it is found just where the Indian impulse ends.

To the east of Cambodia the Champan people established a kingdom in the early centuries of the Christian era. Although bitter rivals of the Khmers, they similarly absorbed the main features of Indian civilization. And their art is similarly born of a conjunction of native and Brahman elements.

But Champan sculpture, although paralleling the Gupta achievement closely at certain periods, departed further than the Khmer in two direc-

tions. First the Indian figure was simplified and synthesized, at times with a beautiful directness. (Witness the *Parvati* now in the museum at Tourane.) Then the Champan genius struck off into a style heavily massive, primitively squared. It was still unrealistic, strictly formalized; but the stylistic affinities can be thought of only as early Chinese or, in the other time direction, as Polynesian. There seem to be unmistakable surface likeness and an affinity in sculptural method to the Mayan.

But many observers will prefer, in the gallery of Champan art, the more "normal" and animated dancing girls from the relief murals at Tra-Kieu. Here one returns to the main Indian tradition. The seductive figures, at once sinuous and voluptuous, the strict formalization without too great strain on natural truth, the striking sense of movement within plastic repose, the melody and the choral enrichment—all these qualities are picked up, epitomized. They afford a text for fitting concluding words about Indian art. This art never lost the feeling of delight in the sense-world, was ever mellifluent and rhythmical and abundant. The sensuous loveliness could be al-most muted, as was fitting, when the artist entered the chambers of spiritual meditation, when he came soberly into the presence of the Buddha. But almost miraculously the balance was held. Here both the soul and the senses are addressed in one evocative harmony, in one sculptural creation.

Dancer and Musician. Figures on a pedestal stone, c. 7th century, Champa.
Tourane Museum, Viet Nam

XI: BYZANTIUM: THE MARRIAGE OF
EAST AND WEST; EARLY CHRISTIAN ART

ONCE only did the Orient come to Europe bringing lavishly its gifts of magnificent color, rich nonrepresentational patterning, and formal stylization. Once only did the Romanized Western world give up something of its logic and its realism and welcome the sensuous and mystic art of the East, accepting for a time an abundant Graeco-Asiatic garment for its newborn and hardly understood Christianity.

Byzantine art is Oriental Christian art. Spiritually and artistically, classic Rome had died. Despite the emphasis laid by later history upon Rome's part in the birth and development of organized Christianity, it is to be remembered first that Christ and the Jews were Asiatic. The background of Christian legendry, ritual, and art was Syrian, Armenian, Persian, and even Egyptian, before it was Roman. It was not a mere wave of influence that carried the color and formalism of the East over a crystallized Western culture; rather the first great Christian culture, the Byzantine, was essentially Oriental in texture, in origin.[1] In the end it is, geographically,

[1] For the general reader and observer this broad use of the term "Byzantine art" seems more satisfactory than any of the limited applications advocated by groups of specialists. Some critics would exclude the earlier mani-

St. Mark's Church, interior. Venice

an art more of Europe than of Asia, but its beginnings and its style-marks are Asiatic.

The common and convenient metaphor for Byzantine art is that it represents the marriage of East and West; but one must remember that the intermixture of blood and culture had been continuing for ages. Such decorative art as Rome had was produced largely by imported artists. Even Alexandria, from which Rome drew so heavily, had lost its Hellenistic character, had absorbed Egyptian and Near Eastern elements.

When, therefore, the Roman Christian emperor Constantine chose the Greek colonial town of Byzantium on the Bosporus for his new capital in the year 330, he thereby gave a name to an art already distinctive, and did not there and then merge the arts of Rome and the arts of the pagan East. Rather there had already developed, on the Eastern shore of the Mediterranean and beyond, where Christianity already had reached a certain maturity, a culture fertilized by immemorially old artistic traditions. The most notable immediate sources were Coptic Egypt—where so many Christian customs and symbols originated, including the first monastic orders, and the official iconography—Syria with its crossed Hebrew, colonial Greek, and Mesopotamian influences; and Persia.

It is illuminating to remember, too, that this Oriental Christian art is half-brother to the Arabian-Moslem art, which was to start its triumphant march across the Middle East and creep along the lower shore of the Mediterranean, even into Spanish Europe, before Byzantine history was half done. Though Christian Europe was to "cleanse itself" of the gorgeous art of the East after a struggle spanning eight centuries, and return with the Renaissance to Roman realism and scientific rationalism, it

festations, even up to the ninth-century flowering, separating them as merely "early Christian." Others would date the development strictly from the designation of Byzantium as the Christian capital in A.D. 330. It seems more useful to extend the meaning to cover the full range of manifestations within the *spirit* of the new culture, with recognition of its two foundations in the Christian faith and in Graeco-Asiatic art traditions, and of its differences from Greek, Roman, and earlier cultures.

tasted this once the sensuousness and mysticism of the Asia that gave it a Christ. It enjoyed for a space the richer beauty of an art related in spirit to the Persian, the Hindu, the Chinese.

The place of the Byzantine culture in the world stream of art is not easily marked off in terms of geographic boundaries or stylistic independence. In duration it extended from the second or third century A.D. to the thirteenth— a span very long in comparison with the Greek, the Roman, or the later European stylistic periods. It lived on in modified expressions, even in pure form in a minor art, till the twentieth century.

It was geographically decentralized in the earliest centuries; was centralized in Byzantium by decree in 330, and in fact from about 500 on; sent its missionaries and its products in a more or less continuous stream, through all its history, to the Western Christian lands, evoking one notable flowering at Ravenna in the sixth century, and one at Venice and in Sicily in the eleventh and twelfth centuries. It crept into upper Italy and France and remained to enrich the otherwise stark Romanesque style. Although Giotto and the Sienese signaled its departure from Western Christendom, it lived on in the Balkan countries and in Russia. The last phase of it persisted in Russia and Greece down to the opening of the twentieth century, in the icons of the Orthodox Church and in the traditional Russian religious architecture.

Stylistically it is the most difficult of the great world art-cultures to define and bound. It grew out of many arts—may be considered almost mongrel in ancestry—and it mixed with so many crossing currents, racial, national, and religious, that what is to one authority its purest issue is to another a bastard product. The two certainties are the Christian purpose of it and the Oriental surface expression. Its monumental architecture resulted almost exclusively in churches; the subject-matter of its mosaics, illuminations, and sculptures was almost unfailingly taken from Christian Bible stories and imagery. But over the churches, the pictures, and the images alike there was the sumptuous glow of the East; and church structure and representational figure are hardly so significant as the nonrepresentational, ornamental aspect of the art. In Byzantium's (twentieth-century Istanbul) Santa Sophia, in Greek churches and monasteries, in the monuments at Ravenna and Palermo and Venice, in Serbia and Russia, there are the color and abundant patterning of Persia and Cathay.

Thus Byzantine art regathered the creative forces of expression in what had been the Hellenized, then the Romanized, eastern Mediterranean world. It turned back the enfeebled classic current. It crystallized a style in the glowing, formalized, abundant way of Asia.

Egyptian Christians: Coptic Art

The land of the Pharaohs, so close to Palestine, is woven into the background of Old Testament history. But European chroniclers have sometimes been less than fair in their accounts of the large part played by Egyptian Christians in the development of the Church and the Christian culture. The Egyptians introduced first an individual asceticism, then the system of monasteries and monastic orders which was to be a feature of Near Eastern and European religious life through all Christian history; which was, moreover, to nurse the more fragile arts through the centuries of intellectual darkness and social chaos in Europe.

The Egyptian Christians are known as Copts. They and the present-day Abyssinians were branches that were cut off from the Christian polity because of one heresy or another. Their ideas and their imagery were ultimately adjudged unorthodox and pagan, which merely means that other sects or branches gained ascendancy.

In any case, in those decades of the third century when Egypt was yielding up numerous Christian martyrs under official Roman persecution, when the earliest monasteries were being built, when Alexandria was a center of theological discussion, dissension, and creed-fixing, there grew up a Coptic art distinctively beautiful. It was Oriental in its ornamentalism. There are catacomb paintings not dissimilar to those in Rome—it is supposed that Alexandrian artists were among the persecuted Christians who decorated the underground burial and meeting places in the Italian cities. But more significant are the frescoes, particularly those in a monastery in Sakkara. For here one can see a blending of Hellenistic picturing with some of the old Egyptian formalism, as well as a strain of full-patterned decorativeness out of the Middle or Far East—a blending of Greek, African, and Asiatic idioms in service of a faith destined to dominate men's minds through century after century in Western Europe.

The flattened compositions, the stiff iconography, the posteresque largeness, and the full color—these are values common to transitional Roman church murals, Coptic monastery frescoes, and early Byzantine mosaics found in cities on the Syrian coast. But the Egyptian paintings are perhaps the most richly eye-filling, more decoratively built up with patterned areas and intertwining linear motives—in the Eastern manner.

If the painted murals are historically more important, the Coptic textiles and decorative sculpture are for the casual observer the more distinctive and enjoyable mementos out of Christian Egypt. The patterned stuffs are among the most engaging and opulent in the world's whole range of designs upon cloth. Outside that development of which they are an integral part —it is not easy to distinguish Coptic from Syrian and Persian relics of the time—there are only the woven stuffs of the Chinese and Japanese, and the textiles of the Peruvians, to dispute supremacy. There is, one notes, a somewhat similar later expression, widely diffused, and found even today in scattered peasant cultures of Europe. They may perhaps be marked as indirect inheritors of Byzantine crafts traditions, or as survivals of parallel cultures starting from the Iranian and Scythian sources that gave character through Persian intermediaries to the Byzantine.

Here are long ribbon fabrics with intricately interlaced, nearly geometric all-over patterning; or richly bordered open fields sprinkled with perfect formalizations of flower sprays or stags or birds; or oftener, panels geometrically divided, the parts filled with conventionalized monsters,

Seated Divinity with Genii and Flowers. Coptic wool tapestry, 5th century.
Dumbarton Oaks Collection, Washington

trees, and men. The animals—they seem direct descendants of the Scythian ones in their vigor and decorativeness—fill out the spaces with an exuberant ornamental fullness. They are replete with movement but perfectly anchored within the design. They leap and pull and prance, yet are flat to the field. All this is suggested in the design on page 246. The colors are at once delightfully harmonious and gorgeous.

For the beginnings of Christian architecture it is necessary to seek in Syria and Persia. The structure from which the elaborated Byzantine church was to grow was probably a simple square hall domed over, with side buildings buttressing against the thrust of the dome. Its origin seems to have been in Persia, and there is a possibility of prototypes in Armenia, although scholars disagree about the evidence. The finest early examples have recently come to light in Syria. In all these regions Christian communities were worshiping in churches while their Roman brothers were still meeting clandestinely underground.

Eastern dome and Eastern vault therefore became the first standard structural elements for Christian houses of worship. The Mesopotamian barrel-vault played a large part in architectural evolution. Even into the twentieth century the Orthodox Church has held to the original cruciform construction with four barrel-vaulted sections pushed out from the domed crossing.

The early Christian churches in Syria and Egypt and Mesopotamia, however, took a wide variety of forms, a few that come within the definition of basilica, but most in varying interpretations of the Eastern idioms. Antioch remained closer to Rome and Alexandria in spirit, a fact also attested by its floor mosaics. In other cities the vaulted construction with domes crystallized in the system that made possible

The Miracle at Cana.
Coptic ivory, 6th century.
Victoria and Albert Museum

the great monument of Santa Sophia at Byzantium. In incidental decorative features also the Syrian churches are typical—blind arcades and occasional inset patterned panels. The column was no longer a main structural element as in Greek and Roman building. Already a long step had been taken toward those unbroken walls on which the Byzantine mosaics were to be spread.

The Syrian monuments of early Christian architecture are not intrinsically of exceptional merit. But they are often pleasingly rhythmic, even majestic. In Istanbul or Athens, in Russia or Spain, you will find churches in the line of descent from these Syriac-Persian vaulted structures. And through the Byzantine the influence came to Western Europe, shaping certain salient features of the Romanesque.

The framework of the new Christian culture was thus being constructed in the East while the West was officially proscribing and persecuting the followers of Christ. Then suddenly an emperor, with true Roman shrewdness, recognized that the only possible way to union lay in the Christian faith and went over to the persecuted. He legalized the Church and laid the foundations of a new "holy Roman Empire" over the territory upon which his old and very unholy one had been progressively going to pieces.

Byzantium Becomes Constantinople

It was in 330 that Constantine transferred the capital to Byzantium, then an unimportant Greek town at the easternmost point of Southern Europe, whence one could look across the straits to Asia. It was a strategic crossroads of trade and tourist routes, and a natural center for an empire designed to amalgamate the Eastern and Western worlds. As a matter of fact most of the West was soon to be lost, taken over by the Northern barbarians. There remained an Eastern Roman Empire, at a time when Rome itself was surrendered to Goths and Vandals. This Eastern Empire really was Roman only in its name and in its imperial ideology. Its language already was substantially Greek; its arts largely Asiatic.

In Rome and Italy, until the legalizing of the new religion, there necessarily had been no Christian architecture. The catacombs had provided hidden meeting places. Sometimes a wealthy convert opened a room or hall in his palace for congregations. When Constantine signed his edict the ban was lifted, and the need for great meeting halls arose. It was then that the basilica, which had been the Roman law court and trading center, was hastily adapted to the purpose.

The old temples were useless, were too cramped. Christianity was the first great religion demanding covered space for large congregations of worshipers. The basilica seemed made to order. The main hall became the nave (symbolically a ship, or *navis*, bearing the believers to the haven of salvation). The apse needed only a table altar to remind the worshipers of the sarcophagus-top which had served for the ceremony of the mass in the catacombs; to these, choir, pulpits, and other features were presently added.

This basilica form was copied in many a distant Roman colony. It was taken by Helena, mother of Constantine, to Palestine, where she caused to be built in classic fashion the Church of the Nativity, over the spot at which Jesus had been born. But at Jerusalem the Church of the Holy Sepulchre was on the combined plan of basilica and Eastern domed church; and throughout the countries bordering on the Holy Land the dome-and-vault church became the commoner model.

Rome had had, too, what is sometimes termed early Christian painting. The catacomb frescoes are little more than amateurish reflections of the rather dull sort of thing to be seen still at Pompeii, interesting as illustration or historical document. Toward the end of the period of persecutions, in the third and early fourth

centuries, there were occasional essays more ambitious and not without artistic merit. In general it may be said that all this tag-end Roman art was dropped from the luggage of Constantine the Great while he was on his way from Rome to Byzantium. What he brought to the new capital was a name—the city was to be known as Constantinople, until the conquering Moslems gave it another name eleven centuries later—and an imperial scale of planning, both political and material.

Constantine personally led in the work of organizing Christendom in one polity before the mortar of his new capital was dry. At the Council of Nicaea in 325 he as emperor, although not yet baptized, presided over discussions that fixed the official creed of Christianity. There and then he pushed the Christian Roman Empire onto the world stage. Soon after he lost some minor churches that had too firmly made up their minds about the nature of God, the divinity of Christ, and ritualistic matters. But he had made the Empire an entity, had united Christians from now beleaguered Rome to Palestine and Persia. He had officially sanctioned the strongest elements and most popular practices out of Eastern and Western pioneer churches: the priesthood, a limited canonization of saints, symbolic participation in the ritual of the wine and the bread. He also had introduced into the church plan the ideas of imperialism, autocracy, and intolerance toward any unorthodoxy.

Architecture: Santa Sophia

It was left to a successor of two centuries later, Justinian, to deck Constantinople out in a splendor fit for the wealthiest city in the world, which had become also an imperial capital. He built Santa Sophia, that incredibly rich monument of Byzantine architecture and decoration, as one unit in a capitol plan. He made the city a center of manufacture and export of those works of art that were to go forth and leaven the sluggish expression of reawakened Europe. Perhaps his empress, Theodora, had something to do with his patronage of the arts and crafts; she had in youth been an artist of a sort, an actress.

Santa Sophia, Istanbul; 6th century with later minarets

It is just as well to pick up the story of actual art products here at the flood, when Santa Sophia was opened, in 537. The structure, at present a Turkish mosque, has for ages been considered the outstanding monument of the Byzantine building art. It is somewhat less than typical in the matter of its display of true Eastern mosaic-work—its walls being more than typically broken up by arcades, galleries, and windows— but it is pre-eminent in its largeness, its breath-taking engineering, and its sumptuous variety of effect. In its own day it was rivaled by the nearby Church of the Holy Apostles, an equally luxuriant expression, but on a simpler constructive system that could be, and was, widely copied in Europe. These two buildings, moreover, should be surrounded, in the imagination, with the complex of regal palaces, colonnades, baths, galleries, administrative halls, gardens, and other apanages of imperial grandeur which once covered the palace grounds from the present church to the sea.

Santa Sophia somewhat belies its name, which means primarily Church of the Holy Wisdom. It is rather a dream come true for a surfeited emperor than a sober expression of spiritual wisdom. It constitutes a gesture to God in the manner of Roman wealth and display, a gesture made at a time when the artistic riches of the East were ready to the builders' hands. The meditative, quietly adorational spirit of Christian worship is somewhat missed. But it turns out to be every man's opportunity to feast upon munificent visual allurements.

More than most Eastern churches, Santa Sophia capitalizes on its structural features, even dramatizes its engineering. The immense domed space—it is, as usual in the old Orient, the interior alone that is eloquent—seems to rest under a floating shell. To this the galleries and arches seem to lift effortlessly. The structure is, as a matter of fact, a superb feat of vaulting.

Santa Sophia is essentially the early cruciform church raised to titanic proportions. There is the same central dome over a square. There are the same "arms" in four directions supporting the outward thrust. The same vaulting in a variety of forms is over all.

It is worth studying out, even in photographs, the way in which the dome of Santa Sophia is carried—its drum resting on four curvilinear triangles of a form known as pendentives, the lower points of these resting on the four piers at the corners of the central square. At all four sides such a domed structure must be buttressed. Here two of the arms are apselike; the main hall extends under half-domes, which themselves rest upon a further complex of apses. At each of the other two sides the pendentives form an immense arch. The wall bounded by the curvilinear arch is generously windowed. Below it is pierced by superposed arcades, beyond which are galleries in the buttressed side-buildings. This illustrates perfectly, with instructive variations, that Eastern system of dome-and-vault building which is the very antithesis of classic post-and-lintel construction. The simple diagrams of pendentives here afford a key to the structural system.

But if the engineering is stupendously impressive, reducing massive and weighty elements to a seeming lightness, it is the decorative profusion that the more certainly evokes amazement and wonder. It is dazzling and inconceivably intricate in view of the simple general impression. It has not the unity of color and gold and fire of some minor Byzantine monuments. It is rather the imperial capital of Christendom frankly displaying its wealth in the large, ostentatiously spreading a feast for the eye.

And indeed the pagan temples of the entire Near East were sacked to provide Byzantium with these porphyry columns and varicolored marbles. Procopius, in his chronicles of the court of Justinian, exclaimed: "Who can tell of the splendor of the columns and marbles with which the church is adorned? One would think that one had come upon a flowery meadow; one marvels at the purple hues of some and the green of others. . . ." The same observer remarks: "It is impossible to describe with accuracy the treasures of gold and silver plate and gems which the Emperor has presented to the church." And he goes on to tell that the revenues of three hundred estates were necessary for the mere routine upkeep of the church. He also names the architects, Anthemius of Tralles and Isodorus of Miletus.

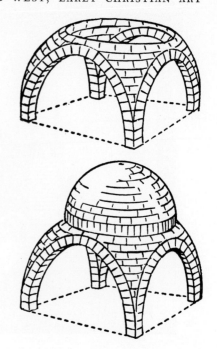

The pendentive. Above, pendentives over a square area, prepared to take a dome. Below, the dome supported

But Procopius gives the emperor prime credit: by selecting "among the men of this profession those most capable of interpreting his lofty conception," he "succeeded in making this church a work of incomparable beauty." Justinian is reported to have said when he entered Santa Sophia on the day of dedication, "Glory to God, who has found me worthy to complete so great a work—and to excel thee, O Solomon!"

The decorative profusion is over a good deal of the space on interior walls, columns, friezes, and doors. It is possible to pick out panels, capitals, and bandings that illustrate the Oriental artist's perfect mastery of all-over ornament and space-filling pattern. The mural enrichment put in by Christian artists and covered over by the Moslems, and finally rediscovered in the twentieth century, is described later on.

There is, however, one cardinal principle but poorly illustrated in Santa Sophia. The Eastern subordination of individual structural members is, at its best, as seen elsewhere, followed by a

Santa Sophia, interior

decorative gain. In churches from Persia and Greece to Ravenna and Palermo there is a frank suppression of incidental columns, cornices, and edgings, to clear the walls for surface decoration. The declared logic of structure gives way before a logic of the unity of decorative lining. To the classicist and the rationalist, this is deplorable. To the lover of glowing garments of color and rhythmic patterning, it is more than justifiable. It led to one of the most glorious manifestations of colorfulness in the whole of world architecture.

Architecture in the West, and the Art of Mosaic

In the Tomb of Galla Placidia at Ravenna and in parts of the glorious churches there, in the chapels at Palermo, and in bits that may be separated by the eye in the Greek monasteries, in Monreale outside Palermo, and in St. Mark's at Venice—in all these one can feel the smoothing of the surfaces to receive the all-important coating of mosaic. Arch flows into wall, pendentive leads

into drum, drum into cupola, with least possible interruption to the eye. The continuous rich lining is the protected feature.

This preparation of the interior surfaces of the building to take easily and effectively a coating of gold and color and mural design is no longer uniformly condemned in the West as an illogical obscuring of structural truth. Rather, there is recognized a different logic, which accepts the mosaic as typically a lining material, thin, flexible, best seen in large areas, and sufficiently precious to warrant the shaping of engineering features to permit its most effective use. In the best manifestations the structural method is less obscured than frankly shaped to the purpose, that is, smoothed down, given a certain flowing unity.

The arches and vaults, to be sure, are there in outline. But they are softened rather than accented at the edges and corners, blunted at the junctures. The eye still sees the larger architectural forms, subconsciously is aware of the complex of weight-bearing elements, of thrust and strain and support; but it is satisfied because the

St. Apollinare in Classe

designers have so frankly declared their decorative purpose, sheering the walls, eschewing columns and frames, molding the structural body to receive the flowing garment. Mosaics added to buildings without this special preparation and declaration are, of course, illogical and superficial. Rounding and smoothing of structure are presupposed. That is the reason why so much modern mosaic, merely an addition to architecture, is unsatisfactory.

At Ravenna on the east coast of Italy, the tomb of Galla Placidia is a nearly perfect miniature example of Byzantine interior architecture and decoration. Built in the mid-fifth century, it antedates Santa Sophia; it is indeed the earliest of surviving full-mosaicked structures. It is perfectly the cruciform building, with dome at center— though the exterior shell over the dome is square, which might be Eastern, or due to Lombard influence at some time of restoration. Inside, above a marble wainscoting, every inch is lined with mosaics. Some parts are pictorial, some traced with abstract or floral ornament. The ceiling is

studded with stars in a field of blue and green. The effect as one goes from the barrenly rugged atmosphere of the brick exterior into this enchanting roomful of color is indescribable. It is, fortunately, only one of the experiences of the exotic richness of Byzantine art possible within a few hours for the visitor to Ravenna.

How art came so richly to this malarious city in an East Italian swamp is a romantic story that cannot be told in any detail here. The malaria helped. For Ravenna was the refuge of those last emperors of the Western Roman Empire, who were harried by the Goths, Vandals, and Huns from the north. Rome lay exhausted, its wealth and its best blood drained away, its morality sunk to worse than barbarian level, its arts run out. Probably the heathen from the north were bringing a manliness and honesty and semi-primitive vigor that were necessary to the regeneration of the Latins. In any case, emperor after emperor had had to compromise with circumstances or run away. Ravenna, a Venice-like island town, defended by water and swamps, was a natural

The Empress Theodora and Her Retinue. Mosaic, St. Vitale, Ravenna

haven. At the worst, too, a hard-pressed ruler and his court could embark there and shortly be in Constantinople under the protection of the brother-emperor who ruled the Eastern Roman Empire—though at about this time even Constantinople was forced to pay tribute to Attila the Hun.

Galla Placidia was the sister of Honorius, one of the emperors who had been, figuratively speaking, chased across Italy. Her gemlike tomb is the only surviving important relic of the first imperial period at Ravenna, when Honorius borrowed native Byzantine artists to decorate the new capital in rivalry with Constantinople. There are descriptions of magnificent churches of this fifth-century flowering, but the larger buildings have been destroyed. Of the second imperial period, however, of about the time of Justinian, there are several surpassing monuments. Ravenna had then, after going the sad way of all Italy, been reclaimed, this time by the Eastern Empire. An exarch or imperial governor had taken residence there, and engaged in extensive building enter-

prises. Two of the immense churches were constructed on the basilica plan, but were decorated in true Byzantine brilliancy: St. Apollinare Nuovo, and St. Apollinare in Classe, the latter outside the town, at what used to be the port. A third great church, St. Vitale, not only was decorated in the Eastern way, but was constructed in typical Byzantine fashion, around a central dome supported by a complex of arches and half-domes.

What magnificent mosaics the imperial artists spread over all available walls may be guessed from the portions that have outwitted time and the destructive proclivities of man. Nowhere in the three churches is there the extravagant glitter of Santa Sophia, or the more unified brilliancy of the nearby mausoleum of Galla Placidia and the faraway churches of Palermo. The two basilicas, of course, in the nature of classic building, offer only limited surfaces to the mosaicist; and St. Vitale is more broken up structurally than the usual Eastern church—and has been despoiled, moreover, of most of its original decoration. Nevertheless, there are rewarding panels and friezes, and occasionally a complete undefiled apse.

In the basilica at Classe the apse and the wall above are adorned with a mosaic composition that sets forth its message with complete lucidity but still remains superb decoration rather than picture. The composition is kept flat, the first requirement of mural design, and the whole has the aspect of rich patterning. Yet here are woven into one composition St. Apollinare leading his flock, an emblematic representation of the Transfiguration, a double procession of sheep going up from Bethlehem and Jerusalem, and a crowning representation of Christ and the four Evangelists. The figuring is as naïve and formal as that on the textiles of the East.

In St. Apollinare Nuovo the long friezes, running the length of the nave, are most impressive. The saints and virgins and martyrs of the processions are conceived as befits an imperial court: they wear rich clothes and bear costly gifts. And the sumptuousness carries over into the mosaic technique.

In St. Vitale the few independent picture-compositions are equally rich in effect; but more comment has been evoked by the fact that here the divinity claimed by secular rulers is made manifest. Not only is the Emperor Justinian set out with a halo, but the Empress Theodora wears one too—and very handsomely. Again the design is flat, the picturing unrealistic, and the decorative effect opulent and glittering—as may be partly seen, partly guessed, from the illustration on page 235.

Mosaic is an art wherein small pieces of stone are set in cement. The method makes exactness of drawing difficult, tends away from realism and the sort of linear niggling that had become standard with the Roman and late Greek painters. It encourages a flat, formalized treatment; and by its resources of brilliant color it perfectly played into the hand of the Oriental decorator intent upon sensuous richness and colorful glow as well as upon religious symbolism.

Beyond the colorfulness and tapestry-like effect there is noticeably combined an angularity of figure with a roundness of handling, due partly to the medium, partly to the bent of the Eastern mind toward formalization rather than imitation. The same carelessness of natural appearance, the same near-abstraction standing for the man represented, the same naïve disregard for background and shadows, are seen in the manuscript illuminations of the era.

The Byzantine mosaics afford a glowing pleasure unique in the history of art. They bring the lavish color and sumptuous patterning of the Orient to Europe in a few monuments surviving from that day when a merging of the European and Asiatic worlds was dreamed of and fought for. If here the monuments at Ravenna have been lingered over, that is not to imply that the mosaic art did not flourish at Constantinople, its source. But the more glorious flowering there occurred later, as is chronicled at the end of the section on Byzantium's golden age.

The illuminations or miniatures in early Christian manuscripts are endlessly engaging. Here there is a considerable body of Hellenistic and transitional work before the Byzantine formalism and "stiffness" prevail; then a long period of typical Byzantine practice; and finally the gradual return toward illustrationalism. But the subject belongs rather to the chapters on medieval art and the treatment of art in the monasteries.

Byzantium's Golden Age

It was the opulent capital, Constantinople, that sent westward the main stream of ivories, colored enamels, illuminations, textiles, and goldsmith's work that was to enrich many a minor court and decorate many a major and minor church far from the Golden Horn; to revolutionize or transform, too, the European conception of the arts until the return to classicism at the period of the Renaissance. There were other great producing centers, for the Byzantine Empire was far-flung, and scores of local administrators, bishops, and lesser monarchs encouraged the arts. Salonika, Antioch, Trebizond, Nicaea, Ephesus, and the cities of Crete afford separate histories of the Byzantine arts.

For Constantinople the years from 330 to the death of Justinian in 565 had been a first Golden

Age. The building art and the decorative crafts had flowered in the Church of Santa Sophia, in the Church of the Holy Apostles, and in the surrounding lavish palace groups. There the magnificence of Roman ostentation had been married to Eastern color and formalism—a much more satisfactory spouse, artistically speaking and in the light of history, than had been naturalistic classic design.

Efforts had been made, nevertheless, to import the masterpieces of classic art and to revive its spirit. Theodosius the Great transferred the Olympic Games to Constantinople in the late fourth century, along with appropriate antiques in the way of statuary and vases. But the Oriental spirit refused to give way. Some say that the Greeks themselves, after their long retirement from creative endeavor during the Hellenistic and Roman eras, had come awake under Eastern nourishment of the spirit, and must themselves be credited as the leading artists of Byzantium. It is known that the streams of influence from Persia—that too-little-recognized fountain of artistic riches—continued to flow through that Golden Age. At Constantinople the forms of Byzantine art had been definitely and unmistakably set, and countless masterpieces had been created, by the mid-sixth century.

Between this and a second Golden Age there was a period of difficulties. Reaction set in, politically and to a lesser extent artistically. Perhaps it was only the inevitable pause that marks the period of paying for luxurious splendor, extravagant overbuilding and overexpansion. There was trouble in the West, where the barbarian forces were overrunning great areas of the Empire and crystallizing their own rival state. To the east the blazing fire of Islam had spread from Arabia to Persia, and had burned away from the Empire the provinces of Syria and Egypt. Even Greece was invaded by heathens of another sort. And the Bulgars, having decimated a Byzantine army—and made a king's drinking-cup of the emperor's skull—swept down to the very walls of Constantinople itself. The threat was removed presently and pleasantly when a succeeding Bulgar king came over to Christianity. In that way too a threatening Russia came under the sway of the Byzantine Empire, and an enormous new field was opened to the Byzantine arts, a field where the style would longest persist.

Now the emperors somehow pushed through to a new beginning, drove away the Moslems, who also had been knocking at the capital's gates, and gradually reclaimed great regions lost to hostile powers. A.D. 843 is the date generally set as the beginning of the second Golden Age and a new beginning for Byzantine art. In the interval, however, there occurred a war over art which is unique in history. What is known as the Iconoclast controversy—the idol-breakers' war—was fought with words, prohibitions, and manifestoes, and finally led to political overturns and actual military actions and bloodshed. Perhaps never before had pictures led men to strap on mail and take up swords.

There had been for many centuries a strain of nonrepresentational art out of the North Asiatic source-land, by which Persia had been strongly influenced through all phases of its art, except in those times when the early world-conquerors modeled their culture upon that of the Babylonians. Abstract motives and near-abstractions based on floral forms were the chief elements of ornamental design; animals entered much more largely into representational arts than did the human figure; even Greek and Roman obsession with the human body failed to affect the Persians profoundly. When humans did appear in picturing, the Oriental habit was to formalize them into hardly more than heraldic emblems and plastic motives. Art was impersonal, stripped of the reality of man's material, anatomical world.

This predisposition toward abstraction and impersonality in art had from the start gone along with the Byzantine way of thinking. It is eloquently evident in the early textiles, sculptured capitals, and manuscript illuminations. Not only does the general disposition of the various elements in paintings and mosaics illustrate it; the very figures in murals and icons have given up their humanness and sentimental naturalism—so much so that they have sometimes seemed to the realists "scarecrows" and caricatures.

Then when Mohammed made his religion out of a miscellany of Hebrew, Christian, and Persian theology and custom, he took over the Mazdean and Hebraic prohibition of imaging. Some say that the Moslems, parading this with other superior cultural conceptions, frightened the emperors of the Byzantine Empire into taking sides with the iconoclasts within their own church. The rulers simply recognized a schism which long had existed, for powerful influences had set themselves against figurative art long before. Chiefly there was agitation against the monasteries that produced a great deal of the minor art. There are even those who believe that the prohibition was calculated primarily to cripple the growing power of the monastic element in the church. Still others give the emperors—Eastern in origin by now—credit for sincerely believing that any representation of the Divine in human form was impious.

On this point the great twentieth-century historian Josef Strzygowski quotes Ter-Mkrttchian's report that there "arose a party which opposed the veneration of pictures as an un-Christian innovation." He quotes also an early historian of Anatolia who in the seventh century wrote that "a great Synod was held in Caesarea, and the painting of pictures in the House of God was sanctioned. Hence the painters grew arrogant, and wished to place their art above all the other church arts." To which the artist-monks sincerely replied: "Our art is . . . the means of enlightening old and young alike, whereas but few can read the Holy Scriptures."

The actual order against images, in 717, had more than artistic and religious consequences. In the East picture-making continued, sometimes in more or less open defiance of the higher powers, sometimes clandestinely; though more energy than before went into illuminated manuscripts, which could be easily hidden, and less into murals. But there was a furious destruction of mosaics, frescoes, and icons throughout the Empire.

The political results, however, concerned the whole delicate relationship of Byzantium and Rome. There had been growing a division of interest between the reviving Western Empire and the troubled Eastern. Christian Rome had got the forms of its art largely from the East. Now in effect the East was repudiating what it had imposed upon the West. Both parties seized upon the question of "idolatrous" art as a convenient issue, and actually fought in the field over it. By 800 the Roman Church had completed the split from the Eastern, thenceforth Orthodox, Church; and through his astute political alliance with Charlemagne the Pope could defy any further attempt to subjugate the West. As a consequence, representational art was to be fully developed as a legitimate prop of religious faith in all the Latin and Germanic countries.

In the East the iconoclasts prevailed for a little more than a century. What treasures of art were then destroyed no one will ever know. The destruction of Catholic art at the time of the Reformation in Flanders and Holland and Germany can hardly have been more catastrophic. But there was one offsetting gain, particularly for Europe: great numbers of artists and craftsmen, more true to art than to the letter of church law, migrated to the centers of Western spiritual and cultural endeavor. Doubtless large quantities of ivories, enamels, icons, and manuscripts were then transported to the Western countries.

When the iconoclasts at last lost their hold on the Eastern ruling power—representational imaging was again legalized in the Orthodox Church in 843—there was an immediate flowering of the typical Byzantine arts. This was the beginning of the so-called second Golden Age. As regards the Byzantine capital, the period is generally dated from 843 to the sack of Constantinople by the brother-Christians of the Latin Church in 1204: three and one-half centuries of almost uninterrupted production of works of art and luxury. Prosperity returned, the sumptuous and extravagant court was re-established, and all the arts flourished.

Again there were the magnificent imperial palaces and the gorgeously decorated churches. The mosaic art was carried on to more spectacular and memorable achievements, always in Christian mythology and symbolism, with the golden background or underlay now standard. As a matter of fact the "later" mosaics as seen in Santa Sophia in Constantinople (or Istanbul) date from the ninth century, when the iconoclast prohibition

St. Mark's Church, Venice: most colorful of Byzantine monuments in the West;
11th century, with later additions

was lifted, to the twelfth century or possibly the fourteenth. As of 1900 the murals had been hidden for hundreds of years under coatings of whitewash or plaster applied by the Moslems when they captured the church in 1453. Gradually, since the nineteen-twenties, picture after picture has been uncovered and so far as possible restored. D. Talbot Rice, most eminent of British scholars in the field of Byzantine art, wrote in 1954, concerning a *Deesis* in the south gallery, that "it is a work of very rare beauty; to the writer in any case it appears as perhaps the most lovely Byzantine mosaic that has come down to us." He suggested a date soon after 1160 and he noted that it represented a "new manner" then introduced.

In Constantinople there were other churches gloriously enriched with mosaic murals. One of the most consistent surviving examples is the Church of the Chora, where the generally clear but sometimes battered pictures are very late, probably of the fourteenth century. (After that, mural painting in general supplanted the art of the mosaic.) The building marked as the finest remaining example of Byzantine mosaic decoration is, however, a church at Daphne in Greece, where the picturing dates from 1100. Many other notable monuments survive in Greece. It was in the late period, during the "renaissance" that lasted from the twelfth to the fourteenth century, that a new wave of influence went out from Byzantium to Italy and Sicily. Especially well known to travelers in southern Europe are the mosaics in St. Mark's Cathedral in Venice, and those at Monreale near Palermo and at Cefalu, in Sicily. At the same time Byzantine artists and craftsmen decorated churches in Kiev and other cities of Russia.

St. Peter.
Enamel, Byzantine.
*Metropolitan Museum
of Art*

Enamels and Icons

The enamels of Byzantium capture the color and vigor of the larger arts to an extraordinary degree. The colors are lustrous and brilliant, though on occasion they are brought to the subtlest balance of nuances, or are misted over and almost muted. The technique, unlike that of European miniature painting, lends itself to broad effect and formalized rhythmic orchestration. The backgrounds are suppressed; the plastic penetration is slight. But nothing could be more vital, vigorous, and elegant than these miniature enamel portraits and icons and decorative medallions.

The Byzantine enamels follow upon an earlier Persian development, which, however, had been distinguished by a lesser mastery. The technique had been perfected in Persia, though the craft had been known to several more ancient civilizations in both East and West. The first known reference to enameling is said to be that of Philostratus, a Greek philosopher of the third century, who reported that "the barbarians of the regions of the ocean are skilled in fusing colors on heated brass, which become hard as stone, and render the ornament thus produced durable."

In the Byzantine work the divisions between colors are in gold line. Gold wire was flattened and fastened, edge-on, to the metal background, forming the outlines of the design. Then the separated areas were filled with enamel (glass powder worked to a paste) and fired. When the surface was polished, the effect was as lustrous as porcelain-painting, but with its own characteristic body-deep coloring and posteresque conventionalization.

In general this was an accessory art; the enamel plaques and medallions were used for enrichment of crowns, book-covers, icon-frames, and altar-fronts—as seen today in the famous Palo d'Oro in St. Mark's at Venice. There are, too, independent jewel-like objects such as the so-called Beresford Hope Cross in the Victoria and Albert Museum. Sometimes the medallions decorated royal or ecclesiastical robes. Again the reliquaries—the coverings for such sacred relics

St. John.
Enamel, Byzantine.
*Metropolitan Museum
of Art*

as bits of the True Cross or saints' bones—were natural settings for this sort of sumptuous bejeweling. But today in the museums there are more of the enamels to be seen separated from their original background and purpose. In no way are they unworthy when facing the world alone, when judged for their self-contained aesthetic merits. The notable series at the Metropolitan Museum of Art in New York is a sheer joy to the eye; examples shown here are the *St. Peter* and the *St. John* medallions.

If the enamels have a certain affinity with the glowing Byzantine mosaics, the small icons are similarly a miniature form not distantly related to both painted fresco and mosaic mural. There were, by the way, small portable mosaic pictures. But the examples surviving today are hardly sufficient to demand extended attention. The one illustrated at the bottom of page 242, in the Victoria and Albert Museum, is especially instructive, showing the elongated and rather dehumanized figures, the unrealistic background, and the all-over ornamentalism. It may be illuminatingly compared with the graceful treatment of the subject by Fra Angelico, shown on page 328.

The name "icon"—meaning merely "image," from the Greek *eikon*—has been narrowed in the public mind to designate the small portraits of sacred personages set up by the faithful of the Orthodox Church as objects of devotion or aids to worship. As a matter of fact an icon can be very large indeed, possibly a panel to be hung on a wall in place of a directly painted mural, possibly a panel to be hinged to others to form an *iconostasis* or altar screen in the church. But the small portable painting, of a size convenient for placing on room walls, is the typical thing.

The usual method of making icons was this: a wooden panel was prepared with a coating of gesso (a mixture of glue or size and what we call plaster of Paris); the surface was polished, then gilded; a tempera paint (with egg yolk as binder) was used for the actual painting. The main outlines were then cut through to the gilt, adding a golden glint to the colors. It is scarcely necessary to say that in the course of a dozen centuries there were innumerable variations in technique and materials. The underlay of gilt was not always applied, but gilt paint was more freely used than it was in other types of picture. The

St. Nicholas the Wonder Worker. Icon, Novgorod School, c. 1300. *Private Collection*

At right: *Annunciation.* Portable mosaic. *Victoria and Albert Museum*

that of a religious reminder. One does not, therefore, expect innovations of subject-matter or sudden changes in style. Nevertheless there is a well-marked transition from the early Byzantine stiffness to a more humanized conception of the characters portrayed. Some authorities are of the opinion that Byzantine conventions were overcome in the East, and especially in Russia, before the Italians in the West, especially at Siena, brought a new tenderness and grace to religious art in the late thirteenth and early fourteenth centuries. One can see how icon-like is the gloriously colorful *Madonna and Child* by Duccio in the National Gallery, London, and also how the early austerity and rigidity of style have given way to a flowing grace and a Franciscan humanism. These qualities are apparent even in the black-and-white illustration on page 319.

The most interesting phases of the history of icon-painting concern the art in Russia. The

"standard" bright coloring seems to have come in as early as the twelfth century. Modern collectors think of the metal covering or "mask" of the portable icon as a typical feature, but this sort of enrichment was a relatively late innovation. The best painting, as such, needed no such heightening of effect as the pierced metal masks afford.

"Icon" or "image" suggests a portrait—though the earliest "portraits" were hardly more than symbols, stiff and dehumanized to a degree—but the subject-matter soon included scenes from Christian legend and story. From the twelfth century to the seventeenth the output of the central Constantinopolitan and the provincial schools must have been enormous. Gradually the center of activity shifted to Russia.

The purpose of the Orthodox icon is primarily

Theophanes the Greek:
The Ascension.
Icon, Novgorod School,
Russia, 14th century

golden age there is considered to have been the period from about 1200 to the fifteenth century. The Novgorod school was then supreme. To Novgorod went Theophanes the Greek, whose name is best known among all masters of icon-painting. After him, and probably his pupil, was Andrea Rublyov, a native Russian. A certain number of icons—as of wall paintings—attributed to these artists survive in Russia to this day, and their style is shown to have been linear, rhythmical, and bright in coloring, with the figures elongated and impressive. Soon afterward Moscow became the center of production, and in the sixteenth century, in the reign of Ivan the Terrible, the Muscovite schools were flooding Russia with icons that were appealing and ornamentally rich, but without the master touch. Even up to the twentieth century and the Communist revolution, icon-making continued, with recognizable marks from the early Byzantine style apparent.

Sculpture in the large was not an outstanding Byzantine art. A certain amount of architectural sculpture—capitals and ornamental columns—may be said to be in the round. But perhaps on second view each piece may prove to be a sort of juncture of several reliefs. The average capital is solidly round, with the typical Byzantine blunted roundness; but from the point of view of decoration it is one more place for a low-relief composition.

A World Peak in Ivory Carving

The deeply incised but carefully unified panel-carving more often associated with the Moslem flowering, which culminated in the arabesque, was originally a Persian-Syrian-Christian art. In Coptic Egypt, in Syrian monasteries, in Santa Sophia in Constantinople, in the Ravenna churches, at Monreale and Palermo, similar richly carved friezes and capitals and pilaster-

Christ Crowning Romanus and Eudoxia. Ivory.
Bibliothèque Nationale, Paris

panels are to be found. The vitality combined with intricacy, the vigorous movement combined with delicate tracery, persist through an extraordinarily long range of examples.

But the unique Byzantine achievement within the art of sculpture is in the small ivories. It may be that the sentiment that discouraged the making of images precluded the cutting of monumental statues; [2] but there was no such prohibition of miniature reliefs. The typical Eastern

---

[2] There are a few exceptions, notably a colossal statue of an emperor, with later arms and legs, now at Barletta in southern Italy, and a high-relief group decorating an outer corner of the Treasury of St. Mark's, Venice; and there are numerous transitional examples, of the time when artists tried to assimilate Roman and Hellenistic portraiture to Oriental method. But the idea of monumental sculpture simply did not prevail.

flatness is here continued. (It will be remembered that the Scythian animals, in the rare instances when they are in the round, are partly flattened toward a wafer-form.) Here too the characteristic Byzantine formalism rounds the outlines, places the subject-elements with decorative near-symmetry. Among the accessories are typical Byzantine architectural elements: the round arch, the column traced over with abstract patterning, the arabesque panel.

The ivory carvings, indeed, are perfectly in the spirit of the enamels and the icons. There is the same mastery of space-filling, of melodic disposition of figures, of answering ornamental rhythms; something, too, of the same elegance and—insofar as this uncolored medium can be said to have it—colorfulness.

The ivories, like the enamels, were considered oftener as accessory decorations than as independent works of art. Although they were common as semi-independent diptychs and triptychs for altars or private chapels, they usually ornament bookcovers, caskets, even thrones. The plaques, sometimes obviously single leaves detached from triptych or polyptych, are found today in all the larger museums, and in great abundance in the treasuries of Catholic cathedrals and churches, whither they were brought in ancient days as gifts of the faithful or as spoils carried home by the Crusaders—who were first-rate looters as well as avengers of infidel blasphemies. The output of Constantinopolitan ivory studios must have been enormous in the Golden Age, and other centers are known for specialized types within the craft.

The ivory carvings, of course, deal primarily with Christian iconography, though there are excursions into glorification of the emperors. A favorite subject was Christ crowning the emperor and empress, as in the beautifully balanced decorative plaque in the Bibliothèque Nationale at Paris. Sometimes the subject is an out-and-out celebration of the ruler alone, without religious attributes or significance; but more common are the icon-like images of the Virgin, or the Virgin and Child, the Christ, or the apostles—often in groups, sometimes in a full episodic composition, though treated with the conventionalism of heraldic emblems.

From these individual pieces the relics range to such a composite work as the bishop's throne or cathedra of Maximian, still preserved in Ravenna. This veritable monument of the ivory-carver's art dates back to the sixth century and is ascribed by experts to Syrian or possibly Egyptian craftsmen (certain details suggest eastern Mediterranean geography and fauna). The chair is actually a composition of carefully joined ivory plaques. As usual in the better Oriental work, the design bears inspection either as a whole, as a synthesized unit, or as a number of perfectly conceived and executed panel-compositions or patterned areas.

The decorative colorfulness of the miniature mosaic, enamel, and ivory plaque can be found throughout a wide range of "minor" arts. There are metal works of the artificers in gold, silver, and bronze which are every bit as masterly and engaging: crosses and chalices and platters, and ornamental shields richly figured. There are metal icons; and all through the later centuries Russia carried on the tradition of shrine-figures on painted board-panels enriched with metal plates, often in repoussé designs and with precious stones set in.

The textiles may serve to complete the roster of arts in little which partake of the larger colorfulness and decorativeness of Byzantine genius. The figured cloth of gold, the embroidered robes, the woven linens are of that general family that looks to Persia as source. Their special beauty, largeness of conception, vigorous floral and animal designs, and rich coloring have perhaps been sufficiently described earlier in the chapter, where Coptic textile art is analyzed and illustrated. The true Byzantine work is perhaps a little less distinctive, more directly derived from Sassanian Persia; but the artisans went on later to special types and variations, and the elaborate vestments of Christian priests of both East and West seem descended from the opulent textiles of the Byzantine workshops.

The story of Byzantine art is literally never done. The reader should be reminded specifically of the treasuries of typical works at Venice and in the cities of Sicily. But it is more important to recall that never before or after did a great school

Maximian's Throne. Ivory, 5th century

of art send forth streams of influence and of actual works to so many countries and through so long a period of time. It was in the third and fourth centuries that Rome began to show mosaics in the Eastern style. It was seven centuries later that the Romanesque art of northern Italy, France, and Germany was brought forth, on foundations more Byzantine than classic or "barbarian." Again in the fourteenth and fifteenth centuries there was a renaissance in the territory still belonging to the Eastern Church.

Until recently mural painting had known scant mention in histories of Byzantine art. Nor were

Western scholars other than loath to concede a derivation of Italian painting from the Byzantine. It was considered more seemly that European religious art be shown forth as a reflowering of the classic. Eyes educated to naturalism saw the Eastern product as impossibly stiff and coarse, and in no way worthy of recognition as the ancestor of Sienese and Florentine loveliness. To-day the decisive influence of the East is recognized, and every evolutionary step from Byzantine iconographic painting to the Western art developed by Duccio and Giotto can be illustrated. The special methods and idioms had been brought to, or echoed in, Rome, Ravenna, and Venice at various dates from the fifth century to the twelfth; and there is evidence of even more direct lineage in the actual half-century during which Cimabue and Duccio were active: records tell of Greek painters' coming then to Central Italy.

On their own account, moreover, the strictly formalized Byzantine frescoes and mosaics are found to be characterized by the virtues of intense plastic life and rich decorative figuring. The later paintings have recently excited lovers of formalized art, as examples have been rediscovered in Greece, Macedonia, Crete, Constantinople, and the Balkan countries. Western students are finding it worth while to make pilgrimages to a church at Nerez in Macedonia, where the walls were painted in the twelfth century, and to Mount Athos and Mistra, where the later Byzantine renaissance is illustrated. In Constantinople, in the Kahriyeh Djami, which was once the Christian Church of the Chora, the painted murals, like the mosaics, dating from the fourteenth century, are not less than masterly. Thus is made known a monumental art, grown up beside the little icon, which like it combines the virtues of the arts of East and West.

Coptic textile

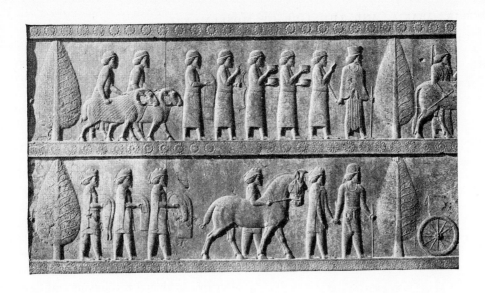

XII: PERSIA, ARABIA, AND
THE TIDE OF MOSLEM ART

IN THE DRAMA of art as it has been recorded, Persia has had a stepchild's role. Seldom given major credit, looked down upon from the eminence of classic culture, neglected by historians because the body of its art is scattered, Persia nevertheless has done more of the hard work of origination, crystallization, and transmission of the spirit and style of the art of the Orient than any other civilization. The Persian name turns up casually in the chronicles of every culture from Spain to China. Persian style-marks, even identifiable motives, can be traced in works scattered from Baghdad to Arles and Kairwan and Cordova; in the other direction from Ispahan to India, Cambodia, and Polynesia; and only a little less directly to Sakkara in Egypt, to Kiev in Ukrainia, and to Byzantine Athens. A silken banner treasured by the Japanese in a shrine at Nara since the ninth century bears a Persian design. Charlemagne was wrapped for burial in a Persian shroud. A Persian architect was spe-

cially summoned to design Tamerlane's tomb. It may be added that the Persian rug or its derivative is still standard on European and American floors.

It is only within the past generation that art historians have recognized Persia's part as other than secondary; but gradually a devoted group of investigators has brought to light the evidence that makes mandatory the assignment of a major role to this country. From the role of the low and unassuming stepchild, Persia is recast as protagonist in the play and counterplay of Asiatic cultural development. It may be that Iran will yet be recognized as the mother of the Oriental arts.

After the decay of Babylon and the disappearance of her realistic arts, the Persians became the outstanding builders and the most accomplished craftsmen in Asia. An invasion from Persia gave India the Brahman caste and therefore the Brahman and Buddhist arts; and this influence went

Tribute-bearers. Stone relief from the palace at Persepolis, Persia

Vase with Figures. Bronze, Luristan.
Collection M. and R. Stora

stamp that is upon the wares of Samarkand, Baghdad, Damascus, Cairo, and Tangier.

In a sense the Mohammedans conquered Persia; but at the most the Persians took over an incipient Arabian-Mohammedan art based on their own, reshaped it, and sent out designers and craftsmen for the glory of Islam. In this matter of Persia and Islam, the former may, indeed, be thought of as the ages-old fostering civilization. For twelve centuries, from the first Iranian conquest of Egypt, Lydia, and Babylon to the founding of the Moslem religion, the Medes and Persians and Parthians (Iranians all) had been developing a tradition and a way of art. Racially of one stock, and culturally of one type, after the incidental revolutions and assimilations they had fixed a recognizable style and nurtured out of it cultures far and near. Islam, on the other hand, was a sudden raging fire of faith and evangelism, which picked up this typically Oriental art and respread it over half the known world.

From an absolute view Mohammed and his Bedouin followers had no art. Their nearest associates, the Jews, although finely literary, had no large gifts of architecture, ornamentation, and craftswork to hand on. Persia, richly endowed with the sensuous artistic spirit, quickly embracing the new religion when invaded by the fanatic Moslem hordes, had the creative faculty that was complementary to Arab faith. Persia again was originator; Islam was instrument.

to shape the surpassing sculpture of Java and Cambodia and Siam. Through a northern route the Iranian and Indian cultures were welcomed into China, where actual Persian compositions are found in figured silks. Tibet, Turkestan, Armenia, Syria—these all drew from the same center; Arabia, too, and even Christian Egypt and Abyssinia, in a corner of Africa that has affinity more with its Eastern than with its Western conquerors. Finally it was Persia that determined the Moslem arts, whether arch and dome, or wooden or stone arabesque, or textile or pottery or metalsmithing. It is essentially an Iranian

The Forming of a Persian Style

The background of Iranian culture might be likened to one of those matchless Persian rugs in which smoldering fires of color are more important than any definite design; in which elusive themes are discovered, lost, and rediscovered. Through it all, too elusive yet for actual recording, is an element of the Eurasian steppe art, the animal art known also as Scythian, from the Russian-Siberian plains country to which Persia is a natural southern gateway. Only once did this northern Oriental art appear in Persia in its purest, nearly primitive form: the Luristan

Rearing Lion. Bronze, Luristan. *Collection Edward M. M. Warburg*

bronzes are as distinctive as the actual Siberian works or as the Far Eastern examples from the Ordos Desert which adjoins China's Shansi Province.

Recovered from the tombs of ancient warriors in western Persia, the Luristan relics are vigorously decorative. The motives are usually animal figures conventionalized far toward abstraction. The intent of the artist-craftsman is invariably decorative rather than illustrative. Here appear the style-marks that will be met again and again in Iranian history: the vigorous, virile, strongly accented main movement, in a composition only slightly asymmetrical; and the introduction of contrasting areas of formalized patterning.

The Persians first appear in recorded history in their descent from the Iranian highlands to menace the Babylonian communities. As told in an earlier chapter, Cyrus and his immediate successors in the sixth century B.C. toppled over one after another of the overexpanded or exhausted nations of the eastern Mediterranean:

Lydia, Egypt, Babylon. By 525 B.C. the Persian Empire was the greatest in extent known to human history up to that time. The conquering Achaemenid Dynasty, which established the first recognizably Persian culture, lasted two centuries —until in 330 B.C., after a failure to break through the westward barrier set up by Greece, it in turn found itself exhausted (and perhaps overluxurious) and fell before the triumphant march of Alexander.

The Achaemenid artists had proved more adaptive of foreign notions than independently creative; though what they took from Babylon and Egypt, and later and less notably from Greece, was respoken with a Persian accent and flowed ultimately, in more colorful and more abstract form, into a distinctive national expression. As noted in the chapter on the ancient Near East, the Achaemenids had seen the great palaces of their vassals, the Mesopotamian kings, as they had seen the vast hypostyle halls of the conquered Egyptians, and had believed that their own greatness as world conquerors should be celebrated by equally impressive structures. The resulting regal palaces and audience halls at Persepolis and Susa, as judged today in fragments and partial restoration, exhibit at once the mixed nature of their derivation and a distinctive Persian contribution, evident chiefly in a feeling for grace, stylization, and integrity of ornament, with colorfulness.

In the sculpture there was less realism, more formalization, than in the Babylonian prototype (as illustrated on pages 36 and 37). In architecture there appeared a greater elegance, an advance toward a dignified "system" of building. Already in certain sculptural accessories and bits there had resulted a combination of virtues destined to lie at the heart of Persian art through all after-centuries: a masterly sense of space-filling, with vigor of movement preserved within rich all-over effect.

There followed several centuries of rule by invaders, first the Alexandrian Greeks, then the Parthians. It is supposed that when Alexander came he brought his own sculptors and artificers, and that he left them to practice in the cities he founded. In Babylon, on the way back from his Persian adventure, the great dictator died. When the Alexandrian empire immediately, and naturally, fell to pieces, the Iranian lands were allotted to the dead emperor's general Seleucus, who established in Persia the non-Persian Seleucid Dynasty; but the immigrant sculptors and the efforts of the alien rulers to bring in Western culture seem to have had little effect. Instead of showing the influence of Hellenistic naturalism, the next marked phases are more strikingly than before decorative and near-abstract. The point may be that the Persians were artistically more civilized than their conquerors. At any rate it was their culture that persisted.

As early as 256 B.C. the Parthians, a people of the northeastern steppe group, began to exert pressure on the Seleucids, and in 140 B.C. they in turn took over all Persia. The succeeding Parthian Dynasty was, one might say, Persianized Scythian. To one who knows the Scythian or steppe art, and later Persian art, it would seem that this is a major link in the chain that was to

Ibex. Bronze, Achaemenid period.
Collection Oscar Raphael

result in Sassanian pottery, textiles, and metalwork, and so to influence the Byzantine and Moslem cultures. The relics are rare but eloquent.

Here history deals briefly with periods that actually cover centuries. It is best to pick up the thread of art with the important Sassanian era (A.D. 226–641), which is marked by the enthusiastic recapturing of the old mastery. The works are of a characteristic sort, and they indicate that the ideals of the Achaemenid emperors, as developed at Susa and Persepolis, had been more or less consciously fostered by artists and craftsmen in the intervening troubled

Horse. Bronze, Sassanian (220-650 A.D.), Arabia. *Dumbarton Oaks Collection*

centuries. Ardashir, the founder of the Sassanian line of emperors, claimed descent from the Achaemenid house. He established a capital at Ctesiphon in old Babylonia—and again the arts flourished.

The brilliant brocades of the time may be taken as index of the luxurious yet refined culture of the reviving empire. There are experts who place them as the supreme expression of man's genius in the textile medium. The compositions are broadly conceived. The figures are large yet are held within rigid and delicate mathematical patterning, in circles or diapered webs or intertwined bands. The figure-dominant or subject-motive may be a formalized animal or flower or a heraldically summarized human being. It is this that affords the vigor, the plastic livingness. The patterned frame and traced-over

Silk tissue with griffins, 11th or 12th century.
Textile Museum of the District of Columbia

In his work there is always something of the carpet, the tapestry, the flat-lying field of contrived design; little of the realist's window upon life. There is the bowl-shape to be remembered, the panel to be filled, the surface that cushions the eye to be respected.

The Sassanian stuffs beautifully illustrate this way of conceiving the design, of filling space colorfully, even luxuriously. There is close affinity with the Syrian and the Coptic cloths of the same centuries, and it is probable that the origin was in Persia. In any case the centers of manufacture were closely related, and from them went out the designs and the craftsmanship that determined Byzantine design. There are legends of the extravagant quantities of Sassanian stuffs ordered by the late Roman emperors of the West and records of lovely Persian fabrics taken to Europe by the Crusaders. The great French authority Mâle is willing to credit the glory of the windows at Chartres partly to the inspiration of Sassanian tapestries.

The animals as they appear in Persian silks —as also in pottery and metalware—are worth special study. They are gorgeously spirited, nobly alive. The links between these and the Luristan bronzes are still lost; one may go back instead to the bulls of the Susa sculptured capitals, to the possibly related horses and stags of the Sanchi gates, India's oldest sculptural monument. In latest and in earliest manifestations there is a virility seen in the Chinese Han animals.

Subjects aside from animals, when representational rather than abstract, are likely to deal with objects and scenes appropriate to the restrained luxuriousness of the art-using classes: with gardens and hunting episodes and courtly routine. The visual arts accommodated themselves to a way of life, reflected a poetic or lyric aspect of gentle living. There is, too, a geographic and climatic correspondence, an appropriateness to environment, as fitting as the lushness of Hindu art is to its fecund land. The Persian park-like landscapes and the palace gardens immemorially celebrated by the poets are implicit in these designs.

Where the picture element, as a document

areas act as a confining field and a decorative restraint. Despite the essential vitality, there is a lyric delicacy or fastidiousness in the handling. The splendor is made a quiet one.

One stresses this particular Persian stylization because the Western road of art led directly away from it. Whether in silks or in pottery or in figured metals, the Persian design seems to say: Art must be vital, living, colorful, instinct with movement; but the art of a cultured, poetic people must be, no less, strictly formalized, rhythmic, restrained.

The Persian's is the craftsman's approach, not that of the limner who sets out to copy a naturally beautiful object, or to idealize one less beautiful, or to celebrate a person or a god. Up to a certain controlled point, the Oriental finds motives in representation. But as artist he is at the far pole from the anatomical, idealizing representational art of the Greeks.

It is nature's business, says the Persian, to create the natural; the artist's business is to create new plastic forms, new rhythms, conditioned by the special virtues and potentialities of the medium he is using. He never forgets the abstract order, the rhythmic vitality, the melodic fullness, characteristic of the decorator.

Figured silver dish. Sassanian period. *The Hermitage, Leningrad*

from nature, sensibly exists, the drawing is formal and summary. There is no perspective. There are no shadows. The designs are not the less full and vital on this account. Rather, line carries a greater burden of expressiveness. Contours become marvelously energetic. The more delicate features are traced with rare feeling and subtlety. All-over patterning is used exceptionally for enrichment and variation.

In a collection in Leningrad there are Persian silver platters and vessels which are counted among the foremost treasures of figured metal in all the world. Into this art the Sassanian craftsmen have carried over the vigor, the decorativeness, and the colorfulness we have noted in textile design. The process is in general that

known as repoussé, in which a relief design is punched or hammered up from the back. The compositions, as before, are notable for virility of design and for the true Persian minor rhythms in formal patterning.

Note in the figured silver dish illustrated here the vital force of the man, the horse, and the rearing lion; the "impossibly" conventionalized trappings, such as the bow and the helmet; the enriching effect of the lions' manes, of the drapery over the saddle, and of the six ornamental harness-disks.

The same distinctive virtues are found within the limitations of the jeweler's medium, in a gold armlet which forms part of the same "Treasure of the Oxus" in Leningrad. The

Rock-cut tomb of Darius, Naksh-i-Rustum

enamels have been lost out of the cloisons, but the piece could hardly have a greater effect of rich ornamentalism than it does now. And here again are the spirited animals. The whole is finely simple yet intricately decorative. Persian cloisonné works are fairly rare, but Persian artists at this time perfected the ancient Egyptian technique and handed it on to Byzantium and to China.

Sassanian monumental art is but poorly represented, comparatively, in surviving statues and buildings. This circumstance is partly due to the fanaticism of the invading Moslems. They destroyed a great deal of sculpture because of the Koran's prohibition of human representation in art. Seven centuries later the Moguls razed entire cities. Most of the important sculpture remaining is badly defaced, as on the rock-cut tombs of the emperors at Naksh-i-Rustum. Even the finest works of the minor arts might be similarly little known to later collectors had not the products of Persia been sought after in bordering countries, and even as far as Italy and China. The collection of figured vessels and jewels in Russia is supposed to have crossed the border in trade for northern furs.

A further reason for lack of figures comparable to those of Egypt, India, or Gothic Europe lies in the nature of the Persian Zoroastrian religion. This enlightened faith discouraged the making of devotional images, although not prohibiting representational art in other than religious channels. The sculptural impulse was turned into metalwares, minor crafts, and near-abstract decorative accessories for architecture.

The great vault of the palace at Ctesiphon is the chief exhibit indicating the original grandeur and magnificence of Sassanian architecture. Although the structure was almost destroyed and was looted of fabulous treasures in the way of furnishings, the immense vault of the throne room and the adjacent walls afford mute testimony to the monumental luxuriousness of sixth-century Persian building.

The ruins, however, are such that they appeal historically rather than intrinsically. How much of the way of building is Persian, in the sense of being an original growth of this land, is problematic. Structurally this is an architecture of arch, vault, and dome. From it was to develop the Moslem system of building, after the invasion. Something of the sort is also the ancestor of the early Christian church upon which the Byzantine style was founded. There are investigators who prefer to divide the credit between Persia and Syria. Others trace the

Plate. Kermanshah, 9th-10th century. *Metropolitan Museum of Art*

development, though as yet on hardly sufficient evidence, to ancient Babylon, where the barrel vault was known. But in the light of recent investigations Persia, with Armenia contributing, seems the likeliest source of both the Byzantine and the Moslem architectural impulse.

Islamic Persian Art

The art of the Mohammedans, commonly thought of as Arab art, was not originated by the culture for which it is thus named, nor are its centers of production or its masterpieces to be found importantly in its "native" land. Although that land gave a name to its outstanding decorative feature—the arabesque—it was else-

where that Islamic art had its roots and developed its distinctive flower. The roots, as we have seen, were largely Persian. The full flower is less to be observed in Mecca and Medina in Arabia than in Ispahan and Baghdad, in Damascus, Samarkand, Cairo, Granada.

A century before Constantine founded his Eastern capital and enfolded the Christian masses within the Byzantine Empire, Ardashir had established the Sassanid Dynasty in Persia. Long before Justinian built Santa Sophia, Persian artists had created the Sassanian masterpieces of silken brocades and silver vessels and enameled jewels. The two bodies of art, Persian and Byzantine, had grown side by side. But politically these two empires had, off and on for generations, been at each other's throats. By the opening of

Islamic ewer. Bronze, Mosul, 13th century.
University Museum, Philadelphia

and plotting, won over his own Arabian people and daringly set out to subjugate the world for Allah.

It is related that in 628 Mohammed sent identical notes to the emperors of the two vast empires to the northward of his unimportant state—if one can call the wandering Bedouins and the clusters of traders' houses on the caravan routes a state. The notes were in the nature of an ultimatum. They called upon the two emperors—and indeed upon all the rulers of the earth—to change heavenly masters and to serve thenceforward the One and Only God. They were signed "Mohammed, the Prophet of God." Heraclius is not known to have replied, but Kavadh of Persia was outraged. The incident is thus succinctly reported by H. G. Wells in *The Outline of History:*

> At Ctesiphon they knew more about this Muhammed. He was said to be a tiresome false prophet, who had incited Yemen, the rich province of Southern Arabia, to rebel against the King of Kings. Kavadh was much occupied with affairs. He had deposed and murdered his father, Chosroes II, and he was attempting to reorganize the Persian military forces. . . . He tore up the letter, flung the fragments at the envoy, and bade him begone.
>
> When this was told to the sender, far away in the squalid little town of Medina, he was very angry. "Even so, O Lord!" he cried; "rend thou his kingdom from him."

Within a decade Persia had been subdued and added to the Islamic state. Even more quickly the Prophet's followers snatched at the edges of the Byzantine realm. They took Syria from the tired Christians without serious effort, even to Antioch. Shortly they had got up into Armenia and down into Egypt.

It does not matter here just how the fire of Islam spread. Groups of Arabs within Persia and Byzantine lands, who had been nominally Christians, or who had accommodatingly professed themselves Zoroastrians or Manichaeans, went over easily to their brethren's faith. But most important was the inadequacy of the ties that held vanquished peoples in "loyalty" to one

the seventh century both were exhausted with the drain of repeated wars. Chosroes II of Persia had conquered Egypt and Syria and Asia Minor, and had brought his armies to the gates of Constantinople; he had, moreover, terribly affronted the Christians by marching into Jerusalem and marching away again with the most venerated Christian relic, the cross on which Jesus had been crucified. Then the fortunes fluctuated and turned temporarily to Heraclius, the Byzantine emperor. It was at this moment that Mohammed, after his years of patient and impatient dreaming, studying,

emperor or the other. The new conquerors were fired with an ardent faith of the sort that breeds leaders and martyrs. Armed opposition melted before their kind of holy crusading. Most of the population merely drifted over.

Mohammedanism began with puritan belief in the simple things. The Caliph Omar, within a decade after Mohammed's death, heard that one of his governors had occupied a luxurious palace on the old imperial Persian model. Immediately he ordered the offending one to tear the palace down; and he inquired acidly if the governor really wanted to be like the magnificent infidel emperors, and to follow them to hell. Wells retells an equally pertinent episode about Omar's entry into Jerusalem:

Jerusalem made a peculiar condition for its surrender. The city would give itself only to the Caliph Omar in person. . . . He came the six-hundred-mile journey with only one attendant; he was mounted on a camel, and a bag of barley, another of dates, a water-skin, and a wooden platter were his provision for the journey. He was met outside the city by his chief captains, robed splendidly in silks and with richly caparisoned horses. At this amazing sight the old man was overcome with rage. He slipped down from his saddle, scrabbled up dirt and stones with his hands, and pelted these fine gentlemen, shouting abuse. What was this insult? What did this finery mean? Where were his warriors? Where were the desert men? He would not let these popinjays escort him. He went on with his attendant and the smart Emirs rode afar off—well out of range of his stones. He met the Patriarch of Jerusalem, who had apparently taken over the city from its Byzantine rulers, alone. With the Patriarch he got on very well. They went round the Holy Places together, and Omar, now a little appeased, made sly jokes at the expense of his too magnificent followers.

Here was religion cutting out some of the rank overgrowth about the tree of art.

If Islam then quickly conquered Syria and Persia, it is equally certain that the Islamic state, culturally considered, moved over to Syria, then to Persia. The puritanic impulse hardly survived two caliphates. The desert cities, without tradi-

Lusterware tile. Rhages, 11th-13th century.
Freer Gallery of Art

tions of art and luxury, could not hold the leaders of a phenomenally successful world movement. Besides, the little Arabian capital was the scene of the pettiest sort of bickering and intrigue over the succession, with murders and womenfolk's jealousies and rival ambitions breeding a very provincial atmosphere.

The next political capital was Damascus, from which the Caliphs soon were ruling a vast territory extending, though not continuously, from the westernmost tip of Europe to the borders of China. The push across Africa had ended with the conquest of parts of Spain, but the Pyrenees proved a permanent barrier, protecting the rest of Europe for Christ and Rome; and the Eastern wave had reached Turkestan, hitherto an unsettled region but more civilized than, say, the Britain or Germany of the time.

Art blossomed again, however, only in the eighth century. Then, after a carnival of massacres and assassinations, a new line of caliphs, the Abbasids, set up the Islamic capital at Baghdad, within a stone's throw of the mound

Capital. Islamic ornament of the Moors in Spain.
Metropolitan Museum of Art

where Babylon had been, and of Ctesiphon, the last native Persian capital. Those followers of the puritanic Caliph Omar who had slipped so easily into magnificent clothes, and that governor who had built the first Moslem-Persian palace, were now vindicated—and surpassed. The Persian arts began to serve sumptuously the new Arabian masters. The palace of Ardashir at Ctesiphon, built seven centuries earlier in an attempt to revive the glories of Persepolis and Susa, had been destroyed, but it found a worthy successor in the palace of Harun al-Rashid, the Abassid caliph who ruled Islam in the years on either side of 800. The architecture was that of vault and dome and encrusted ornamentation. One has only to recall the setting of the *Arabian Nights* stories to have the luxurious and splendid atmosphere of it re-created. This palace was the actual setting of the tales.

Invasion and absorption of foreign strains in her culture were no new thing to Persia. Heir, by right of conquest, to the Babylonian tradition, she had taken something of that permanently into her architecture, though not the Assyrian naturalism in sculpture. From the northeastern steppes, probably the prehistoric homeland of the Medes and the Persians, came, we may believe, that bent toward vigorous decoration with subtle

formalization which is central to her style. Perhaps the invading Parthians, from this same northland, had renewed the strain of conventional and decorative as against realistic art. While they were masters of Syria and of Egypt at times, the Persians doubtless received from them in lesser ways. It is to be remembered, too, that when Justinian closed the schools of Athens as prejudicial to Christian doctrine the fugitive teacher-philosophers had been invited to the Sassanian capital. There were recognizable crossroads of Persian and Chinese art in Eastern Turkestan. Thus, in the Central East, Persia had accumulated from all directions, had made Oriental art her own.

The Arabs, intellectualists, foremost scientists, and artists in literature, but lacking in the visual creative sense, contributed one new element to the decorative arts. They brought with them to all the countries that became Mohammedan a language that lent itself beautifully to calligraphic ornament. Mohammedanism had ridden out across Asia on the hoofs of its cavalry; but its later strength was in obedience to the word of the Koran, and the word came as Arabic. Wherever Islam went, the holy text went. Arabic became the standard devotional language of the Moslem world. It was twined into the ornaments of architecture, pottery, and illuminated manuscripts, all the way from Spain and Morocco to India and Turkestan. Whether on the enriched walls and screens of the Alhambra at Granada or on a lavishly engraved urn picked up in a stall at Samarkand or Delhi, the decorative Arabic calligraphy will be found embedded within the fields of ornament. (See especially the architectural example on page 264.)

It would be idle to think that the Arabs added nothing more to the art which now enfolded their faith. They could not have made the outline of the mosque recognizably the same in Algiers and Cairo and Damascus if they had not stamped on the minds of their Persian and Syrian architects and craftsmen a conviction about life and religion, a philosophy that does intangibly control artistic expression. There was, too, the matter of images.

The taboo on images and on representation

Islamic ornament, detail from the Hall of Ambassadors, the Alhambra, Granada

led to modifications in Persia—and to destruction of earlier works of art. There was a further swing toward abstraction in ornament. The figures were to come creeping in again, to give accent to panel compositions, to afford a center of interest to the bowl or the brocaded shawl. And indeed, by the opening of the ninth century the prohibition was more honored in the breach than in the observance. Sir Mark Sykes, in *The Caliph's Last Heritage,* says that "Harun al-Rashid himself was a wine-bibber, and his palace was decorated with graven images of birds and beasts and men."

Nevertheless, one's first recollection of Islamic art is of gorgeously rich panels of ornament composed out of purely or essentially abstract elements: the field is geometrically parceled out in diapers or circles or ovals, but pulled together for the eye by the interwoven linear tracings, the bands and tendrils and ribbons. The Mohammedan artist—be he Persian or Syrian or Egyptian, or mayhap the Arab himself—is, under the Koran's precept, a great geometrizer of natural form. The leaf, the flower, the twining vine, lose natural identity, familiar eccentricity; but the swelling leaf form, the floral roundness, the twining curves, appear distilled to their purest terms; and, repeated, they build up seductive pattern and tracery winning to the eye.

In architecture the walls are encrusted with these flat panels of abstract design, which reappear on cloths, on pottery, on copper. They are the normal, the typical mark of Islamic decoration; and so "arabesque" is not a misnomer for the final manifestation of controlled patterning. If it is merely the Arabian working-out of a thing that had haunted Eastern art for a thousand years, already implicit in Persian and Indian decorative sculpture and shawl, and long since passed on to Coptic Egypt and to Christian Syria and to the Byzantines, it yet belongs perfectly to Islam. The fretwork screens, the carved-wood panels, the stucco friezes, the pierced metal vessels, are lasting evidence of Mohammedan mastery. Sculptured or cut pattern has never elsewhere been so alive and opulent.

There are Western critics who dismiss it all with a wave of the hand as mere "frosting." It is meant, they say, to beguile the eye momentarily, and has no other significance. Rather, one should remember that this can be rightly an integral part of the enrichment of palace or place of devotion, of ivory chest or embroidered gown. It is then a part of the grace and allure and atmosphere of a building or a costume or a cherished casket. That arabesque and related forms of surface decoration were wrongly used in countless cases, obscuring architectural integrity, adorning dishonest or negligent structure, is hardly pertinent. No more are the debased designs of the later centuries, when the creative spirit had fled, and copying had flooded the world with lifeless imitations and cheapened replicas of the authentic works.

To close one's mind against an art because it is frankly, purposefully, and even eloquently a thing of surface manipulation is to cut oneself off from enjoyments legitimate and good—so at least it would seem to this observer. The pleasure is sensuous; the values are melodious and harmonic rather than contrapuntal. Within the range, the special conception, Islamic low decoration is incomparably graceful, eye-filling, elegant.

It is worth the time to pause over a carved panel or a capital and to trace out the mathematical system underlying the work, the skeleton of the pattern; then to note the larger symmetries and the variations. There is marvelous ingenuity, and a subtle balance of mathematical and free elements. The geometric, repetitive plan controls; yet the free contours are virile and the rhythm is marked. This is the space-filling, decorative, pattern art at a summit. It is worth noting, too, how perfectly in the inscribed designs the calligraphy is blended into the ensemble.

The arabesque is sometimes interpreted as a symbol of the mysticism of the Arabian mind, of the people of the desert. In its ultimate or purest form the arabesque is said by the symbolists to be a design in which there is no beginning or end. The motives appear and disappear in such near-anonymity that there is no point at which the eye comes to rest. It seems more likely that the development is out of man's normal and unceasing search for fresh devices that will delight the eye. Nor is it true that the best designs are restless.

The spirit of typical Islamic art is light, in the best sense, delicate, colorful. There is a strong mathematical undercurrent, as in music. There is hardly a hint of realism in it; indeed, the arts which so often run off into realism—painting and representational sculpture—were in the earlier centuries little known to Islam. The logic of the architecture is weak; but the decoration of interiors and courts reaches a new culmination in subtlety, richness, and enchanting colorfulness.

Persian Pottery

If Persia gave to the Arabs the formula for the arabesque, she had also gifts of freer design. One of these she developed to new heights of expressiveness in the early centuries of Islamic culture, carried it through a cycle of successive triumphs, and by it inspired Spanish, Turkish, even Italian craftsmen to creative innovation. In the design and decoration of pottery there is no culture that surpasses the Persian. China alone rivals the achievement.

In some ways the Persian pottery transcends the Far Eastern, merely by reason of adherence to basic virtues. Chinese porcelain has more

Bowl, 11th or 12th century. *Collection M. Larcade*

technical refinement, and particularly excels in fabrication of the very hard and translucent wares, and in their shaping to perfect roundness. The Persian product is more frankly clay, hand-shaped, with the marks of manual freedom upon it, in contours, texture, and painting. The Far Eastern decorated porcelains have often the atmosphere of the hothouse. In Persian wares the freshness is of the open garden, of the flowers dew-covered and sunlit.

On Persian soil has been found some of the most sensitively figured prehistoric pottery known; there is, in these vases and bowls, an extraordinary decorative elegance. No continuity with later developments has, however, been proved. Indeed, a second prehistoric, probably pre-Iranian, age yields designs less formalized,

tending toward realism. In early historic times, too, that part of Persia on the border of Babylonia fell under the Sumerian-Babylonian influence and showed no originality. But once Persia was firmly established as a nation there developed a ceramic art with a distinctive and unmistakable loveliness. Throughout its course there are the typical Middle Eastern decorative richness and seductive color; but there are also a simple dignity and a melodious grace.

As a guide to enjoyment, the story is best picked up well along in the Persian-Moslem period, under the Abbasid caliphs of the ninth and tenth centuries. The traditional local product then blossomed within the general flowering of the arts and luxuries. Some of the vigor and the full decorativeness of the vases and bowls

Bowl with figures, 12th-13th century. *Parish-Watson Collection*

of the time is directly in line with the plastic virility of the preceding Sassanian luxury-arts. Incidentally the old preoccupation with animals and birds, when dominating "motive" appears, is again evident.

Lusterware is a first outstanding variety within the group of distinctive potteries native to Persia and Eastern Mesopotamia. In this an evanescent sheen is added under the glaze, by applying and burning away a coating of metallic oxides over the already decorated ground. An iridescent but fleeting overtone thus enriches the soft browns, golden yellows, and olive greens of the painted decoration, adding ruby or orange tints. The lustrous beauty of this ware made it a favorite through several centuries, during which it was produced side by side with other types. It was copied extensively in Egypt—from which country the Persians of fifteen centuries earlier may have learned the finer techniques of enameling and glazing. It is found, too, in Turkestan to the east and as far as Spain in the west, all within the Islamic empire. Examples are to be enjoyed today, of course, in all the larger museums of Europe and America. Some of the most beautiful of the tiles used in enrichment of Moslem architecture are in this lusterware.

The nominal prohibition of images continued; and there is indeed in pottery, as elsewhere, a large body of abstract or near-abstract patterning and design. But as often, except in Turkestan, the compositions run to freer design, with

Dish with figures, Rhages type, dated 1210.
Eumorfopoulos Collection, British Museum

animals predominating, but not wholly avoiding the human figure either. Perhaps the chief effect of restriction, as regards pottery, was that the wealthy turned to this art more generally for the enrichment of their halls, harems, and garden courts, in the absence of figure-sculpture and painting. Certainly the arts sometimes considered "minor"—textiles and metals and pottery—were in Islam exceptionally glorified.

For a time vessels of gold and silver had also been under a ban, as out of keeping with the simplicity of living enjoined by the Prophet upon all true Moslems; but the metal arts were merely given pause thereby, to become again a foremost Eastern way of craftsmanship.

The figures came back, in the eleventh and twelfth centuries, in a sort of pottery that is, for some observers, the very type-example of Persian art. In the more refined and delicate vessels the exquisite virtues of later Oriental miniature painting seem crossed with the decorative richness of earlier ceramic art. The Rhages pottery is perhaps the most conspicuous part of the display. Rhages, near Teheran, was, until it was destroyed by Genghis Khan in 1213, one of the most noted of Persian centers of production. Its wares are known in several variations, all vigorous, some with decorations in relief, some with the luster adding iridescence. But the bowls and plates and vases upon which picture-compositions are perfectly combined with abstract ornamental accessory, against a generally

Typical Islamic architecture.
Mosque at Ispahan

free ground of creamy white or turquoise blue, form the culminating exhibit. This is a case of the potter become painter of figure-scenes again —painter with an extraordinary sense of appropriate formalization and with all the old Persian mastery of decorative space-filling.

There is no more glamorous display of the colorist's art than in a group of Rhages bowls with geometrically disposed free figures of riders on horses and elephants, or of lovers or huntsmen.

There are so many periods and types of surpassing achievement in richly decorated pottery that it would require a large history of the art to give them proper relation and emphasis; but even the most summary of lists must include mention of the thirteenth- and fourteenth-century wares produced at Sultanabad, the new

Persian-Islamic capital under the Mogul emperors, whither perhaps the conquerors had taken some of the expert potters of the sacked Rhages. The Eastern Mogul influence is detectable in a certain retreat from the delicacy of the twelfth-century figured vases. There is a lusher, more lavish decorativeness, with a return to all-over patterned effects, and a full-bodied ornamentalism. The arrival of new Eastern influences revived, too, the animal emblemism.

There are wares especially prized by collectors, from Turkestan, from Armenia, and from other regions that were taken into Islam as parts of the Persian empire. Related cultures more distant from Baghdad and Sultanabad—in Egypt and Spain and Turkey—justly find place in specialized accounts. It should be added that Persian pottery

Mosque and minaret
at Kait Bey near Cairo

enters the story again in a later chapter, when the perfected arts of miniature-painting and carpeting will be accompanied by the production of porcelain-like wares, delicately decorated, with a finesse not unrelated to the Chinese. But the essentially Persian, at the same time typically Islamic, elements in the art, as manifested from the ninth to the fourteenth century, have perhaps been sufficiently outlined and illustrated to indicate the brilliant quality of ceramics at this time, justifying the opinion that hardly ever again, at any time or place in history, was pottery so beautifully conceived and produced.

Architecture

The mother art, architecture, as it was shaped in Islam into new uses, and into a new variation of the already established mid-Oriental style, is best illustrated in the palaces that followed on the early Persian ones, and in the mosques, which owe much structurally to the Christian domed and barrel-vaulted churches. In Persia the monuments are less conspicuous than those in farther Mohammedan lands: there are no world-famous exhibits to rival the mosques of Cairo, or the Alhambra in Spain, or, in the other direction, the Taj Mahal in India.

It is well established that Syrian and Persian artisans went out on the heels of the Arabian conquerors to the far corners of the empire. There local influences modified architectural expression, though seldom turning a large building away from the basic vaulted construction and the concentration of decorative effect upon the rich, often incredibly rich, "lining." It is this double idiom that is most typical of Islam: the plainly finished but rhythmically pleasing exterior, with domes, rounded or pointed arches, and accenting minarets; and contrasting lavishly ornamented interior walls and courts.

In Persia the early buildings have rarely survived even in a ruined condition. The Mogul invasions in the thirteenth century were disastrous, wiping out not only individual monuments but entire cities. It was partly the savage sacking of the country that caused artists and craftsmen to flee in numbers to other lands where Mohammedanism was still the religion but under independent dissident governments—particularly to Spain and Egypt.

Of Persia's determining influence, one building is eloquent. The remaining portions of the Masjid Sheikh Luft Ullah in Ispahan—though out of line chronologically—are instructive as illustrating the purest exterior forms of Islamic architecture and, in the "opened" sections, where ruins have been cut away and the skeleton exposed, the usually concealed engineering features.

In passing through Syria, so to speak, on the way to Cairo, it is worth while to recall momentarily the strange history of this land where the roads of trade, religion, and military conquest had so often and so confusingly crossed and recrossed. Partly out of its own history, partly out of Persian example, Syria had contributed to the establishment of the typical form of the early Christian church. The local development had gone on, too, with the maturer Byzantine, so that some historians say that at the time of the taking of Syria for Islam the invaders found Byzantine buildings ready to hand. In any case, here, as in Egypt, Christian halls were adapted by the Moslems with the necessary *mihrab,* or niche toward Mecca, added.

But it is at Cairo that one comes upon the mosque in its truest example and atmosphere. Here are the great rectangular halls surmounted by domes, bare outside except for the occasional clustered arches. Sometimes the dome exterior above the drum is encrusted with a simple but intricate patterning, as in the mosque at Kait Bey, illustrated on page 265.

One can trace in surviving Egyptian mosques, indeed, the whole history of Islamic architectural forms, from the early rudimentary sanctuary, derived from Christian churches or chapels taken by chance and rebuilt with colonnades added on the side of the hall or court toward Mecca, to the fullest expression, to the elaborated structure in which a rich ornamentalism spreads not only to such features as the *mihrab,* the pulpit, and the tribune, but to large areas of interior wall, door, and window-grille. It is probable that the pointed arch developed locally, out of contact of the invading style with Coptic Egyptian art.

The Mosque of Sultan Hassan in Cairo, built in the mid-fourteenth century, is an example of the elaborated religious edifice, in this case with school facilities added. It has the immense built-up portal, and four great pointed arches echo its opening where the arms of the cross open into the central court. A fountain of ornamental architectural design marks the focal point of the court. The eastern or sanctuary recess or arm (the mosque proper) is, exceptionally, the one part ornamented riotously in truest Moslem fashion.

The magnificence in decoration is better seen, perhaps, in less complex structures. At Kait Bey outside Cairo is a cemetery group known as the "Tombs of the Caliphs," dating from the times of the later Mamelukes, about the fifteenth century. There the characteristic domed buildings exist in purest form. In the combination tomb-mosque of Sultan Kait Bey the simple outlines persist, but all surfaces are lavishly decorated. The arabesque areas on wall and window-grille and dome, the stalactite ornamentation on minaret and portal archway, the crenellated wall, and the general aspect of rich carving and encrustation—all these find illustration in one building. There are, too, the idioms of the horseshoe arch, of the striped walls, of alternating dark and light stone, of the mosaicked niches, and of color added by marble veneering, by glass windows, and by stucco inlaid with more precious substances.

As the Mohammedans pushed across northern Africa they built in their own manner, leaving such monuments as the famous Mosque of Kairwan in Tunis. But it was in Spain that Islamic architecture reflowered, with its Eastern richness not only preserved but pushed to a new summit of lavish decorativeness. For a time the Spanish Visigothic and Byzantine forms persisted in combination with those of the invading style. Older buildings were torn down so that the columns, capitals, and stone blocks might be used in construction of mosques and government buildings. At Cordova the Great

Court of the Lions, the Alhambra, Granada

Mosque, begun in 786 but enlarged many times, is less a building erected by traditional or logical plan than a record of compromise between a sought effect and available materials or existent walls. Nevertheless the encrusted ornamentation and added features give it an Oriental appearance.

The Alhambra at Granada is the greatest of Moslem palaces. It is a complex of open courts, colonnades, halls, and rooms bewildering in extent and in variety. The structural forms are logical enough and fairly pleasing; but ornamentation as such has run away with the architecture. Intricacy and delicacy of pattern have never elsewhere in Europe been so beautifully exploited. There is an unparalleled series of sumptuously embellished halls. The courts are arcaded; the floors are of marquetry; every doorway and window is elaborated into a marvelously contrived show of artistry. The whole takes on an air of fancifulness, is like a fairyland in which the realities of life are unknown—though the exterior is as grim and fortresslike as that of any medieval castle.

The Court of the Lions, the Hall of the Two Sisters, the Hall of the Ambassadors, the Court of the Myrtles, and the baths, are widely known in description and illustration. They touch an ultimate point in what the Western observer is likely to appraise as "romantic" architecture. To suggest that the Alhambra is all dignified and well-considered art would be to overpraise. It is generally accepted, however, as one of the most charming and seductive displays of "light" architecture in world history.

Meier-Graefe sums up eloquently another view of Islamic architecture, that of the purist, when he writes in *Pyramid and Temple:* "No mosque allows you to forget that it is a travesty of a church. . . . The nature of a mosque is incompatible with our [Christian] architecture; it sweetens and softens forms whose charm lies in their acerbity." Again he exclaims: "Not the faintest idea of the functions of a column. Everything structural turned to ornament"; and: "The Arabic style was marked out as the perfect decoration for Turkish baths."

The great German critic was comparing the Islamic monuments with the Egyptian pyramids, which was perhaps a bit unfair. When we are not immediately concerned with the profound types of building, there would seem to be a place in appreciation for the opulent ornamental sort too, so long as the manifestation has its own unity and integrity, in relation to intention, technique, and materials. Certainly Mohammedan decorative art is incomparably rich and delicate.

The Spanish adventure of the Moslems ended, after some centuries, in retreat. The architecture of mosque and encrusted palace has remained alien among the buildings of Western Europe. But the West retains a heritage from the Moslems that might be sought in hidden influences or discovered patently in examples of the minor arts, particularly in pottery, textiles, and metalwares. The Hispano-Moresque wares constitute perhaps the most prized type of ceramic art

known to Europe; and there were derivative products in Italy, most notably those named majolica.

The Mohammedans, then, carrying forward a Persian opulence of expression, created on their own ground a great body of rich and seductive art, and they also influenced the decorative ideals of Europe, in a gift discounted and unappreciated during the long Renaissance and neoclassic eras, but now again recognized and counted a corrective—for something of the arabesque was needed in the too stark, too restrained decorative practice of the West.

The Islamic manifestation is a phase of that art which had had the Luristan bronzes as its first expression, which went on to the Sassanian brocades and silverwares, and then to the Rhages bowls and the luster tiles. It flowered differently, perhaps more superficially, in the arabesques and encrustation of Cairo and Granada. But there was to the end something in it of the Iranian method of embedding a vigorous dominant motive within an opulent field of pattern.

XIII: BARBARIANS, MONKS, AND KINGS, AND
THE ART CALLED ROMANESQUE

IT USED to be that every chapter about Romanesque art—about, that is, the first named Christian art of the West—was fitted with a frontispiece showing the portal of St. Trophime at Arles. It was thought that the wide round arch, the symmetrical disposition of incidental columns and pilasters, and the profusion of built-in sculpture afforded an index to this "style"—which has been, at the hands of various authorities, (1) denied existence, (2) hailed as the peer of Gothic, (3) hailed as the triumph of the Roman tradition over barbarian and Oriental incursions,

and (4) hailed as the triumph of barbarian and Oriental creative impulse over the run-out Roman tradition.

There was a time when the present writer, living for a season at Arles, passed St. Trophime day after day; and he studied the porch and portal and got to wondering how this building —derived, if the name signifies, out of Rome— came by the vigorous decorative animals, so inevitably suggesting a connection with Persia or, farther back, with Altai-Iran; and the panels of sculpture in almost Indian profusion; and the

Portal, St. Trophime, Arles

269

typical "fat" Byzantine rounding of the garmented figures. There, puzzlingly, too, were the split columns right out of Rome, and the acanthus; even an egg-and-dart molding folded into the arabesque-like tympanum-border.

The truth is that the Europe of the time covered by the Romanesque period—say, from the sixth to the early twelfth century—was a battleground of warring cultures or, in the peaceful interims, a crossroads of trade routes and religious currents, and a meeting-ground of mutually alien aesthetic aptitudes. The portal at Arles provides an extraordinary visual summary of several ingredients of the style—as may be seen in the illustration on page 269. The subject, as apart from the manner, is the Last Judgment. The closely packed frieze figures on the one side represent the saved; on the other side are the damned. Larger figures of the apostles appear below. Perhaps most truly a key to the influence of Byzantine art on the medieval sculptors is the pictorial or otherwise informal nature of the capitals and bases above and below the columns.

The people of the countries north of Italy were those generically known as barbarians. Although they were being gradually Christianized and doubtless would, if they could, have embraced the arts as well as the religion of Rome, once they became enlightened their instinctive ways of expression were those of the northern and eastern motherlands, utterly different from anything in the Graeco-Roman tradition. Through one-half of Europe the Latin tongue prevailed as the basis for new dialects. This is the one valid reason for the name "Romanesque"; although the territory ultimately Teutonic is as large as that wherein the Romance languages are spoken.

In any case, to define Romanesque as "the art of Romanized Europe"—as has often been done—is unsound and misleading. As archaeological evidence accumulates, as the West escapes from the classic obsession, it becomes progressively clearer that in the Dark and Middle Ages the barbarian and Eastern art impulses dominated and all but submerged the Latin. The great adventure that was Romanesque and Gothic was as far as can be imagined from the Graeco-Roman spirit.

The Northern peoples continued to practice sporadically their formalized crafts; and they treasured, as of their own sort, the works borne in from Byzantium—the figured silks, ivories, enamels, metals. Finally, in a fusion of Gothic and Teutonic elements with Byzantine and Syrian and Persian, the accent and stamp of Rome were well-nigh lost, except in an occasional molding or capital or realistic interpolation. Not until the Italian scholars of the dawning Renaissance triumphed in central Italy was the tide of European art to be turned again into Roman ways: to the rational classic manner of building, to the realistic, informal, documentary grooves of "typical Western" painting and sculpture.

Meanwhile, within the development still called Romanesque, there is historic reason for recognizing that the animals of St. Trophime and of Vézelay and Souillac have affinity more with those of Siberia, and thus with those of China, than with anything out of Athens or Alexandria or Rome. The round arches and certain sculptural motives and rhythms, moreover, as seen in St. Ambrogio in Milan, at Poitiers, at Brunswick, even in the crypt and a porch at Canterbury Cathedral, may be as easily of the Near Oriental as of the Western persuasion.

These long fugitive elements and motives and symbols, hidden under the Romanesque name, have since 1900 brought Romanesque art into a place of significance in the history of European culture. One might almost say that until recently historians had treated Romanesque art as a doormat to the Gothic. Today it is considered, on its own account, one of the richest fields of exploration and enjoyment in all European art. The name "Romanesque" is likely to persist, inadequate as it obviously is; the confusion of motives and sources remains; but there is opened an exciting new experience of art in the popular rediscovery of such monuments as Vézelay, Autun, and Souillac. Nor is the reawakened interest in Norman art, from Sicily to Britain, unconnected with the same shifting of critical values and of appreciation.

As regards architecture and sculpture, there is a school of historians willing to dismiss all the

Tympanum, detail,
Autun Cathedral

art of the Dark and Middle Ages as merely tentative and preparatory until the French genius suddenly unified it and taught it the magnificent gesture by which the Gothic cathedrals seemed to raise all eyes to God. There are even those who would add the best of Romanesque to Gothic (a name also imprecise, meaning merely "barbarous") and then rename the whole development "the French style." This simplification, like the one that summarizes Romanesque art as the art of Romanized Europe, seems to demand a blindness to realities. Whatever the European Christian art of the medieval centuries may or may not be called, it will remain a thing of mixed ancestry, changing aspect, and fused styles. But within the confused web of it is beauty, distinctive and appealing.

The peoples who overran Europe in the centuries during the decline of classic Rome, who sacked the city as early as 410 and as late as 1084, were to contribute in large part to the stock from which present-day inhabitants of middle and northern Europe sprang. It is well to examine their arts as the first background fabric of Romanesque culture. These barbarians, of whom the names Goths, Teutons, Franks, Germans, Lombards are used to indicate a generic likeness or special divisions, brought art aptitudes of their own; but, being less settled, they seldom ventured into the truly monumental arts. As they came from the forest lands, they naturally built in perishable wood. Not centered in permanent home-regions—having, perhaps, the persisting nomad instinct—they had no appreciable sculpture in stone. The most that we have of theirs for appreciation today is in jewelry, weapons, and ceremonial objects, chiefly in precious metals.

Barbarian Arts

In a chapter on "Germanic or Barbarian Art" in his *History of Art*, Pijoan, who made a special study of this field, included illustrations of the votive crown of Recceswinth, Chilperic's sword, the crown and appended cross of Theodolinde,

Spear ornaments from a grave. Vermand, France. *Metropolitan Museum of Art*

Theodoric's cuirass, and the so-called "iron cross" of the Lombards; to which he added various golden fibulae (safety pins), baskets, vases, crosses, and bracelets, along with some later architectural reliefs identified as Visigothic and Merovingian.

The most illuminating fact brought away from an examination of these relics is that the Frankish Chilperic and the Visigothic Recceswinth and the Lombard Queen Theodolinde spoke one language of art. The aspect of all the crowns and weapons and Christian crosses is of the sort we have come to speak of as Oriental. The typical patterning is of the Eastern, rich, all-over sort, and incidental animal figures are in the vigorous steppe-art tradition. There is evident a great range of cultural stages; the use-values of the objects would indicate stages of social organization from wandering tribe to ceremonial court; and the several provenances of the finds, from Hungary to Ireland, from Scandinavia to Spain, indicate successive tides of immigration and extensive diffusion. There is, nevertheless, the generic likeness among them, the general non-Latin aspect.

The most probable explanation is that the barbarians of Europe, in the time of Byzantine Christianity in the East and Rome's struggle to become the seat of Christian power in the West, were of a single racial stock that had pushed westward from the Russian and Siberian plains, through the Danubian gateway in the south and across Poland in the north; and that back in the Scythian homeland certain basic elements of art expression had been early fixed. Germanic and Visigothic and Celtic or Gallic workmanship and design seem to indicate that they have a common origin with the Scytho-Iranian or Persian style, which had so strongly affected both Byzantine and Moslem art.

Indeed, if in Europe and the Near East there could be marked two main streams of art practice and art principle, one would be the Graeco-Roman or classic, tending constantly to rationalism and realism, and to an idealism based on observation of the natural; the other the Persian or Oriental, careless of reproductive reality, ornamentally formalized, richly decorative. Romanesque art was a meeting-ground of these two world currents: the sluggish surviving classic impulse, and the stream of nonrealistic decorative art. Within the latter flow, two currents, originally from the same source but long separated, were coming together: the stream of Byzantine arts from the Eastern into the Western Christian empire, and the native racial art still practiced by the northern "tribes." The Germanic craftsmen were essentially brothers of the Byzantine artists who met them in the Christian West.

Most of the barbarian relics justly so named date from about A.D. 350 to the end of the seventh century. These were manufactured by the still untamed invaders, the uncivilized attackers of Rome. In the Metropolitan Museum in New York there is a collection of their safety pins and rings and brooches and earrings, together with parts of weapons and scabbards. The motives are geometrical and near-abstract. The method is that of dividing the object into "fields" of flattened relief. There are, of course, many routine utilitarian objects not too expertly designed. But there are also exceptional trinkets and orna-

The Oseberg ship.
Oslo Museum

ments that have the vigor and decorative rich-ness of near-primitive adornment.

A set of spear ornaments in gilt-finished silver, recovered from a fourth-century grave at Ver-mand in France, indicates a craftsman's impulse or tradition closely akin to that of the Viking woodcarvers and, in floriations that escape iden-tification with any real flower, to that of the Irish. There are similar metal objects, designed vigor-ously and with the characteristic all-over pat-terning, from points in Germany, Austria, the Balkan states, Switzerland, and Scandinavia—pins and pendants, bracelets and chains, pocket-ornaments and buckles. An especially rich show-ing of this sort of crafts-art is to be seen in the great archaeological museums in the larger Swiss cities—where sometimes it seems that the manu-facture of safety pins was the outstanding bar-barian industry. The artist will note the vast number of these pins that retain a faint reminder of the bird-form—both the simpler types and such works as the elaborated Celtic brooches illus-trated on page 275. The French historians are inclined to make a special subject of this sort of Gallo-Roman art, attempting to isolate barbarian craftsmanship as it developed in Gaul during the early Romanesque (and immediately preceding) centuries from the general Celtic complex. But

only the specialist is able, or needs, to separate the characteristics of Gallic, Celtic, Lombard, and Visigothic art.

There are, however, two outstanding national developments of pre-Romanesque art in Europe which will speedily impress the observer's mind. In Scandinavia the Viking civilization has left monuments finely decorative and obviously re-lated to the Eastern source-art; and in Ireland the distinctive relics are stylistically reminiscent of the same origins, but more eloquent of a settled and independently creative civilization. Some authorities insist that both bodies of art are sur-vivals of Neolithic cultures that cannot on any evidence in hand be connected racially with the Germanic barbarians. Others hold that the Celtic culture, superseding the general late Stone Age culture, of which the Swiss lake-dweller tribes were the most memorable part, marked an East-ern-Iranian invasion preceding the Germanic, and of the same stock. Certainly the motives and methods found in the art works would seem to confirm the theory that there was one Scythian source. In any case the Norse or Scandinavian development and the Irish are notably alike, and in turn have affinity with the later Gothic and Frankish expressions.

The Norsemen or Normans, the Vikings of

Irish sculptured cross. Drumcliffe

Norway and Denmark, were in the ninth and tenth centuries known unfavorably at every seaport from the Baltic Sea to Gibraltar and Palermo. Their piratical exploits and their invasions changed history in England, Ireland, France, Spain, and Sicily. Their early art is best known in connection with the ships that made the sea forays possible. For the Viking chiefs were by custom buried in their galleys. Two of the vessels have been unearthed. The richly carved keel of one of these (now in a museum at Oslo) is ornamented with the intertwined forms, geometrically spaced but expressive of vigorous animal life, which came from the East. The larger decorative form of the ships, moreover, is a link with the tradition of the Iranian steppe-peoples.

One need but trace the virile outline of the prow (see illustration on page 273), and one sees the spirited contour for which so much else was sacrificed in the Luristan bronzes, the Ordos figures, and the Persian textile-motives. It is the virile, formalized line that was eased out of Greek art in favor of symmetrical masses and observed natural detail and refined finish. It is eloquent of the craftsman's approach, the decorative intent, as against the representational and the realistic.

What is oftener known as Norman art is the architecture of a later period, which emerged after the Northmen had settled in western France (still called "Normandy"). Going from there to England, they took with them a Norman-Romanesque way of building; but this later art is better treated as a part of the story of Romanesque architecture, which appears later in the chapter.

The Celtic art of Ireland affords one of the most enjoyable episodes in the early history of Europe. The architectural monuments are in ruins, but the stone crosses are often intact except for the more delicate detail. The best of them are original in form, strong and simple in outline and mass, and extraordinarily rich in abstract and figured sculpture. They are not gravestones but celebrative monuments, often dedicated to saints. Some of the panels with figures are scenes of Christian legendry. Perhaps there converge in the crosses elements of the old Celtic stone-worship and the iconography of the Christian Church.

The proportioning of the shaft to the base and to the actual circled cross is often masterly. No less masterly is the way in which the surfaces are paneled off and in which each is filled with a composition decorative on its own account but contributing to the total lavish ornamental effect. If we had not become familiar with the crosses in their Irish setting we should be likely, upon a first meeting, to mark the intent as Oriental, the decorative manner as un-Western.

There are other Irish relics as distinctive. The reliquary of St. Patrick's bell is a rather sophisticated expression of the earlier abstract patterning and floriations. The bronze and gold brooches vary from those simple in form and sparingly decorated to extremely involved examples like the

Brooches. Bronze and silver on bronze. Celtic, Ireland. *Victoria and Albert Museum*

celebrated Tara Brooch of the seventh century, with elaborated outlines and intricately adorned surfaces. The ornamentation is of the sort that seems derived from the plant world but strictly reduced to abstract tracery.

There is a return to simplified forms in the Ardagh Chalice, in which the extensive areas of plain silver are played against rich bands of interlaced patterning on gold, studded with accenting enamel beads. There are many other ritual objects that testify to the Irish love of opulent ornamentation and to the persistence of the Celtic type of decoration: crosses, crosiers, bookclasps, and ceremonial vessels.

From these one might go on to the illuminated manuscripts produced at the Irish monasteries. The famous *Book of Kells* is one of the most elaborate examples, and the decorations from its pages afford the typical instances of Celtic ornament most often reproduced.

It is a temptation to linger over the episode of Irish art, for its story forms one of the most fascinating chapters in the cultural annals of the peoples of the British Isles. It is replete with romantic figures—not the least that of St. Patrick, who wisely founded Irish Christianity partly upon the learning and organization of the Druids;

who, legend says, dropped the somber habiliments of Rome to ride in white clothes behind two white stags; and who encouraged the continuation of Northern art.

There is something appropriate in the legend that St. Patrick used a bell given him by the Pope to call the Irish people together and to help him charm them away from other religions. There is another legend to the effect that he threw a clanging bell into the midst of an unresponsive and hostile group of barbarians and thus frightened them into submission. The Irish still treasure five bells reputed to have been Patrick's.

It is said that symbols of the pre-Celtic civilization survived in the circles of huge stones around the early Irish monasteries, reminiscent of the cromlechs or menhirs of the Stone Age sanctuaries. That Ireland should have become at one time the only settled home, even the refuge, of Christian faith and education in Europe, in those ages when barbarians were fighting Christians for possession of France and Germany and surrounding territory, and even devastating Italy itself; that it should have carried the torch, even while practicing its own vigorous and distinctive crafts without giving an inch to Roman art, is one of those happy incidents too rare in history.

Borderline Cultures
and Splinter Styles

The reader, after a preliminary look at the mixed character of Romanesque sculpture and architecture, and after a brief review of the small arts of the barbarian invaders, including the pure Northern styles of Scandinavia and Ireland, will now understand the confusion among historians and the well-nigh impossible task of laying out a schema for a showing of Early Christian, Byzantine, Teutonic and Celtic, and finally Romanesque art. There just is no easily marked chronological line, no one area of mergence, no continuous tradition. Europe was replete with borderline cultures, with splinter styles.

In France, as has already been suggested, a special subdivision may be made of Gallo-Roman relics of the early time when Rome actually did subjugate, or make peace with, the barbarian peoples. The suggestion of stark Roman portraiture and the fullness of the panel reliefs on Roman sarcophagi come through in certain medieval church sculptures. Cities such as Arles long continued to have schools of artists which had been established in the Roman era. There are authorities who mark the Calvaires of Brittany as a last product of the Roman spirit. (The Calvaires are outdoor sculptural monuments, often very elaborate, depicting scenes from the Passion of Christ. They survive mostly in Breton towns, always close to churches. They cannot be dated with any assurance before the fifteenth century. The heavy conventionalized handling of the stone is scarcely to be marked as Roman-derived.) There is a good deal of conjecture in all this evidence. More confusing are the mixing currents in Spain, where the Visigothic gradually gave way to the Byzantine (rather than the Roman), after which the area was inundated by Moslem art, then succumbed gradually to the fully matured Romanesque and the Gothic from France.

Farther north, where the Germanic or Frankish peoples were separating into two language groups which were later to give outline to the present French and German nations, with Flemish, Dutch, and Swiss connections, there was a less confused intermingling. By the time of the Merovingian kings, just before Charlemagne—in the eighth century—the Byzantine and Roman conjuncture with Germanic elements can be visibly traced in individual works. Basically, in church building, the basilica of the Western church was adopted, along with Byzantine ideas of decorative enrichment. Under Charlemagne the various forces were finally brought into some sort of focus. It is from "the Carolingian renaissance" that historians generally date the entry of the French spirit into European art.

The northern barbarians had had no architecture of their own. Roman writers mention the lack of cities and towns, and the comparatively mean nature of the scattered houses—when they were not caves. Paris was most like a crossroads camp of the Parisii. After the so-called pacification of Gaul, Roman cities were built in the "provinces" of northern Europe, but with the withdrawal of the Romans in the fourth and fifth centuries these were more or less abandoned. The medieval castles on the hilltops along the Rhone and the Rhine are symbolic of what happened. The barbarian, even when enlightened and wealthy, wanted isolation. The monasteries, particularly those of the Irish, were the truer homes of settled culture.

When a tribal chief became a king and needed a court from which to direct larger affairs, he must therefore draw upon the more established civilizations, and it was here that each ruler had to make an important choice. Should the models be Roman or Byzantine?

In the late fifth century the Ostrogoth Theodoric, having conquered Italy and having become, in the absence of any other, "King of Rome," setting up a court in Ravenna, adopted for his palace the Byzantine style, which had become acclimated there during the rule of the Western exarchs. On the other hand, when Theodoric thought about his tomb he decided it should be like those of the great Roman emperors; and the imported Roman architects did their best to supply their new barbarian king with a noble classic monument. This tomb at Ravenna is a remarkable and instructive compromise, somehow heavily Roman in aspect, yet

Leaf of diptych. Ivory.
Spain, 12th century.
Metropolitan Museum of Art

touched faintly with rich ornament that might be Germanic or Byzantine. The builders had lost the Roman knowledge of dome-construction and had not yet mastered the Eastern; so they imported an immense single stone slab and rounded the top to look like a built-up dome.

When it came Charlemagne's turn to set up a court from which he was to rule the Frankish territories, he chose Aix-la-Chapelle (now Aachen) as his capital. His subjects were then, to put it as accurately as one can, more or less Christianized. But when he drew a circle of advisers around him, wanting perhaps Christians but not Romans, he chose an Irish bishop, a Visigothic bishop from Spain, lately driven out by the Moslems, and sundry German supporters. Whatever these counselors may have contributed to the execution of Charlemagne's dream and plan to revive artistic as well as political glory in the new Holy Roman Empire, it was Byzantium to which all looked for models.

And indeed the chapel in Charlemagne's palace at Aix is after the plan of St. Vitale in Ravenna, a complex of arches and vaults around a domed central hall. The columns were actually brought from Rome and Ravenna, with the Pope's permission; and the mosaicists who set out to enrich the walls in the Eastern fashion are supposed to have been called from Constantinople. Charlemagne could not write, perhaps could not read, and his advisers, coming from the Church, the one remaining treasury and fountain of learning, naturally shaped his artistic tastes as well as his theology and politics; but he kept his authority too, changing the wording of the orthodox creed, collecting the old Frankish songs (later to be destroyed as pagan by his son and successor Louis the Pious), and ordering such works of art and furnishings as his fancy dictated.

After the loss of Italy to the barbarians, the papacy at Rome had been re-established, but had continued only on the sufferance of the Byzantine emperors. Now, by Charlemagne's alliance with the Pope, the Western Church was able to defy the Eastern power and at the same time rid itself of the threat of some still unsubjugated barbarian remnants. It is to be doubted if Rome at this time retained any considered allegiance to classic art as distinguished from Byzantine. Latin Catholicism, after the abandonment of Italy, had practically died, and had re-stemmed from Byzantium. In any case, when the Pope in 800 set a crown on Charlemagne's head and gave Church sanction to his position as successor of the Caesars and Emperor of the Holy Roman Empire, the event tended to stabilize Europe politically but did not change established trends in the arts.

The Emperor's architect built, besides the structures at Aix-la-Chapelle—soon called "the new Rome"—a number of buildings in Germany. Charlemagne's bishops and lieutenants, too, encouraged the arts and crafts throughout the empire. At Cividale, near Udine, in Italy, there are church decorations that are not only rewarding intrinsically but instructive as indicating a mingling of Byzantine, Irish, Germanic, and Roman influences.

The feudal system in some measure explains the diversity continuing through the following two centuries. Petty kingdoms and principalities, even local overlords with small castle-courts and bands of vassals, resisted the central or imperial authority. In the eleventh century France still was a patchwork of practically independent polities: Normandy, Aquitaine, Burgundy, Flanders, etc. This was not yet an age of local initiative, but a time of crossing currents, as was indicated further by the marriage of Otto II, German Emperor of the Holy Roman Empire, to a Byzantine princess, and his importation of a number of Byzantine artists and craftsmen to found schools and workshops in Rome. His son Otto III cherished even grander schemes for restoring Roman glory in culture and the arts. His influence in Germany is noted in the story of Bernward of Hildesheim on page 283.

Monasteries: the Real Home of the Arts

The religion of the time affects art expression fundamentally; and indeed one can scarcely understand Romanesque culture without recalling the function of the monasteries as refuges of learning and workshops of art, without recalling, too, the constant come-and-go of far-traveling pilgrims, and then of Crusaders. The widespread and worshipful treasuring of sacred relics led to a ceaseless movement of the devout back and forth across the Roman Empire and as far east as Palestine. The procession of worshipers meant continual circulation of the diverse currents of the empire, and especially a flood of relics, gifts, and spoils from Byzantium and the Asian holy cities. A little later the same spirit led to the building of churches and cathedrals out of all proportion in size to the needs of local worshipers. Of course the architectural glorification of God—the building of a house for the Divine Spirit and a treasury for sacred objects—called for something monumental; but a more practical consideration was that the structure would need to shelter vast numbers of pilgrims.

The first monasteries to become centers of art production were Egyptian and Syrian. The Copts were the earliest to bring the monastic system into Christianity. Asceticism is an element of the Eastern rather than of the Western spiritual faiths. It had been practiced by the Hindus before Buddha, and to a limited extent by Greek and Jewish cults. It was natural that the Asiatic and Egyptian Christians should be the first to withdraw into sacred communal retreats. The libraries and studios of Alexandria, with the tradition of Hellenism persisting, doubtless had much to do with the development of the schools of scribes within the newly formed monastic establishments.

In the West the monastic system took firm root with the founding of a series of monasteries under St. Benedict early in the sixth century. After completing his own period of mortification in a hair shirt, within a cave retreat on a rocky precipice, he turned back to more practical Western ways of demonstrating Christian piety. He organized and directed a chain of a dozen monasteries in Southern Italy and insisted upon a gospel that included, along with faith, brotherhood and charity and a regimen of hard work. The brothers who did not go out on missions to convert the pagans—practically all the nearest neighbors were heirs to the late Roman cults—were constrained to labor within the monastery walls. The perpetuation of learning and the practice of the arts and crafts constituted a major activity of the inmates.

The central Benedictine monastery at Monte Cassino, south of Rome, became a refuge for all of Western Christianity. It was at times a lonely asylum, during the troubled period when Rome itself was repeatedly sacked and lost to the unlettered barbarians. Within a half-century of Benedict's death one of the Benedictine monks had become Pope—Gregory the Great—and had been instrumental in establishing the Benedictine order through large parts of Europe. The Irish monasteries were linked with the Italian center, and the Irish Benedictines stood firmest for Christ and Rome when political chaos and intellectual darkness had come on the Continent.

In Italy, Cassiodorus was greatest of the early monastic leaders. He particularly set up treasuries and schools and crafts-rooms. Perhaps his Syrian ancestry and his patrician derivation had something to do with his reverence for the intellectual and artistic heritage of mankind. He is said to have founded the first monastery devoted exclusively to the transcription of manuscripts.

The art work of the monks was, of course, directed into those channels which led to glorification of God and the spiritual enlightenment of mankind. Copying and embellishment of the holy books came first. But under a broad-minded superior the manuscripts might extend to lay works on the borders of science and philosophy. And the immediate church arts—particularly when popes and bishops had fallen heirs to the titles and traditions of emperors—could be carried to the most elaborate and sumptuous expressions in goldsmithing, ivory-carving, and vestment-embroidery. Yet it is significant, on the other side, that what is traditionally known in the book arts as "monastic binding" is the sort tooled without gold.

Toward the end of monastic leadership in the arts, in the early twelfth century, Suger, Abbot of St. Denis, defending himself against charges of worldliness brought by St. Bernard of Clairvaux, was to write a line that well sums up the case for the craftsmen in the monasteries. From being scholar and crafts-worker he had become head of the abbey and a national ecclesiastical and political leader in France. He wrote: "If the ancient law . . . ordained that cups of gold should be used for libations and to receive the blood of rams . . . how much rather should we devote gold, precious stones, and the rarest of metals to those vessels destined to hold the blood of Our Lord?" This was the spirit in which goldworkers fashioned chalices and ritual crosses, candelabra and reliquaries.

Cassiodorus himself in his writings expressed something of the spirit in which the copyists of manuscripts worked. The monk, he says, "may fill his mind with the Scriptures while copying the sayings of the Lord; with his fingers he gives life to men and arms against the wiles of the devil; as the antiquarius copies the word of Christ, so many wounds does he inflict on Satan. What he writes in his cell will be carried far and wide over distant provinces." If the monk happened to be a trained and gifted artist as well, he carried on the world traditions of aesthetic expression, even while thus finding satisfaction in a consecrated task.

The manuscript illuminations or illustrations comprise a miniature history of Christian representational art. Here can be traced the beginnings and development of style and method, of icon and symbol. The whole cycle of change, from Greek-influenced picturing, through crystallizing Byzantine formalism, and into the varied European decorative embellishment, may be seen in a well-chosen collection of manuscript illuminations. The highly stylized practice is followed by realistic illustration, then is touched with fantasy and the grotesque, the realist's substitutes for naïveté and formalism.

From the pageant-like changing pages can be selected some of the most spirited and enjoyable miniature paintings in all human history. Each illumination *was* a painting, though then as always the greater portion of painters copied or adapted from a few true masters among them; and the creation of a single manuscript and its illustrations and decorations might consume many years of a miniaturist's time.

In the early Christian manuscripts may be found perfect analogues of Roman and Hellenistic painting, of the Pompeian house paintings and the catacomb murals. All the exactitudes and weaknesses of the realistic illustrator are here. But soon one finds the decorative impulse gaining ascendancy. The Oriental method gradually replaces the classic. The scenes are laid out without background; the figures are formalized; and almost throughout the thousand-year history of Christian illumination the two Oriental canons prevail: rich bordering floriation and richly ornamented panels, and a neglect of "the natural realities" of the human form and all representa-tional elements in favor of plastic aliveness and rigid stylization.

The fifth, sixth, and seventh centuries marked the height of achievement in Byzantium and in the monasteries of nearby lands. Then the iconoclast controversy burst over the Eastern Church, and Constantinople forbade all images. The Western Church, however, carried on Christian iconography and illustration, in the method already set in the Eastern lands. Indeed it is supposed that great numbers of the monk-artists then deserted the Byzantine monasteries of Greece and Syria to escape the prohibition, joining the chapters of their orders in the West.

During the centuries that followed there were tentative and at times notable thrusts toward realistic documentation, but they were the exceptional, not the typical thing, up to the thirteenth century. In the miniatures as in metalworking the stream of influence out of the East, when it had gone from Egypt and Syria to Byzantium and thence to the monasteries that gave political allegiance to the reconstructed Roman authority, met that other stream from the north, bearing influences from the original Iranian-Asiatic source. Thus the Irish formalized ornament found perfect understanding and acceptance among monk-artists accustomed to the ways of the Asiatic scriptoria.

For full appreciation of the miniatures one should have an eye as emancipated from representational necessities as that demanded for enjoyment of Chinese landscapes or Persian miniatures. An early work like the *Gospel of Rossano,* a Syrian or possibly Egyptian manuscript in Greek, of the sixth century, was not yet crystallized into the full Byzantine formalism (or "stiffness"), but already the picturing is flat, decoratively spaced, and stripped of background and detail. The one feature of the treatment of the halo about Christ's head might be noted as indicating the unclassic approach of the artist-monk. It is a decorative scheme in itself. In the Byzantine scripts of the following centuries the patterning instinct, which led the miniaturist to grasp every opportunity to spread a rich all-over design on Christ's or emperor's robe or on architectural column or frieze, is apparent in count-

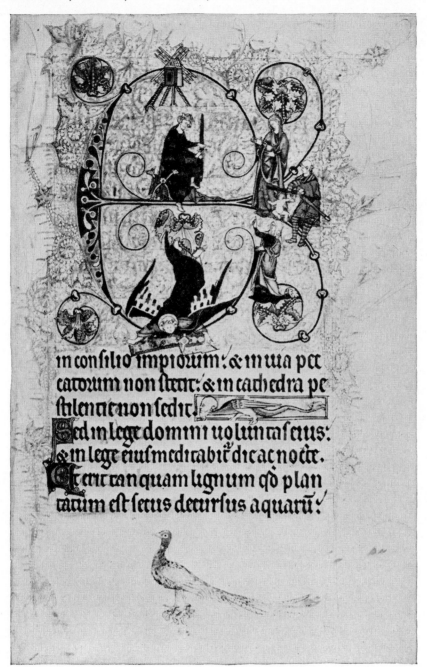

Illuminated page from the Windmill Psalter. England, 14th century.
Pierpont Morgan Library, New York

less manuscripts. The other sort of formalization, which led to treatment of the representational elements in rigid stylization, is as evident in manuscripts as in mosaics and in mural paintings of the time. Then the interest in the "natural" begins to reassert itself. There are examples at

Cover of manuscript
of *The Gospels*.
France, 9th century.
*Pierpont Morgan Library,
New York*

every stage of evolution from stiffened emblem-figure to almost photographic delineation. There is a lesson to be learned from that fourteenth-century English Psalter in the Morgan Library in New York, wherein actualized human beings are presented against areas of abstract patterning. A single page bears a realistic study of a peacock and a fanciful winged figure heraldically formalized. This work was done at the very end of the history of illuminated manuscripts.

From the miniatures as individual precious works of art, and from the vellum manuscripts as a whole, harmonizing calligraphy and decoration, one might go on to the rich bindings as worthy relics of the arts matured in the monasteries. The leather bindings with elaborate tooling are a later development; but the Byzantine examples of sumptuous jeweled book-covers have perhaps never been surpassed. Some of the finest ivory carvings of the Byzantine and Ro-

manesque eras were in the form of panels to be set into bookboards.

The bookbindings, moreover, yield up numerous beautiful examples of enameling, although this craft was incidental also to goldsmithing and to the other metal arts. Enamel picture plaques were set into crosses, votive crowns, and altar-fronts. There are reliquary caskets entirely covered with gold-set enamel sheathing, as illustrated in the opulent example opposite.

While the splendid Byzantine works seem to have influenced the German and French enamelists in the middle era, the early examples lack the fire and glow of Eastern products. But there are in the European things a solemn richness and a distinctive muted harmony of coloring. The process of filling gold-fenced depressions or cloisons with the enamels is here abandoned for a less difficult and costly one known as champlevé, in which the cells for the colored paste

Reliquary with champlevé enamel decorations. Limoges, about 1200.
Metropolitan Museum of Art

are cut into a metal back; and opaque enamels usually replace the translucent ones. The Western medieval enamels can be traced back, in general, to schools or crafts-shops centered at Limoges, Liége and neighboring towns, and Cologne.

A diverting sidelight on the relationship of the monastic artist and the "Northern civilization" is afforded by the stories told of Bernward of Hildesheim, who became bishop in A.D. 993. From being a scholar and a craftsman he progressed to being a leading protector and patron of the arts; and he made his German city a continuing treasury of crafts-works. He personally designed many of the sumptuous accessories and fittings of the cathedral, and the workers under his direction, particularly the goldsmiths, achieved international fame. His own cross and candlesticks are a bit on the florid side, although perpetuating the Germanic synthesis of decorative patterning and incidental vigorous animal forms. The Hildesheim appointments include straight Byzantine designs, and also some obviously transitional works, with elements of realism and a worldliness of subject-interest (even nudes) entering in. There is a strain of ancient Roman naturalism mixing in here, for the bishop had studied the sculptures of the Eternal City as guest at the palace of Otto III.

But Bernward is symbolic. In a time when the arts were still monastic and remote from common living, he gave them wider life, new civic significance. He was painter, scholar, engineer, architect, worker in precious metals; and bishop and fighter as well. He was canonized two centuries later. He is one of the few artist-saints.

Suger, Abbot of St. Denis, who was born about 1081, similarly became patron of the crafts, and defended the monastic artists against the charges of un-Christian lavishness in decoration.

Christ on the Cross. Relief panel.
Metropolitan Museum of Art

Theophilus, a monk and crafts-instructor, probably of the eleventh century, wrote an encyclopedic work on the crafts processes entitled *Upon Divers Arts.* He strove to inspire the monks with a holy zeal, exhorting them to "believe in entire faith that the Spirit of God has filled your heart when you have adorned His house with so great beauty and so many arts." He also assured the workers special rewards in the life to come —where artists of many ages and places have *had* to place their hopes of recompense.

Theophilus' instructions regarding technique and materials are often clear and sound, though some of his instances are very strange, and his chemistry is deplorable. He is very broad in his review of the sources of his crafts knowledge, mentioning the metal-chasing of Arabia, the mosaics and enamels of Tuscany, the windows of France, and the works of "industrious Germany" in metals, wood, and stone.

The Persian-Byzantine tradition in silks and embroideries continued in the centuries of Romanesque crystallization, as one would expect in territories where imported Oriental stuffs had long been among the most prized of gifts and possessions of the wealthy. As we have noted, Charlemagne was buried in a Persian shroud. Sacred relics in the church treasuries were commonly wrapped in bits of rich figured embroidery; robes of bishop and king and chief were opulently decorative. Of native French or English works there is one that transcends all other surviving examples: the so-called Bayeux Tapestry. It embraces a series of seventy-two connected pictures of the Norman Conquest of England, embroidered on a strip of linen 231 feet in length and twenty inches in width. The drawing is spirited and posteresque, and the whole uniquely effective as formal design.

He is the better known for insisting that more French craftsmen be trained and fewer experts brought from Byzantine art centers. He too ran to magnificence and touches of free naturalism, in decorating the monastic church he had built.

It may be only a coincidence, but the traditional formalism began to go out as art became secularized. Not far distant loomed the time of the guilds, the lay organizations of artisans who were to take the crafts, as also the theater art, out of the hands of the Church brothers. The guilds were to grow up at first within the rather precarious stability of the social structure determined by the feudal lords. At the time of Bernward and Suger, however, it was still the church rather than the palace or castle that was the protector and treasury of the arts.

Romanesque Architecture

It is likely that the architects who went to Ravenna to do Theodoric's bidding in the sixth century considered themselves privileged Romans, temporarily deposed, if not Roman nobles. Their art was secular. When Charlemagne built in the ninth century, his architects were servants of the Church; and important European architecture for six centuries following was destined to be ecclesiastical. Romanesque architecture is essentially an art of the Christian Church.

Romanesque is a heavy style. It confesses outwardly the thickness of its walls. The thrust of its vaults led to buttressing either by masses of stone or by side-buildings laterally disposed. In this the style goes back to the pre-Byzantine churches of Christian Persia and Mesopotamia and Syria, of which the cruciform domed structure was an outgrowth. Byzantium played with the form, did daring feats in spreading the dome over complexes of arches, vaults, and apses. Islam had its turn at elaborating and decorating the type. But in France, and thus in England and Germany, Christian church-building turned serious, took something from old Rome, and built heavily on the soil; then became, in a sudden burst of creativeness on the part of the builders, a new expression of man's aspiration and imagination.

Italy had long been barbarian, too, at the dawning of the eleventh century; and Lombard Italy poured into France some of the energy that brought about the Romanesque efflorescence in stone. It is necessary to remember always the continuous streams of pilgrims on the roads of Europe, and particularly the network of monasteries with one spiritual and artistic outlook, from Monte Cassino to Fulda in Germany, and the British communities. The Benedictine monks were a sort of international fatherhood determining the like forms of Romanesque building throughout Europe.

The church of St. Ambrogio in Milan is a landmark in the development of Romanesque, and the more notable because a certain synthesis of lingering Roman elements and Byzantine and Germanic is indicated, even while a new and determining structural feature is involved. In a certain purity of form it is unique among the buildings of Italy. Almost invariably the edifices elsewhere bow to ancient Rome or to Byzantium in their structure, or are studies in decoration—like Pisa Cathedral—over a basilica framework. St. Ambrogio is pure Romanesque.

There are legends, to a certain extent docu-

St. Ambrogio, Milan

mented, regarding the unique mastery of vaulting on the part of the ancient brotherhood of masons, the *Magistri Comacini*, resident at Como above Milan. They invented or revived a variation of roof-structure in the groined vault. In this system the space under the more usual barrel vault is cut into squared segments by transverse arches. Each square is then covered by a vault crossed by diagonal arches or ribs. Among other results, the thrust of the vault is transferred from the lateral walls of the squares to the piers at the four corners. From this circumstance came the clustered columns of the high Romanesque and Gothic periods. There was in the ribbed vault, too, the seed of Gothic separation of structural skeleton and "skin."

The main hall of St. Ambrogio is built over four main squares in the nave, sixteen minor squares in the aisles, and seven in the atrium or portico. To the credit of the Lombard architects, they externalized their novel way of building instead of concealing it. There is a frank

French Romanesque vaulting. Bayeux Cathedral.
Drawing by N.-M. J. Chapuy, 1845

monuments in Italy might be noted as resting within the meaning either structurally or decoratively. But it is St. Ambrogio that is outstanding, by reason of its originality and its vigor, its Germanic forthrightness and its Italian melodious rhythms. Especially there is the new type of vaulting. Here is implicit Italy's contribution to the flowering of a medieval architecture of the North.

Burgundy was the first home of the French genius. From there the spirit swept into Normandy, where French sensibility crossed with Viking vigor. But the amazing thing about the eleventh-century architectural advance is the blazing rapidity with which it covered every part of the old Gallic province. The year 1000, feared by the faithful as likely to bring millennial disaster, had been safely passed. Christian enthusiasm suddenly reacted from a blighting awe and dread. Interest was shifted from the after-life to an immediate future-in-life.

There is a school of criticism that grants less influence to the Burgundians, whose claim is based on the spread of moral and aesthetic impulses from the monastery at Cluny. Earlier the scattered Benedictine abbeys had been independent, but in the tenth century a league was formed, and Cluny became a center of authority and leadership. Soon the Benedictine order held sway over a vast European territory, extending into Spain and Britain and Germany. The building of many of the greatest Romanesque churches was fostered by the monks sent out from the central abbey.

The abbey-church at Cluny, however, was destroyed during the French Revolution. It had been built, or rebuilt, in 1089, and it was then the largest church in the Western Christian empire. It is said to have been so beautiful that no mortal architect could have planned it. St. Paul, according to the faithful, came in a vision to the artist-monk charged with the designing, and gave him the plans. A dissident group of monks, reacting against a growing ornateness and an unnecessary pretentiousness in building, as also against the display of wealth and the relaxation of discipline among the Cluniacs, established in A.D. 1098 the Cistercian order.

squareness, an engaging honesty of expression, in the edifice. The enlarged piers are structurally decorative. Ornament is of the sparest. There is a rhythmic simplicity in the arcades which is Italianate; this feature did not go to France and England. With the lift of Norman Romanesque the lingering southern horizontality disappeared.

It would be misleading to argue too much importance into this one church, as if there were no other Romanesque monuments in Lombardy, no major relics of eleventh- and twelfth-century building in the rest of Italy. In many parts of the marvelous Lombard country there are fascinating hunting grounds for lovers of architecture, from the hill towns against the Alps down through the cities of the Po Valley. And farther south there are the varied achievements at Pisa, Florence (where San Miniato is especially notable), Pistoia, and Lucca. In view of the generously inclusive nature of the term "Romanesque," many of the medieval

Porch of St. Peter's
at Aulnay

St. Bernard of Clairvaux, who in the twelfth century became the greatest churchman and saint of his time, wrote in 1127 a famous letter enumerating the excesses of certain Cluniac establishments. He chided the builders for erecting structures too high and too large. He said that in adding sculptured horrors and abnormal monsters they were introducing alien and pagan features that could only disturb Christian calm. He managed to keep the architecture of Cistercian abbeys simple and unpretentious. But the *typical* French Romanesque church or cathedral continued on its way to grandeur.

There are classifications of the French Romanesque, based on locality, on influences brought in by varied building materials, and on the degree of independence shown in handling the type-structure. Provence and Burgundy were in close affinity. (Both were on the highways from Lombardy.) Farther west, in Toulouse, Auvergne, and Aquitaine there was perhaps more of independent experiment and invention. A new logic comes clear in large structures, and there is a greater profusion of sculpture.

An early church, Notre Dame du Port at Clermont-Ferrand in Auvergne, is transitional in that it combines groined vaults over the aisles with a nave covered by a barrel vault. The thrust of the barrel vault had to be met by flanking half-barrel vaulting over the triforium galleries (the half-stories above the aisles). Under the necessity of providing this direct buttressing, the clerestory windows were squeezed out. Part of the impulse to the development of matured Romanesque came from the desire to increase the amount of light that could be admitted without reducing stability and safety. In St. Sernin at Toulouse, one of the most impressive early medieval churches, the continuous side-thrust of the barrel vault was modified by the insertion of transverse arches at regular intervals; but there still was too little chance to pierce the heavy walls for illumination. Not until the groined vault was further tested and perfected, so that it could be used over the nave, was it possible to achieve the impressive height desired and at the same time to have clerestory lighting.

Before that consummation—that is, before the system developed at St. Ambrogio in Milan was accepted in the North—there were many compromise or transitional structures. At Angoulême the cathedral was built without side-aisles; the nave was roofed by three domes, and the crossing by a fourth one, raised on a drum pierced by windows; but the main façade, decorated with heavy arcading, with corner towers added, had taken on a distinctly Romanesque aspect. St. Front in Périgueux is modeled much more on the Byzantine plan—being notably like Justinian's Church of the Holy Apostles in Constantinople, or its derivative, St. Mark's in Venice—than on Roman and Lombard lines. But its Eastern vaults and domes fail to remove it from the general category of Romanesque building. Similarly it is impossible to say how much in the façade of Notre Dame la Grande at Poitiers is Byzantine, how much Romanesque. A long series of churches, like St. Trophime at Arles, returned toward horizontality. The structural forms and the decorative features lean toward the traditions of Italy and of Byzantium.

But the church that is considered typical "high" Romanesque has those characteristics that could develop only with the perfecting of the groined vault. A basic identifying feature of the style is the round arch. But gradually the pillars pushed upward under the corners of the vault—and the vertical accent that is the second distinguishing surface feature of Northern Romanesque was established. Thus came, too, the increased aspect of mystery that is of the essence of late Romanesque and of Gothic building.

St. Etienne at Caen in Normandy is perhaps the most characteristic example of the high Romanesque phase. The long central nave and the flanking aisles afford a basic form not too changed from that of the ancient Roman basilica. The addition of transept wings, a feature from the East, modifies the plan and renders it cruciform—at a meeting-point of utilitarian considerations and symbolism. There are high clerestory windows, here appearing above a second row of arches giving onto galleries over the aisles. The basilica apse area has been greatly enlarged; not only do the aisles continue around the sanctuary, in what is known as the ambulatory, but the small apses or chapels flanking them are joined in one encircling structural unit.

The interior proclaims at first glance the method of construction: with groined vaults supported by clustered pillars. The arches have not yet given up their roundness, nor is there any attempt to lighten the generally "serious" effect with a profusion of ornament. The sense of mystery, of grandeur, of heaviness—perhaps of a sort of impressive sorrow that derives from Christian ideology—is evoked by these round arches and sturdy piers and by the twilight atmosphere. There is more of rest, of quiet, here than in the more decorated and fragile Gothic. The Romanesque exteriors of the North, too, are comparatively plain, homely and forthright, though many, as at Caen, were later given Gothic spires.

To England the Normans carried from France the knowledge of mature Romanesque design and craftsmanship. The early English cathedrals were constructed in this style, and there were numerous Norman castles. It is said that no fewer than seven thousand churches were built in England in the century following the Norman Conquest of 1066. There had been a native Anglo-Saxon architecture, which was of heavy, sturdy type, and this contributed some minor features to the new expression.

English Romanesque is usually known as Norman architecture. Durham Cathedral is the largest monument in which the original Romanesque character has persisted through later accidents and "improvements." But some of the most impressive bits of Romanesque construction are to be seen in the crypt of Canterbury Cathedral, in the transepts of Winchester, in the crypt of Worcester, and in parts of Peterborough. In general the English cathedrals had longer transepts than those in the typical buildings in France and a main tower was added over the crossing.

In the German Romanesque churches there is more of the old basilica, and of surviving Carlovingian features as adapted from the Byzantine by the architects who built for Charlemagne at Aachen (Aix-la-Chapelle); and there is a special affinity with the Lombard forms with which the Romanesque technically began. But again diversity is a first characteristic of the churches grouped under the style name. The plentiful wood of Germany often led the archi-

Tympanum of abbey church, Vézelay, about 1130

tects to roof the naves with that material, and therefore there was no rapid transition toward the church marked by the idioms developed from the use of the groined vault. Nor was there an influx of Norman ecclesiastics and workers as in England. Nevertheless, the cathedrals of Worms, Mainz, and Speyer, and the Church of the Apostles at Cologne, are among the typical vaulted edifices with consistent round-arch construction. Certain minor features set off the German Romanesque from other varieties— notably, plans with apses at both ends of the church and, on the exterior, a profusion of arcaded galleries and round or octagonal turrets. In Germany more markedly than elsewhere Romanesque architecture was made into something consistent, distinct from the Byzantine on the one hand and from the Gothic on the other. But as an elaborated style, as seen in the larger monuments, it is somewhat dull, with virtues that lie in the perilous realm of the picturesque. Some of the best of it in Germany is appropriately in "romantic" half-ruined castles. And indeed, throughout Europe the thick-walled,

turreted, and almost windowless Romanesque way of building was employed for castles, forts, and city walls.

Sculpture

Sculpture in Europe from the beginning of the Christian era had included: (1) some slight continuation of the late Graeco-Roman naturalism, as seen particularly in reliefs on sarcophagi, with Jonah and the whale, Daniel and the lions, and other Christian characters treated in traditional illusionistic technique, marking the final stage of decadence in the classic method; (2) Byzantine practice, from which monumental statuary had disappeared, but including exquisite ivory carvings, in which Eastern abundant patterning and Eastern rhythmic formalization took on something of Greek grace; (3) sporadic continuation of the Northern "barbarian" art, which crystallized in a few outstanding manifestations such as the Celtic crosses of Ireland and the Viking carved ornamentation, and then was

St. Peter.
Figure on portal,
Moissac

diffused into varied crafts manifestations through northern Europe, Spain, and Lombardy; and (4) a great many isolated examples of production where barbarian, Roman, and Byzantine currents crossed, resulting in ornamental sculpture of the most confused characteristics.

In this period between late Roman realistic practice and the emergence of a first recognizable type of medieval sculpture—which occurred at about A.D. 1100—the Byzantine small sculpture must be considered the standard product in Europe as well as in the Eastern Christian realm. An exceptional development is to be marked in Germany, where in the eleventh century a realistic strain came into evidence. An example is the cathedral doors at Hildesheim, made under the supervision of the craftsman-bishop Bern-

ward. He, as we have seen, had studied the ancient monuments in Rome. (He had been for a term of years tutor of the boy prince who was to become Emperor of the Holy Roman Empire as Otto III.) There is reason to believe that the famous "Bernward column," with its spiral reliefs, was suggested by an examination of Trajan's Column. In any case there entered into German work of 1000-50 a realistic note, and this brought about an unusual mixture of dramatic images and care for natural detail. The intention is obviously pictorial and documentary.

By the opening of the twelfth century, however, the truer forms of medieval sculpture had been established. Two main types can be detected. The general drift of critical opinion is that the Graeco-Roman tradition had then

Figures on west portal,
Chartres Cathedral

run out, and that both types are resultants from essentially Northern or barbarian forces transforming a substantially Byzantine tradition. One type is distinguished by rounded forms, by flat paneling of figures, and by a snug fitting of sculptural to structural parts. The other is distinguished by great vigor, by elongation of forms, by sacrifice of realism of statement to the necessities of rhythm and pattern.

Both types developed as adjuncts of architecture —unlike sculpture in the classic tradition. Both tend to be "unnatural." The approach is intuitively aesthetic rather than intellectual; there is strong feeling for the formalized design, and a corresponding carelessness about observed nature. In other words, medieval sculpture is strongly expressionistic.

The rounded type is, of course, nearer to the Byzantine product; and indeed it is impossible to draw a line between the art that is reflective of practice in the Persian-affected Eastern Empire and the Romanesque of Lombardy and Provence. In general this rounded variety is to be seen in northern Italy and in southern France. In France the richest single exhibit is at Arles. There are ornamental sculptures with comparable flat formalization in Germany and Spain, and England had a great amount of it in the Norman period.

The exterior sculpture of the church of St. Trophime at Arles, concentrated almost entirely in and around the porch of the Romanesque structure, is an exceptionally rich example. Here the influence of classic art may have entered in to an unusual degree, for Arles had been famous as a center of Roman provincial art. There are classic pilasters and moldings folded into the typically Oriental aggregates of figured panels, ornamental bands and edgings, and accenting figures, as in the illustration on page 269.

The recessed porches, constructed of joined arches in diminishing size, are a standard mark of Romanesque, as at Aulnay. Already at St. Trophime the portal thus elaborated had become a chief repository for sculptural illustration and adornment. In the later Romanesque churches the porches were at times to take on a greater unity and a closer texture of patterning —these were preparation for the great ornamental portals of the Gothic cathedrals—but at Arles the individual panels and figures already had a mature refinement of technique and an unsurpassed richness of light-and-shade effect.

The incidental sculpture of many a North Italian church—say at Bergamo, Ferrara, Genoa, and Brescia—will be found to have the same fullness and rounding, often with a sort of conventionalized patterning, or again a playing with arabesquerie, which suggests a partial return to the Byzantine. Similar bits occur at points as far separated as Ripoll in Spain, Brunswick in Germany, and Ely in England.

In the second type, as seen particularly at Moissac, Vézelay, and Autun in France, it is the Northern influence that has prevailed. This might be called the virilely elongated style of medieval sculpture. Forms are drawn out and angles sharpened for vigor and dramatic emphasis. Linear methods come into play, for accenting edges and for the creation of contrasted pattern-areas. For a moment the incomparably virile and eloquent line which we remarked first in the Luristan and Ordos bronzes, which reappeared in Viking art, lives again in Romanesque sculpture. The tympanum group at Vézelay (page 289), and even more forcefully the saints' figures on the jambs at Moissac, mark a summit of sculptural art in Europe. Nature has been violated, her forms twisted and distorted; but the composition lives with an intense plastic vitality.

If the religious monuments of Norman England had not suffered so greatly at the hands of time and the iconoclasts, there might be English parallels to the sculpture of Moissac and

Fragment of relief from Easby Abbey, England, 8th century. *Victoria and Albert Museum*

Autun and Vézelay. There are literally thousands of remnants of medieval carved figures and ornaments upon the walls of cathedrals and churches, and although the workmanship would seem to have been less expert than that upon the Continent, the vigor and the opulent patterning persist through a greater number of examples than elsewhere. No major monument survives unimpaired, but there are many fascinating bits, such as the illustrated panel from Easby Abbey. The relationship to earlier Anglo-Saxon and Scandinavian art is here beautifully suggested.

The whole history of medieval sculpture might be traced in relation to the illuminations or miniatures which were the standard picturing art

Christ on Cross. Swabia, about 1200. *Germanic Museum, Nuremberg*

of the age. When sculpture was needed for the enrichment of the churches, at a time when the tradition of monumental sculpture had died, the carvers often enough turned to the manuscripts treasured in monasteries, not only for subject-matter but for methods of treatment. And so the various phases of Byzantine, Romanesque, and Gothic illuminating were echoed in the progress of sculpturing. The end of the road was, of course, realism.

In the general confusion surrounding the subject, making difficult any classification of the products as well as the uncovering of sources, the dividing line between Romanesque and Gothic sculpture is well-nigh lost. Some leading authorities believe that the Romanesque label can be attached where the approach is mystic and formal—or expressionistic—and that Gothic is marked by increasing realism and intellectualization. If so, there is a good deal of Romanesque sculpture in Gothic cathedrals.

The sculpture of Chartres Cathedral tells the story of the transition. The figures in the west portal are stylized and elongated to bring them within the architectural unity, and they have a certain purity of feeling, an almost primitive restraint. The Eastern or Northern concern for decoration as against illusion prevails: the abstract is still exploited at the expense of the concrete and the natural. But a change is already intimated. There is some little characterization in the faces of these elongated, straightened figures. The respect for the pattern and for the architectonic integration is destined soon to weaken. In the later adornment of Chartres Cathedral the figures are pushing out into importance on their own account and taking on naturalness. They also spill off their individual piers. The sculptors knew more anatomy and tried for more story interest and lesson, and they gradually lost decorative control and pattern effect.

In a great artist's hands the increased reasonableness and humanness of saint or Virgin or Noah or Lazarus did not mean a loss of stylization and sculptural feeling, although the values were different—less vigorous and less dynamic than in the Vézelay figures. Gothic art is rich in groups and bits that claim immediate admiration. Outstandingly popular are the *Gilded Virgin* of Amiens and the *Smiling Angel* of Reims, though sophisticated appreciation is likely to run off to diverging things like the gargoyles of Notre Dame de Paris, and—of special interest because it indicates the intrusion of profane subject-matter—the famous "temptress."

The French cathedrals are extraordinarily rich fields of exploration for the lover of sculpture, and museums the world over are filled with single religious figures, richly carved choir stalls, and decorative accessories. Never before or after in Europe did the sculptor practice at one time in so many media and in so many fields: in stone and wood and metal, in monumental composition, architectural decoration, votive statue, miniature furnishings, and caskets.

Nor is the geographical spread of the style less remarkable. Spain and England and Germany afford rich monuments. In Italy alone the Gothic is hardly more than an incident. There the path to neoclassic realism was being opened at the very time of the building of the cathedrals in the North. Milan Cathedral, with its untold thousands of sculptured figures, is a monumental exception. Its character is explored in the first of the chapters on Italian art.

In Germany the medieval spirit lived on until the opening of the sixteenth century. Although German scholars have constructed a framework of dates and styles, it seems to the layman often that Romanesque and Gothic expression in sculpture persisted side by side for almost three centuries. A Christ of the fifteenth century may have all the naïve feeling and abstract formalization of early medieval expressionism, whereas a neighboring Virgin and Child are realistic, human, and knowing. The Germans were exceptionally masters of sculpture in wood, and the gallery of carved figures of the period 1200-1500 affords an extraordinarily varied and beautiful, and until recently unappreciated, display.

The naïve woodcarvings of Germany, the sculptures—superficially seeming so different—of Moissac and of Arles, the crypts of Norman England with short fat piers, the high-vaulted churches of Caen and Bayeux, and the lower arcaded structures of Lombardy, all add up, strangely, to something called a style. Still more strangely, that style, which drew generously upon the barbarian North, and upon the Asiatic East, and had lost wholly the accent of classicism, is called by a name derivative from Rome.

XIV: GOTHIC ART AND
THE CHRISTIAN APOGEE

GOTHIC ARCHITECTURE is the clearest flame of the Christian spirit. It symbolizes the nobility and aspiration of the soul, the mystery of Christian worship, the sense of the immanence of the Divine. Gothic art emerged indeed at that moment when the spiritual genius of the European people escaped the prison of Roman authority, when popular enthusiasm and faith transcended the quarrels of popes and emperors, to be expressed in communal and aesthetic achievement.

Byzantine art had been an expression of the Christianity of the East. But the people who had there become Christianized already had stable art traditions, Persian, Mesopotamian, and Syrian, and these were easily continued and modified into the new religious expression. Constantinople, moreover, had been shaped by rulers obsessed with the ancient idea of imperialism. Roman and Oriental conceptions of worldly splendor met in the Byzantine capital. Nothing could have been less attuned to the gentle, mystic character of Jesus.

The Christian art of the West, in the nine

Statues on the grand portal, Reims Cathedral

Notre Dame, Paris, west façade

man power. Their own chiefs had taken the title of emperor or pope when occasion arose. Finally, capping that progression, the Germanic peoples had made themselves the guardians and the embodiment of the Christian spirit.

It is this circumstance that gives validity to the "Gothic" label as a persisting style-tag. The first application of it in the field of the arts was to come from the Italian Renaissance scholars, who wished thereby to show their disdain, to damn the Northern Christian style with the name of the unlettered barbarian tribes. The later view is that the untutored and unclassical Northern peoples brought creative and purifying elements sadly needed by the Latin Christian stream.

In any case the barbarians—Goths or Germans, Lombards or Franks, as the names are loosely used—had taken over the reality, though not the official framework, of Western Christianity. Their enthusiasm, their imagination, their unswerving faith built the Gothic cathedrals, pushed through the Crusades, and brought forth a new kind of civic and cultural life in Europe. They brought religion back from the realm of the empire-dreamers to the round of everyday life, to immediate communal expression. Their enthusiasm and their faith failed to save the Church, failed to prevent degeneration of the Crusades into political forays and looting expeditions, failed to fix the Gothic style as a lasting European way of art. But there are the cathedrals at Reims and Chartres and Winchester to attest to a flaming leap upward of human aspiration. The builders believed they were shaping God's home on earth, and they poured their souls into their task.

There was a moment in that fateful twelfth century when Christianity, official and popular, Eastern and Western, came to the verge of unification and world rule. The emperors in Constantinople, badly weakened, had broached to the Pope the idea of a reunion and had mapped a consistent attack against the Moslems, now resurgent under Turkish caliphs. There came a coincidence of official vision and popular enthusiasm. The First Crusaders, despite incidental mass tragedy, pushed through to the

centuries from the last Caesars of classic Rome to the Cluniac development, smoldered and occasionally came alive in tiny flames, and was once rekindled in the sustained but somewhat somber glow of Romanesque architecture. But there was the confused light of mixed or still mixing cultures even in the final Romanesque expression. Within this composite and fitful fire Roman, barbarian, but most strongly Byzantine embers were always to be discerned. The flame first leaped up, purified and intensely European, in the Gothic cathedrals.

When the Gothic age opened, in the early twelfth century, it was the Northern spirit that had triumphed in Europe. The barbarian tribes had harassed and fought the Romans in the republican and the imperial days. Later they had fought and repeatedly conquered the disorganized surviving remnants of the Latin peoples and the successive claimants to the Ro-

Chartres Cathedral

Holy Land and in 1099 took Jerusalem from the Mohammedans with accompanying massacre and looting. When Jerusalem was lost again, ninety years later, there still was spirit enough in Christendom, despite the mutual treachery and jealousy of Constantinople and Rome, to send the Third Crusade across Europe in the direction of Palestine. But this time it was led by kings and churchmen; this was the knightly crusade, made romantic by the far-sung exploits of Richard Coeur-de-Lion. The idea of a world union under the banner of Christ had been lost, had been bartered away by politicians and minor Caesars.

The Fourth Crusade, of 1202, was sent not against the infidel but to bring the Eastern Christian empire into the only sort of union understandable to Rome: one ruled by the Roman popes. Constantinople actually was besieged and taken, looted—in a way that meant another flood of Byzantine ivories, icons, and enamels in the West—and placed under a Latin dominion that lasted a half-century. Thus the arc was completed, from naïve popular enthusiasm and faith to trust in the sword and conquest by force.

But what signifies chiefly for art is that there *was* that flame of spirit in the early and middle twelfth century. If it could arm with swords a hundred thousand pilgrims and send them crusading against the infidel Turk, it could arm other hundreds of thousands and set them building churches to the glory of God. This is of moment, too: the Christian realm was no longer being ruled primarily by the Roman Church officials. The popes had often enough been weak, but hitherto the local priests and bishops, and the monasteries, had been the one controlling and related power. During the twelfth century the courts gained and the communes gained. The priests lost their hold; skepticism began its gradual conquest of the European conscience and mind; the people grumbled about paying their taxes to the representatives of Rome. But the spirit of independence that was successively to discredit and weaken and split the Church at the start added up within the sum of Gothic will and impulse.

Figure. Carved oak, Dutch, 15th century.
Metropolitan Museum of Art

Gothic art, then, is Christian art but no longer monastic art. One begins to hear of the lay guilds and of the communes. It will not be long before there is talk of equal representation of the three estates—church, lords, and commons.

The heart of the Gothic phenomenon, one might say, is in the commune still faithful to the idea of Christ behind the Church. Moreover, the unity of Gothic art embraces the beginnings of a new sort of individualism. This individualism, unrestricted in a later phase, was to come near to being the ruin of art, but at first it brought freshness and vigor within the Gothic manifestation.

Inside the Church also there was an occasional

burst of new spirit. The too grandiose monuments of the Romanesque flowering under Cluniac impetus had brought about a reaction toward reserve and logic. Out of Burgundy again came an order destined to shape the new art. The Cistercian monks continued the countermovement in the direction of unity, thoughtfulness, and thorough organization. Thus one more steadying influence was added to the complex of forces driving France on to Gothic expression.

The Character of Gothic Art

The place of Gothic in the world organism of art is precise. It is as distinctive as the Greek architecture, but unlike it in that it flowered suddenly, then faded entirely, leaving neither branch nor seed in the Europe that immediately after was reclaimed for classicism by the rationalists of the Renaissance.

Gothic architecture is an isolated expression, approached in kind only by the late Romanesque. In some superficial or general ways it is like the Greek—in the thought-out logic of its way of building and in a certain noble solidity. In colorfulness and tendency to richly patterned surfaces it has affinity with the Persian-Scythian expression. But if those two, the classic and the Iranian-Oriental, are to be considered as the outstanding manifestations of Western art, the Gothic is further from both than any other recognized European style. A seeming paradox of Gothic art is that within one of the greatest achievements of mystic expression in the building art there is a strain of fresh realistic expression, based on observation of nature.

The cathedrals hold within their walls almost the whole body of surviving Gothic art. They rose by a new logic of building, a thought-out architectural rationalism which made possible walls of lace and glass, framed within a forest of separated supports; but this rationalism was used in a magnificent gesture of faith—which many will call irrational in itself. There was, in short, a new sense of a fixed plan of organic building, but it was only fragmentarily, even emotionally followed out. There is not extant a single complete drawn plan of a medieval cathedral, although partial plans are numerous. The builders, convinced of the feasibility of building in this new way, foreseeing the perfect adjustment and articulation of the complex whole, yet proceeded bit by bit, adding patch to patch, permitting vagaries to this master mason or to that sculptor. Often enough the system changed between one tower and another —witness Chartres and Rouen and Lincoln.

Realism and logic—they are here, undeniably. But the total result is as unrealistic and illogical as a Mohammedan mosque or a Chinese temple. It is only by an effort of will, by a forced return to reality, that one actually *thinks* about the function of the lacy buttresses and clustered columns. For at first one is lost in the wonder of the soaring height of the building, its dark mystery, and the sudden glory of light in its colored windows. The creative, mystic, and plastic values, even sensuous values, crowd in first; then the rationalism, the logic, can be distinguished as the mind asks for functional justification. And the realistic bits of flower and animal life so much written about in the art books must be sought out, discovered as incidental notes within the sculptural expression.

The logic is there, in other words, in a sort of material framework. The natural leaves and tendrils and the gazelles and local maidens are there. But these artists in their hearts recognized a larger celestial framework of life determined by God; and art might better busy itself crystallizing the feeling of that, in terms appropriately breathtaking and supramundane.

As for the animals and flowers, they had been rediscovered, no doubt, with a sense of delight. Now they would be poured into this treasury of impressions of God's world. But the sculptor's intention was not realistic in the Italian or the Flemish way. He merely widened his net till it caught the things that *are*—and mixed them among the things that (in art) have been, and others that might be. There is a mingling of everything from abstract ornamentation through the stiffest distorted formalism to selective realism, and even an occasional naturalistic bit mirrored from surface life.

St. Paul. Carved oak, Flemish, c. 15th century. *Metropolitan Museum of Art*

The Crusades are an index to the life of the times. The religious enthusiasm of the people was equal to any task, any challenge. The loyalty was not directly to Rome, and no longer primarily to the monasteries; the local bishop was the leader who could stir the common folk to pour in the treasure necessary to erect a surpassing cathedral, and to bring in the guilds of artists and laborers.

Just where the artists were coming from, what was their position in this ferment of new life and building, are questions not fully to be answered. The monasteries were still the chief training grounds, but they had extended their educational classes to include laymen as well as

Tympanum of church, Moissac

monk-artists. There was as yet no hint of that extreme individualism in art that was some day to lead the sculptor to sign his work, or to fix an architect's name in the histories. From the monastic communes there was a gradual transition to civic communes; in both, the artist and artisan remained anonymous. The finished work was the reward, though a faithful artist might also look forward to special favor at the Last Judgment.

Ralph Adams Cram, the American architect, was representative of many people who believed that Gothic art was an expression of life at the highest point reached in human civilization—where, hand in hand, went liberty and obedience, individualism and discipline, humor and courage, faith and intelligence, a profound trust in divinity and a noble humanism. He noted approvingly in 1914 that there were in the Gothic era no industrial suburbs. "From the top of the battlemented walls one could look down into the crowded city, all gold and color and glimmering spires and turrets and dizzy gables, with all the people as gay as tropical birds, in their bright raiment, or, from the other side, into fields and gardens with groves that spread around like a green sea, broken only by the white towers of monasteries amidst their orchards, gray castles crowning hill and headland, and perhaps lines of pilgrims, religious processions with bright banners, knights in shining armor, or a band of

spearmen passing on the winding roads. . . . The world then was a place of rampant beauty, and it is no wonder that the ruins that remain to us should be of such beauty as was hardly before, and certainly has never been since."

Of course one may take an opposite view, remembering the lack of sanitation, the dark alley-streets, the mud and slime, and the mean huts of the poor. Plagues were periodically taking a frightful toll of human life in all "civilized" countries, and doubtless the accelerating urbanization hastened these calamities.

Between the view that Gothic art was a sweet flower grown miraculously out of a dunghill or mudhole and the picture of it as part of the most beautiful way of life man has ever known, there is room for a middle view, for the belief that mankind then struggled for beauty in the ways of life, achieved it for limited classes of privileged citizens, had to close its eyes to the miseries of other classes. The standard was bettering. Perhaps for a time every submerged proletarian and beggar might join in great public works and have a gratifying sense of identification with civic pride and progress.

What one can be sure of is the opening of channels for artistic expression. Somehow the artisan, the builder, the sculptor, the glass-maker, had his living, was able to devote his time—joyously, if the sheer beauty and occasional humor in the work may be taken as evidence—

Notre Dame, Paris. Detail, etching by Charles Meryon. *New York Public Library*

to creating the orchestral poems at Chartres and Reims and Paris. His faith fed his vision. As foundation for his service to the Church, his devotion to the cause, organized religion paid his bills. The people of a community gave their donations to the cathedral corporation; the corporation consulted with the masters of the guilds; the guilds' artisans and artists were employed wholesale, in a sort of obligated freedom seldom paralleled in the story of world art. There are eighteen hundred statues on or in Chartres Cathedral, and they must have kept a small army of artists busy through many decades.

The Gothic Cathedrals

In architecture Gothic art was summed up. Never else did it so deserve the title "the mother art." The cathedral is the key to the understanding of Gothic art as a style. The cathedral is the treasure-house of sculpture, glass, goldsmithing, and minor arts—all these existing most nobly as ornaments integral to one organic fabric, to one distinctive way of visual appeal.

One steps into Amiens or Chartres or Notre Dame de Paris, and instantly one's everyday consciousness of the world is blotted out. Thought is stilled. The common and immediate senses are overwhelmed, cease to grasp detail and to report impressions in the usual way. A flood of emotion sweeps the inner faculties. One is suffused with feeling. There comes the mood of mystic participation, of art possessing one's being. To the man sufficiently prepared the experience may rise to a state of spiritual exaltation, of quiet ecstasy.

If the building is Chartres or the Sainte Chapelle, the special sense-avenue to the mood is obvious. It is that most gratifying, most impalpable means of the artist, color. No other element or instrument so possesses and enchants the human faculties. Yet there are sober, somber, quieter cathedrals, too, which hold one as breathless and wondering, with little actual color. England especially has churches of this sort.

Amiens Cathedral

In the end it is the interplay of all the elements, structural and decorative, that creates the overwhelming effect of these Gothic piles. The architectural upward thrust and massing; the profusion of sculptured forms, enriching, accenting, and pulling together the vast fabric; and the coloring that spreads patterns high on the walls or stabs brilliantly into the mysterious shadows or spreads opalescent pools of crimson and gold and azure at one's feet—the sum and synthesis of the complex web is the first source of delight.

Christianity is among the world faiths that perpetuate the mystery religions of primitive peoples: in the communion, the congregation's periodic attendance at rites, the atmosphere of miracle and candle-lighting and sonorous invocation. The cathedrals are embodiments of this ritualistic, emotional, and mystic spirit of Christianity, particularly of medieval Christian piety and ecstasy. The silent spaciousness and the brooding obscurity, the shadowy loftiness and the warm suffusing color, the mysterious soaring vaults and rounded bays—all these are atmospherically right, perfectly attuned to the medieval way of worship and to the thought and devotion of the time. The Eastern or Byzantine Christian churches had been colorful, gorgeous, inspiring admiration for a brilliant outward magnificence; in Amiens or Chartres the effect is both colorful and mysterious, dramatic and other-worldly.

The outward, recognizable marks which to the layman's eye make a separate style of the Gothic are these: a sustained accent on the perpendicular, as seen in the vertical structural line and in the elongated sculptural figures; the pointed

Amiens Cathedral.
Engraving by B. Winkler
after R. Garland.
New York Public Library

arch, which carries the eye up but, unlike the rounded arch, does not bring it down again; and an emphasized skeleton structure of supports, integrated through myriad clustered pillars and buttresses, and, hovering above, a complex of ribbed vault-ceilings, with screenlike walls between supports. There is a resulting lightness of effect (in contrast with the similarly perpendicular but heavy-walled Romanesque); and, aiding the airiness, not to say laciness, a breaking up of masses and areas with sculptural patterning and ornamental variation. There is a rich complex of recessed panels of figures, lace-like edgings and perforated gables, and spires and finials that never approach their end straight but always push out sprouts and points and crotchets. Within this broken, patterned effect there is the division of window areas by means of tracery.

A different sort of wonder is found when the nonarchitectural mind delves into the technical and functional aspects of Gothic building. It is then apparent that the long thin piers, the pierced walls, and the airy flying buttresses are not decorative additions to the structure but are themselves exactly calculated structural features. Indeed the Gothic cathedral skeleton is the prettiest mathematical solution in the history of human building. The structure is organically alive in every part, equilibrated, articulated, with an exquisite play of pressure and support.

The possibility of distributing weight-thrust in arch-architecture goes back to the perfecting of the ribbed vault by the *Magistri Comacini*, the guild of master masons of Como. The vault pressure was lifted from the solid masonry walls and carried to the four piers at the corners of the area covered; and therefore the piers were enlarged and broadly buttressed. In French Romanesque buildings the heavy piers remained, although a part of the thrust of the central nave vaults was

Amiens Cathedral. Diagram showing
vault thrusts and buttressing

on the piers. But as these are in a wall too fragile to sustain the pressure, the large pier buttresses of masonry are built outside the aisle walls, and flying buttresses are constructed as carriers of the pressure at each vault corner. In some cases—most notably at Reims—there is a double series of the supporting half-arches bridging space. Seeming to the uninitiated merely a remarkable achievement in adding decorations in perfect keeping with the architecture, they are in reality of the very bone of the building, vibrant with structural life. They are essentially props, albeit refined into highly ornamental arcs and bridges.

The removal of the weight from wall and interior pier to distant buttresses permitted the lightness so typical of Gothic design. The walls are mere screens set in between the piers. Large areas between the slender uprights were given over without further thought to compositions of colored glass within delicate traceries. At the front the upper nave was made glorious by the great rose window. Lesser windows terminated the transept wings, over the side porches. Indeed it may be said that the Gothic idioms in general grew out of the effort to elaborate the old nave-and-aisle church form, under ribbed vaults, in such manner that there would be generous window areas in façade, side walls, and clerestory walls.

The most beautiful cathedrals are clustered in Northern France. This was royal France, as distinguished from monastic France. That is, Gothic art burst into flower where the court and lay elements in public life had measurably strengthened. The ecclesiastic had weakened, yet art still served primarily religion. At Amiens and Beauvais, Rouen and Chartres and Reims, and at Paris in two utterly contrasted expressions—the monumental Notre Dame and the miniature Sainte Chapelle—the spirit flamed and architecture became again a glory.

Of the period known as high Gothic, Amiens Cathedral is the most consistent expression. The plan is the usual one, not unlike the Roman basilica in elementary outline and divisions, but with the Eastern modification of transept, resulting in the appropriate cruciform design. The nave soars to a height of 150 feet, and the aisles

carried to the walls outside the aisles. Still the effect was essentially heavy. The windows were small and infrequent, and the piles of weight-carrying masonry obviously massive and cluttering.

The Gothic builders, seeking to lift the cathedral roof ever higher and to lighten the aspect, arrived at a system of thrust and counter-thrust that is a marvel of ingenuity. The downward push and lateral pressure of roof and vault are carried by living members to piers outside the walls, even to ones set at a distance from the building proper. The flying buttress is the key member in this Gothic fabric. It carries the thrust across space, over the aisle roofs, to supports that are out of the way.

In the diagram shown, the weight and the thrust of the vaulted roof, at right, are gathered

are exceptionally lofty (as shown on page 303).

If symbolism is to be read into the cathedrals—and seldom have second meanings been so obviously folded within architecture—the larger significance is the opposite of that of the Greek temple. The ancients, enamored of reason, had capped the aspiring line of the columns. The emotional upward lift was tempered by intellectual restraint. Thus was typified the Greek discipline of impulse by reason, in the uprising pillars bridged by the downbearing mass of entablature and roof. Others saw the temple as a symbol of human aspiration leveled by fate.

The medieval symbol is the aspiring line unbroken, the reach toward Heaven unstayed, gloried in. The basic idioms are the pointed arches and the spires. When the building leaves off, a thousand fingers point to God. Victor Hugo said: "The horizontal is the line of reason, the vertical the line of prayer."

The lesson of the upward-pointing towers and spires was the more effective because the building was dominating and ever-present in the medieval community. The bulk of the cathedral or church rose above the town, above the landscape. This was the city-crown, the symbol of God's kingship.

In countless ways—besides the actual picturing in windows and sculpture—the ideas of Christian worship were embodied in the architecture. The cruciform plan of the building was fundamental. In coming to church at all, the worshiper was returning to the Cross. The nave of the church was the ship (navis) that bears the faithful to the haven of security and final rest.

The orientation of the cathedral equally had its meaning. The main façade faced the west, to the setting of the sun, to take the last light of day. On the larger sculptured area, the tympanum over the central doorway, it was usual to picture the Last Judgment. The priest facing the altar thus faced east, toward Bethlehem and Jerusalem, and equally toward the rising of the sun. North porch and south, cold and warm, were more or less symbolic of the Old Testament and the New; at the south would be pictured the coming of Christ.

Farther afield the symbolists find other, more subtle meanings. The Gothic cathedral, in its multiplicity of parts and forms and decorative details, is a mirror, so they say, of the medieval mind, in which all experience was valued, nothing rejected, and all brought within a Christian synthesis. The Greek had had no place for eccentricity, for curiosity, for the unreal. The Gothic mind attempted to bring a harmony out of the material and the spiritual, the real and the imaginative, the sublime and the grotesque. The concrete dissolved into the symbolic, the natural into the mystic, the logical into the yearning for God.

It is when one arrives at actual sculptures that one finds symbolism confusingly mingled with a fresh realism. The twelfth century was three hundred years before the invention of the printed book, and long before any general diffusion of learning. The cathedral walls are the book of the age. And the illustrations are profuse and often masterly.

Like all illustration that sets forth fact or story convincingly, yet with art, the sculptured panels are filled with familiar figures and are explicit in depiction and narrative, even while formally alive. The story element beguiles one, but the greater marvel is the exhibited mastery of sculptural form—until the formal values are dissolved in a growing naturalism. (Since a dividing line between Romanesque and Gothic sculpture is impossible to draw, the subject, as regards changes in technique and in spirit, has been treated in the preceding chapter. Examples are illustrated in this chapter merely to remind the reader of the close integration of sculpture and the architectural fabric—see page 309—and to indicate the picture-book character of a typical cathedral tympanum and the growing naturalness of individual figures.) The tympanum picture at Moissac (page 300), still Romanesque and expressionist, the four porch figures at Reims, of the high Gothic period (page 295), and the St. Paul (page 299) show the progression to late Gothic realism illuminatingly.

Notre Dame de Paris is one of the fullest expressions of the cathedral idea, although less dramatic than Amiens or Reims or Chartres. It is of exceptional interest to those who like to know

Cathedral,
Freiburg im Breisgau

their early, high, and late periods and methods. The front is of the middle period. It is mature and more reasoned than was usual. It is often cited, indeed, as the "classic" example of the H-form façade. The exuberance of Rouen and Reims is absent. A master builder has brought system, almost a Greek discipline, to play over the Gothic elements. The fact that the spires were never added to the two towers is to be noted as contributing to the atmosphere of sobriety.

The side porches are, in contrast, of the late period, and are agreeably light, lacy, and refined; but they perhaps lack the true Gothic vigor and largeness. Portions of the choir section of the building, again, are of a different age, of a time before either main façade or porches. Here one may see the daring use of flying buttresses in a fine achievement of combined functional and decorative aims.

National Modifications

One of the most interesting studies offered by the play of national temperament upon imported forms is to be followed in the adaptation of Gothic design in the several Christian countries. There are recognizably Gothic buildings even in Asia and Africa, with strange hybrid accessories and sculpture. There is, too, the hardly less mixed expression in the pointed-arch façades on the canals of Venice, and in the Gothic envelope slipped over the Romanesque baptistry at Pisa. From Mexico and Canada to Syria and the

Salisbury Cathedral

Ukraine there are authentic echoes of this style that grew up in the Ile-de-France.

The German cathedrals, except those on the Rhine, near France, are likely to be less decorated, more forthright in their way of pointing toward heaven, as are the ones at Marburg and Lübeck and Trier. But the cathedral at Strasbourg is an outstanding example of the late, obviously decorated phase, with lavish architectural lacework and abundant sculpture. The cathedral at Cologne may well be considered more French than German in stamp. It was modeled upon Amiens, and was under construction at intervals from 1248. Work was stopped in the sixteenth century and not resumed until the nineteenth. The interior of the vast structure is very impressive, and the exterior is rich in effect, although in the late portions the detail and the sculpture are less spirited.

The fine smaller church or Minster at Freiburg im Breisgau is one of the most consistent expressions of the Gothic, also in the recognizably French idiom but exceptional in that it is constructed with a single tower at the front. Because in Germany houses were built in medieval style during several centuries when the Renaissance mode was fashionable elsewhere, the Gothic monuments have an exceptionally appropriate setting at Freiburg and Strasbourg. At Ulm, too, the Minster (page 453) rises up out of a complex of sharp-pointed roofs and towers, with an effectiveness that belonged, one may believe, to the cathedrals in the days when they were centers of worship rather than tourists' landmarks.

Perhaps the most idyllic settings are in England, where cathedrals were built oftener at monastic centers in the country than in congested cities. Salisbury and Lincoln and Gloucester gain immeasurably by their parklike surroundings. As architectural organisms the English structures are less impressive than the French. There is not the close knitting of structural parts, the marvelous articulation of members. The nave is held closer to earth, so that the soaring aspect is less in evidence. Nor do the English builders refrain from using the effects incidental to vaulting and buttressing for display rather than for functional service. These are, nevertheless, great and inspir-

Sainte Chapelle, Paris

ing monuments of the building art, and it is only in comparison with the more consistent French cathedrals that one notes failure to reach the top point of architectonic design and magnificence.

In England the spreading of the vault ribs for decorative effect led to the "fan vaulting" which is a distinctive feature of late Gothic building. It is seen to best advantage in the chapel of King's College at Cambridge and in Gloucester Cathedral. In decadent form the fan vaults grew pendants like stalactites, and finally all sense of architectural integrity was lost.

A central tower rises over the crossing of nave and transept in most English cathedrals. The builders had a marked preference for square forms—perhaps a Saxon survival—and the squarish tower distinguishes the English structures as does no other feature. It forms, as it were, a distinctive and dominating crown, heavy and solid even while delicately ornamented with the usual attenuated buttresses and spires. Thus the vast building is centered as seen from a distance, and given a unity not known elsewhere.

There was a sequence of sub-styles, known as the Early English Gothic, the Decorated Gothic, and the Late or Perpendicular Gothic. The last-named was the most inventive phase on British soil. In it the vertical members were stressed—even added to, illogically—and a compelling pattern was created in which the perpendicular lines dominated in a sort of extravagant architectural embroidery. The outstanding examples are the Chapel of Henry VII in Westminster Abbey, and parts of Gloucester Cathedral.

Westminster Abbey in its general disposition of parts and its structural features is the most French of the English Gothic monuments; but on French ground it would appear uninspired, even dull, lacking sensitive adjustment. It is rather in those buildings that have a distinctive English

Lacy Gothic decoration,
late, detail.
Rouen Cathedral

decorativeness, as at Gloucester and Salisbury and Lincoln, that one finds the country's medieval architecture at its best. Perhaps the most appealing of English Gothic structures are, in the end, the smaller churches, which took on a beauty of form and of incidental decoration that lifts them to a very high place in the annals of religious building. In one's memory of the English provinces nothing else lingers quite so long, and with such intimate appeal, as the lovely church spires.

In Spain there are two main roads of Gothic development: one determined by French influence, brought direct by church officials and by imported builders; the other determined by the mixing of the Northern influence with impulses surviving from Moorish building. The great cathedrals at Burgos and Barcelona, at León and Toledo, are counted among Europe's impressive Gothic structures. Even more interesting, per-

haps, is the Church of Santiago de Compostela, near the northwest tip of the Spanish peninsula. It was a shrine at the end of the French-Spanish "pilgrim road" and is extraordinarily enriched with Romanesque sculpture of a sort allied with the French. As a matter of fact, the church is not rightly to be spoken of as Gothic. The structural parts are Romanesque, and over the main façade there was illogically added, centuries later, a masking screen in the baroque style.

In France as elsewhere the story of Gothic architecture ends in logic forgotten and decoration overexploited. Even Rouen Cathedral, commonly counted among the ten or twelve greatest structures, is characterized by a masklike façade, pretentiously encrusted and lacy, that is a long way from the comparatively plain and sober façades of Chartres and Paris, with their parts and members declaring their functional and structural reasons for being. Amiens and Reims are the two great monuments between, at the point where decoration is elaborate but not yet destructive of architectural integrity.

A gem of Gothic architecture is the comparatively tiny Sainte Chapelle in Paris—perhaps the most loved of Gothic buildings for its color and its unusual intimacy. A reliquary chapel with a crypt beneath, the building is small enough to have complete unity. One enters the main hall (page 308) to encounter a complex of delicate supports framing windows enchantingly colored. Nowhere else is one able to lose oneself so completely in ambient color, to bathe one's senses so in a glory of light. Architect and artist in glass have created more than a building—rather an atmosphere, a feeling. At Chartres the glass is glorious too. But there the poetry of architecture is nearer epic, less sweetly lyric.

The stained-glass window that contributes so much to the richness of the Gothic cathedral was simply one more flower of medieval craftsmanship. The craft was handed on to the Gothic workers with enameling, goldsmithing, ivory-carving, and other miniature arts, with something of the stamp of Persia upon it. Never else in Europe, before or after, did color enter into architecture as in the Gothic piles. Nor was the mastery of the Gothic glassworkers of Paris and of Chartres again approached.

As in the architectural fabric, the larger skeleton of the window design was logically determined to fit within the web of structural members and to withstand wind strain; though the window itself may seem purest fantasy. The method of construction was to lay down the outlines of the broader areas in bars of iron, then to fill in with tiny bits of colored glass and solder them together with lead; and to vary the effect with larger glass areas whereon the designs had been painted and the pieces then fired. Most windows tell serial stories from Old and New Testament legendry. But the drawing carries on Byzantine formalism, without hint of naturalistic intention. And indeed it was as decorators, not as illustrators, that the designers triumphed. What-

ever was the effect of incorporated story and lesson upon the faithful in the thirteenth and fourteenth centuries, in our times a hundred observers glory in the jewel-like patterns and the cloud of color for every one who goes on to the deciphering of the meaning or message. The window is a sort of translucent mosaic, in which color, not subject, is the lasting marvel.

There was in France a Gothic secular architecture, at first in châteaux and fortresses, then in town halls and houses of the rich. But it was rather in Flanders to the north that the burgeoning civic spirit led to the construction of monumental Gothic buildings for other than religious purposes. There the guild halls and municipal halls surpass those of France. Best known are the Cloth Hall at Ypres and the City Hall at Brussels. The style crept into the domestic architecture of the Low Countries and of Germany. The steep-pitched roofs and lingering bits of Gothic ornamentation still afford a medieval aspect in parts of Bruges and Nuremberg and Rothenburg.

But it is the cathedral that is Gothic architecture in its essence. The style there came to a purity within grandeur not achieved in any other. It enfolded, without destruction of unity or integrity, a host of minor arts, so that within its porches and bays are enshrined some of the world's masterpieces of carving, and in its windows unsurpassed glories of decorative picturing art, and on its altars a wealth of gold and ivory and jeweled furnishings. But when the Gothic adventure came to its end there was to be no repetition, hardly an echo. The spirit expressed was gone; the way of life that made expression possible was gone.

Toward the end the gold, the carving, and the coloring had been carried over to castle, to guild hall, to home. But it was a faith, a devotion, now seeped away that had created the synthesis that is Amiens or Reims or Chartres. Very truly the spirit of God had entered into the building of the cathedrals. Now mankind was ready for some other adventure, outside the realm of spiritual imagination and devotional expression.

XV: ITALY AT THE TWILIGHT OF MEDIEVALISM

IN ITALIAN history there is a golden morning, before the full day of the Renaissance, when a clear fresh light suffuses the arts. Northern Europe was then passing into the twilight of medievalism. But in Italy, where the Gothic growth had never been acclimated, the thirteenth- and fourteenth-century religious art is linked in spirit with the most virginal medieval manifestations. In Assisi and Siena and Florence naïve faith and a sunny piety lingered on. Above all, a kindly and personal Christianity was reborn in Assisi. The spirit of the era and of the place may best be termed, from the name of the Assisan saint, Franciscan.

But if the feeling of the time harks back to monastic medievalism, and through it to early Christianity, it also breathes a note of humanism which belongs to the following Renaissance. Contemporary with the later, hardening expression of the Gothic culture, it yet escapes the heavy piety of the North. Foreshadowing as it does the free spirit and human sympathy of the Italian rebirth, it is free within a devotion to God; its humanism is a spiritual one as against the intellectual and pagan sort characteristic of later Florentine and Roman culture.

In short, this rather pale light that shone during the brief golden morning of Italian art may be considered as constituting the dawn of the Renaissance; but at the same time the glow of it

Sassetta: *Christ in Limbo. Fogg Museum of Art, Harvard University*

Giotto: *Resurrection of Drusilla. Santa Croce Church, Florence*

is somehow indistinguishable from the twilight effulgence of the medieval. A fresh, light, smiling aspect came into European art. But it was still of the spirit, in no way fleshly and realistic and knowing, as was to be the art of Masaccio, Correggio, and the Venetians. In being calm and simple, and in a sense consecrated, it was not thin or cold or strange. On the contrary it was colorful and intimately appealing. Seldom in the history of the world has the *warmth* of the spirit been so purely transmitted in works of art.

The spiritual essence is shown sympathetically in depicted human beings, but only in the most innocent types. The Byzantine Madonna becomes a woman; but, as the Sienese writer Scipione Bargagli points out, she is the Sienese gentlewoman, "at the presence of whom the eyes are filled with pleasure, the ears consoled, the spirits restored, the intellect nourished, the abilities made stronger, more refined and more perfect." And he adds, with a glance in the direction of Florence, "She disdains to give herself up all day or all night to dancing as is the custom in some places."

The spiritual symbol of the time is St. Francis. The literary symbol is Dante. The school of painting that expresses most completely the re-

served but colorful character of it is the Sienese, with the simple harmonies and rhythms of Duccio and Simone Martini and Sassetta fixing for all time the naïve faith in the naïve fashion that is sometimes called "primitive." Giotto is the culminating figure, picking up all the resources that make for melody, glow, and fragrance, but moving on toward freedom and full incorporation of seen objects and emotions.

Last belated figure, but personally more representative than any other—in his gentleness, his saintly humanism, and his instinctive expression of the spiritual in sensuous and lyric terms—is Fra Angelico. The young monk-painter might be taken as type-figure of the artist in the Franciscan age. It is recorded that he remained kneeling the whole while he was painting the figures of Jesus and the Virgin Mary; and he wept continuously as he worked on the frescoes of the Crucifixion. His life was so blameless that he was called Angelico, and, after official beatification, Beato, the blessed one.

Art had come to Western Europe first in Italy. Etruria had been its earliest home, then Rome. When the Romans, having dissolved Etruscan art in the borrowings from Greece, established provincial cities in France, Spain, Britain, and

Giotto: *Ascension of St. John. Santa Croce Church, Florence*

Germany, the native peoples of those countries were barbarians with only the most elementary culture. When, after the Roman decline, Byzantium sent successive waves of cultural influence over the West, Italy again profited most, as is attested especially at Ravenna and Venice. When another sort of wave, from the north, brought the independent art and spirit of the Germanic peoples, the Lombards gave Italy its share of the impulse thereof. The Italians were, it might be said, least innocent of the older arts of the European peoples, and they had historically been pioneers in every advance.

It was only in the tenth and eleventh centuries that the torch had been carried to the North. Leadership in Europe then definitely passed to France. The Romanesque and the Gothic styles flowered there and went on to conquer England and Germany. But when the "Italian primitives" found new appreciation after a five-hundred-year eclipse, in the early twentieth century, the fact came clear that Italy had been, even at the zenith of Gothic culture, preparing for another epochal manifestation. The stage was being set for a return to Italian artists as leaders, even in that century which saw the building of Amiens and Reims.

The mysticism of St. Francis was of a sort that valued identification of the individual soul with all life in a God-created unity, yet did not run to physical mortification and withdrawal from the world. The piety of St. Francis was based on a sense of the dignity of the human soul, the immanence of God, the goodness of nature, and the importance of being happy in this world as well as in the next. He wanted joy in men's service to God.

The Franciscan conception of Christianity, thus so godly and so human, marrying the ecstasy of the spirit with delight in the actual physical world, finding love a radiant thing, is perfectly the background of the Sienese panel paintings, so modestly done yet so enchanting in their bright colors and gold, always devotedly Christian in theme yet sensuously lovely. The Christian message is no longer fearsome; rather the subjects tend to be touching. The beholder is reminded to be charitable, compassionate, and loving. Kindliness and charity run like a refrain through the incidents and imagery. Simplicity, calm, clarity, and sweetness are in the line and color of Franciscan painting.

The message of this art comes with the gentle beauty expressed by Giovanni Colombini, the

Piazza San Marco, Venice, showing Doges' Palace

Sienese mystic, in his letters to Paola Foresia, Abbess of the convent of Santa Bonda. To her and the sisters Colombini wrote: "Most dear friends: How can I express the affection and the charity which my heart and soul feel towards you?—charity and affection ardent and burning with the love of the Holy Spirit, transforming everything through devotion to Christ. May it enter your souls like flame, with gentle penetration."

St. Catherine of Siena found evidences of the divine love in nature and in her garden; she cultivated lilies and roses quite as she cultivated the vision of God within the garden of her soul, and she believed that poetry and music and all beautiful things were eloquent of the divine order. She said that life might be conceived of as music. In Sienese painting one feels this music and this mysticism.

If the art of Siena and of Giotto is the true expression of the medieval spirit in Italy, there still are monuments of the Northern Gothic mode scattered in scores of cities and towns throughout the country. It is worth while to pause and to inquire about those which have a particular Italian accent. A few, at least, afford delight in a distinctive and unforgettable way. In other cases the interest is hardly more than that afforded by a strange grafting of one major style upon the stump of another. Nevertheless, the Gothic incidence cannot be overlooked in the approach to Italian Renaissance art.

Gothic Architecture in Italy

One's gondola glides through the canals of Venice, and here and there a Gothic façade adds the richness of pointed-arch colonnades and perpendicular-accent sculpturing to the glow of color and the softening haze that seem to lie over Venetian architecture. Here the Gothic idiom finds its most gracious adaptation to the Italian scene. There is no sense of an alien origin, of a dour Northern note's having crept in.

The occasional palace fronts are sometimes exquisitely jewel-like and colorful—in that magic soft-focus setting. But most engaging, and out-

Milan Cathedral

standing because of its size and civic-historic importance, is the Doges' Palace. The building shines out in Oriental color and loses nothing atmospherically by its position beside the Byzantine brilliance of St. Mark's Cathedral. Yet upon analysis of the detail, one finds at least the outer architectural garment Gothic. There is the typical perforated and pinnacled richness of minor forms —though the massing retains Italianate horizontality. The effect is obtained by letting in a double arcade, gallery over gallery, under a fairly plain wall. A few pointed-arch windows pierce this upper façade, and a top edging echoes the brokenness and variety of the decorated arcades below. There is, of course, no logic in it, in the French Gothic sense; but the eye delights even while the rational mind cautions that it *is* a slipped-on garment one beholds.

But if, as in Venice, Italian Gothic may be superficially enchanting, and sometimes, though rarely, as in the Cathedral of Orvieto, impressive

for a certain organic consistency, it is oftener true that the monuments betray an alien spirit, announcing unintentionally the effort to import a fashion not understood. There are no examples of that daring based on logic that makes the glory of Reims and Amiens.

There are, rather, integrated Gothic structures holding up Italianized façades; or, more often, Italian Romanesque buildings traced over with Gothic lacy and pointed ornamentation. The cathedral at Siena, planned by the Cistercian monks under French influence, has vaults and arches direct from the North; but Italian artists treated the surfaces in their own way. At Como, on the contrary, the cathedral is in frank Romanesque style, on the ancient basilica plan, and there are even hints of a return to classic clarity; but the edges are enriched with high elongated panels of Gothic sculpturing, and pointed spires sprout incipiently at likely corners of the roof. One remembers that the masons of Como three centu-

Duccio: *Christ in the Garden*

ries earlier had perfected the groined vault that made possible the Northern development of the Romanesque, and so of the Gothic. But when the flower is brought back to Lombardy it fails to take root; it is merely on exhibition, and not too happily.

The most monumental Gothic building in Italy, and the truest to Northern principles, is in nearby Milan. The cathedral there, more bespired than that of Salamanca or Cologne, is decked out in Gothic togs rather than basically expressive of the vertical logic. The mass of the building has an un-Gothic spread. The perpendicular towers and the forest of spires are added to a structure essentially low-lying. Whatever the thousands of heaven-pointing pinnacles say, the building is squat, not soaring.

In the glare of the Milanese sun, too, the exterior takes on a little the effect of cake-icing. For florid tastes—the French would say for Italian tastes—it is a masterpiece. For others it is most rewarding at dusk, when a half-light softens the effort to ornament every square foot of surface. And always there are genuine and heart-stilling experiences to be had within, where miracles of color are met in the profound silence of the nave, among the immense trunks of the inner piers.

French architects, then German, then Italian, are known to have worked on the structure. That fact might be offered as a key to the lesser importance of the Gothic architecture in Italy. It was halfheartedly imported, briefly accepted as a fashion. It was to suffer eclipse under the Renaissance, and indeed no architect or decorator of the *quattrocento* was to scruple to destroy Gothic works or replace them with the revived-classic.

At Pisa the great group of ecclesiastical buildings is sometimes cited as Italy's outstanding Gothic exhibit. But the effect again is one of surface manipulation. The plans and structural methods of the cathedral and the baptistry are nearer Roman, Byzantine, and Romanesque than Gothic. The Campo Santo is structurally a Lombard cloister. The campanile, or detached tower (better known as the Leaning Tower), is unlike anything in the North of Europe. But there *is* considerable built-on Gothic façading, as decoration of both cathedral and baptistry. Indeed nothing could be more eloquent of the vacillation of the Italian city-states over the acceptance of the French style than this group of hybrid erections inescapably impressive yet palpably patched together out of a half-dozen successive fashions of building. There are classical capitals and columns within the basilica-like cathedral, probably taken by the Pisans as spoils from some conquered Sicilian city. The original architect of the cathedral is supposed to have been a Greek, who would have been Byzantine-trained. The main structural forms are Romanesque. Finally Gothic ornamental features were added.

It is not to be overlooked that many incidental virtues are to be uncovered in a study of the Pisan monuments, and fascinating bits found on every hand. Every art-conscious traveler remembers his days spent there as crowded with excitement and rewarding discovery. John Ruskin, the English critic, wrote eloquently of the symphonic nature of the architecture of the cathedral and especially stressed the relationship of the rhythms of the superimposed arcades of the façade to the proportions of the whole. The interior arcade of the Campo Santo achieves more simple harmony, with its graceful Gothic tracery inserted into wide Italian arches. Perhaps we should, like our Italian friends, explain that the virtue here, as generally in Italian Gothic, is in variety rather than in logical unity.

Such was the halting Gothic adventure in Italy. Venetian, Lombard, Tuscan had recognized the medieval style of the North, had played with it fitfully, had settled back to enjoyment and employment of older idioms. In architecture the next step was to be that epochal adaptation of the antique Roman forms that ushered in the full Renaissance. But long before the building of the Milan Cathedral or the decoration of the Palace of the Doges, there had been born in Assisi the saint whose spirit was to inform another art, painting, and to evoke during this twilight of the Gothic an expression truly Italianate, and best understood as Franciscan.

Sienese Painting

The Sienese painters were the truest artists of the Franciscan spirit. At first something of the preceding Byzantine stiffness persisted. It is to be remembered that the art of the Eastern Roman Empire had spread and respread over Italy. Thus the icons were implicit in the early Sienese manner. But even in Duccio, who began to paint late in the thirteenth century, a fresh harmony and an enlightened naïveté are evident.

It is not difficult to detect in Duccio's pictures a considered linear felicity and harmony of parts without Italian precedent. The figures and faces also have a human grace unknown to the Byzantine artists. Their attitudes express an actual devotion; they are not merely symbols hardened by tradition into set form. There is sweetness in the countenances. The type known as "the motherly Madonna" replaces the Byzantine abstraction. It is not to be inferred that the medieval style lacked virtues of its own. On the contrary, the Byzantine panels are distinguished by a fine largeness in design, with strong plastic vitality, that was destined to be lost, lamentably, in later Italian painting. It is Duccio's merit that he preserved measurably the pictorial architecture of the Eastern style even while adding this other felicity and freshness.

The citizens of Siena were fighters and patriots as well as churchmen. And if religious passion inspired their work, there is in it nonetheless a reflection of civic pride. The independent position of the city-states of this time, and the new importance of the citizen as such, were partial causes of the advance out of the traditional ways of expression. Perhaps the freedom of the individual is the framework within which the artist can be more effectively faithful and devoted than ever before. The Statute of 1355 in Siena bound artists to be "by the grace of God revealers of those marvelous things which operate by virtue of Faith." It added that the artist must possess "ability, knowledge, and earnest desire."

A contemporary of Duccio describes an incident indicating at once the civic feeling and the religious devotion of the people of Siena. The painter had completed an altarpiece for the Duomo, or cathedral. The account of its placing is thus transcribed by Piero Misciattelli: "The picture was carried to the Duomo, accompanied by a worthy and devout company of priests and monks, the Signori del Nove, all the officials of the Commune and the general public. The procession walked around the Campo, while all the bells of the city rang out a joyous peal in honor of such a noble picture, which was made by

Duccio di Niccolo, painter, in the house of Muciatti, outside the gate of Stalloreggi. And all that day was given up to orations; all the shops were shut and many alms were given to the poor, while prayers were offered to God and His Mother who is our advocate, beseeching that we should be defended by His Mercy from adversity and every evil, and from the hands of traitors and enemies of Siena."

This was no common picture, and the celebration was, of course, in honor of the Virgin Mary, whom the painting portrayed. She was the Queen of Siena (just as, for a time, Christ was officially King of Florence). But the fact remains that art thus entered into the common life and the religious passion of the people. Between the lines of the account, supposed to be from the hand of an eyewitness, may be read many of the background facts, of the setting for the emergence of the art of fourteenth-century Italy: the joint celebration by churchmen and citizens, the love of Mary and the prayer for destruction of Siena's enemies, the devoutness and the thought of alms-giving, the joyous pealing of bells and the holiday orations celebrating a gold-and-color tablet from a craftsman's studio.

Duccio's altarpiece is a perfect example of the transitional painting, to which cling formalisms unmistakably Byzantine, but within a freedom already Italian. The figures are flattened and separate, almost geometrically disposed, in true icon fashion. But already the faces have been humanized, and if the bodies are not confessed as flesh-and-blood realities beneath the garments, at least the draperies themselves escape the traditional stiffness, and even lend their folds and edges to linear harmonies. Mary is a woman, a mother; is studied, one must believe, from those very Sienese women who followed the picture in the procession and prayed before it in the church.

On the back of the altarpiece Duccio painted forty-four smaller scenes, of the Passion and of church festivals, in the same transitional manner. But the works live in their own right. The flat mural technique, with fields of gold taking the place of later landscape vistas and architectural compositions, and the obviously rhythmic disposition of the figures, afford continual delight to the eye. Duccio's special touch of outlining the folds of garments in gold adds an element of linear counterpoint to the simple melodies. The device is well illustrated, along with the lingering Byzantine richness of patterning and the particular Sienese delicacy, in the *Madonna and Child* altarpiece in the National Gallery, London. The *Transfiguration* on the same walls is a marvelous example of simplification for the sake of majestic calm and uninvolved decorativeness.

Duccio died about 1319. His family refused to accept his estate because it was overburdened with debts. But he had written his name in the annals of world art.

Simone Martini carried on even more beautifully a splendor of color transmitted by the Byzantine painters from the Orient. His pictures almost invariably are enriched with gold-encrusted and sumptuously patterned areas. One sees them in the Virgin's robe, in throne-panels and hanging stuffs, even added arbitrarily as tracery and arabesque within the haloes and along the sleeve-edges. The feathers of an angel's wings become frank decoration; the aureole around a saint's head or enclosing the enthroned Virgin becomes a field of goldsmith's patterning, with the golden ground incised and pricked in intricate design.

By reason of the greater surface enrichment, Simone Martini's pictures lose something of the singular simplicity of Duccio's. But the figures are presented without background. The Renaissance concern with perspective and scientific anatomy is still far off. The composition is flattened, and the sense of distance is gained in the manner of the Chinese, who "lay up" the several elements in a painting. The mural in the Council Room of the Civic Hall at Siena, celebrating the Virgin Mary as queen and, in a sense, setting her up as presiding officer of the City Council, is a glorious example of art serving several functions: pious in its iconography and symbolism; finely, even Orientally rich in decorative effect; and breathing a majestic largeness, as befits civic art.

There are traces of Gothic feeling and idiom in the work. And indeed Simone Martini, unlike his teacher Duccio, was an international figure, known at the French court in Naples

Duccio: *Madonna and Child. National Gallery, London*

and resident for a period at the Palace of the Popes in Avignon at the time when the papacy had been transferred to the Provençal city.

With two brothers, Pietro and Ambrogio Lorenzetti, Sienese painting moved another stage away from Byzantine formalism and toward Italian realism, though not so far that there fails to be an unmistakable naïve primitivism, treat-

Simone Martini: *Annunciation*. Side panels by Lippo Memmi.
Uffizi Gallery, Florence

ing a reality still dreamlike. The gold and the flat compositional pattern remain, but the earlier geometric disposition of figures gives way to more natural grouping. And Ambrogio studies the human face and endows it with a precise though hard realism, and adds background vistas somewhat pictorial. It is not these qualities, however, that arrest the eye and hold one breathless, but rather the glow of color, the flowing grace of line, and the wealth of movement—with a hint of that pageantry in painting which will flower a century later on Florentine walls.

It is still the fashion among certain historians to dilate upon the insensitiveness of the Sienese artists, and to stress the retrograde spirit that permitted the city to lapse back and die out of the drama of Renaissance worldly progress. The city of death, Siena is called; partly because the artists failed to see and paint the pageant of life that was passing in her own streets and was staged in her festivals and fighting; and also because they failed to give ear to the new scientific knowledge that was revolutionizing painting in neighboring Florence. But it should be enough that Siena was herself to the last, preserving the fresh faith and mystic fervor and the sunny humanism of the age of Francis.

In Siena the lover of Chinese painting is more at home than in any other field of European art. There are similar repose and harmony and otherworldliness in the two manifestations. And, indeed, even among the lesser Sienese artists of the late fourteenth and early fifteenth centuries one is continually discovering Crucifixions and Madonnas and retellings of the Passion incidents and the saints' stories that sing with color and weave melodious rhythms of line, and so still the mind and fill the heart with contentment.

Most exquisite in workmanship, and most fluent in composition, is Stefano di Giovanni,

Ambrogio Lorenzetti:
Incidents from the story
of St. Nicholas of Bari.
Academy Gallery, Florence

better known as Sassetta. He is one of the most satisfying of the secondary masters, and he carried on the Sienese tradition undefiled until his death in 1450. Giovanni di Paolo and Sano di Pietro continued to produce the panel pictures for thirty years longer. If their art loses a little of the primitive simplicity, of the strong formal manipulation and patterning, their paintings, nevertheless, as seen in Siena or as far away as in New York or San Francisco, afford a deep and a lasting pleasure—each picture made rare with the author's own distinctive sort of naïve charm. (See the Giovanni di Paolo *Madonna,* page 322, and an exceptionally fine Sassetta on page 311.)

Giovanni di Paolo:
*Madonna
with Child and Saints.*
*Maitland Griggs Collection,
New York*

The Florentine Painters

But Giotto was the golden one of the early morning of Italian painting. In him the sensitive coloring and the simplified approach to storytelling, the fresh Franciscan faith and the budding humanism, the abstract formalism of the East and the unfolding spirit of freedom of the West—in him these met. In his work is the first monumental expression of European painting. He initiated a major era.

Giotto has often enough been called the greatest European painter. And indeed no other is quite so fitted to please the taste of realist and formalist alike. He is at once a superb illustrator and an ingratiating decorator. His storybook of the life of St. Francis in the Upper Church at Assisi touchingly brings to visual actuality the events and the message of the life of the saint. Mural art elsewhere was seldom so purely handled as here and in the Arena Chapel at Padua.

Giotto was a simple man of the people and of the faith, in close affinity with the Sienese artists. But he added urbanity—without sophistication. He was still medieval-minded, though after him could come only the full Renaissance and its expression rooted in science. He was the first of the Italian artists who, like the Greeks, were to be interested primarily in people. He saw God and Mary and the saints through his knowledge of men and women. Yet his faith and humility survived. And his plastic sense remained

Giotto: *Presentation in the Temple. Isabella Stewart Gardner Museum, Boston*

that of the decorators, the arrangers of abstract figures on a two-dimensional ground. His painting takes on additional depth; his figures have volume; but the painter does not yet puncture his background with perspective vistas, or sacrifice pattern to elaboration of statement. If he impinges upon the Renaissance, he is also the last to exploit nobly a Byzantine heritage.

Giotto's immediate background was not Sienese but Florentine. But, if one may venture the thought, Florence was not yet Florence. Giotto was only ten or twelve years the junior of Duccio. His teacher was Cimabue, who had but slightly softened the austerity and rigidity of traditional Italo-Byzantine painting. At this time the Sienese and the Pisans rather than the Florentines were the pioneers of a new experimental humanism and freedom in art. In them the spirit of Francis seems to have stirred first a new vision of the service of art to God and the Church. In this earliest Florentine period Sienese painters were called to work side by side with the local artists. There was as yet no hint of the intellectual and scientific evolution so soon to come. Cimabue was called to Assisi to help decorate the Church of St. Francis, and took the boy-artist Giotto with him. Cimabue's own murals there, although badly defaced, indicate a memorable gift for majestic composition within the Byzantine iconographic method. But soon Giotto's harmonious and compact designs were to mark the pupil as the greater master.

Giotto, without confining himself within the Byzantine conventions, the stiffness of the separated figures, the strictly geometrical disposition of elements, and the flat laying-up of planes, carries on the glow of gold-and-color and a decorative linear emphasis. In giving a greater sculpturesque fullness to the figures, he yet remembers the Eastern mural technique, the conception of the picture as a decoration, with plastic completeness of its own, a poised and powerful movement-life within a strictly bounded depth-range.

But his humanistic innovations make his work epochal. He introduces believable, persuasive human beings as protagonists—not yet strongly individualized, not anatomically impressive, but observed from life rather than copied from traditional approximations. To these, too, he adds a believable movement-flow, a sense of varied, richly textured life. And over all is the essentially Italian spirit, now for the first time crystallized in painting—a manner gracious, lazily colorful, sunny. It is as Italianate as the rhythmic round-arched cloisters.

Born to pastoral surroundings, in the Tuscan hills, he came naturally, perhaps, by his easy-going, sunny qualities. The legend tells plausibly how Cimabue, already famous, came upon the boy tending sheep and at the same time making drawings upon a smooth stone, and was so struck with his talent that he straightway took him to Florence to be his pupil and apprentice. There in Cimabue's *bottega,* or street-shop, no doubt the youngster learned to grind colors, to prepare the panels of poplar wood that then did service as "canvases," to carve and gild frames in the Gothic style, and a hundred odds and ends of the craft and business of being a painter. There would be lessons in drawing, too, then in coloring, in the slow tempera technique, using sticky egg-base paints on the gesso panels. And finally would come instruction in the fresco medium, so difficult because strokes once made could never be altered; a misstep meant often the scraping away of the entire plaster panel and re-laying a wall.

But Giotto learned quickly and soon was given commissions of his own. His fame grew steadily, and before many years city after city, church after church, was calling for his services. Wherever the most ambitious projects for building and decorating cathedrals and chapels were conceived, the talented planners and the wealthy patrons wanted this successful painter. He went to Assisi, at first to assist Cimabue with some decorations in the Upper Church, which means that he was transported to the very center of advanced art experiment. He stayed on to add a series of panels of his own. At Padua he spent three years filling the Arena Chapel with his murals. At Florence, at Rome, and at Naples he accepted commissions and left his distinctive works. In the end he had become the intimate of princes and bishops. The King of Naples recorded with pride that Giotto was his friend and guest.

The main surviving monuments to his genius are at Assisi, Padua, and Florence. In the Upper Church at Assisi, built over the tomb of St. Francis, Giotto painted scenes from the life and legendry of the great mystic. Other walls had been painted by Cavallini and by Cimabue. But Giotto best translated into pictures the simple, lovable spirit of the saint.

Whereas the earlier artists, held to traditional themes of the Passion, the Madonna, and allegories of the Church, and trained to a traditional method, had made little progress beyond recognized idioms, Giotto created his own versions of the incidents, out of his emotion and his observation of the people, men and women exactly like those who had entered, hardly more than a century before, into the actual Franciscan drama. It was he who fixed the method of Franciscan illustration for a whole school of followers. In short, a generation of painters was to imitate and adapt his creations, substituting them for the types and attitudes and groupings which had for centuries been the Byzantium-derived currency of painting. There is not, let it be noted, unanimity of opinion among the historians and critics regarding this early Assisan series. Some even deny Giotto's authorship, though whom else to name is a puzzle.

Giotto: *Deposition from the Cross. Arena Chapel, Padua*

The origin of the Arena Chapel at Padua is illustrative of the strange ways in which some of the noblest works have been given to the Western world. One Enrico Scrovegno had died and left the reputation of having made his fortune out of shameful usury. There was ample ground for questioning his status in purgatory. His son, reckoning that his own position could not but be bettered by gift of a princely chapel in the service of religion, and to the glory of that highest intercessionary figure, the Virgin Mary, while his father's chances would be improved thereby, had built what is now sometimes known as Giotto's Chapel. Whether or not the gift brought repose for the soul of the elder Scrovegno, countless Christians have uttered something like ecstatic prayer as they left the church after feasting their eyes and their souls on one of the most moving and gracious art exhibits to be seen anywhere.

The church is simple in form, with a single hall, infrequently pierced by windows, covered by a barrel vault. Giotto cut the interior into rows of panels between painted columns, and he and his helpers painted in all thirty-eight pictures, covering the entire wall space. The total effect is colorful and eye-filling, without the overpowering, organ-thundering tones of Michelangelo's Sistine Chapel wall and ceiling, but equally moving in a melodious way. The subjects are from the life of the Virgin Mary and the life of Jesus—a continuous serial story, tragic but tenderly conceived, humanly believable, persuasive.

The compositions are notable for that simplicity which Giotto carried over from the Byzantine and Sienese methods. All his life he

Taddeo Gaddi: *Presentation in the Temple. Santa Croce Church, Florence*

remained a master in unifying and setting out the figures of his actors, freed of cluttering circumstance. Architectural backgrounds are frequent, but they are frame and setting, not added subject-matter played up in scientific perspective and competing emphasis. Landscapes, when they appear, as rarely they do, behind the figures, are laid up in curtain fashion. The mountains are shaped walls, and the trees are as flat and conventionalized as those in a Persian miniature. But the bodies are round and sculpturesque, and the faces emotionally alive.

Some of the finest of Giotto's murals, although they were once whitewashed over and badly restored after the uncovering, are in the Santa Croce Church in Florence. Here the mature Giotto, expert illustrator and superb muralist, is represented by pictures a little fuller, with greater depth, than in Padua (pages 312-13).

After being honored at the court of Naples, Giotto was called back to Florence in his old age. The city fathers, wanting a city architect and superintendent of public works, and desiring also the honor accruing from Giotto's presence, secured his return and bestowed on him publicly the title "Great Master."

As if the highest honors in painting were not sufficient to memorialize his genius, the artist turned to architecture and designed the campanile beside the Florentine Cathedral. It is unique in its decorative features, obviously echoing the Gothic language of the North, but add-

Bernardo Daddi: *Vision of St. Dominic. Gallery of Fine Arts, Yale University*

ing Southern sensuousness, grace, and rhythmic repetitions. Every visitor to Florence has been haunted by its mysterious loveliness. Beautifully it accents the cathedral group of Santa Maria del Fiore—Our Lady of the Flower.

Just as the lesser painters of Siena afford exquisite pleasure within their little field of melodious panel-pictures, so the Florentine followers of Giotto created a garden rich in unexpected and lovely, at times even gorgeous, paintings. Sometimes they harked back to the Byzantine formalism, approximating the gold-and-color ornament of the Sienese artists who so often

painted side by side with them in Santa Croce or Santa Maria Novella; or again they echoed Giotto himself along the road of humanized and simplified artistry; or, more exceptionally, they added an individual charm of coloring or composition or emotional feeling to the typical product.

Taddeo Gaddi is rather too great a creator to be mentioned merely in a list of Giottesque painters. During twenty-four years he was Giotto's pupil and helper. He elaborated his own backgrounds but not to the point of adding vista-like scenes demanding a change of focus on the observer's part. He held to Giotto's masterly sim-

Fra Angelico: *The Annunciation. San Marco Museum, Florence*

plification in figure organization, and he carried on an Eastern sensuous coloring. His murals in the Santa Croce Church are widely admired.

Bernardo Daddi leaned more definitely toward the miniature virtues. Like the Sienese, he was poetic, decorative, charming. His panel crucifixions and saints, golden-toned and melodiously rhythmic, grace walls in many European and American museums.

Lorenzo Monaco, born in Siena but master of a studio in Florence, carried over something of the miniature ornamentalism and color of his early homeland, and established the Sienese fragile formalism as a variety within early Florentine practice. He harked back to Simone Martini and Duccio in his use of sensitive and decorative line and controlled plastic melodies. It was he who handed on the Franciscan manner to Fra Angelico.

Andrea da Firenze gave way somewhat to the fashionable overloading of the wall with figures, though continuing in the tradition of primitive flatness and incidental bejeweled ornamentation. Spinello Aretino is known as painter of the

frescoes in the sacristy at San Miniato, and for colorful panels in many museums. Giottino (Tommaso di Stefano) returned to Sienese linear rhythms and simpler, more powerful composition. He seems not to have been one of the successful artists of his time, for one of the few details recorded of his life is that even his paints and a stone for grinding colors were finally taken from him by his creditors. It is probable that the stories about him, like the paintings attributed to him, pertain to two or even to three artists.

It was fifty years after Giotto's death that Fra Angelico—he who was named by his associates "the angelic one" because of his humility and piety—was born. Until his death in 1455, when Florence had made the full swing into realism, learning, and paganism, he carried on painting in the Franciscan spirit, with unmistakable idioms out of the medieval manner.

Fra Angelico has a gentleness and a sweetness of his own. If there were violences and agonized moments and worldly episodes in the Christian legendry that was his only theme-book, he found a way to sublimate them. Adoration, sacrifice,

Fra Angelico: *The Nativity.*
Metropolitan Museum of Art

heavenly glory—these are of the very mood of his art. He was adept at creating a linear harmony and a discreetly colorful melody with his richly draped but simply disposed figures, then at echoing the rhythms in simplified architectural backgrounds.

There is something of the cloistered monastery spirit implicit in his art. It is as if he, a friar, made a garden out of the scenes of Christian legendry and forgot, so far as a gentle soul may, the devils and executioners and tormentors, peopling it instead with demure Madonnas and saints and Magdalens, among whom there is a Christ radiant and victorious. In his work martyrs are beheaded without bloodiness. Even the damned in hell are pictured without too distressing sufferings. Perhaps the interweaving plastic melodies soften the reality of these underworld scenes, as certainly they build up into a joyful rhythmic paean the depicted gardens of heaven.

No one is known to have lived so completely the Christian ecstasies and thoughts and sorrows while painting them. Weeping as he re-created the Crucifixion scenes, kneeling in adoration as he painted the Virgin enthroned, were only two among the familiar reverences which made his painting career a long act of devotion. He painted many of his finest frescoes on the walls of the bare cells of his fellow monks; not in order that art might color and ease their environment, but that each brother might awaken upon his pallet and open his eyes to the lesson of the Annunciation, the Adoration, or the Nativity.

His art was a work of love; his love was that of

the innocent-minded. Every painting grew out of a faith that had simplified the world to a few values. Each is endowed with a distinguishing tenderness and naïveté out of his own saintly character. That he carried on, into an era that had come to value more robust and less spiritual virtues in its art, the simplicities and archaisms and the tapestry-like composition—with paper-flat trees and figures hardly more than two-dimensional—is evidence of the vitality of certain aesthetic qualities of primitivism. He closed an era that left to Europe, within the field of painting, a heritage more graceful, sensuously more enchanting, and more musical than any other.

Filippo Lippi: *Mary Kneeling before the Infant Jesus. State Museum, Berlin*

XVI: FLORENCE AND THE REBIRTH OF INTELLECTUALISM

IN 1345—a year after Simone Martini's death, eight years after Giotto's—citizens of Siena dug from the earth a Roman statue of the Goddess of Love, perhaps a copy of the nude *Venus Anadyomene*. Wonder at the beauty of the figure—"at so great a marvel and so much art," as a reporter of the time put it—ran high.

The pagan goddess was carried in joyful procession through the streets and set over the fountain in the city's central piazza. There for twelve years Venus ruled, in the very city whose citizens had so often spoken of the Virgin Mary as their Queen and a generation earlier had similarly carried Duccio's portrait of the Madonna through

Verrocchio: *Colleoni Monument*. Venice

the same streets with shouts of acclamation and prayers for protection.

But Siena did not prosper under Venus' rule. Misfortunes of every sort were visited upon the city. The plague scourged her, woefully thinning the ranks of her people. Civil war set brother against brother with the sword until anarchy was nearly reached. Then enemies from without savagely invaded Siena, burned and murdered. In 1357 the citizens gathered at the fountain in the piazza and smashed their beautiful pagan goddess into tiny bits. Nor were they content until they had transported the fragments out of Sienese territory and scattered them on ground belonging to Florence. Thereafter Siena knew pagan art and the pagan world only as works of Satan.

Florence at this time already was awakening to her neo-pagan destiny. The *Venus Anadyomene* would lie forever untroubled on her ground. Florence, "the Flower," was opening to an emancipation from medieval notions of reverence, from fear of Satan. This new state of mind is called by some *freedom*, by others *skepticism*.

Leonardo da Vinci is generally considered the typical figure of the Florentine Renaissance. In his own life and work he summed up its intellectual curiosity, its passion for scientific research, its calculated realism. He entered into the romantic mood of its patriotism and its civic pride —signed himself always "Leonardo the Florentine"—and joined in the spirit of its pageantry. He was gracious yet dignified, independent yet ready to take orders from the tyrant-princes. He failed to fall in with the fashionable woman-worship of the time, and thus was somewhat apart from the network of personal intrigue and licentious adventure that formed a web upon which the political (and religious) history of the era was woven; yet his own sort of sexual aberrancy, in one so universally honored and praised, is a symbol of the extent to which Florentine custom had reacted from Franciscan innocence. As to faith, Leonardo's cold skepticism was even more modern than the contemporary paganism of the princes and courtiers and merchants, who could wholeheartedly embrace Church custom while holding to the morals of the thug and the

libertine. But skepticism is the master-key to an understanding of the Renaissance.

Behind the decay of faith was the constructive use of the intellect. The scientific spirit emerged. Even art was based upon a way of knowing rather than upon a way of feeling. It was intellectual research that brought art back to the ancients and established a neoclassicism.

Florence is at the heart of the Renaissance. Few cities, hardly Athens itself or Byzantium, have been so favored, so strategically placed and so determining, in the pageant of Western civilization. "Miraculous Florence" . . .

Architecture and the Revival of Learning

The Italian spirit had regarded Gothic architecture as an aberration. The Italians had been the ones to dub it "Gothic," meaning to discredit it for all time as something uncouth and alien to cultured art. It had found little foothold in Italy; it was practiced only superficially, as an imported fashion of ornamentation. Nor, in the centuries of the Gothic culmination and decline in the North of Europe, was there a crystallization of any other style of building in the Italian city-states. There was no extension of the Franciscan spirit to the building arts. Pisa, with her mixture of Romanesque, Byzantine, and Gothic motives and methods, spells the story of late medieval uninventiveness and vacillation.

The monuments of Florence at the moment of Giotto's death were the Baptistry and the San Miniato Church, both in the variety of Romanesque known as Tuscan; and some fortress-palaces of a very plain and utilitarian sort, even rudely designed, with a few high windows and tall battlemented towers. To these Giotto had added his Gothic-accented campanile, and he had attempted to bring to completion the half-built and styleless cathedral. The campanile is a lovely thing, affording a colorful delight; but it breathes no hint of an emerging Italian type of architecture. Rome in Giotto's time was still a century away from peace and the opportunity to foster architectural innovations. It was to be almost a century before Florence, recognized by all

Italian cities as leader in the arts—and holding in actual subjugation Siena and Assisi and Pisa—knew the first Renaissance architect, one Filippo Brunelleschi.

The Florentines must have been asking themselves often in the fourteenth and early fifteenth centuries, when the "new painting" was being practiced on every side, when the Pisan sculptors had revived classic realism and were handing a lighted torch to Ghiberti and Donatello: "What is the comparable new way of architecture? How shall we have a style of building at once splendid, rational, and beautiful?"

Perhaps if they had asked only for rationalism, a *logical* sort of construction, and a consequent beauty, all would have been well—a new style would have been born. Instead the impulse expressed itself as a *re*birth, a Renaissance. The demand for splendor reminded the learned Florentine scholars of Greece and Rome. As the prince-tyrants must have their pageants and their theatricals in approximations of Roman theaters, and in settings supposed to be characteristic of the classic stage, entirely innocent of the traditions of the medieval Christian theater, so the search for an architecture of sufficient splendor to memorialize the civic pride and princely courtliness of Florence carried the builders directly back to Rome. The revival of learning had meant the uncovering of the monuments of the ancient civilization. Antiquity was now worshiped in the arts no less than in the revels of the upper classes.

A talented imitation, with an exercise of native taste in variation, was here substituted for creation. Architects delved into history, seeking excellencies of effect that they might imitate, instead of beginning with a new purpose, new building inventions, and new imagination.

The Renaissance architect arranged his findings from antiquity, says Charles Harris Whitaker, "just as a palaeontologist might arrange old bones in a search for some possible variety of animal that Nature had overlooked." Actually the animal he patched together looked a good deal like the Roman. The larger bones were the Roman arch and columns; the lesser ones were the pilaster and half-columns which the uncreative Romans in turn had acquired by

splitting the really functional and therefore rational Greek building-bones.

In short, the architect now began to work from inherited models and from a set of rules, not from human necessities and his own feel for tools and materials and suitable plastic forms of building. As for the rules, it was found that a late Roman builder named Vitruvius had conveniently codified them back in the first century A.D. He had been certain that Rome had established the one true, orthodox, and final way of constructing and decorating the chief types of architectural monument necessary to man. He explained in detail every method and step, and doubtless believed he had fixed the outlines within which the architecture of cultured man would be practiced for ever after.

Centuries later the Renaissance scholar-architects took him at his own word. The authority and supremacy of the "orders of architecture" were re-established, and no one will ever know the extent to which creative building art was damaged in that submission. European and American architecture was fixed in the neoclassic mold—not without pleasing and ingenious variations, but essentially without original inventiveness—for the entire period from 1420 to 1920.

Even in Brunelleschi's time, before the rediscovered monuments had really been dusted off, and certainly before the practice of a recognizable Renaissance architecture had been established, theorists had analyzed and interpreted Vitruvius. Manuals of architecture were circulated, were ready for duplication and international circulation when printing was discovered in this same fifteenth century.

There is something fateful, almost sinister, in the spectacle of these scholar-architects leading and controlling the building architects. Few art influences can be so neatly traced as this one: the revived classic style pushing its way out to every court in Europe, to Jacobean England, even to South and North America, everywhere causing fashionable kings and bishops and burghers to throw aside all former styles and to build palaces, churches, banqueting-halls, and state capitols in one not very vital idiom.

Inigo Jones, the famous English architect, carried the Italian treatises back with him to England, where he turned the tide of building into purest Renaissance. The books are to be seen in the library at Worcester College, Oxford, today. Farther afield, as an instance of the wide diffusion of the Florentine influence, there is in the library of the Santa Barbara Mission on the Pacific Coast of America a copy of a Spanish edition of Vitruvius's *De Architectura* from which the priests were able to transmit to their Amerindian workmen enough of the way of Roman arch-and-column building to afford a touch of classic style to the mission church façade. Thus in all directions and over great distances the Renaissance manuals of architecture went out to determine the appearance of buildings in the Western world. (In America, somewhat later, New England and Southern Colonial architecture echoed the influence, received by way of Georgian England.) Thus came the spread of that "paper architecture" which for centuries was more evident than inventive building.

Paper architecture triumphed in another sense also. The swing of the pendulum away from medieval communal effort to the extreme of individualism meant the emergence of the architect as a personality distinct from the master builder. Previously there had been no architects in the modern meaning of the word, as denoting a separate designer, a self-consciously artistic planner. This separate and separated artist now began, with Vitruvius and the rule-books derived from Vitruvius at his elbow, to make pictures of the building-to-be on paper.

The architect was no longer in any sense builder. The builder was no longer architect; indeed, he lost the sense of the whole and was content to have a chart and specifications of his own bit, his own job, be it masonry foundations or interior paneling or a roof. This separation was to last from Florentine days down to the thirties of the twentieth century, and was carried to unprecedented extremes as the Industrial Revolution gathered momentum following the mid-eighteenth century.

As for the craftsman who had been independent but profoundly interested in the whole fabric of the cathedral or the guild hall in medieval times, he too in Renaissance times was separated from any large concern with the building to which he contributed. His faith and loyalty and imagination had been, in the Gothic centuries, keys to the understanding of the poured-out wealth of sculpturing, coloring, and furnishing at Chartres and Reims and Paris. He was one of a commune, building in group self-expression, one within a brotherhood of artificers who kept a collective eye upon the total rising structure. Now he was to work at a point increasingly remote from the constructive and inventive center. This separation, like that of architect from builder, had much to do with the decline of the creative arts incidental to building, and the lack of any architectural synthesis comparable to the Gothic and the Greek during the four centuries following 1500.

In the decades just before and after that date Florence was teeming with woodcarvers, sculptors, painters, jewelers; but thenceforth the statue and the painting and the silversmith's trinket were to be seen less and less in the old architectural setting, more and more as individually displayed artistic items. And so began the struggle of artists and craftsmen to maintain their position in a world that no longer valued their work communally. Thenceforward the creator was not given a living for his recognized contribution to a commonly inspired monument. He was instead put at the disposal of "patrons," and later, failing that, was at the mercy of something called "popular demand." At first, if he had personality and originality and a sound technique, he fared well; for the Italian merchant princes and bankers and cardinals were inordinately rich and avid of ornament, as were the French kings after them, and at times the German, the Spanish, the Russian monarchs afterward.

All this—signalizing an epochal change in art in the Christian countries—followed upon the decay of faith and the final separation of the artist from monastic protection, upon the reorganization of society under the rule of bankers and merchants. The Medici "princes" of Florence afford the typical example, being actual bankers and soon actual rulers of their city—and of its

Cathedral of Florence, with Giotto's tower and Brunelleschi's dome

arts. Architecture was the art that suffered most from this new state.

This is not to say that there are no pleasing Renaissance buildings—they exist in great number—or to challenge the claim that neoclassicism is, in the breadth of its profusion over the earth and the extent of its practice in time, a major world style. It is only to qualify the nature of that style, to suggest that it is the least original of the major types of architecture, the least organic, and the least exciting. There is no Renaissance building that can conceivably be mentioned with Amiens or Santa Sophia or the Pantheon or the Parthenon. Mostly the monuments exist in parts which must be enjoyed separate from the building as a whole: there is a dome, a façade, a cloister, or a portico of importance.

The dome of the cathedral at Florence is Brunelleschi's monument. It is known universally as "Brunelleschi's dome," almost the first tribute of the sort to an individual architect. It is a beautiful thing in its own right, though wholly unrelated stylistically to the structure of which it is the crowning feature. Fortunately the main building is largely lost to sight from almost any point of view, near or far; the dome and Giotto's campanile near by stand up like independent creations.

Brunelleschi's dome is medieval in type, rather than Roman; the dressing-up with the architectural language of split columns, arcades, and pediments has not yet come in. But there are a capturing of clarity and an attainment of rhythmic simplicity which signalize a return to the classic ideal. There is something flower-like in the bulk of the dome as seen from without— appropriately, since this is the Cathedral of Our Lady of the Flower. One who has lived in Florence can testify how often, in varied light and from numberless vantage-points, the composition has evoked a pleasurable and distinctive response.

The full return to Rome and the real begin-

Brunelleschi: Pazzi Chapel, Florence

ning of the revival of classicism are marked rather in the conformist Pazzi Chapel, which Brunelleschi placed in the cloister area of Santa Croce Church. The columns, arches, entablatures, pedimented doorway, and pilasters—and the general studied look of the façade—are in the spirit of the neoclassic development. The building is charming; even today it loses nothing by comparison with later work, after five hundred years of Renaissance conformity and variation. If the beauty is only that of a garment, not deeply related to the organic truth of the structure, one nevertheless accepts it thankfully.

Here, as in the cathedral dome, there is a certain freshness, and this is apparent again in the portico of the Foundling Hospital in Florence. The round-arched arcade, so simply rhythmic, open, and reposefully horizontal, is an example of the use of arcading as a major decorative feature, which will become idiomatic in the Renaissance style through all Europe. (One of the most pleasing illustrations of it is in Fra Angelico's painting of *The Annunciation*, reproduced on page 328.)

The Pazzi Chapel, dated 1529, may be offered as a key exhibit, forecasting Renaissance practice in its two main aspects: as returning to Roman appearance-dominants, and as introducing a fresh harmonious lightness and clarity. In other monuments, notably the Churches of San Lorenzo and San Spirito, Brunelleschi followed ancient models more closely; they are Roman basilicas with only slight decorative innovations.

When Brunelleschi designed the Pitti Palace in Florence he modified, not too successfully, the older type of urban fortress-dwelling-place, using Roman ornamental forms. The palace as a type is better studied in the examples designed by his pupil and follower Michelozzo Michelozzi. Brunelleschi, however, by reason of the inventiveness shown in the cathedral dome, and the distinctive note in the lesser monuments, takes rank as one of the three or four foremost Italian architects.

The Medici Palace, long known as the Riccardi Palace, but recently labeled again with the name of the famous builders, was constructed from plans by Michelozzo in 1430. It is prototype

Michelozzo:
Medici Palace, Florence

of the urban palace as it was to be constructed in and out of Italy for two centuries. It retains certain medieval features, particularly the rough stone or "rusticated" lower walls, and the windows divided by pillar-mullions. But the determining idioms are those borrowed from Rome: the horizontal accents between stories and the heavy overhanging cornice at the top, in place of medieval battlements; and the window-spacing suggesting superimposed arcades. An interior court escapes the severe overheavy look of the exterior and is one of the pure expressions of Renaissance taste and method. The details of capital and entablature are copied from an ancient model. The total effect is graceful and learned, if a bit dull. The fragile aspect of the columns has been remarked as out of keeping with their function, and the general lightness is antithetical to the aspect of the rest of the building.

Later palaces are more of a piece, because the fortress-like aspect was gradually eased out of the exterior façades and because later architects gained a certain facility in the manipulation and harmonizing of the Roman ornamental language. The Strozzi Palace was to carry on directly the architectural form fixed in the Medici Palace, with some of the lingering medievalisms designed out, but this was not to be accomplished until considerably later. Meanwhile the Palazzo Rucellai introduced another Roman way of ornamentation in three rows of pilasters adorning the three stories of the façade, tying it together and lightening its appearance. From then on, for centuries, the useless pilaster was to be an incubus upon Western architecture. It set the seal of Rome firmly upon what was until the nineteen-twenties called "modern" building.

The man who reintroduced the pilaster was Leon Battista Alberti, a scholar-architect who had pored over Vitruvius and sought to render Florentine building orthodoxly classic. At Rimini he shortly afterward draped an imitation of a Roman triumphal arch over the front of an old church. This was typical of the spirit of "creative" building as it was now being initiated in the most progressive cities of Italy. The success was repeated at Mantua and elsewhere.

The Florentine antiquarians had done their work so well that imitative adaptation had by 1500 driven out every vestige of invention. The intellectual concept of a revived classicism had then utterly triumphed. In summary, the early Renaissance had known no change in architecture; the middle Renaissance saw a progression from the partial Romanism (still subject to original variation) of Brunelleschi to the full academism of Alberti. The high or late Renaissance, of the sixteenth and seventeenth centuries, was to see architects vying with one another in rearrangements of the now sanctified Graeco-Roman motives. All façades were to be topped with cornices and graced with (1) rows of pedimented windows or (2) superimposed arcades, real or blind—with often a framework of pilasters or engaged columns, and the occasional introduction of a larger complex of features such as the triumphal arch. The curious thing here is that the paper design is reasoned, rationalized, intellectualized over; but the structural elements are unreasonably and irrationally obscured under the studied mask. There were to be many pleasingly masked buildings in the sixteenth century, but no movingly organic ones.

Sculpture

The Medicean aristocrats of the fifteenth century used to fill their gardens with exhumed ancient statues, and the local sculptors were invited thither to study and to be imbued with the classic spirit of realism. But two centuries earlier an Italian sculptor in another city had already rediscovered the Roman monuments and initiated the revival of antique forms. Nicola Pisano, whose life fell wholly within the thirteenth century, practiced particularly the art of high relief in crowded panels of figures unmistakably suggested by the narrative sculptures of imperial Rome. He doubtless had felt, too, the influence of the naturalism which was then entering the

Gothic sculpture in France, though it was there held strictly within a larger formal synthesis.

Long considered by scholars a Pisan by birth and training, Nicola Pisano is now known to have come from Apulia in Southern Italy and thus to have had opportunity to see Roman statues where they most abundantly survived. Then, too, the enterprising Pisans had sacked many a Sicilian and other Mediterranean city and had carried home sculptured marbles along with unsculptured, for the building and adornment of their cathedral and baptistry. Some of the figures and groupings in Nicola's panels can be traced directly to the Roman sarcophagi and carved vases still standing in the Pisan Campo Santo. One of his angels obviously wears a Roman toga, and the Virgin in the *Nativity* is in an attitude said to be traceable to Roman-Etruscan conventions. In any case, in this one artist's work there is a sudden complete reversion from the current Byzantine and Romanesque decorative sculpture to Roman conceptions and method.

At Pisa, Nicola carved the pulpit in the baptistry, one of the most celebrated sculptural works in Europe. The architectural elements are amazingly mixed; but the dominating sculptural panels are straight Roman, crowded with figures, realistic, dramatic. The pulpit ensemble and the individual panels are effectively rich, opulently decorative. There are hints of some true Renaissance modifications in the way of storytelling—but the whole is essentially revival.

Straightway the Pisan pulpit excited admiration and envy throughout Tuscany, and Nicola Pisano was invited to design and carve a pulpit for the cathedral at Siena. The result is somewhat more elaborate, equally inconsistent architecturally, but equally eye-filling and dramatic. Here the revived antique panel sculpture is seen in several varied interpretations; for the master had brought along assistants and had taught them, each according to temperament and ability, to follow the pattern. Soon, from this center, the influence went out in a dozen directions.

Nicola's son, Giovanni Pisano, returned to Pisa to do a pulpit for the cathedral, and later did another for Pistoia—engaging works both, but overdecorated and occasionally melodramatic

Nicola Pisano:
Pulpit in baptistry, Pisa

in subject-matter. It was Arnolfo di Cambio rather who carried the impetus on into the full tide of the Renaissance, for he was a Florentine and thus was able to convey the message of a revived classicism into an atmosphere soon to be charged with a very passion for antiquity.

Arnolfo seems for a time to have trembled on the verge of a sculptural art expressive of the Franciscan spirit, fragile, melodious, and formalized. But his pupils diverted the humanistic trend into other fields. Just as all painting after Fra Angelico must be judged for a set of virtues different from those of the colorful, decorative, plastically controlled panel-painting of the Sienese school—rather by an illustrational and "natural" canon—so Florentine sculpture, from Ghiberti to Desiderio da Settignano, must be assessed primarily as realism.

Indeed, from any point of view except that of the devoted realist, the sculpture of the early and middle Renaissance is generally inferior to that of the great eras of direct carving in stone. Nevertheless, in all the virtues except the most profound, this body of popular Renaissance busts, panels, figurines, and medals represents one of the greatest upsurgings of the art on European soil, and is characterized by grace, skill, and prettiness to an extraordinary degree. One of these early practitioners, Donatello, was a born sculptor and suffers only when put beside a giant like Michelangelo. To be sure, nothing in the whole range of art has been so widely and lavishly praised as the works of Ghiberti, Donatello, and the della Robbias. Now, at a time when the tide of realism has receded, it becomes clear that no school of sculpture has been so overpraised.

Vasari, a gossipy writer of the sixteenth century, whose biographies of Renaissance artists have been very useful to later scholars despite inaccuracies, prejudices, and a provincial sort of

Ghiberti: *Creation of Adam and Eve, The Temptation,* and *The Expulsion.*
Panel in baptistry door, Florence

nationalism, tells the story of Lorenzo Ghiberti's winning of a competition held to determine what sculptor should design the doors of the baptistry in Florence at the opening of the fifteenth century. Ghiberti's trial design for one of the twenty-eight panels exists in a Florentine museum along with one by Brunelleschi; both are so realistic, pictorial, and theatric that there can be no doubt about the full triumph of illustrationalism at this time.

Brunelleschi withdrew—to become the foremost architect of the era. Ghiberti spent the next twenty-two years designing and casting the pair of doors. So pleased were the Florentines that he was then commissioned to execute another

pair, to take the place of some then deemed old-fashioned; and he spent another term of twenty-two years on the job.

Andrea Pisano, a follower of Nicola and Giovanni of the same name, though unrelated in family, had done that earlier pair of doors for the baptistry seventy years before. They were moved to a less conspicuous portal, but they remain, when judged by architectural and sculptural standards, more competent and pleasing than the more celebrated Ghiberti compositions. Ghiberti, however, introduced marvels of a sort unprecedented in the art of sculpture—and very popular. He treated each panel as if it were an easel picture. The amount of narrative and action

Ghiberti: Bronze doors of baptistry, Florence

and casual detail incorporated into the four doors is extraordinary. Trees, mountains, streams, clouds, ships, armies—all are expertly manipulated for pictorial effectiveness. The newly discovered scientific perspective is worked to the utmost for agreeable and surprising effect. The reader can satisfy himself regarding these points by studying the illustration opposite, and the one above.

The sculptor himself, writing of the second pair of doors (each bearing five picture panels instead of the fourteen on each of the earlier pair), records that "in some of these ten reliefs I

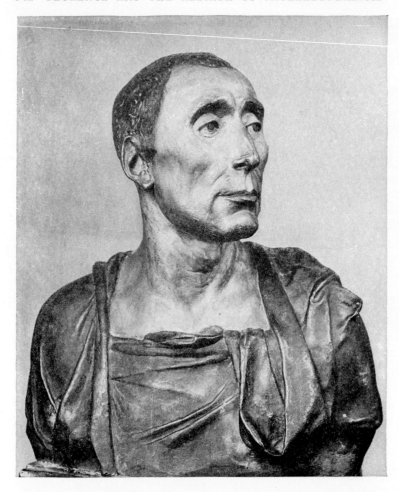

Donatello:
Bust of Nicola da Uzzano.
National Museum, Florence

introduced more than a hundred figures, in others fewer. . . . Observing the laws of optics, I succeeded in giving them an appearance of such reality that when seen at a distance the figures seem to be in the round. The nearer figures are largest, while those in the further planes diminish in size, as occurs in Nature."

In the matter of verisimilitude this is a notable advance over the ancients. Western relief sculpture theretofore had presented the figures in equal size except for the arbitrary purpose of emphasizing the importance of a king, as in Assyria, or Christ, as in Byzantine art, or a similarly symbolic figure. Even Nicola Pisano had enlarged the Virgin Mary. But with Ghiberti scientific naturalism is exploited and brought conspicuously into sculptural art.

Vasari described parts of the second doors as "the most beautiful work that has appeared in ancient or modern times." The Florentines have traditionally called them "The Doors of Paradise," as being worthy to grace heaven itself. Nor has the chorus of similar hyperbolic praise from those partial to realism ceased at any time since.

If one grants that to accomplish in one art the technical feats pertaining to another, that to achieve in bronze the effect of linear flow and spacious background natural to painting, constitutes an artistic triumph, Ghiberti's panels are masterpieces. It is easy to mark in them the pictorial and illustrational virtues: pleasingly natural settings, well-grouped figure compositions, and plentiful, simply organized action. To these may be added the virtuoso manipulation of the space-effects, and a newly competent handling of anatomy—if as yet without marked sense of char-

Donatello:
The Gattamelata Statue, detail.
Padua

acterization. But when all is said, the compositions are rich in just those values that are most alien to plastic unity, sculptural roundness, and three-dimensional vitality. The future may yet judge them a marvelous show of misdirected inventiveness.

Incidentally, in Ghiberti's work the return to paganism, or to a neo-pagan humanism, is signalized by one other detail—the frank and caressing treatment of the nude figure. Since Christian puritanism had initiated a millennium of denial of the body there had been precious little picturing of the nude for its own sake. Occasionally Christian mythology had permitted the portrayal of the naked—and usually ugly—bodies of temptresses, imps, or sinners roasting in Hell. Francis of Assisi, in combating asceticism and mortification of the flesh and teaching the beauty and holiness of the natural, had paved the way for a return to appreciation of the human architecture.

One way and another, there is a considerable collection of personable and inviting nymphs in Ghiberti's holy picture-panels of the baptistry doors. We shall see the holy elements rapidly diminish and the sensuously seductive ones increase in Florentine art in the decades following. Curiously enough, although the doors have given Ghiberti the reputation of being an artist "of one masterpiece," he left a number of treatments of the Madonna and Child, in the full round, which are superior to the illustrational reliefs. They add to the tender and sweet realism a felicity of line and a gracefully flowing treatment of sculptural mass that are legitimately of the stone or metal art.

Donatello surpassed even Ghiberti in the piling-up of natural detail when he turned to relief art, though he was less fortunate in the matters of pictorial composition and suave dramatic flow. His outstanding achievements are in the round.

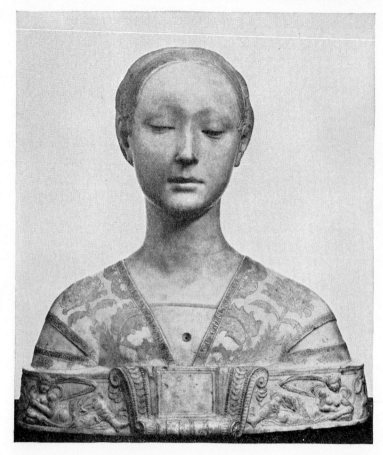

Laurana:
A Neapolitan Princess.
State Museum, Berlin

With him the realism out of rediscovered Rome and the realism that had been growing out of the late Gothic nature-interest had met. Renaissance sculpture was then fully emergent.

The portrait busts of Donatello are hardly less revealing than those left by the surpassing realists of Augustan Rome. For a moment the art based on anatomical study and intent observation seems about to pass over into that modern sort based on psychological analysis. The type-figure that ruled in the sculptural art for a dozen centuries has been overthrown in favor of character portrayal.

Donatello had spent years of study in Rome, but after his return to Florence in about 1406 he seems to have clung for a time to certain medievalisms. Ten years later, however, by the time of the "bald pate" or Pumpkin-Head statue in a niche on the campanile, he had adopted every idiom of Roman realism, including the wooden drapery (naturalistic treatment of drapery in stone or metal cannot but result in a heavy, stiff effect), the exact reproduction of every anatomical idiosyncrasy, and a general air of cruelly analytical recording. In the same vein, and more arresting because the interest is concentrated in the head, is the polychrome bust which may be of Cicero or of one of Donatello's fellow citizens named Nicola da Uzzano (shown on page 342). In it Renaissance sculpture reaches a culmination of exact portraiture.

Donatello was equal to the task of carrying the new passion for naturalism into every sculptural field. A relief of the Annunciation in Santa Croce Church shows the Virgin as a perfectly transcribed gracious lady of the *quattrocento* listening to a very human angel. The piece is inordinately praised alike by Vasari and by twentieth-century writers who consider lifelikeness the prime quality in art. It is an instructive

Desiderio da Settignano:
Bust of a Young Woman.
Bargello, Florence

example of the dispersion of sculptural values. More can be said for the famous reliefs of the choir gallery in the cathedral at Florence. The architectural features confine better the complicated, even exuberant, movement of the panels, and afford a rich impression in the tradition of the antique Roman sarcophagi.

The full-size equestrian statue of Gattamelata in Padua by Donatello is lifelike in a slack way, and is beautifully placed, so that the mass of it silhouettes decoratively against the sky. But as a whole it lacks the spiritedness of Verrocchio's counterpiece at Venice, with which it is most often bracketed. The fact is that as a whole Donatello's monument is a bit awkward and squat, partly because of the smallness of the man in relation to the horse. Nevertheless the head of Gattamelata (page 343) is an extraordinarily fine portrait. It has all the best traits of

neoclassicism—characterful reality, clarity, force.

There are enough of these clear, lifelike, and impressive pieces to mark Donatello as the outstanding figure of the early Renaissance group. He was indeed recognized as leader by his contemporaries. He stands the perfect neo-Greek. Truthfulness to nature, a logical idealism, harmonious grace—these he seems to take naturally from the Romans and the Greeks. He adds often a sweetness of his own, and certainly a special extension of the quality that may be considered Greek clarity. The sweetness may run off into sentimentality, even into a cloying taste for *putti* or cherubs, oftenest arranged in panels but also spilled into the backgrounds of Madonna-and-Child plaques or set out independently as single figurines. Sweet in the better sense, and in every way clear and fine, is the full-length statue of *St. George,* once at Or San Michele and now in

Pisanello: Medals

Florence's Bargello museum. A companion piece, *St. John the Baptist* (the *young* St. John), is sweetly expressive, too—again, the head is very fine—but there is greater concession to the contemporary ideal of "pictorial" sculpture.

To the writer the statue most universally praised among Donatello's works, the youthful *David*, is, despite the pretty body, insipid as sculpture; it is sentimentally literary, overdetailed, weak. The incidental relief on the helmet of the severed head of Goliath deals with the triumph of love. This unrestrained indulgence in detail for its own sake—the ivy leaves on the hat, the flowing tresses, the piled-up trophies at the base—is, according to the judgment of today, unsculptural. The same fault is carried to its ulti-

mate excess in the famous *Judith and Holofernes* in the Piazza della Signoria in Florence.

"Perfection" is a word commonly used to describe Donatello's works. There is enough evidence to warrant a limited use of it. But it becomes clearer year by year that Donatello's importance is that of a culminating figure in an age of sculpture devoid of massive and lithic characteristics. He is a master when sensitivity and grace have been substituted for harder, more vigorous and rocklike qualities.

The faults of oversweetness that had developed with many sculptors find their apotheosis in the wholly feminine sculpture of Luca della Robbia. The realism of the time no longer has the surprise of character revelation. The natural-

Luca della Robbia: *Virgin and Child*. Glazed terra cotta. *Philadelphia Museum*

ism is standardized. All the cherubic children—and they abound—are alike. The Madonnas and angels seem to have been studied from one local girl. The panel picturing of Ghiberti, already weakened in Donatello, slides even further into a frank wash-drawing technique.

Luca della Robbia at first worked in marble, devising a choir gallery with reliefs of singing boys that rivals Donatello's in the Florence cathedral. "The most wonderful singers imaginable: you can almost hear them," commented the American sculptor Lorado Taft. Later Luca developed the pretty art of polychrome ceramic sculpture which is more especially associated with his name. Luca's nephew Andrea carried on the tradition, and, although less accomplished as

a sculptor-picturer, he did some *bambini* and Madonnas that became immediately popular and have been duplicated endlessly. Della Robbia plaques are to be seen in the original in every museum great or small, and in competent reproductions in every "art shop." An illustration here shows one of Luca's early and comparatively strong compositions, the *Virgin and Child* in the Philadelphia Museum.

A contemporary of the della Robbias, Andrea del Verrocchio, returned to a scientific realism and preserved a certain masculinity. His *David* is a bonily boyish boy, as contrasted with the prettily androgynous figure by Donatello, though it is equally far from typical sculptural cleanness and hardness. His masterpiece is the over-life-

Jacopo della Quercia: *Creation of Adam. Church of San Petronio, Bologna*

sized equestrian statue known as the *Colleoni,* in Venice, one of the finest things of the sort in European art history. Here there is a return to sculptural massiveness. The simple relationship of parts and the dynamic organization are notable. The dramatic strength has served as inspiration to generations of makers of equestrian monuments. It is illustrated on page 331.

Contemporary with Ghiberti there had been at Siena a figure more important than any of the Florentines as a forerunner of that one genius of Renaissance art-in-marble, Michelangelo. This was Jacopo della Quercia. He saw sculpture as a monumental rather than a pretty art. Even in devising the reliefs currently so popular he maintained a largeness of conception and strength in modeling. There is an amplitude in the panels around the doorway of San Petronio Church at Bologna which is repeated in some rather battered fountain figures at Siena; the whole exhibit marks this exceptional artist as one of the few born sculptors of the Renaissance.

Jacopo had been one of the competitors for the commission to design the baptistry doors at

Jacopo della Quercia: *Expulsion of Adam and Eve. Church of San Petronio, Bologna*

Florence; and one may wonder whether Italian sculpture might not have followed a more creative course if so masculine an artist had then been chosen instead of the maker of miniature pictures. It is known that Michelangelo, the transcendent artist of the following century, studied to good purpose Jacopo's works at Bologna. His virtues of massive sculptural conception and plastic vitality seem not to have been discovered by the other and lesser Renais-

sance artists—or by critics for many generations.

In Florence the best was past long before the end of the fifteenth century. The della Robbia family continued to capitalize on the popularity of the colored plaques. The Rossellinos, Bernardo and Antonio, continued their production of both free-standing statues and picture reliefs. Some of the most natural angels known are found among their works. Mino da Fiesole and Benedetto da Maiano practiced in that tradition too, but are better known for certain portrait busts done in uncompromising neoclassic accuracy. Pollaiuolo completed the destruction of truly sculptural values in free-standing statues, adding melodramatic stress and strain to observed anatomic realism. He is vivid, but sculptural amplitude and quietude have fled from his work.

Recently there has been an appreciative revival of interest in the low-relief harmonies of Agostino di Duccio. His panel pictures with raised figures exhibit an appealing linear grace, and his sense of space-filling composition is better than that of his contemporaries. But the values are largely those borrowed from another art, and he plucks the sentimental note to excess, according to present judgments. Less overdone is the feminine appeal in the plaques and statuettes by Desiderio da Settignano. They depend upon the grace and sweetness of the model, but they retain sculptural integrity. If he had left no more than the lovely *Bust of a Young Woman* in the Bargello, shown on page 345, his fame would be secure. Another who worked the stone with appealing smoothness and fluency was Francesco Laurana, who is sometimes placed at the very head of the list of successful Renaissance portraitists.

In summary of the disservice of the later Florentines to the art of sculpture it may be said that they progressively weakened and feminized it. Except when Michelangelo came back from Rome to work on the Medici tomb figures, the art was not to be heard of again in the city on the Arno—unless one counts the trinkets manufactured by Cellini, and a statue or two of his.

If one disregards size, perhaps the best thing in sculpture of the *quattrocento*, excepting Jacopo della Quercia's works, is a series of medals by Pisanello of Verona. He was a world master of miniature relief design. With him style was born again. The intention is frankly decorative—as seen on page 346. The problem of filling space, of the abstract architecture of the design within a given area, is beautifully solved. The main motives are strong, dominating, and dynamically contrived. After reports of so much weakened

and washy sculptural design, it is pleasant to end the account of early Italian sculpture on this note of an art which, if small, is stiffly stylized, masculinely strong—and everlastingly attractive.

It may be instructive to add a quotation on the broad way in which the artist worked in the era of Medicean magnificence and patronage of the arts. As contrasted with the simple straightforward devotion of the Gothic sculptor to a single task or a single type of art, a picture of the hustle and bustle of the artist's life in fifteenth-century Florence is significant. It is taken from Rachel Annand Taylor's colorful book entitled *Leonardo the Florentine,* and describes the life of Verrocchio as sculptor-in-ordinary to the Medici:

Much employed by Lorenzo, he made Piero de' Medici's beautiful tomb in San Lorenzo, red porphyry and green marble on great lion's paws with twisted, thorny bronze foliage. He had wrought on the Forteguerra tomb. He lifted the ball of gilded copper on the dome, and set the Cross over the ball. . . . For the Medici he was always at work, tombs, statues, armour, pageantry, ex-votos, busts of both brothers, Giuliano and Lorenzo—Lorenzo with graven harpies on his breast. He did many things cheerfully, for, oppressed by poverty and duty to his kin, he had known himself so thwarted that he could not even ply for want of metals the trade of goldsmith. He fashioned the silver hind for Giuliano's helmet; he had made breastplates for Galeazzo Maria Sforza; he painted standards and devised gilded steel for the tournaments; he cast a churchbell for the monks of Vallombrosa. In an inspired and radiant mood he charmed from some garden-nursery of Olympos that inimitable *putto* with the dolphin for Careggi, and he restored the antique red marble bust of Marsyas, using the white veins in the stone for the sinews. He made clasps and cups with devices of foliage and fabulous beasts, acanthus and pinions alive and lovely, but with that hint of natural malice in them which becomes a conscious threat of danger in Leonardo's spined wings and leaves. . . . He had much of his pupil's versatility, but none of his disdains, for he was a goldsmith and intaglio-maker, even bell-caster, as well as painter, musician, and geometrician.

XVII: FLORENTINE PAINTING:
THE SCIENTIFIC SPIRIT AND THE PAGEANTISTS

Giotto had already established painting as the outstanding art of Italy before the Renaissance had been fully initiated. His humanism had brought to the picturing art a new emotionalism out of familiar life. Yet he is more often termed a late medieval artist. The stream of Franciscan painting, with its simple, intimate depiction of Christian subjects within the formalism and glow inherited from Italo-Byzantine practice, continued in "the School of Giotto" in fourteenth-century Florence, and even through the first half of the fifteenth century in the lovely but lonely creations of Fra Angelico. Nevertheless, humanism had then taken a turn, particularly under secular patronage, toward a fuller portrayal of man on the one hand, and toward a fuller celebration of his emancipated neo-pagan way of living on the other. Progress may be traced along the two lines: scientific naturalism and a joyous pageantism. The lines flow together at times, in an Uccello or a Botticelli. It was science that won in the end.

The scientific spirit was in the air. It acted upon painting generally as an impulse toward the recording of life "more truly," and specifically as an impulse toward the study of anatomy, of light and shade, and of perspective. Knowledge of the bones and muscles and sinews under the skin, it was thought, must add to truth. Soon the painters were to pose figures in attitudes that made for a knowing display of muscle and bone articulation. Likewise, perspective backgrounds were to be insisted upon till the two-dimensional picture field was sadly punctured and violated. Shadows would be sketched naturally.

If the new knowledge of anatomy and optics at first all but destroyed the painting as formal organization, it represented a step toward the artists who would masterfully combine realism *and* organization: Michelangelo, Titian, and Tintoretto. And there are a thousand things to delight the eye and satisfy the mind in the Florentine painting of the revolutionary and transitional fifteenth century. Indeed, no century has pro-

Gentile da Fabriano: *The Flight into Egypt. Uffizi Gallery, Florence*

Masaccio: *Expulsion from Paradise.*
Santa Maria della Carmine, Florence

oratively conceived. And indeed the young Masaccio vacillated between his new-found photographic realism and the pictorial conventions of his predecessors. He might have been one of the greatest of European painters if he had not died at the age of twenty-seven, in 1428. As it is, he is known as the initiator of Italian scientific realism. He was almost the first artist to define subjects by natural light-and-shadow.

Tonal Representation and Dramatic Painting

Up to this time contour, as emphasized by line, had been the major means of representation of solids in a painting. Giotto had introduced sculpturally rounded figures, but without regard to the science of light, and he had continued to play linear harmonies in the mode inherited from Duccio. Now Masaccio compared existing art with nature—and could not find any justification for lines. He set painting in the way of tonal facsimile representation.

Masolino, who painted before Masaccio and is supposed to have been the latter's teacher, made strides toward "natural" statement, particularly in nudes—though possibly Masaccio had shown the way, for teacher outlived pupil by two decades. Altogether Masolino was hardly a first-class painter in either his earlier, more or less medieval style or the later realistic one. He is significant chiefly as the possible co-originator of scientific naturalism. An occasional Giottesque panel, like the *Crucifixion* in the Maitland Griggs Collection, is an exception, affording deep visual enjoyment through the linear harmonies employed by Giotto and Bernardo Daddi.

Andrea del Castagno was next to learn the lessons of anatomy and optics. He continued the methods of representation by natural shading and mastered perspective—of which he made too much show—but his treatment was wooden as compared with the subtle tonalities of Masaccio. And he is overshadowed by Filippo Lippi.

Nothing could be more illuminating, as showing the conflict between the old artistic (and ecclesiastic) traditions and the new ideals of

duced in one place so many artists destined to world fame. Between 1400 and 1450 the mature works of Fra Angelico and Filippo Lippi appeared, as also of della Quercia, Ghiberti, and Donatello—and the experiments of Masaccio, Uccello, and Pisanello. After 1450 came Botticelli and Leonardo da Vinci.

Adam and Eve in the *Expulsion from Paradise* by Masaccio, first of the great Italian realists, are just a naked man and woman, reproduced in facsimile, showing all the signs of grief, he with hands over eyes, she with distressful upturned face and hands stretched to cover those parts of her body of which she has just become guiltily conscious. The human actors are real, observed. But the gate behind them is still a medieval symbol, and the angel above is dec-

Masolino (attributed to):
Crucifixion.
Maitland Griggs Collection

liberalism and realism, than the story of this natural libertine cooped within the walls of a monastery and constrained to paint instructive church pictures while his heart was devoted to the fleshly world outside. The reader may remember how Robert Browning's poem "Fra Lippo Lippi" summarizes the conflict and brings out the painter's Florentine philosophy. He has been out on the streets making a night of it (his amorous adventures are fully chronicled by Vasari), and, being taken up by the police, explains how he painted the monastery walls with Bible pictures, but incorporating "every sort of monk" and "folks at church" and "some poor girl." But—

The Prior and the learned pulled a face

And stopped all that in no time. "How? What's
    here?
Quite from the mark of painting, bless us all!
Faces, legs, arms and bodies like the true
As much as pea and pea! it's devil's-game! . . .
Paint the soul, never mind the legs and arms!
Rub all out, try at it a second time. . . ."

And Fra Lippo is made to summarize his passion for the real in these words:

The beauty and the wonder and the power,
The shapes of things, their colours, lights and
    shades,
Changes, surprises—and God made it all!
. . . Why not do as well as say—paint these
Just as they are, careless what comes of it?
God's works—paint anyone, and count it crime
To let a truth slip. . . .

Filippo Lippi: *Virgin and Child. Pitti Palace, Florence*

In Filippo Lippi's paintings it is not only that the interest in the real detail and in individualized people gets in the way of creative conception, but that a certain mechanical marshaling of parts is evident, and a rather too hard exactitude of rendering. Among the most appealing of his pictures is an early one of *Mary Kneeling before the Infant Jesus,* owned by the State Museum, Berlin. The Virgin is obviously an observed local girl—she might be the "sweet angelic slip of a thing" of the poem—and God and Joseph are photographically exact characterizations of real old men. But a freshness about the whole and an organizational unity lift it above the general run of Filippo Lippi's work. One look at the Virgin figure indicates

the extraordinary advance since Giotto's time in realistic rendering (see page 330). In others of Filippo Lippi's pictures, particularly in the *Virgin and Child* in the Pitti Gallery, there is evidence that the monk-artist had studied well the new science of perspective.

The scientific tendency found its culmination in the very exact works of Piero della Francesca, who was not a Florentine at first but came as a young painter to spend a few years at the center of experiment and progress in his art. He mastered anatomy, perspective, and the new tonal method of representation, and he often added extensive landscape backgrounds or elaborate architectural ones. If this were all, he might be dismissed as merely a link between

Gentile da Fabriano: *Adoration of the Magi. Uffizi Gallery, Florence*

Masaccio and Leonardo. But Piero added to these advances in naturalism an exceptional gift in the field of abstract picture-design. That he consciously studied balance, weight distribution, and space division at a time when formal design had badly retrogressed and the virtues of "the natural" had been substituted is made obvious in numerous paintings—so much so that recent studies in pictorial composition and plastic organization have greatly increased his reputation. Undramatic as his work generally is, there are subtle adjustments and a sort of pictorial architecture that afford an exceptional pleasure. Some portrait busts, perfectly set in the frames, with melting landscapes in the background, are outstanding.

In some of Piero's canvases and frescoes there appear bits of ornamental enrichment and processional pageantry which suggest the advisability of pausing in this chronicle of growing Italian realism to trace the second stream of development —that which was termed, at the opening of the chapter, "pageantism." If the naturalism of Masaccio and Filippo Lippi and Piero was a direct outgrowth of the Florentine scientific spirit, this other superficially decorative tendency is traceable to a pagan philosophy and a sumptuous way of life in those circles wherein the artists found patronage.

Back in the time of Giotto's immediate followers, in the mid-fourteenth century, a painter-sculptor-architect known as Orcagna had turned a little away from the emotional humanism of Giotto and toward a dramatic building up of crowded patterns of figures. The device was not new. It was in line with the decorative tendency out of Siena, and indeed the Byzantine-derived glow of color was continued in it. Several of the Giottesque painters had leaned in this direction, particularly Andrea da Firenze, and so had Ambrogio Lorenzetti; but it was an Umbrian, Gentile da Fabriano, who first carried the rich panoramic method to a culmination. His only major surviving work, the *Adoration of the Magi* in the Uffizi Gallery in Florence, shows some incidental absorption of the realistic tendencies of the painter's contemporaries. The Sienese and Giottesque stiffness is gone. But

Pisanello: *St. George Liberating the Princess of Trebizond.*
Church of Santa Anastasia, Verona

something of the grace, the flowery freshness, and the embroidered richness remains. To this Gentile adds movement and the quickness of life. The pageant is still of the Church, but it is alive with the energy of Florentine secular "society." Gentile could do an episodic picture, too, one not unworthy to stand beside those of his gifted contemporary, Fra Angelico, as is to be verified by the *Flight into Egypt* of the predella of the *Adoration,* illustrated on page 351.

Paolo Uccello was the next great figure in the line of dramatic painters. Uccello became, however, so doctrinairely engrossed with the problems and effects of scientific perspective that his pictures are likely to ask the eye—so to speak—to pause and marvel at the clever way in which a complex of lines leads up to an accent in deep space, or at an animal perfectly foreshortened. It is said that Donatello remonstrated with Uccello, saying: "Ah, Paolo, with this perspective of yours you are sacrificing the substance for the shadow."

Before going on to the last great figure among the panorama-painters, Benozzo Gozzoli, it is well to recall an individualist, already noted as a master of medal-design, Pisanello of Verona. He has generally been underestimated by historians. His work gives notable pleasure to the observer whose faculties are open to an appreciation of highly stylized art. His rich decorativeness is combined with consummate delicacy of touch, and his method of laying up the elements of the picture flat mark him as kin to the painters of the Far East. The harmonious miniatures of Persia and the formalized landscapes of China are hardly more expertly flattened.

Someone has said that Pisanello was a master painter of individual figures and objects but that he had little sense of composition and organization. Rather, his tapestry-like disposition of simplified and emphasized figures, with incidental patterned areas, is a departure from realistic practice but beautifully effective. Whether in the sumptuous frescoes in Santa Anastasia Church at Verona, or in a narrative panel, or in the simple portrait of Lionello d'Este at Bergamo, the rare qualities of the rare pictures by Pisanello afford a distinctive and full-bodied enjoyment.

Fra Angelico, even while remaining his own inimitable self, a rare last Franciscan lingering on

Benozzo Gozzoli: *Journey of the Kings. Medici Palace, Florence*

into Medicean days, borrowed from both the realism of Masaccio and the pageantism of the panoramists. It was, strangely, one of his pupils who went over the whole way to the pageantists, in the fullest secular interpretation. Benozzo Gozzoli, instead of carrying on the still faintly medieval courtliness of Gentile da Fabriano and Pisanello, undertook illustrational recording of the actual pageantry now being staged in the daily lives of the social princes of Florence.

Every visitor to that city is taken immediately to the Palazzo Medici to see the paintings of the story of the *Three Kings* in the private chapel constructed for Piero de' Medici (the Gouty) by Michelozzo in 1444-52. Here Benozzo Gozzoli spread on three walls processional pictures of the journeys of the Kings to Bethlehem in clever panoramic illustrations. The presentation is of a pageant in which local celebrities take part, and every detail is studied from the environs of Florence and from the people of the Medicean circle. There are no fewer than five members of

the Medici family among the nobles of the cavalcade, and Lorenzo (later to be "the Magnificent") is one of the Kings.

Thus the pageant-painters of the early Renaissance traveled the distance from the remote and formalized imagery of the Lorenzettis and Simone Martini to depiction of the actual panorama of neo-pagan Florentine life. The *Three Kings* marks arrival at a new sort of courtly realism. The art of it is rich and artificial because the fashionable life of Florence is so, not because the artist enriched and formalized and thereby rendered the picture artificial.

As a matter of fact Gozzoli is a distinctly second-rate painter in any ultimate creative sense. He scores heavily by reason of the wealth of interest in the life he has illustrated. He presents the pomp and circumstance of his time spontaneously, with a great deal of red-velvet coloring, and with page boys and lap-dogs added. Others less celebrated are perhaps superior in invention—Domenico Veneziano among them.

Ghirlandaio: *Nativity of the Virgin. Church of Santa Maria Novella, Florence*

Some artists are known almost wholly for their paintings on the *cassoni* or trousseau chests which were fashionable as presents to young girls; or for decorated salvers presented when a young mother gave birth to a child, or for "wainscot panels" specially hung during festive occasions. The very nature of these settings afforded the artist an excuse for finally escaping from religious imagery into a treatment of themes in keeping with the luxurious and decorative court life.

The subjects on the *cassone* panels are scenes from sporting life—racing, jousting, and hunting —and from allegorical or legendary episodes, and from actual pageants and parties. The salvers may duplicate these themes, or treat birth itself symbolically or in a historical instance, or celebrate love. The "triumphs" that formed a main motive in Florentine poetry and drama, immortalized by Petrarch and made visually eloquent in pageant and tableau on the Renaissance ballroom stages, come into painting here. They were to be exploited in larger paintings by Piero della Francesca, Mantegna, and many others. *The Triumph of Love,* or *The Triumph of Beauty,* would be exceptionally in place on a

bride's *cassone;* and *The Triumph of Fame* on a salver celebrating the birth of a Medicean heir. Pesellino's paintings on bridal chests in particular are rich illustrations of luxurious Florentine custom and of colorful triumphal processions.

At this time there were artists who were carrying on the work of scientific investigation and recording, while others were bringing together the naturalistic and the decorative currents. Pollaiuolo introduced a nervous and at times melodramatic realism, and is widely praised by the intellectualists for taking a further step in accurately reproducing life as it is seen. He was the first to dissect corpses for the advancement of art. Verrocchio was less at ease as painter than as sculptor; his rather hard style of realistic picturing is the better known because he was the teacher of Leonardo da Vinci, whose mannerisms are foreshadowed in the elder man's figures.

Where the two currents flow together Andrea Mantegna, not a Florentine but a Paduan, stands prominent. His documentation is convincing but overexact, and his effects of crowded richness are obviously obtained by the loading-in of architectural detail, garlands, banners, and rich stuffs. There is a wooden fixity in his faces and figures—

Piero di Cosimo: *Hunting Scene*, detail. *Metropolitan Museum of Art*

almost like woodcarvings—albeit they are faithfully studied from life. Nevertheless, in a picture in the tradition of the masquelike "triumphs," the *Parnassus* in the Louvre, he transcends his own usual limitations and brings to a culmination realistic picturing of classic legendry. His color sometimes approaches Venetian opulence. Luca Signorelli suffers from a similar hardness of manner, though less bound by the limitations of the line-draftsman.

Domenico Ghirlandaio completes this trio of contemporaries who academized the realism which had been introduced by Masaccio. There is too much in nearly all of Ghirlandaio's frescoes and panels, even in simple portraits. Perhaps the best single work of his is the so-called *Nativity of the Virgin,* a fresco in the Church of Santa Maria Novella in Florence. But it is significant that the nativity incident is pushed to one side and chief place given to a portrait of Luisa Tornabuoni, daughter of the donor of the frescoes, and her retinue. It is obvious, too, that the stairway in perspective was of more account in the artist's reckoning than any religious sentiment that might have been conveyed. It is illuminating that elsewhere Ghirlandaio transported the nativity of Jesus out of the traditional humble place, manger or cave, and stageset the

incident amid the decorated columns of a ruined palace. (At this time no landscape gardening was stylish unless it included some architectural ruins.)

Toward the end of the fifteenth century there came such a wealth of competent, if uninspired, painters that none but a specialist need pretend to remember their names. There are critics who are partial to Filippino Lippi, son of Filippo, for his showy and glamorous compositions, which later slipped over into sentimental and melodramatic effusions, in a darkened painting method. Piero di Cosimo was more solidly constructive, particularly in some vigorous portraits, which might be cited as epitomizing the century-long progress toward persuasive reproductive reality. In another direction, where he gave play to his imagination, he created some strange and charming mythological scenes. Cosimo Tura, when he restrained a tendency toward overelaboration, often achieved a dryly finished technique—and remains a world master of exact drawing.

Lorenzo di Credi more definitely sacrificed plastic values to an indulgence in perspective vistas and overexact depiction, but his carefully posed figure compositions are graceful and pleasing, and his coloring is less harsh than that of

Botticelli: *Primavera. Uffizi Gallery, Florence*

many of his contemporaries. Pietro Vanucci, better known as Perugino (because he was from Perugia), was in the main line of scientifically studied advance, his mechanical composing and intellectual mannerisms being particularly marked. He helped to develop landscape, though there was as yet no separate landscape painting in the Western world—only background settings for figure compositions. One of Perugino's pupils, Pinturicchio, was to refine upon this feature, and to move forward also in a graceful if at times overfeminized figure treatment. But a much younger apprentice of Perugino, Raphael, was to overshadow all others on that road.

Meanwhile, Florentine painting had reached the fifteenth-century culmination in two figures: Leonardo da Vinci, who summarized in a slight, exquisite body of works the achievements and limitations of the intellectual method; and Botticelli, who picked up the exactitude of drawing and the emotionalized humanism of his predecessors and went on to poetize his subjects, and to clothe his aristocratic nymphs in lovely Grecian garments. These two men may be considered the ultimate figures in the two main currents of Florentine advance.

Botticelli
and Leonardo

When Savonarola, the Dominican monk and preacher of reform, was cruelly burned to death at the stake in the Piazza della Signoria in 1498, Sandro Botticelli, it is said, swore he would never again paint portraits of the mistresses of the Medici princes, and he hurried to burn all his nude studies. During the lifetime of the great Dominican prophet Botticelli seems to have sided with the *Arrabbiati,* or foes of the churchman. Perhaps he had heard Savonarola, in sermons from the cathedral pulpit, castigate the dwellers in courts and palaces that "give shelter to ribalds and malefactors." The preacher had denounced the love of oratory and poetry, adding: "In the mansions of the great prelates and lords . . . you will find them all, with books on the humanities in their hands, telling one another they can guide men's souls by means of Virgil, Horace, and Cicero." Savonarola exhorted the Florentines to turn back to Christ instead. Speaking approvingly of the older pictures on the church walls, he indicted the later ones—"images of false gods or

Botticelli: *The Birth of Venus. Uffizi Gallery, Florence*

portraits of the first women you meet in the street." And he exclaimed: "Painters, you do ill, you bring vanity into the churches, you vest the Blessed Virgin as if she were a common woman. . . . And what shall I say to Christian painters who represent nude figures?"

There had come a day thereafter when the Medicean overlords were driven from the city, and Savonarola briefly ruled, although, as the inscription on the Palazzo Vecchio had it, "Christ is King of Florence." Even public celebrations were made religious, and the carnival in 1497 ended with a huge bonfire acclaimed as "the pyre of vanities," upon which were heaped all the symbols of worldliness—and books, statues, and pictures. Still Botticelli seems to have been unregenerate. Only the shock of the killing of Savonarola a year later, when the fanatic preacher had pointed out that the papal court was corrupt and licentious, could arouse the fashionable painter into realization of the real evils intertwined with his success.

Botticelli had been in especial the painter-interpreter of the cult of neo-paganism, of the life of those who triumphed by the intellect, who consciously worshiped beauty. Plato was their mentor—Savonarola had said pithily: "An old woman knows more than Plato about Faith" —but at the court the Greek ideals were not much more than a cloak. A certain artificiality and a superficiality lie over even the loveliest of Botticelli's allegories. There is this to be said, however: if a revived classicism had made architecture and sculpture dull and imitative, it imparted to this painter's work a welcome lightness and freshness. The architects and sculptors had actual Greek—or, oftener, Roman—models to copy from. There were no Greek paintings. So Botticelli drew his art from some dream of his own, bathed it in the glow of the imagined art of Athens and Elysium and the Greek Isles. It is redolent of the fresh spirit of Greece, not of Greece's exhumed relics. It is the sweetest and most exquisite flower of neoclassicism out of all the periods of revival.

In the allegories and tableaux and festival pieces Botticelli disposes nymphs and goddesses on Parnassian hills and fields, or shows Venus rising from the sea. But the figures and faces are those of well-known Florentine ladies—oftenest Simonetta, mistress of Giuliano de' Medici. (Of the meeting of Sandro Botticelli and this lovely Simonetta, and of how she consented to pose for him in the nude, one should read the pretty and

Leonardo da Vinci: *St. Anne with the Virgin and Child. Louvre*

highly romanticized account in Maurice Hewlett's *Earthwork out of Tuscany*.) Sometimes the pictures were painted in memory of some actual tableau seen on the stage of the palace ballroom, and in these cases the portraits of courtiers and courtesans would be in the day's work. *Primavera* or *The Allegory of Spring* is supposed to have been such a memento of a pageant episode. In others it was a matter of the artist's paying compliments or hiding double meanings behind classical allusions. At least once portraits of Giuliano and his lady-love appear in the guise of Mars and Venus—because, forsooth, the lady was still another man's wife and a formal portrait of the two would hardly have been proper.

Except for a sort of golden glow, Botticelli's color is not important. He was rather a draftsman, a master of line (see the *Head of Venus* in color). But a great deal of his work is fresh and pretty—and immensely popular. When he turned to religious painting, after the burning of Savonarola, his style hardened somewhat—but at last, if only briefly, Greece measurably served the Church. Two years after his resolve and the burning of the nudes the artist stopped painting altogether, perhaps went into a monastery.

Leonardo da Vinci: *Mona Lisa. Louvre*

"The perfect painter," "the flawless artist," "the first universal man," "godlike," "incomparable"—these are phrases used in description of Leonardo da Vinci, the painter who in his own life and work epitomizes the Florentine intellectual search for beauty, who most effectively harmonizes science and art. He is not at all representative of the sumptuous side of Florentine activity. He designed pageant episodes and settings or ballroom decorations and richly jeweled costumes, but their spirit did not creep into his paintings as it had into Uccello's and Pesellino's. The ornamentalism of Gozzoli and the poetized classicism of Botticelli alike passed him by.

Leonardo was the final product of the spirit of scientific research and intellectual refinement which comprised the sounder half of the Medicean cultural revival. More than any other artist he set to work to perfect the painter's means of expression, to find a formula for exact documentation with the brush. Whereas the efforts of Botticelli led to a dead end, Leonardo perfected a method that profoundly affected the course of painting as an art. He completed Masaccio's task of achieving tonal and atmospheric realization. He led on to Fra Bartolommeo, Raphael, and Andrea del Sarto.

For one, like the present writer, who is not fully convinced of the universality and supremacy of Leonardo's genius as artist, and yet is faced by an almost unanimous chorus of praise, it is well to take refuge in quotation in order to be sure of giving the man his due. A passage from Théophile Gautier, the nineteenth-century French writer, indicates the extraordinary range of Leonardo's mind and his inventive production, and at the same time records the common view of his art: [1]

It was he who led the way to that pitch of perfection which has never since been surpassed. To be thus the leader and the unexcelled in art seems enough of glory; yet painting was but one of Leonardo's talents. So all-embracing was his genius, so endowed was he with every faculty, that he might have been equally great in any other domain of human effort. . . .

Having created the one most beautiful of portraits, the one most beautiful picture, the one most beautiful fresco, the one most beautiful cartoon, he was content and gave his mind to other things—to the modelling of an immense horse, to the building of the Naviglio Canal, to the contriving of engines of war, to the invention of diving armour, flying-machines, and other more or less chimerical imaginations. He suspected the usefulness of steam and predicted the balloon; he manufactured mechanical birds which flew and animals which walked. He made a silver lyre fashioned in the shape of a horse's head, and played upon it exquisitely. . . . He invented the camera obscura. He planned the great works of engineering that have controlled the courses of the Arno and the Po. He walked beside the sea, and understood that the waters were composed of countless molecules. . . .

No man was ever more human, more lovable, or more fascinating than this same Leonardo da Vinci. He was witty, graceful, polished. His bodily strength was so great that he could bend an iron horseshoe like lead. His physical beauty was flawless—the beauty of Apollo. Great painter

that he was, painting was but one among his splendid gifts.

Such is the orthodox view. By way of restoring the balance, one may suggest that it was the diffusion of Leonardo's energies and inventiveness over so many fields that prevented a surpassing success as painter. The very fact of his extraordinary intellectual powers, moreover, may have precluded exercise of any passionate creative faculty. It is said that he was the first to reconcile the real and the spiritual in art. But his approach was from what his mind conceived of as real— the observed, dissected reality—and he penetrated toward the spiritual only a very little way, in a literary manner. He made his landscape backgrounds and the expressions on portrayed faces "mysterious," but of the truer mystic values there is scarcely a trace.

There are very beautiful qualities in Leonardo's paintings, within the field determined by his approach and by his method. He was above all a superb draftsman. He brought in a consistency in the dramatic treatment of reality. In a revealing treatise on the art of painting he wrote: "What should be asked first in judging whether a picture be good is whether the movements are appropriate to the mind of the figure that moves." His own advance in this matter can be illustrated by comparison of his *Virgin of the Rocks* or his *Last Supper* with treatments of similar themes at the hands of Ghirlandaio, Verrocchio, and Perugino.

Leonardo made advances also in compositional effectiveness, though his pyramidal construction suggests a single formula rather than a universal principle. Similarly he idealized the human face, but in a single type. He completed—to an extent never surpassed—the conquest of light-and-shade as a means of exact delineation. His emphasis by lighting, although not so dramatic and plastically alive as Rembrandt's was to be, is precise, harmonious, and appealing. There is a grace about everything he touches.

Two of the most famous paintings in the world are from Leonardo's hand: the portrait in the Louvre known as *Mona Lisa,* and *The Last Supper,* a fresco on the wall of the refectory of Santa

---

[1] Quoted from the *Masters in Art* monograph dealing with Leonardo da Vinci, dated February 1901, published by Bates & Guild Company, Boston.

Leonardo da Vinci: *The Last Supper. Church of Santa Maria delle Grazie, Milan*

Maria delle Grazie in Milan. Only two other major works undisputedly by him are extant: the *Virgin of the Rocks,* in the National Gallery, London, and the *St. Anne with Virgin and Child* in the Louvre. Of these four the *Mona Lisa* is least interesting, but the enigmatic expression on the lady's face has teased observers into writing miles of speculative comment. One may study here Leonardo's one form of compositional structure, the pyramid; his one atmospheric landscape background; his one idealized face. There is less sharpness in the drawing, but no less the usual delineation by lighting. The *Virgin of the Rocks* and the *St. Anne* are equally typical of his perfection of statement, his compositional method, and his lighting technique, and more illustrative of his psychological and dramatic planning.

But it is in *The Last Supper* that the dramatic action is supremely exemplified. The way in which individual movement is worked into the plan of composition is masterly. The architectural features also aid in centering the observer's attention on the head of Christ. It is a masterpiece of scientific and mechanical picture construction, and of realistic religious illustration.

Remembering, for example, Botticelli's pretty interpretations, one would say offhand that Leonardo da Vinci was only slightly the man of his era. But on second view it will appear that the courtly painters are representative only of a passing activity, painting a reflection of the life of an artificial, removed class society, decorating an unstable and already doomed social circle. Deeper down, even in the Medicean palaces and studios, is this other serious concern with science, law, and psychology.

Leonardo's path wove in and out of the superficial pageantry of the palaces, but within himself he was devotedly and coldly concerned with knowledge and natural law. He dissected cadavers and calmly sketched the mangled victims of war and assassination. No one else so refined upon the methods of research and observation. No one ever believed more firmly that laws could be discovered under every phenomenon—even under art.

That Leonardo came to the end of his life disillusioned and frustrated is perhaps an illustration of the eternal tragedy of the materialist in living, the realist in art. It is enough of fame for one man, no doubt, that for centuries he was recognized as owning the greatest intellect in history; that he foreshadowed a dozen generations of skeptics; that he turned man's eyes to nature, not to the Church, for authority; that he incalculably advanced scientific research and invention.

By that token, which gives him warrant for the title "the perfect Florentine," he is excluded from the rolls of those in whose art the creative values transcend the illustrational ones. With him formal values are secondary. Mystic overtones are unknown. He is elegant, dignified, learned, and graceful. He also is literary, sentimental, academic. According as one's tastes are for the formal and creative or for the realistic and intellectual, one will judge him the brainiest dilettante in the history of art, or the most perfect painter. He was a worldly success, the protégé and companion of princes and dukes, and he died, metaphorically if not literally, in the arms of a king. Even the kings had come to science.

The Handicrafts

Crafts products in the early Renaissance were works of art as much as were the paintings and sculptures, and were often from the same hands, or at least from the workshops of the same masters. The greatest creative workers did not scorn to serve as artists-in-ordinary to their ruler-patrons and to turn artisan on order. This was true in all the great cities—Milan, Rome, Venice—but Florence was the most famous center. There superlative taste was fostered in particular by Lorenzo the Magnificent. There the industrial arts achieved one of the high points in world history.

Unlimited supplies of rich materials were available—precious metals, precious stones, ivory, bronze, iron. Rare colors were imported from the East, particularly from Persia, for fine enamels and pottery; and craftsmen were brought in who could teach the weaving of velvets, damask, and brocades. Above all, there were the artists, filled with the new spirit of experiment, given freedom to create. There were, too, innumerable buyers.

Palaces and churches became treasure-houses filled with precious objects, and as such have been celebrated for all the centuries since. Within the palaces friezes were inset with masks and wound with wreaths; pilaster panels held medallions, heraldic shields, and festoons. There were terra-cotta lunettes in colorful reliefs of fruit and flower, all somehow unified and made to form a harmonious whole. Outside, great doors of sculptured bronze were set in frames of carved marble, with intricately wrought lanterns and torch-holders beside them, and before them iron screens and gates that were often one airy patterning of flowers and foliage.

Verrocchio might serve as the typical figure of the artist-craftsman. He was not above decorating a washbasin for his patron, setting up a pageant for the jousts, or shaping a little *ex voto* for the ruler's propitiatory moments. His neighbor, Pollaiuolo, struck medals in the Roman fashion for the famous Medici collection, as did many other followers of Pisanello. The young Leonardo "fashioned cups and clasps" and damascened armor, and Michelangelo is credited in the guidebooks for the iron and marble well-head in a monastery garden near the city.

But as time went on craftswork tended more and more to become overornamented. The decline can be traced in Cellini's designs, from the crystal and silver casket made for the marriage of Catherine de' Medici and offered still as one of the masterpieces of the Pitti Palace collections, to the gold and enamel salt-cellar of Francis I (now in the History of Art Museum, Vienna), the celebrated candelabrum in St. Peter's, and the famous key to the Palazzo Strozzi. The bronze base alone of Cellini's *Perseus* on the Piazza della Signoria in Florence, however, shows graphically enough the decline, and the outcome of a mania for ornament that lasted almost to our own time.

XVIII: ROME, THE NEO-PAGAN CHURCHMEN, AND MICHELANGELO

VASARI recorded that an Italian primitive painter, the thirteenth-century Margaritone of Arezzo, in his seventies was "regretful that he had lived until a different form of art arose, new artists being honored for their innovations." Centuries later the French writer Anatole France inserted into a diverting satire, *Penguin Island,* a chapter entitled "The Arts: The Primitives of Penguin Painting"; and he used Margaritone for his principal character. As sometimes happens when fact and fiction are combined, France brings out, in a diatribe put into the old painter's mouth, a truth which illumi-nates a whole era: in this case the age of primitive and Renaissance painting. The following passage is ostensibly quoted from a leading Penguin art-historian:

Margaritone, full of years and labors, went one day to visit . . . a young painter who had lately settled in the town. He noticed in the studio a freshly painted Madonna, which, although severe and rigid, nevertheless, by a certain exactness in the proportions and a devilish mingling of light and shade, assumed an appearance of relief and life. At this sight the artless and sublime worker of Arezzo perceived with horror what the future

Correggio: *Leda and the Swan. State Museum, Berlin*

of painting would be. With his brow clasped in his hands he exclaimed:

"What things of shame does not this figure show forth! I discern in it the end of that Christian art which paints the soul and inspires the beholder with an ardent desire for heaven. Future painters will not restrain themselves as does this one to portraying on the side of a wall or on a wooden panel the cursed matter of which our bodies are formed; they will celebrate and glorify it. They will clothe their figures with dangerous appearances of flesh, and these figures will seem like real persons. Their bodies will be seen; their forms will appear through their clothing. St. Magdalen will have a bosom, St. Martha a belly, St. Barbara hips, St. Agnes buttocks; St. Sebastian will unveil his youthful beauty. . . . Where will painters stop in their indiscreet inquiries? They will stop nowhere. They will go so far as to show men and women naked like the idols of the Romans. There will be a sacred art and a profane art, and the sacred art will not be less profane than the other.

"Get ye behind me, demons," exclaimed the old master. For in prophetic vision he saw the righteous and the saints assuming the appearance of melancholy athletes. He saw Apollos playing the lute on a flowery hill, in the midst of the Muses wearing light tunics. . . . He saw Auroras scattering roses, and a multitude of naked Dianas and Nymphs surprised on the banks of retired streams. And the great Margaritone died, strangled by so horrible a presentiment of the Renaissance and the Bolognese School.

If the Florentine *quattrocento* had already witnessed a steady decline from the spiritual to the materialistic and worldly in art, it yet remained for the following century, and for Rome, to fulfill the last implications of "Margaritone's vision." From the realistically inclined experimentation of Masaccio's *Adam and Eve,* through the reportorial limning of common people in Filippo Lippi's presumably religious pictures, to Botticelli's Florentine Venuses, the early Renaissance had swung a long course directly away from Byzantine impersonality and remote Franciscan innocence. But it remained for sixteenth-century Rome to push immeasurably further along the road of profane art.

It was really a provincial, Correggio of Parma, who signalized the final triumph in capitalizing on the lure of the flesh. Could Margaritone have seen, just once, one of Correggio's sumptuous, voluptuous, melting nudes, it might well have proved to be that "horrible . . . presentiment of the Renaissance" which finally strangled the aged artist. It would not have eased his mind that some of the most enjoyable of Correggio's undraped figures are shown as angels floating in the clouds of the Christian heaven.

This matter of "clothing the figures with dangerous appearances of flesh" is but one sign of arrival at the "high" Renaissance. It is perhaps most typical because it intimates a whole train of consequences: luxuriousness, an officially endorsed paganism, drama, color. All these belong to the Roman half-century. But also the passion for antiquity passed into a new phase. Whereas Florentine academies and artists had played with classicism, it was now made into ruthless law. The old monuments were restored, measured, set up as the only worthy models. Aesthetics became a scholars' plaything. Intellectualism decided upon rules of creation.

The artist became fully dependent upon the wealthy patron. That bankers and merchants took over the papacy is a circumstance immensely significant to Christian art. A wealthy spendthrift pope brought the foremost artists to Rome to decorate the Vatican Palace, to build pleasure pavilions, to stage pageants and plays. The popes themselves were foremost in advocating a Christianity wide enough to include the Roman ideals of pagan wisdom and worldly pleasures.

The encouraging thing about art, of course, is that in such a time, full of energy and enthusiasm, there will come an unpredictable artist who will ride above all the generalizations, all the laws, all the specifications laid down by patrons. Michelangelo was such a one. For him the long procession from abstract and spiritual symbolism to human and worldly representation meant only freedom to use the human body as he wished. By creative manipulation of it he traveled the other half of the circle, offering it to us in compositions made timeless by those mysterious formal elements which are not to be distinguished from the spiritual. He took what he needed out of the discoveries incident to the revival of learning, gaining classic monumentality without being bound by classic naturalism. As to the patrons, he fought a lifelong battle with them, and won at least to the extent of bequeathing to all later ages an uncontrolled revelation of his unique vision.

Other artists, of course, better express the routine of the age: Raphael, the politic conformist, the perfect delineator, master of grace; the fluent and overperfect Andrea del Sarto; the competent but uninspired Bronzino. But it is Michelangelo who at once expresses and transcends the times, who picks up the impulse of the age and carries on to ageless achievement.

Rome was now heir to the worldly magnificence and show which had been characteristic of Florentine upper-class life in the fifteenth century. The Holy City drew away the artists by offering greater opportunity for display—and more money. Against the background of a general moral degeneracy that reached even into the papacy, and within the flow of violent, corrupt, and unhealthy life in the secularized "religious" courts, this unhappy fact about art stands out: the painter or sculptor or architect could be bought and set to work to decorate the surroundings of ruffian-rulers and capitalist-churchmen. Celebrated artists were considered part of the pomp and swagger of a court.

Further in the background was the struggle between the Church and secular emperors and princes for the power to rule over Europe. The actual churchmen had already lost, as they were certain to do in a time when freedom of thought and intellectual research were becoming major human objectives. This opening quarter of the sixteenth century was the very time of the free-thinking Luther in the North, and the beginning of the Protestant rift.

The churchmen had lost, too, by giving way to personal ambitions, to the lust for worldly power, and in many cases to licentiousness. They had thus failed to establish a kingdom of God in Europe because of blindness, bigotry, and moral weakness. But the Church framework was immovable, was the one fabric binding Europe. What happened was that secular and commercial princes temporarily took over the papacy. There were even to be Medici popes.

Whether this in a sense saved the Roman Church, or further discredited it, thus resulting in the great schism of the Reformation, is beside the point here. What signifies for art is that Pope Leo X capped the process of political-religious change by which Rome became the center of Renaissance worldly energy and spending. The Vatican was made the greatest palace in Italy. The trappings of the richest courts were brought into the Church itself. If pagan subject-matter and the antique spirit were the fashionable things in secular art, the Vatican too must have representations of Parnassus and Athens on its sacred walls. St. Peter's must be rebuilt on palatially magnificent lines.

The impulse to decorate the church opulently and to provide a luxurious palace for the representative of God on earth was by no means a new one. Since the age of Constantine, when the Eastern Christian establishment had taken on the habiliments of imperial Rome, a measure of sumptuous decoration had been deemed fitting. Already in the fifteenth century cardinals had vied with petty princes and banker-overlords in ornamenting their palaces with works of art. The earlier popes had brought painters to Rome: Masaccio had died there while executing a commission, and Piero della Francesca and Fra Angelico had been among those bidden to add to the glory of the older Vatican buildings. Pinturicchio had been called by the Borgia Pope, Pius II, to decorate his apartments.

Under Alexander VI, Pinturicchio, joined by his teacher, Perugino, had painted frescoes in several Roman churches; and they were joined by Botticelli and Ghirlandaio in decorating the Sistine Chapel. But it was Julius II, the della Rovere Pope, who was to bring this tendency to its climax; who was to set Michelangelo and Raphael to their tasks in Rome; who was to plan the new St. Peter's, which remains to this day the world's foremost example of a church adorned in the palatial spirit. Even the ancient Romans had not built structures more overloaded with ornamental encrustation and sculptural adornment. (See the picture on page 507.)

Raphael: *Madonna of the Chair. Pitti Palace, Florence*

Raphael

"Raphael, the most beloved name in art"—so Bernhard Berenson, the great twentieth-century art critic, sums up, not wholly approvingly, the nineteenth-century idolization of the greatest of all Christian illustrators. Of Raphael's Madonnas the German art scholar Wilhelm Lübke said: "They exist for all time and for all mankind because they present an immortal truth in a form that makes a universal appeal." Lübke believed that Raphael's *Sistine Madonna* "is, and will continue to be, the apex of all religious art."

But today the air of sanctity and homage built up around the *Sistine Madonna,* which for decades hung in a hushed chapel-like room in a Dresden gallery, enshrined apart from other works of art, is beginning to be clouded by doubts if not actually disturbed by smiles. To many people the picture, despite its obvious merits, is most significant as a memento of the sentimentalism and superficiality of appreciation in a long period of academic-realistic obsession. How many observers have recalled uneasily those eye-rolling, wooden cherubs!

Raphael Sanzio is the illustrator-painter *par excellence.* He simplifies, makes obvious, prettifies. He deals largely in children and pretty young women, though he can sketch a characterful portrait on occasion. He dramatizes his subjects subtly and unobtrusively. His exactitude of drawing is sufficient to satisfy the most highly trained realist. No one before him so wonderfully

Raphael:
Pope Leo X with Cardinals.
Pitti Palace, Florence

portrayed the texture of velvet, of brocades, of a caressable skin. It is all virginally done, however, with none of the sensuous relish and glow that Giorgione and Titian will introduce, in Venice, during the same half-century.

Raphael's whole technique, indeed, seems to match some feminine reticence, the sentimental temperament, within himself. It is, like his attitude toward life, sweet, smoothed, calculated not to challenge or disturb anyone. His composition is facile, appealingly effective, balanced. As the subject-matter is easy to understand, so the pictorial composition is always attractive, delectably rhythmic, at first glance.

No one ever had such a popular vogue as Raphael. And that is greatly unfortunate and a little unfair to the artist. It is probable that he knew he was no creator in the Michelangelesque sense. He had started in his native Umbria as a pupil of Perugino, and soon was outdoing that near-master at his own trade of realistic religious painting. He early painted faces not to be distinguished from those by his teacher. But he picked up from Fra Bartolommeo a trick of figure-grouping, and from Leonardo the science of pyramidal surface composition. (Very beautifully he used it, too.)

All these influences, as also that of the antique Roman statues just then creating such a furore, he assimilated to his own facile style. Later, when he saw Michelangelo becoming his one rival in popularity, favored over him for an unaccountable vigor, grandeur, and formal aliveness, he was misled for a moment and attempted to incorporate that giant's virtues also into his own—and utterly failed. He remains the great Renaissance eclectic, able to imitate or absorb all the fashionable, effective traits developed by his predecessors, up to the capacity of his understanding; failing only in the sphere of the greatest genius among his contemporaries. The feminine charm and sentimental thoughtfulness of his work remain his claim to attention.

Born in 1483 in Urbino, of a father who was both minor painter and minor poet, Raphael was precocious and already successful at an age when he might well have been doing an apprentice's work. It was Perugino who introduced him into the cultural center at Florence, and here he picked up those other influences, out of the innovations of Leonardo and Fra Bartolommeo, which flowed so easily into his "manner." In 1508, when he was twenty-five years old, he was invited by Pope Julius II to go to Rome to decorate some apartments in the Vatican. He so pleased his patron with his preliminary figures that commissions already given to Signorelli, Perugino, and Sodoma were withdrawn and entrusted to the brilliant newcomer. During the following twelve years, until his death at the age of thirty-seven in 1520, Raphael never lacked for work or for money. He lived like a prince (quite unusually, like a self-respecting and highly moral prince), and numbered cardinals, poets, and artists among his intimate friends.

His masterpieces may be divided into three groups. The first consists of the popular Madonnas and other ingratiating religious story-pictures —balanced, polished, a bit sentimental. They are graceful, melodious, rounded for popular appeal. In color alone they are likely to be a little harsh and unnatural. Second is a group of portraits, competently lifelike, well set in the canvas, with considerable character. If they sometimes exhibit too much concern with the accurate and brilliant delineation of such details as the bell and book in the *Pope Leo X with Cardinals* (page 371), it is not a surprising fault in one who has learned that he can do a realistic bit with more *éclat* than could any preceding painter.

Finally there are the murals in the Vatican. The "Raphael Rooms" there contain the painter's most mature and masculine work. It is not all his own; Vasari recorded that when Raphael started out to work at the court he trailed along fifty assistant painters and craftsmen. But in the Stanza della Segnatura one has him at his best, particularly in the two grand murals known as

The School of Athens and the *Disputa* or *Triumph of Faith*. On adjoining walls are the *Parnassus* and the *Jurisprudence*.

Here a certain monumentality is added to the painter's talent for graceful illustration. The arrangement and thought are academic and learned; and the plastic movement is lax, if one bears in mind Michelangelo's symphonic murals in a nearby chapel. But *The School of Athens* is a perfect example of a picture thoughtfully conceived, with great numbers of interesting figures well disposed, painted suavely and with naturalness. It is arranged, tasteful, eclectic painting at its best. It is an example, too, of the bringing of Greek subject-matter to Rome, and of the externalizing of harmonious Greek idealization. Raphael prettified paganism and left to more sensual artists such as Correggio the amoral pastoral joyousness.

Toward the end of his life Raphael felt too keenly the overshadowing genius of Michelangelo, and he who had been able to absorb all the popular qualities of his other contemporaries set out to incorporate also sculpturesque largeness and plastic vigor. His mind was not equal to understanding the nature of Michelangelo's mastery, much less was it capable of duplicating it; and in trying to do so Raphael put into his final works a good deal of theatrical pose, and figures flabbily obese rather than ones throbbing with power. His reputation rests rather on the Stanze story-pictures, on the portraits, and on the appealing Madonnas. There he is adequate, graceful, master of all the minor and normal perfections of the art.

When painting in the tradition of Perugino and Raphael was more popular than it is now, Fra Bartolommeo used to be paraded as a less sensitive but more successfully "sublime" painter. His sort of rather artificial sublimity has gone out of fashion, and the obviously posed figures are accounted wooden. Nevertheless, Fra Bartolommeo's method of figure-grouping was often effective, and he gave this to Raphael. More lastingly popular is Andrea del Sarto, known in his own time as "the perfect painter," and still notable as one of the great technicians among Italian painter-illustrators. Better than any biography of him is Browning's poem "Andrea del Sarto," wherein the determining weakness of the man and the fatal facility of the artist are illuminatingly set forth in a monologue addressed by the painter to his beloved but unfaithful wife. He was a Raphael betrayed by a commonplace mind and given to disagreeably candy-like coloring.

At this time—and therefore sandwiched in here between the two great figures of the era, Raphael and Michelangelo—there were still other thoroughly competent but not greatly inspired artists. Bronzino did attractive portraits, although he showed mediocre imagination and invention whenever he essayed the sort of monumental story-picture produced by Raphael and Fra Bartolommeo and even by Andrea del Sarto. Pontormo, too, was more successful as a portraitist. All of these painters were Florentines.

Rome, indeed, had no school of art except in that the patrons there drew in artists by the prodigality of their pay. The spirit of the age was Roman, and the major works in architecture and painting were accomplished there, but Florence still bred or attracted artists and remained a creative center until the mid-sixteenth century, although the star of Venice was already rising. At Parma, Correggio was practicing his own profuse variation of "the grand style," but he became involved in glorification of the human body as a sensuously lovely object. His pagan allegories and Jovian love-incidents are among the most engaging things in all erotically inspired art (as illustrated on page 367). His murals, denying architectural control, were a bad influence on his followers and had something to do with the descent into baroque. But because he sums up one line of Renaissance development, intimating a major change in the direction of European art, and affording a pleasure particular to his own achievement, it is worth while to quote John Addington Symonds' pithy description of him in his work, *Renaissance in Italy:*

Correggio created a world of beautiful human beings, the whole condition of whose existence is an innocent and radiant wantonness. Over the domain of tragedy he held no sway; nor could he deal with subjects demanding pregnancy of intellectual meaning. He paints the three Fates, for instance, like young and joyous Bacchantes. . . . It is enough for him to produce a gleeful symphony by the play of light and color, by the animation of his figures, and by the intoxicating beauty of his forms. His angels are genii disimprisoned from the chalices of flowers, houris of an erotic Paradise, elemental sprites of nature wantoning in Eden in her prime.

Michelangelo: Painting and Sculpture

In coming to Michelangelo one meets the first overwhelming genius in painting since Giotto. Despite the extraordinary advance in the art, and the long procession of notable figures from Masaccio and Fra Angelico to Leonardo and Raphael, they are lesser men as compared with this unaccountable creative genius. Painting only under protest, insisting that he wanted only to practice his own art of sculpture, he yet outdid all his contemporaries in originality, vitality, and sheer compelling mastery in the mural art. A single figure by Michelangelo seems to today's modern artists and critics to have more plastic vigor than all that artists such as Perugino, Bronzino, and Fra Bartolommeo ever created.

For one thing, while everybody else was busy introducing Greek harmony and grace and idealization, and prettifying painting, here was an imagination that remembered that Christianity had a Hebrew-Biblical as well as a pagan inheritance; here was a man who could thunder like Jeremiah and praise mightily like the Psalmists, and be profoundly troubled by immediate life. In his re-creation of the Greeks, too, he saw through the current sentimentalization and weakening of the classic heritage. The romantic sweetness of Raphael and the ecstatic eroticism of Correggio fade from memory when one meets Michelangelo's Greek Sibyls.

One may well ask which among the sixteenth-century artists is the truest symbol and voice of the age. The cultured circles had found refuge in the revival of learning and in visual arts that put on the face of a romanticized classicism. For more than a century the patrons, establishing academies and financing the uncovering of ancient monuments and the publication of treatises

Michelangelo: *The Temptation* and *The Expulsion. Sistine Chapel, Rome*

about them, had encouraged this neoclassic, reflective picturing. It progressed not without a new scientific acumen and a freshly reasoned understanding of optical law and of the structure of natural forms. But the classical was a refuge from all the larger realities of Italian life in that time. In the midst of murder, violence, and the shocks of war and overturned states, the current of "harmonizing" art flowed on.

Leonardo brought to a final expression the intellectualized attitude. Botticelli epitomized the pageant-like neo-pagan unrealities of the courtly classicism. Raphael equally avoided any but pleasing reality, while capping the procession toward facsimile statement. These painters expressed the spirit of the pedagogues and the aspirations of the rich patron-princes of their time. They were busy shaping a new Greece in a wish-formed likeness of the old. But may it not be that Michelangelo, thinking on Dante and Savonarola as well as on Plato and the Muses, giving up sweetened harmony and obvious charm for a passionate outpouring of emotion and a half-tamed cry of defiance, was the truest expression of that turbulent sixteenth century?

Personally Leonardo and Raphael had been cultured, graceful, not a little feminine—true courtiers, every inch. Michelangelo was rough in manner, troubled in mind, sharp-spoken. But his was no cramped, mean outlook. If his faculties

refused to discount the miseries of the world and the immediate troubles of living, they nonetheless embraced a great passion for the joys of work and for the wonders of human aspiration. There is joyousness incarnate in the figures of the Sistine vault. The zest of living and the grandeur of human endeavor have never else been recorded with such relish—and with such galvanizing effect. As Michelangelo synthesized the Biblical and the Greek elements in Christianity, so he brought into one expression the world's woe and its joy, human tribulation and human glory. If he lived in tempestuous pain—and he recorded often that he did—he knew the other face of that experience: he emerged into a rapture and contemplation beyond the capacity of any of his neo-Greek contemporaries. In his own right he was philosopher, prophet, creator.

Michelangelo was born in 1475, in the mountains above Florence, of middle-class parentage. He early decided for himself that he would be an artist—against the wishes of his father, who, however, came to see the light when, in 1489, the lad's talent attracted the attention of the reigning Medici overlord in Florence and thus secured patronage for both himself and the family. In the Medici gardens he studied antique statues at first hand, and he was taken into the house of Lorenzo, where he met artists and scholars, poets and professional antiquarians. It was the time of

Michelangelo: *The Drunkenness of Noah. Sistine Chapel, Rome*

Savonarola's fiery denunciation of worldly luxury and art, and the lad seems to have absorbed the evangelical influence with the courtly. He was himself silent, sensitive, and moody, and never came to proficiency in the politeness of the drawing-room. When Lorenzo de' Medici died and his son was driven from Florence, the young artist's exposure to the influences that shaped so many of his contemporaries was over. In 1496, at the age of twenty-one, he went to Rome. "Here," wrote Symonds, "while the Borgias were turning the Vatican into a den of thieves and harlots, he executed the purest of all his statues—a *Pietà* in marble." (See page 379.)

It was thus that Michelangelo's first masterpiece was born, after perhaps a half-dozen trial statues. For many years thereafter he was destined to live in Rome, a paradoxically Christian temperament among pseudo-Greeks; a reserved, introspective contemplator of the historical comi-tragedy of man, among all the bright intelligences and the eager limners of the papal entourage.

Michelangelo stood his ground with popes and princes, pitting his dignity against their imperiousness, his solitary assurance against their whims. And yet it was a pope, Julius II, who overbore him in the matter of the decorations of

the Sistine Chapel, forced him to take the commission for painting the ceiling vault, when what the artist solely wished was to be left to practice in peace the sculpture which he knew to be pre-eminently his art.

As Michelangelo was a superman, self-disciplined to the point of austere asceticism in an age of indulgence, broodingly mystical when everyone around him was trying to be bright and rational and open, so the figures he painted in the Vatican chapel are superhuman. The obvious largeness of aspect is matched by sublimity of conception and character. And—rarest of phenomena—the sheer plastic vitality of the paintings is similarly vast, inescapable.

Other artists had painted the side walls of the chapel. It was in 1508 that Pope Julius II decided that the ceiling, too, should be done and that Michelangelo was the man to paint it. At best the task would have seemed a thankless one, even to a practiced muralist. The vault is nearly a hundred feet above the floor—a curving surface, a half-cylinder in shape, 133 feet long. For this Michelangelo, gently setting aside the Pope's suggested scheme, devised a series of pictures and figures and architectural accessories which constitutes the greatest single exhibit of the

Michelangelo:
The Last Judgment, detail.
Sistine Chapel, Rome

painter's art in Europe—though difficult to see.

The conception is as audacious in the vast range of its subject-matter as in its organization. There are shown not only the creation and history of man, in the Christian interpretation, but the ancient prophets, Greek as well as Hebrew, who foretold Christ's world, and a host of supporting personages from legend and imagination. No observer could then or can today take in the full significance of the total work. Certain scenes, set off separately, may be studied as single pictorial entities, such as the *Creation of Man* (see the color plate), or the colossal figures of the *Sibyls* and *Prophets*. But the amazing thing is the sense of vigor and grandeur that runs through major and minor parts of the composition. There are 343 figures in the ceiling. After trying out assistants, Michelangelo painted the

entire 10,000 square feet of surface himself. In a famous sonnet he complains of the discomfort he experienced in painting while lying on his back on the scaffolding.

It took him four and one-half years to complete the job. After the scaffolding was down and the work had been greatly admired, the Pope suggested that the artist enrich the composition with additions in bright colors and gold, to which Michelangelo replied that the prophets and the holy men pictured there were rich not by reason of that sort of wealth. Nor has the world since doubted that here a painter created richness that is without measure, beyond gold.

That Michelangelo the painter gained from the studies of Michelangelo the sculptor is not to be doubted. No other painter has accomplished figures so swelling with power, so statu-

Michelangelo: *The Holy Family. Uffizi Gallery, Florence*

esquely monumental. But the means he used are those legitimate to painting art. On the two-dimensional plane he created the space-volume impression by line, chiaroscuro, color, texture. Greater plastic mastery is not to be found in the whole range of painting. Powerful, rhythmic, profoundly animated is the impression. Each figure is living, abounding with life, and the throng of figures is gorgeously orchestrated, symphonically related. Never else has the human body been so sublimely utilized, so woven into poems epic and heroic.

It was twenty-one years after the completion of the Sistine ceiling—a period during which the artist did no painting—that Michelangelo was called by another Pope, Paul III, to paint an immense mural for the rear wall of the chapel,

above the altar. For seven years more he labored, and then in 1541 *The Last Judgment* was unveiled, and a masterpiece of extraordinary vigor and originality was given to the world.

Again Michelangelo made his own rules. He had learned all that the Renaissance perfecting of the picturing medium made possible by way of clarity of statement and truth to light-and-shade appearance. But—stirred perhaps by the degradation and corruption of life around him, by the tragic decline of Italy and the crumbling of human character—he fixed a conception of the final judgment of man which is medieval in its uncompromising rectitude and somberness. It is no pretty picture, and perhaps too violently animated for architectural "decoration." But it is surpassingly moving, plastically alive as a whole and

Portrait of Michelangelo.
Possibly self-portrait.
Uffizi Gallery,
Florence

in every part, and its allegory, its picturing of the divine judgment scene, stirs the mind. As the Chinese say, it has its own movement of life. As the Europeans say, it instructs and makes men better.

Unlike the ceiling decorations, *The Last Judgment* is laid out as one picture; but the surface is so vast—forty-three by fifty-four feet—and the troops of figures are so crowded, that ordinarily appreciation is directed to this or that part. One who has become adept at creating his own frames, picking an arbitrary section of the whole and mentally isolating it for study and enjoyment, will find a score of profoundly stirring pictures (some of them subtly marked off by Michelangelo himself, though without disturbance of the total effectiveness).

Even in photographs one cannot fail to realize the power, the imaginativeness, and the superb draftsmanship of these detached fragments. Unfortunately the smoke and dust of four hundred years have almost obliterated the color. There has been also some damaging "restoration" attempted at times. It is said, moreover, that at the unveiling certain figures appeared too naked for the sensibilities of the Vatican ecclesiastics, and clothes were added by a minor artist who was known ever after as "the breeches-maker." Michelangelo himself was so incensed by the remarks of one of the prudish courtiers, a certain Biagio da Cesena, that he painted the man's portrait into the group of sinners in Hell.

Michelangelo the painter is known almost exclusively by the two works in the Sistine Chapel

Michelangelo: *Pietà*. Stone. *St. Peter's Church, Rome*

at the Vatican. He apparently had no interest in easel-pictures. In the only one that survives complete, the early *Holy Family* now in the Uffizi Gallery (page 377), he proves that he can pack into the smaller space a generous measure of that power so evident in his murals and his sculptures. The rhythms are strong and vital, and the drawing masterly. There is, however, concession to the fashion of sweet finish, which is not known in the more monumental works. Two or three un-

finished pictures, with great virtues so far as they go, but still incomplete, are the only other paintings credited to him. There is, however, a portrait of the artist so fine, so rugged, and yet so sensitive, that it is difficult to avoid the inference that Michelangelo at least helped to paint it if he did not completely do so.

One of the main lines of Renaissance progress in art had been scientific, and one of the sciences perfected in this era was anatomy. Giotto had

Michelangelo: *Day*. Stone. *Medici Chapel, San Lorenzo Church, Florence*

attempted no revelation of the human body beneath the voluminous garments of his figures. But Ghiberti and Donatello were already accomplished revealers of bone and muscle, and Masaccio individualized the anatomy of his nudes. Leonardo pursued the unusual aspects of the body, even to sketching the peculiar hunching and muscular sag of a corpse recently hanged. Thus was science in art pushed to an ultimate point.

But Michelangelo, evidently knowing anatomy to the last physical detail, went on to that other half of the study of the human figure, learning as never did anyone else to fix the expressiveness of attitudes and movements. He used the body as an unsurpassed medium for the communication of emotion. Passion and heroism, despair and transfiguration, contemplation and exaltation, all are expressed by this one bodily means. It is said that toward the end of his life the beauty of the human form so obsessed him that he brooded continually over the ways in which the great truths of the life and aspiration (and tragedy) of mankind might be interpreted through it.

The little extras that Ghiberti and Donatello and the della Robbias had put into their sculptures—borrowing the perspective vistas of the theater designers and the landscapes of the painters to add variety to their reliefs—were here forgotten like toys gone out of fashion. In sculpture, as in painting, the body is Michelangelo's supreme material, the body set out free of all encumbering circumstance, the body alone speaking for the dignity and sorrows and triumphs of the human soul.

Where the eloquence of the body leaves off and pure sculptural eloquence begins, no one can say. Of the abstract values of the art on its own account—if it could be freed from subject-matter—Michelangelo proved himself a master not only unrivaled in his age but unsurpassed by any artist in the whole history of Europe. Only the anonymous creators of the Parthenon figures had grasped so much of mountainous strength and exalted vigor. The sheer plastic vitality of his single figures is enormous. There is in them a hint of cosmic order and elemental power.

In that early work, the *Pietà*, done at twenty-

Michelangelo: *Night*. Stone. *Medici Chapel, San Lorenzo Church, Florence*

four, so much more graceful and harmoniously rhythmic than Michelangelo's later things, there is already also an amplitude, a power, that heralds the arrival of a sculptural genius. Immediately the art is lifted out of the field of reproductive activity, of naturalism and sentimentality, to which the later sculptors of the *quattrocento* had degraded it. In the *Pietà* one does not have to look at the expression on Mary's face to feel the sentiment of the incident, and one does not remark the truth of the modeling or the marvelous exactitude of treatment of this or that part. The whole thing breathes the sentiment: the largeness of the enfolding feminine figure, the play and counterplay of mass and direction, the ample, sheltering completeness. (See page 379.)

This largeness of conception, this powerful movement, is instinct throughout Michelangelo's sculpture. A few pieces sacrifice a little of it to more realistic statement of the observed figure and attitude, particularly the famous *David*. But almost always there is preserved the sense of the life of the stone block, the push of elemental energies, the poise of vast forces held in tension.

If, as some modern critics believe, every sculptural composition is an organization of volumes in space with relation to an indicated field or frame, Michelangelo is the supreme Western master, both in indication of the frame and in bold manipulation of the contained volumes for plastic vigor with repose. In the massive, voluminous ampleness of his works he rivals those world-masters the Egyptians and the Chinese.

Most of Michelangelo's statues are left to posterity as single figures, although planned originally as parts of great tomb compositions which never took more than fragmentary form. Long and bitter were the quarrels the artist waged with his patrons over these commissioned projects, and grievous was the loss of his time in balked effort. But even unfinished, with only seven of the score of planned figures in place, the mausoleum room of the Medici family in San Lorenzo Church in Florence takes rank as a major shrine of the sculptural art in Europe. The four figures known as *Day, Night, Dawn,* and *Evening* are huge tomb guardians with an extraordinary appearance of confined movement. Here nudity

Michelangelo:
Madonna and Child.
Medici Chapel,
San Lorenzo Church,
Florence

lends itself to dignity and grandeur, and each single body is made to breathe the feeling of majestic power. The figures are not natural—heaven forbid! Rather they are superhuman conceptions, dramatized and superbly "artificial."

There are other celebrated works: the *Moses* in Rome; two slaves breaking their bonds, planned for a grand tomb in St. Peter's, upon which the Moses, too, was to have been an item; a relief plaque of the Madonna and Child; and a bust known as the *Brutus*.

Michelangelo lived to be eighty-nine years old. In the end art itself failed to satisfy his longing to serve mankind. Having lived the most blameless of lives, as mortal standards go, he yet further denied worldly interests and gave his mind to God. His last statue was a *Deposition from the Cross* made for the cathedral in Florence. It pleased him to portray himself as Joseph of Arimathea, sorrowfully handing down Jesus'

body to the Virgin Mother and the Magdalen below. The dejected yet dignified and loving figure was symbolic of what the world was to mean to him in the decade before his death in 1564.

Sixteenth-century sculpture, outside the product of this one genius, is weak if not trivial. If only for his unique character one artist cannot, however, be overlooked, although his statues are hardly more than the elegant trifles of a *pasticheur* in bronze. Benvenuto Cellini is one of the most engaging braggarts in art history. His autobiography throws light on the violent and corrupt life of the times in a way that is enormously interesting and valuable. But his boasting about his work is not justified by the evidence of the bronze statuettes, bric-à-brac, and salt-cellars credited to him. His one major statue, the *Perseus with the Head of Medusa*, in Florence, is an unsculptural picture-piece, an enlarged version of a goldsmith's conception of the new "natural" art of sculpture. It stands on a base almost incredibly overadorned with this and that. Nevertheless, when the statue was set up sonnets and odes to Cellini were tacked on pillars around the square, and he has been accounted a leading European sculptor by all the ornament-enamored generations that have intervened.

Some of Cellini's bronze statuettes are pretty mantelpiece ornaments. The workmanship is marvelous for its delicacy. But increasingly the art student turns to him to enjoy not his art but the unique and racy chronicle of the life of an artist-craftsman, who put down his exploits as murderer and seducer as illuminatingly as he described those in the field of goldsmithing, and set the whole against a background in which currents of dark medieval credulity mingled with the new scientific elements in the common mind.

At this time there came into European sculpture that strange mixture of truth to observation and unimaginative academic manner which was to stultify the art for nearly four hundred years. Every sort of unsculptural, spiky, and dispersed effect was tried, until one has to believe that the sense of a proper relationship between subject and medium was wholly lost. The realism of Cellini's contemporaries and followers is seldom exciting. The artist known variously as Giambologna or Giovanni da Bologna (*not* Jean de Boulogne), a Frenchman identified with the school of Florence, is outstanding among the makers of bronze statuettes. Replicas of his *Flying Mercury* used to be in every home.

There was at this time a Paduan school of sculpture which was especially prolific of small bronze groups. The Paduans followed the most theatrical aspects of Florentine fashion, but occasionally turned out a less involved statuette with spontaneous charm and unmistakable grace. Andrea Riccio and Francesco da Sant' Agata are most significant. At Venice, near Padua, Jacopo Sansovino was both popular sculptor and leading architect. His statues are essentially good "fillers" for architectural niches. One of his followers, Alessandro Vittoria, was the designer of some portrait busts in terra cotta which preserve sculptural largeness—are truly impressive—but are the

Unknown Italian sculptor: *St. Sebastian.* Terra cotta. *Metropolitan Museum of Art*

more wondered at for a marvelous representation of brocaded robes and other detailing. Exceptional is the rhythmic grace of a *St. Sebastian,* now in the Metropolitan Museum in New York, by an unnamed sculptor.

The truth is that in Europe from 1550 to 1900 there was precious little sculpture that transcended the limitations of a pleasing naturalism. The one exceptional "school" is the baroque. The baroque style developed first in architecture, when such eccentricities as twisted columns and bulging silhouettes were introduced. It was to dominate seventeenth-century Italian sculpture, especially in the figure of Lorenzo Bernini.

Dome of St. Peter's Church, Rome

Architecture

Michelangelo, called to architecture, as he had been to painting, against his own desires and judgment, acquitted himself worthily in one monument, St. Peter's dome—and, for the rest, joined the routine Renaissance architects in re-arranging the decorative remnants derived from a misunderstood classicism. The academies and the architect-scholars had declared for a complete return to antique virtues, and henceforth all monumental Italian building was to wear the semblance of ancient Rome. The rebuilders of the sixteenth-century Holy City could visualize its aggrandizement only in terms of the capital of the Caesars.

Bramante was the architect most responsible for fixing the stamp of old Rome indelibly on the products of the new "Roman school." He had been a successful practitioner in Milan when Pope Julius II called him to Rome to plan a St. Peter's Church intended to be a worthily magnificent capitol of Christendom. In some minor works Bramante showed his taste by adopting the less ornamental and more constructional features of ancient architecture, preferring the Doric order to the Corinthian. His plan for St. Peter's was the sort of compromise one would expect when an eclectic is faced with a new vast problem to be solved in the idioms of a long-buried past. His death intervened between the time of the clearing of the site and that of the building of the church. His plans were so altered by his successors that he is to be little blamed for the somewhat scrambled aspect of the present building.

St. Peter's is so typical of a certain indeterminateness or inadequacy of Renaissance architecture that it is well to give it greater attention than its merits as a work of art strictly warrant. Renaissance architecture is, in the sum, the collection of ways in which builders enamored of classic ornamentation spread the borrowed decorative elements over their structures. In St. Peter's all the façades lack style and are in general dull. The interior, on the other hand, is brilliantly alive and vigorously ostentatious.

After Bramante, Raphael had been called to supervise the structure, and with him Antonio da

Sansovino: Library and loggetta, Piazza San Marco, Venice

Sangallo, and they may or may not have improved the original plan. Finally Michelangelo was forced to take over the work. Vasari says: "There were various opinions, but His Holiness, inspired, as I believe, by God, resolved to entrust the building to Michelangelo. . . . The Pope commanded him to accept, and he was obliged to take part in the work against his will."

It is not necessary to review in detail the changes Michelangelo made, mostly by way of simplification. There are rear wall-sections as he designed them, although a baroque upper story was added later to negate their simple dignity and largeness. In any case the dome is the one addition worthy of the great artist's genius, and at the same time the one feature of the immense structure which adds to the world's store of architectural masterpieces. To this day it is a joy to the eye on the Roman skyline. And it has been the model for countless crowning domes on churches, libraries, and state-houses throughout Europe and the Americas. In silhouette it is sensitive yet powerful.

Although St. Peter's Church is the showpiece of Renaissance architecture, and supremely important by reason of Michelangelo's crowning feature, there are lesser monuments which are more consistent examples of stylization; that is, of consistent adaptation of the ancient "motives" to façades. The Farnese Palace in Rome, by Sangallo, is one of the purest adaptations, with its symmetrical rows of pedimented windows and its huge cornice. Incidentally a great deal of the usefulness of the building was sacrificed for the antique effect. There are other examples, ranging from the rather severe Palazzo Massimi to the overburdened rear façade of the Villa Medici, with a triumphal arch as central motive and a collection of actual relics of the ancients embedded in the surrounding paneled walls.

The more attractive buildings of the late Renaissance were to find homes in the northern cities, particularly in Vicenza and Venice. Vignola, to be sure, did some notable monuments in the neighborhood of Rome, particularly the Farnese Palace at Caprarola, which has an interior court perfectly typical of heavy Roman re-creation; and at Florence there are musty academic façades by Vasari, the painter-architect-writer whose histories of art are usefully quoted by all later generations. But at Vicenza, Palladio brought a new refinement to the manner of re-arranging columns, pilasters, arches, and pediments. He came nearer than any other to being a creator while using the antiquarian language which the custom of the time ordained. There is a certain magnificence in the Municipal Palace of Vicenza, and an unaccustomed dignity without heaviness in the Villa Rotunda. It was from Palladio that Inigo Jones chiefly took his Renaissance variation into England; therefore Palladio was an ancestor to the American "colonial" style.

At Venice, Sansovino succeeded in giving a lighter touch to adapted forms, particularly in the loggetta at the foot of the campanile. In the library nearby he gained a more heavily decorative effect with two superimposed colonnades and a generous measure of garlands, statues, and other incidental ornamentation. In both these buildings—both recognizable as Renaissance work at its best—there is a traceable source in antiquity for every structural and ornamental feature. They sum up, as it were, the slight inventiveness and the great learning of the Italian architects. They point up the way in which Renaissance architecture, even while being made gracefully rhythmic, departed from the functional law of the art. The latest view is that all the grace in the world, and all the learning from celebrated past periods, could not wholly redeem buildings that were actually one thing but *seemed* to be another. Engineering truth is here disguised, or, worse, is distorted to fit within "paper" façades. It was this mode of building that prevailed for three more centuries. Even up to the nineteen-thirties architectural students were commonly taught how to design columns and moldings and pedimented doorways out of books written and illustrated by Vignola and Palladio. We begin to suspect that the Renaissance style was one of the most gigantic frauds ever perpetrated within the practice of a major art.

In Sansovino's Venice at this time there was, in another art, an originality of an extraordinary sort, along with splendor and authentic opulence. Painting, which had declined sadly in Rome after the completion of *The Last Judgment* in the Sistine Chapel, had been brought in Venice to a glorious pitch unknown before. Within a century the city of the canals saw three of the greatest geniuses of Western art: Giorgione, Titian, and Tintoretto. What happened later in Rome is hardly more than a pendant to their story.

XIX: VENETIAN PAINTING:
ORIENTALIZED ITALY

IT IS TOLD of one of the earliest Venetian painters, Gentile Bellini, that he was invited to take up residence at the court of the Sultan Mohammed II at Constantinople. Having greatly pleased the monarch by the skill and perfection of some portraits, he was commissioned to paint also a series of religious pictures in the Western manner. A *Beheading of St. John* seemed particularly praiseworthy to the Sultan, who, however, criticized what seemed to him a slight anatomical inaccuracy. The neck of John, he thought, would not look exactly that way if a head had just been severed from it. When the artist demurred, his kind patron summoned a slave whom he had an attendant behead on the spot, thus being enabled to justify his opinion. From that day, it is said, Bellini lost his taste for court life and longed only to return to Venice.

Having made, as soon as possible, a plausible excuse, he was released back to his own city, loaded down by the appreciative Sultan with honors, recommendations, and gifts.

Bellini is a symbol: he stands for a conjuncture of forces, a meeting of influences, destined to shape Venetian painting. Inheritor of the Italian traditional technique and manner—his father, Jacopo Bellini, had been an assistant of Gentile da Fabriano and had traveled in Florence and Rome, and Mantegna was his brother-in-law—inheritor thus of a Western way of art, he yet had the East in his blood through the Oriental nature of the Venetian-Byzantine environment, and through actual contacts such as that at the court of Constantinople. The incident is a reminder, too, of the violence which artists had to witness, as a shaping circumstance of that age.

Giorgione and Titian: *Sleeping Venus. State Gallery, Dresden*

Giorgione: *The Pastoral Symphony. Louvre*

The background out of which emerged Giorgione, Titian, and Tintoretto thus was half Italian, half Eastern. The atmospheric glow of the Orient had taken Venice for its own—St. Mark's is no less colorful and melting than are the mosques of Baghdad and Cairo and Samarkand—but Venice was, too, a part of Italy, where the revival of learning had turned the direction of the Renaissance art current back to ancient Greece and Rome.

The Sienese painters who had so notably exploited the legacy of color and sumptuous design from Byzantium had now disappeared. Of the two ways of art in the world, Florence and Rome had fully established the classic or Western way, rational, realistic, and intellectual, as the European norm, and had rejected the way of the Orient, emotional, sensualized, and formalized. After Michelangelo, Florentine painting was thin, natural (except for its artificial, hard coloring), no more than agreeable; but there was yet one meeting place of East and West. In Venice the two diverse ways were richly brought together.

In Venice there had already been a long-established tradition of luxurious living and splendid pageantry, and a wealth of public art. The most celebrated trading center in Europe, rich with the imports from both East and West, the city was stored with the spoils of countless collecting expeditions. There had even been laws forcing every returning ship to bring some object for the adornment of public buildings or *piazzas*.

Free from civil strife and seldom embroiled in foreign wars, the community was ruled as a nominal republic by a group of commercial barons. They had vied with each other in building and furnishing sumptuous palaces, and in contributing funds for the decoration of the churches, guild-halls, and community palace. For a long time architects and artists were imported, as had been, long centuries before, the builders and mosaicists of St. Mark's. But it was time for the flowering of a local "school."

The routine of life, too, was shot through with

Titian: *Bacchus and Ariadne. National Gallery, London*

colorful elements. The calendar had an extraordinary number of holidays, and carnivals and processions and ceremonial meetings were continually before the eye. Here the first great opera houses were built. There was drama in the air. Life itself was a festival. In the setting of the city, moreover, there were glamorous glow, opalescent color. Who shall say whether the marble and fresco and gilt of the buildings lining the canals, or the soft sunlight on the water, cause the golden haze that lies over Venice? Symonds speaks of "that melodrama of flame and gold and rose and orange and azure which the skies and lagoons of Venice yield almost daily to the eyes."

These so to speak local and geographical influences could not alone create a consummate art. From the other direction, from the Italy that is more of the West, drained the impetus to a free sort of painting. If the culture of Venice escaped

the sometimes blighting effect of the return to classicism, nevertheless it gained immensely by those other major Renaissance changes: the emancipation of the mind for free thought and experiment, and the push forward into an exuberance of expression. The neoclassic incubus evaded, this one city profited enormously by the spirit of liberalism which had grown so notably in the Florence of the early *quattrocento*. But here, late in that century and during the sixteenth, there was no knuckling under when scholars set up Athens and Rome as the only orthodox models. The approach did not become academic and literary—as with Botticelli, Raphael, and Andrea del Sarto. There was no fealty sworn to science—that science which had so absorbed Leonardo that he departed from painting except for practicing it as a sideline. Nor was there in Venice even a nominal obligation to the Church:

Gentile Bellini: *Miracle of the Holy Cross. Academy Gallery, Venice*

the Venetian merchant princes were content to remain merchant princes, not annexing the titles of cardinal and pope.

In other words, here was a market for painting that was rich in technique and devoted to a subject-matter in keeping with the atmosphere of carnival and luxury and drama. Giorgione, Titian, Tintoretto, and Veronese answered the demand of the merchant princes. They were indeed of their time and spirit, and they pushed the painting art to new achievements of gorgeous expression.

Color was the typical, the salient resource that was freshly capitalized on and made to serve in unprecedented ways. No longer a mere addition to the painting, or a means of harmonizing, it became a leading element in the plastic orchestration. But it is to be noted, too—since it has been overlooked in a great many critical estimates—that in the matter of composition in space, of formal organization, the Venetians pushed far ahead of the Florentines. After the Sienese decorative formalism died out, the school of Florence progressively lost the abstract values

of structure and the plastic richness of the early expression, dispersing the formal synthesis under the new concern for anatomical truth, light-and-shade reality, scientific perspective, and general "naturalism." Florentine composition may be expert in the surface aspect, but it is increasingly lacking in the deeper three-dimensional, self-contained power of movement. Raphael, though a marvelous composer in the surface elements, is not a symphonic painter in the Venetian sense. With Andrea del Sarto and Guido Reni the abstract and contrapuntal values have disappeared.

The school of Titian and Tintoretto beautifully revived the pictorial compactness, the structural soundness, of painting. It went on to unparalleled achievements in volume-space organization. It made painting a symphonic rather than a melodic art. It is from this source, moreover, that El Greco picked up the impulse to his superbly contrapuntal art; El Greco, who was to preserve and utilize the abstract and mobile elements in painting, and to become—so masterly was he in this matter of plastic creation—the

Carpaccio: *Episode in the St. Ursula Legend. Academy Gallery, Venice*

idol of the twentieth-century moderns. In Venice, Titian and Tintoretto (with whom El Greco studied) matched a certain energy and largeness of outward statement and of portrayed life with this other inner life, this symphonic grandeur.

Yet color *is* the outwardly striking characteristic. A sort of sensuous glow lies over Giorgione's *Pastoral Symphony,* Titian's *Venuses,* and Veronese's sumptuous banquet scenes and allegories. The color exists partly, no doubt, in the accessory subject-materials: rich brocades, glamorous garden backgrounds or canopied interiors, jewels and shining armor, the crimson and scarlet of ceremonial robes. Yet these may all be absent, and color, in a deeper sense, still suffuses the picture. It is inbuilt, is of the fabric of painting as such, not dependent upon subject.

Early Venetian Painters

The Italian roots of Venetian painting can be traced back to Florence, to Verona, whence Gentile da Fabriano and Pisanello were called to Venice on commissions in the fifteenth century, and to nearby Padua, where Squarcione had a famous studio-school and Mantegna was practicing. The earliest local painters who left creditable work were Giovanni d'Allemagna—or John of Germany—the two Vivarinis, who had served an apprenticeship at Padua, and Jacopo Bellini. This last artist is less important as a creator than as an

absorber and transmitter of influences. He was a capable, industrious painter. He was strongly influenced by Mantegna, who became his son-in-law. This is a main link with the standard Renaissance realism, for Mantegna owed much to Florentines who had sojourned in Padua, particularly to Donatello and Uccello. Jacopo Bellini's workshop, moreover, was a point of experiment where the secrets of the new medium of *oil* painting were being uncovered.

In a transitional group, Carlo Crivelli showed individualism but did not become one of the great painters. Nevertheless there is a hint of later Venetian opulence in his mechanical and overlinear compositions. A Sicilian, Antonello da Messina, schooled in Flemish naturalism—once a student at Ghent—gave further impetus to the drift toward exact illustration and so-called scientific means when he came to Venice in 1472 and practiced in a manner that may have seemed miraculous to his fellow artists. Dürer, from another part of the North, sojourned in Venice in 1505-1506, and beautifully demonstrated another sort of naturalism.

It is as illustrators of the first rank that one must take the next two artists—sometimes termed "the first important Venetian painters"—Vittore Carpaccio and Gentile Bellini, son of Jacopo. In their pictures the pageantry and social activities of Venice come to life. One has exact and endlessly interesting records of civic and religious processions, ceremonies, shipping, and social life.

Giovanni Bellini: *The Feast of the Gods. Widener Collection,*
National Gallery, Washington

Gentile Bellini's contribution, being the earlier —he died in 1507—may be placed first. His panoramic pictures, while unmistakably representing the Venice of his time, are the more likely to have religious themes. His marshaling of many actors into intelligible groups and his meticulous attention to detail are notable. Of its kind the *Miracle of the Holy Cross* is as great a picture as one can find in all the European output. It is reproduced on page 390.

Carpaccio learned to crowd in even more of circumstantial detail, with an atmospheric reality seldom equaled. In *St. Trephonius Exorcizes a Demon* he surpasses the Florentines at their own game of creating perfectly believable, minutely detailed records of people and places. Carpaccio almost miraculously gives us sixteenth-century Venice: the palaces and the canals, the campanili and the bridges, the doges and the patricians, the

bishops and the courtesans, the gondolas and the galleons, the Orientally rich costumes and the pet dogs. One may recall, however, that the undertaking here is to *illustrate* the pomp and pageantry and color of Venice. Next the richness and splendor entered into the actual painting medium, and thus came the true Venetian art.

It was Giovanni Bellini, younger brother of Gentile, who first suffused his painting-medium with the city's golden light. He reverted to Madonnas and Crucifixions, and his panoramic work runs to idyllic interpretations of the mountain country above the lagoon city rather than to illustrations of its buildings, squares, and canal-streets. But the color and atmosphere and opulent grace characteristic of the place and its life are at last entering into the medium itself. Giovanni Bellini, incidentally, lived to the age of eighty-five, painting actively to the end, and was then

Giovanni Bellini: *Sacred Allegory. Uffizi Gallery, Florence*

the venerable, honored, and chief figure in the midst of a group of renowned artists that included Titian, already thirty-nine years old. Bellini had taught both Titian and Giorgione. The latter had died before the master, at the age of thirty-three, in 1511.

Giorgione, Titian, and Tintoretto

Giorgione of Castelfranco, native of a town in the Alpine foothills above Venice, but sent early to study with Bellini, may have carried with him throughout life some nostalgic affection for the beautiful country of his nativity. Or the Arcadian note in his painting may be a visual echo of the pastoral poetry that gained such great popularity in the Italy of 1500. In any case, he ushers in a delicate lyricism that is not at all uncongenial to the Venetian spirit of luxurious languor and holiday relaxation. More important, he carries color to a fresh degree of emotional expressiveness, and his superb picture-building is the first marked manifestation of the typical Venetian mastery of form.

Less known than Titian, and author of comparatively few authenticated works, he nevertheless possesses a fame that has grown continuously in the twentieth-century decades of reappraisal. Giorgione is seen as that miraculous figure, the man who frees himself of contemporary fetters, of rules and influences and academized ways of statement. He cut the ties that were holding Venetian art bound to the Florentine and Paduan tradition. The trend had been away from formal organization, toward illustrational documentation, but he returned the painter to a search for formal expressiveness. He practically gave up religious picturing—the famous *Castelfranco Madonna* is the one notable exception—and struck out into a realm of allegory and fancy; and he evolved a plastic method that is poetic, even musical, without violating the limits natural to the painting art.

It is, indeed, Giorgione's greatest original contribution that he restored the formal unity, even the formal grandeur, of painting. Everywhere just then, in Rome, in Flanders, in slowly awakening Germany, the dispersal of formal structure, the weakening of the basic design element, was under way. The structural organism was being forgotten in the haste to be scientific, realistic, natural. Giorgione restored the three-dimensional framework. He organized the move-

Giorgione: *Soldier and Gypsy. Academy Gallery, Venice*

ment elements, orchestrated the volume-space contrasts, the linear directions, the tension and thrust, and the inward-outward fluctuations. Each picture achieves a main rhythm, and then is enriched by minor counterplay. Few things in painting are at once so compact, so strongly alive, and yet so varied as *The Pastoral Symphony*, shown on page 388.

The Concert (probably worked on by Titian also) is deprived of deep thrust; rather it is flattened and orchestrated in planes. Its area-relationships are as expertly adjusted as those in the most studied of Piero della Francesca's works.

In the so-called *Soldier and Gypsy* the depth element, the penetration to plane after plane of interest, yet all within a related structure, is again beautifully contrived.

The student not fully trained to recognize this symphonic-structural element—which is the key to the modernist's "search for form" in the twentieth century—should be directed to Giorgione's canvases, and after that, to Titian, Tintoretto, and El Greco, who variously carried on the impetus that the genius of Castelfranco initiated.

The Pastoral Symphony, even in black-and-

Titian: *Sacred and Profane Love. Borghese Gallery, Rome*

white reproduction, indicates a sort of colorfulness unknown to European painting up to this time. It is not the decorative richness built up, as in Byzantine and Sienese painting, by adding together gold and crimson and patches of profusely ornamented surface. There is usually in that decoratively formalized art—enchanting in its own way—a certain loss of depth, a sacrifice of the stronger rhythms of sculptural forms disposed in space. Giorgione picks up the space painting of Florence, organizes the volumes and planes with fresh strength, and then proceeds to build the color into every part. He even adds color within shadows—an unprecedented thing.

The painters who had discovered light-and-shade as a means of representation had always considered it a technical resource practically separate from color. The lighted portions of any volume might receive a coating of color, objective color: trees green, flesh pink, sky blue, and so forth. But shadows were darkened with a gray-brown overlay. It was Giorgione's discovery that shadows harbored mixed color. He varied color in both lighted and shaded areas. His treatment gives a warmth and glow to his pictures, a colorfulness perfectly attuned to the ceremonial gaiety and opulent display of Venetian life, at the same time that it expresses Giorgione's own character and temperament.

Titian, born a year before Giorgione, likewise a native of the Venetian hinterland and a student of Giovanni Bellini, lived to be nearly a hundred years old. A plague took Giorgione at the age of thirty-three. It was also a plague that took Titian at the age of ninety-nine, but this was sixty-five years later, in 1576. Thus Titian's work-life may be figured as five times as long as Giorgione's, and certainly his paintings are five times as numerous in the world's galleries.

Although Giorgione was by a year the younger man, he was very truly the master from whom his more renowned associate learned. In their painting firm in Venice, Titian was the junior partner. At that time, moreover, Titian's method and style were unformed and hardly notable. Giorgione is the true initiator of the typical Venetian picture: secular, poetic, majestic. After Giorgione's death Titian seems consciously to have made the decision to abandon all other paths and to follow the one opened by his gifted associate.

Titian—or, more exactly, Tiziano Vecelli—was the most soundly magnificent painter in history. Sane, sober, dignified, he yet was inspired, colorful, and far-riding. He had none of Tintoretto's passionate and imaginative impetuosity, little of Michelangelo's extravagant outpouring of power. Yet he belonged with those titan figures by virtue of strength, largeness of conception, and sureness of touch. Of the half-dozen greatest masters of European painting, he was the most even-tempered and dependable. Although proud, opulent, and brilliant, like all the late Venetians, he stands a little apart by reason of a steadying balance and a native orderliness. Whether the picture is monumental or seemingly casual, there

Titian: *Venus of Urbino. Uffizi Gallery, Florence*

is an unfailing sense of command, an aristocratic and unfaltering firmness.

Titian is, indeed, the type-figure of the Venetian artist. Well born, he studied in just those places which would shape an expressive style: first with a mosaicist, then with Gentile Bellini, and finally with Giovanni Bellini. After that came the all-important partnership with Giorgione. He was by no means precocious. Practically every one of his important pictures is dated after 1517, when he was forty. But soon after that he was the intimate of dukes, princes, cardinals, and literary men, and commissions were urged on him by faraway kings and popes.

His earliest important work outside Venice was at the ducal court of Mantua in 1523. From then on through fifty years he was to go forth, between successes at home, to triumphs at Milan, Ferrara, Augsburg, and other courts. The Emperor Charles V, whose "German" empire just then included almost half of Europe (and technically most of America), bought Titian's services with large payments of money, generous

honors, and titles and pensions of dubious value (the artist's correspondence is picturesquely filled with duns and complaints about this). The imperial interludes resulted in expressive portraits of the Emperor and his aristocracy.

At home Titian had his own palace-studio, from which he carried on diplomatic relationships with patrons among neighbors and abroad. He painted for the Venetian Council a large historical picture for the Doges' Palace (though he finished it only under threats twenty-one years after receiving the commission and advance payments). At the same time he produced religious allegories and lovely Venuses to the market demand.

Despite his wealth he seems to have been abstemious and careful in his personal tastes as compared with his fellow Venetians. Music was his only passion outside painting. Widowed early, he was apparently only an observer of the buxom women whom he painted as Venuses and nymphs. These are Venetian through and through—of a mature, opulent type, sex-conscious without self-consciousness, nobly erotic.

Titian: *Rape of Europa. Isabella Stewart Gardner Museum, Boston*

His house seems to have been a noted center for entertainment and merriment, and something of this is implicit in his rich painting method. However, when Titian, nearing eighty, was deprived of most of those dearest to him, and his home was bereft of gaiety, he merely took refuge in more intense application to his art. Curiously enough, the great religious pictures of his last period are interspersed among some of the master's loveliest and most sensual nudes. His final picture, however, was a *Pietà*, and in it the artist painted his own figure reaching out to the Christ.

As painting pure and simple Titian's work is most notable for the perfection of those qualities which he took over from Giorgione. No one else is quite so sure in the arrangement of compact, strongly impelled forces, in the showing of powerful movement confined in closed rhythms. And his painting has a glory of color within an abiding fullness of all surface-sensuous elements.

These values inhere most gorgeously in the mythological pieces and in some of the monumental religious compositions. For a study of picture-building as such there is hardly anywhere in history (unless it be in El Greco's achievement) a "run" of paintings so important as Titian's pastoral and mythological scenes with nudes. The *Sacred and Profane Love*, comparatively early and very Giorgionesque in conception and in detail, is less compact and unified than the lovely *Venus of Urbino* and the *Venus with a Mirror*.

In the same vein but even more dynamic, and impinging upon the baroque, are such late masterpieces as *The Rape of Europa* and *Bacchanal*. Some historians trace the inception of baroque art to the unexplainable individualistic works of Michelangelo, and to such paintings by Titian as *The Rape of Europa*.

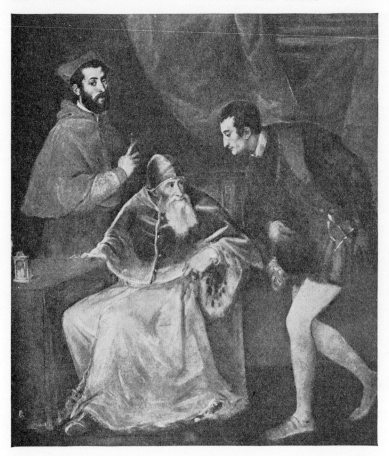

Titian:
Pope Paul III and His Nephews.
National Museum, Naples

Certainly some of the most obvious baroque characteristics are here seen in essence: the diagonal emphasis in composition, the opulent curving forms, the fluttering movement. Among Titian's late religious pictures the plastic rhythm is exceptionally strong in the *Madonna of the Pesaro Family,* and again, with more variation, in the *Assumption,* which critics used to account one of the greatest pictures in the world.

Titian was no less the master when he addressed himself to the simpler task of the portrait-painter. The early *Man with the Glove* is a superbly contrived thing, apparently as exact as photography could have made it, but built on as expert knowledge of pictorial engineering as is the *Venus of Urbino.* Thirty years later Pope Paul III was no less beautifully stabilized in a frame, and was given more solidity, was made sculpturally three-dimensional. As psychological portraiture, too, this is very fine. A

superb portrait is that of Frederick of Saxony. (See page xix of this book's Introduction.)

Incidentally, *Pope Paul III* is one of Titian's paintings that afford a hint of certain technical means which he was presently to hand on to his pupil El Greco—not excluding what the realists call "deformations" of head and hand for expressive purpose. This very portrait is known, moreover, to have affected Velázquez' manner when he studied it ninety years later. And Titian is the master from whose works the renowned Flemish portraitist Van Dyck was to learn his trade. The Venetian need not fear the comparison. His works are the profounder, the more solid. A certain magnificence in the *Pope Paul III* carries over to the less subtle portraits of Aretino and into a self-portrait; and also, with greater reliance upon colorfulness of surface texture and accessory "properties," into the celebrated picture of the artist's daughter Lavinia. Another

Tintoretto:
Portrait of Jacopo Sansovino.
Uffizi Gallery, Florence

famous portrait is *The Man with the Glove.*

Titian is oftenest described as the most musical of painters, and the adjective commonly used is "symphonic." The description is more than usually apt, particularly now when the moderns speak of formal orchestration as the basic virtue of great painting art. One might expect that when this great master had gone Venice would have been left with composers of only a secondary and reflective genius—such indeed were a half-dozen decorators and portraitists who may be found in the museums. On the other hand, there is another painter who, if not for all tastes the equal of Titian, is one of the titans. He lacks the melodic clarity of the elder man, and also the glamorous, joyous, openhearted directness. But the term "symphonic" belongs equally to his work, and he surpasses the other in imaginative vigor and in compressed animation. Titian oftener devotes his genius to the sensuous, and even carnal, aspects of life. Tintoretto reaches for insubstantial glories and mystic hidden overtones. By that token his color is more somber; but

he achieves an equally marvelous luminosity by his flamelike patterning of light and shade.

He was known as Tintoretto because he was the son of a dyer. His real name was Jacopo Robusti. There is a legend to the effect that shortly after he was sent as a pupil to the studio of Titian the master happened upon a group of his sketches and straightway ordered that the boy should never be permitted to enter the studio again—some say that he was jealous of what the sketches promised, others that he could not stand the wild impetuosity and quivering, leaping animation in them. The youth therefore studied in his own way, moodily following this and that impulse to investigation. It is as well, perhaps, that he became no one's apprentice and follower. Instead of permitting a certain isolation, which was his through life, to embitter him and handicap his art, he threw himself the more impetuously into hard work and individualistic experiment. He emerged with a technique and a vision wholly distinctive, and achieved one of the most amazing personal

Tintoretto: *Bacchus and Ariadne. Doges' Palace, Venice*

triumphs in the annals of the painting art.

His fellow painters—good commercialists all, and rightly, since that was the spirit of the time —disliked him because he would give away canvases or sell them for a song, and thus weaken the market. Once he was asked, along with a distinguished group of artists that included Veronese and two eminent Tuscan painters, to enter a competition for a mural to be placed on the ceiling of the School of San Rocco, the subject being *The Glory of San Rocco*. When the day of the decision came, and the other painters hopefully brought in sketches, they were surprised to find that in the brief time allowed Tintoretto had worked feverishly and finished his painting, and had, moreover, caused it to be inserted in the actual ceiling panel the better to display its worth. The question was raised whether he was not unfairly winning the commission and the fee, and he retorted that he knew

no other way to work and settled the financial insinuation by giving the painting to the school. Incidentally, he had pushed his style, more than had been his custom, over toward the baroque manner just then becoming fashionable in Florence, in order to forestall criticism from those who might wish to turn the commission to his two Tuscan competitors.

Tintoretto seems always to have remained a solitary among the artists of Venice (although at home he had a wife and eight children). Perhaps the memory of Titian's repudiation of him as a youth never quite faded away; he was urged from within constantly to push his work forward and to force every opening. Public recognition of his genius could not be long delayed, and yet it was often grudging.

Pietro Aretino, that picturesque literary-political ruffian who had taken refuge in Venice and who was an intimate of Titian, gave his

valuable endorsement to the then young Tintoretto. Later he reversed his attitude and joined
in depreciating the man, for which Tintoretto
took his own sort of revenge when the vain
Aretino decided that after all he must have his
portrait done by so famous a master. After placing the writer on the model-stand, Tintoretto
got out a great pistol and ostentatiously waved it
about his startled and apprehensive sitter, but
ended by explaining that he was using the
weapon as a measuring stick and that Aretino
was three pistols high. He never heard criticism
from that quarter again.

If such incidents indicate a temperament and
a manner incurably individualistic, tending
toward eccentricity, in a time when artists were
in general diplomatic, social, and eager to please
patrons and public, there is nonetheless a quality
in Tintoretto's work that is essentially Venetian.
There are idyllic figure pieces which could have
been done only by a painter following on the
advance made by Giorgione and Titian. There
is everywhere the luminosity that belongs to
this school, and certainly the exuberance of
statement is of the time and the place. The
opulent life is expressed by Titian in one way,
through the sanest and most balanced of temperaments. It is the same life that is responsible for
the largeness and colorfulness of the younger
man's outpourings, but expressed through his
subjective impetuosity and inspirational method.

For all his individualism, it is well to remember
that the youthful Tintoretto once stated his ideal
as "the drawing of Michelangelo with the coloring of Titian." It may have been only a schoolboy
precept, chalked on his studio wall after some
vision had come to him of a work to be done,
but it is clarifying even today. Only Michelangelo was ever quite so prodigal; no one else
so beautifully understood the arbitrary use of
the human body in the creation of plastic rhythms. It is significant that in going to Rome for
tutelage Tintoretto was fascinated by Michelangelo alone, totally overlooking the Raphaelesque neoclassicism.

Here, then, is the third of the giants in the
Venetian culmination, most imaginative and
most dramatic of all. Hugely prolific, he suffers

often from the inevitable faults of the inspirational worker. Some canvases too obviously
betray the impatience of his nature and the
hurry of his method. There are pictures confused,
windy, even chaotic. The patterns of light are
too tempestuous, exciting without finally spelling
compositional repose. But in an extraordinary
range of works the herculean energy is brought
under control, the excitement is held in bounds,
the vast plan is unified, the multiple rhythms
are confined within a visually comprehensible
—and gorgeously stimulating—pictorial achievement.

Tintoretto is, indeed, the equal of Giorgione
and Titian when he cares to limit his composition
to a few figures related in tension and balance.
He can be as neatly compact as anyone in dealing
with strong movement and heavy volumes suspended in equilibrium. His *Bacchus and Ariadne*
and *Adam and Eve* and *Mercury and the Graces*
are outstanding examples of orchestration around
the main motive of a few dominating volumes
in space. Master of lighting that he is—one of
the greatest—he often enough arbitrarily puts
light and shade where he creatively wants
them, out of tune with nature no doubt, but
aesthetically justified. In his nudes, as in the
Bacchus and Ariadne here, he shows none of
the inviting sexual attitudes and implications
known to Titian. Bodies are beautifully sculpturesque and luminous, but solid rather than of
a melting voluptuousness.

Impersonally considered, the human body is
utilized by Tintoretto with a virtuosity equaled
only by that of Michelangelo. The man or
woman is foreshortened or lengthened as may
be compositionally right, and may be seen from
any arbitrarily chosen angle, if the volume
rhythm or linear pattern is thereby served.
Tintoretto made up wax figures and studied
them from all angles, and placed them in boxes
so shuttered that light would strike them from
one direction after another. He was studying
the body not for individuality or for revealing
attitude but for its place in creative organization
of volume, line, and light-dark patterning.

The result is seen in the very simple *Bacchus
and Ariadne* at Venice, in the more varied *Mars,*

Tintoretto: *Christ with Mary and Martha. Alte Pinakothek, Munich*

Venus, and the Three Graces at Chicago, and subtly in the very different *Christ with Mary and Martha* at Munich. This last is a symphonic picture if any exists. There are major and minor movements, contrasting yet related, with the arbitrary bending of the figures creating the central full-volume rhythm or compositional theme. Nor, beyond these abstract, purely

Tintoretto: *Fight of the Archangel Michael and Satan. State Gallery, Dresden*

aesthetic values, appealing subconsciously, is there any lack of spiritual truth and objective interest. In fact, the Bible parable is conceived with originality and stated explicitly.

Tintoretto is the better known for the more ambitious and monumental things for churches and public halls. His *Paradise* in the Doges' Palace is literally as big as a house, actually the

Veronese: *Feast in Levi's House. Academy Gallery, Venice*

largest painted canvas in existence. It really is too large to be seen as a whole. Enjoyment of it —though one does definitely feel a cosmic magnificence—comes down to the matter of studying "passages" one at a time. No other painting approaches so closely to Michelangelo's *The Last Judgment* in the pleasure it affords in this manner. Group after group among the hundreds of figures will be found to have compositional unity and dynamic effectiveness. The *Paradise* was painted, incidentally, after the artist had turned seventy, and he scandalized his fellow painters by refusing as excessive an extra fee voted to him by the city fathers after the unveiling and the popular acclaim.

There is no painter upon whose merits and demerits the critics so disagree, and the works chosen as masterpieces vary greatly from critic to critic. Most popular, perhaps, are *The Origin of the Milky Way,* in London, a superbly opulent decoration but somewhat crowded, and *The Miracle of St. Mark,* in Venice, which is characteristic but on the tumultuous side. The great panoramic pictures like the San Rocco *Crucifixion,* the *Massacre of the Innocents,* and the *Battle by Land and Sea* please some; others, seeking more severity and clarity, go back to the *Bacchus and Ariadne.* Recently the school of appreciation which finds form-organization basic in the evocation of aesthetic pleasure has turned attention to Tintoretto's extraordinary handling of light-and-dark patterning, in conjunction with his marshaling of figures in space. The swirling volumes of his main rhythms and the contrapuntal play of flamelike draperies and light-streaked edges afford a formal effect paralleled only in El Greco. And new attention is directed to pictures like the *Fight of the Archangel Michael and Satan* and the *Christ with Mary and Martha* for observation of these virtues.

It is eloquent of the imagination and reach of Tintoretto that he could score so variously. That the quality he handed on to El Greco is being revived in the twentieth century as an animating principle of modernism is but one sign of his transcending genius. Incidentally he was a very great portraitist, though definitely a notch below the supreme Titian.

Veronese and "Minor" Venetian Painters

There is yet one more artist to be mentioned as adding to the glory of Venetian painting, although he is hardly worthy of a place beside Titian and Tintoretto. When Paolo Calieri of Verona, later to be known universally as Veronese, went to Venice in 1555 he was already an accomplished artist, successful at twenty-seven. Perhaps if he had gone at seventeen instead he would have absorbed the one thing he lacks out of the typical Venetian equipment—

Veronese: *The Rape of Europa. Doges' Palace, Venice*

form-understanding. As it is, his work is external and not a little flat. The spirited color is that depicted from the subject, rather than that which is inbuilt. He is all on the surface. His magnificence is that of gay costume, architectural grandeur, and processional movement.

Let us not make any mistake: Veronese's pictures are decorative; they are charmingly alive; they are full of brilliant passages and gaily decked backgrounds. The "furniture" is unfailingly grand. At times he can trick a picture in the sound tradition of ordered form till one would swear, except for the signature, that Tintoretto had had a hand in it. But the characteristic things are the loosely constructed murals seen at the Villa Maser, and the banqueting and pageantry scenes common to all art-history books —sumptuous, colorful, Venetian. But in them there is an atmosphere of artificial stage-setting, of contrived grandeur. One is getting back to the opulence illustrated, not imparted out of the painter's soul and craftsmanship. Hence the sub-

jects are usually ceremonial occasions—or historical episodes ceremonially treated—within halls richly colonnaded and banner-hung, with crowds of gaily costumed people.

Such are the ceiling piece in the Doges' Palace, called the *Apotheosis of Venice*, and, most famous of all, the *Feast in Levi's House*, as magnificent a piece of contrived scenery as one could ask. Just there is the point: on his own superficial decorative ground Veronese is supreme. But he is theatrical where Tintoretto is dramatic. The latter's imagination and conviction are absent, and of the sober poetry of Giorgione and Titian there is no trace. Above all, the painting-structure is relaxed, weakened.

Once one has passed beyond the work of Giovanni Bellini one finds the succession of giants—Giorgione, Titian, Tintoretto—so overwhelmingly important and absorbing that there is danger of overlooking artists who are called "minor" only because of the shadowing eminence of these geniuses. If he had appeared in

Sebastiano del Piombo: *Venus and Adonis. Uffizi Gallery, Florence*

any other than this golden age, Palma Vecchio would be accounted a considerable figure. It is true that his virtues seem derivative: he followed, rather than helped to initiate, the rich glow, the luminous patterning, and the full but balanced compositions of his contemporaries Giorgione and Titian. But in *The Meeting of Jacob and Rachel* and the *Sacred Conversation,* favorite canvases, he adds a distinctive softening fluency in a manner agreeable and catching. It is only after analysis that one notes that the figures are rather obviously posed and the scenery insubstantial.

A pupil and associate of Palma, Bonifazio, is likewise a respected painter of the second rank, whose best pictures are in the Giorgionesque tradition, though without the masterly compactness and fullness. The *Diana and Actaeon* at Oxford is outstanding. Paris Bordone, who lived, as did these other two, entirely within the lifetime of Titian, failed to absorb either the poetry of conception or the sound plastic means distinguishing the great Venetian art of the time; but he painted one outstanding and very popular showpiece, *The Ring of St. Mark Presented to the Doge.* It is justly starred in all the guidebooks to Venice. It is notable among historical

ceremonial works of art, and its stage-setting grandeur fails to distract one seriously from the successful figure arrangement. It is a fine, superficial, story-telling piece of invention.

More solid, but with an unfortunate woodenness, is Lorenzo Lotto's variation of the current way of painting. He had more originality than the other minor artists; the *St. Jerome* in the Louvre is notable as an experiment in arranged, superimposed planes (almost in the twentieth-century cubist method) and as a distinctly advanced study of landscape for its own sake. There is, of course, no landscape painting as a separate category in Renaissance times. In portraiture Lotto pushes on also toward the goal of exact documentary representation. The canvas known as *The Sick Man* is one of the most convincing realistic portraits painted up to Lotto's time, having sound pictorial structure along with exact statement and psychological insight.

Whereas Lotto was introspective, religious-minded, and apart from the main Venetian current, his contemporary Sebastiano del Piombo floated with the stream. Working frankly in the Giorgionesque manner, he painted one picture obviously in the master's style, but as obviously

Moroni:
The Bergamask Captain.
Worcester Art Museum

without the master's sensitive adjustment: the famous *Venus and Adonis* of the Uffizi. Having gone from Venice to Rome and gained a sense of monumental painting construction from Michelangelo, he did some religious pictures which at least are more commanding than the contemporaneous products of the School of Rome. But Sebastiano's better claim to notice is in his solidly impressive portraits, which are not without Michelangelesque implications.

As a portraitist, however, there is one other—last of the sixteenth-century Venetians to be mentioned—who excels in a distinctive way. Precisely because he is the ultimate Renaissance realist, Giambattista Moroni occupies a prominent niche in all leading galleries. He laid out the main areas of his picture with a sufficient under-

standing of surface composition, but other values were sacrificed to a meticulous, representational exactitude.

Even Titian noted that Moroni's likenesses were more "faithful" than his own, and when he could not take portrait commissions he urged his clients to go to this first of all the truly camera-eyed artists among the Italians. Not an attitude or a gesture, not a whisker or a wrinkle, not a button or a minutest fold of embroidered goods escapes notice and immortalization; as you may verify from *A Tailor* in London, or *The Warrior* in New York, or *The Bergamask Captain* at Worcester. These pictures are beautifully lighted, too, and often glamorously colored. All they lack is the element that would make them live as paintings rather than persist as exact portraits.

Guardi: *View of the Lagoon. Poldi Pezzoli Gallery, Milan*

As it is, the sitter is miraculously fixed, perfectly perpetuated.

It was more than a century later that the same painstaking realism was brought into service in the production of picturesque "views": in *vedute* art, as the Italians succinctly have it. In the canvases of Antonio Canale, commonly called Canaletto, who was born in 1697, the Venetian canals and shipping are glamorously and faithfully portrayed. His painting is a revival, in a sense, of Carpaccio's topographical and documentary art of two and one-half centuries earlier, but with the ease of manner and luminous atmosphere possible after the color-synthesis achieved in Titian's century. A nephew of Canale, who also took the name Canaletto, carried on acceptably in the *vedute* tradition. But it was Francesco Guardi who gave a fresh turn to the genre, adding a sparkling lightness and brilliant contrasts of light and shadow. Here realism, helped immensely by the natural picturesqueness of the Venetian scene, is further enhanced by a brilliantly staccato accenting and an opalescent veiling. This is souvenir art at its best.

Canale was the son of a painter of stage-settings but escaped into service of the real. A contemporary of his, Giovanni Battista Tiepolo, on the other hand, avoided the slide toward realism and reverted to what is often little more than theatrical decoration. He owes something to Veronese—not a safe model—but is more capricious, sketchy, even slapdash. There is freshness of color in his works; there is unbounded verve; there is virtuosity. But there is too little sound foundation in design.

Tiepolo used to be called "the last of the great succession," and his murals were noted for "splendor" and "drama." But today it is clear that a sickness had overtaken Italian art. Tiepolo's canvases are generally empty of serious design, his effects are stagy, his colorfulness is superficial. The form-organization of Giorgione and Titian has disappeared: the movement is dispersed, the organism shattered. Figures float about, unrelated in any architectural scheme; picturesque bits of nature are casually dropped in.

The date, of course, is now well down in the era that is called baroque elsewhere—but this is not baroque art of the stamp of Rubens and Bernini. Other chapters, tracing the Renaissance impetus in Spain, Flanders, and Germany, intervene before we turn to that development.

Having touched upon realism, however, as one of the two directions of decline, one may add here

El Greco: *The Assumption of the Virgin*. Detail suggesting influences of
Titian and Michelangelo. *Art Institute, Chicago*

a note upon the end of Renaissance "scientific" painting in depictions of everyday people and incidents, as practiced not in Venice but in Rome and Naples. Caravaggio is the great figure—an outstanding innovator in that he challenged those who were carrying on the pretty neoclassicism popularized by Raphael, and particularly the "grand manner" of Giulio Romano and the Caracci. But when Caravaggio had mastered the natural light-and-shade technique, and had gone to the streets and taverns for characters and incidents, he failed to create an art more profound than that of his pompous enemies. He took refuge in forcing his lighting and melodramatizing his everyday scenes—and here is the beginning of the art of Ribera and Murillo. He made an enormous success in his own time, and appropriately died as the result of a brawl, without learning that he had led painting into a side-pocket, not into a main vein. After him, Salvator Rosa found material for the new natural art in nature (which Caravaggio had somehow overlooked); and the next phase is picturesque landscape. He specialized in ruins and stormy skies and craggy shores.

Many historians, however, place the blame for the ruin of Italian painting less upon the realists than upon the Bolognese eclectics. Particularly they mark the artists of the Caracci family as having made a formula for fine painting, partly out of antiquarian study, partly out of Raphael's surface mannerisms, and partly out of a misunderstanding of the grand style, which they thought was apotheosized in the rather slack Correggio.

The Caracci founded an academy and school, and their influence soon went out in all directions. There is no doubt that Caravaggio's realism was in the air and helped to determine subsequent proceedings. Perhaps mutually antithetic ingredients—nature, melodrama, and a sublime manner—were being poured in together. In general the Caracci effort passed off in overvigorous action, sentimentalization, and pompousness.

Since the Caracci had determined to incorporate into their art the most desirable qualities of the preceding masters—the largeness of Michelangelo, the superb color of Titian, the balanced figures of Raphael, and so on—they became known as the school of Eclectics. But as they tried to reproduce the special *manner* of each master, and inevitably produced only a caricature or affectation, they ended by being known as the mannerists. The term covers more than the members of the Caracci School, because

earlier a number of unimaginative artists, particularly followers (at a distance) of Michelangelo, had thought to copy in the same way. In sculpture Giambologna is identified as a typical victim of mannerism. In general it may be said that the mannerist effort ended in an art too large, too vigorous, pictorially too complicated.

After the Caracci themselves—Agostino and Annibale—Guido Reni and Domenichino are the only still popular names. The former did a fresco —the *Aurora*—which is endlessly reproduced. The latter reverted sufficiently toward the ideals of Perugino and Raphael, with a little of the recent influence of the Venetians, to be accounted a belated and sometimes rewarding idealist.

But Domenichino was so much out of his time that the realists of Naples conspired to silence him by murder—in 1641—and either actually poisoned him or drove him to the death of one frustrated and broken by overwhelming opposition. Therein is more than a hint of what was happening to dignified and imaginative art in that turbulent seventeenth century when blood flowed almost as freely as paint.

If the Renaissance be reckoned—as it is by critics enough—as marking saliently the rediscovery of "reality," as being the turning-point into modern realism, the first cycle is now complete. Venice has had its day, perhaps the most glorious one in the calendar of Italian art. Its artists stayed the current which had earlier set in toward science and rationalism and documentary reality, and restored and heightened the formal values, even to the point of gorgeously symphonic expression, with the added glory of color out of the East. Giorgione, Titian, and Tintoretto had made painting live with a fullness not known in Europe before. It was their disciple, Domenico Theotocópuli of Candia, known as El Greco, who alone was to carry the full splendor of the painting art into the next era.

XX: EL GRECO AND CATHOLIC SPAIN

Since the Bronze Age the Spanish Peninsula has been a melting-pot of diverse peoples. It is fitting, then, that the foremost artist of Spain should be a Greek born in Crete, tutored by the Venetian colorists, and brought to Toledo in Spain by way of Rome.

In the Spanish background are the blood-strains of Iberians, Phoenicians, Romans, of Vandals and Visigoths, of Moors, and of those Frenchmen who in the eleventh and twelfth centuries poured over the Pyrenees in the Holy Wars against the Saracens. The language is Latin as modified by successive invaders. The arts consti-

tute Europe's most vivid illustration of the mixture of cultures: Oriental and Western, Christian and pagan. Utterly different monuments of purest style stand side by side: an early Christian church of substantially Syrian form, an Arab mosque, and a Gothic cathedral. In other examples the styles are inextricably mingled: there are buildings that can be called neither Byzantine nor Saracenic and yet are both. In one period the Lombard motives are grafted onto the already mixed "native" design. At one end of the shelf of Spanish pottery are pieces proclaiming themselves purest Persian, along with apparently

El Greco: *Christ in the Garden. Toledo Museum of Art, Toledo, Ohio*

411

Coptic and Moresque examples (the latter with Arabic inscriptions decoratively used); and toward the other end panels unmistakably della Robbian, faïence of French type, and finally porcelain statuettes that speak exactly the language of Meissen in Germany.

In that post-medieval time in which we are taking up the story of art in Spain, in the early sixteenth century, the Spaniards were more than ever internationally minded. The Moors had been conquered after five centuries of wars, and Spain itself was united, though its blood was mixed. The king was German, a Habsburg. His viceroys and overlords ruled Naples, Sicily, and the Netherlands. The crown owned the Americas. There was free intercourse with the Italian art centers, through Naples on the one hand, and through the German court which claimed dominion over half of Europe on the other. The king's walls at Madrid bore proudly the masterpieces of Titian, beside the works of van Eyck and van der Weyden and Bosch.

And yet, subjected to so many varied Renaissance influences, Spanish art remained almost broodingly Spanish. In a time when the Church of Rome was most slack and undirectioned and all the rest of Europe was torn by religious schism and war, Spain characteristically remained fanatically Catholic. This rectitude was of the nature of the mountainous and rock-bound country—and of its art, too. Spain is, indeed, the most extreme example of a country invaded by heterogeneous styles and peoples, yet forging the local and imported materials and impulses into a generally recognizable national style.

The Renaissance, at first an Italian development, then a movement that pushed into all the central North European countries, was slowest in spreading over Spain, and its influence was thin. If one considers only the cultural aspect, it is doubtful whether there was a Spanish Renaissance. The commercial and explorative expansion which accompanied the cultural awakening elsewhere was stirringly present in the conquest and exploitation of the Americas. In religious progress, on the other hand, Spain was reactionary. There was no sympathy with the Reformation here. On the contrary, Spain begot the Catholic Reaction.

The Spaniards led in forcing the Vatican to purge itself of corruption and worldly paganism. The Jesuits, organized by St. Ignatius of Loyola in 1541, were foremost in re-establishing the authority and enterprise of Catholicism, whether by education and reform or by the burning of heretics. Where the Northern reformers had not undermined Romanism beyond saving, the Jesuits entered to build new churches and establish schools.

The backwardness of Spain in the figurative arts is more than a little due to the uncompromising puritanism, not to say the fanatic bigotry, of the Church fathers, and to their moral control over king, courtier, and citizen. When Italy was glorying in pagan allegory and Parnassian idyll, and lovely Venuses paraded in the galleries beside coy and lifelike Italian mistresses, the nude was strictly forbidden in Spain. Even study from the undraped body was considered a sin. Until the time of Velázquez in the seventeenth century there were no nude females—and then for two centuries there was only his one lonely *Venus*.

The Church had, indeed, precise regulations for pictures. It prohibited such heretical representations as angels with beards, imps of hell with wings, or the Virgin Mary's robe in any style other than that declared by the Church to be historically truthful. It was heresy to show the Virgin's feet. There was a censor, an officer of the Church, to watch art and report violations to "the Lords of the Inquisition."

Every artist is irked by the very thought of censorship, and most art-lovers will concur in the opinion that art eventually is destroyed by censorship, whether religious or political. Another view, however, is that the burning faith itself fed the ardor of the artist, that the painters of the time probably did not feel themselves unduly shackled. They worked within the faith, and the overwhelming preponderance of religious subjects is a reflection of their interest—at least until they had traveled in Italy. There are many reports of artists' partaking of the sacrament before commencing a painting, and even of preparatory shriving and penance.

Nevertheless, intolerance does impede the free diffusion of art, and Spain, descending to the

St. John the Evangelist and St. John the Baptist. Retable, detail, early 16th century.
Hispanic Society of America

most oppressive period of the Inquisition just at the culminating moment of the Italian Renaissance, definitely set up barriers to the free activity of the aesthetic spirit. The story is told that the renowned Italian sculptor Torrigiano, a contemporary of Michelangelo and Benvenuto Cellini, having made a statue of the Madonna for a Spanish aristocrat and then disagreeing with his patron over the price, smashed the figure into fragments, whereupon the Inquisition condemned him for impiety. The sculptor starved himself to death in his dungeon cell rather than be burned alive.

It is illuminating that the neck-ruff and billowskirt came into fashion in Europe out of the Spanish effort to hide the natural body as completely as possible. Figuratively the iron corsets of the fashionable gentlemen bound art too.

The early painting of Spain shows the general European diversity; from the twelfth century to the beginning of the fifteenth there was effort of various kinds—illuminated manuscripts, murals, and countless religious panels and shrines. While a new art of painting was budding in Siena, Avignon, and Cologne, there were many local schools of artists in the two main divisions of Spanish territory, Castile and Aragon. In the first, Northern influences were earlier felt; in the other there were continuing contacts with Italy and other Mediterranean centers of commerce and culture. Farther back the traditions were those of the rest of Christian Europe: most notably of Byzantine iconography, and of the art of illumination that had been originally Byzantine but was now being gradually Gothicized.

Aragon might have developed religious painting as distinctive as the Sienese—and even more Orientally colorful, since the Saracens had brought in a second wave of formalized color art out of the East. But the surviving works are, with notable and welcome exceptions, curiously lacking in the naïve virtues that Duccio and his contemporaries were attaining in Siena at the end of the thirteenth century. There is early a sophisticated elaboration about them. They are ornamentally florid or, as pictures, overdetailed. Incidentally, they soon come to be loaded with excessive molasses-like color. The simple linear harmonies, the naïve directness of statement, and the transparency of color so notable in the works of the gentle Franciscans are missing in the Spanish gallery. Whereas Duccio edged draperies delicately with a line of gold, the Spaniards built up wide gilded borders.

It becomes clear as soon as one has seen the typical Spanish pre-Renaissance painting that a Northern current of illustrators' naturalism has been crossed with the local native stream. The tie with the Netherlands was not alone political. As early as 1429 Jan van Eyck, Flemish innovator, had visited Castile, Andalusia, and Granada. Thenceforward there was a steady flow of Flemish paintings into Spain. Native craftsmen hastened to absorb the surface characteristics of this fashionable imported art. Nearly a century later one encounters the first often-mentioned Spanish painter, Pedro Berruguete, to whom is ascribed a three-part altarpiece at Avila. It is competent and well managed as illustrational painting, and the Northern idioms are obvious.

At about this time a renewed tide of influence set in from Italy too. All through the sixteenth century the advocates of the Flemish manner waged war with the invading Italians, or with the Spaniards who had been tutored in Italy. In general the two parties worked to a single end, since the Flemings had been realists from the start, and the Florentine and Roman Italians were just completing the cycle from naïve decoration to neoclassic realism. The differences were more of method: one worked for exquisitely detailed and finished verisimilitude; the other tended to a more monumental effect and an appearance of facile lifelikeness.

When these two reference points have been established, there is a certain interest in tracing individual artists' loyalty to one school or the other. Juan de Juanes leaned more to the Italian, though adding a Spanish intensity of feeling;

and Luis de Morales had the Flemish enamel-like finish, very shiny, and miniature fidelity. He is the most appealing and the most considerable painter up to his time. The native note in his unfailingly religious pictures is sorrowful rather than agonized. The Spaniards have called him "Morales the Divine." His heads sometimes suggest the elongation later to be noted as a mannerism of El Greco. A third sixteenth-century painter, Pedro de Campaña, combined the Flemish and Italian influences at first hand, since he was born in Brussels (though of Dutch extraction, originally named Kempener), passed his apprenticeship in Rome, being a disciple particularly of Raphael, and spent his mature artistic life in Seville, a city then wealthy and enterprising because of Columbus' discoveries. But he lacks something of Spanish fire.

Another effective Italianizer was Luis de Vargas, a Spaniard who spent twenty-eight years in Rome before settling down to spread the Raphaelesque gospel at home. That he remained more Spanish than Italian in spirit, and more medieval than Renaissance, is indicated by stories of his asceticism and self-scourging. He kept an open coffin by his bed and lay in it often, that he might remember the lessons of death. By contrast, one may recall the sunny spirit and the resultant radiant art of such Italian painters as Giotto and Fra Angelico, who lacked nothing of religious faith, but were joyous about it.

There were, besides, actual Italian artists of the second rank who were brought by King Philip II to decorate the Escorial Palace and its chapels. Titian, too, was here more briefly as visiting court painter. As an influence in the other direction there was one Antonio Moro, a Flemish portraitist who also was resident at the Spanish court, where he did tight, natural likenesses. His pupil, Alonso Sánchez Coello, became a famous painter in this specialty. His precise and overdetailed portraits are treasured in the great museums today. He in turn had a pupil-successor at the court, Juan Pantoja de la Cruz, who is a shade less convincing. This line was to lead on to Velázquez, who transformed the naturalism into an agreeable selective realism in beautiful technique.

El Greco: *Portrait of a Man. Metropolitan Museum of Art*

El Greco

But with the painting of Pantoja de la Cruz one has crossed into the seventeenth century. By 1600 El Greco had been twenty-five years in Spain. He was so immeasurably greater a figure than anyone else mentioned in the chapter so far that everything before his time seems like preparation. Not a Spaniard himself, and probably thirty years old at the time of his arrival in Toledo, he somehow made himself the most Spanish of painters—and a master worthy to stand beside such giants as Michelangelo, Titian, and

Tintoretto. His artistry is supreme, whether in simple portrait or complex story-picture.

Born in Candia, Crete, where Byzantine art had survived in its purest expression—where indeed he may have begun his art studies in a school of icon-painting—El Greco went to Venice early in life. There, too, he could dream in glowing Byzantine chapels. The earliest known mention places him as a pupil in Titian's studio. While Titian's organizational genius and certain slighter mannerisms are to be detected in El Greco's canvases, the younger man seems to have abandoned consciously the sober and clarified statement of that master in favor of the more imaginative reaches and mystic manner of that other Venetian, Tintoretto. Probably Tintoretto and El Greco both gained a plastic vitality, a sense of rhythmic structural organization, from Titian; but Titian has less affinity with either one than the two have for each other.

There is no direct evidence that the young Greek worked in Tintoretto's studio, but a half-hundred canvases suggest the probability, intimate a spiritual tie as well as the direct transmission of a passionate, flamelike, medievally intense way of working.

El Greco is next heard of in Rome, about 1570, where indubitably he studied the works of Michelangelo (there is a portrait of the latter inserted, along with one of Titian, in a religious picture by El Greco now in Minneapolis), though he rejected much of Michelangelo's method in favor of Tintoretto's. After his long sojourn in Italy, during which he thus had had some sort of contact with three of the greatest painters of the Italian Renaissance, El Greco went to Spain, probably in 1575. It is part of the measure of his genius that, after his long experience of Venice and Rome, his art could not possibly be mistaken for Italian. He was incorruptibly a personality; spiritually he became a part of Spain.

Aloofness and pride seem to have been in El Greco's character along with the mystic's self-effacement in the search for God. Living in Toledo, stronghold of chivalric Catholicism, home of the most tortured asceticism, a city so irredeemably medieval that the royal court, slightly liberal in thought and outlook, had moved from there to Madrid, he was the familiar of Inquisitor and grandee.

A Spanish writer of the generation after El Greco's says that "Domenico Greco"—thus, in the Italian form—"came to this city with a high reputation. . . . His nature was extravagant like his painting. . . . He used to say that no price was high enough for his works, and so only gave them in pledge to buyers, who willingly advanced him what he asked for. He earned much money, but spent it in great pomp and display in his house, even keeping paid musicians to entertain him at his meals. . . . He had few disciples as none cared to follow his capricious and extravagant style, which was suitable only to himself." He had a pupil and helper, however, in his son, who was not a genius.

The artist's library of Greek and Italian classics bears further witness to his cultural breadth and his discriminating love for the other arts. The enriched life thus indicated, combined with the man's predilections for solitude and contemplation, may be considered in some sort a key to the combination of intensified sense-appeal and austere abstraction in his art. No one else has overlaid his subject-matter and inner design with so rich a play of moving, rhythmic forms, with so fiery an orchestration of visual elements. Yet underneath is the soundest plastic structure, the most nearly infallible handling of the skeleton of abstract elements, known to Western painting.

For forty years El Greco worked in Spain, almost continuously, so far as is recorded, in rocky Toledo, of which he made one of the earliest European masterpieces in the landscape genre. (The Chinese were past masters of the "view" at this time.) The *View of Toledo*, now in the Metropolitan Museum of New York, besides having this historical distinction, is a gorgeous example of El Greco's symphonic composition and richly rhythmic surface expression, as well as a revelation of the spirit of the city and its countryside (see Color Plate IV).

Once only, it seems, the Greek of Toledo trembled upon the verge of a fashionable success with other than the Church corporations and dignitaries. At the direction of King Philip II in 1580 he painted *The Legend of St. Mauritius* for placement in a chapel in the Escorial. A quarter-century later a Father Siguenza, commenting upon the presence of the picture in a minor room of the palace, noted that "it was designed for the altar of the saint, but it did not satisfy His Majesty. It is not much, because it satisfied few; though they say it has great art, and that its author has much knowledge and that excellent things can be seen from his hand."

In other words, the King, surrounded by Flemish and Italian fashionable painters, was mystified and displeased by the work of this man who

El Greco: *Crucifixion.*
Prado, Madrid

expressed the soul of that other Spain, and he gave no more commissions to El Greco. The court had its several echoers of Raphael and Romano, and it had Coello and Pantoja. It was soon to have Ribera, then Velázquez.

The Greek was remanded to Toledo for life. It was probably one of the most fortunate failures in art history. At any rate, among the fervid clerics and fanatic hidalgos of the ancient capital, remote from the fashions and politics of the court, he found just the nourishment to bring his individualistic genius to flower. He died in Toledo in 1614, and his works entered into a period of obscurity which lasted well into the twentieth century. Probably the King and courtiers first spread the story that his art was what it was because of insanity.

It is no longer necessary to defend one's enjoyment of El Greco's works, or even to inquire why they so offend the realist and materialist. But it may be helpful to explore briefly the ways in which he obtained his effects. Fundamentally, as a "builder of pictures," he is supreme in the Western galleries. That is, he handles the abstract values, the structural principles and the instrumental means, of his art for effects of unparalleled richness, vitality, and variety. He orchestrates the movement elements into a symphony marked at once by grandeur and by tenderness, by clarity and by opulent overtones.

He creates with fullest use of the primary assets of the painting artist, volume-space organization, construction by planes, play of line. Color alone, of the major resources, he utilizes less generously and less creatively than did his Venetian teachers; but he mutes this element, and along with it incidental pattern, only to achieve the same sort of visual enrichment by an extraordinary surface play of light-and-shade. No one in the records of painting has so intensified the visual effectiveness of the design by light-dark manipulation. The flamelike swirls and elongated streakings of white contrasting with somber backgrounds are the most striking external earmark of his art. It will not escape the symbolist that the accent is vertical, aspiring; that the method adheres to the medieval, the Gothic logic, rather than to the Italian or classic.

This modeling by light, this patterning of light, this building of spurts of light into an exciting visual fire, this distortion of light for emotional impact—all contribute to the most provocative personal style in European practice. The *Crucifixion,* whether the one in the Louvre or that at Philadelphia, or one at Madrid, sets up the body on the cross in pitiless white light, in a strong main rhythm that dominates the plastic organization. In the first version, the balancing donor and priest at the foot of the cross complete the figure composition, but the sweep of clouds, with moving masses of dark against the light, creates an impression of almost turbulent grandeur and emotional power. In the second, where the Christ figure is more elongated, the two minor figures are crowded to one side of the cross; a balancing landscape with groups of figures is touched in by delicate streaks of light in the opposite corner; and the main background is varied by only a few clearly delineated shreds of cloud (very voluminously treated, however, where tension is needed). The movement effect is no less compelling. In the third version the artist crowds the canvas with figures, even placing two angels directly under the outstretched arms of Christ; yet the protagonist's figure again dominates the composition, and the play of light on drapery edges creates a counterpoint as rich and strong as that in the other pictures.

Because he so usually employs light in this way, as binding element, as the chief means to patterning, El Greco utilizes less than usual the "natural" backgrounds common to most religious pictures of the era. Clouds, rocks, draperies are substituted and frankly manipulated for contrapuntal variation and intensification. Incidentally, the nude Christs of these three pictures are a sufficient answer to those who carelessly assert that the Greek did not excel in nude painting. The nude that is an objective transcription of soft feminine loveliness, in erotic mood, is absent from the list of his works. But there are a score of undraped figures that have both convincing truth and a beautiful fitness to their artistic purpose.

The same ascending flamelike lighting and even greater virtuosity in manipulation of swirling clouds and draperies are seen in the several versions of *Christ in the Garden.* And indeed few paintings in the world so repay study of the abstract design and the method of obtaining fullness of rhythmic play and counterplay of forms. These are, of course, favorites of the expressionists, who find special pleasure in richly orchestrated plastic elements, even at the expense of distortion of natural aspects.

But it is notable that, when El Greco leaves the field of complex picturing and turns to such a simple problem as a portrait bust, he is likely to build up his composition with similar light patterning, modeling the elongated head with streaked light and repeating the rhythms in voluminous robes over the shoulders, and—final touch—echoing the method in supersensitive modeling of the hands.

Just what is the hidden rhythm, the order, that he puts into these simple or complex organizations is the artist's secret, the unexplainable creative addition. The mechanists offer the explanation that certain mathematical arrangements, in terms of balanced weight, proportioned areas, and symmetrical juxtaposition of volumes, please the eye, and that El Greco cunningly hides these geometrical adjustments within his picture. The observers who grant a mystic insight and a more imaginative inventiveness to the artist speak of El Greco's work as echoing the not-to-be-explained melodies of the divine order. They see in these canvases a fixation of cosmic design, an extension of cosmic movement.

The portraits as a group may serve as a point

El Greco: *Christ in the Garden. Private collection, Budapest*

of departure from the study of El Greco's artistic means to an analysis of his success in handling his subject-matter as such. Does he, in building his picture for plastic strength and richness, sacrifice that fidelity which may fairly be considered a prime virtue of portraiture? He does not; rather

El Greco: *St. Dominic*, detail.
Museum of Fine Arts,
Boston

can he be placed in the very first rank of por-traitists—with Titian. The faces are alert and living, though they show the reserve of the aris-tocrat or ascetic.

El Greco distorted natural aspect, certainly. In general he narrowed the faces, elongated the fore-heads, dwelt upon the flamelike lights of the head, and refined the hands, too, until they be-came sensitized indicators of emotion and char-acter. This applies especially to the imperious churchmen and the proud grandees who were his usual sitters; in elucidating the pride and fire and aspiration in the Spanish character, he showed himself a forerunner of modern psychological portraiture. The distortion, the departure from camera truth, is not only for rhythmic and sensu-ous effect but for the truthful revelation of char-acter.

That the method is equally employed in El Greco's long series of "invented portraits" of the apostles and saints is explainable on the same grounds. El Greco, in re-creating historic char-acters, took models, in so far as they were neces-sary to complement his inner images, from the holy men around him. Spain was the scene of the intensest religious activity of the time, and Toledo the very center of Christian ardor. There

is a spiritual truth in this transmutation of char-acter into forms that writhe like fire. There is a basis in material truth, too, for scientists have noted a small-headed, long-limbed type of man as native to the Toledo region; though he is not, of course, nearly so attenuated as the artist's figures.

The picture generally considered El Greco's masterpiece is a panoramic painting in the Santo Tomé Church in Toledo, *The Funeral of Count Orgaz.* It is truest El Greco, yet it recalls the painter's apprenticeship to Titian and Tintoretto: Titian in the earthly scene of the lower half of the composition, with its superb portraits, superbly related; and Tintoretto in the heavenly apparition above. Yet just as certainly neither Italian could have painted this mystically in-spired picture. The conception is said to have come to El Greco in a flash, as a vision. Count Orgaz had founded the Church of Santo Tomé in the fourteenth century. So great had been his piety that when he died and was ready for burial two saints came down from heaven and gently lifted his body and placed it in the grave.

The lower half of the picture beautifully repre-sents the event, with the church pageantry suf-ficiently woven into the central group, before the

El Greco: *St. Paul.*
City Art Museum, St. Louis

congregation of aristocratic mourners. In contrast with this scene, which is devised with more calm horizontal accent than is usual with El Greco, there is placed, above, the representation of the reception of the soul of the deceased in heaven, in a panoramic composition that is one of the most liquid, aspiring, and audacious achievements in the whole range of the artist's work. (Unfortunately the salient values cannot be illustrated with any success in a book of ordinary size.)

Undoubtedly the sober, stable, earthbound character of the scene below is purposely played against the melting, joyous, and exalted rhythms of the celestial scene above. Here are all El Greco's favorite distortions and intensifications: the lightning-flash lighting, the folding involutions of clouds and drapery, the elongated bodies, the fluctuating counterpoint of dark-light answering a strong main rhythm. All these are manipulated to build up to the Christ figure enthroned, with Mary the Intercessor at one side and the naked soul at the other. Echoing hosts of angels

are disposed with beautiful variety in the clouds around.

The celestial half of the picture is an utter negation of classic ideals and Italian methods. It reminds one of El Greco's Cretan origin. The disposition of elements harks back to the Byzantine: in the strong, simple organization; in the dependence upon abstraction rather than upon verisimilitude; in the suppression of background. Similarly in El Greco's simplified and rhythmic portraits there is a hint of the forthrightness and abstraction of the Byzantine icons. To have gone back to the Byzantine, to icon and mosaic, in any idiomatic way would have been retrogression. But El Greco seems instead to have restored to objective Western painting a strength and a profound rhythmic flow out of that earlier Oriental style. His work is as near to a fusion of Oriental and Occidental ideals and methods as anything in art history.

If the Greek sacrificed any major resource of Western painting it was perhaps in the field of color. Like Titian, he is not content to add his colors objectively; rather he builds them in. El Greco, however, prefers a cool color range, in contrast to Venetian glamour and warmth. A pale or dull green, cool blues, lemon-yellow or ocher, wine-red—these predominate, though often kept secondary to browns and grays with touched-in light.

Perhaps in the orchestration the partial muting of one instrument was necessary to permit giving full play to the others. Not until the time of Cézanne was an attempt to be made to achieve, in terms of color, nuances of form-expression as rich and delicate as those in El Greco's canvases. Nor, until some twentieth-century master fuses the newly understood color potentialities with the other elements, will anyone be able to record that the Spanish painter has been surpassed. Where painting touches upon the ecstatic and the supernal, he is master above all others.

Spanish Art after El Greco

The painters who took the center of the stage in Spain after El Greco, except the visitor Rubens, were steeped in realism, sometimes of the frightful, sometimes of the saccharine variety. Until the star of Velázquez rose there was only a secondary activity, though critics enough have listed Ribera among Spain's greatest masters.

Born in Valencia in 1588, Ribera made his way as a boy to Rome, all but starved on the streets there, went to Naples, and studied with the violent realist Caravaggio. He spent most of his life at the court of the Spanish viceroy in Naples, although he was well known in Madrid, too. The Neapolitans called him El Spagnoletto, and occasional canvases are so labeled today.

Ribera's drama, unlike El Greco's, is of the most obvious, outward aspects of life—often drifting into melodrama—and his method is realistic. His one virtue is that he returned to nature and seldom pretended to more than a transcription of incidents that interested him among picturesque beggars, gutter boys, hermits, and the like; though he branched out into monumental religious art in his own factual way. He especially loved to paint martyrdoms. He was one of the earliest slum realists, outdoing even Caravaggio in the lowness of his tastes. He became rich and associated with the aristocracy, but he seems to have remained at heart a bully and a low ruffian. He was leader of the secret society, the Camorra, that brought about the death of Domenichino and of others who stood up against the organized Neapolitan realists.

For all that, he could paint a head or hand with surpassing verisimilitude and make a theatrically lighted face live vividly. In accounting for Ribera one remembers that the Spanish primitives often made too much of the blood spouting from the Christ's wounds. Ribera added that note to Italy's new detailed naturalism.

Ribera, following on Caravaggio's success in showing out figures vividly lighted against deeply blackened backgrounds, became with his master a leader in the minor school sometimes known as the Tenebrists—from the Latin *tenebrae,* meaning darkness, or shadow. In this school the contrasts of light and dark must be violent, like much else in the picture.

More agreeable but less important, intrinsically and as an influence, was the religious painter Francisco de Zurbarán. He caught something of the effectiveness of Caravaggio's and Ribera's delineation by shadowing. His carefully lighted scenes and figures are executed with unusual round softness, albeit his outlines are precise—pretty, but without strength.

Alonzo Cano was, like Ribera and unlike the monkish Zurbarán, one of the high-living, violent figures of the time, mixing art with intrigue, murder, and bitter penance. The punishing Inquisitors ran his hand through a mangle but had the grace to mutilate the left hand because he was an artist. As a painter he was a clever eclectic, never achieving an individual manner but agreeably imitating the fashionable Italians and Van Dyck, in a dry vein. Some of his pictures have the effect of having been put together out of the work of several painters. As a sculptor he was a facile eclectic too. And that may be considered reason enough for inserting here the few words that need be said about the art of sculpture in post-Gothic Spain.

The great sculpture of Spain is almost wholly

A Prophet. Wood, detail. Spain, 15th century. *Ridgway Collection*

pre-Renaissance in date. The country had fostered the art through the Byzantine, Romanesque, and Gothic eras, sometimes with native artists, more often with imported ones. The fifteenth century had witnessed an invasion of Burgundian sculptors as aids to the international Gothic builders. Very beautiful statues survive from the Dark and Middle Ages. But the tastes of Charles V were soon Italianized, and thereafter, say from 1530 on, fashionable Florentine realism was standard. The Italian sculptor Torrigiano had already died in a cell, to be sure, prisoner of the Inquisitors, who found Italian ideas too liberal. But the King made Leone

Leoni a court artist—and saw himself immortalized, naked and naturalistic, in the true manner of Roman imperial sculpture.

Leone's son Pompeyo carried on with competent lifelikeness. He was aided and abetted by other Italians, and shortly by native Spaniards educated in Rome and Florence. Of these Alonso Berruguete is most typical. There is an illuminating tribute to Berruguete by the historian Cean Bermudez (as translated by Pijoan): "He was the first Spanish teacher who disseminated in the kingdom the knowledge of correct drawing and the proper proportions of the human body, magnificence of form, expression and the other sublime attributes of sculpture and painting." Nevertheless, the *early* Spanish sculpture is so magnificent in comparison—especially that to be seen still upon the walls of the Church of Santiago at Compostela, a Romanesque structure—that the body of Spanish Renaissance carving is dwarfed. The fragment shown on page 423 retains something of Romanesque-Gothic magnificence.

Among a group of sculptors who turned away from what had been a sound nonrealistic Spanish tradition, Gasparo Becerra is notable as having retained, although a student of Vasari, a native independence. He initiated a fashion of polychrome sculpture peculiar to Spain. (The Italians, of course, had arrived at colorlessness because that was the state of the exhumed Roman statues.) Martinez Montañes is especially known for his polychrome religious statues, which are still reverently carried through the streets on days of processions. They are in keeping with the rich pageantry fostered by the Spanish Catholic fathers—although artistically far inferior to the Byzantine-influenced crucifixes known to the Spaniards of some centuries earlier.

Through Montañes one comes to his pupil Cano, and in turn to Cano's pupil Pedro de Mena, who is at once so naturalistic and so sentimental that Spanish Renaissance sculpture may be marked as then arriving at the pitch of sweetness and feminine softness reached long since by the last della Robbias in Italy.

Velázquez and Murillo

Most appreciated among Spanish-born artists is Velázquez (more fully, Diego Rodríguez de Silva y Velázquez), a coldly truthful painter and, at his best, one of the most exquisite and admirable of realists. He was exceptionally prolific; perhaps no other acclaimed master is so widely represented in the world's museums by canvases sometimes good, frequently mediocre, and occasionally downright bad. From 1622, when Francisco Pacheco, the artist who for six years had been his teacher in Seville, sent him to Madrid to seek favor at the court of Philip IV, until his death nearly forty years later, he was successful, a favored courtier and a renowned purveyor to the aristocracy.

The works he had done when he went up to Madrid at the age of twenty-three—he took a homely study of a water-carrier as sample—were competently naturalistic genre studies and religious pictures, very much like imitations of Caravaggio and Ribera with the violence curbed. They caught the attention of the King's favorite, then of the King himself. From that moment Velázquez never lacked for patronage and honors. His own character, too—for he was upright, quiet-mannered, and faithful, if unspirited and over-pliant—contributed to make his position secure, his career materially successful. He was not only the King's painter—there are forty portraits of Philip IV from his brush—but the King's familiar companion. Philip himself took to painting under his tutelage.

Velázquez' last painting before an Italian journey which was to prove an epochal influence was *The Topers*, an ultra-representational, studio-posed familiar group, which has had an enormous vogue. It was Rubens, then a visitor at the court of Madrid, who insisted that the young man go to Italy to broaden his outlook and see the latest fashions. After leaving Madrid in 1629, he spent two years in the sometime haunts of Titian, Tintoretto, Raphael, Michelangelo, and Caravaggio. He also studied the disinterred classic statues. He was not the man to resist fashionable currents, and he seems to have studied Caravaggio and Ribera even too well; though in another direction there is Guido Reni's influence in his too smooth middle-period portraits. Fortunately other pictures bear witness that he turned back to Titian.

An academic hardness is evident just after Velázquez returned from Italy to the court at Madrid. There follows a long period in which portraits claim his attention almost exclusively. He adds a certain dash and freshness to them. There is a moment in the sequence when he goes back to study El Greco. His one notable historical scene in paint shows the influence. It is the famous *Surrender of Breda*, which is full, animated—and Spanish.

The spirit of Spain otherwise enters hardly at all into Velázquez' way of painting. There is

Velázquez: *The Surrender of Breda. Prado, Madrid*

nothing of the fire, the pride, and the mysticism which are said to be of the very essence of the national character in his transcriptions of life around him. In the mature period of his art, indeed, there is hardly more than an objective record of people seen within the narrow confines of court life: transcriptions of its characters, costumes, and oddities.

What does signify in the history of art is that Velázquez refined the painting medium and the current realism to a new degree of clarity, reaching forward to a modern freshness and directness of coloring; and that his portraits afford a caressing pleasure to the eye. He knew compositional structure, too; although in the surface, Raphaelesque sense, without ever once approaching the symphonic fullness and three-dimensional solidity of Titian and El Greco. His portrait heads and full-length figures sit nicely in their framed fields. But especially the delicate, controlled coloring, the atmospheric freshness—plus,

of course, faithfulness to a model—are the things that count.

Already in the time of the *Breda* picture the painter was studying light effects and advancing beyond the technical formulas developed by his predecessors. There is steady progress thereafter toward a thinning of medium. The brushwork as such disappears. Color creeps into the faces, and there is unprecedented delicacy in the nuances. The portrait becomes alive, subtly appealing, in a new way—foreshadowing, indeed, the sweet harmonies of Whistler and Manet. Because he advanced beyond Titian and El Greco in detecting varicolored vibration in shadows, which were still, in general, painted black, Velázquez has been called "the first impressionist." But whereas the nineteenth-century leaders of impressionism were to develop a method of painting in "pure color," without a marked structure of dark-light, thus achieving a brilliant vibrancy unknown before, Velázquez developed his color-harmonies within a scheme almost somberly dark. His virtue is in a freshness and transparency of color veiled in harmonies of gray and silver and pearl.

In general his portraits are outwardly conceived, objective. He presents his subjects without analysis or commentary. But on rare occasions he did get down to psychological reality, even to criticism. During a second sojourn of two years in Italy, 1649–51, when he had been internationally recognized as a leading portraitist, Pope Innocent X insisted upon sitting to him. When the artist had finished a preliminary oil sketch, revealing the shrewd, hard character beneath the outward visage, His Holiness winced and then exclaimed, "Too true!"

As so often happens when an artist is obsessed with the idea of verisimilitude, the two extant sketch paintings of Innocent X are superior in some ways to the finished and elaborate version. The head in the National Gallery at Washington and the head-and-shoulders sketch in the Gardner Museum at Boston come near to being in the very first rank of portraits. The completed painting, in the Doria Palace, Rome, suffers from the meticulously exact treatment of chairback, hands, paper, and lacy apron. Something of the unity and concentration is there lost.

Unfortunately it was naturalism that most often controlled Velázquez' hand when he painted his celebrated gallery of characters at King Philip's court—particularly the buffoons and dwarfs, the hoop-skirted ladies, and the armored gentlemen. An interesting novelty is Las Meninas in the Prado Museum in Madrid. It is a view of the artist's studio during a sitting of the King and Queen for a portrait, though the picture is centered upon the Infanta. It is interesting as a visual "arrangement" and interesting as a puzzle—for the observer must discover or be told that Their Majesties appear only vaguely, in a mirror.

In the end it is best to return to the simplest heads, or to bits in the larger canvases, noting the fresh-air aspect and the flower-like coloring, the sometimes exquisite arrangement and the felicitous smoothness. Ultimately, indeed, the joy to be had in Velázquez will assuredly be found in the "slighter" pictures, with their silvery and grayed tonal effects and their exquisite adjustment of parts.

Very famous, however, is the so-called Rokeby Venus in the National Gallery, London, the only female nude known to have been executed in Spain up to this time. The picture was painted after Velázquez' second Italian visit, and obviously under the influence of the Giorgione-Titian school. It fails by a very great deal to match the works of the Venetian masters—although no one can fail to see that the young lady as such has excellent points. In this late period of his life, too, Velázquez returned to religious story-pictures, not very happily.

Originality, indeed, had never been this artist's forte. Aside from the development of that one individual virtue, his fresh-colored, pearly manner of painting, Velázquez did little to rank him above the average successful court painter. For a time, in recent generations, other painters were inclined to find a "faultless purity" in his method. But it was a thing of method rather than of substance.

Velázquez seems to have been forgotten by the world within a quarter-century after his death in 1660, and his fame slept until well into the nineteenth century. Then the proponents of impressionism rediscovered his innovations, and a generation avid for realism in all its forms raised him to a place beside Raphael and Vermeer, among the foremost popular masters. Now again fewer pilgrims are to be found at his shrine. He is today accounted high among the masters installed a notch below Titian, El Greco, and the other titans of painting.

If Velázquez suffered eclipse, his contemporary Murillo, also a Sevillian and younger by a few years, had better luck until the twentieth century. Enormously popular during his lifetime, he held his own during the eighteenth and nineteenth centuries. He specialized in two types of art precious to the sentimental-minded: sweetened versions of religious story-painting, faultlessly natural; and genre studies of gutter life.

The religious canvases are likely to be laid out in the tradition of the grand manner; but the Madonnas are local girls—very sweet and appealing, too, though given overmuch to rolling their

Velázquez: *Pope Innocent X. Isabella Stewart Gardner Museum, Boston*

eyes heavenward—and the cupids are chubby, perky babes out of the home cradles. In the later periods the *Immaculate Conceptions,* of which there are twenty, exhibit the figures floating in vaporous mists in what used to be considered a poetic vagueness.

The gutter studies are done with a purpose quite opposite to that of the slum realists of Naples. Although the children are obviously gamins, they are miraculously washed and pretty. The method is naturalistic, with every grape and toenail separately and completely limned, but all that might be unpleasant in the background is omitted. Life for Murillo, whether that of the Madonnas and angels or of the town orphans, was something to be sweetened by paint. No other romantic ever put into canvases so many girls and babies and cupids, so many lambs and doves.

Today the bubble of Murillo's fame has burst. It is seen that the figures are posed, that the subjects are sentimentalized; the "masterly" painting is recognized as surface craftsmanship of an academic order. No other painter so long praised as immortal has fallen into eclipse with such rapidity. One hears oftenest now the adjectives "insipid" and "superficial." At least two histories of European art have appeared without picturing his works, and one fails even to mention him. His two-hundred-year reign as an accepted master is, however, in itself a phenomenon not a little illuminating; as also are the places of honor still given his canvases in not altogether provincial museums. He lacks, more than any other recently revered artist, the plastic strength and the imaginative content by which the modern observer judges visual art.

For the rest, there was in seventeenth-century Spain Velázquez' son-in-law and helper, Juan Bautisto del Mazo, who was next in line as court painter, a competent but uninspired portraitist and one of the earliest Spanish landscape painters. His name has been the more bandied about by critics because he made copies of many of Velázquez' pictures, so that great difficulty has arisen over which canvases are from the master's hand, which from the clever copyist's (and which, perchance, are to be attributed to both).

The next court painter, Juan Carreño de Miranda, has more claim to mention for his own work. But already Spanish painting was comparatively lifeless, and was certainly unoriginal. When the Bourbon kings displaced the Habsburgs, in 1700, imported artists were to take the court position; and well into the eighteenth century there was no notable painting. Goya blazed across the Spanish sky before the century was done—but he belongs to a later era, a foreign tradition.

In architecture Spain continued to follow the changes in style of general European practice, but with a stubborn clinging to national singularities. It will be remembered that the church at Santiago de Compostela was (and is, in the interior features) one of the great monuments of Romanesque building, though the façade is now veiled over with a Spanish baroque fabric of a later period. The Gothic expression, too, had been adapted and generally dissociated from the "pure" French style. The Cathedral of Seville, the second largest Gothic church in the world, is of special interest on account of the detail work in the Spanish-Moorish tradition—and indeed the contribution of the Mudejar Moslems was determining through several generations. When Italian architecture was made over in the name of classicism, during the Renaissance, Spain accepted the style very slowly and—except when a monarch imported Italian designers—grudgingly. The most important development was a mode of design called "plateresque," from the word for silversmith, *platero,* signifying the fineness of the carving. In this agreeable style certain areas of a building were adorned with compositions, especially around and above doorways, divided into many panels separated by pilasters and moldings. Each panel was filled with low-relief sculpture, abstract or heraldic, conventional or freely pictorial. The all-over effect was richly decorative. As seen on the walls over the main portal of the university at Salamanca, the plateresque is at once distinctively Spanish and recognizably in direct lineage from Italian Renaissance forms. In the interiors of Spanish churches a special feature is the altar screen, and the plateresque principles contributed to making the screens appropriately flat but eye-filling and intricately delicate.

XXI: FLEMISH ART AND THE SPREAD
OF REALISM

IT WAS Michelangelo, a very great artist but little known as a critic, who gave expression to this illuminating estimate of Flemish art:

The paintings of Flanders please any pious person more than the paintings of Italy . . . not because Flemish art is effective or excellent, but because of the capacities of good people. It seems beautiful to women, especially to the very old and very young ones, as also to monks and nuns, and to a few persons of quality who are blind to rhythmic values. It is an anecdotal and sentimental art, which aims only at success and

obtains it easily, not by values of painting, but by the subject-matter. The painters select things that gladden one, particularly saints and pious figures, for which tears are always ready.

In Flanders, too, they paint to deceive the external eye. They delight in showing actual stuffs: bricks and ruins and rags, and grasses, and the shadowed fields with trees, rivers and bridges —these they call landscapes—with a great many figures here and there. All this is very popular: the least artistic intelligence can find therein something that appeals to it. An interest in facts, and two eyes alone are necessary. But, although

Van der Goes: *Four Shepherds*, detail. *Uffizi Gallery, Florence*

some people delight in it, in truth it is done without reason or art; it lacks rhythm or proportion; it shows no care in selecting or rejecting; it is innocent of artistic body and vitality. . . .

I do not consider all Flemish painting bad—in some other places it is far worse—but it tries to do too many things at once, each of which if attempted alone would suffice for a great work, so that it fails to do anything really well.

This opinion, we are told, was expressed in Rome, at a discussion held in the year 1538 or 1539, and Michelangelo's lovely Platonic friend, Vittoria Colonna, "undertook the defense of the religious and consolatory art of the North." That is fitting, too, for the great sculptor-painter had once said that oil painting was a less virile art, good only for women and sluggards. What is useful today—in the absence of Vittoria Colonna's rebuttal—is to note how infallibly Michelangelo put his finger upon every weakness of Flemish art.

Allowing for Michelangelo's stormy nature and his overpowering conviction as a creative artist, remembering that his own genius was for those very qualities that the Northern painters lacked —grandeur, plastic aliveness, and symphonic fullness—granting therefore that he may have overlooked a certain virtue that lies in doing smaller things surpassingly well, one may accept his criticism of Flemish art as extraordinarily penetrating—as the best, if negatory, introduction to it.

For the truth is that the widely celebrated paintings of the van Eycks, van der Weyden, and Memling *are* small, external, and only minutely realistic. The early Flemish painters were so interested in doing a little thing well that they entirely overlooked some of the big things that go to make up supremely effective art. Their aim *was* to deceive the external eye; their subjects *were* chosen to please easily; they *did* put in so many little things, and so fail to choose any for emphasis, that interest often wastes away in a sea of perfections. But they were geniuses in their chosen miniature mode.

If it be womanish to delight in these delicate and transcriptive things—and, one notes, it is

seldom men who gaze through the magnifying glasses sometimes placed beside the van Eyck canvases in art museums—then let us remember that there are women enough among museum-goers. Nor has anyone, despite the lesser place commanded by realism in recent art appreciation, established the point at which devotion to realism makes painting negligible.

Realism was the established European type of art from the fifteenth to the nineteenth century. Flemish art affords material for an early and a determining chapter in the record of this type. It is to be remembered, in taking up the painting of the van Eycks, that one is returning to the year 1400, when in Italy only the sculptors had cultivated the "camera eye." Although the painters of the South were to take a full century thereafter to perfect "the new vision" (Masaccio's dates are 1401-1428, Leonardo's 1452-1519), the van Eycks seem to have leaped forward to the most meticulous documentary illustration during the actual afternoon of Gothic practice, at the very beginning of the fifteenth century.

It is to Gothic practice that one turns to detect the promise and the beginnings of this triumph of the natural. There are roots in two arts, manuscript illumination and sculpture. The miniatures of the thirteenth century, in general, held to their formalism as inherited from Byzantine iconography and abstraction. They were on the side of decoration, symbolism, and convention. But in the fourteenth century pictorialism and naturalism had crept in.

Just as in late Gothic sculpture an objective interest had entered, based perhaps upon a newly awakened delight in the works of nature, so in illuminations one begins to see, in the fourteenth century, geometrical lines branching and bursting into leaf, and latticed fields splitting to admit here a bird, there a mermaid—often unrelated to anything in the text. As these fanciful but "real" innovations became commoner, the old sense of the miniature as decoration progressively disappeared. The idea of space-filling as a fundamentally plastic art weakened; the idea of faithful illustration advanced.

A hundred illuminated texts might be brought

Miniatures,
Turin Book of Hours.
Ascribed to Jan van Eyck

into exhibition, showing every step from abstract and conventionalized design to naturalistic, detailed illustration. But two masterpieces will serve as well at the moment: one, an English psalter of the fourteenth century, instancing the decorative mode elaborated and embellished with natural figures, flowers, and birds (see page 281); the other a page from the *Turin Book of Hours,* wherein illumination has become illustration—probably at the hand of Jan van Eyck. The panel picture reproduced above is crowded with detail. The people are "real."

Sculpture—which in Italy, it will be remembered, in the innovations of Ghiberti and Donatello, had anticipated the Masaccian advance by a century—had in France also turned natural to a measurable extent. In Burgundy the late Gothic carvers had eased out of their art the medieval "distortion" in favor of rational state-

ment. The Low Countries were in 1400 a part of the Burgundian domain, and intercourse between Dijon and Bruges was close and frequent.

From the rudimentary Flemish frescoes and panel-painting of the thirteenth and fourteenth centuries there was evidently little influence; but the *opportunity* to push realism to a new exactitude did come from development within the art, from technical advances. For some generations experiments had been made with oil as a color-base, as against the stiffer and more sticky tempera. The van Eycks—long reported to have invented oil painting, but now known to have picked up a medium occasionally used by earlier painters—perfected the method and were the first to utilize it in the service of the new vision, to which its fluidity and smoothness particularly suited it.

Their own effects, so jewel-like, may have

Pieter Brueghel: *A Dark Day. Kunsthistorisches Museum, Vienna*

been influenced by the enamels so popular in medieval Europe. The hard, brilliant finish and, in the portraits especially, a lingering flatness of composition, would suggest some vague affinity. Nevertheless, of all the influences cited to account for the comparatively sudden emergence of the early fifteenth-century oil painting of Flanders, one must go back to illumination as standing first. A glance through any collection of fifteenth-century panel-paintings suffices to emphasize the likeness to the advanced miniatures of the books of hours, psalters, and missals of the preceding hundred years. Indeed, the virtues of illumination—now become illustration—are exactly those of the independent painting: minute depiction and colorful picturing, documentation exhaustively detailed, and homely characterization. It was not until the time of Bosch and Brueghel that these values, essentially those of a small art enlarged by artists still small-minded, were notably transcended.

Flanders, for the purposes of art history, is that part of the Low Countries today embraced in Belgium. The Dutch, differentiated in later records as belonging to Holland, the present Netherlands, richly contributed to the Flemish flowering of art before their own cities supported schools and studios. Of the fifteenth-century group of "Flemish masters," Dirk Bouts and Gerard David and Petrus Christus were born Dutchmen. They naturally went to Bruges, as the art capital of all the Low Countries, for schooling and apprenticeship first, and then for a market.

Bruges was a rich and progressive city, one of the great seaports of the world, a center of commercial intercourse and a scene of pageantry and colorful ceremony. Flanders boasted other prospering cities, Louvain, Ypres, Brussels, and Ghent. A little later Antwerp was to rise as Bruges declined. All these communities knew the glories of Gothic art. They had long since been recognized as manufacturers of the most popular tapestries of the Western world.

Here democracy (of a plutocratic sort) was more advanced than in the war-torn Latin countries. The third estate already was strong; there was a burning civic pride; and on holidays a large number of burghers swaggered about in the vel-

Dirk Bouts: *Madonna and Child. Bache Collection, Metropolitan Museum of Art*

vets and laces once reserved to nobles of the royal courts and to church dignitaries. In short, there was a bourgeois aristocracy and it was ready for art—especially for realistic art.

It happened that the Low Countries belonged to the Dukes of Burgundy. In late Romanesque days, and in Gothic, the Burgundians had been noteworthy artists; we have already seen them as

Rogier van der Weyden:
Philip the Good.
Antwerp Museum

far afield as Spain. The court was art-conscious, and there was an interchange between Bruges and Dijon. Matching this royal example at the top, there was at the bottom a guild system that worked not only to stabilize conditions (and profits) for the artists but to insist upon honest materials—lasting colors, for instance—and to assure the soundest craftsmanship, based on a normal seven-years' apprenticeship. In short, art was a worker-controlled industry within a prosperous community numbering both royal and rich-burgher patrons.

The Renaissance was, of course, in the self-sufficient Flanders of the fifteenth century, nothing more than a rumor from the South. There were no classical ruins to be dug up; hence no confusing cross-currents of theory, demanding Greek harmony or Roman lifelikeness. Nor had the scientific passion been awakened in the workaday Flemish breast. The realism here was

Gothic, childlike, external. The painting grew direct out of Flemish and Burgundian illustration, in a way shaped by the forthright character of the stolid citizenry.

The Nature of Flemish Art

Here, then, are neither the sweet melodies of the Sienese nor the symphonic grandeurs of the Venetians. Michelangelo, who had said, "Painting is the music of God, the outpouring of His radiant perfection," found Flemish painting empty of everything that makes art transcendent. It is not that the Flemings neglect the religious themes; their most ambitious works are altarpieces and reliquary panels and church paintings. But they fill them with *Hausfrauen* and Low Country burghers and peasants in their Sunday clothes, and trees, flowers, grasses, dogs, carpets,

Petrus Christus: *Dionysius the Carthusian. Bache Collection, Metropolitan Museum*

furniture, and buildings, all so meticulously portrayed that there is no room for the larger conceptions and aspirations. We may well believe that their eyes were directed downward as they shaped their *Adorations* or *Crucifixions*; that their interest really was in those accessories which

Jan van Eyck:
Portrait of the Artist's Wife.
Communal Museum, Bruges

they depicted so minutely, in the texture of hair and velvet and armor, in the hang and lie of drapery, in the leaves of the tree, the swelling hills, the distant towers—which together "they call landscapes."

All emphasis is on what is seen with the intent outward eye, and on the precision with which that can be recorded. This painting is the commonplace discovered and glorified with competency by artists with good consciences and good digestions. It is the earthy made to seem fresh because observed with a new and clear-eyed accuracy and presented with unparalleled delicacy. If it is petty, at least it has the virtue of the homely and familiar. One is disarmed by the very cleanness and unpretentiousness of it.

If Italian art had not slipped so soon into grandiosity and futile academism one would say confidently that the Italian was incomparably the better way. But at least these Northern painters did not go into art in the self-conscious manner that is proclaimed by most of the second-rate reborn Italians, that led to a sterile rhetoric. The Flemings observed honestly; their intention was small; in small and honest effects they are supreme.

It is not only the emphasis on objective detail that announces the littleness of their intention and interests—that, too, but with it there is a neglect of larger coherence. For though a wrinkled face and a workworn hand may both be depicted with consummate documentation, there is no reality in the relationship between them. The face is essentially a face and not part of a three-dimensional head. And when, rarely, the Flemings attempted a nude, it is—well, terrible. It is an added-together record of the variously observed parts of some local man or woman, usually overfed or broken down, without sense of a dignity of the whole, without a rhythmic beauty of the body that artists elsewhere have recognized and sometimes immortalized. (The very celebrated St. Bavon altarpiece at Ghent was known in its own time not by its right name, *The Adoration of the Lamb,* but as the "Adam and Eve altar," by reason of the unusualness of the two naked figures, depicted in side panels, and the

Hubert van Eyck: *Adoration of the Lamb. St. Bavon Church, Ghent*

fascination they evoked among the worshipers.)

Beyond this objective shortcoming there is that of method and plastic manipulation. The painters *built* their pictures small-mindedly. They did not know how to compose in the large. The central panel of the St. Bavon altarpiece, by Hubert van Eyck—which has other virtues—is laid out with only the most elementary symmetry, and it is plastically negative: without focus, with no main motive, with no indicated track for the eye. There is nothing in the composition to draw attention to the whole before the parts become apparent and are counted over. Either the bits are equally played up or the emphasis is by chance. It is because of this lack of rhythmic generalization, of plastic organization, that the small pictures, portraits particularly, are likely to please us more than the ambitious religious paintings—except in the case of those among us who especially value minutely documentary and complexly representational rendering.

It is noteworthy that, although this is realism of the extreme sort sometimes termed naturalism, it differs in both conception and method from the slowly emerging realism of the Renaissance Italians. The Flemings advanced by copying what they saw with a marvelous fidelity and with meticulous craftsmanship. In Italy, instead, it was the intellect that was awakened, more than the natural eye. Masaccio and Pollaiuolo and Leonardo were off on a search for *laws* of representation; and science was worshiped, particularly in the names of anatomy and perspective. One does not hear that the Flemish artists dissected cadavers. Their knowledge was objective, their art compounded of many seen things added together.

There is something uncritical, trusting, and childlike about Flemish painting, and one does well to approach it, for enjoyment, in that spirit or not at all. If one is going to retain memories of the organ tones of Michelangelo or Tintoretto or El Greco, or of the melodic and spiritual inspiration of Duccio and Fra Angelico, the paler virtues of these homely panels will dissipate. But granted the many-sidedness of art, and of the enjoyment it affords, anyone can find a pleasure in the faithful patience, the impeccable miniature craftsmanship, and the diverting characterizations.

At its best—say, in Jan van Eyck's *The Madonna of Chancellor Rolin* or in van der Weyden's *Portrait of a Lady* or Petrus Christus' monk —this art is characterized by an appealing fragile loveliness. Once, in his picture of *The Marys at the Sepulcher*, Hubert van Eyck transcended the limitations of his school and produced a complex picture with adequate relationship of large and small, with organizational strength added to a rich array of minor facts. And in a final phase, when realism was no longer self-consciously insistent, a genius, Brueghel, was to enlarge the Flemish idiom and paint local pictures with universal sweep and organizational power.

The very little known about Hubert van Eyck affords scant light on the reasons for his artistic eminence and tells nothing of the sources of his inspiration and artistry. He was born about 1365, it is thought, in a remote village beyond the Dutch border, named Maaseyck, whence his name. He probably received training at a studio in nearby Maastricht. He seems to have moved early to Ghent, and there he died in 1426.

Jan van Eyck was supposedly twenty years younger. It is known definitely that he moved from Bruges to Lille in 1425 by order of Philip III, Duke of Burgundy; he was then *"varlet de chambre et peintre de mon dict seigneur."* And of Jan there are numerous records, many in regard to payments from the duke, sometimes for his work as painter, sometimes for secret or open missions to foreign countries. (It will be remembered that he introduced Flemish ideals and methods into Spain in 1429.) There are notations also of payments from the municipality of Bruges for painting and gilding statues and tabernacles on the front of the city hall, and an entry concerning completion in 1432 of the polyptych of *The Adoration of the Lamb,* upon which Hubert had been engaged at the time of his death six years earlier. Jan died in 1441, an honored and widely known artist.

The paintings left by the brothers afford the more eloquent record. They testify that the two artists leaped forward, at a time when painting around them was still "primitive" and conventional, to camera-eye naturalness. They partook of a new curiosity about nature and they perfected a means of expression flawless and superficially brilliant. In the foreground of Hubert's *The Marys at the Sepulcher* the various little flowers can be recognized by the botanist as nettle and iris, mullein and teasel, so exact is the rendering; and every bit of cloth, embroidery, metal helmet, or marble surface is perfectly characterized as to texture and "feel." No less distinctly detailed (though historically a poor guess) is the

city of Jerusalem in the distance. There is even a flight of geese across the cloud-flecked sky.

One remembers, too, that in the picture there is a Roman soldier asleep against the front of the tomb. That he is studied directly from a local peasant is obvious, but the greater significance is in the fact that he is thoroughly individualized. At this time in Italy the faces in Masaccio's pictures still were type studies. They had begun to show appropriate emotion, but all were variations of one model, or of a generalized conception of Man. Filippo Lippi's characters, two or three decades later, caused a stir because they were "like the Prior's niece," or suggested the breathless fellow "fresh from his murder," or "folks at church." But here already in the North the van Eycks had come to this familiar characterization and were far more true to the exact surface individualization of it than Fra Lippo would ever be; and they added botanical and geological and sartorial exhibits, equally exact in characterization, to the human.

The Marys at the Sepulcher is now generally ascribed to Hubert van Eyck rather than to Jan, for reasons more important to the experts than to the casual student. If the ascription is right, Hubert was the superior artist, for seldom did an early Flemish painter so well contrive the structure of an ambitious picture. The relationship of figures, the concentration of interest, the transition from foreground group to background elements—all these are managed with mastery hardly hinted at in most of the complex panels of the era. The background, moreover, is an advance upon anything in the art of painting in Europe up to this time: there is nowhere, so early, a landscape so detailed and in itself so handsome.

Of other paintings ascribed to Hubert the most celebrated are the center panel of the St. Bavon altarpiece, known as *The Adoration of the Lamb;* and two panels depicting *The Crucifixion* and *The Last Judgment,* now in the Metropolitan Museum of New York. All three are typical in their minute naturalism and their microscopic dexterity. An illuminating note in the Museum catalogue indicates how revolutionary was the advance Hubert van Eyck had made from the old symbolic-formalistic painting: "The Cruci-

Robert Campin: *Annunciation. Brussels Museum*

fixion is conceived as an execution, with the brutal or curious or idle onlookers which such a spectacle would attract. The Mother of God is a poor, broken old woman whose son has been put to death before her eyes. There are countless figures in the picture and each is a real person actuated by his particular feelings and circumstances."

Jan van Eyck depicts the wrinkles of an old face or the threads of an embroidered edging even more painstakingly, if that is possible, than does Hubert. He is more than likely, however, to let a bit of patiently and lovingly worked out detail draw attention from those parts on which the eye might better be focused. In *The Madonna of Chancellor Rolin,* one of his richest paintings, the floor detail in the foreground, the windows at the sides, and the elaborate vista at the back all suc-

ceed in pulling away the gaze that earlier or later painters want concentrated upon the middle-ground figures. It is a picture full of a great number of things extraordinarily well painted, but its very virtues disperse its compositional unity. It is rather in his portraits that Jan van Eyck is happiest. Hugo van der Goes, born in the year of Jan van Eyck's death, carried Jan's exactitude of facial rendering to the pitch seen in the plate on page 429.

Robert Campin is sometimes bracketed with the van Eycks, his contemporaries, as an initiator of Flemish realism. He lacked nothing of their characteristic minuteness of depiction; he is also a victim of his own sharply drawn minor detail; and there is a suggestion of woodenness in many of the works ascribed to him. He is sometimes identified as "The Master of Flémalle," or as

Rogier van der Weyden: *Portrait of a Lady.*
Mellon Collection, National Gallery, Washington

"The Master of Mérode," and there is some doubt about the attributed pictures. In any case *The Annunciation* at Brussels is one of the most rewarding things of the period.

It was Rogier van der Weyden, a pupil of Campin's, who introduced a fresh note. His *Portrait of a Lady* in the Mellon Collection marks a distinctive achievement within Flemish painstaking

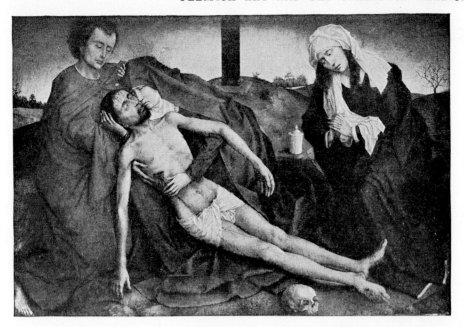

Rogier van der Weyden: *Deposition from the Cross. Brussels Museum*

portraiture. Here is masterly planning of the larger areas in relation to the frame. There is a generalized harmony and a sweet linear grace. While there are not many things in van der Weyden's work, or in surviving Flemish painting, that approach the felicitous harmony of this portrait, the quality is implicit if less marked, in a number of the artist's other compositions: notably the *Madonna and Child* in the Huntington Collection, and the *Portrait of Philip the Good* at Antwerp (page 434). Even in a larger religious composition, the *Crucifixion* in the Johnson Collection at Philadelphia, one finds the same fresh crispness and rhythmic grace. One notes, too, that the background is washed clean of all those supplementary details so much insisted upon by Jan van Eyck.

Van der Weyden's advance is graphically illustrated in two versions of *The Deposition from the Cross*. The later one, in the Brussels Museum, is simplified, rendered coherent, and, as a painter would say, generally pulled together, as compared with an early, more detailed rendering. It is instructive to note how the background vistas—so beloved by most Flemish painters of the time, and so destructive of the formal structure, of

focus—are suppressed, how the minutiae of the costumes are veiled, to what extent detail disappears. It is an object lesson in the way of a master who picks up the valuable knowledge uncovered by his associates, but integrates it to his own vision and selects from it to his own ends.

A new way of art was born with the van Eycks and was thus beautifully enlarged and refined within a quarter-century by van der Weyden. The half-dozen painters who were their contemporaries or followers repeated, in general, their achievements, sometimes slavishly, occasionally with distinctive variations. There was in Flanders an unusual tradition of what Sir Martin Conway, the English art historian, terms "systematic borrowing." Dirk Bouts fails to suppress detail—is too often a victim of the current naturalism—and his figures are likely to be angular or attitudinized; but the gallery-goer now and again stumbles upon an interestingly rewarding picture of his, such as the *Madonna* illustrated on page 433.

Petrus Christus in his larger pictures is likely to lose his protagonists among accessories; but there are portraits from his hand which have simple grace and a smooth elegance. He is more than usually, too, a builder of inner pictorial structure.

Hans Memling:
Legend of St. Ursula:
Arrival at Basel.
Hospice of St. John, Bruges

It has been suggested that both van der Weyden and Petrus Christus gained, in this matter of compositional solidity, by contacts with Italian painting. Certainly some broadening influence had entered by the time of van der Goes, who in turn influenced the Italians. But it was Hans Memling who did most to reconcile the ideals and methods of the two schools. He was the foremost Flemish artist of the second half of the fifteenth century.

Memling, who may have been a German by birth, and perhaps also by training, lacks nothing of the Flemish microscopic fidelity, but he fuses one set of details to another with a fresh suavity. He softens the whole surface of his canvas with a sort of pervading hazy light, and his feeling for broader compositional values is distinctly Italianate. Nevertheless he remains primarily a Northern illustrator. There is a special serenity and a tenderness in his religious pictures. Favorite

among his works is the series of six reliquary panels illustrating the life of St. Ursula, at the Hospice of St. John in Bruges—given, legend says, by the artist because the nuns had nursed him back to health after he had crept to the hospice doors as a wounded soldier. The panels adorn a casket. The artist has rendered them as illustrations that might as gracefully adorn the pages of a contemporary manuscript of the lives of the saints. The ships and castles and cathedrals and city gates are those of Cologne and Basel.

The first cycle of Flemish painting closes with Gerard David, a follower of Memling who brought Dutch seriousness and placidity to his religious pictures. Bruges had declined as a commercial center, and artists were congregating in other cities. There is, however, a definite continuity of spirit and method from the van Eycks through van der Weyden and Memling to this last artist of the line. Almost any one of Gerard

Hans Memling:
Legend of St. Ursula:
Arrival at Cologne.
Hospice of St. John, Bruges

David's works, up to a late Italian period, will indicate how closely he adhered to the original minutely naturalistic method, how close is the spirit of this art to that of the fourteenth-century illuminators.

A New Cycle: A Larger Vision

Antwerp succeeded Bruges as the center of Flemish art endeavor, and at the time of the rebirth in the sixteenth century the typical Flemish realism had been further modified by Italian influences. The actual materials, as seen in architectural backgrounds up to this time, had been chiefly Gothic (as had been also the decorative picture-frames, with traceries that often encroached upon the picture field). Now the round arch and the classic molding crept in. There was a corresponding change in the conception of the picture, as examples by Quentin Matsys and Mabuse (otherwise Jan Gossaert) would testify, or others by Joos van Cleve and Adrian Isenbrandt.

As so often when national traditions are crossed, the result was in general destructive of conviction and distinction. And paintings enough from Matsys' hand, marked by the traditional Flemish accuracy and homely truth, seem only to dissipate those qualities in a pseudo-Italian grandeur. But occasional portraits, too impeccably craftsmanlike to be Italian, too strong and vital to be directly derived from fifteenth-century Flemish tradition, prove Matsys' mastery when he was not too receptive to the alien currents of fashion. More Italian is the *Mary Magdalen* of the Antwerp Museum, or the *Laying in the Tomb* of the same gallery. His larger compositions fail to reconcile the old minuteness with the new and ampler intention. He seems, from their evidence,

Joachim Patinir: *Rest on the Flight to Egypt. Johnson Collection, Philadelphia Museum*

to have got from the South an alien formula rather than an applicable inspiration.

Mabuse likewise adopted a great deal of Italian manner without understanding the true Renaissance spirit, and his Southern sojourn, in the train of Duke Philip of Burgundy, failed to bring warmth to his rather cold draftsmanship and frozen composition—perhaps because he studied especially the works of Leonardo da Vinci. He muffed the nudes, too, when he attempted them in the Italian fashion. It is necessary to go to his simple and sympathetic portraits to find undisturbed and distinctive enjoyment. The *Self-Portrait* at Liége is one of the best. In historical accounts he commands a place larger than that justified by his surviving works because he is a pivotal figure, symbolic of a change creeping over Northern art.

Lovers of landscape painting—of, say, Constable, Turner, Corot, and Cézanne—are sometimes surprised to learn that the genre hardly existed before the seventeenth century (except, of course, in the far Orient, then unknown to the West). The first great school of landscapists

was the Dutch, but incidentally the Flemings and Germans did most to establish the form. In particular Joachim Patinir, a contemporary of Matsys and Mabuse, and like them a member of the Antwerp school, detached, as it were, the topographical composition from the cluttering figure-groups, and glorified landscape on its own account.

It will be remembered what a long step Hubert van Eyck had taken, in *The Marys at the Sepulcher* and in his miniatures; that he had already given dignity and lifelikeness to the open-air backgrounds. Throughout the following century the landscape vista or backdrop held its place in Flemish painting; at the same time it was more slowly creeping into Italian, Spanish, and German painting. But Patinir's are the earliest "natural scenes" commonly accounted masterly and widely treasured on gallery walls. They have a distinctive clear coloring and a luminous atmosphere—and altogether a charm that has brought them a very special critical following.

In some of Patinir's landscapes there is a fanciful treatment of cliffs and trees, or of rivers and

Hieronymus Bosch: *The Prodigal Son. Boymans Museum, Rotterdam*

figures, which seems out of keeping with the sober Flemish tradition. It may be that Patinir got it from Hieronymus Bosch, a slightly older painter; or perhaps the debt was the other way round. In any case Bosch is the most unaccountable figure in the history of the Low Countries. He mixes the local realism with fantasy and invention, the sacred with the obscene, the accurately truthful portrait with the caricature, a primitive "distortion" with amazingly sensitive exactitude, the amusing with the sublime. Until recently he had been numbered foremost among the willful bad boys of art and generally dismissed by authorities with a line—"Too bad he wasn't serious." Perhaps his greatest claim upon our attention lies in his mastery of formal organization—a value generally neglected throughout the history of Flemish art. Suddenly, in this one artist's work, there is a return of design, of solid structure and weighted order. Few paintings are more compact, more securely interrelated in parts, than the best of Bosch's. They have, besides, sensitive finish, even a seductive fluency.

In some of his canvases there is a nightmare of confusion; there are also a great many creatures of an unnatural and invented sort known seldom outside the troubled realms of dream. But nothing could be more sober and reposeful than certain of the religious illustrations. Yet again a serious *Adoration* or a *Christ Carrying the Cross* may be peopled, off at the sides, with humorous rustics; or attention may be taken from the protagonists

Hieronymus Bosch: *The Garden of Eden. Art Institute, Chicago*

by the argument of two minor characters, satirically treated. Bosch's paintings were enormously popular not only at home but as far away as Madrid and Lisbon. Subsequently he was forgotten, and one may read a good half of the older art histories on library shelves and not encounter his name.

If Bosch ran off into hallucinations and artistic disorder at times, a greater master came, with a similar genius for pictorial organization, and took something of the satire, the sly or lusty humor, and the fancy, without the grotesqueness and the diableries: Pieter Brueghel. He was born about 1525, and, like Bosch, was a Hollander. He spent most of his working life in Antwerp and Brussels. Like the truest Flemings, he was first of all a painter of the time and for the people. They liked seeing themselves portrayed, gaucheries, foibles, and all; and they enjoyed his wit and his homely moralizing. But kings and courtiers appreciated his canvases, too. The Holy Roman Emperor Rudolf II became so enamored of them that he offered the weight of any of the artist's pictures in gold. The Vienna Museum therefore has fifteen of the most covetable of them to this day.

Truly Flemish, too, is Brueghel's bent for story-telling in pictures, with a great deal of minute detail. In other words, he was an illustrator. But his painting is illustration with a difference. For he was a visual constructor of surpassing imagination and skill. He transformed his anecdotal, literary, and documentary materials into superb pictorial orchestrations. So much was added, indeed, that Abraham Ortelius the Flemish geographer was led to remark: "Brueghel painted many things that the painters cannot paint."

Brueghel translated every scene into local idiom, and sometimes apparently forgot the parent idea almost completely. In the very fine *Icarus Falling into the Sea* (see page 448), the observer can by diligent search discover, down in one corner, Icarus' legs just disappearing into the water. But what a glorious seascape! And with what loving interest—and what broad yet sensitive artistry—is the foreground scene, with its familiar plowing and shepherding, accomplished! When Brueghel did the *Christ Carrying the Cross,* now in Vienna, he all but hid the figure of Jesus, while the characters in the crowd and the holiday-like bustle of the extraordinary

Pieter Brueghel: *The Hired Shepherd. Johnson Collection, Philadelphia Museum*

event are illustrated with much spirit and relish.

Although a painter of man in the widest and yet the minutest sense, Brueghel is one of the giants in the succession of artists who developed landscape. Even so broadly moralistic a picture as *The Blind Leading the Blind* shows the characters against a tenderly painted panoramic scene. In *The Hired Shepherd* one is likely to overlook the significance of figure and title—the literary and social, not to add humorous, values—while the luminous and spacious landscape is enjoyed. Before that, indeed, if the training in purely aesthetic values has been adequate, the observer's faculties will have leaped to intuitive pleasure in the sheer plastic values of the picture; for seldom are abstract elements of volume and plane, chiaroscuro and texture, more cunningly adjusted for visual rhythm and melodious movement.

Let the student of pictorial structure study well the compositional function of each of the three trees, as linear elements and as accenting three successive planes in recession (not missing the fact that each vertical has its corresponding horizontal line across the canvas at its base); the way

in which a diagonal line intersects the horizontal at the foot of the far tree; the corresponding diagonal formed by the bird on the branch, the wolf, and the shepherd's staff, reinforced by the darkened furrow; and finally the weight relationship between the figure and the distant copses, with the harmonious complex of lines interconnecting them. Brueghel's work is filled with this sort of organizational rhythm and counterpoint, marvelous to the art student, and for the rest of us appealing and melodiously satisfying.

If here a single figure dominates the canvas, other pictures—such as *The Massacre of the Innocents* and *The Wedding Dance*—exhibit scores or hundreds. Nor does the artist lose his way or impair the unity of impression. He accomplishes this partly by a device better known to Chinese than to Western painters: by adopting "a high viewpoint." The horizon line is raised and a panoramic effect is achieved, with greater pictorial compactness and security. *The Wedding Dance* (among the plates in color at the opening of the book) shows one of these panoramic scenes laid up in a fluid design, along with abundant human

Pieter Brueghel: *Icarus Falling into the Sea. Brussels Museum*

interest and humor in the detail. The devices suggesting movement are worth studying out.

If mural decoration had been a Northern rather than an Italian art, Brueghel would have been a master of fresco. One may call in testimony the *Adoration of the Kings* in the National Gallery, London, with its expert disposition of figures and its resolute holding of the eye to a shallow depth-range: an exceptional example of contrived organization. Here again, on the content side, one finds a serious story—one in other times and climes considered too sublime for any but idealized treatment—brought to terms with everyday, individually imperfect human beings. There is a world of interest in secondary things: in the king apparently nettled at kneeling, yet gingerly offering his gift, in the intently gazing soldier, in the boggle-eyed peasant at the right, and especially in the side drama of Joseph and the whisperer. The religious sentiment evaporates, of course, when one has gone the rounds of these character-bits; but one returns to the gorgeous rhythm of the whole with renewed interest. Since it fails to convey the theme-sentiment effectively, the picture *is* inferior to many another Brueghel canvas; but it illustrates exceptionally

the artist's mastery of space-filling, of mural technique, and his characterization that grows out of the original Flemish homely and naturalistic tradition.

There were several later Brueghels, but Pieter the Elder was never equaled, though his son of the same name left some pictures that approach his in panoramic interest. For the rest, some artists turned back to second-rate van Eyckian depiction, others imitated the Italians, and of course Bosch and Brueghel had their lesser followers. But the names are unimportant—until at the opening of the seventeenth century a youth trained in Antwerp by Italianized Flemings brilliantly pulled together several influences and manners which would seem mutually alien and unmixable and became the darling of all the courts of Europe: Peter Paul Rubens. But he was truly an internationalist, belonging to the Era of Great Kings, and he opened what is sometimes termed the Modern Age. He will grace better a chapter not concerned first with the humble if acute vision of Hubert van Eyck, and laudatory of the peasant witticisms, honest landscapes, and uncourtly grandeur of Brueghel.

If in the end one has said nothing of Flemish

Pieter Brueghel: *The Adoration of the Kings. National Gallery, London*

sculpture, it is because there had been little with distinctive character. From the thirteenth century on, endless figures had been carved, and around 1400 the Flemish sculptors had been called, with the illuminators, to France to work on schemes of the Dukes of Burgundy. Their products in general were unoriginal and inferior to those of the French. But the Holland-born Nicolas Gerhaert of Leiden was an outstanding figure among them, and in 1462 or 1463 went on to become master of the sculptors decorating the Strasbourg Cathedral. He came as near as anyone to establishing a thoroughgoing late Gothic realism. In Flanders excellence is to be looked for in the fine craftsmanship of relief carving, and in the pleasing all-over designs the figures are usually subordinated. There are rood screens where saints and angels seem to emerge amid delicate lacelike traceries of stone, and there are tombs where the effigy is seen merely as a central motif. But it was in the carving in wood of altar screens that sculptors produced their most notable works. Workshops in Brussels and Antwerp in the fifteenth and sixteenth centuries, when this expression attained its highest level, became celebrated and received commissions from churches all over Flanders, and from France, Germany, and the Scandinavian countries. Many of the screens were triptychs with a high central panel, and were set into a framework of carving of flamboyant Gothic design, often gilded. The panels were divided into numerous scenes with high-relief figures only less realistic and varied than those in the painted van Eyck altarpiece. The figures were often colored or enameled. Jan van Eyck comes into history as a colorer of such figures, and van der Weyden recorded going to Brussels to gild and color the carvings in the Carmelite church there.

In architecture the Gothic impulse continued into the sixteenth century. Some monuments in the style were then added to the treasure of medieval building, and some original solutions were arrived at in transitional Gothic-into-Renaissance design. Among the cathedrals, one of the most impressive is Ste. Gudule in Brussels, which is, however, mixed in early and late (flamboyant) design. The cathedral at Antwerp, largest of all, has one magnificent tower, terminated by a spire that is among the tallest in Europe.

Among the great town halls upon which the traditionally free Flemish cities of the Middle Ages continued to lavish money and loving care, that at Brussels represents the most logical design, and it, too, has a splendid spire which terminates its central tower. Town halls at Bruges and Audenarde are impressive but less consistent in design, and that at Louvain, adhering to sound basic principles of Gothic architecture, is fantastically overloaded with decorations. Even greater initiative and wealth were expended on the vast market halls of Flanders from the twelfth through the fifteenth century. Weaving was among the chief sources of Flemish wealth, and half a dozen rich industrial cities served as the trading centers for the cloth industry of all North Europe. It is not therefore surprising that the great cloth halls should survive as the most original type of Flemish building. The Cloth Hall at Ypres is still generally considered the world's most beautiful example of Gothic civic architecture.

For most art lovers, however, what comes to one's mind at mention of "Flemish art" is a type of painting, born in the literal exactness of the van Eycks, flowering in the harmonious and appealing Madonnas of Dirk Bouts and Rogier van der Weyden, and ending in the compositions, symphonic and yet earthy in a special way, of Bosch and Brueghel.

XXII: GOTHIC SURVIVALS AND
REFORMATION DEVELOPMENTS: GERMAN ART

IT IS SAID that when a Flemish painter visited Venice toward the end of the fifteenth century, and demonstrated the accuracy of delineation possible to the oil-painting medium as employed in the North, Giovanni Bellini, then the foremost master in the Italian city, disguised himself as a gentleman and sat to the visitor for his portrait. Thus the Venetian learned by observation the secrets of the Flemish method. He was particularly pleased because after that he was enabled to make human eyes look more natural.

When Albrecht Dürer of Germany went to Venice in 1506, the elderly Bellini observed that another Northern school excelled in a different detail of naturalism. He had never seen hair rendered with the exactitude and delicacy evident in the works of the Nuremberg master. Dürer having with native graciousness begged that he be permitted to cooperate with the Venetian artists, Bellini asked outright for the special brush he used in the painting of hairs. Dürer

was constrained to take up his common brushes and demonstrate then and there that it was the mastery of the hand and not of the instrument that made possible the effect. "I wouldn't have believed it if I hadn't seen it," commented Bellini —and he painted more believable hairs the rest of his life, and gained something else, too, for his followers Giorgione and Titian.

To complete the triangle, one may note that Dürer spent a considerable term in Antwerp, absorbing more of those influences which had already been felt in Cologne and Ulm and other German centers. Thus is made clear the internationalism of art at this time. The brief hour of German mastery occurred when this interchange of knowledge and impulse among the Christian nations of Europe was beginning. The Flemings had perfected the new miniature realism; Venice was giving fresh release to the spirit of the Italian Renaissance; and each culture was curious about the other. And Germany was on the trade

Cranach: *Double Portrait, Electors of Saxony. Uffizi Gallery, Florence* routes that lay between Antwerp and Venice.

German art, restricted and only locally important before 1475, retained a native character during the next sixty years, but became peculiarly the expression of an impulse common to all of Northern Europe; was an extension of the typical Northern Gothic, if you like, worked upon but not absorbed by Italian Renaissance ideology.

Dürer was the foremost artist of the time. But for the student he is even more. Dürer the internationalist is also Dürer solidly and incorruptibly Germanic. He is, incidentally, one of the most gracious personalities in the annals of art.

There was a moment when German art trembled upon the verge of a great synthesis. Had the wars of the Reformation not cut off the possibility of continuance, driving artists to other lands or destroying in youth those who should have been painters and sculptors, the German tradition instead of the Italian might later have prevailed in Europe, from the late sixteenth to the nineteenth century. As it was, the true German spirit found expression, in any manner important to the rest of the world, in only a single generation. The work-life of every memorable native painter— Dürer, Cranach, Baldung, Grünewald, Holbein —falls within the period 1495-1550, barely over a half-century of accomplishment. Then the Protestant-Catholic disorders and finally the Thirty Years' War bathed the country in blood, made Germany inimical to art. The reformers were not content to curb further production of pictures; they fanatically burned and smashed vast numbers of paintings and statues.

In that half-century, however, a distinctive national mode of expression had been established. Cranach was an essentially German painter, and so were Baldung and Grünewald. Dürer and the Little Masters at the same time created copper-plate prints never rivaled for brilliancy and vigor. Holbein and his fellows added a capital chapter to the history of wood-engraving.

All the sources were drawn upon: Gothic France, Franciscan Siena, independently creative Flanders, and the cities of Renaissance Italy. Nevertheless, there is in, say, Dürer's *The Four Horsemen* or Grünewald's *Crucifixion* something patently German, something of the vigor and the directness of statement that had characterized the art of Central Europe in the Dark Ages, when across this territory passed the tribes that fertilized the art of the North in Scandinavia, of the West in England and Ireland, of the South in Lombardy and Spain. If Gothic is the name given especially to the development that centered in France, Germany was earlier the home of the Goths and carried on the style after French medievalism had given way to the siren spirit of the South.

The German cities were medieval in character, and the German painter was just another craftsman, not the honored celebrity that the Flemish artist had become, or the Venetian. It is from Dürer's journals that the clearest light is cast on the conditions of the time. Many are his references to the higher position he was accorded when away from his native land. "Here I am somebody," he exclaims in Venice, "while at home I am counted a parasite." But back he goes to his own community and his accustomed work, his eyes opened to new vistas, but without foolish notions that German art must be Italianized.

Again, he records the details of a trip to Flanders. He has worked hard on his engravings, and his wife has hawked the prints from stalls at the fairs, for which he has received a few coins. But in the Low Countries he finds himself fêted and honored. He is astonished at the lavishness both of the banquet and of the praise heaped upon him in Antwerp, when the painters there entertain him at the Guild Hall:

On Sunday night, the fifth of August, the painters invited me to their house together with my wife and her maid. The entire service was of silver and there were other handsome decorations. . . . The food was most costly. All the wives of the painters were present at the company. I was seated at the head and they, at either side, as though I were a great lord. All did everything possible to be agreeable to me, and when I was seated thus with such honor the magistrate of Antwerp came with two servants and presented me with four jars of wine in the name of the city council, offering me every good wish. Afterward came the master of the carpenters and presented me with two more jars, offering

View of Ulm, with Minster Church, illustrating persisting Gothic aspect

me his good offices. Thus we passed a pleasant evening until very late, and all the company accompanied us to our lodgings with lanterns in great honor.

Nuremberg, with its gabled houses, its crooked streets, its markets, and its guilds, may be visualized as the typical city of Germany at the time of art's awakening: still a medieval city in every lineament. Here world paths crossed, to be sure, but life went on in the old ways; the craftsman did his work well and remained anonymous; the community was piously Catholic—although there was already some agitation against the licentiousness and godlessness at Rome.

There are paradoxes and puzzles here. The Protestant spirit retarded the spread of Renaissance culture in Central Europe; yet the intellectual independence of the revolting churchmen can be seen as resulting only from the mental freedom that is essentially of the Renaissance. The Northern churchmen distrusted the artists, if only because the Popes had made such showy —and often profane—use of art at Rome, in the Vatican Palace and in St. Peter's and in a dozen

cardinals' palaces. Yet Dürer with his prints, and the cutters of woodblock illustrations, probably did more to popularize Christian illustration than any other artists in history.

Such is the confusion encountered when one asks what were the forces, social, religious, and political, which expressed themselves in the works of Altdorfer, of Dürer, of Cranach. There was medievalism quickened by something out of the Renaissance, but resisting everything that the Italian Renaissance had become; a distinctive native expression vital and original enough to place the people among the foremost creators of art, yet an expression that was cut off in a single generation.

Perhaps it is that in this brief hour the German mind escaped the old mental fetters, just at the moment when German craftsmanship came to full flower. For a moment the freedom to think, the freedom to criticize, was attained, and the creative release came. Then too quickly the Reformation was accomplished and other prohibitions settled upon the artist.

As for the German *land*, it is implicit in this

Christ in the Garden,
by an unknown artist,
Lower Rhine School,
about 1500.
Johnson Collection,
Philadelphia Museum

art: particularly the forests and the Rhineland— the curiously broken landscapes, the winding rivers, the hilltop castles, but, above all, the forests. Gothic art had always retained something of the forest spirit. Dürer carried that on. When he discovered nature as an aid to art, as its new source—as the Flemings had so suddenly discovered their fields and flowers and trees, as the Italians had haltingly discovered theirs—he put into his pictures the actual crags and castles and woodland trees. But the forest is in his pictures in a deeper sense. Its upright line, its dark and shade, its restless minor movement, all have a counterpart in his method and conception.

The German city, too, whether Nuremberg or Rothenburg or Augsburg, is in the graphic art. Look from the high-gabled houses, the crooked streets, and the angular walls to almost any one

of Dürer's engravings, and you can note the same wandering line, the identical angular movement and vitality. By contrast, place a German engraving beside a photograph of an Italian arcade or a neoclassic palace façade, and note how utterly unlike is the spirit of one work from that expressed in the other.

German art remains through its flowering a Northern art. It is still Gothic, yet born anew out of its own land, in perfect keeping with its architectural environment and its landscape. Nowhere in it, except possibly in Holbein, who alone forsook Germany, is the serene horizontal line dominant. The poise of the German picture is that born of complex movement delicately organized, with more of vertical than of horizontal accent.

Behind it all, no doubt, are the dark German

Cranach:
*Night in the Garden
of Gethsemane.*
Art Institute, Chicago

philosophy and the German intellectual restlessness and analytical curiosity. The sensuous and formal values are not lacking—else in the modern view this would not basically be art—but they commonly and essentially subserve idea and subjective statement. This art is emotional—degenerating into sentimentalism in later centuries—or it is philosophical. Nowhere else is the *Dance of Death,* with its juxtaposition of bright and macabre themes, so common a subject. It is art exploring life, with death often enough walking beside life; seldom art contrived to soothe or to

Cranach: *Adam and Eve. Antwerp Museum*

afford escape or to be art merely as ornament.

It is mystical to the extent that second meanings are inbuilt. Beyond the trees is the murmur from the depths of the forest. Above the portrait is a whisper of the seriousness of living. There is a good deal of the Faustian ever-seeking, in both canvas and print. A body of art could hardly be farther from Greek (and Italian) clarity of statement and simple interest in the human form and idealized types. Equally alien to its analytic spirit is that other Italian development, "the grand style," with its empty rhetoric and windy decorativeness.

There was in Germany, of course, the late Gothic or early Renaissance awakening to the beauties of nature, which was common to all Europe. The native curiosity gave this swing to realism its own special direction, so that the German development of accuracy in depicting flower and bird or landscape or human features is neither the microscopically observed, localized naturalism of the Flemings nor the science-derived and then prettified actuality of the Italians. It stands midway between, with something of the detailed, patient truth of one, and a breath of the larger imagining and humanism of the other. On one hand is the Northern minuteness and complexity; though the German seldom loses himself in the minute view as did the van Eycks, and seldom takes refuge in portraying facial curiosities and aberrations as did later Flemish painters. On the other hand is a certain large dignity of the South, and an emphasis on human significance.

How much more generalized is the German humanism than the Flemish is announced by any one of Cranach's naïvely charming Venuses, so confident of their loveliness and so rhythmically synthesized. One involuntarily remembers with distaste the Van Eycks' *Adam and Eve* and Mabuse's unsuccessful imitations of the Italian things—which turn out nakeds, not nudes.

It is Dürer, nevertheless, who typifies the broad curiosity and the serious humanism of this amazing generation of Northern artists. He mastered all that could be learned about the graphic arts in his own land. Then he traveled, observed, wrote, and philosophized. His hand lagged in cunning, dragged behind his intellect, when he painted. But his prints are a sensitive index to a mind curious and erudite, almost encyclopedic. His art is deep, serious, studied. He rose above his fellows precisely by his ability to set out so much of observed life and of learning clearly and with technical brilliance, yet with profuse detail. Again one remembers the Gothic cathedral with its main lines coming clear out of multiplex columns and an intricate pattern of living ornament.

That Dürer was minutely concerned with rocks and rivers, with pigs and dogs and horses, with faces and bodies and wings and armor, appears constantly. These prints and portraits and occasional religious paintings hold their place in the very front of the realistic advance now going forward in Europe. Perhaps the German love of nature, as such, is the most genuine of all. The Flemish view of nature is near-sighted, the Italian likely to be scientific—or erotic. Perhaps there is a clue in the innate pantheism of the Teutonic temperament.

In the South, man—or often enough woman—was the measure of all things. The North admitted no such measure. The old abstract ornament of the Dark Ages, and the animals in its art; then the medieval cathedrals that soared until they dwarfed man—these are signs of a different approach. The Germans of 1500 were broad enough to listen intently to the poems of Man as composed south of the Alps. But their own art is not cut to the logic of anthropomorphism. Again, they were on the Gothic side, with God an infinite distance from the earthbound human being.

The Art of Painting in Germany

Painting is not by nature a medium agreeable to the Gothic ideal. The failure of the Germans to score heavily in that art is perhaps thus explained. Their black-and-white arts, particularly those dealing basically with line, transcend their painting. Before 1500 such painting as Germany had—sharing the misnomer "primitive" with Sienese and other early schools—was secondary to architecture and woodcarving. The picture was often enough merely an incidental panel in some large altarpiece which gave chief prominence to sculpture. And the painter was a subordinate worker.

It is, then, no matter for surprise that, when the one generation of painters had passed, again architecture, woodcarving, print-making, and the minor crafts absorbed all original talent. The communal arts, the craftsmanlike arts, triumphed. Even for the half-century of Cranach and Grünewald and Baldung one gains only an indistinct vision of the working painter, of his patrons and his market, or of the pictures themselves gracing walls. But memory leaps up of the craftsmen's shops, of woodcarving and goldsmithing and heraldic emblems; of churches filled to overflowing with richly carved shrines and furnishings, ornamented tombs, and choir stalls; of house gables carved and touched in with gold and red

and blue. The arts of wood were common above all.

In painting, the artistry is that of men accomplished in other directions. The method is overlinear. Even in Cranach, where the effects are apparently achieved flatly and fluently, the exquisite rhythmic contours count for most. Dürer's edges are oversharp, and one actually looks for cross-hatching in his shadows. He loves to put an old stone wall, wherein every block can be outlined, behind his characters, and he lavishes extraordinary care upon flowing tresses and luxuriant beards.

The exquisite expressive line is Holbein's first virtue. Line is so overused by Altdorfer that one almost feels him to be a draftsman wandered into the painting field by mistake. It is well to recall that the invention of printing in Germany was preceded by a century of marked activity in wood-engraving, resulting in a body of black-and-white works of extraordinary vigor and variety. The block-books constituted a first attempt to give the masses an art medium corresponding to the illuminated manuscripts so long accessible to the learned and the rich. On the foundation laid by the block-book designers was raised the structure of late fifteenth- and sixteenth-century painting.

Germany had known one school of "primitive" painting comparable to that of Avignon, and reminiscent of the school of Siena. At Cologne an activity and a style developed not unconnected with the groups of mystics of the Lower Rhine territory. They, in their effort to reach back to a direct and simple communion with God, had found it expedient to resist the building of magnificent churches. But they approved the art of painting "which would kindle men's hearts toward God."

There is in the paintings a sweet, nature-loving, tenderly humanistic note, suggesting the teachings of St. Francis. Whereas other primitive artists—in Spain particularly, but also to a degree in France—had insisted upon, nay, gloried in, the wounds and sufferings of Jesus, urging men to self-scourging, these early Germans emphasized His lovingness and the harmony of man's life when devoted to Him. The pictures are, like the Sienese, colorful and sensuously appealing.

Conrad Witz:
The Annunciation.
Germanic Museum, Nuremberg

These qualities, however, are not mentioned in the earliest report of the school that has come down to us. The Bimburg Chronicle of 1380 says: "There was in Cologne at this time a famous painter named Wilhelm whose like could not be found in all the land. He portrayed men so cunningly it seemed they were alive."

But Wilhelm of Cologne, praised thus in his own time for his realism, is only midway between Byzantine formalism and the coming free style; that is, if the attribution of the *Madonna of the Bean-Flower* is to stand. Of another Cologne master more is known, for he lived to 1451: Stephan Lochner. His works have less of the simple linear harmonies and uninvolved backgrounds. The panel is filled with a number of enriching things. But it is worth while to note how the typical face has persisted in this Virgin who has about her a dewy purity and a gentle grace. How much of increased naturalness came

in the next generation may be guessed from the figures by the Master of the Bartholomaeus Altar, in a panel from his major known work. The bodies have even begun to throw visible shadows!

There is a picture by the Master of the Upper Rhine which seems to sum up the service of the mystics in turning men's minds from the sufferings of the world. It is entitled *The Garden of Paradise,* and it depicts naïvely all those gracious things which he who gives himself to God will enjoy in the after-life. Here are birds and trees, flowers and fruits, a spring of fresh water, musical instruments and books—and the company of very aristocratic-looking saints.

The devotional, quietistic, and even joyous aspect is less evident in the works of other early German schools; although there is a gentle beauty about the pictures by Conrad Witz, who worked in Constance during the second quarter of the fifteenth century, and apparently a studied avoid-

Master of the Life of Mary: *The Annunciation. Alte Pinakothek, Munich*

ance of the distressing episodes and details of the pious legends he illustrated. In addition to these virtues there is in *The Annunciation,* shown here, a fine example of picture-building, of formal organization. There were centers in Northern Germany, and even in Switzerland and Tirol; in Augsburg, where the activity was to lead on to the emergence of the Holbeins; and in Colmar, which gave to Germany a truly great traditional figure: Martin Schongauer. He was noted in his own time (he died in 1491) as the leading German painter and as an innovator.

Schongauer's panels retain a good deal of primitive formalism; they are stiffly posed, and the draftsmanship is heavy; but they reach forward to detailed depiction, and there is an occasional landscape background or individually characterized face. The stiffer things are perhaps the best, for he seems to make decorative capital out of the rigid lines and the mathematically disposed figures. But it was in his engravings that Schongauer was most the master. More than any other

artist he lifted the medium to the estate of an independent art, established the engraver above the anonymity that had been his, and left a mode and a technique of engraving ready for Dürer's hand. He produced prints worthy to stand in company with Dürer's. (See over-page.)

Albrecht Dürer

"What beauty is," Dürer wrote, "I do not know; but it adheres to many things." Therefore, he continued, the artist must inquire widely so that he will have "a mind well stored." The beautiful figure he makes, then, is not to be called wholly his own; it is partly acquired and learned from understanding of many figures. Nevertheless "the secret feeling of the heart" also is manifested in the image, and thus a new thing, not in nature but created, is brought into the world.

One might easily read into Dürer's words a

Martin Schongauer: *Christ Carrying the Cross*. Engraving.
Metropolitan Museum of Art

statement of aesthetics very similar to the most modern credo. The insistence upon the independent and invented quality of the work of art, beyond a transcription from nature, is especially "up-to-date." Nor is insistence upon close communion with life as it is alien to the most advanced theories. Yet Dürer's own works are evidence that with him the observing eye and the controlling brain were given more sway than "the secret images of the heart." The formal excellence of his work, the abstract structure or pattern, is always conditioned by a scrupulous fidelity to seen aspects and reasonable objects. The overtones and unreal meanings are not those obtained by the "distortions" of Tintoretto and El Greco, or the naïve simplifications of Duccio and Simone Martini. Dürer's is a philosophical and intellectual conception.

Trained in his early years to be a goldsmith, like his father, he decided that painting was an art he "more esteemed." He records, in his direct way, that his father was not pleased. Nevertheless he was apprenticed to one Michael Wohlgemuth, and he spent three years learning to do the many things required of a crafts-man-painter. Wohlgemuth was also preparing wood-engraved blocks to illustrate the books which were being made by the new invention of printing from movable type. Dürer's training for goldsmithing and his early experience in book-illustrating conspired to direct his attention to the engraver's arts, which often took him from the painter's easel for considerable periods.

Wandering through Germany—and once perhaps as far away as Venice—during the next four years, the youth stored up impressions of people, places, and things, and gained a wider outlook on life. He returned home to Nuremberg to marry a neighbor's daughter. Her handsome dowry and his own industry secured him a modestly prosperous position in the community. His exceptional intellectual endowment and gentle manners brought companionship with the leading figures of his time.

In this first productive period at Nuremberg he worked in a spirit obviously inspired by lingering medieval ideals and traditions. The marvelously vigorous print *The Four Horsemen of the Apocalypse*, dated 1498, immediately proclaims its more Northern and Gothic character

Dürer: *Melancholy*.
Engraving.
*Fogg Museum of Art,
Harvard University*

when placed beside prints made after the artist's Italian sojourn, such as the *Mary in the Temple*.

The former is filled with vital movement, with upward drive; is, for all its compact composition and clear motivation, almost nervously animated. The latter has gained roundness, simplification, and repose. Perhaps the earlier manner was the better for the purpose Dürer had then: to illustrate in popular prints the Christian testaments and legendry, for a medievally pious audience. That his sympathies were on the Reformist side, although he was never openly zealous in Luther's cause, is indicated in one of the engravings of the *Apocalypse* series, the Pope and cardinals appearing among the wicked.

It was in 1505 that Dürer went to Venice. A plague was then distressing Nuremberg, and artists were hard put to it to secure work. Having borrowed money for the trip, he was gratified to find himself honored in the Italian city, not only by the large German colony there but by the Venetian aristocracy. The Doge and the city fathers offered him an official post if he would become a permanent resident. But after a year and a half he returned to Nuremberg. Although he was in general wary of criticism, he recorded in his diary that the Venetian painters "spend their time mostly in singing and drinking." Of the elderly Bellini, however, he wrote affectionately, and with naïve pleasure at his own success: "Giovanni Bellini praised my work, before celebrities and nobles. He wishes to own one of my paintings, even though he pay for it. He is an excellent man."

Dürer: *Self-Portrait.*
Alte Pinakothek, Munich

Back in Germany he carried on as before, painting when he felt he could afford it, keeping the pot boiling by the making of prints. The Italian influences were absorbed, changing a little his way of statement, perhaps broadening his sense of composition. But he seems never to have been tempted to go over uncritically to the Italian fashion—as the Flemings of this period, Matsys and Mabuse, were doing, and as the Germans after the Reformation were destined to do. Just how much it meant for German art at this moment to have a leader who had gained an insight into Italian methods and ideals, yet resisted any national surrender to the Southern style, is impossible to estimate. It is something of a miracle that Germany could already know so much of the Renaissance splendor, yet develop artistically along her own lines during the half-century before serious art was wholly cut off.

The larger spirit is evident again and again in Dürer's journal. When he journeys to the Low Countries he finds friends and inspiration among the artists there, praises sincerely, and exchanges knowledge. Of Patinir he characteristically notes: "Master Joachim, that good landscape painter, asked me to his wedding and showed me all honor." And he speaks reverently of "the great master, van der Weyden."

Most revealing and unusual is the enthusiasm he shows over examples of Aztec or Mayan art which had been brought overseas to Antwerp from newly discovered America. "Never," he exclaims, "have I seen things which pleased me so much. Besides their art, I was surprised at

Dürer: *Portrait:*
Hieronymus Holzschuher.
State Museum, Berlin

the subtle ingenuity of the people of those strange lands." Thus he added another to the impressions with which he had stored his mind, not being put off by the strangeness of objects that are known to seem repellent to some museum curators even today. It was the other face of this idea of open-minded inquiry that led, no doubt, to Dürer's readiness to give everything possible to other artists, and to impart to the people by the art that teaches while it pleases.

Dürer died in 1528, and it is fitting that so great a countryman as Luther should have written an epitaph filled with something of the same spirit of well-wishing and generosity: "Christ gave him grace, and has removed him happily from among the present tempests, and mayhap from worse ones to come; that he who

was worthy to know only the best might not be subjected to the worst."

Of Dürer's painting it may be said only that he could do a faithful portrait well, with Flemish truth to the model, with more than Flemish largeness and synthesis, but without inspiration. The best ones are those not too far from drawing. Such is the head of Hieronymus Holzschuher, or the half-length portrait of the artist's father, or the *St. Jerome.* The religious pictures are likely to be a bit wooden in feeling, with curious reversions to overuse of line. Many historians list *The Worship of the Trinity* and *The Adoration of the Kings* among world masterpieces; but it would seem better to fall back upon the smaller paintings, or upon the engravings, which constitute a treasure nowhere surpassed in linear art.

If one seeks in Dürer's paintings likeness to the

art of other nations, the portraits will be found to approximate those of the later Flemish realists; there are elsewhere affinities with the Italian paintings not of Giorgione and Titian but of Mantegna and Signorelli. That he expended painstaking care on his pictures, in the Flemish way, is indicated by the inscription on a celebrated altar-panel done for the chapel of the German Exchange in Venice: "Albrecht Dürer executed this work in 1506, in a period of five months."

That Dürer's prints, fresh from the presses, should have been hawked from a stall at the Nuremberg or the Frankfort Fair, as a poor man's art, gives us pause today, when every slightest thing from his hand is treasured by connoisseurs. Because the artist was a master the print takes on a larger dignity, even a splendor, not before granted to the engraving. There is true magnificence in *The Four Horsemen* or *The Battle of the Angels,* and brilliant technical display, even scintillation, in the print called *Melancholy* (see page 461).

Whether the medium is woodcut block or engraved copperplate, there is an effect of richness not before achieved in black-and-white. The brilliancy of an original print of the little *Angels with Veronica's Veil,* or the *Rider, Death, and Devil,* or *St. Jerome in His Cell,* or *The Angel Stilling the Wind* is unprecedented and nothing less than marvelous. The technique of it Dürer was to pass on to a group of "Little Masters" destined to leave to later generations a treasure of miniature prints. But none again equaled his achievement of grandeur with delicacy, of intense vigor with a jewel-like sparkle.

Perhaps with Dürer the prints were a sideline, secondary to what he considered his important work of painting. They were necessary to do because a large edition paid immediate and continuing returns. Certainly the brilliance of his technique was built up for cheapness. Before his time it had been customary to use the woodcut print for outlines and then to color over it, by hand or stencil. Dürer actually did away with coloring and obtained as rich and sparkling an effect by the manipulation of black lines only.

Dürer's Contemporaries

Lucas Cranach, born a year later than Dürer, is more significant as a painter, and a less important master—though still a master—of engraving. Of all the German artists he was nearest to a pure painter, and most individual in style. Little is known of his early life. Later he was everything that Dürer was not: he clung to certain primitivisms; he was joyously pagan in his apprehension of the beauty of the nude; he was a court painter (to the Elector Frederick the Wise). He lived in Wittenberg, Luther's city, and before his death at eighty-one he had been many things besides artist: pharmacist and ambassador, bookseller and burgomaster.

Some people affect to see an element of humor in all Cranach's nudes; and indeed there is a pertness about his ladies that faintly amuses. But there is so much of sheer rhythmic loveliness, of sensuous charm and plastic coherence, that today—when the attenuation of figure, which used to be termed "distortion," is recognized as necessary to the particular plastic effect intended —his pictures are again given prominent place on gallery walls, with devoted pilgrims always before them.

Without approaching the Italian way of regarding the nude—at this time considerably erotic—Cranach's work suggests an attitude very different from Dürer's: so much so that the two artists may be taken to illustrate the two extremes, psychologically, within the German innocent delight in life. Dürer, despite his openmindedness, was self-conscious where nakedness was concerned. There is a line in his diary recording that when a near-nude girl appeared in a pageant at Antwerp he looked long and hard, being, as he took pains to explain, an interested painter. In contrast with Dürer's self-consciousness and rather ponderous seriousness are the frank delight of Cranach and his presentation of the body in its most melodious and decorative aspects.

There is nothing quite like his Eves and Venuses in the whole range of Western art.

Cranach: *Venus. Art Institute, Frankfort-on-Main*

That Eve and the pagan goddess are shown so alike as to be indistinguishable without the labels—or a hint of serpent or apple with the one, a Cupid with the other—does not sit well with those who want religious picturing to be piously instructive. Nevertheless, just *as paintings* the *Venus* at Frankfort, the *Eve* of the Uffizi, the *Adam and Eve* at Antwerp (page 456), and

Grünewald: *Crucifixion*. Central panel from the Isenheim Altar. *Colmar Museum*

the *Venus* of the Louvre are so seductive and appealing, in a naïve, other-worldly way, that this sometime neglected artist seems likely to come into increased rather than lessened favor. He is not a "large" painter—there is something cramped about his style—but he has a charm of his own.

There are portraits from Cranach's hand that retain something of primitive conventionalization even while indicating close study of Flemish realism (page 451). They have, too, a delicacy and freshness that is an original innovation, a special sort of linear preciseness that will be seen later in Holbein's works. Cranach's larger pictures painted for religious purposes seem to

this observer less successful—unless a picture of *Paradise* must be considered by its very nature religious. His wood-engravings, however, repay study, even though they are considerably less brilliant than Dürer's.

Two other painters escaped almost completely the linear incubus from which Dürer never freed himself: Mathias Grünewald and Hans Baldung. Grünewald, more than any other German, approaches the spaciousness of Italian painting. He uses light-and-shade composition effectively, almost melodramatically. His major surviving work, the Isenheim altarpiece now in the museum at Colmar, verges on the theatrical in the strained posing of the figures. But the *Crucifixion* is

Baldung: *Crucifixion*.
Altar painting in the cathedral,
Freiburg im Breisgau

compositionally an extraordinarily sound accomplishment, and its coloring is expert and rich.

The subject-matter is set forth with unexampled and unforgettable vividness and intensity of emotion. It is not pretty, is even insistently terrible. But there are those who feel that it transcends distressing reality, emerging in the realm of sublime tragedy. Unfortunately there is almost nothing else by Grünewald surviving, though some attributed pieces have rugged strength and expert finish. Nor is there more than a scrap of information about the painter's life: only the fact of his having lived at Mainz, saddened and lonely because he was the victim of an unhappy marriage.

Hans Baldung never matured into mastery of those special gifts of spaciousness, drama, and emotional intensity evidenced by Grünewald. He is more akin to Cranach in a certain ingenuous departure from realism. When he

essayed a portrait, however, he was hardly less microscopically accurate than the van Eycks. He had a favorite color, green, and his name appears as often as not in the form of Hans Baldung Grien. But color is his least happy accomplishment. He was, in his feeling for the disposing of figures in space, and in mastery of the brush, a born painter. His best-known work, the altar series at Freiburg im Breisgau, is alone sufficient to raise him to the first rank of German painters.

For a very long time Hans Holbein the Younger has been listed as the second artist of Germany, coming after Dürer alone. To the literalist, Holbein is the most accomplished German painter and perhaps the world's greatest portraitist. Recently he has declined a little in popularity, owing to the frequently mechanical nature of his composition and technique. He is the most limited in range of all the artists recently accounted world masters. He is known

Holbein: *Portrait of a Woman. Cook Gallery, Richmond, England*

almost exclusively for portraits. In them he is undramatic, unimaginative. Yet within his elected specialty, in spite of his rigid limitations, he is unmatched.

Holbein the Younger was born in 1497 at Augsburg. His father was an artist of no small ability, but without the son's talent for naturalism and his polished method. Times were hard for the artist family in Augsburg, and as a youth the son went to Switzerland. He made illustrations for book publishers in Basel, returned briefly to

Germany, then settled in Basel. From illustrating, engraving, and craftswork he graduated into easel painting, specializing in portraiture. His few religious pictures, of which the once esteemed *Meyer Madonna* is most notable, are hard and academic and overdetailed.

Times being troublous in Switzerland as well as in Germany, Holbein went to England. He carried a letter of introduction from Erasmus, the Dutch scholar, whom he had painted in Basel, to Sir Thomas More, then a favorite of

Holbein: *Portrait of Dirk Berck*, detail.
Metropolitan Museum of Art

Henry VIII and powerful at the English court. Holbein was successful in giving his British sitters the sort of natural and attractively colored likenesses they wanted; and so, after finding Switzerland again disturbed by the controversies over religion, and the air not healthful for so partisan a Protestant as he had become, he moved permanently to England. By 1532 Henry VIII had made him court painter and had given him a studio in the palace of Whitehall with ample means for a living. He died in London in 1543, a world-renowned artist in his chosen field.

As a painter Holbein is at his best in simplest portraiture. There his extremely sensitive draftsmanship shows to advantage. His besetting sin is overlaboring of detail, so that—considered as art organisms—many of his portraits are improved when accessories in background and corners are covered. Occasionally he concentrated the interest, laying out the field in large masses of dark and light, and suppressing detail except in head and hands. There the shading and lining are marvelously delicate and exact.

Holbein's claim to attention is as a realist with a miniaturist's technique. He could, with pen or brush, outline a nose or a cheek with masterly expressiveness. He worked up the hairs with a crow-quill pen rather than with a brush. It might almost be said that to the end he worked as a drawing master rather than as essentially a painter. This genius for microscopic truth appealed to upper British circles, and Holbein has left to later generations a record of Henry VIII and his favorites and officers which is of great historic and human interest. One knows just how the Archbishop of Canterbury looked, or the Astronomer Royal, or the King's falconer. There are likenesses, too, of most of the ladies whom Henry VIII married or merely had a mind to marry. One who refused the King— possibly with the oft-quoted line, "I should be delighted if I had two heads"—was the sixteen-year-old Duchess of Milan. The simple and dignified portrait is now in the National Gallery, London. (See the characteristic double portrait facing the title page of this book.)

There is an anecdote that neatly sums up Holbein's mastery and its limits. He called at the studio of another famous painter, who proved to be away. Holbein tarried long enough to paint a fly on the surface of a picture which stood on an easel. The other artist when he returned tried to wave the fly away, then to brush it off. When he saw what it really was, and the exactitude of its rendering, he knew that none other than Holbein could have been the visitor.

There were painters in Germany during Holbein's service abroad, and during the decades after. But his flight is symbolic. Christoph Amberger, also of Augsburg, carried on the tradition of German realistic portraiture, with only a little less of mastery, in the second half of the sixteenth century. Bartholomaeus Bruyn of Cologne also was a very accomplished portraitist, somewhat influenced by the Flemish painters. Mention may be made, too, of Hans Maler, born in Ulm but long resident in Tirol. He painted portraits attractively combining naturalism with a posteresque simplification. After the mid-century the Protestant hostility or indifference to art was fully felt. There was not another internationally known painter until the neoclassicist Mengs, of the eighteenth century, who elected to live in Italy and Spain.

After the triumph of the Reformers, indeed, the more stolid arts flourished, particularly sculpture in wood. But naturalism had long since injured the sculptural art. The best in Germany occurred where the medieval tradition persisted. By 1600 the baroque spirit had pushed up from Italy, although its worst excesses occurred after 1750, when the appearance of flight was actually attempted in sculpture. What had in Dürer's time seemed the true, sober German spirit had then been dissipated, and up to the twentieth century there was to be only a rather weak reflection of successive developments from foreign centers—in general, all within the march of realism.

Bartholomaeus Bruyn: *Portrait of Gertrud Voss. Wallraf-Richartz Museum, Cologne*

XXIII: REMBRANDT
AND THE HOLLANDERS

Holland affords the first example of a national art truly democratic, escaped from priestly, kingly, and aristocratic domination; and for the partisan of democracy the result is deplorable. For the Dutch exhibit, aside from the works of one genius, is the most prosaic, unexciting, and earthbound in the annals of greatly celebrated art. The light of Rembrandt's surpassing genius gives splendor to this national display in the early seventeenth century, and afterward there is the exquisite but pale glow of Vermeer's artistry. All the others together—there are very many of these Dutch painters, as befits democracy—emit only a dull, routine, and almost negligible light.

Ever since we first encountered "civilized" society, back in Sumeria in the thirty-fifth century B.C., art has been the apanage of a top class, the possession usually of royalty or of the higher priesthood. Always the elect have patronized the artist and controlled his product—in Babylonia, the emperors; in Egypt, the priests; in Greece, for a brief season, the free nobles; in Rome, when the first great republic was born,

Rembrandt: *The Night Watch. Royal Museum, Amsterdam*

471

Rembrandt:
Man in a Gold Helmet.
State Museum, Berlin

before the advent of the emperors, the patricians and military victors. Then again there was an immense period when church rulers and royalty vied with each other to control life and art; or church and court merged, as often happened, so that the artist served a cardinal-prince.

In Spain at this very time of Holland's emergence as a nation, in the sixteenth century, all art served the magnificent court at Madrid or the churchmen and grandees in lesser cities. In Venice and Flanders the rich merchants and traders had pushed forward as socially significant, and as patrons; but in one case the pictures were obviously painted for palaces, as attesta-

tions of grandeur; in the other they were still either church decorations or portraits of the well-to-do, with only an occasional hint of tavern scene or household life. They began to be filled, it is true, with familiar detail of flower and field, of cloth texture and homely facial expression; but these common things were fitted into pleasure pictures for the rich or showpieces for the religious shrines. Flanders, indeed, in her great period of art production had been a Burgundian royal domain, and very Catholic. In Germany, too, despite the creation of a popular art of prints, beautifully practiced by Dürer, the larger arts were still for the old

Rembrandt: *Portrait:*
Nikolaus Bruyningh, detail.
State Gallery, Cassel

patron-classes. Cranach was a court painter, and Holbein, last of the great Germans, took up the single work of immortalizing the features of kings and aristocrats.

It is only when the story of Holland is reached that the fisherman and the humble housewife, the windmill and the cow—yes, the turnip and the beer mug—seriously sit for their portraits. The Flemish realism of method, perfected when Holland and Flanders were socially and politically one, is here joined with that other realism that brings art down to the lower levels of living for its choice of subject-matter. The painting reminds man of his own houses and fields instead of heaven and legendary saints, flatters the doctor and the captain of the guard and the bulb-grower instead of king and duchess.

Holland, freed heroically of king and overlord, freed of the influence of the Roman Church, jealously assertive of the common citizen's rights, thus democratized art. Bourgeois taste demanded its new types of painting. The burgher patron wanted himself immortalized, or his surroundings (though he wanted, too, the courtly extravagance in picture-*frames,* the rich encrustation and the gilt). Painters responded in hordes.

But democracy was not a success *for the artist.* Paintings were overproduced and were soon underpriced. A canvas sold for hardly the price of a day's meals. Dealers appeared, to buy pictures low and await the chance to sell high. The patrons, too, were fickle, more fickle even than kings and churchmen had been. A painter who had enjoyed a period of acclamation and popularity might be cast aside if fashions changed or he dared an unfamiliar manner. Hals was thrown on charity toward the end, and died a pauper. Rembrandt was sold up for debt, lived out his life in neglect, and was buried not as a recognized artist but as an obscure and beggarly ghetto character. Jan Steen ran a pub to eke out a living, and de Hooch turned manservant. Nevertheless these unfortunate artists created the style or mode that the new public wanted. An art was born, and with it a new way of living for the artist. This was, of course, the beginning of the story of the artist in the modern capitalist state, just as it was the beginning of the seventeenth-eighteenth-nineteenth-century picturesque and genre painting.

Rembrandt transcended his times. He rose above all the restrictions put on him, at first by popularity, then by cramping poverty and neglect. He created a body of art that constitutes nine-tenths of the entire Dutch significant achievement. He *is* the art of Holland, for the rest of the world. He stands for a national achievement more singly than does an artist in any other major country. (Spain has Velázquez and Goya in addition to El Greco.) But the others created the local, typical Dutch thing. And theirs, the first democratic gallery of art, is the levelest and dullest of all.

Before Rembrandt was Hals alone, a realist until recently widely acclaimed as a world master, but then eased out of the top list with Murillo and del Sarto and Guido Reni. Before Hals's time the Hollanders had generally trooped off to Flanders when they felt the call of art, or later had practiced at home a pale imitation of the Italian "grand style," or picturing in the classic manner. And after Rembrandt, even while he worked, except for his own contribution the level was that of routine filling of demand: an extraordinary output of uninspired portrayals of common surroundings; endless "views," pictures of cows in meadows, boats on the canals, ruddy girls and self-satisfied grocers, household interiors and family incidents, taverns and drinking. Some names are remembered for happy lighting effects accomplished or for trifles of homely sentiment recorded: ter Borch and de Hooch—and Vermeer lifts the mode to beautifully arranged and exquisitely finished transcription; while landscape is at last cleared of man's presence and rendered natural by van Goyen and Ruisdael and Hobbema.

When the Hollanders defied the foreign kings, while their blood-brothers in Flanders bent the knee, a new chapter of political history was opened. A small people by heroic struggle and superb self-reliance fought its way to independence and then to commercial supremacy. The citizens freed themselves from paying taxes to resident or absentee monarchs or to privileged princes and regents. They opened the way to a free and extensive foreign trade. They destroyed the last vestiges of control of the conscience from Rome.

The revolt started in 1567; a declaration of independence is dated 1579. The wars dragged on until 1609, and recognition of the Dutch Republic was not fully granted until 1648, at the Peace of Westphalia. Thus Hals (1580-1666) began painting before fighting had ceased, and carried on into the most settled and prosperous era of national life; whereas Rembrandt, born in 1606, hardly knew the time of war at all. If the nationalist critics are right, the era just following the attainment of independence, hard upon heroic deeds and economic and territorial expansion, should have produced great art, reflecting heroism, aspiration, and spiritual advance. But there is little sign of anything of the sort in the Dutch galleries.

Some observers feel that the Reformation was a backward step, removing men from refreshment at spiritual sources, and that it is Protestantism that renders routine Dutch art so materialistic and dull. Certainly the Protestant states have failed to produce any large art expression, and none at all that reflects a new spiritual consciousness—there is no Protestant art that rivals the Catholic, or, for that matter, the Buddhist, Mohammedan, or Taoist—but Catholic art since the Reformation has been equally uncreative and unexciting, even more superficial and tasteless. We may therefore have to fall back upon the fact that art all over Europe became comparatively uncreative and impotent, in Catholic and Protestant countries alike, while the third estate was gaining power, while the upper crust of the bourgeoisie, the money-makers, were becoming the patrons. The few geniuses are outside the lines of national developments, of traditional styles and schools.

In any case the decay of faith is not to be overlooked as a factor. For thirteen centuries the great body of European art had been religious, whether in painting or illumination, in sculpture or enamel, in architecture or minor craft. The cathedrals are matched by the paintings of Giotto and Michelangelo and El Greco. The artist had been a man of faith, sharing a common conviction and an inner fire with the men he worked for. Now the conviction was gone on both sides. The artist, in escaping Rome, had lost his mightiest incentive. No artist since Rembrandt (who alone in his time clung to religious themes) has found a spiritual reason for his picturing, to take the place of naïve Christian devotion.

The cry was that art henceforward would serve man instead of God. Heroes would be glorified instead of saints. A peaceful earth would interest citizens more than a hypothetical heaven. But art apparently paid a staggering price for this freedom, this descent from God-worship to man-regard.

Perhaps the answer is that the painters of Holland simply were not great enough. They were enabled to portray but not to glorify their own people and their own country. The collective portrait is interesting and pleasing, just as the homely ways of this self-respecting, clean-living people are interesting and pleasing. But one looks at the gallery of paintings as one would at a photographic record of equally attractive landscapes and persons. It is homey, intimate, appealing. But it is prosy, unexciting, colorless.

A country's physical aspects to a certain degree shape its art. This painting without eminence (the nation, incidentally, had no sculpture, and no original architecture until the twentieth century) is perhaps in accord with the horizon-hugging landscape, the level dikes, and the rainy climate. The character of the thrifty burghers and frugal housewives, too, is in the clean and tidy pictures, in the neat craftsmanship and undramatic documentation—a transcript of Holland, perfectly literal or slightly sentimentalized, but nowhere dramatized or uplifted.

Of course this exact representation of familiar things, of cow-strewn fields and sails against cloudy skies, of an old woman combing a child's hair, or of a pair of topers, was a novelty and therefore something to marvel at in its own day. But it faded into an exhibition of craftsmanship and a bondage to one small corner of nature as the outward eye records it. Rembrandt alone brings to it the two elements that may lift any content to the realm of great art: the subjective "second sight" which enables the artist to perceive more than common folks do in (or beneath) the object; and the understanding of plastic organization.

Dutch Painting before Rembrandt

Back in the days before the separation of Holland and Flanders, when the Low Countries constituted a single political unit, it had been a custom for art students from Harlem and Leiden and Utrecht to go to Bruges, and later to Brussels and Antwerp, for training, and then to practice. One went where masters already were, where buyers came. While Flanders was still Gothic in spirit, although establishing the methods of the new secular realism, several of the most talented artists had emigrated from the Dutch cities; most notably Dirk Bouts and Albert van Ouwater. They were followed later by that strange genius Hieronymus Bosch, by Gerard David and Mabuse, and finally by the great master Pieter Brueghel. Because they spent their working years in the Flemish cities they all are treated by historians (except by the Dutch) as Flemish painters.

But to indicate that Holland was not without an art life of its own one may mention Geertgen tot Sint Jans (known also as Geertgen van Harlem), who stayed at home and gave importance to the school of Harlem. He left more than a dozen pictures which show him to have departed a little from the current Flemish ex-

Lucas van Leiden: *Adoration of the Kings. Art Institute, Chicago*

actitude of statement. He broadened the technique of the Low Countries art and is even, with cautious reservations, mentioned as a forerunner of Rembrandt. Dürer was so enthusiastic when he first saw Geertgen's work that he exclaimed, "He was a painter before he left his mother's womb!" Geertgen was another of those who advanced landscape painting—although not yet, of course, in the fifteenth century, as a separate or separated art. Had he lived to maturity—he died at twenty-eight—he might have been one of the very great figures. His influence was wide: upon Gerard David among the Hollanders who went to practice in Flanders; upon Jan Mostaert and Jacob Cornelisz, painters of a slightly lower rank who close the story of the school of Harlem as such. They contributed competent pictures that are found today on the walls of leading museums.

There followed a school of Leiden, of which Cornelis Engelbrechtsen was the first notable figure. His pupil Lucas van Leiden is the better

known, less as a painter than as an engraver second in ability and fame to Dürer alone. He met the master of Nuremberg when both were visiting in Antwerp in 1521, and Dürer gave him prints and drew a portrait of him. Lucas gained immensely by the contact. His copper engraving is brilliant, and his realism is less Gothic than the German's: it suggests, in fact, a breath of Renaissance clarity and freedom. His prints mark the highest point touched by pre-Rembrandtian art in Holland. His painting *The Adoration of the Kings* at Chicago is bright and appealing and pictorially well constructed; but it is easy to see even in the reproduction here the intrusion of the method of the detail-minded engraver.

At this time one encounters a real wave of Italianization flowing over the Northern countries. The painters who were washed along by it are unimportant, although they imitated the Southern manner more successfully than did their Flemish fellows. Some of their nudes even

Frans Hals: *Regents of the Old Men's Home*, detail. *Frans Hals Museum, Harlem*

are believable and attractive. More interesting as an individual, however, and as a symbol, is the painter whom the Dutch call Antoon Moor van Dashorst. He is that accomplished portraitist whom we met in Spain under the name Antonio Moro, who in England was Sir Anthony More. He had been born Dutch, and trained with Jan Scoorel of Harlem; then went to Flanders, then to Italy; he served the Habsburg Emperor Charles V, progressed in turn to Spain, Portugal, and England, and became court painter to Philip II at Madrid. He finally returned to Brussels under patronage of the notorious Duke of Alva, who carried the methods of the Inquisition into the Low Countries, prosecuting the campaigns known as the Spanish Terror.

Moor's career affords a sidelight on the interconnection of the courts of Europe at the time, and the distribution of both the works and influence of such masters and near-masters as Titian, Holbein, Velázquez, and Murillo. There were to follow other great figures in the paths of royal art: Rubens and Van Dyck. But Antoon

Moor, like all those, is outside the real story of Dutch art, outside the republican spirit and the burgher painting. The book of his portraits, however fascinating historically, is an international gallery of kings, queens, dukes, and knights, of the Tudors and Habsburgs, and of Alva himself—all hateful to the Hollanders.

Frans Hals signalizes the transition from court portraiture to citizen portraiture. Born in 1580 to parents who had been and were later to be residents of Harlem, but who were temporarily driven by the war to Antwerp, he early knew of Holland's troubled fortunes at first hand. But as painter he rode in on the wave of civic enthusiasm and self-satisfaction that came with virtual though not final victory and independence. His direct method, flattering "splash," and freedom from inspirational flights fitted him perfectly to serve the new citizen masters.

His well-advertised habits of tippling, which got him charged with wife-beating, would hardly claim attention if it were not for a corresponding gusto and expansiveness, not to say recklessness,

Frans Hals: *The Jolly Toper. Royal Museum, Amsterdam*

evident in his method of painting. Some say he could not paint without being near-drunk. One might add as the moral of the tale, however, that Hals never escaped a certain coarseness of statement. His work is characterized by extraordinary dash and bravura, considering that he retained the true Low Country realism as a base. But there his eminence ended.

He was well esteemed by his fellow citizens, and well patronized. It may have been personal weakness rather than public apathy that put him into bankruptcy and, at the end, permitted him to die a ward of charity. While he prospered, none was more popular. He specialized in single portraits and in "corporation pictures." The corporations were like guilds, but usually military in character: they were organized companies of citizens who had fought together in the wars against Spain; or they might be groups of hospital regents or guilds of doctors or drapers.

The military corps in particular entered importantly into the civic and social life of the day.

Each one had its clubhouse, and the walls must be adorned with pictures which would feed the vanity of the members—and the officers. The corporation or company picture resulted. Each member whose portrait appeared in the group paid a proportionate share of the cost. The painter received a stated amount for each head and an additional sum for each hand. (The hands are, in number, out of proportion to aesthetic needs in many of the examples.)

Who better for this new social art than the convivial and flattering Hals? He had the verve, the sense of display, and the theatrical touch. Through his brushes all the company members in every corporation turn out dashing gallants. The picture itself is brilliantly alive and contagiously spirited—just the crowning ornament for a social room. It is not to be overlooked that as portraiture, too, beyond the trick of flattering elegance and dashing brushwork, these canvases are essentially truthful, with a fleeting expression caught and fixed effortlessly.

But the excellences are within the range of documentary statement and technical virtuosity. Of the art in its deeper aspects of expressive organization Hals is comparatively innocent. A French painter once exclaimed, "No one ever will paint better than Hals." But one remembers that Hals's great reputation was built up in an era when truth to model and a flashing style were the first tests. Increasingly a superficiality and a coarseness have been recognized in Hals's achievement. He is known today as a diverting painter—hardly more—for his hearty materialism, his swaggering virtuosity with the brush, and a strain of sympathetic humor. His is portraiture with a disarming gusto and a dazzling spontaneity. After the pleasure of the first impression, the observer is conscious of the perfunctory organization, the rather shallow understanding, the journalistic shortcutting.

It was during the brief stay in Leiden of those dissenters who are called in America the Pilgrim Fathers that a child was born there and given the name Rembrandt Harmenszoon van Rijn, or Rembrandt son of Harmens of the Rhine. The year was 1606. Harmens was a comfortably prosperous miller with four other children. Rembrandt was to have been a scholar and accordingly was sent to the Latin school. But, having proved by indirection that he was good for nothing except art, he was apprenticed at the age of fifteen to an obscure local painter named Swanenburch. After three years he was sent to Amsterdam to study with Pieter Lastman, then fashionable because he could paint in the manner of the Italian classicists, which had not quite given way before the craze for local naturalism. Since Lastman himself had studied with a German in Rome, he doubtless gave Rembrandt a curiously mixed dose of internationalism. The effect was evidently beneficial, for Rembrandt became the only painter of Holland who transcended national limitations, the only Dutchman who was universal. The training was good because it broadened the young man's outlook without setting his feet on the path to Italy. It is not known that he ever stepped outside the borders of Holland.

The Genius Rembrandt

He began independent practice of his art in Leiden, but after a few years decided upon Amsterdam, then a thriving commercial city, as a more favorable field. He was twenty-five years old when he settled there. Within a short time he was the city's leading artist, specializing, as did his rivals, in portraiture. He was already a master of the etching medium.

In that biography of Rembrandt entitled *R. v. R.*, purporting to be a work by the artist's physician, one Joannis van Loon, but written—with a great amount of local color, collateral history, and incidental philosophy—by Hendrik Willem van Loon of our own century, the author affords a picture of the prosperity of Amsterdam at this time, and of the citizen patrons of art. The physician is speaking:

I had in the meantime seen a great many paintings. Our city was full of them. It sometimes seemed to me that our town would burst from sheer riches, like a sack too heavily loaded with grain. Our harbors were more crowded than ever. The streets near the Exchange gave one the impression of a continual county-fair. During the morning hours, when the musicians played on the Dam, one saw as many Turks and Germans and Blackamoors and Frenchmen and Britishers and Swedes, and even people from far-away India, as one did Dutchmen. . . .

They [my neighbors] would retire from the business of storming the gates of Heaven and Hell and would turn respectable and they would buy themselves large and comfortable houses in one of the newly laid out parts of the town . . . and of course they must show their neighbors how rich they were (what is the fun in having bags and bags and bags of money if no one knows it?) and so they filled their houses with elegant French chairs that weighed a ton and with Spanish chests that only a mule could move and with pictures—rows and rows and still more rows of pictures. . . .

As a result, wherever I went, whether my patient happened to be a simple butcher from the Volderstraat or a rich Indian merchant living on the fashionable side of the Heerengracht, I found myself surrounded by miles and miles of colored canvases. Some of them were probably very good and a few of them were undoubtedly very bad, but most of them were of a very decent quality, as the Guild of St. Luke maintained the highest possible standards and no one could hope to qualify as a master until he had spent years and years in a very exacting and very difficult apprenticeship.

Rembrandt prospered with the rest, and his art grew. Then a great happiness befell him. He had been, perhaps, something of a plodder and so extraordinarily wrapped up in the pursuit of his art—at which he worked day and night with a passionate absorption—that he had failed to acquire the usual social graces. Besides, he *was* the son of a miller. But suddenly he fell in love with a beautiful girl of both social position and moderate wealth. They were married, after some skirmishing with her outraged relatives— she was throwing herself away on a fellow known to be not only an artist but a low-born one at that.

Rembrandt adored Saskia, at least when he was not absorbed in that very important business, painting and etching. The two young people

seem to have had grand times together, and some of their joy is reflected in the portraits he painted of her. Using his own earnings, now large, and her dowry, Rembrandt showered upon her the sorts of finery to which artists' wives are not accustomed. At the same time he indulged his own taste for art works, building up a collection made notable by paintings of Raphael, Giorgione, and the van Eycks, besides many works by Dutch artists whom he admired or wanted to encourage. He bought, too, a large house, in the Jewish quarter of Amsterdam.

But the years of his happiness with Saskia, and of material prosperity, were few. He had gone deep into debt; Saskia's relatives made trouble; and with one thing and another he found himself on the road to bankruptcy. Two catastrophes overtook him within a single year: Saskia died; and he alienated his patrons and the public. Although the second event helped to wreck his immediate fortunes, it signaled the saving of his artistic soul, and so it is not to be regarded as catastrophe but as good fortune for the rest of the world. What Rembrandt had done was defy popular taste, which had held him, in his market output, to the standard realistic portraiture. He had raised realism to its highest level, to be sure, but without imagination, or sacrifice of "reasonable" surface truth to plastic necessities. Now he chose to go beyond truth as the casual eye sees it, to expression of his own inner vision.

The actual painting which marked his change of direction, which turned the public from him, was that most famous of corporation pictures *The Night Watch,* more correctly known as *The Sortie of the Banning Cock Company.* The members of the company had expected a canvas upon which exact and prominent likenesses of all the individuals would be brought together in a single group-portrait, and no foolishness about artistic organization, pattern, emphasis, and all that rot. Rembrandt eight years earlier had painted a prime picture of the sort for the guild of doctors, known as *The Anatomy Lesson.* But now he chose to consider his art problems more important than squaring his work with the vanity—or rightful demands, if

Rembrandt: *The Anatomy Lesson*, detail. *Royal Picture Museum, The Hague*

you will—of his customers. He produced a picture that was a masterpiece as a composition, a daring arrangement of light accents in a darkened field, an imposing *tour de force* in light-dark manipulation. But imagine the dismay of certain company members at finding their own portraits half obscured, or smaller by half than those of the fellows up front.

Then and there Rembrandt's standing as a popular painter was destroyed. This finest of all company pictures was defaced, its balance and fullness of effect badly impaired by the cutting of two figures from one side and the cutting off of strips at top and bottom. The offended corporation had adjudged it unfit for the intended place of honor in the club hall, and thus callously cut it down to fit it into an anteroom. Even so it retains today an exceptional effectiveness. It is perhaps as celebrated as any work from the master's hand. It is reproduced on page 471.

Rembrandt: *The Syndics of the Cloth Guild. Royal Museum, Amsterdam*

So Rembrandt lost his market, except for a few devoted friends. He seems to have cared less than might have been expected. He found more and more consolation in working passionately at his two arts, pushing further and further into understanding of the potentialities of painting and etching. He had some sort of home life, not without its contentments and its protective effect upon his work. One Hendrickje Stoffels became his housekeeper, if not legally his wife, and took good care of Titus, the only surviving one of the four children born to Saskia. Hendrickje was loyal to her artist-master and should perhaps be credited with the management that postponed the catastrophe of bankruptcy for a further term of years—during which Rembrandt produced many of his masterpieces. It was in 1656, when he was fifty, that his creditors sold him out—took his house, and auctioned his own and his collected paintings for pitiably small prices, for such a mere fraction of their value that he was left under a burden of debt and a succession of minor persecutions that clouded the rest of his life.

But still he had his art, and mercifully some copperplates had been left to him. He took a house farther inside the ghetto. For one moment he re-emerged into the popular world. An old friend got him a commission for another corporation picture, and he painted it with a fine balance of artistry and portrait-exactitude. Indeed *The Syndics of the Cloth Guild* stands with *The Anatomy Lesson* in the very first rank of works of this genre. But this success was a flicker. No more commissions came. Hendrickje died. Rembrandt seems in the years that followed never to have been in actual physical want, although doubtless poorly nourished. Nor could he feel unhappy or defeated continuously, so long as he had his art.

His dignity and self-discipline were especially remarked when he saw his son Titus follow the others of his loved ones to the grave. He went on painting. His eyes had been overstrained long before in his etching work, and his portfolio of prints was therefore closed. In this last period he painted self-portraits that contrast strangely with those of the early days when he had shown himself in princely costumes and endowed with almost arrogant self-confidence. But the late

Rembrandt:
Portrait of a Man.
Metropolitan Museum
of Art

things have a notable human dignity, too. He died in 1669. Holland had long before forgotten him. The parish officials put him down on the mortuary records as "a painter on the Roozengracht, opposite the doolhof," in order, says Louis A. Holman, "that he might not be confounded with some other old man."

In the ultimate view the forgotten old man needed no recompense for neglect. He had kept his integrity. It might have pleased him to know that in later ages his works would be considered incomparably the greatest gifts of Holland to the larger world. Apparently no artist ever had less interest in the reaction to his paintings, or more in the process of conceiving and producing them.

Even the swiftest glance through a gallery of his works indicates that he outdistanced every competitor in all those branches especially characteristic of the Dutch: the intimate, forthright portrait; the corporation picture; the genre bit, even the landscape. He took the current fashionable thing in portraiture and landscape and made it more vital than it had been, injecting something of his philosopher's insight and adding values out of his equipment as creative plastic artist. He went on to add achievements in fields closed to his fellows. He carried on religious painting—was indeed the last master in that realm. He did not hesitate to attempt a classic subject if the mood struck him. There are critics who believe that *The Mill* is the greatest landscape ever painted. If some casual observer dissents, he should at the least be forced to go and live with the picture for a time—until the mysterious power and the ordered life in it reach his consciousness. It is perhaps not the greatest, but very, very great.

In portraiture—Rembrandt stands with Titian, El Greco, and a very few others in the first rank —he added to his instrumental artistry a deep psychological insight. His interest ran to people of character, to faces eloquent of philosophical adjustment to living, particularly to those marked by struggle and sorrow. The face chiseled by experience—this gave content to the superb portraits, the character studies of the persecuted Jews in whose quarter the Rembrandts lived, and the sympathetic and penetrating portraits of the artist's mother and other old women, kindly, or gravely quizzical, or bravely submissive. There is, too, a mellow richness of technique —which ages beautifully—as may be seen especially in the head reproduced among the color prints at the opening of this book (a reproduction made before the painting was cleaned).

The means upon which Rembrandt exceptionally relied in arriving at pictures of intense formal vitality was lighting. Whereas other masters had orchestrated their works with the full quota of plastic instruments, with volumes disposed geometrically in space, with related planes, with textures and the interplay of colors, he studied especially the play between light and dark. He is the foremost master in the manipulation of chiaroscuro.

In the single heads the highlighted features stand out almost startlingly from the bed of dark; although as the eye searches the canvas the shadows gradually give back a rich though muted accompaniment of detail. The golden browns and yellows and darkened reds are opulently varied yet blended. In the larger canvases the main composition forms a pattern of related lights on the dark ground, with half-illumined figures and touched edges of drapery or jewels or wall affording contrapuntal enrichment.

Rembrandt's lighting is artificial and forced, say some literalists. But the forcing has added measurably to the expressiveness of his canvases. They are rendered dramatically vivid; they are

thus given unity, coherence, and emphasis. The thick shadowing is Rembrandt's method of suppressing the detail that appears in nature but is unimportant or destructive in a picture. It permits him to stress the essential in subject even while providing a sensuous glow and splendor.

As draftsman in line, too, he is the outstanding master of Western art. His drawings are tense, economical, richly expressive. In that purest of the linear arts, etching—where the line is traced with a needle-point—his achievement is unsurpassed.

At twenty-two he had already proved himself a master of etching. A portrait of his mother dated 1628 is one of the prints most sought after by collectors. From the "pure etching" method used to achieve this trifle two and one-half inches square, he went on to extend the boundaries of the art until it encompassed effects of tonal contrasts, of massed lights and darks, not before considered possible to the medium, in plates measured in feet. Nor has anyone since his time matched in etching the impressiveness and sheer pictorial brilliancy and grandeur of the *Hundred-Guilder Print*—so named because the unprecedented price struck the popular imagination—or *The Three Crosses*. These mark a climax in black-and-white picturing not less notable than Dürer's achievement in engraving or Hokusai's in brush-drawing.

Rembrandt's method is more individualistic than is usual among the great masters. He stands apart from his school, from the painters of his own nation—whereas Giotto, Titian, and even Michelangelo fit into some traceable sequence of preparation, culmination, and decline within a phase of art. Rembrandt had no notable follower, as he had no important predecessor.

In this fact the historians have found reason for a broad generalization: Rembrandt was the first true modern painter because he was the earliest great individualist. From his time on schools of painting were to be feeble, comparatively indeterminate. Individual genius and independence from tradition counted more. A roll call of the great names of the eighteenth and nineteenth centuries supports the thesis: Goya,

Rembrandt: *Christ Healing the Sick.* "The Hundred-Guilder Print." Etching.
Knoedler Galleries, New York

Daumier, Cézanne, Blake, Turner—these are names outside the clear paths of tradition and expectation. Goya alone might be fitted into a national and traditional reason for being; but he, too, is independent of most of the historical Spanish traits.

Rembrandt the individual was Rembrandt passionately devoted to his art, absorbed in its problems, neglectful of all that failed to touch vitally the work he was doing. He was not heedless of what other artists had done. He studied diligently the pictures of the great Italians. Although little given to reading, he had his copy of Dürer's treatise on perspective. But in general his approach to painting was exceptionally personal and each of his solutions was unique.

After Rembrandt

The artists who came after Rembrandt, and those who were his contemporaries, are sometimes called the "Little Dutchmen." It is not only that their talents were small as compared with those of the one master, but that they specialized in painting little things and little effects. The literally little things include children and dogs and vegetables and milk jugs. The little effects are those of cunningly lighted interiors, meticulously detailed, of a windmill against a gray sky, or of trees along a canal. The little incidents of family life, too, are pictured in endless variation: the doctor's visit, the writing of a letter, the music lesson, cooking dinner.

It is not that these subjects had never appeared in serious art before. On the contrary, masters had made them incidental to great painting again and again. But never had they been exploited for their own sake and with such loving care for detail. Never had familiar sentiment been so turned to account. Somehow painting itself, the instrument that had compassed Michelangelo's fugues and El Greco's symphonies, was brought down also to little methods, to miniature prettinesses, to petty purposes. Thus was genre painting—"scenes from ordinary life"—first popularized and brought to its own sort of perfection.

If the subjects and the medium are slight, the

De Hooch:
In the Pantry.
Royal Museum, Amsterdam

list of accomplished and popular painters is big out of all proportion. The museums are full of canvases by Brouwer and van Ostade, by Metsu and Maes, by ter Borch and Jan Steen, by de Hooch and Vermeer and Gerard Dou. It is not necessary, in tracing the main current in the world stream of art, to pause over each of these men, whatever their fame in schoolhouse and museum. Some never rose above a competent sort of illustration. Nicolaes Maes catches something of Rembrandt's magical lighting, but uses it to less noble ends and does not, on the other hand, arrive at the miniature mastery of ter Borch or Vermeer. Gabriel Metsu, also influenced by Rembrandt in his early years, developed a distinctive type of middle-class genre painting, with exceptional polish.

Pieter de Hooch was one of the earliest of the Little Masters of Dutch interior painting. His household views with a few well-placed figures indicate a competent sort of surface composition. He could handle a subtle problem of natural lighting with the best of his fellows—except for Vermeer, from whom he learned something of the trick of it. More original in theme are his rare garden scenes, detailed down to the last leaf on each tree, the last blossom on each bush.

Gerard ter Borch, better born and widely traveled, arrived at a miniature achievement which is sure and pleasing. During one of his several visits abroad he met Velázquez, and he doubtless absorbed something of the Spaniard's technique of thin-paint use and of pearly coloring. He learned to eliminate, too, a good many accessories and details that his contemporaries felt constrained to cling to—retained as part of the "truth" of household naturalism—so that his little pictures have an agreeable atmosphere of simplicity and coherent harmony. There is much to be enjoyed in his exquisite portraits and genre bits. The *Boy Hunting Fleas* is typically atmospheric and harmonious and exact.

Most prolific of the Little Dutchmen, and least likely to be himself, or his best self, through any considerable run of his paintings, Jan Steen is the eclectic of the group. His tavern scenes have

Ter Borch:
Boy Hunting Fleas.
Alte Pinakothek,
Munich

long been favorites; his lively and crowded illustrations of lower-class home life are faithfully instructive and often amusing; and he used to be considered the peer of ter Borch and Vermeer. But it is increasingly recognized that his gifts were primarily those of a spirited illustrator. He was one of those who found capitalistic democracy unkind to art. He suffered hunger and went through bankruptcy, and toward the end turned his house into a tavern as a means of keeping alive. His work is most uneven, ranging from exquisite domestic scenes to mediocre and commonplace depictions of trivial and sensational incident.

It is Vermeer of Delft who transcends the others and lifts genre to a region of exquisite perfection. One of the lost and forgotten painters through several generations, he was rediscovered in the mid-nineteenth century, when the devotion of a French scholar brought his contribution to public attention and established him as painter of many works then ascribed to others. His reputation has grown steadily until today he stands second to Rembrandt alone as a master among Holland's artists.

No one has equaled Vermeer's delicacy in handling natural light. He commonly places his figures, preferably single, in an enveloping crystal-clear atmosphere, softly but palely warm. He clears out the clutter of detail and accessory that destroys unity of effect in so many Dutch interiors; or rather he organizes the canvas into an arrangement of a few detailed units against cleared backgrounds. In the end it is arrangement that spells his success. He is master of arranged surface composition, expert in adjusting line and mass with balance and grace. He loves to play with texture as such, fixing all its appealing values, whether in a caressable skin or in clean linen, or in glazed pottery or in polished

Vermeer:
Girl Reading a Letter.
State Gallery, Dresden

metals. Patterned stuffs, rugs and tablecloths and laces, exquisitely reproduced, add incidental richness at just the right point. His coloring is harmonious, cool, and agreeable. But always the telling over of his virtues brings one back to contrived but apparently natural lighting.

These many perfections found in Vermeer's canvases are, of course, fragilely refined. They tend toward the precious and the over-exquisite. It is not to deny his standing, which is at the very top in one miniature field of art, but only to restrain a too enthusiastic acceptance, that one points out the artist's total lack of imagination and the exclusion of everything that will not fit within a single formula of rather shallow plastic composition.

Obviously the Dutch did not want painting that went deep in either sense: as subjective expression, or as abstract orchestration. As regards the surface painting which they liked, comprehensible at a glance, flatteringly familiar, admirably representational, Vermeer is the perfect artist. His expressiveness goes further than that, is inward in that his own method perfectly represents the clean Dutch ways, the bright, polished neatness of the Dutch household, the tidymindedness and thrifty economy of the Hollanders. There is something choice, something sweet and fresh, about each of Vermeer's too rare canvases as one meets them in the museums. A little flame of joy leaps up as one recognizes on the walls their delicate manner, their discreet touch, their pure atmosphere.

Landscape painting had been developed in

Vermeer: *A Woman Weighing Gold.*
Widener Collection, National Gallery, Washington

Flanders and Germany, and toyed with in Italy, and so was not an invention of the Dutch. But they were the first to glorify it and place it among the foremost popular categories of art. Holland saw the first great school of landscapists, the earliest group of artists who devoted themselves exclusively to the out-of-doors scene.

There had been Dutch experimenters and pioneers some time after the advances made by Patinir and Altdorfer and Brueghel. Rembrandt did a few landscape canvases such as *The Mill* in the Widener Collection at the National Gallery, Washington, and the *Landscape with Obelisk* in the Gardner Museum, Boston, which have more vigor and largeness than any by the later Dutch specialists. Before him had been one Hercules Seghers, who is credited with teaching Rembrandt something of etching and of landscape composition.

But it is the group of specializing painters somewhat younger than Rembrandt who constitute the so-called Dutch landscape school: Albert Cuyp, Paul Potter, Philips Wouwerman, Adrian van de Velde, Jan van Goyen, Meindert Hobbema, and Jacob van Ruisdael. Not one of these but was competent to represent an observed

Vermeer: *Portrait of a Young Girl. Royal Picture Museum, The Hague*

interesting landscape truthfully and even attractively. But Ruisdael did a great deal more.

Van Goyen had brought to the outdoor scene something of the quality or element that Vermeer had added to interior views: arrangement. For all the natural "look" of his picture, it is found upon analysis to have gained by an adjustment of parts that is artificial, an augmentation out of his reasoned or intuitive grasp of abstract composition. Ruisdael had the sense of arrangement, and he

Ruisdael: *The Jewish Cemetery. State Gallery, Dresden*

added a richness or fullness of expression that lifts him above all his fellows.

Hobbema, for instance, had a good eye for well-balanced bits in nature—an alley of trees centered between diversified fields and buildings, or a group of houses in an island of trees between river and road. But there is this difference: one feels that Hobbema *found* picturesque materials and faithfully transcribed them, whereas Ruisdael was able to create them.

With the latter the materials are nature's and Holland's, but the compositional garment is Ruisdael's. There is a communication of felt mood and character, too. The atmosphere of a wet sky and drenched field, or the strange subdued-brilliant light from a sun just setting, or a vapor-softened marshland, is delicately conveyed.

Uneven in his work, Ruisdael occasionally attempted more than he could compass, and he changed over to a less congenial but fashionable style toward the end, when neglected and in want. He left many unimportant canvases. But there is a sufficiently large body of superior pictures marked by his special amplitude and his atmospheric felicity, based on a good grasp of abstract order, to warrant his rank with the earliest true masters of the landscape. In *The Jewish Cemetery*, for instance, a student may find exceptional materials for instructive analysis: first, in the organizational elements, the use of line and plane, of volume and space, of light and dark, and of textures, to create a firmly locked formal unity, with full and varied counterplay of main and minor rhythms; and second, in the distilled feeling of cold and desolation, of a tomb-like sadness. Most popular and pleasing, of course, are the familiar broad landscapes, filled with movement but beautifully calm; which might so often be better called skyscapes, so extensive an area is given to the sky and its masses of living, moving clouds.

Ruisdael's talents were too powerful and too large for the public of his time. He, too, died in the poorhouse.

There are puzzling and curious aspects of the art history of Holland, of the first annals of democratic art. First, there is the appearance of a single genius, apparently without ancestry, and certainly without progeny, a lonely, removed figure. Second, there is the birth in a single generation—one might almost say the spawning in one batch—of more popular painters than ever before or after appeared at one time in one place: within fifteen years, 1617 to 1632, were born ten of the important Dutch painters, men known to every museum-goer, including Vermeer, Ruisdael, ter Borch, de Hooch, Steen, Cuyp, Potter, and Maes. Third, there is the sudden cessation of the line, for after Hobbema, who was born in 1638 and died in 1709, there were no more celebrated Dutch painters, even of the "little" variety, until late in the nineteenth century. Fourth, there is witnessed the curious phenomenon of thousands of Dutch citizens, in that prolific seventeenth century, speculating in pictures, buying great numbers of prints and paintings, selling or trading them at fairs, bargaining with the artists for lowest prices (and trading on the frequent dire need of the producers), generally making a gambling commodity and an instrument of materialistic gain of what should be, some impossible

idealists have suggested, a companion to man in his nobler haunts and his least commercial moments. And there is—final circumstance—the Hollanders' consistent neglect, not to say social abuse, of every artist who showed talent above the second rank: the neglect of Rembrandt and Vermeer, the toleration of bankruptcies that embittered both Hals and Rembrandt, the obtuse disregard that drove Steen to alcohol and Ruisdael to the poorhouse.

These strange phenomena accompanied the beginning of art in the modern society that is democratic and bourgeois-controlled. No wonder some recent commentators, finding the twentieth-century artist hardly more secure in the social structure, have extolled the virtues of old-fashioned royal and aristocratic patronage.

But the artist, when he can be brought to consider politics, is likely to be the most devoted advocate of democracy. Perhaps it is the *kind* of democracy that is to be blamed. Perhaps a sort will be devised that will permit painters to be painters. There are, of course, people who go about saying that artists do their best work when close to starvation; the Hollanders must have said it first. It is just possible that some other system would prove that the world has lost more of transcending art than it has gained by moving the artist's studio over within sight of the poorhouse. Rembrandt would have shrugged at the thought, would have kept right on brushing his canvas till he was dragged to a pauper's grave.

XXIV: FRANCE AND
THE INTERNATIONAL BAROQUE ART

FRANCE was disunited and torn with wars in those decades during which the van Eycks were, with almost incredible swiftness, emancipating Northern art from its medieval fetters and establishing realism as painting's normal mode of expression in Europe. At the same time Masaccio and his fellows and followers in Florence were initiating the scientific reforms which were to provide a bridge from primitive formalism to representation in accordance with "the modern vision." France, geographically between these pioneering and originating nations, was then busy fighting or recuperating to fight again. This is the explanation of the centuries of artistic impotence between the era of Romanesque and Gothic art and the appearance of the French school in the seventeenth century.

The work done by the French courts and armies after the Gothic period was not without influence upon the arts. The feudal lords were then put down; the bourgeoisie emerged as a power but was reconciled to the most ornamental monarchy in Western history; and the machinery was established for standardizing the crafts styles internationally. But very little surpassing art came out of France in the period 1350-1600.

Those were the greatest centuries of the painting art in Europe. The fourteenth century belonged to Siena and Giotto; the fifteenth to Florence and Flanders; the sixteenth saw the brief rise of Germany's star, and the glory of the Venetian school and of El Greco in Spain. The seventeenth, too, was to see greater names than those of France: Rembrandt and Rubens, even

Watteau: *The Embarkation for Cytherea. Louvre*

493

Velázquez and Van Dyck. If one presses, for France, the names of Poussin and Claude Lorrain, magnifying their stature, there is certain to be the rejoinder that both were lifelong expatriates, and that Lorrain was more German than French in all respects. Nevertheless, with them the true French tradition begins; although it was the mid-eighteenth century before European art leadership fully returned to France. It was exercised for a time to spread a courtly sort of art that is the least profound and least honest of the European international styles. Only in the nineteenth century was the nation's genius to be soundly and creatively world-influencing. Then the French became the leaders in art among Western peoples.

In short, France disappears from the story of art as the Gothic spirit fades, and is heard from only in minor channels through three centuries, establishes a sort of ornamental leadership in the era of Versailles court grandeur, and true creative leadership after the Revolution.

At one moment during the Flemish advance —sometimes counted by French historians a French movement—Flanders and its art had almost fallen into the lap of Paris. But Philip the Hardy, himself a prince of the true house of France, the Valois, having become Duke of Burgundy and married Marguerite of Flanders in 1369, turned enemy to his brother, the French King, just when signs pointed to a renaissance for the united nation—a renaissance that could only have had a strong Flemish stamp. In any case the Burgundian dukes continued to take Flemish artists to the capital at Dijon from the vice-capital at Bruges, whereas the rest of France was plunged into devastating warfare.

The start made by the King of France and a third brother, the Duke of Berry, toward a court-fostered art was brief-lived. Civil war, then defeats at the hands of the English, shattered all stability. Aside from the school of Burgundy there persisted only some small effort in Provence and Touraine, where a primitive tradition survived. This gave way to a school of miniature-realistic portraiture which is of interest, which has its little masters, but which has only passing international significance.

Supposed portrait of *le Dauphin Charles,* son of Charles VIII. *Louvre*

When the country was truly united, late in the fifteenth century, the court turned for culture to the South, and a pale reflection of Italian Renaissance art guided French taste. So Italianate was the following century that all the chief names are of French artists resident in Italy or of Italian artists imported to Fontainebleau, Paris, and Versailles. It was France's adaptation of Italian Renaissance and baroque forms that determined the national style when finally Louis XIV decided to make Paris the art capital of the world and began to send out the courtly palace influence to every great kingdom or petty duchy of Europe.

And indeed when France was fairly established as an originating nation the keynote of its first

Pietà. Ascribed to an unknown painter, school of Avignon.
Helen Clay Frick Collection, New York

gift to the world was courtliness. Witness the opera houses and ballets and tapestries as well as Watteau's bonbon-box painting. Of course there was a counter-current of revived "classical" art too. But artistic France, up to the Revolution, was essentially monarchical, concerned with a baroque decorativeness. The influence was on the side of an insubstantial, fashionable courtiers' playtime art.

Painting from the Primitives to the Portraitists

When a pope made Avignon the official residence of the Holy See, abandoning a too disorderly and discredited Rome in 1305, he built a palace in the Provençal city and of course wanted the latest adornments for it. Among the artists called from Italy to decorate its walls was no less a figure than Simone Martini of Siena. Thus was introduced an influence colorful,

rhythmic, and graceful. France had, of course, its schools of miniaturists; but when a French type of primitive painting appeared, it was marked by characteristics not a little reminiscent of the Sienese.

The present-day knowledge of French primitive artists is defective. There is a school of Avignon—best represented by the famous *Pietà* in the Louvre—which exhibits typical Northern traits along with certain of the Italian idioms. And there are scattered panels known as Franco-Italian which are among the most intriguing of late medieval paintings. A characteristic work is the *Pietà* which is to be seen in two versions, with and without the donor, in the Frick Collection, New York. In this, as in the Louvre panel, it is fairly easy to detect something Gothic, certainly some quality that is not to be found in the graceful Sienese pictures. The transition in Italy had been direct from Byzantine to the linear melodies and sunny colorfulness of Duccio. In the panels typically French

—though the phrase may not be wholly warranted—there is a stiffer or more angular effect that is essentially French Gothic. Even the Cologne primitives are nearer the Italian type.

There are fugitive examples in France of nearly every transitional mode, and some strange hybrid things besides. There are pictures painted, apparently, after the makers of miniatures had seen and admired a Sienese masterpiece, or, a little later, a Flemish oil-painted panel. There is a Master of Moulins whose works are nearer to the German type, or perhaps, like the German, strongly influenced by the Flemings. Artists of the so-called school of Provence, on the other hand, suggest Italian affiliations.

Of named artists not far from the old formalism but already aware of the van Eyckian search for exactness of statement, Malouel is most notable. He had gone from Flanders to the Burgundian capital; but if the attributed *Madonna and Child* is really his, or the panel, *God with the Virgin and St. John Weeping over the Body of Jesus,* in the Louvre, then one may know that he had taken a direction away from the Northerners—his own, or possibly one to be signposted as French.

One of the earliest named painters is Enguerrand Charonton, who did a panoramic altarpiece for the Church of the Chartreux at Villeneuve-lès-Avignon in 1453: a marvelously mixed work, perhaps because the artist and his assistants divided up the several parts. There are unmistakable Italian influences apparent in the heaven portion, showing the Virgin being crowned; and signs of Flemish exactitude in the view of Rome (which is depicted as a Northern medieval city) and in the hosts of lesser figures. There are fascinating bits in the painting, but what is exceptionally instructive, as indicating the artist's way of working at this time, is the extant contract between the wealthy patron-donor and Charonton. The document binds the painter to deliver an altarpiece upon which "first there shall be the representation of Paradise and in this Paradise shall be the Holy Trinity." It goes on thus (in the translation by Guy Eglington):

And between Father and Son shall be no dif-

Jean Malouel: *Madonna and Child*

ference; and the Holy Spirit in the form of a dove, and Our Lady, before. . . . Item: By the side of Our Lady shall be the angel Gabriel with a certain number of angels, and on the other side Saint Michael with such number of angels as shall seem best to the said master Enguerrand. Item: on the other hand Saint John the Baptist with other patriarchs and prophets. . . .

Item: after the heavens the earth, of which shall be shown a portion of the city of Rome. Item: on the side of the setting sun shall be the form of the Church of Saint Peter of Rome, and the front of the said church at the portal has a cone of copper and ilex, [whence] one descends by great steps into a large square leading to the bridge Sant' Angelo. Item: on the left side of the said square is a portion of the wall of Rome and on the other side are houses and shops of all manner of men; at the end of the said square is the castle of Sant' Angelo and a bridge over the Tiber which is in the city of Rome. . . . Item: on the left side will be Hell . . . and on the

Fouquet: *Virgin and Child*, detail. *Antwerp Museum*

side of Hell will be a greatly deformed devil on the mountain, turning his back on the angel and lying in wait for certain souls in Hell, which, by other devils, are driven toward him. Item: in Purgatory and Hell will be souls of every estate according to the judgment of the said master Enguerrand. . . . Item: the said master Enguerrand shall use all his science in the Holy Trinity and the Blessed Virgin, and the rest according to his conscience.

And so on, through many paragraphs itemizing subject-matter. Even the colors, which might otherwise not be up to first quality for luster and permanence, are specified.

It is Jean Fouquet, however, who is commonly marked as the first significant French painter. He combines the influences—is known to have visited Italy, and worked side by side with imported Flemish miniaturists—yet has distinctive qualities of sensitivity and tasteful objectivity which are not quite attained elsewhere. He is an illustrator, of course, as are all the French and Flemings in this mid-fifteenth century, as will be most of the Italians within a generation or so. But he brings a moderately expert understanding of plastic organization to his pictures, whether still actual manuscript-illustrations or larger panels. He is not far behind the van Eycks and Dirk Bouts in exploration of the outdoor scene for background effects: the landscape of the *St. Marguerite* in the Book of Hours of Etienne Chevalier is already landscape not only well observed but attractively realized. (The so-called French landscape school will stem from another growth entirely, some generations later.)

But it is as a portraitist that Fouquet particularly scores. The *Portrait of an Unknown Man* in the Lichtenstein Gallery, Vienna, is one of the

Diane de Poitiers. Ascribed to François Clouet. *Worcester Art Museum*

best, recommended by its very simplicity and its utter honesty of statement. Some prefer the *Charles VII* in the Louvre as more characterful. It is when Fouquet leaves straightforward documentation that he betrays his limitations as a picture-maker. The famous *Virgin and Child* at Antwerp is but badly served, formally, by the background cherubs (which nicely fill one side of the canvas but let the eye slip off the edge at the other). The Virgin, nevertheless, is beautifully done, perhaps because it is a portrait—a likeness, it is said, of Agnès Sorel, the actress and favorite of King Charles VII.

Any roomful of early French pictures will show how Fouquet's work led to the portraiture of the elder Clouet, in the next generation, and of his son or sons in the next. France was portrait-mad at this time. There are 341 portraits listed

Corneille de Lyon:
A Nobleman.
Johnson Collection,
Philadelphia Museum

among the effects left by Catherine de' Medici, queen of Henry II, at her death in 1589. Miniatures and enamels were fashionable as well as the Clouet type of painting. Enameling, for many centuries a French art centered at Limoges, may be put down indeed as a source of some of the qualities realized by Fouquet and his followers.

Jean Clouet, the father, probably from Brussels, was an excellent draftsman and he knew how to frame up a bust or half-figure effectively; although, like most of the middle-period Flemings, he was likely to destroy concentration of interest by his too scrupulous attention to detail in all corners. Such portraits as the *William of Montmorency* at Lyons or the attributed *Elizabeth of Austria* in the Louvre are individually rewarding to study. The gallery of Clouet likenesses affords an extraordinary record of the people of courtly France at this time.

If the names of the Clouets and of Corneille de Lyon occur surprisingly often on museum walls and in private collections, it is because something like a portrait factory was organized to exploit both the products and the trademarks, with many artists as assistants. Jean Clouet and his son François were less concerned with the very small portraits (which are not quite small enough to be technically miniatures). These were rather the specialty of Corneille de Lyon. The beautifully finished little plaques from his hand (and those of what assistants we know not) approach the richness of the contemporary enamels and provide one of the very pleasurable spots in an otherwise arid period.

There was, no doubt, some little influence from the world-popular Holbein upon the later developments under the names of Clouet and Corneille de Lyon, in sensitive and expressive use of line, and in a method of paling facial shadows to give a blond aspect to the flesh areas, these being further brought into contrast by nearby masses of black. But the Frenchmen were little masters in their own right.

Poussin: *The Baptism. Bridgewater House, London.*
(By permission of the Earl of Ellesmere)

The Italians at Fontainebleau, and Poussin

France at the time of the Clouets was, as the chapter so far reveals, artistically provincial. To the north the later group of Flemings was again breaking new ground, with at least one world master in Brueghel. The Germans were completing their half-century of distinctive achievement. In Italy, Michelangelo had capped the progress of Florence and Rome, and the school of Venice was entering upon its most glorious period. The French King and courtiers recognized Italy as the new fountain of culture. They patronized their own portrait-makers, but portraiture seemed a tame display when placed beside the great pictures of the Italians. There began, about 1530, a process of borrowing, based on a recognition of cultural inferiority, that was to mean within a century the complete Italianization of French art.

France in troubled days had entertained Italian masters. Leonardo da Vinci, then an old man, had accepted the invitation of Francis I to take up residence at Amboise near Blois in 1516, but rather promptly died there. Andrea del Sarto had served the same monarch briefly, too—served him ill, incidentally, since he took back to Florence a purse of money and failed to deliver paintings as agreed. Later Benvenuto Cellini was to visit the northern court.

But the story of French art as such is bound up rather with the lesser Italians who became fixtures in France, and with two Frenchmen who (this was a little later, after 1600) went to Italy to spend their working life. The most important of the artists who were bought and brought was Francesco Primaticcio, a decorator who represented the run-out Florentine tradition, or the new Bolognese extension of it. He and his associates and assistants set up a veritable Italian island in the heart of France, at Fontainebleau.

There are no important works surviving, nor any names worth remembering, from the school of Fontainebleau. But it is well to note that in the un-self-reliant French court there was established, in the fifteen-thirties, this center of influence, and actual examples of Italian grand-manner ornamentation. All the later Renaissance

Poussin: *Orpheus and Eurydice. Louvre*

mannerisms and devices were demonstrated by Italians who soon called themselves Frenchmen, and by the French artists who gathered round and imitated them. And this had a bearing on what was to be French taste and a French style one hundred and fifty years later.

Architecture responded almost immediately, and so did the art of the theater; but painting retrogressed, became the strange mixed thing which is perhaps to be expected when a frozen classicism crosses with sensuality and love of display. The paganism of glorified nudity was perfectly to the taste of the triflers of the court, was fitted to express the special society for which art was now set to work. But the academic grandeur and the habit of veiling realism behind mythological allegory hindered formation of any real style. A borrowed rhetoric prevailed.

In exception, there is a freshness about the anonymous *Flora and Attendants* which lifts it above Bolognese posed and forced monumentalism. Almost it suggests a possible happy meeting of Italian rhythmic lyricism and the Fouquet-Clouet sort of cleanness and polish. But it is a very rare sort of exception.

The school of Fontainebleau, then, is to be counted no more than preparation and fertilization. But of the Frenchmen who went to Italy

to study and stayed, one, Nicolas Poussin, was successful in establishing a way of art that was to be picked up by later generations and made basic to a French tradition. That Poussin had something creative to give is proved, perhaps, by his success in adding a significance to the late Florentine-Roman classicism when the Italians themselves were finding it only a road to futility.

Poussin turns out in the end to be always a trifle hard, his effects calculated, his approach intellectual. But at the far pole from intuitively felt, spontaneous, and emotional painting, where rationalism and intellect control, he is nearly supreme. He had studied, obviously, Raphael and the antique statues and Domenichino. He put together several derived manners—but emerged with one of his own. Beneath the manner is something most unusual in this seventeenth century: a calculated display of pictorial structure. There is mathematical distribution of parts, a play and counterplay of balanced weights, of arranged planes, of answering lights. Once one gets over the obvious unreality, the too scholarly artificiality, one's eye begins to find a subtly rhythmic order in the compositions. The volumes, planes, and textures, the chiaroscuro and the sparing color, are orchestrated cunningly and with great sureness.

Claude Lorrain: *Marriage of Isaac and Rebecca. National Gallery, London*

Poussin is almost the only artist successful in just this way. He permits himself to become a slave to classic notions of purity, grandeur, and remoteness, yet he goes on to capture a large measure of plastic aliveness, of melodious movement. His canvases ought, by evidence of one's first glance, to be as empty as those of Giulio Romano or Anton Raphael Mengs, and observers enough still dismiss them as static, cold, and pedantic. But with the modern sharpening of the eye for abstract rhythms and plastic order, new recognition has come to the expatriate Frenchman. His orchestration, to be sure, never carries him near the grand formal effects of a Michelangelo or an El Greco; but in his own shy and restrained way he is a structural master.

The scholarly Poussin did not find the France of his day congenial and he spent his life in Rome. The painters still in the run-out tradition of the school of Fontainebleau were carrying on what they thought to be the true expression of neoclassicism, modified further toward the sensual and the magnificent by the conditions of royal living, in which courtesans and their affairs had undue weight. At the same moment Poussin, away in Rome, was developing this other classicism, with its sound architectural foundation, which may be called typically French because the essence of it was to appear again and again in the French non-courtly painters: most notably in Chardin, in the classicists who reacted toward purity and sound structure in the era of the Revolution, in Ingres, and finally in France's most original painter, Cézanne.

If Poussin faintly chills—with his tombs and ruins, his long-dead Greek philosophers, his over-delicate pastoral shepherdesses, his too literary legends, and his rather colorless method—one yet may enjoy his sure, slight melody and know that here the French tradition is at last established. He initiates a pictorial *discipline* which is definitely national.

Claude Lorrain: *Landscape with a Piping Shepherd. William Rockhill Nelson Gallery*

The men of Poussin's generation or slightly after—except Claude, of whom more in a moment—are almost negligible; though Eustache Lesueur is treated seriously in most of the books. He was honestly rather than displayfully classical; but he departed from the colder methods to gain something out of his own warm sympathy for the life around him. A simple and plain man, son of a carpenter and father of a grocer, he was unpretentious and content with his small triumphs. It may seem strange, considering his predilection for classic and religious subjects and his low station, but he had a quality of airy grace in painting which contains more than a hint of the Watteau-Boucher prettiness of two generations later.

At the same time a wave of Low Country naturalism again swept France. Best known among the practitioners were the three Le Nain brothers, whose popular works are scenes of peasant life, done with Dutch honesty but without the redeeming delicacy and compositional consistency of ter Borch or Vermeer. At the other extreme of method and interest was Charles Le Brun, grandiloquent, soft, facile, and decorative. His paintings are less significant to us today than is the fact that he was the first head of the French Royal Academy and thus connected with an institution that has been considered in "liberal" opinion a bulwark of anti-art.

Claude Gelée remains an authentic figure whether for pure enjoyment or for his place as initiator. Not French except by accident of birth, he nevertheless is commonly counted as in the French tradition, even as an originator of it. He seems to have left his birthplace in the border province of Lorraine, whence the name Claude Lorrain by which he is commonly known, at the age of twelve, to live with a brother in Germany. He later went to Italy and eventually made Rome his permanent place of residence. He not only never visited Paris and the courts but probably never set foot in any part of France except Lorraine. His teachers and his companions, too, were

Italian and German. Yet his work *is* French; partly by reason of some quality more Gallic than anything else; partly because, with Poussin's, his example led directly to a French "picturesque landscape" current and influenced scattered painters from the dry Hubert Robert and the courtly Watteau to the Barbizon landscapists and the impressionists.

Claude Lorrain bridged, so to speak, from classicism to observed open-air realism. His classicism is incidental rather than fundamental: at times is a none-too-fitting ornamentation, at other times a specious affectation. It consists, on that side, of introduced goddesses and shepherdesses, of antique ruins and Greek statues and urns. But in his work, too, are a calm, a discipline, and a rational structure which are on the true classic side. Claude's greatest service to art, however, lies in the discovery by him of the out-of-doors as subject-matter, and an advance in atmospheric lighting. He puts the sun, the glamorous southern sun, to work with effect. Like Poussin—and all would be futile without it—he expertly uses pictorial architecture, arranged structure; though apparently by instinctive grasp rather than with forethought.

Altogether this limited and—they say—downright ignorant man, who oftener than not hired someone else to paint in the figures of his landscapes because he could not manage them correctly, pushed forward the art of painted views in the South, much as the Hollanders were doing during his lifetime in the North.

The art of Poussin and of Claude is a meaty episode in a tale thin and unnutritious. Claude was born in 1600, and his working period was two centuries later than Fouquet's—and what a dearth of names between! After the two Roman Frenchmen there was another empty period. French art was to reappear importantly at the court of Louis XIV, about 1700. But it would then be seen to have one root not indicated in either the false classicism of the Fontainebleau episode or the real classicism developed in the South; nor again in any of those minor manifestations, Clouet miniature portraiture or Le Nain genre or Le Brun academism. It was introduced into France by a celebrated internationalist who

was a favorite at all the great courts of Europe in that century—Rubens. Since there is just here a natural pause in the French story, opportunity is afforded to go back and inquire into the phenomenon of the baroque style, which alone can explain Rubens and the later French art of Watteau and Fragonard.

Rubens more often than any other eminent painter confines within his pictures a great deal of nervous movement, of fluttering light, of interweaving curved lines and sinuous forms. He is at the far pole from classic repose, clarity, and horizontality. He is the typical baroque painter.

The Rise and Triumph of Baroque

Baroque, as a style, developed first in architecture, not in painting. It followed upon the disintegration of Renaissance neoclassic architecture. While there is no consistent logic in the Italian version of classic building design, it had been marked, under Bramante and Palladio and Vignola, by strict laws governing the design and placing of ornamental features, particularly columns and capitals, pediments and cornices. The logical structural reason for these elements was gone, but they at least pretended to a certain functional look and position. One illogic breeds another, and builders without academic reverence for Vitruvian rules began to mix the ornaments, to tamper with the severe classic outlines and the traditionally fixed detail. Soon they were twisting the columns, bulging out the straight silhouette, wreathing the capitals with garlands. They broke the pediments at the center to admit statues, and they piled up heaps of mixed ornamentation at every likely transition point or terminal.

Under most baroque architectural envelopes there persist classic outlines, marked by pilasters and columns, by grouped windows and arch-of-triumph doorways, by cornices and string courses. But all the original Greek horizontal repose and mathematical clarity has disappeared. The building is restless, loaded, self-proclaimingly dressed up.

It is possible that even the better minds among

Church of Santa Maria
della Salute,
Venice

Italian architects recognized that they had rigged up only a too little expressive thing in the standard Rome-derived Renaissance building. The avowed purist Palladio had recombined the classic forms, putting large and small columns side by side, and multiplying cornices and balustrades. Sansovino further enriched façades with wreathings and intricately sculptured panels and rows of crowning statues; although he kept the building's divisions and outlines clear. (See page 385.) All this led to a more theatrical and unconsidered straining after magnificent effect, after variety and profusion. Soon parts were swelling out like overripe fruit. Severity of outline gave place to broken silhouette. Opulent, even frivolous streamers of ornament clambered over every foot of wall space. The style had got out of hand.

This is not to say that baroque design is all overblown or tortured. A few architects—then sculptors, then painters—recognized a certain fitness in the curved line and the swelling form, an appropriateness to the regal pretensions of king and bishop, and they saw a chance to dramatize contemporary life in their own way. They measurably tamed the style and left many churches and a few palaces that please the discriminating eye; along with very little sculpture —and Rubens' painting.

The name baroque—which seems to have the very look of the manifestation in it—is as difficult to trace to an origin as is the style itself. It may have been derived from the Portuguese *barocco*, defining a pearl irregularly shaped; or it may be traced to the Italian *verruca*, "wart"; or, again, to the Greek *baros,* "heavy." All three ideas, irregularity, wartiness, heaviness, seem to belong to the architectural manifestation.

Of church exteriors the most celebrated in the style is Santa Maria della Salute in Venice. The main portal is a Roman triumphal arch; the dome emerges fairly clear as the Renaissance type; and there is the standard assortment of classic pilasters, pediments, cornices, and balustrades. But what a jumble, all the way up to the drum of the dome! How illogical, how unfunctional! Yet somehow, how beautiful! For the pile has *great* beauty when seen from a distance—though the glamorous Grand Canal has something to do with it.

The interior of St. Peter's Church in Rome had been designed originally by Bramante and Michelangelo in the late Renaissance style. It was transformed by Bernini and Maderna into what is today undoubtedly the most ambitious and resplendent display of Italian baroque. Lorenzo Bernini (1598-1680) was the director of building at St. Peter's for forty years (under eight popes) and his authority was almost absolute. Like most of the builders of his time he was sculptor and decorative painter as well as architect. He designed the pontifical throne and its sunburst backing. His also is the astonishing ninety-foot *baldacchino* or ornamental canopy over the altar, supported by four immense tortured columns. These compositions, which are not so much architecture as sculpture and dazzling bursts of decoration, are among the most controversial designs in Europe. The forecourt of the church, St. Peter's Piazza, is Bernini's outstanding architectural achievement. The double curved colonnade which encloses the Piazza is a quarter-mile in length, with nearly three hundred enormous Doric columns, topped by sixty-odd statues.

Carlo Maderna was Bernini's chief associate architect in the work at St. Peter's, and when he died Francesco Borromini was appointed to take his place. In Borromini the climax was reached in the use of fantastic detail. What had started as a reaction against the continuing use of dull classical mannerisms in building reached undreamed-of extremes of eccentricity in his work. The reaction had begun as far back as Michelangelo's

time in little dissatisfactions and little revolts that already were apparent in his San Lorenzo Chapel in Florence. The Church of the Gesú, Mother Church of the Jesuits in Rome, originally planned by Michelangelo, was replanned with a restrained baroque façade by Vignola; but it was Giacomo della Porta who finally designed the façade as it stands today. It is considered one of the earliest and best examples of the baroque style. Of the late Italian baroque masterpieces, the most characteristic example is perhaps Borromini's San Carlo alle Quattro Fontane.

Bernini so long remained practically a dictator in Rome that he was for a time the most celebrated architect in Europe. He was called to Paris by Louis XIV, and was given a brilliant reception. If his new designs for the Louvre, his portrait of the king, and his sketches for sculptural works for Versailles were later discarded, it was because the French, once wholly dependent upon Italy for leadership, at last desired only a French neoclassicism. There came to be jealous avoidance of foreign contributions. Many influences were at work that were to lead, after a long period of architectural decadence in Italy, into another and less ornate phase of recurrent classicism, the neoclassicism of Canova's era.

Meantime the baroque style had been adopted by the Jesuit leaders of the Counter-Reformation, who became the most active educators in Europe, and active builders too. Thus it pushed especially into Spain, where more good façades are to be seen in the style than in any other country. It developed there into a special form known as the Churrigueresque. José Churriguera (1650-1725), who gave the style that name, was not the first architect of Spanish baroque building, and the extravagantly overelaborated work that came to dominate the style in his name was of a later period. The year before he was born, Alonzo Cano had made a triumphal arch, after Borromini, for the entry of Doña Maria Ana of Austria into Madrid, and a generation of followers of the Cano brothers worked in the manner and spirit of the Italian baroque long before Churriguera planned his great doorway for the new cathedral at Salamanca, or his catafalque for Queen Marie Luise de Bourbon. His followers and imitators finally

St. Peter's Church interior, Rome, as seen by the eighteenth-century painter
Giovanni Panini. *Louvre*

destroyed all architectural logic and created a welter of ornament. Curved lines, twisted columns, spiraled brackets were everywhere. Statuary, medallions, carved draperies, festoons, foliage, even Moorish arabesques spread over doorways that literally expanded to cover whole façades. The Cathedral of Nuestra Señora del Pilar in Saragossa ranks among the most lavishly ornamented of the great Spanish baroque buildings, but none excels the old Romanesque Cathedral of Santiago at Compostela as redesigned by Fernando Casas y Novoa. In silhouette it is a complex of towers, obelisks, brackets, and volutes. Its façade is a screen of all-over patterning. But the church interiors offer the richest massing of detail, on choir screens, on tombs, in the vaulting of the naves, and especially on the retables, or altar screens. None excels the altar screen of St. Tecla, in Burgos Cathedral.

From Spain the special Spanish sort of baroque traveled to the colonies in America, and flowered in churches all the way from Mexico to the extremity of South America. One may find the inordinately enriched doorways and towers and altar screens in Cuzco or Lima, Peru, or in Quito, Ecuador, or in almost any ancient Mexican city. In much of the free-standing sculpture as well as in the architectural decoration there is the Spanish love of movement, swirl, and concentrated grandeur, even of theatricality.

In many European church interiors today one may trace just how the original Gothic structure was modified or refitted when the Renaissance influence was felt; how, then, the baroque wave followed, with the introduction of a third crop of architectural or decorative features. In Bavaria, Tirol, and Switzerland there are churches consistently in the baroque style, gorgeously if not overwhelmingly decorative. Salzburg is particularly proud of its baroque monuments, and many

Bernini: *Ecstasy of Saint Theresa.* Santa Maria della Vittoria, Rome

an out-of-the-way Tirolean village has monasteries and chapels adorned in this fashion.

The baroque obviously was a style for palaces. There are examples scattered from the originating point in Rome to the petty courts in Germany and even to Russia and Sweden. It is no surprise to find Italian architects—like Italian stage decorators—invited to distant courts to design this or that palace or opera house or pavilion. France, having imported Italian builders, became jealous of foreign influences and developed her own restrained variation of baroque. In its late phase it was called "rococo." Several great architects, the Mansarts and Perrault among them, designed parts of the Louvre and the palace at Versailles.

Today's architects, now that they are returning to a structural rather than a decorative basis for their art, begin to claim that baroque design was no architectural style at all; that rather it was

what a group of decorative sculptors evolved when they mistakenly thought they were architects. Indeed, baroque is more a style of ornament or decoration than a mode of structure.

Bernini had been first a sculptor, then architect and decorator. Baroque sculpture may almost stand or fall by one example of his work (above). It shows how the baroque theatricality and the baroque profusion, when translated into metal and stone, resulted in a rich, flamelike sense of movement but at the expense of sculptural repose and plastic unity. The spiky, dispersed effects of Benvenuto Cellini had pointed in this direction. After Bernini, sculpture was a secondary art for two hundred years. The baroque feeling is one of sketchiness and fluidity, and sculptors affected by it practically gave up the stone for clay. Not until the twentieth century was the fallacy of that choice recognized, and return made from facile modeling to the basic stone block.

Rubens: *Rape of the Daughters of Leucippus. Alte Pinakothek, Munich*

Rubens and the Opulent Style; International Baroque Painting

From the building art there is sometimes carried over into discussions of painting the analogy of horizontal-accent and vertical-accent architecture. Giotto, when he was emerging from medievalism, showed his drift toward a neoclassic ideal in nothing so much as his reposeful, horizontal spread of figures. Giorgione introduced the low, undulating line, with all its peaceful connotations, into his pastoral pictures, and Titian followed him when dealing with classic themes. El Greco, however, returned to Gothic verticality and got his unforgettable movement-effects out of the aspiring line and flamelike forms. (Only his great mastery of plastic structure enabled him to hold his undulating lines and planes in a compact structure that is more Gothic than baroque.)

In accent upon the diagonal line, instead of horizontal or vertical, some theorists find the essential mark of baroque painting. Rubens, they point out, not only fills his canvases with nervous movement, thus achieving somewhat the effect of the broken silhouette and the poured-in ornaments of baroque architecture; he also stresses main diagonal lines. Witness the *Rape of the Daughters of Leucippus* herewith. Curved lines,

Rubens: *Coronation of Marie de' Medici. Louvre*

diagonal emphasis, and opulent, wavering forms are of the essence of the baroque painting method.

Perhaps Caravaggio's streaked lighting had some influence; perhaps the piling up of forms by the Caracci. Rubens studied and copied Titian and Veronese. But he is so outstandingly the representative of the baroque style, both its first great practitioner and the agent of its spread to Central and Northern Europe, that the style may be said to stand or fall with his achievement.

Born in Germany in 1577, of Flemish parents temporarily exiled, Peter Paul Rubens was brought up in Antwerp and at the early age of twenty-one became a member of the guild of painters there. But the call of Italy was strong among Low Country artists, and two years later Rubens was studying the Venetian masters in their own city, and soon after became court painter to the Duke of Mantua. He undertook diplomatic missions for his master, going to Florence and again as far abroad as Madrid. He was soon the great internationalist of art, speaking eight languages and traveling from country to country, from court to court.

Antwerp, however, became again his home, and he is generally accounted as belonging to the Flemish school; but it is to be noted that he built himself an Italian palace there. Trained by the Jesuits, he furthered the identification of baroque art with the Catholic Counter-Reformation, and particularly with the spread of baroque church architecture in Spain. (Some authorities describe Rubens as essentially a Spanish painter; a certain justification lies in the fact that Flanders at this time still belonged to the Spanish crown.)

Seldom has an artist been more industrious— he rose at five o'clock every morning—and never did a painter turn out a greater acreage of canvases. To ascribe all to Rubens' hand exclusively would be patently rash. As a matter of fact he is known to have had a horde of assistants, who often would paint a complete picture from the master's sketch, to be merely retouched by his hand. The method accounts for the great unevenness in the canvases passing as his work. Nor can anyone be sure how much in a competent or even beautiful piece may be by such a talented assistant as Van Dyck. Nevertheless, there can be no serious questioning of Rubens' surpassing talent as a monumental and vigorous decorator. He is also a masterly portraitist—in the range just below Titian and El Greco—and upon occasion a very fine landscapist. If one's taste runs to the magnificent and the exuberant,

Jordaens: *Fecundity. Brussels Museum*

one may choose Rubens as first among painters. For soberer tastes and more reposeful enjoyment, he is inferior to a dozen other masters. There are delicate-minded women who simply cannot endure being in a room with his pictures—partly because of the clash and turbulence of his diagonal method, but oftener because of the sensuality of his over-fleshly nudes. His color is often disturbing, seldom soothing or even harmoniously coordinated. Nor is he always able to distinguish the dramatic form from the melodramatic. At the age of fifty-three Rubens married one Helen Fourment, who, although only sixteen years old, was very plump, even opulently womanly; and thenceforward even his Madonnas had the physical roundness which proves disturbing to fastidious observers.

In the balance on the other side may be placed a genius for monumental vigor and extraordinary animation. Many of his pictures are superbly spirited. In the best of them he confined the strong movement within a planned compositional structure, amply justifying the dynamic power

and the overflowing abundance of materials.

Rubens is the greatest of the painters who lived contented in the physical realm, without intimations of mystic forces beyond the seeable world, without attempting poetic overtones or spiritual communication. He is earthy, virile, invigorating. His *joie de vivre* is contagious and compelling. There is great surface richness, too.

But to return to the baroque in his art: he had grasped during his long stay in Italy the essential nervous movement of it, and the profuse ornamentalism. Although he all but banished line as such in his later phase, the curved line as contour was his mainstay. The diagonal composition is in the great figure-pieces, sometimes even in the landscapes and portraits.

This art, capitalizing movement to a degree unprecedented, was demonstrated by Rubens at Madrid, at Paris, at London. Marie de' Medici of France had herself immortalized in a series of twenty-one panels from Rubens' hand. The flamboyant series is now in the Louvre. A baroque object-lesson was thus set up at the very heart of French court life. In Madrid it was Rubens who insisted that Velázquez get rid of his provincialism by studying in Italy; but Velázquez himself prudently returned to Titian after a time, although the baroque fashion proved just the dish for the lesser Spanish illustrator-painters. Whether Rubens actually brought about the fluttering weakness of eighteenth-century British portrait-painting is open to question; but the faults are of his kind—display, dispersion of volumes, overnervous or overloose composition.

In Antwerp itself some closer followers definitely aped the master. One, Jacob Jordaens, carried the sensual note and the dashing sinuous technique to a further extreme. The celebrated *Fecundity* from his brush (page 511) is opulent and brilliant; but one seems to see the virtuoso behind it. David Teniers the Younger, of the generation after Rubens and last of the usually named Flemings, had no talent for grandeur. He took what of the looser movement and animation he could assimilate to his intimate pictures of tavern life and peasants dancing.

Van Dyck, a second Fleming who became an international figure, was as a youth closely associated with Rubens; he entered the latter's studio as pupil and stayed as assistant. But he early shook off the more extreme mannerisms of the baroque. He learned a great deal from Titian's works—he is not notable as an initiator—and he went on to be an agreeable and exceedingly popular portraitist. He was a born courtier, and he worked almost entirely among aristocrats and princes. After five years in Italy and four in his native Antwerp, he was called to be court painter to King Charles I of England, and spent the next nine years laboring to keep up with the ever-increasing orders for portraits. He died of overwork, or at least of overexertion, leaving a great number of competent canvases and a few excellent ones.

His finer portraits are solid, restrained, and graceful. From the charming *Marchesa Cattaneo* or the sober *Cornelius van der Geest,* both in the National Gallery, London, one would never infer that Van Dyck had worked in the baroque tradition. But the *James Stuart* in the Metropolitan Museum of New York, fluent, opulent,

Van Dyck: *James Stuart, Duke of Lenox.*
Metropolitan Museum of Art

and superficially brilliant, slips over into the mannerisms of the style. It was this type of thing that led on to the courtly art of Reynolds and Gainsborough, and certainly to Lawrence. The best of Van Dyck seems to lie in the other direction, in the territory least touched by Rubens' influence, though the young man so perfectly imitated the master at one period that certain of his canvases may be taken at first glance for the master's.

There was no great successor to Rubens. It may almost be said that there is no other first-rate baroque painter in history. Delacroix, the ro-

Van Dyck: *Cornelius van der Geest. National Gallery, London*

manticist, was to attempt to found a school upon Rubens' methods two centuries later. In Italy, Tiepolo made superficially brilliant use of the swirl and the billowed forms (and did an occasional solid picture, too); but he goes back rather to a separate lineage, in which Veronese is important.

Although a horde of Italian painters answered the call of Bernini, who laid out vast plans for decorating the Jesuit churches, and for palaces, few were other than misled by the passion for movement and show. They ended in theatricality. One cannot overlook, as an exception, Alessandro Magnasco, whose canvases, as one comes upon them rarely in museums, give back a definite and quiet pleasure. He tamed the baroque style, achieved an individualistic interpretation of its diagonal-accent composition and brilliantly stac-

Magnasco: *Arcadian Landscape. Art Institute, Chicago*

cato handling. The *Arcadian Landscape* at Chicago illustrates his method of patterning by highlights, with generous use of dark masses for contrast.

It was, then, the *spirit* of baroque rather than the individualistic Rubens technique that lived on to transform French painting at the end of the seventeenth century, and then English painting. Perhaps without the background of court display, of the taste for brilliant make-believe living, the light spirit of it might have died within a generation. But France was on the verge of the most glittering exhibition of courtly manners and artificial culture in Western history; and the mannerisms of decadent baroque, and the titillating superficial play of it, were precisely to the taste of fop and courtesan. Watteau caught, in the small, the sense of surface movement, the nervous vibration, and the loose structure. Even earlier Largillière and Rigaud had brought over the sartorial aspect, the swish-swash and swirl of dashing clothes—as seen here in a typical aristocratic portrait by Largillière.

French Courtly Art

Grandeur without seriousness, elegant manners without sincerity, a continual pursuit of gaiety, a court life like a perpetual masquerade —such were the background and motivation of art in *le grand siècle*. The center of courtly activity had been shifted from Fontainebleau and "the château country" to Paris, where the Louvre was, by 1650, a pretentious and expansive palace; largely through the initiative of Henry II, spurred on by his favorite, Diane de Poitiers; somewhat through that of Henry IV and Richelieu. The Luxembourg was a second Italian-French Renaissance palace in Paris, built by Marie de' Medici, queen of Henry IV, and there were other notable centers of courtly activities, including the Tuileries and the palace of Richelieu.

The typical palace of the age of the great monarchs is, however, the suburban one at Versailles. It had been until the accession of Louis XIV a

Largillière:
*The Marquis
of Montespan.
California Palace
of the Legion of Honor,
San Francisco*

petit château, really a hunting lodge and hideaway for the Sun-King's moody predecessor. But the greatest Louis (except the Saint) set about to construct the most magnificent of royal residences. He once was chided by his minister Colbert, who preferred to see the Louvre further glorified, in these words: "This house contributes more to the pleasure and distraction of Your Majesty than to your glory. . . . If Your Majesty should seek to find in Versailles the five hundred thousand crowns which have been spent there in two years, you would have difficulty in finding them."

The King was merely spurred on to further expenditure, to creating at whatever cost an unexampled regal setting for the court pageantry. A mere palace, however magnificent, was not

enough. André Lenôtre laid out the surrounding gardens, which have been a model for park designers ever since, and they were enriched with accessory temples, fountains, grottoes, and statuary. The spirit of fêtes and pageants was externalized everywhere, inside and out, so that the dandies and the courtesans might never be without cushioned salons and boudoirs, romantic love nooks and rustic bowers.

The great art of France centered here, as well as the dilettante activity; the dramatists and actors came to the palace theater and staged masques in the gardens. Here French opera was born, and the ballet developed (under imported Italian masters). Here poets and architects and painters met and conversed and drank.

It was the courtesan element that triumphed

in painting and architecture. Nowhere else have the names of women entered so persistently into history as in the France of the late seventeenth and the eighteenth centuries. Certainly nowhere else has visual art been so feminized. It need not for that reason alone be frivolous art. But the nature of the women who advised and led the French kings was of a sort to influence the artist toward the make-believe thing, toward ostentatious artificiality and light ornamentalism. Interior decoration was soon transformed from baroque to rococo—the rock-and-shell style—and then to a delicate and not unpleasant boudoir version of neoclassic design. Watteau, Boucher, Fragonard were the painters of the time.

Some people are willing to credit two or three royal mistresses with the will to superfluous ornamentation which determined styles in furnishing (and these were to persist as elegant fashions down to 1920); and they believe it was the mischievous taste of these women that turned French painting away from the lead of Poussin and Claude and toward the trivial fêtes-galantes ideal. It is a more likely guess that, because baroque was in the air, any court determined to be gay and fashionable, whether mistress-ridden or not, would have arrived at walls lined with delicate curves, and flower-strewn, and at paintings painstakingly sweet and frivolous, without solidity or sincerity.

The best painters of the time are not to be dismissed as only and always concerned with frivolities and furbelows, and their intentions should not be condemned as consistently trivial and insincere. One wisely takes into consideration that all men have their light moments; one bows, moreover, before the inescapable historical fact that up to the early twentieth century the tradition persisted of art as a commodity especially contrived for ladies, or for festive and inconsequential occasions. Many histories, indeed, list Watteau and Fragonard among the greatest masters. For the rococo environment—and what long-established museum escapes some faint suggestion of it?—they are perfect.

The virtues of Largillière and Rigaud are obvious from almost any simple example. The picture is like the sitter's dress: satiny, befrilled, an honest reflection of sartorial magnificence. But Watteau and Boucher and Fragonard pretend to more than that single-minded exaltation of vestments. Besides, there *aren't* any clothes on a good many of the bodies they portray.

Antoine Watteau was first of the *galante* school. His lack of physical robustness may have had something to do with the extreme delicacy of his painting method. His death came at the age of thirty-seven, from tuberculosis. He is at his best in the exquisite illustration of dressed-up courtiers as they stroll, play games, dance, make love, or embark for the enchanted isles in an environment of festooned parks and gardens and pastoral fields. For this light business he had just the right fluttering touch. His colors are appropriately fresh and sweet. Occasionally he pulls together the composition, too, until one feels a pleasant pictorial compactness. (But one really dare not defend him, once judgment is put upon the basis of plastic organization, for the unity and controlled movement which Giorgione and Titian had beautifully managed in the earliest important pastoral scenes are here badly and finally dissipated.)

Watteau painted the Italian comedians successfully in a truthful record exciting to students of the theater; and there are individual portraits. But one comes back always gratefully to the brittle enchantment of *The Embarkation for Cytherea* or the *Fête Champêtre* or *The Garden of St. Cloud*. (See illustration, page 493.)

Watteau was born of Flemish parents, but he took on Parisian refinements until, in his last period, he was considered the most French of painters. The Academy, however, still pretending to a "classic" standard, received him (in 1712) under the designation *"peintre des fêtes galantes."* Incidentally it is illuminating to know that Watteau had little to do directly with the court at Versailles. There was by this time a circle of secondary courts, of state officials, cardinals, social pretenders, and visiting nobles, which patronized the rising fashionable artists, and of course demanded just as lightsome fare as the royal entourage consumed. Watteau was never official court painter. He gained his living by catering to the eager lesser aristocrats.

Watteau:
Fête Champêtre.
National Gallery
of Scotland,
Edinburgh

In the end he destroyed such of his paintings and sketches as seemed to him too erotic, and he painted a *Crucifixion* for the pastor of the town in which he was dying. The incident reminds one that painting of nudes had taken a turn for the worse in the hothouse courtly atmosphere. Never before had there been such a teasing display of breasts, such a frank parading of female haunches, and, on the other hand, such a gallery of characterless faces. In many earlier eras the nude had served art beautifully, especially in Greece and Italy. Even the erotic note had been integral and acceptable in the noble mythological pieces of Titian. Nor had the frank sensuality of Rubens' fleshy women been as disturbing as these slyly carnal French things. This was the climax, however, so far as leading painters are concerned. There was a reaction toward the puritanic when the monarchy fell, and similarly, of course, in the British school.

And nineteenth-century nudes were to return to innocence when not forgotten in the artists' return to a search for formal excellencies.

Nicolas Lancret and Jean-Baptiste Pater seem to belong even more completely than Watteau to the world of dalliance and light amorousness. The former frankly copied Watteau's manner; the latter had been his assistant. Jean-Marc Nattier returned a little way toward the older methods of portraiture: he developed a style of portrait painting that is midway between Largillière's costume glorification and Watteau's dainty illustrating. Maurice-Quentin de la Tour, chief among a considerable group of pastelists of the time, succeeded in making portraits that were showy, even flashy, and yet speakingly alive and truthful.

The great figure next in succession to Watteau is François Boucher. His method of painting is more solid, but his morals are considerably

Boucher: *Jupiter in the Guise of Diana, and Calisto. William Rockhill Nelson Gallery*

flimsier. No one in these days, of course, asks that art have a prime concern with morals. But Boucher's canvases so preponderantly—and so prettily!—deal with the lusts of the flesh that his very anti-morality demands notice. His subjects may pretend to be Greek goddesses or shepherdesses from remote times or just "models"; but they are all in actual fact up-to-the-moment Parisiennes displaying lovely bodies or very frankly provoking an erotic response. Within the limits of the rococo atmosphere, Boucher was a competent decorator; he did not relax the design element as had Watteau, did not entirely fritter away the structure. He was a different sort of purveyor of pretty trifles—and in the final accounting a less interesting one. He became President of the Academy and *Premier Peintre du Roi*, and was appropriately the favorite painter of la Pompadour, mistress of Louis XV.

But Jean-Honoré Fragonard, of the following generation, born almost exactly a half-century later than Watteau, is the finer—and the final—flower of French baroque impulse. For elegance, dash, and superficial brilliance he is unsurpassed. He is intimate and trivial and deft. At the same time he is unreal, remote from life, and his backgrounds are theatrical scenery. He could decorate a salon or a boudoir more smartly and more seductively than anyone else; and did, for the du Barry, a later mistress of the King (though once by her rebuffed), and others.

Fragonard failed to die before the monarchy was overthrown. When the tinsel world of Versailles and the Tuileries collapsed, and heads began to fall, the reason for his art was (at least temporarily) gone. He was even in some personal danger. Some of the stricter revolutionaries wanted to do away with him as a useless survivor of the *fêtes-galantes* world. But, long before, he had happened to do a favor for one Louis-

Fragonard:
Love Letters.
Frick Collection

Jacques David, who in the reversed order of things now turned up as art dictator.

His life spared, Fragonard still could not paint, however, in the new serious manner. In 1806 Napoleon had him turned out from his studio in the Louvre (with all the other artists working there), and he promptly died. In his work he epitomized an era which now was—not unjustly and not unfortunately, perhaps—terminated.

Academicians and Others

"Old men," wrote Anatole France, "hold far too obstinately to their opinions. That is why the Fiji Islanders kill their parents when they show their age. In this way they facilitate evolution, while we retard progress by founding Academies."

Art academies are continually under fire from creative artists, and yet they exist in all the countries devoted to culture in a serious way. In the kingdoms they are "Royal"; elsewhere, "National." They are the strongholds of old artists who seek to protect tradition. Sometimes they do good, slowing up revolutions not well prepared for. In general they retard progress by controlling exhibition halls and museums and denying entry to the younger creative men; controlling also art education and the art press. Every so often the revolutionary stream becomes so strong that it washes over the academy, sometimes overturning it, oftener leaving some of the new ideas within the fortress walls—when a new tradition is set up, congealed, and defended. In France for a long time, Academy membership had the advantage of securing jobs, and sometimes a clever politician-artist could get his son elected, and thus financially cared for, for life.

The French Royal Academy of Painting was founded in 1648. A simple guild no longer seemed adequate when the artists were working practically hand-in-glove with the King and his courtiers. In general the important members were at first the decorators who had built on the tradition brought from Italy. The now debilitated classic style was the thing to be defended.

Sometimes, of course, all the greatest artists belonged to the Academy. A body of practitioners that has the sanction and actually the ear of the King is not lightly to be flouted. But an occasional creative painter rebelled and stayed apart. When a "light" painter such as Watteau was admitted, it must be in a lower category than that of the "history painters." Nothing was taught in the official art school other than "history painting" —in the grand manner.

Charles Le Brun had been the real organizer of the Academy, and in painting it had remained at about his level, or even lower. But in another direction it had served France well. Le Brun had worked in close cooperation with Colbert, the minister of Louis XIV. While Colbert had opposed the King's vast expenditures at Versailles, he believed that a court's and even a country's importance could be measured by the grandeur of its artistic monuments. He set out to adorn Paris to the extent of rendering it beyond challenge the artistic capital of the world. Concurrently he encouraged with grants such establishments as those producing Gobelin tapestries and Sèvres porcelains.

The Academies (there were those of architecture and music also) were to Colbert a part of the regulatory and fostering machinery. That he was successful in establishing France as the arbiter of European taste, and in rendering the court of Louis a model for that of every kingdom and principality, cannot be questioned. The chairs we all sit in, the mantels over our fireplaces, or the curtains in our bedrooms are likely to bear the mark of Louis XIV or Louis XV, or of the post-Revolution emperors.

Of course the demands Colbert made on the artists were in many cases impossible of fulfillment. He ordered the architects to create a French order of architecture as distinctive as the Greek; but there is no recorded consummation of this feat. He naïvely thought the rules of painting could be permanently codified, and that out of a fostering academy a national school of great painters would automatically result. The academicians undertook by a series of *Conférences*, now famous, to formulate the rules. However far they got, it was not far enough to encompass the creative element in art. They and Colbert had better luck, however, in forming a royal collection of paintings, which they set up in the Louvre: twenty-four hundred pictures in all, the basis of the collection there today.

Truly creative artists are apt to froth at the mouth when an academy is mentioned (although they have often been known to quiet down when invited to membership); and the controversy over the usefulness of the institution rages today as in the era of monarchy in France. In any case the academies provide an incident not to be overlooked in the chronicles of visual art.

While Paris and Versailles were witnessing the two developments side by side—an academic, rhetorical, moribund painting, and a baroque-influenced, sentimental, boudoir-and-bonbon-box painting—a single artist was going his way, unconcerned, honest, independent. Jean-Baptiste Chardin has left to posterity from the era of the Great Kings a group of unpretentious, humbly simple paintings which is today valued beyond the beguiling things of Watteau, Boucher, and Fragonard. He was not without an appreciative, if unfashionable, audience in his own time. He then suffered almost total eclipse for a century. Today he has come into his own.

It is now seen that Chardin, alone among the host of eighteenth-century French painters, picked up the structural values known to Poussin, revived the lapsed tradition of consciously ordered design in painting. Beside the *fêtes-galantes* artists he is solid, sound, and an honest craftsman. In his sympathies he was closer to the Dutch and Flemish contemporaries than to

Chardin:
Lady with a Bird-Organ.
Frick Collection

French or Italian painters—in his craftsmanship, too. But he had personality enough to make his own distinctive—and in that country wholly exceptional—contribution: he painted a body of pictures formally creative, depending very little upon subject-matter for their lasting appeal, and untouched by any breath of frivolity.

Chardin was, through and through, a bourgeois. Born the son of a cabinet-maker, he remained throughout his life an associate of carpenters and petty craftsmen and tradesfolk. The longest trip he ever made seems to have been that from Paris to Versailles. He studied with routine painters. Then he came under the influence of a dilettante artist-collector who had studied in Amsterdam, and it may have been that this taught him to look for subjects in his own intimate bourgeois environment. He was presently doing genre studies in the Low Countries fashion. He even deceived some of his fellow painters into taking his work for Dutch. He lived uneventfully; he was a hard worker and a respected neighbor; he really cared only for his painting and the homely pleasures of the lower bourgeoisie.

For many years he painted housewives and children and people gaming and letter-writing and contentedly working at their unspectacular tasks. During the last quarter-century of his career, until his death in 1779, he did only still-lifes. His genre pieces were and are, of course, the more popular. One can imagine how in their own day they delighted the people they portrayed. For these modest canvases are like mirrors held up to the workers in kitchens and parlors and bedrooms, so accurate is Chardin's seeing, so careful his craftsmanship.

Yet what makes them today much more than mirror-art—superior, for instance, to the genre of de Hooch and Steen and Teniers—is a quality or value hidden by Chardin within each picture. It is because this quality has to do with design rather than with subject-matter that the artist dropped from sight for a century or so. It was Cézanne who brought a new significance to it, leading to a reconsideration of all art, who unknowingly put Chardin on the way to being rediscovered.

It is said that Chardin saw common things magically. It may be more accurate to say that he arranged with a magic of the imagination what he saw. He put into his simple interior scenes the organizational order, half mathematical, half mystical, that Poussin put into grand landscapes. It is the design element, sweetly balanced, harmoniously adjusted. There are, too, other virtues in Chardin's work: his sure lighting, his playing over lovely textures for their own sake, his reserved but ingratiating color.

Chardin is not one of the giant figures of art. His field is small. His triumph is that of a man doing a lesser thing supremely well. In his field he affords a sure but delicate pleasure. It was his distinction to be utterly honest, wholly unassuming, when fashionable art around him was all on the side of insincere pretense and rhetorical bombast. It might be argued that Versailles, for all its surface magnificence, for all the popularity of its decorative painters, was the accident, the departure from normal French art; that the humble and unfashionable Chardin marks better the path of the French genius, midway between Poussin and Cézanne.

Although sculpture had become, after Bernini, a secondary art (as noted earlier in the chapter), there was in France in the seventeenth and eighteenth centuries a progression of very productive and competent sculptors. There was, at the beginning, one who linked directly with the Italian school, since he had been an assistant to Bernini at Rome: Pierre Puget, whose dates are from 1622 to 1697. But France did not wholly give in to the fashionable clamor for the baroque.

In the stupendous projects of Louis XIV, the sculptors were scarcely to be regarded as independent artists; in general they worked on the same footing as the gilders and the muralists, and were often the same men. Ancient statues were bought and brought back to the court from classical Rome, or were reproduced by French artisans when they were not acquired. These were insisted upon as models, and the royally imposed Manual dictated the manner of their execution. The result was, of course, heavy, dull, and generally allegorical. Thus—as had been the case in architecture—French taste set up against the baroque a solid sort of classicism. French sculpture through several generations maintained a style that avoided the excesses of violence and dazzling grandeur that had developed in Italian baroque, remained closer to earlier Renaissance neoclassicism and prettified naturalism.

The names, except Houdon's, are not greatly important. The French historians parade the works of Antoine Coysevox, Guillaume Coustou (the Elder), and François Girardon as those of great figures in the time of Louis XIV. It was Robert Le Lorrain, a little younger, who reached the ultimate in feminized court sculpture, in a wash-drawing technique. Among portraitists Jean Baptiste Lemoyne (1698-1762) left more acceptable works than any other. Two sculptors of this period put somewhat more of baroque feeling into their statues; they are remembered especially for what may be termed bathroom nudes. Indeed on the one score of pretty bodies immortalized, Étienne Maurice Falconet and Claude Michel, better known as Clodion, were supremely successful. They best represent France's rococo period and the taste of the time.

Jean Antoine Houdon (1741-1828) was, however, the most original and most talented French sculptor between the late Gothic masters and Rodin. He served especially to hasten the establishment of realism (or naturalism) as the standard sculptural style of the early nineteenth century—that is, in advanced circles, after the neoclassicism of the David and Canova sort had already been challenged as lifeless and as the echo of the echo of an art. His famous bronze *Diana* in the Louvre had the mark of truly understood antique classicism. But it is in his fine psychological portraits that he appears substantially a product of France and a forerunner of Rodin and Despiau. His robed figure of Voltaire in marble in the foyer of the Comédie Française is justly celebrated, but it is rather in the portrait busts that his originality and power come out most strongly. Among them those of Napoleon at Dijon and of Voltaire in the Louvre are outstanding, as is the Franklin, also in the Louvre.

One admonition of Houdon to his pupils marks him as prophet of the era that follows: "Copy, keep on copying, and above all, copy exactly."

XXV: PORTRAIT, LANDSCAPE, AND
STORY-PICTURE: THE BRITISH

OUTSIDE England the name best known in the annals of British visual art is not that of a painter, a sculptor, or an architect, but that of a nineteenth-century theorist and critic, John Ruskin. The circumstance is eloquent of a truth regarding the approach to art in Britain: it is literary, associative, and thoughtful, rather than intensely creative or experiential.

Ruskin, in a chapter of *The Two Paths* entitled "The Deteriorative Power of Conventional Art over Nations," wrote as follows:

Wherever art is practiced for its own sake, and the delight of the workman is in what he *does* and *produces,* instead of what he *interprets* or *exhibits,* there art has an influence of the most fatal kind on brain and heart, and it issues, if long so pursued, in the *destruction both of intellectual power* and *moral principle;* whereas art, devoted humbly and self-forgetfully to the clear statement and record of the facts of the universe, is always helpful and beneficent to mankind, full of comfort, strength and salvation. . . . Review for yourselves the history of art, and you will find this to be a manifest certainty, that *no great school ever yet existed which had not for primal aim the representation of some natural fact as truly as possible.* . . . [The italics are Ruskin's.]

Leave, therefore, boldly, though not irrever-

Constable: Stoke-by-Nayland. Art Institute, Chicago

ently, mysticism and symbolism on the one side; cast away with utter scorn geometry and legalism on the other; seize hold of God's hand, and look full in the face of His creation, and there is nothing He will not enable you to achieve.

He proceeded then to note the complementary need for "the gift of design"—which he interpreted as intellectual:

That collateral necessity is *the visible operation of human intellect in the presentation of truth,* the evidence of what is properly called design or plan in the work, no less than of veracity. A looking glass does not design—it receives and communicates indiscriminately all that passes before it; a painter designs when he chooses some things, refuses others, and arranges all.

It would be unfair to let the excerpts stand for Ruskin's theories without noting qualifications which he elsewhere set down, particularly as regards the need for composition and the necessity to see down to the *organism* of nature. Nevertheless, the central thought of the few sentences—their insistence upon *veracity* and upon *intellectual control*—is at the heart of British aesthetics down to the opening of the twentieth century. The foundation of practice is naturalism; the method is that of the rational mind, which distrusts mystical and formal elements, valuing instead literary allusion, associative sentiment, and instruction. English art, when it is not merely attractive portraiture or landscape, more than any other national manifestation favors anecdote, incident, and moral reflection.

Ruskin is one of the most interesting figures in art criticism. Let no one mistake his importance—even his constructive importance at the time he wrote. The impassioned plea for a renewed contact with nature was sorely needed; it followed upon an era given to some very negative sorts of artificiality. But in the longer view Ruskin seems wrong-headed and mischievous with his "veracity" and intellectual choosing and moral principle. Certain immediate truths he found and admirably fought for; but there was a larger truth he missed.

There is apparent everywhere in the serious art works of England the intellectual good intention. But generally they turn away from what should after all be a goal of creative art; the attainment of a self-sufficient, inbuilt formal vitality. Rhythm, organization, all that the modern painters and critics mean by the term "expressive form," is weak or lacking in the popular portraiture from Reynolds to Lawrence. It is well-nigh lost in the topographical landscapes from Wilson to Cotman. Blake alone richly felt and expressed it in his remote, almost miniature contribution—and, at times, Turner.

At its best, art spiritually expresses peoples and lands. But there is no visual art deeply expressing England. There is little painting that gives the feeling of the lovely English countryside or the bleak coasts or the idyllic hamlets; none that expresses the virile life, the inquiring spirit, the dogged fighting temper, and the magnificence of empire-building.

The literature of England is magnificent, is such a monument as no other modern nation has erected. The poets from the age of Spenser, Marlowe, and Shakespeare to the opening of the twentieth century have known how to express English thought, life, and feeling in accents lacking nothing of formal beauty. But among British painters there are no Shakespeares and Miltons and Shelleys. Literature is the art of England, as music is (after the sixteenth century) the art of Germany.

Let us begin, then, by admitting that there is here no one to put beside Titian and El Greco and Giotto; not even a match for Velázquez or Poussin or Goya. There exists, nonetheless, an interest for the world in the English school, as there is an interest in the "Little Dutchmen" or the Romans.

What, the student may well inquire, is the reason for this lack of top-ranking artists in three major arts—for architecture and sculpture are in the same case—among a people obviously world-leaders in material enterprise, in scientific advancement, and in a different branch of art? Can there be such a thing as a nation that is form-blind, or a race unaware of sensuous loveliness? Is it inhibition from within, or some outward binding circumstance that is responsible?

Puritanism is one reason given. The Reformation brought to England and to Scotland a wave of intolerance and iconoclasm intense and bitter beyond even the developments in Germany and Holland. The rich medieval arts of Britain, painting, sculpture, and ornamentation, which had survived through the days of the Tudors and the Stuarts, were wiped out as at a stroke. A single entry in the records of a "visitor" appointed by Parliament in 1643 to demolish "the superstitious pictures and ornaments of churches" reads: "Clare: we brake down 1000 pictures superstitious." The tradition of Puritanism continued through many generations and confused the sensuously beautiful with the "sinful" sensual pleasures. The beginnings of the arts in colonial America, too, suffered under this inhibiting influence.

The British court, however, soon escaped into pastures decorative and even licentious. The fact dovetails nicely with the next conventional explanation of the lack of deeply creative activity: painting for a century and a half after the Restoration in 1660 was a *class* art, designed exclusively (with the exception of Hogarth's works) for the peerage and squirearchy. At first the court circle held all the patrons, and there was a period of imported painters. When Reynolds broke through the prejudice, by the sheer merit of his competitive work, and when the circle of patrons widened, there was a cycle of fashions in fulsome portraiture.

For a long time portraits were all that picture-buyers wanted. Art was a feeder to pride and a means to signalize gentility. And of course the sort of portrait wanted was the flattering, prettified, showy thing. Three generations of the best talent in England seem to have been diverted into this fashion-serving business. Some blame the artists who gave in to a stultifying demand. In certain conspicuous cases they made great fortunes and lived a socially glittering life. Others blame what they are pleased to term the English hostility to genius and blindness to formally rich art. The occupants of that camp declare that the artists, to avoid starvation, were forced to give in to the demands of patrons short-sighted and insensitive. They point out that Richard Wilson, "father of British landscape," *was* permitted to starve.

Or again the blame is carried to the Royal Academy and the spirit of conservatism and regimentation which it represents. The Academy has been continuously strong in Britain since its founding in 1768. The tendency to hold habitually to the rhetoric of the past, or at least to ideals a half-century outgrown, so that the academicians seem invariably to be fighting against the art that is living in its own day, is even more marked in England than in France. It has ever been the British public's way to respect authority; and an establishment with the royal sanction is accorded a popular esteem, if not reverence, hardly matched elsewhere.

The Academy's first president and leading spirit was Sir Joshua Reynolds, proponent of the "grand style," who said that nature should be understood first through a study of the great masters—among whom, to the misfortune of his followers, he placed Lodovico Caracci. Even today most of the British academicians might subscribe without embarrassment to the bulk of Sir Joshua's pronouncements. In any case, historically the popular support of academism and its hold upon the art schools even to the opening of the twentieth century help to explain the lack of formal creativeness and imaginative invention in British art.

These are, no doubt, generalizations not a little dangerous. But one records them precisely because one hopes to avoid that larger and even more dangerous generalization: that an entire national or racial group is constitutionally insensitive to formal values—that the British (or the Anglo-Saxons) are deficient in feeling for the sensuously lovely and the plastically vital elements in art.

England's serious art, then, is of the camera-eye and the brain. There is also an immense popular audience for the whimsical and the roguish. Everything leads to literature in art, away from pictorial structure, plastic rhythm, and the architectonic virtues.

In a very great deal of British appreciation it is the collateral literary, social, and historical

Lady Margaret Beaufort.
Anonymous, 15th century.
National Portrait Gallery,
London

significance that most counts. Without recognition of this associative factor, one cannot approach English art with understanding of the country's own reaction to it and love for it, and the common ranking of Reynolds, Gainsborough, and Romney among the greatest masters of all time.

Portraitists, Imported and Native

In early British art formal values were not unduly sacrificed. In certain crafts practiced in the monasteries the English workers led the world—most notably in embroidering. Examples are to be found in the treasuries of Continental cathedrals today. But the iconoclasts left few examples of native Gothic painting. Nor is it certain that the chief relic of primitive painting

now existing in England, the Wilton Diptych, is from an English hand. (It has been variously attributed to British, French, Flemish, Italian, and German masters.) It is a lovely thing of its sort, more finished in aspect and in craftsmanship than the usual exhibits offered as primitive in France and Flanders.

There is no traceable British school in the fifteenth century. A picture of about 1485, however, the portrait of Lady Margaret Beaufort, claimed for an anonymous English master, is marked by an exceptionally sound pictorial sense, has an expert structural solidity. It proclaims stylistic affinity with Flemish portraiture.

In the following century, when the tide of Renaissance cultural influences flowed strong from Italy, the native painters were definitely overshadowed by the imported masters. Holbein was in England from 1526 to 1543. From Moor

Martha, Wife of Joshua Horton of Sowerby. Possibly by John Riley.
National Portrait Gallery, London

to Van Dyck there was a procession of able foreign-trained portraitists. Of the English, the ones oftenest named are Nicholas Hilliard of the Elizabethan era, and John Riley, who lived from 1646 to 1691.

Hilliard was primarily a miniaturist. He copied too directly for his own good the popular manner of Holbein. Riley, if he is the painter of the portrait, *Martha, Wife of Joshua Horton of Sowerby,* which is ascribed to him by half the authorities, had an original and noteworthy talent. It is an admirable bit of characterization, and it also is beautifully managed as a pictorial entity, with weight, mass, and dark-light pattern-

ing expertly used. Nor is it to be overlooked that this seems a typical English thing, proclaims itself of the Puritan period, with no breath of the superficial brilliance and glitter which the imported artists had made fashionable among the aristocrats. More on the showy side is Riley's celebrated portrait of James II in the National Portrait Gallery in London.

There are scattered anonymous portraits from the Elizabethan, Stuart, and Restoration periods which indicate a continued competent production. An occasional one is decoratively appealing in a way common to minor French, Flemish, and Spanish portraiture of the time. Particularly

Gheeraerts:
Queen Elizabeth.
National
Portrait Gallery,
London

effective are the figures or busts enriched with detailed delineation of lace and embroidery accessories, so that the main areas of the picture are traced over with intricate patterning. The mode may have come in first with the minute depiction of textures cultivated by the early Flemings. It was only slightly modified in France by the school of the Clouets. In Spain it became popular after Antoon Moor was appointed resident painter at the court of Madrid, and was carried on by his pupil Coello. Moor helped to establish the vogue in England. It resulted in even more appealing variations when men less accomplished in naturalism took it in hand. Then the naïve, frankly artificial intention yielded a result more ingratiating than the exact imitation.

A Fleming who spent his entire mature life in England, Marcus Gheeraerts the Younger, was particularly happy in this milieu, as the *Queen Elizabeth* shows. Cornelius Johnson,

born in England of a Flemish father, made excellent incidental use of a flattened pattern of laces and accessories in contrast with the full modeled face. His medallion of Lady Waterpark is charming and sound. Before 1700 this type of portraiture, based on minute realism but happily modified by naïvely decorative intention, had found its way to America, and the twentieth-century interest in "American primitive" has resulted in admission of a number of ornamental if rather stiff portraits into the public galleries.

All this time the British court circles and fashionable society had been patronizing the foreign masters whom the kings or powerful ministers and merchants invited to England. After Holbein, who was court painter to Henry VIII, had come Antoon Moor. In 1629 Rubens arrived in London on a diplomatic mission, and stayed for a time to paint. In 1632 Van Dyck became court painter to Charles I. It was upon the work of Rubens and Van Dyck, perhaps unfortunately, that the later group of English portraitists was to base its practice: the celebrated school of Reynolds-Gainsborough-Romney.

Before the time of Sir Joshua, however, two other spectacular foreigners dominate the London scene. Sir Peter Lely was a Hollander who became extraordinarily popular during a lifetime spent in England. He constructed his pictures well, but there is a flamboyant nervousness and generally a superficiality about his effects. His successor was Sir Godfrey Kneller, a German who had studied in Amsterdam. His sitters are given more of three-dimensional solidity, but in general it is the showy, essentially baroque element of Rubens or Van Dyck which is carried on, to have effect upon Reynolds (who was born in the year of Kneller's death, 1723).

From the Miniaturists to Hogarth

It will not have escaped the reader that the entire story of English painting to this time has been that of portraiture. France also had been portrait-mad in the two and one-half centuries between Fouquet and Largillière; but on the Continent other types of painting had not been entirely crowded out. Landscape, "historical pictures," and genre all had found practitioners and public response.

In Britain the single mode sufficed. A special form, the miniature, was added to the larger categories. The word "miniature" as applied to earlier painting is used to designate the illustrations in illuminated manuscripts. But from the sixteenth century on—illuminating having been neglected as an art after printed books became common—the name is transferred to the tiny portable pictures, usually portraits, painted on ivory. The size is small enough for the pocket or for the palm of the hand; a true miniature will be marked also by an appropriate minuteness of depiction and a delicacy of method.

The first portable or detached miniatures had been painted on vellum—had been, indeed, merely a version of the miniature likeness of king or donor found on the dedicatory pages of manuscripts, or even on illuminated proclamations, charters, etc. Sometimes the portraits were done on the backs of playing cards. Then came ivory specially shaped for the purpose. It is likely that the first great popularity of miniature portraits dates from the fifteenth-century French wars, when knights and fair ladies, honorably separated, carried consoling likenesses next their hearts or on necklaces. Although France initiated the custom, England made the miniature her own.

William Hogarth was most English of the Englishmen in his purposeful approach to art, his literary documentation, and his moral aim; most English, too, in his weak grasp upon pictorial structure and formal concentration. But he is completely out of line in that he abandoned portraiture for the story-picture. He was the only British artist of consequence in four hundred years who failed to devote himself to portraits and landscapes.

A great independent on so many scores—he disdained and pilloried the fashionable foreign painters and those who aped them—and gifted with wit and courage, he might have been England's greatest artist if he had had the picture sense of Hokusai, Brueghel, or Daumier. As it is, he interests the world by his mordant social satire—and draws closer attention as an artist of caliber by at least one picture, *The Shrimp Girl*.

Born in 1697, of middle-class parents, to a somewhat cramped environment, Hogarth never outgrew a certain limited view. He had, as he said, "a naturally good eye," and he trained it to retain impressions, so that he was able later to dispense with models. He had the Englishman's pride in bluntness, the self-made man's dogmatism, and the literalist's scorn for all art that was not illustration. He raised popular illustration to a socially and politically significant activity; and by his engraving he brought serious art to the English masses.

Hogarth invented an art form new to England: the serial story-picture. He painted and engraved satires on the depraved life of "high society." He adopted the technique of the theater, which he loved (not forgetting the heavily underlined moral that was a part of the play).

Hogarth:
The Shrimp Girl.
National Gallery, London

Indeed he said that his intention was "to give in his pictures all that an actor can do on the stage"; and he spoke of "men and women my players." His three series, entitled *Marriage à la Mode, The Harlot's Progress,* and *The Rake's Progress,* are among the classics of pictorial satire. No less interesting as comment, or lampoon, are such single pieces as *Taste in High Life, Gin Lane,* and *The Distressed Poet.*

The artist's pictures are so diverting as illustration and as social comedy that one is likely to forgive his overcrowding and the fact that he makes concentration impossible by his overattention to detail. The portraits are, in the final analysis, just a little insensitive, even wooden. His version of the "conversation piece" (of which more in a moment) is lively and diverting, but superficially posed. The story-pictures—"dramatic paintings," he called them—with few exceptions sacrifice everything to story, or to propa-

ganda. In the end one comes back to two fugitive and uncharacteristic things, the virile and dashing sketch of *The Shrimp Girl* and the well-composed *Calais Gate,* wherein for once Hogarth disciplined his materials and fitted them within a coherent pictorial scheme—conveying, too, his contemptuous feeling about the "depraved" life of the French. Elsewhere he was so intent upon depicting and sermonizing about the vices and foibles of his contemporaries that he forgot that his pictorial medium should have an architecture and an organic coherence.

If British painting is, as we suspect, over-literary, Hogarth is its accomplished pamphleteer. He adds the controversialist's overemphasis to story materials. A curious sidelight is thrown on Hogarth's approach by a book he wrote under the title *The Analysis of Beauty.* Having made a popular success in illustration and satire, he desired at the end, of course, the one sort of recognition his achievement did not warrant: he wanted to claim pre-eminence as "pure artist." He rightly hated "the grand manner" and made rich fun of the artists who professed a devotion to the "sublime"; and he considered the proposal for a British Academy silly—"a ridiculous imitation of the foolish parade of the French Academy." But the grand-manner people had something—if only, in England, a prettiness—that he wanted to understand and master. His vanity led him to publish a treatise "Written with a view of fixing the fluctuating Ideas of Taste," and explaining "the fundamental principles of Beauty . . . Fitness, Variety, Uniformity, Simplicity, Intricacy, and Quantity." One of his generalizations, that there is a "line of beauty," a curved line found oftenest in silhouettes of the female human body, has survived for discussion in later books on aesthetics. For the rest, Hogarth's precepts went the way of his unfortunate attempts to equal the "sublime" painters on their own ground.

The "conversation piece" is a typically British variation of group portraiture. It shows, in a not too serious vein, an English family at one of its routine gatherings—at table, in the garden, in the drawing-room—conversing. It is intimate in atmosphere, and artfully artless, with figures carefully posed as if they had casually fallen into the attitudes. A master of this minor mode was John Zoffany, a German-born painter. He documented the polite world of his time with an unassuming simplicity which is appealing and especially refreshing after a session with the heavily satiric and moralistic pounding of Hogarth. Not unconnected in intention with the conversation piece is that other English specialty, the sporting picture. It has had no masters in any sense other than illustrational and sentimental.

One artist besides Hogarth touched a high mark in satire and caricature and was equally unafraid of the sordid and the brutal: Thomas Rowlandson. He belongs chronologically to the era of the later portraitists and of Blake, and so is out of line here. But his slender and isolated genius is linked, if at all, with Hogarth's. His restless curiosity and a moralizing impulse led him in the direction of popular print-making and routine illustration, and in the end he was an accomplished draftsman, master of expressive line, rather than a picture-maker in the fuller sense. Not long after, there was to be an engraver on wood, Thomas Bewick, destined to become famous for his "white line" engravings, which are much prized by connoisseurs.

But these have been excursions from the main path of British painting, which continued to take fashionable artists into one activity, portraiture, in a direction which the criticism of the time considered classical. There had been, in the early eighteenth century, the so-called Classical Age of English literature, adorned by the poetry of Pope and the essays of Addison and Steele. Architecture had become neoclassic, in a version adapted from Italian Renaissance models, had wavered toward the baroque, and now under Robert Adam had returned to the classic idioms. The furniture styles of Hepplewhite and Sheraton were soon to supplement Adam's building and, not long after, the drawings of John Flaxman.

But British painting escaped every adjective in the definition of classic. It had fallen heir, rather, to the baroque tendencies of Rubens and Van Dyck. The youthful English artist paid homage to the Italian masters upon his "grand tour," but it was a debased neoclassicism that now passed current in Rome and Naples. Nor can one believe that England escaped a certain influence from the light ornamentalism of Watteau, Nattier, and Fragonard, in vogue across the Channel.

From Reynolds to Lawrence

Whatever the sources, whatever the inventive additions, British portraiture of the grand period began in a realistic intention. A surface naturalism of facial aspect is basic to it; but there is superadded the baroque artist's liveliness and glitter, by means of glorified clothes and stage-setting backgrounds and a feathery technique. The classical busts and urns and ruins so frequently inserted into the backcloths of Reynolds' portraits are no more than ornamental theatrical properties. They really have no relationship with the actors. They are as innocent of any connection with the spirit and method of the painting as are the negligently sketched trees and parks and lawns among which they appear. The portrait's the thing; the rest is dressing.

Sir Joshua Reynolds was the first of the line of fashionable native painters. He was a man of robust tastes, of affable social address, of wide culture and cosmopolitan contacts, of shrewd commercial and political ability. He was well fitted to express the age of Britain's economic expansion, to be head of its Royal Academy, to be himself a sign of the arrival of British art at maturity and sophistication. He was the premier interpreter of the materialism and display of the age. But he stood virtuously above its profligacy.

A chance meeting with the owner of a sailing vessel, after Reynolds had had an average training, permitted him to go to Italy. For ever after he called Michelangelo his god; but, true first to principles he had already had from Rubens and Van Dyck, he added certain traits out of lesser and later Italian masters. He believed thoroughly in eclecticism. Back in London, in 1752, he made an immediate popular success. Thenceforward he was England's favored portraitist, arbiter of artistic controversies, and member of the literary-social group which included Goldsmith, Johnson, and Garrick.

Never did a leading artist more successfully preach one sort of art and practice another. The particular ideal set up in Reynolds' famous *Discourses* is "the Grand Style." There are wisdom and common sense in some of his pronouncements, particularly in those by which he tried to make young painters realize the necessity for seeing objects in full volume, with light around them. But in others there is an indication of that haziness, not to say insincerity, which landed his own paintings on the side of superficial grandeur and virtuoso theatricality. He was a realistic painter of silks and satins, of fashions and masks, within an artificial framework faintly classic.

Of portraiture he wrote: "He who in his practice of portrait painting wishes to dignify his subject, which we will suppose to be a lady, will not paint her in the modern dress, the familiarity of which alone is sufficient to destroy all dignity, and therefore dresses his figure something with the general air of the antique for the sake of dignity, and preserves something of the modern for sake of likeness." And curiously he seems to mix expedient sophistry and truth in this observation: "Well-colored pictures are in more esteem and sell for higher prices than in reason they seem to deserve, as coloring is an excellence of a lower rank than the qualities of correctness and greatness of character."

When Van Dyck had been court portraitist in London he had himself painted the faces of his patrons but had let assistants paint in their clothes—the costume being left at the studio for the purpose. For the hands he had studio-models, so that he could add those lesser details at odd times. Some other painters are known to have posed sitters so as to hide the hands, to save working at a problem beyond their capacities. Reynolds probably painted the hands in his canvases —but they might be largely from one model. It is certain that he had assistants, known as his drapers, who added backgrounds and accessories. He sometimes painted his parts of a portrait in four hours.

Grace, color pleasing up to a point, good taste: these can be granted. We enjoy his adequate likenesses of fair women and innocent children. We admire his stage direction and its results. But about it all there is a childish sort of make-believe. If Reynolds thought that he was serving to carry British art out of its insularity, if he believed that he was achieving the Grand Style, and if by the Grand Style he meant the great European tradition of Titian and Rubens, of Michelangelo and Rembrandt, he utterly failed. He lost completely the sense of organization, the structural order, the formal vitality that are implicit in the pictures of those creators. Beside them Reynolds is undisciplined and sketchy, is concerned with literary and sentimental trivialities—and with clothes. His method has more affinity with Watteau's than with that of any solid European master. At first glance his paintings are brilliant, bright, aristocratically elegant. But the effect turns out to be dazzle rather than a steady light, dash rather than spirit. And the

Reynolds: *Jane, Countess of Harrington.*
Huntington Art Gallery, San Marino, California

apparent solidity of *Mrs. Siddons as the Tragic Muse* or *Nelly O'Brien* turns out to be based on unimaginative symmetry. The figure of *Jane,* *Countess of Harrington,* if taken alone seems a superior accomplishment, though the background could hardly be more stagy, with its balustrade,

Reynolds: *Lord Heathfield. National Gallery, London*

its urn, and a backcloth landscape. There are lovers of eighteenth-century portrait-painting who gain more pleasure apparently from this sort of "dramatic" limning than from the gallery of Titian's portraits or El Greco's. But it is a significant fact that the museums generally make less of the British rooms than they did a quarter-century ago. In the midst of so much that is over-feminine in interest and so soft as art it is a pleas-ure to encounter in Reynolds' work a portrait that is as firm and masculine as that of Lord Heathfield. This is a picture, in the National Gallery, London, that seems to have genuine feel-ing, spontaneity, and candor. If the background is still stagy, it does not intrude.

Reynolds was nevertheless a man of his age, one of the greatest "successes" in the history of art. He was appointed court painter and was for

Gainsborough:
*The Artist's
Daughters.*
Worcester Art Museum

twenty-three years President of the Royal Academy. He had a coach with gilded wheels and pictures painted on it. He was knighted and had liveried servants. He earned an immense fortune, just out of painting, and he had one of the grandest funerals ever known in London, with three dukes and three earls among the pall-bearers, and ninety-one carriages in the procession to St. Paul's.

Thomas Gainsborough, who came to popular success more slowly, but just as surely in the end, possessed a more solid talent. Moreover, he played two instruments, portraiture and landscape, whereas Reynolds played but one. He studied only intermittently, but through an advantageous marriage was enabled to continue his practice and experiment, unhampered by the problems of supporting a family, until he found his market. He spent fourteen years painting in Bath, most fashionable and gayest of English resort cities, before he went to London in 1774. In the capital he shared the field with Sir Joshua as purveyor of portraits to the elegant world. He asked and got princely sums for his pictures—except the landscapes, which cluttered up his house and studio until visitors could hardly get around.

In a great many of Gainsborough's portraits there is a freshness, even a sincerity, generally lacking in the fashionable school. If any of the portraitists approached mastery of plastic values, it was he. There are canvases enough from which one would not guess it. But there are sound construction and nicety of adjustment in some of the

Gainsborough: *The Blue Boy. Huntington Art Gallery*

favorite pieces: the several portraits of his daughters especially, *The Blue Boy,* and the early landscapes.

From a study of Rubens and Van Dyck, Gainsborough had taken the better courtly qualities: a certain dignity, a glamorous sparkle. His backgrounds and his landscapes suffered from a fluttery touch which he got partly from Rubens but more especially from a minor painter of the Watteau school. But in his eclecticism he was more fortunate than Reynolds. He had a sort of intellectual independence, too. When Reynolds proclaimed that blue could not be used successfully except as a minor color in a picture, Gainsborough painted *The Blue Boy* to prove otherwise. To that extent it is a thesis picture. But it would hardly have become the celebrated work it is if the artist had not given it an unmistakable quality, a unique freshness which was a gift out of his temperament.

Gainsborough loses less of the sitter's personality, however, by asserting his own. The distinctive loveliness of English womanhood and girlhood is nowhere else so truthfully and winningly conveyed as in the gallery of his portraits. There is less of the masquerade element than in most of the elegant portraiture; more of simple statement and native beauty. If there is any point at which the rather feminine British method of painting is fully justified, it is in Gainsborough's better pictures. This gracious portrayal of English womanhood is happily to be enjoyed in American collections—at Worcester, Massachusetts, and Washington, D. C., and most notably in the Huntington Gallery at San Marino, California—as well as in the English galleries.

The Gainsborough landscapes are in general a less fortunate exhibit. The qualities that make for brilliant portraiture are likely to seem artificial in outdoor views. Many landscapes from Gainsborough's hand appear to have been studied from stage scenery rather than from nature. The Watteau nervous touch is much in evidence. There is to be credited to the artist, however, a freshness in the use of color, achieved by a method that anticipated the "pointillism" of the impressionists. In construction and depth, strangely enough, the very early landscapes are superior to later ones. If he had not made such a complete and exacting success of portraiture, diverting his talent into that direction, he might have been among the foremost inventors of modern landscape art.

The other portraitists, except one, Lawrence, fall below distinctive achievement. George Romney, born in 1734—eleven years later than Reynolds, seven later than Gainsborough—is often put down as one of "the great trio." But his picture-making as such is definitely inferior. He had just enough talent to enable him to grasp the formula for "best-sellers." A sufficient reality is joined to a deceptive freshness or clarity. He could set down a pretty face charmingly—as in *The Parson's Daughter* and in some of the studies of the fascinating Lady Hamilton. Sir Henry Raeburn, a Scotsman, was a more literal portraitist, although not without the affectation of a sketchy brilliancy, and sometimes a forced dramatic note. John Hoppner leaned to the other side, with less reality but with more feminine prettiness. He did a soft portrait nicely, particularly if the sitter was a girlish matron or a pert child.

Sir Thomas Lawrence divided honors with Hoppner in the fashionable circles of London at the end of the century—a full generation after Reynolds and Gainsborough—and he carried the brilliant artificial manner to its ultimate triumph and its end. In his hands facile brushwork and attenuated grace became hardly less than ravishing. He was a precocious artist; he made a living by crayon portraiture at the age of twelve and exhibited some of his later celebrated pictures when he was hardly out of his teens. At twenty-one he painted a portrait of the Queen. The Royal Academy elected him an associate when he was twenty-two and a full member three years later. He was then already the darling of the court and of society. He was duly knighted and eventually became President of the Academy.

Lawrence's portraits, which constitute his whole achievement, are so self-proclaimingly what they are, with no attempt to veil their theatrical virtues behind pretensions of classic composition or psychological penetration, that one is likely to prefer them to the reputedly solider pictures of Reynolds and Romney. The facile elegance and frank artificiality of *Pinkie* or the *Archduke of Austria* are more ingratiating and leave a more pleasant impression than does *Mrs. Siddons as the Tragic Muse*, or the equally

Lawrence: *Pinkie.*
Huntington Art Gallery

famous *Nelly O'Brien,* or *Lady Bunbury Sacrificing to the Graces.* Lawrence's work is superficial painting at its very best; possesses, at the least, immediate charm, fastidious fragility, and consummate fluency.

With Lawrence the story of native British portraiture is done. His death in 1830, less than eighty years after Reynolds had started practice in London, closes an era made notable by a larger group of popular and competent purveyors to fashionable demand than had been known in any other time or place.

Somewhat earlier two American painters had entered into the English scene. Benjamin West (1738-1820), a precocious young Pennsylvanian, in London at twenty-five, won royal patronage and for many years all but dominated the official British art world. He served as president of the British Royal Academy from Reynolds' death in 1792 until his own death. Although he painted portraits, his more serious efforts went into religious and mythological subjects. They survive today chiefly as reminders of the deterioration of the grand manner. West's influence was tremendous, and his London salon was a mecca for all ambitious young Americans. John Singleton Copley (1738-1815) was a mature artist when he went to visit West in 1774. He, too, became a London favorite and never returned home. Gilbert Stuart entered West's studio in 1777, and also won wide favor as a social portraitist. He returned to America to become celebrated especially as painter of the new country's first president. Over a hundred portraits of Washington have been ascribed

Lawrence: *Archduke Charles of Austria. Windsor Castle.*
By gracious permission of the late King George VI

to him. America from 1640 on had developed artists who catered to the colonists' demand for portraits in the European manner; but the greater interest for collectors today is in the school of home-taught "primitive" painters, who often achieved a naïve charm in their folk likenesses.

Crome: *Windmill on Mousehold Heath. National Gallery, London*

The British Landscape School, Turner, and Blake

Richard Wilson, born in 1714, is called "the father of British landscape." He is more significant for pioneering in England in a type of art then known by the imported canvases of Claude Lorrain and the Dutchmen—and from "views" by the visitors Canaletto and Guardi—than for a distinctive originality. His early works are tinged by classicism of the sort developed by Claude and Poussin in Rome. But, back in England after an Italian visit, Wilson followed his own course, portraying the English countryside with honesty and a certain attractive realism. He never rose to imaginative vision, nor did he have the power to endow the canvas with a vitality of its own, as Poussin had done, and, in a different way, Ruisdael. He was a prose painter. Wilson's personal story is a pathetic one: he gave up portraiture, in which he might have scored a success, to initiate a sort of art in which he had a passionate faith, and he was permitted to spend his best years all but starved in an attic.

It was slightly before Wilson's death in 1782 that a single decade saw the birth of England's three greatest landscapists: Crome, Constable, and Turner. John Crome was self-made, unlettered, and provincial. He was a lover of nature in

Constable: *The Haywain. National Gallery, London*

her severer and grander moods; and that love is measurably conveyed in his better canvases, with a native dignity exercised within a borrowed Dutch formula. He is a rare figure in British art in that he made no capital of the picturesque and sought out no sentimental associations. He seems by instinct to have achieved in an occasional canvas a structural order or spatial rhythm. The *Windmill on Mousehold Heath* in the National Gallery, London, is outstanding.

John Constable was, however, the typical English landscapist. He dwelt with loving care upon every least detail of the picturesque countryside; but he had enough of genius to convey its atmosphere and spirit, too. He stuck to the topographic truth—he would not be essentially British if he greatly violated it—but he had an eye for the large effect of storm, of light-and-shade movement under scurrying clouds, of contrasted dark woods and sunny open fields. The heaths, the slow rivers, the cottages, the fresh wet farmlands—these are his materials. His is an honest record of the peculiar outdoor loveliness of England. There is little inspiration in most of his canvases, only a peculiarly sensitive documen-

tation. But occasionally he becomes almost passionately alive and direct and revealing.

Constable was one of the earliest artists to insist that landscapes be painted from nature, and his storm pictures are perhaps the earliest to warrant the name "impressions." One feels the swift pleasure of his discovery of an evanescent light-dark effect; and the best of his work resulted when he did not spend too much time finishing the picture in the studio afterward.

Some of Constable's precepts regarding the significance of the immediate impression and the importance of freshness foreshadowed axioms of the impressionists, actually so called, of a half-century later. He was before them, too, in the discovery of reflected light as varied color on all objects, and even in shadows; although he did not exploit color in the lavish if not reckless manner of the eighties. He does, however, warrant being called a colorist. Constable and Turner were the only Englishmen ever to influence deeply the main European visual tradition. (Lawrence had enjoyed a vogue on the Continent, but it led only to disaster.)

Unfortunately Constable is not to be seen in

Constable: *Landscape with Mill. Worcester Art Museum*

this fresh mood in most galleries. He could paint as literally and woodenly as any academician might ask: he did indeed labor his canvases and give them excessive detail for a public that was put off by the unconventional appearance of the "impressions." He had no such reputation as Turner, and his enterprise and originality, as seen in the freer pictures, were not similarly applauded. The museums mostly have treasured the academic and larger-scale works. At Worcester, Massachusetts, however, is the swiftly realized sketch of the *Landscape with Windmill*, with its transparent airiness and fresh spontaneity. The "finished" painting from this, also very fine in a heavier way, is in the Neue Pinakothek at Munich. Of the larger canvases *The Leaping Horse* at Burlington House, London, is one of the cleverest and most animated, and at the same time most solidly structural. The sketch for it is in the Victoria and Albert Museum, London, which has also the vivid water-color *Stoke-by-Nayland*. A more frankly documentary piece in the National Gallery, London, *The Haywain*, is better known than any of these; is, perhaps, the national favorite (see page 541).

Joseph Mallord William Turner, born in 1775, was destined to pick up the tradition of English landscape, as established by Wilson and enlarged by Constable (who was actually a year younger), and to develop first a typical mastery of it, then go on to the one great flight into abstract painting known in British annals. A prodigious producer of pictures, a strange, unsocial man, an uneven genius, he ended by being the one true giant of English visual art. At his imaginative best—when the images do not become vaporous and vague—he was a magic artist, doing almost incredible things with paint. Before he came to that wonder he covered the whole lower range, from literal transcripts of the picturesque, and the usual pretty English detailed views, through the constructed thing that parallels the Dutch

Turner: *Ulysses Deriding Polyphemus. National Gallery, London*

achievement and Claude, to the romantic interpretation and finally the near-abstract visual invention. It is illuminating that he bridges two literary eras, that of Wordsworth and the romantic one of Byron, Shelley, and Keats.

Turner was a Cockney and a barber's son. He made his way without social favor, by sheer ability and persistence. He remained through life almost a recluse, and his asocial ways and unattractive habits earned him the reputation of an eccentric. Nevertheless, he exhibited at the Royal Academy when he was fifteen. In his late years he became a favorite artist of Ruskin, then the most powerful and gifted critic in England— who, indeed, overpraised him to the artist's own ultimate disadvantage. Turner's only interests were in his painting and in a career. He gave himself wholly to increasing his knowledge of nature and to the business of picture-making. By being solitary he came to know more of nature than any artist had known before. He had a knack of retaining in visual memory every aspect of tree, rock, grass-blade, and water, along with a phenomenal ability to reconstruct a fleeting larger effect.

At first (after obviously juvenile experiments)

his views were literal and topographic. Then he went into a period of solidly constructive painting, for which he learned much from Claude Lorrain, and gave the world many favorite transcripts of the English countryside, among which *Crossing the Brook* and *Richmond Hill* are outstanding.

By 1830 Turner had come to his second method. He cast aside the restraints of "normal" sight. He turned from the literal to be romantic and dramatic. He recognized new pictorial potentialities in light and color exploited for their own sake. Soon he was painting pictures far more "impressionistic" than Constable's. At their best, as in *Ulysses Deriding Polyphemus* or *The Fighting Téméraire*, these canvases have a gorgeous play of light, and a spontaneous grandeur, even while built on sound plastic principles. At other times the structure is dissipated with the subject-matter, as somewhat happens in the famous *Rain, Steam, and Speed*. This almost nebulous picture marks one of the earliest recorded attempts to paint a subject typical of the industrial age. Turner was like that: trying to make sheerest poetry out of a railway train, when everybody else was certain that machinery was destroying romance and beauty. Equally he delighted in painting dirty boats and wharves, littered streets and untidy markets.

In the end his love of color as such ran away with his judgment. There are too many of the large late pictures that are spineless, structureless, even chaotic. One remembers vast Venetian canvases that seem formless and lurid. But in the field of water-colors the lyric impulse resulted in the loveliest opalescent trifles in the entire range of Western painting. The series of Alpine views includes examples of ethereal handling of colors and composing in abstract shadowy fabrics which are utterly delightful. Their luminous, fragile, insubstantial beauty is hardly surpassed even in Oriental portfolios.

Perhaps one must have retained a childlike, romantic tenderness of mind to enjoy these things that are "all mist and mystery"; or it may be, as some of us believe, that occasionally an artist does, by means of color and pattern, plane and volume, manipulated as near-abstractions, speak directly to faculties nearer the spiritual than the intellectual centers of our being—and that Turner in his most felicitous water-colors achieves this aim. The transcriptive value, the familiar or picturesque aspect of crag and cloud, waterfall or tree, has little to do with our response. Rather the enchanting color melodies and the slight formal rhythms form a tissue of visual delight, apart from all associative thought.

It is only right to record that some of the soundest modern critics put down this sort of appreciation as self-intoxication. They believe that Turner created a realm in which the yearning can wander and indulge their own daydream fancies. To this observer it seems rather that Turner has afforded, in a minor mode, a rarely felicitous and legitimately enjoyable experience. Fortunately the water-colors are to be seen in a great many galleries.

At the time of his death in 1851—after, characteristically, some years in which sordid drinking bouts in the lowest surroundings alternated with periods of feverish creative work—Turner had traversed a mighty arc. From sheerest prose he had gone on to Wordsworthian nature-interpretation in simple words and familiar images.

Then he had turned romantic—was, as he himself wished, the Byron of painting. And finally, in the insubstantial lyricism, the ethereal unreality of his most personal work, he showed affinity with Shelley. His work is England's one major release from literal and earthbound painting. If, in the attempt to be imaginative or lyrical or musical, Turner often lost contact with "objective truth," he nevertheless occasionally fixed in color a rare quality that speaks with a sure if quiet accent to an increasing audience.

There was in England, even in Turner's time, a painter-mystic who might, under slightly changed conditions, have been one of the greatest visual artists of all time. William Blake, driven partly by poverty, partly by ascetic preference, to avoidance of painting in the larger manner, possessed the surest pictorial sense given to any Englishman. But he had, or made, no opportunity to create pictures in the monumental or even in the standard fields.

A mystic, a seer, a born rebel (in the materialist view), Blake was furthest from the stream of national development, least touched by English practicality and literal-mindedness. Seeing all things from within, counting imaginative vision the truest reality, the sight of the physical eyes a lesser actuality, he penetrated to meanings not vouchsafed to other men. Standing once with Constable before one of the latter's canvases, Blake said, "Why, this is not drawing, but inspiration." And Constable, whether through shrewdness or literal-minded misapprehension answered, "I meant it for drawing." Blake looked for hidden significances and cosmic revelations—and, so far as mortals may, he trafficked in these values.

Blake was the author of a relatively small body of small pictures. They are, indeed, hardly more than colored drawings. There is in them, nonetheless, the soundest spatial sense, the most powerful plastic movement, known to British art. He fixed in his unassuming compositions an extraordinary degree of formal vitality or "order." His pictures, presumably illustrating Bible stories, narrative poems, and world epics, yet the more surely illustrate the artist's own central vision and search.

Turner: *Simplon Pass. Collection Edward W. Forbes.*
Courtesy Fogg Museum of Art, Harvard University

One saying lies at the heart of his philosophy and guides his art: "He who sees the infinite in all things, sees God." Once he wrote: "If the doors of perception were cleansed, everything would appear to man as it is, infinite. For man has closed himself up. . . ." To Blake the artist's business was that of opening men's perceptive faculties to a sort of truth that is commonly hidden.

There are other points at which Blake's philosophy—and his drawings—are more like the Oriental than the Western. The need for stillness within, the waiting for a spiritual intimation or distillation, the belief that abstraction may serve to reveal more truly than realistic representation—these are reminders of an approach un-Western and alien. He seems to say that there is a divine unity that interests him more than all the pretty and obvious faces and places and things in the world. In his drawings there is the majesty of that which is remote—and, for those who prefer their pictures familiarly depictive and intellectually definite, a strangeness and often "distortion."

Blake's biography is uneventful but illuminating. Born to a home in small circumstances, son of a hosier or draper, he learned engraving at fourteen. God and the angels he reported seeing repeatedly, from early childhood, and Christ and the prophets. He experienced visions in which the Bible characters appeared to him quite clearly, and this he found very convenient since it enabled him to dispense with models. He made his insecure living by writing poetry, by engraving his own designs and selling his illustrated writings, and by engraving the works of other artists. At twenty-five he married a woman as poverty-stricken as himself, illiterate, but a satisfactory mate for him. She had beauty of looks and of character; she believed implicitly in his visions; and she learned to be his assistant in engraving and coloring. With Catherine at his side, Blake wrote his poems as "spoken by someone in eternity," and designed and engraved happily "with a ladder of angels reaching from the heavens to his cottage." When he died he was so little esteemed that he was buried in some place lost to record.

Blake:
*When the Morning Stars
Sang Together.*
Engraving, from the Book of Job.
Metropolitan Museum of Art

There are a few known tempera paintings from Blake's hand. Otherwise the list is of water-colors, usually with line, and of engravings with and without wash or color. Blake's method was what we today would term expressionistic. He freely violated nature; indeed he wrote that "natural objects always did and do weaken, deaden, and obliterate imagination in me." And: "A man puts a model before him, and paints it so neat as to make it a deception. Now I ask any man of sense, is that art?" In blunter words, Blake distorted. He eliminated detail and background. He further intensified expression by emphasizing abstract rhythm, building structural patterns. Whether it is the engravings for *Job* or the *Christ and the Woman Taken in Adultery* or *The Procession from Calvary,* the pattern and rhythm and

order engage one's eyes before the "meaning."

The obvious linear method immediately links Blake with the Gothic style, which was, of course, out of fashion. That his first assignment in his apprentice days led him to make drawings of the medieval monuments in Westminster Abbey is not without significance. He is known also to have studied reproductions of works by Michelangelo—that Florentine master who was too great to be held to the Renaissance formulas, who was passionate and Biblical as well as Greek. Like Michelangelo, Blake—and Tintoretto alone to the same degree—manipulated the human body, its directions and weights and postures, for arbitrary effect. Many of his drawings are poems of movement, told wholly in terms of bodies rhythmically disposed. In the art of purest line, engraving,

Blake: *The Procession from Calvary*. Tempera. *National Gallery, Millbank, London*

Blake is perhaps the greatest master after Dürer. As the sixteenth-century Germans marked the end of Gothicism on the Continent, so Blake is an isolated throwback to the "Northern" style in England.

William Blake, despite the modest physical dimensions of his works, is accepted by the twentieth-century moderns as England's most original and most rewarding graphic artist. The direction taken by art theory in recent years gives his picturing more than intrinsic significance, even a prophetic importance—although not without raising paradoxical questions. The moderns—and we all tend to become moderns—believe implicitly in the basic importance of the formal structure in art. They believe that the experience of order, movement, and rhythm should come before the pleasure of familiar subject-matter and lesson and associative recollection. Particularly they discount art that is overliterary, and they have been known to be caustic about Britain's partiality to anecdote and sentiment. It is a paradox then that today's moderns have rediscovered Blake; for no other British artist is so inextricably bound up with literature.

The explanation is that his creative drawings are so endowed with the plastic values that it little matters what subject-matter lies beyond. The moderns, after all, do not demand that the abstract design element be divorced from representational elements; only that it be in the picture whether objective nature or symbol or narrative is emphasized or not. Blake happens to include literary illustration without impairing in the least the rhythmic and formal values; indeed he makes spatial order and vitalized design reinforce concrete meaning.

There is a huge gap between Britain's earliest orthodox master, Sir Joshua Reynolds, and Blake. Neither the theories set down in Reynolds' *Discourses* nor his fashionable practice foreshadowed in the slightest this mystic, whose works were considered in his own time "unintelligible" and "the effusions of a disordered brain." Blake on his side wrote that Reynolds had been "hired by Satan to depress art." After reading the *Discourses*, Blake jotted this note in the margin: "The Enquiry in England is not whether a man has Talent and Genius but whether he is Passive and Polite and a Virtuous Ass." Yet this impolite critic and unorthodox genius was born English and never spent a day of his seventy years outside Britain. If Reynolds and his fellows failed in their objective of overcoming insularity, of bringing British art into the great European tradition of creativeness, Blake strangely overrode all traditions and touched on forms of expression that are universal and eternal.

Architecture

Renaissance architecture came late to England, and not until long after the "new learning" from Italy had transformed the social and intellectual life of the Elizabethan court. Only gradually pillars, columns, and porticos were added to older buildings, and interiors were designed with classic detailing. Until well into the seventeenth century the spirit of British architecture remained essentially medieval.

Two names are important above all others in the Renaissance building art that finally came to Britain, those of Inigo Jones (1573-1651) and Christopher Wren (1632-1723). Inigo Jones returned from study in Italy with a knowledge of ancient classic architecture and a skill that had already won him royal commissions in Denmark. He was soon to win the title "the English Palladio," and his life was to be devoted to clearing up confusions in current building ideas and averting the growing menace in the curved lines and broken pediments of Italian baroque. He gave the country its first clear conception of the classic style. He built a few great country houses and some public buildings. In the service of James I, he made the plans for a royal palace at Whitehall intended to be the largest residence in Europe. Only the banqueting hall was built, and stands a nobly proportioned and distinguished structure. These plans and his writings made him the outstanding influence upon a later generation.

Christopher Wren was an Oxford professor who had already become architect-in-chief to the King before the great London fire of 1666. After the fire had destroyed most of the city, he rebuilt St. Paul's Cathedral (begun in 1675, and completed in 1710) and fifty other churches. The characteristic feature of St. Paul's is the great dome, originally inspired by the Pantheon in Rome. The interior as finally completed represents compromises with older cathedral design. In one way and another many baroque idioms were incorporated into the cathedral's fabric. The smaller churches became distinguishing features of the landscape, particularly because of their slender towers terminated by delicate spires.

The influence of the Wren churches (and those of his follower James Gibbs) upon the builders in the American colonies was beyond calculation. In New England especially the richest and serenest architectural experiences are to be had, even to this day, from such town squares and village greens as have been preserved from colonial times, dominated by the classic-detail churches. Hardly less important are the colonial houses of English Renaissance inspiration. This is not to say that, after the Revolution, America did not experience Roman-revival and Greek-revival phases, through influence from other countries, and achieve a different sort of Renaissance style.

One later architect in England, Robert Adam (1727-92), with his brother James, designed beautifully in the Renaissance spirit. He was indebted to Jones and Wren, and to the French Empire style, too, but his excellence was in a classic purity of design gained by new knowledge of ancient Greece. The Adam style was widely affected in America, in furniture as well as in building; and painted panels, niches for sculpture, medallion insets, and other antique motifs as he used them are still among the hallmarks of the Adam style amply in evidence in "period" interiors.

XXVI: THE MARCH OF REALISM:
THE NINETEENTH CENTURY

IN THE HISTORY of painting the nineteenth century is known as the era of revolutions. In Paris, then the center of the arts of the Western world, there was a series of cycles, each marked by advance, consolidation, revolt, and overturn. From 1800, when Davidian classicism had firmly established itself, to the rise and decline of impressionism three generations later, excitement followed excitement; "schools" developed, gained international vogue, and were discredited; old revolutions were lost in new.

Only in the nineteen-fifties was proper perspective gained on the four "decisive" movements, dated roughly at 1790, 1830, 1855, and 1875: the classic or neoclassic, the romantic, the realistic, and the impressionist. Now, in retrospect, it is

seen that all were parts of a single more extensive phenomenon, the maturing of the Renaissance realism. It turns out that, of the four, impressionism alone is epochal. It rises measurably above the others for two reasons: it marked the final fulfillment of the scientific and realistic aims initiated by Masaccio and Leonardo centuries before; and it has left a body of works inventive and lastingly effective, signalized particularly in the canvases of Pissarro, Monet, and Renoir.

There is, further, this readjustment being made: the one overshadowing revolution of the century took place at the point where impressionism as a dogma was abandoned, where a new slope was entered upon by men no longer bound by realism, by the tyranny of appearances; men

Géricault: *The Raft of the Medusa. Louvre*

who, while accepting the heritage of scientific color from the impressionists, turned their backs upon the "reality" sought in all the centuries from Raphael to Monet, seeking instead a return to formal excellence and structural integrity.

The reorientation in the light of the post-impressionism (or expressionism) of 1880–1950 shows the movements of 1790–1880 to have been merely phases of that other type of art. The insurrections and doctrines so exciting and so discussed even within our own memory sink back into the routine of past history, as part of a grayness of minor difference and minor manner. The men who had seemed giants—David and Ingres, Delacroix and Géricault, Courbet and Manet, once compared with Raphael and Rembrandt, with Dürer and Velázquez—lose a little in stature, are seen as epitomizing variations within that one historic type or phase of painting. It is a man outside all schools and outside France who emerges as the finest flower of avowed realism: Goya. After him the really great figures are Cézanne and van Gogh.

The nineteenth-century spectacle is still brave and gripping when humanly considered. The incidents are stirring, the characters dramatic. While the cannon are still firing in France and severed heads are dropping into baskets, David overturns the structure of courtly decorative art, destroys the Royal Academy, and "purifies" expression. Then he is exiled by a restored monarch, and Baron Gros, to whom David entrusts the authority and sanctity of classicism, fails as custodian in the face of romantic successes and is so contrite that he kills himself. Delacroix puts through his revolution in the name of Romance, destroying heroic classicism perhaps forever, but is recognized a half-century later as less a creative insurgent than a reviver of baroque ideals.

Courbet then strides through the polite halls of French painting, which are still romantic or lingeringly classic, as a disillusioned and savage materialist, bringing the camera eye to bear mercilessly on sea and woods and animals, on workers and prostitutes and sportsmen. Corot and Degas steady a little the gains for clear-seeing naturalism, bringing a new measure of constructive craft; although it is Degas who opposes the turn

into impressionism, who in his north-lighted studio eloquently turns up his coat collar at mention of the radicals who work in the open air. Then Pissarro and Monet, vilified and excluded, turn out to be the real victors in the long campaign for scientific seeing and exact statement, capping Renaissance progress.

After them all comes Cézanne, who did not sell a picture till he was forty, whom society would not have permitted to paint if he had not happened to be the son of a banker, who started as a faithful impressionist but recognized that the realists had thrown away a quality of form that was essentially *the* creative element in picture-art —Cézanne, who terminates one age and initiates another, who ushers in a school that overshadows all those of the preceding two centuries.

It is the continued march of realism that is important historically in the era 1790–1880, whatever the labels. It is realism under four masks, but always with the literalist essentially controlling. With the classicists a correct, Greek-hallowed mask is put on, but beneath there is nonetheless the painstaking statement of outward truth, the reverence for verisimilitude. With the romantics the mask is that of emotionalized, theatricalized statement and a loose technique, but without violation of nature as excitedly observed at home or as reported from exotic climes. When the Courbet group arrives—and it temporarily runs away with the label "realist"—there is a show of dropping all masks; it seems to clear the way to the *realest* truth. But it is discovered that something noble and desirable is hidden—or lost—by these materialists. Finally the impressionists fit up their atmospheric mask, behind it devote their effort to aspect-of-the-moment reality, to views fixed according to the latest discovered laws of optics.

In short it is at last recognized that beneath the four masks is the same reverence for things observantly viewed and cleverly transcribed. It is seen that when Cézanne and van Gogh adopted new *expressive* aims (aided by Whistler and Gauguin, who adopted new *decorative* ones) they accomplished the true modern revolution, because then for the first time the direction of effort that had prevailed for three hundred years was reversed. And so the nineteenth-century phases, still labeled for convenience classic, romantic, realistic, and impressionist, are tumbled into one basket tagged "varieties of realism."

Realism

Realism was supposed by some for a time to be typically the art of democracy, of leveled classes, and therefore typically the art for the republican age. It was said that the "honest" vision of Courbet and Millet and Manet was to be expected and applauded in the time when the kings and courts had been expelled and destroyed, as in France and America, or disciplined and rendered powerless as in England and Belgium.

The lines are not so easily drawn as that. The revolt of the current modern artists *against* realism, for instance, came in places and in periods most devoted to democracy. But there is considerable pertinency in the linking of nineteenth-century naturalism and sentimental realism with the rise of the middle class and the triumph of materialistic philosophies.

The men made rich by the industrial revolution became in the nineteenth century the sustaining patrons of art. They came to control not only buying for home decoration but official museum collecting. Indirectly they came into control of the academies and art schools. It was, too, at this point that the present system of salons and periodic exhibitions was established: great displays of art-produce spread before the bourgeois buyer, inviting the new seeker after culture to look and to express his opinion. The artificial structure of shows, dealers, critics, and connoisseurs was thus set up in an effort to meet the needs and wishes of a new and often untutored class of purchasers.

For the patron art became sometimes a new and sincerely valued way to pleasure; oftener it was a means of conspicuous display. In the other direction, that of the artist, the adjustment of product to demand was, in general, deeply injurious. Buyers, even critics, demanded art intelligible to the least trained faculties. In some

countries, in England particularly, the familiar, sentimental, and dexterous thing was so thoroughly exalted over any deeply creative expression that three-quarters of a century passed with hardly a mentionable name in the annals of national painting and sculpture.

The thrifty, prosperous, and—according to his lights—honest manufacturer or banker or merchant-prince has made his way up by unimaginative hard work and shrewd calculation. When he spends his money upon works of art he wants pictures that seem honest and clever and unmysterious. He wants art true to familiar aspects of environment, and dexterously contrived. Storytelling in paint he can easily understand, and a bit of affecting sentiment is not out of place in an activity that is, after all, a sort of Sunday and holiday thing. This is the reason for nineteenth-century anecdotal and reproductive painting and sculpture.

It is not out of tune with the scholarly and popular philosophy of the era. Materialism was being put forward as explanation of existence and as guide to personal living. Success philosophies as shallow as the art of Landseer and Frith abounded. (It was their predecessor Sir David Wilkie who candidly said, "To know the taste of the public, to know what will best please the employer, is, to an artist, the most valuable of all knowledge"—a far cry from the creative independence and the wholehearted passion of Rembrandt or El Greco.) In general the academies got into the hands of the painters who purveyed to the middle-class demand.

It was a long time before science, which through the inventor's laboratory and the application of mechanical power to manufacture made possible the machine age, was visibly reflected in works of art. Until the opening of the twentieth century the new and exciting structure of architecture was carefully hidden behind masks fashioned from building styles long since dead. The new mass-produced commodities, which might have been expected to take on a characteristic beauty out of the nature of the shaping tools, and out of the ways of living in the machine age, were instead ornamented with motives faithfully copied from the superseded manual crafts. And in the figurative arts, until the very end of the nineteenth century, subject-matter could not be taken from the life of the times. It was not until after World War I that typical mass interests, such as the life of the workingman or the lessons of socialism, were considered suitable themes for painting.

The technique of the impressionists marked the one point at which the graphic arts received a notable impetus from the scientific laboratory. When color was understood by artists as broken-up light, a new resource was discovered and developed. The impressionists then pushed the logic of the camera-eye and the understanding of natural lighting to a conclusion impossible in any earlier era, and therefore typically of the new age. Otherwise the scientific mastery of nature that had been epochal for man in his major activities—war, work, communication, transportation, recreation—had comparatively negligible influence upon contrived art.

Political change and thought were more truly reflected in art at those moments when kings and emperors temporarily came back to power. David's gesture of purifying painting, his destruction of all that was courtly and trivial in French pictures, had been a sincere attempt to express a new democratic ideology. In seeking models for that neoclassic republican art he and his followers actually dressed painting in the idioms of Republican Rome. They depicted the triumphs of democracy in the ancient capital, and thereby symbolically celebrated the victories of the citizens of Paris. But when Napoleon turned democracy into imperialism they as easily slipped over into celebrating in terms of Imperial Rome.

Napoleon wanted his Empire signalized in suitable monuments, and he commanded the painters to create a worthy new style—whence some of the most deplorable heroic-bombastic art in existence. It was the grandeur of Rome that led to his building of the Arc de Triomphe at the end of the Champs-Elysées in Paris.

Louis XVIII and Charles X made feeble attempts to restore the ornamental, even the baroque sort of thing. Charles believed that disaster had overtaken France because Louis XVI had mistakenly given ground to the democrats,

and he set out to restore absolutism, planning a monarchical art to match. But a six-year reign proved too short for the consummation. In general, art and politics may be said to have parted company when he abdicated.

Thenceforth it was, for better or for worse, the age of individualism. In the end art was to gain by the circumstance. But the record of futility, of uncreativeness, over so much of the world for so many decades to follow is evidence enough that the artist did not know what to do with his freedom.

The arts did, however, become international—which may be counted an effect of science—and no longer did climatic and geographic conditions have a determining influence. When the next style of architecture came in, it was recognizably one expression in America and Germany, in France and Russia, in England and Japan. The machine, having spelled the doom of handicraft in all but the most precious forms of manufacture, determined in all the world the style marks of standard designed commodities. Hardly less were painting and sculpture re-created in forms nearer the universally expressive, and less local, than ever before. But that was long after the close of the story of the nineteenth century and of realism.

A bird's-eye view of art in Europe in the year 1800 would reveal that a certain number of minor and since unheralded painters, particularly in France, England, and Holland, had foreseen a market for literal and sentimental realism; that they had ignored alike the millinered art of the courtly and aristocratic circles and the purified sort brought in by the classicists. If their reputations for significance have not lasted, they yet were surpassingly popular in their time, and they should have a special interest for us today because their works were the ancestors of what is still our most popular form of art, appearing annually on our calendars, as pretty girls' heads on the covers of our monthly magazines, as genre studies on the covers of our weeklies. Greuze and Vigée-Lebrun were of this ancestral company in France, Sir David Wilkie in England, and some of the homely painters in Holland.

In Paris in 1800 the Versailles cargo had been

David: *Portrait of Pope Pius VII. Louvre*

safely jettisoned. Fragonard was to die of neglect and a broken heart in 1804. David had already been dictator for a decade. But not one of the neoclassicists was destined to approach the popular success, the bourgeois success long since achieved by that outstanding trifler with paint, Jean-Baptiste Greuze. Even in the days of the Great Kings he had been the darling of the French middle class and hardly less esteemed by the English. He could build up a sentimental bit with irresistible tenderness, and he could slick over an empty or prurient subject with the most virtuous show of artistry. His masterpieces are known in millions of reproductions: *The Girl with Doves, Innocence, The Village Bride,* and *The Broken Pitcher* (see page xviii).

Greuze's sometime pupil, Mme. Marie Anne Elisabeth Vigée-Lebrun, was doing immensely popular sentimental portraits, correct and highly colored, from the later years of the monarchy— she was an intimate of Marie Antoinette— through the period of the Revolution (though outside France, for her health), on through the Empire, and even into the reign of the last restored Louis. She was famous throughout Europe, belonged to four academies, and is still a best-seller in all art's marketplaces.

George Morland is a name from this time still revered in England. He was outstanding in a group of realists who specialized in household and barnyard genre, beside the authentic landscape art of Constable and Turner and the final flare-up of modish portraiture in Lawrence. Morland exhibited at the Royal Academy at the age of ten, and he turned out four thousand canvases before he died young in 1804, of drink and— some say—of contrition over betraying a great artist's talents. His *Interior of a Stable* and *Pigs*

Goya: *The Divided Bull Ring. Metropolitan Museum of Art*

and *The Alehouse Door* are typical. All three are favorites still with that part of the British public that takes to that kind of art.

After him David Wilkie was to carry on the trade in sentimental-natural realism and anecdote-picturing; and these two point forward only too accurately to the loss of all but illustrational values in mid-century, and to the total dissolution of pictorial structure in Landseer and Frith and then in Millais.

These all are artists who did not have to wait for the romantic insurgent Delacroix before knowing how to dramatize painting for popular audiences, or have to await Courbet's pronouncements before painting details of nature "just as they are." The point of the matter here is that there was, wholly outside the succession of recorded nineteenth-century revolutions, an enormously successful industry concerned with the production of sentimental pictures, within any definition of realism. The whole inordinately

popular line, from Morland to Landseer and Alma-Tadema, from Greuze to Cazin and Meissonier, is a middle-class phenomenon, signifying the change of standards due to shifting of picture-buying money into the pockets of a commercial class.

Goya, the Most Masterly Realist

But in 1800, outside all the countries so far mentioned in the chapter, in Spain, there was an artist who had independently developed realism to an unprecedented importance, who stands today as the greatest figure among all who are called realists: Goya. He had a camera-eye, and he was free of all illusions about adorning the truth. But he was a born painter, and he added to accurate seeing and candid statement an understanding of structure of a sort hardly known since Rembrandt.

Goya:
Majas on a Balcony.
Metropolitan Museum of Art

Goya is outside the routine history of the painting of the eighteenth and nineteenth centuries as surely as is Greuze or Morland, but for an opposite reason. He forestalled Courbet and taught Delacroix, and he practiced something very like impressionism before broken color and scientific optics were heard of. He overrode all the varieties of realism which were later to be the noted discoveries of French and therefore of European art, before the controversial distinctions were made. He was the most vital realist of them all. Whereas others were to be devoted to verisimilitude for its own sake, he made it an instrument (the realist's only legitimate excuse for being). He had a native interest in character; he added satire; he made brilliant images.

Francisco Goya was born as early as 1746, but he seems not to have come to the maturity of his artistic power until well along in life. Then by sheer vigor and pictorial honesty he pushed aside the weak native and imported court artists in Madrid. He had earlier done a great deal of hack work, ending with years given to making cartoons for tapestries.

Personally—and it shows in his art—he was a libertine and a reckless and violent adventurer, an audacious egotist and a skeptic. In youth, at Saragossa, he defied the authorities of the Inquisition and was forced to flee from the Churchmen. In Madrid he got into love-scrapes time and time again, and once was stabbed by a jealous rival and left for dead, but revived and fled the police. In Rome he barely escaped execution after he had been foiled in an attempted abduc-

Goya:
Don Francisco,
Son of Carlos II.
Escorial Palace

tion of a girl from a nunnery; he was exiled back to Spain instead. He seemed on the way to settling down and married the sister of the then court painter at Madrid. But soon his relations with the court ladies were so notorious that one of them, the famous Duchess of Alva, was banished. Goya loyally followed. But the King missed him and recalled the pair, and Goya was made court painter.

With the fall of the House of Bourbon, Goya seems to have gone over easily in loyalty to the French invader, Joseph Bonaparte; although he then painted and etched the world's most sincere and most terrible pictorial exposé of the horrors of warfare, after the siege. He equally facilely turncoated to the side of a restored Spanish king, who said he knew he ought to guillotine so traitorous a subject but guessed he wouldn't because the painter's art was so good. So Goya resumed his duties as court painter. A short time later he asked permission to visit in France; there he settled, and died in 1828, too old to care about the controversies over art then raging. He had made himself a greater figure than any painter then living.

Something of the violence, vividness, and audacity of Goya's way of living carries over into his painting and etching. The scope of his subject-matter is immense: from orthodoxly religious pictures to the most savage satires on the Church; portraits of every sort, from innocent children to ornamental royal groups and slyly cruel revelations of the characters of prominent but vicious people; story-pictures that castigate

Goya:
*Don Ignacio Omulryan
y Rourera.*
Nelson Gallery

mankind for its follies and bestiality; nudes, bull-fights, balcony pieces, cartoons, caprices. He observed and brooded, and scorned mankind, and put down in paint a record of what he saw and thought.

His portraits of the Spanish King and Queen are among the curiosa of painting. He apparently maliciously showed up the rulers for what they were: the King a stupid and lazy incompetent; the Queen Maria Luisa a greedy and hardened courtesan. Here psychological penetration and cruel satire came to a remarkable union. Apparently the liberty of the artist was fully respected. He remained a court favorite. And at least Goya was no less honest in painting himself. The same cunning hand could, however, depict a little boy with tenderness and insight.

Portraiture of a different but hardly less masterly sort is the *Maja Nude,* a figure as voluptuously felt and transcribed as any in European painting. The companion picture of the *Maja Clothed,* also a portrait of the Duchess of Alva, is equally voluptuous and winning. This same lady, as well as others discarded, was later savagely held up to ridicule. Indeed, when Goya did not like a model he was as candid in advertising the sitter's shortcomings as he had been in glorifying the savored charms and beauty of the duchess.

In this depreciative direction one may easily be sated with his cruelty and his nastiness. There is a plethora of voluptuaries and harlots and fiends in his later pictures. They deal fully and mercilessly with cannibals and idiots, firing squads and torturers, cripples and executioners, corpses and fetuses. One could make from his works a terrible album of perversion and unhealthiness. Yet there runs through his dealings with abnormality and the vicious such a burning scorn for the stupid and the avaricious that one comes away from the exhibit with some of the purged emotion that follows great tragedy. And Goya has just enough of poetry of statement to justify the descent into the terrifyingly evil and gruesome.

His war pictures, in both painting and etching, are among the most moving and horrifying documents about man's inhumanity known to art. At the time of their making, the artists of France were competing to glorify the Napoleonic Wars for their hero-master. Goya forgot heroes and rulers, showed the bleeding, shell-torn bodies, the piles of nauseating corpses, the captives being shot down, even the women being violated. The grandiose and patriotic fiction of war is punctured, the sordid reality set forth grimly, truthfully. He nowhere sets himself up as moralist; but no one would remember, after perusing his *Disasters of War,* the copybook sentimentalisms about dying gloriously for one's country. Cruelty, butchery, and gore—these persist in the memory.

There is a great deal of Goya's art, nevertheless, that escapes the terrible or the unhealthy note. There is plentiful satire with the humor stressed, not without a biting contempt for man's intentions. There are canvases in which the normal and the beautiful are intensified and glorified. And through it all run an admirable vigor and an inescapable vividness. Goya's canvases are outstandingly *alive* in any gallery.

And finally—what makes him an artist beyond so many who have verisimilitude and vividness and nothing more—he rises at times to a beautiful mastery of the architecture of picture-making. In a figure-piece like the *Majas on a Balcony* there is notable plastic organization. In some of the war pictures there is the same expert handling of volume and space, of plane and depth. The pictures of bullfights are disposed on the canvas with extraordinary deftness, with a formal balance (page 554), yet with full validity given to every illustrational requirement. The portraits vary from a great many negligently put down figures (too often paraded indiscriminately as masterpieces now that Goya's name is celebrated) to likenesses expertly disposed in the two-dimensional field. With the portraits

one always comes back to the exceptional living-ness of the face and figure.

And so this genius a little takes off the edge of novelty from the realism of the French of the nineteenth century. This vitally realistic yet cunningly constructive painter was, at the beginning of the age of individualism, already a giant. Spanish painting had been all but dead since Velázquez, when suddenly Goya appeared. He is said to have been Spain's brainiest man in that century of trouble and degradation; and certainly he was her most passionate, most furious, most accomplished commentator in paint.

Neoclassicism to Romanticism

One has only to place (or imagine) a vivid Goya canvas beside one of David's frigid pictures to know how sterile was the so-called classicism of 1800 in France—and, for that matter, in Germany, and later in England.

Jacques-Louis David has his historical place. He rode in on the wave of public indignation and intolerance that demanded destruction of everything suggesting the old court life. He was able to destroy the Watteau-Fragonard tradition. But when he became art dictator he decreed a type of painting just as narrow and special and unconnected with full-blooded living. He had studied at the French Academy in Rome and had a scholar's vision of what noble art should be.

David and his fellows had the best intentions in the world. They could see that the glittering, baroque, and erotic art of Versailles represented only a fringe of society, a fringe now happily gone. They did not see that in purifying art according to the ideals of ancient Rome they were throwing out not only glitter, insincerity, and pretense but also all living content and social significance. Their painting is hard, cold, mechanical, and intellectual. They took the Roman bas-relief as their model for the "effect" a painting should have. They suffered also from the insistence of the political authorities that every picture be patriotic.

The heroic story-art might be varied with portraits or with bits illustrating the Revolution,

Ingres: *Mlle. Rivière. Louvre*

like David's often-reproduced *Death of Marat.* The equally famous *Mme. Récamier* in the Louvre has the merit of novelty, is superior to the lifeless—yes, the insupportably bad—celebrated things such as his *Paris and Helen, The Sabines,* and *The Crowning of Napoleon.* Some observers profess to see in David's canvases a mastery of plastic architectonics similar to Poussin's, and therefore feel that he deserves a major position in the annals of creative art in France. Rather his place would seem political and pivotal, his contribution intrinsically second-rate.

Others who tried with intellectual might and main to wed classical mythology and antique purity to revolutionary impulse—or, later, to Napoleonic propaganda—were Gérard, whose *Cupid and Psyche* is still seen commonly in reproduction, and Baron Gros, a born panoramic illustrator, who could put the more military feeling into his canvases because he had been to war. He specialized in celebrating the exploits of Napoleon. It was he who, charged with up-

Ingres: *Portrait of a Gentleman. Metropolitan Museum of Art*

holding the banner of classic purity after David's exile, felt that he had been lax in enforcing authority and so lay down in a ditch and drowned himself, leaving art to shift for itself.

Pierre Prud'hon softened the sculpturesque classicism of his fellows and was less political-minded. He orthodoxly returned to approved archaeological fields for his subject-matter, but he had a Correggio-like taste for the voluptuousness of the flesh. He was the author of a painting which became prodigiously popular in the late nineteenth century, *The Zephyrs Carrying Away Psyche*.

But it was Ingres, a late follower of David

(born in 1780 and living until 1867), who brought the greatest talent to the neoclassicist group. He had hardly started his career when the tide of romanticism broke over artistic France, and he became the bulwark of conservatism in its fight to keep "the youngsters" from ruining art.

Probably the reactionary position forced on Ingres hurt his individuality and inventiveness. In any case his early pictures are the more original, the portraits of 1805–1807 touch the top mark. The *Mlle. Rivière* (page 559) and the *Mme. Rivière*, both in the Louvre, and the *M. Granet* at Aix-en-Provence—as also the *Portrait of a Gentleman* in the Metropolitan Museum—are marked by an exceptional sense of architectural design, with a fine understanding of arranged planes. But too much contact with actual survivals of ancient art—he lived in Rome and Florence nearly twenty years—evidently hardened his technique and apparently lessened his feeling for plastic order. When he returned to Paris in 1824 he became very popular by painting, on the one hand, pseudo-classic pedantic allegories, and, on the other, photographically exact nudes such as *The Source* and *The Turkish Bath*. This was the period of the daguerreotype, and even a classic realist must meet the competition of the camera.

There was one other neoclassicist who gained an international reputation, the German Anton Raphael Mengs. He was an intimate of the archaeologist Winckelmann in Rome, and his return to Roman purity antedated that of David. (Chronologically Mengs belongs to the age of the baroque, since he lived from 1728 to 1779.) But his paintings are generally recognized today as hard and academic. They are a perfect parallel to the equally celebrated sculptures of the Italian Canova and the Danish Thorwaldsen, who fixed the men and women of their time in the attitudes of Greek gods and goddesses and lovers, with a strange mixture of antique stiffness and modern photographic exactitude.

Canova occasionally rose above the rather frigid level of the neoclassic sculpture, and there is an illuminating sidelight to be had from study of his "portrait" of Paolina Borghese, Napoleon's sister. It is rigged with a portrait head, a Greek goddess's body, nude to the thighs, and a period couch with photographically treated pillows, in marble.

Architecture, of course, had its share in the classic revival, and churches and capitols, homes and banks and railway terminals, were to revert occasionally throughout the nineteenth century to Greek temple prototypes. Then, too, the plague of Roman arches of triumph reappeared and spread.

David said in his last years that he well knew that his sort of painting was too severe to please the French public for long, and he prophesied the return to a style more colorful and familiar. Already in 1820 the question was being bandied about: "Who will save us from the Greeks and the Romans?"

When the reaction came it swung all the way from the coldness and impersonality of David and Ingres, and from their emphasis upon expressive linear draftsmanship, to overemotional, heated, and confusedly dramatic statement, and to melodramatic theme. Not all the pictures, of course, are overdone; but the effort seems, in the average, to have been for color, movement, and drama at any cost.

Eugène Delacroix and Théodore Géricault, the two leaders of the French romantic movement, owed a great deal to studies in England, where the romantic poets were then ascendant. They graciously acknowledged a debt, moreover, to Constable; and the young British painter Bonington, who died untimely at twenty-six in 1828, was their companion in Paris.

Delacroix is the towering figure, having left a great number of illustrational pictures, some almost as monumental in dimensions as those of the Davidian heroic school. He shamelessly theatricalized his subjects. In manner of painting he reverted to the baroque tendencies of Rubens and the nervous touch of Watteau.

Today many of Delacroix's canvases seem forced and turgid. He seldom brought the tumultuous movement into a poised framework. He is seen to have capitalized upon movement for its own sake, on the surface, failed to curb its pull and strain within plastic order. In that particular he falls short of Rubens' mastery or Tintoretto's. He is an exciting figure in his reckless insurgency, and he opened doors that had been injuriously closed by the classicists. He has a place in the second rank of nineteenth-century masters, but he is no longer held in the almost fanatical reverence that was his a generation ago.

There has been a determined effort among the moderns to exalt Géricault as the more important initiator of the romantic revival, at the expense of Delacroix. But the pictures do not seem to warrant such reranking. Géricault was hardly less literary and no less sentimentally

Delacroix: *The Bark of Dante. Louvre*

emotional than Delacroix. He put forward the free use of color and helped bring vigor back to painting. *The Raft of the Medusa* (see page 549) is sheer melodrama. There are few major canvases of his, indeed, in which one can take even that measured sort of pleasure that may be had from a score of Delacroix's things— say, *The Bark of Dante* in the Louvre, or the *Christ on the Sea of Galilee* in the Walters Gallery at Baltimore, or the *Oriental Lion Hunt* (more melodramatic) at Chicago. Very exceptional, and a masterpiece in its slighter, impressionistic way, is Delacroix's portrait of Paganini to be seen in the Phillips Gallery at Washington. In the other direction he turned, in his search for rich color, to the Orient, and found movement and drama in the harems and the desert warriors and the exotic hunts. This was the beginning of a sort of journalist Orientalism that has been much exploited by minor painters and major dealers ever since.

There were followers of the two romantic masters, but they count little. Perhaps more to be preferred than any of the lesser Frenchmen was the German Adolph von Menzel, if only because he accepted the baroque implications of the romantic manner and used it theatrically to memorialize the regal splendor of the Kaiser's court. In England, Turner was painting until the mid-century, and remains the most authentic romantic of them all.

The labels are inexact, of course. The Germans are likely to speak of "the romantic classicists" to distinguish the later group who warmed up their figures, rendering them less frigidly statuesque than David's. Even Ingres pushes over into a variant category. And it is easy for any eye to recognize that between romanticism and what the Victorians called realism there is no sharp dividing line. There are artists who affect the freedom and color and movement introduced by Delacroix and Géricault, who yet curb the passion and tumult and go on to exact statement and "commonness" of theme.

Millet: *The Goose Girl. Walters Art Gallery, Baltimore*

One of the transitional figures is Chassériau, who studied with Ingres, was strongly influenced by Delacroix, and had independence enough to push ahead in his own way. He might have been a very great decorative painter if he had not died in early middle age; and indeed he was the teacher of Puvis de Chavannes, who was destined to become France's lone important muralist of the era just before the triumph of impressionism (of whom more on page 610).

Landscape Painting and Corot

Jean-François Millet similarly bridges two schools; but the romantics taught him, the new realists claimed him. In the end he summed up neatly in one precept the error of the Delacroix school from which he had stemmed: "Keep away from the theaters!"

Millet never rose to a secure sense of picture-building, and he is known rather for his honesty and sentiment and homely truth. He was born of a peasant family and he loved the earth, particularly in its calmest moods. When he did not labor the social or literary allusion he was honestly affecting. For our sentimental moments he is one of the most agreeable of painters. *The Sower, The Angelus,* and *The Gleaners* continue to be favorites, and *The Man with the Hoe* has exceptional interest because it inspired one of the most popular poems of a generation ago.

Millet is sometimes counted, because of his associations in later life, a member of the Barbizon group, which is more correctly known as a school of pure landscape painters. The name is taken from the village of Barbizon at the edge of the Forest of Fontainebleau, just outside Paris, where a band of lesser artists made the discovery of an intrinsic and transcribable loveliness in nature.

Landscape painting for its own sake had been practically unknown in France—had been, up to 1830, a specialty of the Low Countries artists, of the Germans, and of the English. The only Frenchmen involved in its history, Poussin and Claude, had been expatriates in Rome; and in their day landscapes were not painted from nature but constructed out of stereotyped parts in the studio. They saw nature, moreover, through the haze of Arcadia. The gardens and parks peopled with courtiers and mock shepherdesses from the brushes of Watteau and Fragonard are hardly within the definition, and the classicists had found nothing in the out-of-doors to remind them of ancient virtues.

The studio painter of Paris—all the Barbizon brethren were Parisians—found in his way, as regards direct portrayals of nature, barriers hardly to be understood today. An artist then simply could not see the landscape in its own right. To observe a tree was to observe how it illustrated Claude's "treatment," or Ruisdael's, or Constable's. Landscape could be thought of as a state of mind, as a scene of dramas of love, or as a "construction"; never as the thing seen daily with the common eye. The British were far ahead in this. Constable is reported to have said of his Parisian contemporaries, "They know no more of nature than cabhorses do of meadows." (But only a few years earlier Constable had been constrained to place a violin against foliage in the open to prove to his British contemporaries that trees were not all a rich brown.)

When the Barbizon members accomplished the epochal advance of depicting actual places, actual trees, actual lighting, they were, then, introducing a novelty. In 1830 to carry one's easel into the open air was plain insanity.

Théodore Rousseau, the good rebel who led the fight for the new outdoor art—there was a fight, of course, and in this case there was incredibly stupid persecution at the hands of the Academicians—happened to be a literalist, and so Barbizon got off to a naturalistic start. But others of the school were at the far extreme of lyric and twilight statement. There is, indeed, every shade of realism within the membership, from prosaic botanic accuracy to misty and moody "interpretation." In short, the new realists and the old romantics—now the recognized conservatives—were, in the out-of-doors, friends and co-workers.

If Corot is essentially a Barbizon painter, then Barbizon is poetic. Lately there has been a disposition to treat Corot as a separate phenomenon, a master above all schools; and since his figure-paintings, long obscured, are now considered to constitute his larger claim to genius, he deserves more than a paragraph incidental to a school. His work is described presently.

Within the circle, Daubigny followed Rousseau in his fidelity to the tree and the brook as outwardly seen; and Diaz went to the opposite extreme of mysteriously shadowed landscapes accented with light-flecked trees. Jules Dupré was a middle-of-the-road figure, occasionally poetic, more often literal, but with a tendency to set out the calmer effects of nature.

Constant Troyon specialized in animal-filled landscapes; and indeed he was so successful with them that he set up a studio-factory in which he painted groups of oxen or cows or sheep and hired assistants to fill out the sky and field backgrounds. Nevertheless, there is pleasing pictorial composition to Troyon's credit in a few canvases in the vein of the *Oxen Going Out to Plow* in the Louvre. Charles Jacque, one of the last of the Barbizon men (1834–1894), is known especially for his gentle landscapes with sheep.

In general the Barbizon development is historically rather than intrinsically significant, as preparation for the impressionists. The several members opened a road of art that has been much traveled in all the generations since Rousseau proclaimed war on "studio concoctions," in the name of a forest. In a sense the Frenchmen universalized landscape as the Dutch, working in a flat country and a minor key, had not done. The idea was picked up in Germany and Scandinavia and America. And indeed the American George Inness was as near a master of this limited mode as any. He brought a good sense of surface composition, and occasionally built into his transcripts of what he called "civilized landscapes," as against untamed ones, a notable measure of three-dimensional structure.

It is said among the French that Corot was the painter of three thousand pictures, of which ten thousand were sold to Americans. No other artist has been so imitated; no other's works have

Inness: *Evening at Medfield. Metropolitan Museum of Art*

been so commonly manufactured under forged signature. Corot was inordinately popular in his own later life. With the "higher authorities" he was out of favor at the beginning of the new century. Now again, after a resifting of masters, he takes a place just below the top Frenchmen, not because of the popular "poetic" landscapes but because of the figure-pieces that have gradually been brought up out of museum basements and gallery storerooms. They are found to be endowed with plastic significance, a quality largely sacrificed to glamour and softness in the idyllic scenes of woods and lakes and nymphs.

Seldom in history has there been such a Jekyll-and-Hyde performance. On one hand are the compact, soundly organized, plastically orchestrated pieces, usually built around one dominating figure. On the other are those vaporous, hazy landscapes, dripping with sentiment and literary allusion—the very embodiment of the gloaming—and very enjoyable indeed when we are in sentimental mood.

Jean-Baptiste Camille Corot was born in 1796. He did not have any idea of being a revolutionary or an innovator, and he made no violent controversial gestures like those of Delacroix and Courbet. He was spared, too, the poverty, neglect, and deprivation suffered by Rousseau,

Millet, Daumier, and other contemporaries (though not, till he was nearly sixty, by earnings from art).

He wanted only to paint. He happened to have a father who, after some vain attempts to confine the lad within his own draper's business, gave him an allowance and his blessing. So it did not trouble him to the point of starvation or suicide that he could not sell one picture in the next thirty years. He worked much in Italy. But he had a villa not far from Barbizon, and by sympathy and a like aim he came into contact with the Rousseau-Diaz-Dupré group. He lived a quiet life, felt comfortable with little so long as he could paint, received the insignia of the Legion of Honor when he was fifty, and was a popular success at sixty.

Mostly the landscapes are all mood, all alike painted in silvery light, all the expression of one dream of what nature might be. They are not transcripts like Rousseau's or Daubigny's; indeed one cannot place any one of them as French or Italian. Rather they all are Elysian—though the labels spell out *Souvenir of Normandy* or *Breton Landscape* or *Environs de Naples*.

In the typical examples the time is always dawn or twilight. There is usually an impres-

Corot: *The Artist's Studio. Widener Collection, National Gallery, Washington*

tures that prove Corot's plastic mastery—when he did not give in to his twilight reveries.

An occasional landscape canvas marks a return to structural solidity, to planned plastic integration. Such is *The Bridge at Mantes* in the Louvre, which at the same time holds to the atmospheric, blurred-vision method; or the *Villa of the Parasol Pine* at Kansas City. In general the series of views of Rome, much earlier in period, is more architectural and therefore nearer to an initial impulse out of Claude Lorrain.

But it is when the canvas is given up to a full or half-figure, often a *Girl Reading* or a reclining woman, that the melodies are played with fuller exploitation of volume-space relationships, of plane organization, and of textural enrichment. In his understanding of texture or pattern as an item in the plastic synthesis Corot has affinity with Cézanne and Matisse. Corot was one of the earliest of the French to realize that the painter must see the encompassing light and not merely the light-struck object. "Le Père Corot," as he was known to his younger associates—he was the senior of Rousseau by sixteen years, of Millet by eighteen—lived on till 1875, still painting. He was then a great success, getting large sums for repeated variations of his lyric, melting woods-scenes; but he was destined to return to the lists of the masters through the "slighter" figure-paintings then forgotten. Of course the poetical things are the ones that have been endlessly imitated and forged.

The Realists

One might easily argue Corot into either the camp of the romantics or that of the realists. It is said that he was at a loss without a model before him, which sounds like realism. But with his grasp of structure he transformed his pictures into creations not seriously to be confused with the products of those mid-century painters who might best be described as "desperately realistic."

Gustave Courbet was the propagandist and self-conscious fighter for the school. The dullest of the academists were now entrenched in the

sionistic framework of diaphanous trees, and between them a glimpse of lake or river or a dew-drenched field. The foreground is likely to show two or three scattered impressionistic nymphs, very poetically indistinct. (They have something more than a literary function, however. By contrast they give scale to the masses of trees, and often enough a needed accent at the center of interest.)

These vaporous, luminous, misty things are not very deep as art; are not a little tricky, are sentimentally rather than solidly appealing. Still they have a lesser, a shadowy place in our affections. Merely as landscape they surpass in appeal most of the works left by the true Barbizon brethren. And beside them are those figure-pic-

Corot: *Villa of the Parasol Pine. William Rockhill Nelson Gallery of Art, Kansas City*

places of power, and it was one of them who scornfully dismissed something of Courbet's with the epithet "realistic." He immediately wrote up over his studio door: "G. Courbet, Realist." And he vociferously maintained that the whole aim of painting was to set down without reserve what nature presented to the eye.

There can be no doubt that so sincere and ringing a challenge to artificiality had a healthful influence upon French art. In so far as Courbet stood by his own precepts, reproducing as closely as he could all nature's imperfections and violences and chance aspects, he failed to create works of significance (and few celebrated names appear so often in galleries on paintings worthless and empty). Fortunately he was to a considerable degree a born painter, and, forgetting his "mission" and his precepts, he occasionally achieved a canvas with engaging and lasting values. Nevertheless, his greatest service to art may have been in the jolting of men's loyalty free from classic and romantic prepossessions.

To understand how bound up with unnatural effects French painting had been—one says "French" because Goya had opened a way long before, albeit he had been overlooked—it is necessary to go back to the two methods of *seeing* typical of David and of Delacroix. When the classicists, to take a familiar instance, painted the horsemen and horses in a war picture, they studied and got down with unchallengeable correctness the outline of each figure of man or animal, along with exact details of uniform, weapon, saddle, bridle, and mane. They made each part stand still separately for copying. Also, true to memories of antique statues, they set out each individual figure, free of other figures.

The romantics reversed this procedure: they interwove figures—as the men and horses would be interwoven if one were looking at an actual battle. Detail was lost; characteristic outlines were stressed, others obscured. What came clear to the eye was a sense of movement, a lively, colorful illustration.

Nature had been forced to stand still for the classicists; each little piece was "photographed" separately, and the pieces were then

Courbet: *A Real Allegory. Louvre*

assembled coldly, according to a reasoned plan. The result was mechanical, chilling. If one looked intently at any single part of the canvas it was "real," correct; but the reality disappeared once one remembered that it is movement that makes life. But the romanticists forced nature, so to speak, to pass before one's eyes on the run. There was then no mechanical assembling of correctly conveyed static bits. The reality was in the conveyed sense of movement.

In both cases nature had, Courbet rightly inferred, been forced: to an artificial static pose with the Davidians; to an artificial animation and theatricalism with Géricault and Delacroix, and especially with the Orientalists who followed them. There must be, Courbet decided, a still more real way of seeing. The newly popular camera helped to show both David and Delacroix to be wrong. Courbet decided upon camera truth for painting.

Even monumental pictures would henceforth deal with easily observable things, and Courbet consecrated immense canvases to commonplaces. The academicians asked: What is the sense of grandeur in size if the subject is not grand—an incident on Parnassus, an illustration from the Bible, or a historical episode? But Courbet painted huge pictures of weddings, funerals, home life, his own studio. They had an effect, though it is not clear that any one of them survives as a masterpiece. It is, indeed, necessary to search through the smaller canvases to see Courbet intrinsically justified: perhaps best in the self-portrait at the age of forty-eight, or in the *Baudelaire* in the museum at Montpellier or in a long line of modest seascapes.

One of the immense pictures of "common" subjects, *A Real Allegory: My Studio after Seven Years of Art-Life,* is a celebrated curiosity. It indicates how far Courbet was from following his own dicta, such as "I paint what I see." In the picture he shows himself at his easel, life-size, and beside him a nude model, a small boy, and a cat of the just-too-cute sort. On one side are grouped a dozen of his friends, posed much as the artist had portrayed them individually in other canvases. On the other side is a group of "characters" from among his outdoor friends, hunters and the like. Certainly realism is here offered in a strangely concocted medley. *Of course* there was scandal over the nude model and the mixed company—and there were columns and columns in the papers about "realism."

Courbet was peasant-born, a thick-skinned

Manet: *Déjeuner sur l'Herbe. Louvre*

and successful climber, a forceful egotist. He made history; but his pictures may tend to be fewer in the museums. He threw out much of the science of picture-construction along with the artificialities. He studied faithfully for a time, but the masters he chose to copy were Ribera and Hals and Velázquez.

Edouard Manet picked up the tradition of direct seeing, suffered, like Courbet, unqualified abuse from those who wanted conformance to hallowed custom, turned out a very great deal of moderately interesting, substantially illustrative work, and at times added some decorative understanding to his equipment as competent realist. He seems often on the verge of going on to a revolutionary way of art—almost grasps the long-lost principle of mural technique, almost suggests a near-Oriental pattern-based art. But in the end it is only a pleasing individual method he achieves, within the true realistic school.

As picture-maker Manet rises far above Courbet's level; there used to be a room at the Metropolitan Museum in New York wherein his *In the Boat* and his *Woman with a Parrot* hung close by a selection of Courbet's unorganized, actual "views." Obviously Manet was a painter, the other an accomplished transcriber. But one has only to turn and look at a Cézanne (or even a Whistler) to know that design means something else again.

Manet was born in 1832. He was therefore at the impressionable age of eighteen when Courbet threw down his challenge to the romantics and caused a sensation by espousing illustration of things as they are. Manet studied, too, just those past artists bound to reinforce his naturalism: Hals, Ribera, Zurbarán, Velázquez, and Goya. By the time he was twenty-two he was recognized as a fighter at Courbet's side. In 1863 he achieved a *succès de scandale* through the exhibition of the *Déjeuner sur l'Herbe*, or *Lunch on the Grass*. It was neither first-class realism nor good designed picturing, a fact that was wholly overlooked in the excitement over the subject-matter:

two dressed gentlemen and two undressed ladies together in a park. Because the thing was daringly new it enraged the conservatives and equally drew the young radicals to Manet's side. Actually the painter had mixed his new naturalism with some very artificial conventions taken with little understanding from the Spaniards: particularly the excessive black shadowing. And the whole composition, considered in the light of later open-air ideals, is a ridiculous bit of studio-posing against a set-up of stage scenery.

Nevertheless this became the most famous and notorious picture of the nineteenth century, and Manet was thenceforward a figure and a battle-cry. Largely for his sake Napoleon III created the *Salon des Refusés,* so that the public might have a chance to compare radical art with the officially approved sort—a move that gave heart and help to many a shamelessly persecuted innovator, and to plenty of incompetents and charlatans as well.

Two years later Manet again shook the art world to its foundations by exhibiting his almost equally famous and notorious *Olympia,* a nude portrait of a typical Parisian demi-mondaine. Because the elder artists and the moralists were collectively shocked, the young realists were sure again that here was the revolutionary new way. Again it was overlooked that the picture had little virtue beyond fidelity to nature and utter candor. Obviously inspired by Giorgione's *Sleeping Venus* and Goya's *Maja Nude,* it lacked the poetic loveliness and plastic mastery of the one and the transcribed physical healthiness and sensuous charm of the other. A naked, pampered harlot—hardly more.

Manet is sometimes—erroneously, it now seems clear—credited with the introduction of the methods of color-use which are at the heart of impressionism. But it was not until after 1870 that he became impressionistic. That is, he was a follower of Pissarro and Monet rather than a discoverer and their teacher. As the excitement over his "shockers" fades, he is recognized as a good painter in the second rank of avowed realists—of far lesser stature, for instance, than Goya—but author of many direct and arresting portraits and an occasional pleasing and clever figure-

piece. He helped Whistler to an understanding of flatness and simplification as formal assets—thus putting him on the road away from Courbet's insistent naturalism—and that was a service to later art. Like Whistler (and the post-impressionists), he caught a glimpse of a pattern-value that might profitably be restored to picturing; but he was too deeply caught in the aesthetics of materialism to escape often into formally creative pastures.

The third of the triumvirate of realists of the fifties and sixties was Edgar Degas, as individual in his method as Manet, and possessor of a superior sense of design. He is best known for his charming transcriptions of ballet-dancers, on the stage, in rehearsal, in the dressing-room. He goes back a little to the older schools in his care for exact draftsmanship. It does not escape him, however, that his contemporaries are pushing forward toward purer color: his becomes brilliant, luminous, and fresh. But he does not go on to impressionism in the full, melting sense. He is too sound a constructor for that. And very often, out of architectural instinct and clear-seeing, with some sentiment thrown in, he achieves a picture lastingly alive and winning.

Degas studied with the classicists and went to Italy, and thus had a background uncongenial to the innovations of Courbet and Manet, whose gods were instead the Dutchmen and the Spaniards. Perhaps thus Degas was able to temper the new hasty naturalism with something organic to ordered painting, with structure and form. When he chose to be "straight realist" he pushed photographic accuracy to a new level (though in soft focus), as the *Portrait of a Woman* in the Louvre (see the color plate) indicates. This is ingratiating realism at its best. But his fuller achievement is in the series of studies of dancers, often as glimpsed from unusual angles, and sometimes in pastels; in the racetrack views, in which he used a flattened composition with plastic understanding far superior to Manet's; and in various street and café scenes so clearly planned on architectural principles that they almost warrant Whistler's term, "arrangements," as does *The Print Collector* illustrated here. This might be compared with Whistler's *Carlyle,* page 609.

Degas:
The Print Collector.
Metropolitan Museum of Art

Degas, born in 1834, two years after Manet, lived on until 1917, through the decades of the rise and decline of the avowed naturalists, through the entire impressionist adventure, and on to the years when the anti-realists, in the names of Cézanne and Gauguin and van Gogh, had come into favor. In the view of many moderns he is the most respectable and rewarding of the sometime celebrated Frenchmen of the realistic century.

There are other names out of the period, once in all lists of the masters, which today are used only as indices of changes in taste, or, more usually, as warnings against what is not to be enjoyed. Meissonier, in the direct line from Greuze, born about 1814 and living on into the last decade of the century, was famous for his meticulous, almost microscopic treatment of historical episode and genre. No one else was ever so exact in rendering every hair and every button, or so conscientious in gaining archaeological and anatomical accuracy. He was an illustrator in the large with a miniaturist's technique.

Adolphe Bouguereau was yet another who became inordinately popular, only to be accepted later as a useful bugaboo and scapegoat. He erred on the saccharine side. Realistic landscape was picked up by Cazin and sentimentalized *ad nauseam*. He demands mention only because his canvases still cover walls and walls in British and American galleries. He was, in short, a Victorian favorite and yet not quite bad enough to have been eased out of the museums with the bulk of British and American Victorians.

In England there were no masters comparable to Manet and Degas. A literal reproduction of the Derby Day crowds, done with miniature fidelity, proves sensational. But the more usual thing is exemplified in Landseer's animals and

Stevens: *Mrs. Collmann.*
National Gallery, London

in his touching pouting children, or in illustrations of Shakespearean scene or Greek legend.

London, nevertheless, saw a strange intellectual revolt against current standards on the part of a group of painters who called themselves the Pre-Raphaelite Brotherhood. They declared war on what they termed "slosh in art," of which England in 1850 had plenty; although these rebels were inclined to include Rubens and Rembrandt among the destroyers of art. Their substitute was to have been painting as nobly free in execution as that of the time before the academic classicism of Raphael, as nobly spiritual in theme as that of the era before Correggio and the sensual Venetians. They would observe from nature, not follow conventions. They would paint pictures with substance.

Their intentions were above reproach. But it happened that there was not a born painter in the group. They were admirable minor poets and pamphleteers, and, so far as visual art goes, three or four were competent illustrators. The result was that Pre-Raphaelitism slipped into forms of expression no less literary and hardly less sentimental than those of their enemies, the Academicians. In place of Frith's colored photographs and Landseer's portraits of Rover and the monarch of the glen, they substituted English Madonnas and Italianesque Arthurian knights—all from the books—in meadows and castles rendered in a tight naturalistic technique.

Dante Gabriel Rossetti was the foremost poet of the group, William Holman Hunt its most consistent early-Christian moralist, and John Everett Millais its one wholly successful painter-member—who, however, backslid badly and eventually became President of the Royal Academy. Ford Madox Brown and Edward Burne-Jones were talented followers who became distinguished illustrators.

It is unimportant which painters in England detoured more or less into the etherealized pastures opened by the Pre-Raphaelites and swung out again to purvey, a little less sloshily, to the popular demand for anecdote-pictures and calendar chromos; or which others continued full in the road worn smooth by Wilkie and Frith. It barely matters that two belated classicists, cold and correct, turned up in Lawrence Alma-Tadema and Frederick Leighton—except that Queen Victoria made the latter a lord in recognition of his art, marking the first time a brush-wielder had risen to the peerage.

In a single painting Alfred Stevens outdid all the other British realists. His portrait of Mrs. Collmann in the National Gallery in London is a thing to give pause. The subject, so beautifully the gracious Englishwoman, is set out simply and cleverly, with a sufficient reserve of detail to prevent the too usual dispersion of picture-values.

The United States had a realist of the Courbet stamp, Thomas Eakins, who came too late to make history as a pivotal insurgent (for American painting had already split into a half-dozen schools—Barbizonians, impressionists, romantic realists, a return-to-the-Old-Masters group inspired in Munich, etc.—by the time he set up in Philadelphia after his years of study in Paris). But it has been recognized recently that he saw with the true naturalist's curiosity and unemotional detachment, and painted with uncanny directness. It was Walt Whitman, curiously enough, who summed up the whole case for the realist in art, in a comment about Eakins: "I never knew of but one artist and that's Tom Eakins who could resist the temptation to see what they think they ought to see rather than what is."

Eakins too commonly has only the virtues of candid observation and unforced statement—leaving a great body of gallery-size illustrations—but he touches expert surface organization frequently enough to warrant ranking above many a figure more celebrated a generation ago. The artist most praised as bringing a typically American note into painting is Winslow Homer, a vigorous descriptive picturer of rocky coasts, stormy seas, and the lives of fisherfolk. His best work is perhaps in his water-colors, which have an admirable largeness and spontaneity.

The Impressionists

The impressionists could hardly have existed had there been no Courbet to strike out (verbally) for an absolute surface realism. Misty, atmospheric, and vague as are the typical impressionist pictures, they came about in a search for a more exact, scientific, and immediate way of recording "natural" truth. Impressionism is the ultimate phase of realism, the final fling of those dedicated to reproducing what nature discloses to the outward eye.

But if the Frenchmen of the 1870s built theoretically on the naturalism of Courbet and Manet they had before them suggestive works from very different quarters, in which effects foreshadowing a new theory of seeing could have been detected. There were, in particular, the canvases of Constable and Turner, the two British masters who were having not one whit of influence in their own land.

Constable had gone into the open air and had achieved a sparkling effect of light. Turner had ultimately suppressed natural forms until his pictures seemed like improvisations in pure color—very unrestrained and nebulous, but stimulating as experiments in chromatic harmonization. Such a canvas as Constable's *Stoke-by-Nayland* at Chicago (page 523), or any of a hundred of Turner's opalescent water-colors, might have been used to demonstrate a coming vibrancy and freshness of color—and, one might add, naturalness of coloring—unknown to the elder masters and hardly hinted at in Courbet. The beginnings might be found much further back, in certain canvases of Velázquez; and a remarkable foreshadowing of true impressionistic quivering color and atmospheric liveliness had been seen in rare canvases of Goya, not least in some of the portraits.

When Claude Monet began to paint as a disciple of the Courbet group and a friendly contemporary of Manet, he received the influ-

Pissarro: *River, Early Morning. Johnson Collection, Philadelphia Museum*

ence from the Spaniards through Manet; and more than once he confessed a debt to the Englishmen. He became convinced that, since painting is a visual art and all things are discovered to the eye by light falling on objects, a true realism must be attainable through a study of light as such rather than through isolation and study of the object. At the moment new scientific analyses of color aided his theoretical advance: colors were known to be, or to result from, light rays of varying wave-lengths. The whole problem of painting was bound up in the further conquest of light.

And so one more variety of realism was added to the list, this time at the very opposite pole from Davidian classicism. What happened now was an almost total dissolution of solids, and there was a transfer of the painter's attention to the surface play of light over nature and to the hidden color-effects within light and shadow.

Camille Pissaro was as much an initiator of the new methods as Monet, and a sounder painter structurally. But just because Monet carried the principle to extremes he is the more instructive figure; and something may be said for dropping (momentarily) all notions that painting *is* anything else but light-nuances and color harmonies —thus meeting impressionism on its own ground. Then Monet is supreme.

The name adopted by the school came by chance, from a reference—slurring and derogatory at the time—to one of Monet's canvases in the *Salon des Refusés* of 1874, entitled *Impression: Soleil Levant*. Reviewers found the label handy, and soon the painters undertook to defend themselves as *impressionistes*.

One of Monet's principles was that what the subject intrinsically is, really does not matter; only its appearance under light matters. This was not out of line with Courbet's avowals: anything was material for art—not solely ancient legends, large historical events, and religiously

Monet: *Grand Canal, Venice. Museum of Fine Arts, Boston*

hallowed figures. The haystack, the postman, and the railway station now became picture subjects. Impressionism thus continued the tradition of familiar, even commonplace, subject-matter. The fact did not much matter, for technique was soon to swallow up subject or content. In the end it is not the object or event that counts, but the visual impression as caught at a certain time of day, under a certain light. Reality went into a luminous fog.

It is evident from the most cursory look into a museum that from 1870 on there are a freshness and brilliancy of color on the gallery walls that contrast strikingly with the brown-gray look of earlier exhibits. Partly the sparkling effect is due to the suppression of drawing as the basis for painting and to the building of shadows with mixed colors, without blackening. But more especially the impressionist technique promoted freshness and vibrancy of color by juxtaposing staccato touches of pure pigment on the canvas, in the knowledge that the observer's eye at a certain distance would find the hues fused.

Roughly speaking, the orthodox method of painting a purple area theretofore had been to mix red and blue on the palette to the desired purple shade, then to spread the mixture flat. The impressionists discovered (from laboratory scientists) that the color came much more alive and brilliant if tiny dots or smears or lines of the two colors were placed side by side and the mixing was left to the eye.

This is the technique which gave rise to the names *pointillisme*, divisionism, and broken color. The system is no longer doctrinairely followed, but in modified form it contributes to the transparent liveliness of most contemporary painting.

In the hands of the impressionists it all led to a feast of color and to an out-of-doors freshness. And if the extreme practitioners threw away subject-matter as anything but an excuse for light-harmonies, and threw away pictorial architecture as well, Monet—and measurably Pissarro and Sisley—provided a slight color-lyricism that

Renoir: *Boatmen's Lunch. Phillips Gallery, Washington*

sets up a sweet and acceptable song. Their impressions of evanescent aspects, their rainbow melodies, their feminine soft-focus loveliness are closer to our hearts than Courbet's stark journalistic reporting or Delacroix's heated melodramas.

One other gain in understanding of vision came from the impressionists' studies: the painter learned that the observer's eye does not take in outline and detail except at one area at the center of vision. Blurring is natural outside a very restricted area. Whether the painter should paint for a still eye or a roving eye is another question, not yet settled by the modernists, and giving rise to theories of movement-paths in the canvas, plastic orchestration, and rhythmic vitality which belong to expressionism. But certainly within realism there is firm justification for the blurred as against the oversharp technique.

The impressionists so far departed from care for the objective values that they would make a dozen pictures of a haystack, a bridge, or a cathedral front, if only the light was different.

If the atmosphere had changed, a totally different picture would result. The changing nuances of luminous aspect, the shifting chromatic patterns, were the things that counted.

Ridicule and vilification were, of course, poured upon the early pictures of Monet and Pissarro when they began to paint atmospherically, and the painters suffered through times of direst poverty. Curiously enough the academicians and critics included color among the properties the new painters failed to understand. It was recorded in the *Chronique des Arts,* after the group had taken a gallery for its own exhibitions—to which eighteen avowed impressionists contributed, including Renoir, Berthe Morisot, and Cézanne: "They are lamentable. They display the profoundest ignorance of drawing, and composition, and color. Children do better, playing with color-box and paper."

But the little band of pioneers persisted, held exhibitions season after season, and by 1890, a quarter-century after their first challenge, began to sell pictures to a few connoisseurs, and im-

Renoir: *Three Bathers with a Crab. Cleveland Museum of Art*

pressionism was in line to become academic art. It is hardly exaggeration to say that after 1900 Monet was accepted everywhere as an old master. He died in 1926 at the age of eighty-six, widely respected but already considered a little old-fashioned.

It was Renoir who turned out to be the most important—nay, the most luscious—painter of the impressionist group. He was from the start more independent, less tied to demonstrating doctrinairely the formulas of *plein-air* vision and broken color. He held, more than did Monet, to the object in its own right, and somewhat to old-time composition.

There was a feminine aspect to all the impressionist melting harmonies, and the soft beauty of it came aptly to Renoir's hand. He frankly was obsessed by the sensuous and fruity loveliness of the feminine body, and concurrently by the fragile colorfulness of flower-petals. He had

once been a painter of porcelain, had afterwards, while decorating fans, had visions of modernizing the voluptuous picturing of Boucher, and finally fell in with the *plein-airistes*. He could do a surpassingly good landscape in broken color, too, and for a time he painted portraits with competently characterized figures and faces embedded in the new lush coloring. But the feminine nude and the roses more and more absorbed his interest and his genius.

There are a very great many paintings by Renoir which yield little more than a sensuous loveliness. The agreeable impression is exceptionally full, softly seductive—sometimes sickeningly sweet. But Renoir's best canvases have also a structural backbone and a formal rhythm. They then touch achievement above any known to Pissarro and Monet and Sisley. In certain of the nude studies the solid body forms and the vague backgrounds are bound together in a sort of warming color-glow, a glamorous, sinuous interweaving of surface tints and body silhouettes and textural luster.

Simply as examples of masterly use of paint for visual pleasure, Renoir's works are gorgeous. They fill the eye; they caress the senses. There is a quality of iridescence, of luminous fullness, that is Renoir's own.

His method being thus fluid and voluptuous and velvety, it is natural that the artist turned to nature in its most fragilely yet fully delectable manifestations. In a very true sense his nudes are wholly impersonal, uncharacterized. They are so many felicitous mediums for conveying the pictorial charm of a superlative painting method. And of course all drama, all philosophy, all elevated imagination are dropped out of his calculations. Renoir is the great modern pagan, with a little in him of Correggio and the Venetians, a little of Watteau's method and of Boucher's voluptuousness.

It is, perhaps, characteristic of a certain emptiness in realism as a division of art that the last artist of the line should be the one most devoted to surface beauty and natural sensuous values. Renoir made attractive, even seductive, what had been hard and chilling with the classicists, overheating with the romanticists, commonplace with Courbet, and somewhat vague and intangible with the early impressionists. He made realism palatable. Among his contemporaries were men, however, who accomplished the true epochal revolution of modern times, who turned their backs on nature and sought a reason for art in nonrealistic achievement. The next chapter in the history of Western painting must deal with Cézanne and van Gogh, with Gauguin and Picasso.

There were, of course, other creative and gifted men among the impressionists, most notably Armand Guillaumin and Alfred Sisley. But the more interesting point is, perhaps, that at this time two women made secure places for themselves in the ranks of leading painters. Berthe Morisot brought a special feminine loveliness to her modified impressionism, and Mary Cassatt, an American who spent the larger part of her life in France, developed a mastery of the new coloring, within a compositional framework taken from earlier schools, which brought her canvases into many leading museums. These two feminine names are, however, likely to be lonely on the walls of the world's galleries.

A colorful postscript to the story of international realism was added belatedly in the United States, even after Cézanne had made his contribution and had died. A group of painters officially known as The Eight, but soon famous as the Ash-Can School, came to notice in Philadelphia, then New York, in 1908. They served as the Courbet realists had served in France a half-century earlier, shocking the conservative art world and the press by their "vulgar" choice of subjects, broadening the boundaries of art. They protested also the excessive Europeanization of American painting. Robert Henri—a great teacher —was leader of the group. The member truest to its principles was John Sloan, and the titles of three of his most celebrated paintings, *McSorley's Bar, In the Wake of the Ferry,* and *Back Yards, Greenwich Village,* will convey to the reader something of the flavor of Ash-Can School art. Some of the members deserted and painted shamelessly in the French impressionist or neo-impressionist style; but it is fitting that the chapter close with this mention of one more group organized to defend realism and the commonplace subject.

XXVII: THE ORIENT AGAIN;
AFRICA, AMERICA, THE SOUTH SEAS

WHILE the march of realism was continuing in Europe, in the centuries following the innovations of Nicola Pisano and Donatello in sculpture, and of Masaccio and the van Eycks in painting, when Western art was preoccupied with the search for the scientifically true and the literally exact, there were developments of an opposite nature in Asia, Africa, and the South Seas. Nor were these unrelated to the subsequent turn of events in Europe.

At the very time when Ghiberti was putting perspective scenes upon his bronze doors for the Baptistry at Florence, when Jan van Eyck was painting his minutely truthful and painstaking portraits, the Chinese were at the beginning of a very different sort of renaissance in painting, were already practicing the highly stylized art of the Ming period. Japan was then emerging from dependence upon China to produce a distinctive body of painting and sculpture within the formal Eastern manner. Persia re-enters the story with a type of miniature picturing distinguished by a very special fragile loveliness.

All these achievements demand chronicling at some point between the chapters on the Italian Renaissance and that dealing with the revolt against realism in Europe in the late nineteenth century. The works from China, Japan, and Persia affected profoundly the post-impressionists who broke the hold of naturalism upon European artists. There may be added here, too, for lack of any more logical point of articulation with the structure of world history as erected by European scholarship, mention of certain manifestations from more alien peoples, in Central Africa, in the South Seas, and in pre-Columbian America. These, too, have since their discovery influenced a little the direction of artistic effort in Europe, and museums have been known to move out

Burning of the Sanjo Palace, detail. *Museum of Fine Arts, Boston*

whole roomfuls of painting and sculpture of the illustrational era to make way for Mayan sculptures, Negro fetishes, and Polynesian carvings.

China, after the fall of the Yüan Dynasty in 1368, was never again to see such glorious achievements in sculpture as had been hers at intervals through the preceding two thousand years. There was to be, indeed, hardly more than imitation within the older types, and some vigorous but not particularly inventive carving in the service of architecture. Painting, however, knew a renaissance in the Ming era that followed the Yüan. Architecture then came to its most characteristic expression. And pottery was further refined into that delicate white ware which is known as "china" in most parts of the civilized world.

The first of the line of Ming emperors undertook to re-establish art upon a lavish scale. In painting there was re-establishment and rebirth rather than a new creative release along original lines. In an effort to equal the transcending achievements of the Sung era, the rules were tightened and mastery of traditional methods and subjects was rewarded. Very beautiful work was done within limits set by devotion to one old master or another—to Wu Tao-tzǔ or Wang Wei or Ma Yüan. The eclectic and intellectual tendencies finally prevailed, and the Ming effort passed ultimately into sterile and decadent repetitions of old themes and old formulas.

Among other results of devotion to the past was the preservation of the works of painters of the T'ang and Sung periods in copies by artists only a shade less gifted than the ancient masters. Of original works there is a large body concerned with the depiction of trees, flowers, and birds, in which the subject becomes less important than the technique and "manner." There were schools leaning to monochrome painting and others turning to fuller color. Calligraphic line was brought again to a marvelous degree of expressiveness— of vigor and virility on one hand, of sensitive shading and delicate incisiveness on the other. Rules were laid down for handling of the brush and the character of the stroke for willow foliage or pine twigs or eagle's claws.

This effort was to lead on in late times to that sort of painting, so puzzling to the Western mind, which concerns itself with a show of virtuosity in rendering one of four traditional subjects— bamboo, chrysanthemums, orchids, and plum blossoms. These are, of course, treasured plants, and a certain appropriateness exists of treatment to flower; but to the connoisseur the richer pleasure is afforded by the quality of the brush stroke, the felicity of the placing, and the spontaneity or "life" of the impression. The rest of us may be content if we so overcome our unfamiliarity with Oriental painting that we feel instantaneously the more obvious values in a picture such as the *Deer*, by Chou Yüan: the pervading richness of the whole, the contrived rhythms, and the wintry spirit.

In general, painting of the Ming period is closer to Western ideals than that of earlier eras, for there is less of the mystical element, less attempt to express in aesthetic terms the unknowable and the fleeting. Taoism is less a motivating force. But art remains, even so, essentially conventional in method and unconcerned with surface truths. There are works that follow the traditional calligraphic style and accomplish miracles of abstract order. There are others—they are the more likely to have found their way into Western collections—which are less summary, less heedless in their treatment of nature's appearances; which have less of austerity and magnitude and more of intimate grace and human sentiment.

When the end of the Ming Dynasty came in 1644, painting was already a matter of exercises in this or that recognized manner. But when the new Manchu Dynasty was established, another art received encouragement and went on to unprecedented accomplishment. In pottery and porcelain the beautiful wares known to the T'ang and Sung periods were duplicated, even as late as the mid-seventeenth century, and distinctive decorated porcelains were originated.

The ceramic art had been practiced in China with notable mastery as far back as the Han era. But it was during the time of the T'ang splendor that a great variety of products appeared, in every field from small sculpture in glazed and unglazed terra cotta to most delicate, unornamented vase and bowl, extremely sensitive in proportioning

Chou Yüan: *Deer.*
Ming Dynasty.
Freer Gallery of Art

and in porcelain-like finish. In the Sung era (corresponding to the European Middle Ages) the potters went on to a bewildering number of wares of surpassing excellence, and this is known as China's classic period in ceramics. To the uneducated eye the museum cases seem to contain merely a beautifully varied display of attractive pieces: fragilely lovely pale plates and slender vases; solidly realized and sturdily ornamented jars and bowls; and at the end a range of gorgeously decorated vessels in a great variety of techniques and finishes with lavish all-over patterning or elaborate formalized picturing.

The specialists in ceramic history and appreciation have developed an intricate and useful system of classification, but the layman may find enjoyment without more than a casual knowledge of techniques, potteries, and styles; though he will remember as typically Chinese certain early heavy wares, later translucent ones of an extreme fineness of texture and patterning, and, in latest periods, the sumptuously decorated monumental vases, as richly adorned as the Chinese embroidered robes or the lacquer screens or the cloisonné vessels. A few distinctive types will have stayed in mind by name: the jadelike celadon, the peach-bloom, the hawthorn, the ox-blood, certain of the wares with crackle glaze, and of course the "standard" fine white porcelain, particularly the blue-and-white. It was in the Ming period that "white china" emerged as the outstanding contribution of the Chinese to ceramic art, and the town of Ching-tê Chên near Nanking then became world-famous for the products of its potteries. Imperial encouragement of the art was renewed in the Ch'ing period, and inventive design continued into the nineteenth century.

If Chinese bowls and vases have become familiar to Western eyes and so have come to be treasured for their patent excellencies, Chinese architecture is in quite another case. Almost unchanging in general aspect through all its known history and through all types of monumental building, utterly different from European forms, it seems as a style alien and difficult. Nevertheless, a brief study of its effect in relation to materials, use, and the thinking of the Chinese people must lead to recognition of a sufficient logic in it, combined with richness and consistency of decorative expression. It is essentially a decorated architecture rather than one nakedly expressive of function.

The roof is in general the dominating feature. It is supported by stilts, and the whole is held together by an elaborate system of bracketing and tying. The walls are screens between the stilts rather than weight-bearing members (as is true in Gothic cathedrals and modern steel-framed skyscrapers, but is without parallel in other historic Western building). The exterior decorativeness is achieved largely through the elaborated treatment of the roof and its under-eaves supports. The roof edges are commonly given a flare at the corners. In the eight-sided pagodas, or temple towers, the roof overhang is repeated at each story, and a "repeat roof" over a gallery is one of the commonest motives in the design of larger structures.

There are no large buildings comparable to European cathedral or Indian temple. The Chinese—unless one counts the common wall or continuous fortification—have very few single grand structures. Rather they add together, for palace or religious shrine, a series of lesser buildings, placed on courts and bound by encircling and connecting walls. What would be a palace elsewhere becomes in Peiping the complex of buildings and courts and walls, almost labyrinthine in character, known as the Forbidden City.

If the European or American observer misses the accent of simple grandeur that is heralded by the finest of monumental Western buildings—say, the Greek temples, the Pantheon and the Roman basilicas, and the early Gothic cathedrals—one yet may enjoy the Chinese temples, pavilions, and pagodas as an isolated type of decorative architecture, well suited to the nature of the country, narrowly and even monotonously idiomatic, but distinctive and—in its place—eye-filling, satisfying. In certain of the crafts accessory to architecture, especially in woodcarving, the Chinese have excelled all others as consistent and lavish decorators—excepting only the Japanese.

Japanese Art

In Japan the development of art is marked by a series of definable periods in which alternately the artists follow closely the ideals and influences brought in from China, and then settle down to assimilate, and to give a slight native flavor to, the imported ways of expression. Japanese art has a history of its own, but for many centuries the finest manifestations were so clearly a reflection of Chinese practice that they are best explained as parts or extensions of the older culture.

The art works that survive from the period

before the introduction of Buddhism into the country are negligible. The new religion was brought from China by way of Korea about A.D. 400, but only in the mid-sixth century did it find wide acceptance. A second mighty wave of influence came during the expansion of Chinese culture in the T'ang era, and again the art impulse was linked with Buddhist thought and practice. It was then that Japanese art flowered most beautifully in direct imitation of the Chinese masters—in what is known as the Nara period, from the name of the capital city. When a third wave came, during the Chinese Sung Dynasty, it was again Buddhism that influenced expression in sculpture, painting, and architecture. The sect known as Zen Buddhists brought in—often at the hands of priest-artists—an "idealized" type of painting, which reached its fullest development, however, only in the fifteenth and sixteenth centuries.

There is in the early periods no point at which one can pick up the thread of Japanese art and say, "Here began the exquisite craftsmanship and vivid impressionism which are characteristic of the national genius." Rather the distinctive qualities had been developed gradually. At any rate, by the time that marks the opening of the Renaissance period in Europe, there was in Japan ample evidence of a passion for delicate craftsmanship, for preciseness and grace of statement, for decorative effect by sharp contrast—all within the limits of strict formalization in the general Eastern manner.

These special qualities persist through courtly art and popular, through religious and profane. Whether in a painting of the Kamakura period, which corresponds to the late Sung, or in a brush drawing by the people's artist, Hokusai, who lived six centuries later, there is the touch that the Western world has come to know as Japanese.

In Japanese painting there are the conventions known to practically all Oriental picture-art: flatness of composition, with little modeling of figures, with depth suggested rather than emphasized—though "space" is made a living part of the design to an extent unknown in the Western world; disregard of shadows; concentration of attention upon single figures or landscape bits,

with suppression of environmental and incidental detail. All this leads to an art of suggestion rather than of factual statement. But the Japanese passion for precise rightness and for decorative sharpness leads to amazing feats in delineation of those details that the artist deems important to his purpose. There is this duality of strict formalization and devotion to miniature truth in countless works.

The neglect of shadowing, of perspective, of background, is well shown in portions of the roll-painting known as the *Burning of the Sanjo Palace,* one of the masterpieces of Kamakura art, of the thirteenth century. Here are extraordinary vividness and precision and concentration. Each bit when detached by the eye, particularly the leading bowman or the horse and rider, is characterized by spirited action, by exquisitely sensitive drawing, and by superb decorative stylization. (See the detail from this painting illustrated on page 579.)

Landscape the better suggests one of the sources of the Japanese method of laying up the pictorial elements in planes with a vivid contrast of a few striking elements—trees, rocks, silhouettes of roofs or hills—against misty, receding elements. The backgrounds are hardly more than curtains inserted to make the vigorous "forward" bits stand out more vividly. The Japanese countryside is like that. The hazy air softens all that is in distance and gives sharp definition to nearby tree branches and buildings—or, it may be, birds and horses. Thus the artist is bred in an environment that suggests simplification of composition and contrast between foreground and muted distance.

It would be wrong to argue the point too far, for there are, in those types of painting more directly taken from the Chinese, compositions richly complex and filled with fascinating bits throughout the background. This is especially true of certain phases of painting in illustration of Buddhist legendry, where panels are filled with correlated episodes and interwoven groups of figures, like tapestries incredibly lavish in story materials, yet amazingly detailed and sensitive. At the other extreme is that sort of painting that gives pleasure especially by the calligraphic ex-

Korin: *The Wave Screen. Metropolitan Museum of Art*

pressiveness of the drawing and by the exact spacing of the motive on the picture plane. A single tiger or horse or dragon will dominate its panel to the farthest empty corner. Or a sprig of flower or a branch with a bird, sometimes a human figure or a head, will serve as well to bring the field of space to life. Here the Japanese brush-drawn line, like the Chinese, becomes subtly and richly eloquent beyond any consummation known to the art of the West.

Out of this sort of painting there came two developments which largely stand for Japanese art to the casual observer: the folding screens with decorative paintings, and the colored wood-cut prints. The screens, used as movable walls where Western homes have built-in partitions, demand a special decorative style, leaning even more to the conventional and the abstract than the independent or hanging paintings; and it is necessary that the composition be pleasing as a whole as well as that the part appearing upon each panel or leaf should have sufficient unity and coherence.

The earlier screens, of the fourteenth and fifteenth centuries, were paintings in Chinese ink on paper, and the delicacy of tonal transitions and the vigor of the calligraphic drawing counted greatly. In the sixteenth century there came a richer style, nearer to frank ornamentation, and the introduction of fuller colors, varied with areas of gold and silver. Sesshu, Eitoku, and Sosatsu are names particularly known in connection with the screens, and in the sumptuous decorative mode Korin was one of the outstanding masters. He is sometimes called Japan's greatest decorative painter. The screen painted by Korin now in the Metropolitan Museum, New York, with waves vigorously formalized, characterized by powerful movement held securely within the picture field, is typical and magnificent of its sort.

Hokusai: *The Wave*. Wood engraving, from series *The Thirty-Six Views of Mount Fuji. Fogg Art Museum, Harvard University*

The colored prints represent the plebeian picture-art of Japan. Despite their marvelous compositional values, their felicitous drawing, and their sometimes exquisite coloring, they are considered by Japanese connoisseurs an inferior type of art. The technique, determined not by the use of the brush but by the capabilities of the graver's knife (the prints were impressed from woodblocks or planks), is comparatively "hard" and the effect posteresque. Nevertheless, there are carried over into the new medium the exquisite craftsmanship and the feeling for rich pattern; and the sensitive drawing is not so much lost as reborn in a different sort of excellence.

This people's art, which grew out of *Uki-yo-e*, a type of genre painting "picturing the passing world," separate from the Buddhist art and from the types of roll and screen painting which the nobles affected in imitation of the Chinese, became popular in the middle of the seventeenth century, and production of masterly works continued until the middle of the nineteenth century. They are masterly, of course, only in a minor field and are not to be compared with Oriental paintings in the matter of sensuous fullness and plastic orchestration. But there are a gracious intimacy and a charming harmony about them; and fortunately it is an art within the reach of the lightest purse.

After Moronobu (1625–94), who is credited with popularizing the prints—though not with inventing them, for this art, too, had Chinese antecedents—there came a series of artists who specialized in figure pictures. For a full hundred years the prints were made from a single block and hand-colored. Then two blocks were used, and finally, about 1765, a great designer, Harunobu, introduced polychrome blocks.

After him there are the great names of Kiyonaga and Utamaro, and finally Hokusai and Hiroshige, who are the more familiar to European and American collectors because they specialized in subjects to which the Western amateur is accustomed, especially landscape. Both were exceptional masters of drawing and composition on the flat.

Hokusai is internationally known for paintings and brush drawings as well as for prints. No one has been able to express more of vigorous movement and of characteristic feature and gesture in a single stroke. In the *Mangwa,* an encyclopedic series of picture books, there are miracles of expressive statement and endless inspiration for the lover of "free" drawing. But most famous of his works are the prints known as *The Thirty-Six Views of Mount Fuji.*

At the end of his life Hokusai called himself "the old man mad with drawing," and he died saying that if the Powers had only granted him another five years he might have become a real master. Perhaps because he is a little more given to "human interest" and a little more realistic in his drawing than most Japanese artists, his fame has gone round the world, and he is, outside Japan, considered the country's foremost draftsman of all time. The Japanese connoisseur, seeking certain traditional virtues of scholarly allusion and handling, and doubtless a little put off by Hokusai's vulgar choice of subjects, counts him inferior to many another master. Nevertheless, it may be a long time before Japan or any other nation produces an artist with such direct and vigorous statement and yet with such subtle expressiveness in line.

In history the Japanese are known as masters of sculpture. There are very fine religious pieces in all the usual materials, especially in bronze and in dried lacquer, but the most distinctive and subtle expression is in figures carved in wood. Although patently an offshoot of the Chinese (and Korean) growth, the Japanese style was unmistakable, once imported artist-monks had imparted their skill to native artists. In the Buddhist temples at Nara the display of statues achieving a sort of spiritual realization is one of the finest in all the world.

As early as the sixth century Korea, a little China in its wealth of sculptural expression, had given the Japanese the religion of Buddha and actual sculptural figures. The Japanese at first copied the Korean models and worked under Korean mentors, then started on the road that would bring them to national types of their own. Their work, especially known from the figures in wood, became a little less angular, a little softer in impact upon the observer. Thereafter the national genius proceeded in two directions: first, toward a simplification, which centuries later ended in a series of the starkest and most lifelike statues ever known; and second, toward a delicate sort of decorative or decorated figure in which the accessories are exquisitely treated for enrichment of the main motive. The sculptors did not scruple to add a lacy fretwork crown in metal to a figure carved in wood, as a decorative contrast to the simple head and torso. In their carving of wood the great masters showed loving appreciation of the medium. Part of the appeal of the statue is that of the grain or texture of the wood and of the handling of the knife.

The very fine illustration here shows the art as it was brought to the country by the Koreans. The head is a detail from a figure of Buddha, supposed to have been carved in the seventh century by Korean sculptor-monks in Japan. It is now in the Chuguji Temple at Nara. The wood has hardened and blackened so that one might mistake the medium. It is, nonetheless, a masterpiece in its dignity, its fluent yet sharply accented cutting, and its achieved sense of largeness, solemnity, and inner peace. In contrast, there is a widely known thirteenth-century *Portrait of Ashanga,* by the master Unkei. Though beautifully carved, it is familiar, relaxed, unidealized. At the time of Ashanga, a Hindu missionary revered for his work in renewing the Buddhist faith, the Japanese were pursuing a course toward realism. At first theirs was a psychologic sort of realism, intent upon exposing the inner rather than the outer man. In any case, through seven centuries the native carvers had traveled the course from a noble formalism to the most amazing naturalism known to the history of the sculptural art.

In modern times the Japanese have been known as producers of vast numbers of minor sculptures, especially in ivory and wood. The netsuke, used as a decorative costume detail, is known to every collector of miniature carved objects, and in the museums the iron sword guards make up engaging exhibits. In recent centuries the national genius for woodcarving has led to lavish embellishment of architectural monuments (all modeled after Chinese buildings). Temples, pagodas, and memorial gateways are dressed with fretwork screens and grilles, with

Buddha. Wood, detail. *Chuguji Temple, Nara, Japan*

panels carved in high relief, and with beam-ends and false roofs sumptuously sculptured. The effect is eye-filling and luxurious beyond anything known in Western architecture.

At Kamakura there is a sculptured monument that is one of the world's largest single figures, a statue that is known to countless tourists and is pictured oftener than the more subtly beautiful Buddhas in the shrines at Nara. The bronze Great Buddha of Kamakura is just under fifty feet in height. It was erected in the thirteenth century. It is distinguished by a certain majesty, and especially it brings to the beholder a sense of solemnity, a mood of contemplation. Perhaps among the world's colossal statues the figure of the Buddha at Anuradhapura in Ceylon alone

Glazed dish, Persian, 17th century. *Metropolitan Museum of Art*

surpasses it for sculptural beauty and spiritual impressiveness.

In the ceramic art the Japanese have long been world masters. Their work has not the extraordinarily wide range of the Chinese or the Persian, but there is a distinctive loveliness in many of their bowls, and a very high standard of design in their simplest wares. In the decoration of pottery and porcelain their artists show the same surprising combination of vigor and delicacy, of strong outline and subtle tonal variation, which is seen in the painting. Architecture in the island empire is similar to that of China; is, indeed, directly derivative, with differences in detail that become apparent to the Western eye only after study. The buildings run to a greater refinement in carved ornamentation, and to lighter and more graceful effects in the arrangement of the multiplied roofs. These seem to cut the sky with silhouettes exactly fitted to those of the pine trees of the surrounding garden—which is, of course, also a work of painstaking art.

Persia and India

In Persia, where so many of the Oriental arts and crafts had flowered in earlier centuries, there was after the Mogul invasions a renaissance, and there are works in incised bronze and in precious-metal inlays, in pottery and in porcelain, in woven damask silk and in figured velvets, which

Miniature from manuscript of the *Shah-Namah*. Persian, 14th century.
Metropolitan Museum of Art

are not unworthy of a place beside the older masterpieces. But it was in two other arts, not unknown before but less conspicuously practiced, that new history was made in the centuries between 1300 and 1700. In painting a fragilely lovely, exquisitely decorative sort of miniature was perfected. In rug weaving there was achieved a beauty hardly approached elsewhere in all the world.

The Persian miniature is one of those minor arts that have drawn devoted bands of followers who prize the special delicacy, naïve charm, and sensuous colorfulness beyond the more monumental virtues of painting as practiced farther east and farther west. In the field of picturing that is designed as illustration, that is filled with story materials, this is the sort that is most expert and most ingratiating *as decoration.*

The body of Persian painting lies almost wholly within the covers of books. They are exceptionally sumptuous books, but literature is the reason for the miniatures. The manuscript without the pictures would be a work of art, for here calligraphy is a branch of design. The painting often loses when taken from its inscribed borders and "context." Yet some thousands of the miniatures have been removed from the manuscripts and placed independently on gallery walls, and there delight countless eyes.

The special charm of the Persian painting lies in its incisive delicacy of line, its rich yet pale harmony of colors, and its strict formalization of composition. There is an atmosphere of enchantment here: a breath of a world all gardens and forests, all music and play, all romance and poetry. The method is that of the Far East—China had exerted direct influence upon Persia long before the Moguls brought the countries under one rule—with the picture elements laid up in flattened planes, with background suppressed or converted frankly into an area of patterning. There is no roundness in the figures, and there is no attempt at shadowing. In color the Persian paintings are consistently brighter and fresher than the Chinese. This is explained, perhaps, by the fact that the Persian instinct for decorative design had been expressed for a period in Mohammedan arabesque practice and then had been influenced by the art brought by the Mogul conquerors from China. The three elements blend in this enchanting art that is both literary and ornamental, which pictures people yet has something of the curtain quality of the arabesque. The medium is gouache, a sort of opaque water-color.

There are few known names of artists from the earlier centuries. Then in the late fifteenth century the greatest master, Bihzād, is encountered. He had notable followers but none of his own stature. By the opening of the seventeenth

Medallion rug. Safavid culture, Persia, 16th century.
Metropolitan Museum of Art

century the art was well along on its gradual decline.

Even reproductions in black-and-white, without the seductive coloring, may reveal the marvelous subtlety of line and tone, the crisp composi-

tion, and the vivid textural contrasts in the examples of this precious art. Whether it is an apparently inconsequential tailpiece like the bit from a manuscript of the *Shah-Namah* of the fourteenth century, in the Metropolitan Mu-

The Taj Mahal, Agra, India, 17th century

seum, New York, or a gorgeous elaborated piece like the famous *Humay Received at the Court of China* of the fifteenth century, in the Louvre, the picture bears the marks of supreme mastery in one miniature field of decorative art.

Something of the same grace, the same sensuous coloring, the same fastidiousness in design, is carried into the rugs and carpets with which Persian artist-craftsmen have delighted the world in later centuries. While the other arts were declining, weaving knew a renaissance. As the Iranian silks had taken rank as the most ravishing works within the textile art back in Sassanian times, so now, a millennium later, the Persian rug became the typical exhibit of art that is luxurious, enchantingly colorful, exquisite, and formalized. It may be an abstract design in the direct tradition of the architectural or ceramic arabesque, or an "animal rug" with conventionalized beasts strewn in a flowered field, or a "garden map"; but the virtues of a mural flatness, a rich depth of tone, and a marvelously opulent patterning will adhere in each case. These are indeed a

final achievement in the textile art. All the countries bordering on Persia, and those which experienced the contact when Persian craftsmen went abroad in the service of Islam, felt the influence which led to this achievement, and Turkish and Indian rugs are only a little less esteemed than are those from Iran.

In India, too, there were special developments of other textile branches, and some of the most delicate of figured muslins have their provenance in the Indian states. So popular became the commoner cotton stuffs abroad that the native Indian names are found in the dictionaries of many peoples—as in the case of our *bandanna*. The *cashmere* shawl is as distinctively known as is the Malayan *batik*. In India the art of miniature-painting flourished, and if it there lacked something of the highly formalized decorativeness of the Persian, it yet has left a body of works attractive and masterly. In general the illustrational intention draws the artist a little further from abstract patterning than is the case in Iran.

But in summaries of later Indian art it is

Negro sculpture. British Nigeria.
Collection Baron Eduard von der Heydt

neither painting nor sculpture that contributes the most outstanding masterpiece, demanding mention and illustration. A building, the Taj Mahal at Agra, is not only the best known example of Indian architecture but one of the first monuments of all Islam. It is a mausoleum erected by Shah Jahan in the mid-seventeenth century, in memory of his queen. The structure is crowned with a central pointed dome, and this feature is echoed in four small lotus domes at the corners of the building and in miniature domes atop the minarets. The material is white marble. The many arches are pointed, and the wall spaces are traced over with arabesque carving or are inlaid with precious stones. The building gains by its placing in a park, with long pool and garden approaches. But merely as an architectural

design it achieves a wonderful atmosphere of delicate grace and shimmering lightness. It is adorned architecture at one of its most ethereal and luxurious moments.

Africa, the South Seas, and America

It was toward the end of the first decade of the twentieth century that enthusiasm was aroused, particularly in France and Germany, over what had been considered the barbaric and preposterous art of the African Negroes. Because the discovery was made by radicals who were fighting against prevailing ideals in art—ideals which had become overnaturalistic and over-academic—the matter was thrown into the field of the wider controversy, and almost immediately the critical world was divided into two camps on the subject. In one African sculpture was over-praised, almost worshiped; in the other there were condemnation and bitter scorn, and questions, doubtless sincere, as to the sanity of those who pretended to elevate these curios, with all the marks of heathen ignorance and idolatry upon them, above the works of Rodin and St. Gaudens and Meunier.

Within a generation the Negro figures had taken a sure place in the annals and the galleries of creative art; but it is seen to be a not very large place. There is recognition of a limited expression extraordinarily vivid and sensitive, accomplished with unmistakable marks of expert craftsmanship. And a large public has been found to take delight, upon occasion, in the direct imaging, the rhythmic vitality, and the painstaking finish. The appreciative white can never, of course, reach enjoyment of the sort, tinged with religious and racial emotion, which the artist meant to stir in his own people. Fortunately the rich formal and plastic values, and certain subject appeals more universal than local, exist above the symbolic or ritualistic values.

The ancestral figures, masks, and decorated utensils now shown in European and American museums have been brought from various parts of Africa and are the products of cultures widely different in degree of civilization. Of some a good

Stool with Woman's Figure. Wood; Baluba, Belgian Congo.
Musée de l'Homme, Paris

deal is known. Such is the state of Benin, which was visited and reported upon in the fifteenth century, and for which a fairly complete history can be constructed. Others still await exploration and documentation. The wide diversity of ways of expression, the occurrence of metal sculpture in some provinces and not in others, and the divergencies in craftsmanship are, in any case, signs of independent cultural growth.

And yet there is a generic likeness in the body of Negro work. At almost no point does it tend to naturalism. As a group these thousands of sculptures show an exceptional intuitive grasp of the thing that has lately been discussed as the form

Figure known as the *African Venus*.
Collection Louis Carré, Paris

and practice had existed for many centuries before, through what crossings and recrossings of cultures we cannot know; but products in wood disintegrate fairly quickly, and the likelihood is against the survival of more ancient examples. What bits of history there are, some bordering perhaps on fable, indicate the existence in earlier eras of states closer to the European idea of civilization than any existing among the African Negroes today.

If one wondered at first that the bronzes of Benin should have such largeness, such sureness, and such elaboration of ornament, one may know now that this mature sculptural art went with extensive palaces, broad boulevards, and a luxurious way of living. The reliefs and statues are characterized by a perfection of finish unsurpassed on the other continents, indicating a knowledge of the *cire perdue* process of casting. Some critics believe that the technique was transmitted by the Portuguese in the fifteenth century, others that it came to the Negroes from Egypt. A second group of "mature" sculptural works was uncovered by the German explorer Frobenius at Ife in British Nigeria in 1910, and this find lends color to the theory that there was a fully developed Negro art earlier than the supposed Portuguese importation of European influence.

But the Benin and Ifa products are exceptional in the range of African works, and the great mass of ancestral figures and utensils, of masks and fetishes, may be said to lie much nearer to primitive images and primitive craftsmanship. There is simple, direct statement of the essentials of the subject. There is elementary repetition of a few main rhythms. There is grasp of abstract values. There is loving care for the potentialities of the medium, for the polished surface of the wood. Beyond all, there is that mastery of formal organization, of plastic manipulation, which we can explain only as intuitive. These are the works of born sculptors. In no other way can one account for the relationship of volumes in the little figure illustrated here—known as the *African Venus*—or for the lighter rhythms of line and mass in the equestrian figure shown opposite.

At one time the naïve, direct expression, the concentration of interest, and the intensification

element in art, of plastic organization and rhythmic order. The objects throughout have a detached, impersonal quality, a reserve. There is about them no mark of the self-conscious artist displaying knowledge and indulging in flourish.

It is probable that very few of the works surviving were produced more than two hundred years ago, and most are likely to have been made in the nineteenth century. The workmanship and apparently the feeling for plastic expression deteriorated after the Negro's contact with the white races, and recent sculpture often lacks the virtues found in the pieces earlier collected.

It is probably safe to place the time of the preponderance of works commonly studied as between 1775 and 1875. Doubtless the tradition

Horse and Rider.
Negro sculpture.
Collection Louis Carré,
Paris

of feeling count most. Again it may be the felicity of some bit of incidental ornamentation, or the literally polished craftsmanship. The masks afford particularly eloquent examples of near-abstract formalization; they are not carvings in imitation of human features but abstractions of the idea of god or adorer or devil. The structure or geometry of the face remains; the rest is invention or improvisation—an artist's feeling and imaging given concrete form. Note the mask-like face of the figure on page 17. What a superbly direct expression that figure is!

A second field of discovery of unsophisticated art was opened when appreciators of African sculpture turned to the South Sea Islands. Polynesian and Melanesian idols and masks are found to have, though at a lesser intensity, the concen-

trated emotion, the direct statement, the plastic vitality of the work of the Negroes. There is here more elaboration of ornament for its own sake. Some of the masks—particularly those from New Guinea and the New Hebrides Islands—are gorgeously showy. The richness, with suitable reserve, enters into the woodcarving of the Maoris, where canoe prows, oars, and house pillars are sculptured with intricate designs wherein near-abstract patterning is varied with inserted objective figures (see page 10).

Here again the artist is unselfconscious. He approaches his materials and his task with respect, getting fullest beauty out of the wood in which he works, and never forgetting the purpose of his statue or relief in a show of personal virtuosity. The carvings have consistent style; they are

Head of a God. Mayan; Copan, Honduras; probably sixth century.
Peabody Museum, Cambridge, Massachusetts

creations, not copies of nature; they are eloquent of a loving care for the craftsmanship involved.

The Maoris, of course, were far advanced beyond primitive or barbaric conditions of life, and their works are those of a mature (though not especially intellectual) culture. The works from Oceania cover a range from this fairly civilized art to primitive examples in which the simpler geometric forms of decoration predominate, and the likeness of man or totem-animal is of the most summary and formal nature. Throughout the range may be discovered the sense of rhythm, the purely sculptural or decorative vitality, which had been lost from European practice for so many generations when these "heathenish" works were first taken from the ethnographic museums and brought to the galleries by the expressionists.

Yet even in Europe there were traces of this art

Mask of Xipe. Stone; Aztec; Mexico. *British Museum*

that had retained primitive directness and primitive plastic mastery. It was discovered, not without surprise on the part of the critics, that in the most advanced countries a "peasant art" persisted, often with the marks of fresh, clear seeing and instinctive creation upon it. Peasant potteries, textiles, and woodcarvings were gathered from the Balkan countries, from Russia, Tirol, and the Swiss mountain districts. "Unspoiled" art was discovered even in Italy and in Germany.

From study of the peasant arts and the exotic objects from Africa and Oceania a generalization was drawn—and it is not inappropriate to the pages of a history. The long process of civilizing man by systematic cultivation of the intellect had resulted in a certain narrowing of the human faculties to calculated ends. Europe came to inventive, governmental, and intellectual mastery by educating for business enterprise, for scientific advance, for military domination, and for other purposes far from creative aesthetic fields. Men in that process lost contact with nature as simple inspiration, with the wellsprings of intuitive living, with the creative spirit. What some called "the disease of civilization" had to be gone through.

It was worth going through only if the material and intellectual conquest meant leisure afterward in which artists could be released back to their own activities, and in which the obscured threads of aesthetic creativeness could be picked up again. Fortunately some "benighted" peoples had resisted the allurements of intellectual progress, had held to modes of expression near to pristine creativeness. Now it was found, too, that the masses of lower-class people who within civilized countries had been debarred from the intellectual life had retained something of the unspoiled faculty for making images and the natural feeling for craftsmanship of the primitive. Europe, then, and America, must turn back to learn from the peasants, from the African Negroes, from the Polynesians and Melanesians.

Such was the argument by which the artists and critics who rediscovered the folk arts and the exotic arts directed general attention to a body of objects long overlooked, if not scorned. Modern art is not a result of study of the near-primitive and exotic things, but it has gained a great deal from knowledge and enjoyment of them. It was found that what art needed for refertilization was a retreat from intellectualism, from sophistication, and from academism. In finding enjoyment in works near the primitive, in simplicity, in formal vitality, in impersonality, the artists found a spur to pure creativeness, to intuitive imaging and dynamic expression. They are trying today to re-encompass these desirable things within a practice that holds also to the gains made in the name of Western civilization.

One other body of art, though not to be considered primitive or even early, has been paraded by expressionists as superior to the European product of the realistic centuries. The Mayan culture is especially rich in sculpture, both monumental and small. The Incan textiles and pottery rank high in the lists of accomplishment in those two crafts. The entire field of pre-Columbian art in America, not yet fully explored, offers rich reward for the student, whether in the advanced cultures of Peru, Central America, and Yucatan, or in the derivative and nearer-primitive cultures of surviving Indian tribes in Mexico, the United States, and Canada. But it is from the Mayans that the works that might be agreed upon as masterpieces are usually taken.

Mayan sculpture in general was close to architecture, adorning great temples and palaces. The reliefs are almost as profuse as are the ones in the great Javan and Cambodian temples. There are, too, independent stone-carved furnishings, usually of a ritual nature: sacrificial tables,

calendar stones, masks, etc. The mastery of formal design, however, extended through the range of household and personal objects, jugs and plates, cloths and jewelry.

As examples of the expert, not to say surpassing, character of Mayan sculpture, one may study that body of fragments owned by the Peabody Museum at Harvard University (though there are excellent collections in the natural history museums in New York and Paris and Berlin, and most notably in the National Museum in Mexico City). The head illustrated on page 596 may serve to indicate the sculptural largeness combined with sensitive modeling, the powerful plastic "movement" played against reticently patterned areas. The manner is Oriental, unrealistic, conventional. The affinities are with Chinese and Cambodian art rather than with European.

Not Mayan but Aztec is the second illustration, a mask of Xipe (an unpleasant native god), beautifully simple and conventionalized, and retaining the quality of the stone. Incidentally the back of the piece is carved with reliefs, masterly in their own way. In Mexico, besides the Aztec culture, there are the Toltec and the Olmec, yielding as great sculptural treasures as the Aztec (which is better known because it was current at the time of the Spanish conquest of Mexico). All the way from Central America and lower Mexico, where the ancient Zapotec culture was important, to Canada and Alaska, there are "pockets" of Amerindian art that just miss alignment with such small-nation achievements as the Cypriote or the Viking. The Pueblo pottery, the small sculpture of the Mound Builders, the basketry of certain tribes in California, the sculpture in wood of Vancouver and lower Alaska—all this goes to form a body of Stone Age art fascinating in its excellencies and its variety.

This is to be added to the arts brought forward to give support to those who were recently the radicals of Europe's studios, who now are making over Western art in the most far-reaching revolution since the time of Giotto. It is time to turn back to Europe and to the history of the change from realism to expressionism, to the story of "modern" art.

XXVIII: WORLD-WIDE REVOLUTION:
MODERN ART

Two THOUSAND YEARS AGO a puzzled ruler faced by a spiritual prophet asked, "What is truth?" Men today are as far as ever from agreement upon an answer. Three centuries before the time of Pilate a Greek philosopher had ventured an opinion in answer to a question hardly less puzzling: "What is art?" Aristotle had said, "Art is imitation."

Whether the phrase was mistranslated (as some believe) or misinterpreted, there can be no doubt that the idea behind the saying, supported by the great authority accorded Aristotle's name, dominated theories of the visual arts in Europe from the late Middle Ages to the mid-nineteenth century. From the beginning of the Renaissance to the time of Courbet's naturalism there was a steady march of art as surface realism, a gradual refinement of means by which the aspects of nature could be imitated. The great revolution in both aesthetics and practice came when a few radical artists gave up the convention of imitation and reversed the centuries-long trend, moved away toward values other than representational.

Because impressionism had been the last marked phase of the historic march of realism, the critics who earliest recognized the epochal nature of the revolution named the emergent art "post-impressionism." After several decades of development it found a more definitive label, "expressionism," a name that seems destined to live because it throws emphasis back upon expression as against imitation.

Moore: *Reclining Figure.* Lead, 5½ inches long. *Collection William Wilder*

599

Expression of what? The modern artists do not, of course, agree upon an answer. The one generalization that can be made, after examination of the diverse currents of creative painting since 1880, is that all are anti-realistic. The one single thing that no reputable twentieth-century artist does is imitate laboriously effects discovered in nature. Correlatively, the modern does not illustrate. He avoids the literary or anecdotal approach as well as the documentary or descriptive.

As for expression, there are three main lines of argument as to the nature of the thing substituted for transcribed or imitated values. One group of observers claims that it is the artist's feeling that counts, his emotion in the presence of the object, not the object itself. His special way of seeing, his passionate and sensitized brooding over something in nature or life, and the resultant intuitive image: these are to be expressed—without hampering fidelity to surface fact. This leads to the subjective sort of expressionism: the outpourings of van Gogh or Kokoschka, with negligent or deliberate distortion of the camera view.

A second theory is that there are elements of rhythm, order, or plastic vitality securable in a picture or a statue which signify far more, are more profoundly moving to the intelligent spectator, than the values transferred from nature. It is therefore insisted upon that the work of art have a "life of its own," separate from any in viewed nature; that it have what the Chinese of fourteen centuries ago termed "the life-movement of the spirit, or rhythmic vitality." This wing of modernists—with Cézanne as its prime exhibit—brought in the familiar studio talk about *form* as the indispensable creative element in painting—"significant form," in the phrase of Clive Bell, first popularizer of the theory; "expressive form," in the phrase of those who settled upon expressionism as the characteristic name of the development.

In any case, these people who have stressed an abstract design, a formal excellence, as the basic creative element in art have been at the very center of the modernist advance. Some of them have gone on to the conclusion that nature must be wholly squeezed out of the picture, that the true new art is to be wholly abstract—and one then has the "purists" and Kandinski and Mondrian. From Cézannist to ruthless abstractionist, the factions all are known as "form-seeking," and there is talk of "plastic orchestration" for formal effect. There are even those who carry this effort into mystical regions, asserting that the abstract artist sets down a revelation of cosmic order.

A third group, sometimes denied by the subjectivist and abstractionist wings, but just as clearly substituting expressive values for imitative, is that which seeks *decorative* ends. In general the practitioners—of whom Gauguin was chief—have sought less profound effects, have been content to claim new sensuous and melodious values for their rhythmically patterned and richly colored compositions. But since they are as careless of nature as the others, distorting figure or face, tree or flower, for weight or repetitive accent (though generally distorting for mural flatness), they patently belong to the non-imitative school.

These might be said to represent the three main channels of expressionist experiment and advance, although there is every shade of pure and of compromised expression; and a host of individualists have emerged to challenge any generalized statement. Nonetheless, the layman will find the approach to the art of 1880–1930 simplified if he remembers the three stressed ways of expression: subjective or emotional; abstract; decorative.

All three wings hold to one other basic expressive virtue. A special value, a particular intensity of effect, is to be gained out of the use of materials and tools. Thus the sculptor especially expresses stone or wood and the cutting instruments. The painter "declares" his two-dimensional field, his color, and his brush strokes. It is for this reason that one has the granite aspect, the mountainous and hard "feel," of so much early modernist sculpture, and the stressed painty look of paintings. This is intensified expression of medium. Van Gogh piled up gobs of raw paint and reveled in flaming color; but equally Cézanne used paints with utmost regard for the formal value of each stroke; and the third pioneer post-impressionist, Gauguin, gorgeously and daringly enlarged the Western way of utilizing color for decorative ends.

Expression in art means, too, a reflection of environment, of outward life around the artist. It is hardly necessary to point out an exceptional *dynamic* quality in all the arts since impressionism. In the machine age, when living has been intensified and movement accelerated, art has taken on intensity of color and vigor of statement, and where the plastic element is discussed one hears especially of "movement in the canvas." The scientific gains of the laboratory, opening new vistas into stupendous universes and giving fresh meaning to men's conception of order, are not unreflected in the painting that turns its attention to abstract structure.

Art's own revolution is so thorough that it has no illusions about expressing the new age merely by illustrating outward aspects. (The futurists thought they could be modern by picturing automobiles and other moving objects and by stressing their speed lines; and because they were thus holding to the illustrative—that is, the imitative—view they have dropped out of the lists of significant twentieth-century schools.) Expressionism seeks to express the *spirit* of the machine age —which is, after all, folded within the spirit of each artist-seer.

One last word of theory and caution to aid further against narrow-mindedness—in order that more of us may perhaps, in relation to today's radicals, avoid the sort of blindness that led our recent forefathers to starve and persecute successively the impressionists, the first post-impressionists, then the avowed expressionists: let us understand all we can of *abstract* art. They have a very reasonable case who argue that the next release of the creative impulse will be in the direction of revealing more fully the spirit of man in terms plastic but mystic. As we think of generic man continually increasing the scope of his understanding, at present in realms outside immediate sense experience, so we may think of the creative artist as widening his faculties for intuition and imaging, and affording us—if we, too, have widened our capacities—further experience of a realm spiritual and beautiful.

Men have pushed back the frontiers of understanding. The most sensitive seers among them, their artists, may be on the road to the expression of an order beyond common sight, to experience in a realm with a life beyond visible nature's. As music deals aurally with abstractions, so painting may come to deal visually—and create a similar world of delight.

By trying to understand the farthest reaches of abstraction in art, we shall the better understand all modernism since Cézanne, because a structure of intangibles lies within every memorable canvas of the artists who continue history after 1880.

The Revolt against Realism

Paul Cézanne was born in 1839 at Aix-en-Provence. His people were of lower middle-class families. His father, however, moved up from the business of selling felt hats to banking and became the leading citizen and financier of the town. Thus Paul, when he had fought down his father's opposition—he studied law for two years and wasted a third during which he wrote considerable verse—was enabled by income from his family to study in Paris, whither he went first in 1861; and then to live modestly but comfortably through years and years and years during which he failed to sell a picture. He threw in his artistic fortunes with the painters of the *Salon des Refusés,* from which the impressionists as a school were to emerge soon after. His early professional life was spent between Provence and Paris, and he learned directly from Manet and Pissarro before his own further revolutionary ideas made him a lone rebel.

He kept hope for a time that his paintings might gain recognition and reward, even officially, but later became so absorbed in the actual problems of picture-making that he left off thinking of juries and museums and buyers; he might even throw a canvas into a handy ditch, or cut it to ribbons, once the work was done. He deserted Paris periodically for his more congenial Provence and was known to be practically a recluse.

When he was fifty-six years old, in 1895, after a period of eighteen years during which only

Cézanne: *Landscape. Metropolitan Museum of Art*

three of his pictures had been shown in exhibitions, a dealer penetrated his obscurity and arranged a one-man show in Paris. The response was divided, ranging from the summary in the *Journal des Artistes*, "a nightmarish apparition of atrocities," to enthusiastic reviews. The dealer went to Aix and bought a large number of Cézanne's pictures and later made a fortune from them. Cézanne died in 1906. Within the following quarter-century even the most respectable museums put in his works.

Cézanne is first among modern artists by reason of both spiritual leadership and accomplishment in his own art. No one could seem less like a world leader than this strange, provincially ill-at-ease, inarticulate person, yet from stray sayings of his related to hidden elements, or from hints in his paintings, a new Western aesthetic has been built up, schools have stemmed, and a revolution in practice has taken place. His canvases as a group still illustrate best the main drifts of modernism, the search for expressive form, the intentional distortion of nature, the reach for abstraction. Placed in the orthodox galleries before van Gogh's, the canvases of Cézanne proved to many eyes that most contemporary painting was by contrast lifeless, empty, inert. For common appreciators, as well as for artists and aestheticians, Cézanne marked the turn from one major slope into another.

He was the insurgent who turned the waters back upon the impressionists. Practicing with them at first, he recognized the shallowness of their chromatic harmonies and soft-focus surface "photography." He said frankly, "I wish to make of impressionism an art solid and durable like that of the museum masters." He chose to study, however, not the realistic painters but those who had incorporated formal rhythms into their canvases: in particular Rubens—not, perhaps, to be considered a consistent master of formal organization, but author of works overflowing with movement and with at times a close-knit plastic structure—and Tintoretto and Poussin. In these

Cézanne: *Bathers. Collection Mrs. Rutherford McCormick, Chicago*

artists he found a "durable" thing that the impressionists (and the Courbet school of realists before them) had lost.

But never did an artist develop his means less out of the devices of predecessors, more out of his own anguish and vision and study of nature. Although Cézanne violated every law of representation as known to the realists, he clung to nature as a source and inspiration. He searched passionately for the elusive thing he termed "the realization," a fugitive something, partly a sensation, partly an intuition, and partly an image. He glimpsed it perhaps not so much in nature as beyond or through nature. He wanted his art, he said, to afford the feeling of "the eternal in nature." Again he wrote: "The true and endless study is in the diversity of the spectacle of nature." And: "For progress toward realization there is nothing but nature."

Searching, he brought back to painting organized, coherent, structural design. He found,

richly, the rhythmic vitality of the Chinese "spiritual" painter. He brought together nature and abstraction, the commonest object and the deepest revelation of cosmic order.

By means evident to the specialist he fixed this element of structural design more firmly in his canvas than had any other painter since El Greco. The means are of a sort to be mentioned rather than analyzed in a history. They concern superimposed and sloping planes, spiral movement, focal points, volume weight and counterweight, color counterpoint, and textural enrichment. In color-use he far surpassed El Greco, for he fused drawing and coloring into one process. He spoke of reducing all shapes in nature to three fundamental forms, the cube, the cone, and the cylinder; and from later application of this idea came the adventure of the cubists. He, more often than any other modern painter, made the abstract elements speak eloquently.

More simply stated, there is in the creative

Cézanne: *The Card Players. Louvre*

picture a dynamic effect, an ordered construction of backward-forward movement elements, which gives life to the composition—and rhythm to the observer's experience. There is a marked path for the eye, and a counterpoint of fluctuating movement. A Cézanne picture, whether a landscape or a portrait, a still-life or a figure-piece, communicates something of this living abstract "realization," this eternal ordered rhythm, to the spectator who is emancipated from facsimile art.

Cézanne's water-colors mark his nearest approach to pure abstraction. But the more successful part of his achievement is perhaps in those landscapes and still-lifes wherein the distortion of natural aspects is only slight yet the formal rhythm strong. They are probably giving more aesthetic pleasure to a larger art-trained audience than the works of any other painter who has lived since 1700.

Cézanne by example set the survey stakes within which twentieth-century expressive painting was, in the main, to develop. Before turning, however, to those who followed directly in his footsteps—cubists, abstractionists, *fauves,* and a large international group who can hardly be called other than "Cézannists"—it is well to glance at certain "rediscovered" moderns, now recognized as having affinity with the master of Aix; and at correlative movements initiated by his fellows, Gauguin and van Gogh.

Once the retreat from the realistic position began, when a new criterion of formal excellence was being set up, attention was drawn to certain older painters who had instinctively held to "constructed" art, neglected men who indubitably had put into their painting some of the plastic value that Cézanne wanted to preserve out of "museum" art and which he had seen joyously exploited by Tintoretto and used with reserve, covered over with rhetoric, by Poussin. El Greco, of course, affords the classic example of a genius obscured and forgotten, then redis-

Daumier: *The Uprising. Phillips Gallery, Washington*

covered by the moderns. There were others in Cézanne's own century.

Of all the rehabilitated nineteenth-century masters, Honoré Daumier is the most lauded today. He is honored as one of the very great elder moderns. He is the more significant because he is known to have influenced Cézanne at a critical moment. But his pictures are sufficient passport for his entry into the new Pantheon.

Daumier, born in 1808, self-educated in the arts, was considered in his time an effective cartoonist and an accomplished lithographer, but his paintings were officially and popularly thought (except by a few friends) to be without merit.

Those paintings, in today's changed view, are seen to possess the all-important form-quality, the elementary plastic vitality, more richly than the works of any artist contemporary with Daumier. It is considered by some an added virtue that Daumier was at the same time a social historian, that his art reflects life in the Paris of his era, with the color of his reactions to social inequality, bureaucratic stupidity, and miscarriage of justice.

In technique he belonged distinctly to the phase before impressionism. A student when Delacroix challenged the cold and mechanical draftsmanship of the classicists, he rode in on the wave of freer brushing and swift outlining introduced by the romantics, and he preserved something of their dramatic emotion and vigor when he took up with the Courbet realists, with whom he is often grouped by historians. Constrained to work diligently and hastily as a political cartoonist if he cared to eat, he had reason to tie his art to what was close by and familiar. He carried over to his painting something of the broad and simple method of the habitual worker in black-and-white. Indeed many of his canvases are practically without color, and the traces of the rapid draftsman are seldom concealed (see the plate on page ix).

Daumier: *Corot Sketching. Metropolitan Museum of Art*

But his larger pictures lack nothing of sculpturesque largeness, compositional fullness, and vigorous movement. He was devoted to common themes, to what he saw on the banks of the Seine, in the third-class railway carriage, in the theater balcony, law court, or street café. He was one of the earliest to document the struggle of the submerged classes, to dramatize hunger and thievery and injustice. He sometimes carried the cartoonist's barb into the gallery canvas.

Despite these journalistic preoccupations—and this is what matters most a century later—his plastic rhythms are sound and strong. Whether it is a pulsingly alive document-picture such as

The Uprising, in the Phillips Gallery in Washington—which is an extraordinary example of physical movement conveyed but harnessed as pictorial movement, counterweighted and poised —or a light, inconsequential thing such as the *Corot Sketching,* in the Metropolitan Museum of New York, the formal effect is sure, the pattern pronounced. In his forceful use of human bodies Daumier inevitably calls to mind Michelangelo.

It is one of the tragedies of the early era of democratic art that Daumier was permitted to paint only as a marginal activity. It is apparently still a question whether society should exclude

Ryder: *Toilers of the Sea. Addison Gallery, Andover, Massachusetts*

from the opportunity to experiment and create all those not fortunate enough to have inherited incomes—as had Delacroix, Corot, Manet, and Cézanne in Daumier's time. Cramped as he was by lifelong poverty, and comparatively few in number though his paintings were, he yet lives today powerfully, with a sort of grandeur which has gone out of the reputations of many artists widely proclaimed in his day. The state buried him, not from any wish to do him honor but because he died a pauper.

Jean-Louis Forain, a young man of twenty-seven when Daumier died in 1879, also a journalistic commentator by trade, did not succeed so well in pulling his oil paintings up to compositional grandeur and patterned order, but he did reinforce his episode-pictures from law courts sense of balanced movement. He forces his social documents, insists upon pathos or indignation and cafés with dramatic lighting and a sure

or contempt, as Daumier does not; but structurally he is sounder than the academicians on one side of him and the impressionists on the other.

Another rediscovered figure, also an illustrator, is Constantin Guys, who, however, was neither a caricaturist nor a propagandist, but only a recorder of life around him, with a talent that lifted some of his drawings to the estate of masterly design. He is, some believe, the most characteristic illustrator of the latter half of the nineteenth century, with a nervous shorthand style of drawing that got down precise and animated impressions.

A second graphic artist, equally the illustrator but often enough venturing into the field of larger painting, was Henri de Toulouse-Lautrec. A cripple who nevertheless ventured into the places of most lurid excitement in Paris, the cafés and dives, the law courts and dance-halls, the revue theaters and circuses, he turned out records of hothouse metropolitan life that are still exciting. He had studied Goya in particular, but tempered the realistic intention with something learned from treasured Japanese prints. He has affinity with Degas, and is surer in his formal patterning—which is why the moderns turn to him sympathetically; but in the end he must be put down as essentially one who enlarged graphic illustrations to the size of wall paintings, not without unusual decorative mastery. The combination of exciting subject-matter and modern technique brought Lautrec into extraordinary popular esteem in the years just after 1950.

America has come to recognize one of the neglected masters of formal organization in Albert Pinkham Ryder. He had not a whit of Daumier's impulse to satirize or comment upon current life, nor of the passion to illustrate as reflected in the works of Guys and Toulouse-Lautrec. Rather he was remote, impersonal, imaginative. He sought mystically to express truths apprehended beyond the surface aspects of nature, and his one great achievement is in endowing his canvases—generally small in area but massive in treatment—with a communicable sense of abstract order. Whether it is his favorite theme of a moonlit sea, or an open landscape or a scene from legendry or literature, the picture structure is balanced, the pattern effect strong and certain. (See page 607.)

Ryder's technique and his plastic mastery well served the spirit of the content of his art: there is clear expression of his own feeling of loneliness among men, of the tragic grandeur of the sea, of a constantly felt order in the universe. He knew himself for a dreamer, for one drawn aside from what men considered the significant life of the day; he was healthy and philosophical; he was poor, frugal, and the associate of undistinguished and unpretentious people—all of which has left a mark upon his painting. He is the most considerable painter among Americans who had developed up to 1930. In his half-century he was unapproached by any English-speaking artist in mastery of picture-making as such. A contemporary of Cézanne, he independently arrived at that under-standing of the abstract element in painting, the solid structural framework of it, which the Frenchman was destined to demonstrate as the foundation of the new revolutionary art. Ryder's was a slighter but a distinctive achievement, within the new vision and the new rhythmic statement. He supplies concrete examples of that unexplainable thing, mystic visual art.

Another nineteenth-century American who transcended national and school lines, who found a way to put a plastic structure under the realistic-looking surface of his art, was John H. Twachtman. He went to Paris and learned the impressionist broken-color technique, and at first glance his pictures may seem like most fragile Monets. But Twachtman felt the call to realize some deeper order, to use design in expression of abstract rhythm. Belonging by right to the post-impressionist development, he is the oftener catalogued as the greatest American follower of Pissarro and Monet. His luminous, exquisite canvases will be found by those who have an eye for it to be characterized by this other form-value, which lifts him to a place above the very appealing group of American impressionist land-scapists.

The Decorative School

It was an American-born painter, Paris-trained, resident in uncongenial London, who first effectively absorbed Oriental attributes into his art, marking the beginning of that decorative stream that intertwines confusedly with the main current of abstract modernism. James Abbott McNeill Whistler is, indeed, the chief figure after Gauguin on the lighter, sensuously affective side of post-realistic painting.

The decorative school of modern painters might be defined as that which deliberately creates a shallow picture-space, deals generously in linear rhythms and color harmonies, and generally is content with surface melodies rather than with deep contrapuntal orchestration. Texture and finish are here of exceptional moment.

Whistler was twenty years old when he left the United States to take up his art training

Whistler: *Portrait of Carlyle. Corporation Art Gallery, Glasgow*

in Paris. Those Americans who would claim him for their country's art-story have just about as much reason as the French, who trained him, or the English, among whom he practiced. He learned most from Velázquez among the European old masters, drowned out a good deal of that influence in his homage to the Japanese, and ended as a solitary in Western painting.

It is something of a critical fashion today to depreciate Whistler and to deny him a place in the modern scene. The extreme finish of his pictures, and a sentimentalism read into his portraits and nocturnes—directly against his own vigorous denials of other than decorative pur-

pose—have laid him open to attack by the "red-blooded," vigorously dynamic moderns. Of course the moralists and littérateurs opposed him, feeling that his fight for art as its own justification endangered the orthodox tradition. By his provocative propaganda against emphasis upon descriptive and instructive values in painting he fed fuel to the fire raging over art's meaning. And he became involved as a central figure in a controversy over a possible "art for art's sake."

Those who have an eye for richly formalized art find a very special delight in Whistler's canvases, in a field seldom exploited by Western painters. The famous *Battersea Bridge* is as pretty a piece of abstract plane-arrangement and muted color-harmony as any achieved by European (or American) artists. Many a "nocturne" or "symphony" or "arrangement" from the same hand has a similar exquisitely decorative and sensuous loveliness. To call it melodious and musical is not at all unreasonable; although when Whistler chose to label his canvases with titles such as *Symphony in White* or *Nocturne: Blue and Silver,* the British public and critics considered him impudent and idiotic, even maudlin and insane. Unfortunately Ruskin was drawn into the circle of his enemies and penned one of the most famous and most ill-judged indictments of an artist in all history, ending with the words: "I have seen, and heard, much of Cockney impudence before now; but never expected to hear a coxcomb ask two hundred guineas for flinging a pot of paint in the public's face."

A widely publicized libel suit followed; Whistler was further disgraced in the eyes of the orthodox; and art came into headlines as it had seldom before in England. Ultimately Whistler put his thoughts into a brief essay, delivered first as a lecture under the title "Ten O'Clock," which is one of the meatiest and wittiest of refutations of the pretensions of the realists. It equally showed Whistler as concerned with only a small corner of the field open to the artist.

But that corner *is* on the modern side; and such pictures as the portrait of Carlyle, the portrait of the artist's mother, certain of the riverside nocturnes, and such an interior as *The Artist's Studio,* in Chicago, constitute a body of works consistently planned for formal effects. They are instinct with a controlled plastic animation, touched with unfailing fragile grace. Almost invariably cool in color and low in tone, and exceedingly sensitive in compositional arrangement, they have their continuing place among the orchid-like, exquisitely dainty products of post-realistic art. Whistler also was a master of etching; his sensitive touch resulted, particularly in his London river scenes and in a Venetian series, in prints as sought after as any in the history of the art, excepting only Rembrandt's.

The West had lost, centuries before, the secret of mural painting. Naturalism, and particularly the architectural vista in perspective and the deep landscape, clashed seriously with the conventions necessary to mural art. A flattened effect, meaning a reduced range of penetration in space, and a method of arranging the picture elements in simple planes, is at the very heart of wall decoration. In the mid-nineteenth century there began a return to flat painting in the mural technique, and the Frenchman Puvis de Chavannes is remembered as a pioneer. At the same moment the revival of interest in Oriental art and the trend to formalism and abstraction among the pioneers of post-impressionism strengthened the position of the muralists.

Puvis de Chavannes, who lived from 1824 to 1898, is almost the only international figure in the mode, and nothing was to be heard of it again until a wave of interest swept America in the nineteen-thirties, impelled by the achievements of two Mexicans. So Puvis' walls stand lonesome and exceptional, marking the rediscovery of a technique and an intrinsic contribution not very forceful but agreeably colorful and tranquilly architectural. His colors are quiet and harmonious, and his compositions are expertly flattened without "unreasonable" violation of natural aspect. One wishes that he might have had a little more of the courage of the expressionists, sacrificed more of nature to design. But perhaps his chief fault is in a rather mechanical disposition of figures; they sometimes seem pasted to the background without adequate relationship to the other elements.

Nevertheless, it was an exceptional reach forward that a man in the midst of naturalistic painters was able to return to architectonic principles and reaffirm the age-old conventions of muralism, not without a certain pale majesty and a charming colorfulness. The main exhibits of his art are at Paris, in the Boston Public Library, and in provincial museum buildings in France; but sizable panels may be found in many American and European art galleries.

In Germany a single artist guessed the importance of the plastic synthesis as a step to decorative ends. Unfortunately his output was slight; but Hans von Marées deserves mention as

Whistler:
Battersea Bridge.
National Gallery,
Millbank, London

Germany's most gifted and most original visual artist between the generation of Holbein and the twentieth-century expressionists. He spent twenty years in Italy and died in Rome in 1887.

Paul Gauguin is the most famous—and the most spectacular—figure in the decorative wing of the modernist advance. He was one of the original trio of post-impressionist masters (with Cézanne and van Gogh), and because his art is less violently expressionistic and more seductively sensuous, his radicalism found favor earlier. He also drew attention by the picturesque, not to say lurid, nature of his insurgency. He had been a respectable businessman, a stockbroker, when at thirty-five, in 1883, he abandoned business, family, and security to take up painting. He had originality enough to establish, with principles taken to some extent from Cézanne and van Gogh, one of the three lines of anti-realist advance; although his was the least significant of the three.

Gauguin carried his decorative method to a certain mastery during his years in France, but found the more stimulating field for his talents in the South Sea Islands. He did not neglect the opportunity to make his gesture of abandoning decadent civilization a theatrical one, and there was doubtless some sincerity in the action. On the other hand, there were bills owing, and there is some question whether van Gogh did not, in a spell of undoubted insanity, try to murder Gauguin. What with one such annoyance and another, he decided to go where life was simple and primitive. He went to Tahiti.

Gauguin: *The White Horse. Louvre*

His flat-patterning, linear harmonies, and brilliant color were well suited to the Tahitian scene and people. He had returned to a tapestry-like lay-out method, with little regard for per-spective, and he had learned to deform human bodies for volume-weight or repeat-pattern purposes. The semi-nude figures of the Tahitians and the exotic coloring of landscape and of native

Van Gogh: *Night Café. Private collection, New York*

clothes fed his passion for broad, highly colored decorativeness.

He has left a feast for the eyes in a body of formally alive, sensuously lovely canvases. No one else in the West has used color so vividly and recklessly (in the academic view) and yet achieved harmony. No one else has woven color and line into such compelling melodies. There is not the profound plastic order, the symphonic movement, of Cézanne; but within the limits of flattened, decorative organization Gauguin is supreme.

Of course Gauguin's much-advertised "escape from civilization" proved nothing about the artist in modern society. There was sincere protest behind the abandonment of the sophisticated Parisian world at the moment of his going, but something of affectation in his labored barbarism, too. He died in wretchedness in the Marquesas Islands in 1903, just as he would have died in poverty in Paris had he stayed. Considering his flair for the exotic and for the Orientally colorful, he probably painted more beautiful pictures for

having gone to live with "savages." Today leading museums and millionaires compete in purchasing his works at fabulous prices.

The Individualists

"Madness alone is entirely free from the commonplace," commented the British author William Bolitho in an essay upon the painting of van Gogh. Certainly a streak of what men call insanity seems to have aided this third of the original post-impressionists to achieve a release of the images that formed in the creative chambers of his being. He was the most brilliantly unconventional, the most subjectively passionate, of the pioneer moderns.

There is something of mad intensity, also of primal innocence, about van Gogh's paintings. They are himself poured out. They are his dreams, his feelings, his inner living made manifest in paints. They were strange at first to other men because the spectators were bound up with all sorts of inhibitions and traditions as to what "real" life is, as to what proper painting is. The paintings are now accepted and enjoyed, not because we have all become a little mad but because again the boundaries of experience and of tradition have been pushed out; the field of normal art has been widened. "Yes," we say, "a yellow sunflower *can* look like that, does have that intensity of dazzling color, may momentarily light up a universe as it does this picture."

Bolitho, arguing a special revelation out of the Provençal sun, saw the pictures as he saw van Gogh himself, madly aflame. "His cypress is a green and yellow fire, with a purple glow at its heart, like a conflagration on a stem."

The vivid intensity of his art, the individualistic quality of his vision, the directness of statement, mark van Gogh as the typical early expressionist. "Expressionism," as we have seen, is a generic label for the several anti-realistic schools: the seekers after plastic order and abstract realization; the seekers after decorative loveliness through formalization; and such others as van Gogh, who sacrificed natural aspect to an outpouring of inner feeling and passionate imaging. But it was of the last group that the word was first used (in Germany).

When the sponsors of the first-named expressionists went back to seek pioneers and prophets —as sponsors will—they found van Gogh, still less understood than Cézanne or Gauguin, perfectly illustrating the thesis that art should be an unhampered expression of the artist's passion, of his exceptional way of seeing. He was obviously the great individualist. He had thrown away "finish" and he had distorted trees and human beings and had filled the sky with flames. It was found, nevertheless, that he had expressed something worth expressing. If he had wholly overlooked the Greek (and the current) rule that "art is imitation," if he had overstepped all existing rules as to moderation in color and limits of vigorous draftsmanship, he had done something that in 1910 already gave delight to a few observers. By 1920 he was canonized as one of the three creators of modernism. By 1936 he was in danger of being "all the rage." In that year a retrospective exhibition of his works at the

Museum of Modern Art in New York drew crowds that broke all attendance records; 123,000 people passed the doors. It was a success destined to be repeated many times and in many countries in the following decades.

Vincent van Gogh was a Dutchman, born in 1853 to the family of a minister. He tried business as a salesman in an art shop, teaching, and finally preaching in a small way—as pastor of a miserable mining-section flock. In all these vocations he found himself tortured, and ultimately a failure. He sincerely—and madly—wanted a way of spiritual expression and at the same time a way of unselfish service to mankind. When he was twenty-seven years old he abandoned everything else to give himself to painting. He was further frustrated, again a failure in the eyes of the world; but his fanaticism, which had wrecked his teaching and his preaching, this time resulted in a clear-flamed expression and, as it appears two generations later, an individual and unique service to mankind.

In one of the three volumes of letters to his brother, which form a moving and tragic autobiography, he writes that his only anxiety is "How can I be of use in the world, cannot I be of any good?" His brother sent him the little money he could spare, enough to buy paints and the meanest of shelter and food. Van Gogh lived in Provence during his years of painting, part of the time with Gauguin in rooms at Arles. During a final detention in a sanatorium he committed suicide, believing that he was thus saving himself from total madness. It is not certain that he had sold more than one painting during his lifetime.

The most popular of his works are those flower studies in which he has poured into sunflower and marigold and roses the flaming molten gold of the sun he so loved and almost deified. His landscapes are hardly less sundrenched and dazzlingly bright: cornfields and flower farms and Provençal orchards. But when one turns to the portraits one finds again the brilliant lighting, the reveling in vivid pigment.

Van Gogh's painting method gives a peculiarly brilliant and fresh aspect to the canvas. The impressionist technique is pushed to a new con-

Van Gogh: *Self-Portrait.*
Collection Adelaide M. De Groot

clusion: wiggly streaks of color juxtaposed to make each area a field of sinuous brush strokes, with, in extreme cases, high ridges of pigment catching the light. But he does not, like the other broken-color painters, lose the weight of solids in the luminous surface treatment. He has, moreover, at times an instinctive sense of volume-and-space organization, of structure by planes; and he is among the masters in his use of textures for formal enrichment. Altogether his is a blazingly alive technique—within a madman's unearthly glory of color.

Overlooked in his time, van Gogh's genius is recognized and almost universally praised today, but no one has walked in his steps or made a school in his name. The German expressionists came nearest to doing this. The wildness, the passionate reach, are apparent particularly in the groups that flourished just after World War I. Emil Nolde, Karl Schmidt-Rottluff, and Max Pechstein were foremost, perhaps, in a body of painters striving to pour out emotion in vigorous, even explosive technique. They had their own

German and Northern mentors: one Edvard Munch, originally from Norway; and Lovis Corinth, who worked out of an impressionist manner into a strongly individualized, careless-of-nature way of statement, with notable grasp of plastic animation. But within this development the outstanding figure is Oskar Kokoschka, an Austrian long resident in Germany, then in England, who packs more of virile organization and rugged form into a canvas than does any other follower of van Gogh and Cézanne. There is a quality of ruthlessness in the way in which Kokoschka, Nolde, and Schmidt-Rottluff have sought form—at the expense of natural aspect and finished technique.

In France the greatest individualist in this direction was Georges Rouault. He grasped the significance of the inner abstract architecture of painting, at the same time leaning to the side of the subjective or emotional expressionists. More is said of him—as probably the greatest of French artists since Cézanne—when the story of the School of Paris is resumed a few pages ahead.

Kokoschka: *Double Portrait. Formerly State Gallery, Dresden*

The Modern Primitives

The reversal of the main trend of Western painting after Cézanne, and particularly the efforts of many artists to vault the whole distance back to "instinctive" statement, led to a great deal of talk about a new primitivism. It was then that Negro sculpture was discovered, praised, and overpraised; to which were added South Seas decorative art, Mayan sculpture, and sundry actual savage masks and weapons. Many artists were affected, particularly by the rich formal realization exhibited in African carved figures.

The more noteworthy primitivism is to be found, however, in the works of certain artists native to civilized states who, not having contact with savage peoples or ancient relics, reverted to naïve statement and formal patterning. These exceptional ones, known as "naturals" to their sophisticated brother artists, seem born with an incorruptible child's innocence in their view of the world—never seeking to be effective or showy or learned—and with an intuitive plastic sense, gaining casually some echo of that order which Cézanne with such difficulty struggled to achieve.

Of the early primitives discovered and hailed by the moderns the foremost was Henri Rousseau, a Frenchman who lived from 1844 to 1910. He was a customs inspector—and therefore known oftenest in the records as *Rousseau le douanier*—and so could paint only on Sundays.

Rousseau: *Scene on the Seine. Phillips Gallery, Washington*

Untutored in art, little educated in any direction, he conceived a passion for painting when he was middle-aged. His canvases are likely to be decorative, in which case he beautifully preserves the mural flatness, the tapestry-like treatment in simple planes; or else charmingly naïve depictions of familiar life: his family promenading or in the parlor, the banks of the Seine, or Sunday-afternoon scenes in the park. But what gives validity to them is the formal excellence, which the man came to without that long process of study, reasoning, and experiment which the "regular" painters had to resort to.

There is, in a world still overrun with dull academic and futilely photographic painting, a particular delight in the little unpretentious fancies and occasional sly fresh humor discoverable in Rousseau's work. It is a small contribution, but distinctive and imaginative and ingratiating.

America by virtue of its broad expanse and its remoteness from school centers, with its consequent lack of uniformity and sophistication, developed a more than average share of intuitively gifted formalizing artists; and since the first general recognition of modernism there has been fitful activity in discovering "American primitives"—meaning not the native Indian relics but the works of those painters who carried on European ideals according to provincial understanding. The resultant gallery exhibits from the late seventeenth, the eighteenth, and the early nineteenth centuries are frequently diverting and sometimes richly rewarding in terms of sheer pictorial-plastic experience. There are no outstanding masters, in the world view. But it may be fairly said that in the decades of the great portrait masters in England, say from 1750 to 1830, although the colonial painters were inferior to the homeland artists in glamour and dash and elegance, they were often superior in the feeling for formal structure and plastic solidity. Almost any art museum or historical museum shows examples that are little less than masterly in construction. Even stranger, because without any English precedent, was the painting by Edward Hicks, who practiced from the final years of the eighteenth century to the mid-nineteenth. He combined carriage- and sign-painting with preaching. He is best known for his many versions of one subject, *The Peaceable Kingdom*. More decorative are the few pictures by Joseph Pickett, a carpenter and barge-builder, who did not take up painting until late in life, after 1900.

Other American primitives appeared early in the twentieth century, and if the exploited figures fail to approach Rousseau in stature there are a shy charm and an unconventional freshness in the romantic landscapes of Louis Eilshemius, and in the panoramas of John Kane—which are definitely a "folk art" survival. In the nineteen-forties Anna Mary Robertson Moses, known in the international art world simply as Grandma Moses, became the most popular of America's neo-primitives. Untrained in art, after a life of hard farm labor, in her seventies she took up painting because "it is a lot easier than embroidery," and out of her dreams of life as it used to be on the farms and hills about her she created hundreds of pictures that are charming and slightly imaginative, and intuitively blessed with pictorial structure. Somewhere between a natural's gift and a studied understanding of plastic principles lies the simple and effective designing, in almost stark terms, of Matthew Barnes.

Naïve primitivism is in any case a side-road of modern art, and conscious imitation of antique primitives or of contemporary savages has led only into blind alleys. The effect of Negro (and Mayan and Polynesian) sculpture upon European and American has in general been broadening and beneficial; but only when the artists have not attempted to duplicate actual effects. It takes little study to recognize that the body of modern art has more affinity with primitive than with European realistic art of the eighteenth and nineteenth centuries; as also it has affinity with Italo-Byzantine and Sienese developments, which the realists called "primitive" for their stiffness and formalism at the expense of naturalness. But the affinity is rightly one of principle and structure, not of imitated aspect. One of the lessons learned from a study of "modern primitives" is that copying an Aztec motive or sailing to Tierra del Fuego or Easter Island will not make a sophisticated painter a good formal artist. But knowing the reasons for the excellences of Polynesian or African carving will make easier for the layman the comprehension of values in not only Rousseau but Cézanne and Matisse and Rouault and Kandinski.

The intensely subjective school of expressionists, the decorative wing, and the "naturals" are severally important, but in the end the main path of modernism seems to have run from Cézanne, through the neo-impressionists, the cubists, and the *fauves,* to the varied schools of abstractionists and near-abstractionists. The controversies over the merits of the several schools and over their diverse aims still rage, and the historical account is therefore likely to be confused. Some historians end by heralding the achievement of an absolute art of abstraction. Others were certain for a time that a new school of muralists, conserving abstract values but intensely conscious of social values in their subject-matter, had snatched the torch of creativeness. These two developments, one a steady march toward abstraction, the other a tide of passionately felt socially propagandist art, moved along side by side through two decades. As instanced, say, in the works of Kandinski on one hand and in the painting of Orozco and Rivera on the other, they were of one common body of modern art, and both bound, technically, in a debt to Cézanne.

In the days of impressionist experiment there was an artist who in a small group of canvases attained to a formal mastery that at times rivals Cézanne's, and to a surface technique distinctively individual. Georges Seurat has often been termed a neo-impressionist by reason of his adherence to the broken-color method and especially to the *pointilliste* system of building up areas of color with dots or pellets of pigment. But it has been recognized by later analysts that his painstaking technique went to accentuate an underlying abstract rhythm as nicely adjusted as

Seurat: *The Bridge at Courbevoie. Courtauld Collection, London*

that in a Hiroshige print or a Ming landscape. The arrangement of linear elements, recessive planes, and textural patterning in the landscape of the Samuel Courtauld Collection in London, or in the monumental *Sunday on Grande Jatte Island* at Chicago, will well repay study for gradually emerging rhythm and sub-rhythms.

Even in black-and-white reproduction the landscape indicates how definitely the artist has returned to a concern with design as such as against natural appearances, with consciously manipulated form as against descriptive documentation. It may be added that simply as a tonal study the picture is as subtle as any by the tone-mad impressionists, and yet it has this other, profounder dignity of structure too. Seurat died at the age of thirty-two in 1891. He might, had he lived on, have been one of the universal masters. As it is, the very slight body of completed works assures him praise in every history or analysis of post-impressionist art. Neo-im-

pressionism as a "school" was known importantly only through the works of Seurat, though Paul Signac was as much an insurgent—without the gift for plastic magic. Signac eventually fell back into impressionism of the sort that Pissarro was practicing. It should be added that the neo-impressionists did not insist upon technical *pointillisme* or dot-painting, but opened the way to application of the pigments in juxtaposed wedges or streaks or, eventually, thumb-smudges or palette-knife slashes.

The Fauves

In 1905 there occurred in Paris at once a scandal and a historic step forward for modernism. Up to this time, the reader will have noted, attention had been given to individual rebels and to apparently personal methods of painting. No one had tried to correlate and understand as one advance the innovations of Cézanne, van Gogh, Gauguin, and Seurat. At the *Salon d' Automne* of 1905 a room was assigned to a youthful group of nonconformist painters, a set of unknowns which included Henri Matisse, Georges Rouault, Georges Braque, André Derain, and Raoul Dufy. The exhibition had hardly opened before the room became known as the *cage aux fauves*—the cage of the wild ones—and the artists as *fauves*.

For a few years thereafter the *fauves* stuck together as the central and guiding force within French post-impressionism. The response of the public and the press was almost solidly adverse, hilarious, and vituperative. But in the week of that salon opening the School of Paris was born. The individual *fauves* were destined to be leaders in the international scene from 1908 forward. With a few later adherents (among them the overwhelming Picasso) they were to emerge in the nineteen-forties as the grand old men of French painting.

In 1905 there was not much likeness between the painting method of Rouault, who had then reached the most savage point in his career in both his attack upon canvas and paints and his comment upon social conventions, and that of Matisse, then already in a period of simplification and decorativism; and certainly there was little likeness—ever—between the canvases of Braque and those of Dufy. Yet all these artists were carrying on the tradition of insurgency and in a hidden way were observing the technical advances made by Cézanne. For the first time the leading post-impressionists were banded together and a school of expressionism was widely recognized. The only style that could be marked was in paintings in heavy outlines and contrasting areas of vivid color.

There had been a few years earlier an authentic group of nonacademic painters, literate and vocal, who, as the *nabis,* claimed direct succession from Cézanne. But their success was limited, and the direction of their painting had been diverted from expressionist channels in the full sense to a rather pretty muralism, not unaffected by the study of Japanese prints. The leader of the *nabis,* Maurice Denis, retrogressed into pleasant illustrationalism. No members except Edouard Vuillard, a neo-impressionist in effect, Odilon Redon, who made an individual success in a minor way with his strangely other-worldly paintings and prints, and Pierre Bonnard turned out to be historically important. And Pierre Bonnard alone showed himself a strong artist allied in aims with the *fauves*. He became one of the leaders in the School of Paris.

The one thing that the *fauves*—or several of them—did together before they split into groups or turned into strongly individualistic paths, was to establish cubism as a school or a style. Within a year or two of the emergence of the *fauves,* certainly by 1907, Braque had begun to use planes and volumes in the manner later made familiar by the cubists; though some historians credit Pablo Picasso, who had naturally drifted into the *fauve* group, with establishing actual or doctrinaire cubism with the painting now called *The Demoiselles of Avignon*. Within another year the object, whether landscape or demoiselles, had almost disappeared from the picture and the cubist school was firmly established, representing the left wing of fauvism. Braque and Picasso were the leaders, but Derain went along with them; a few younger Frenchmen joined with the group, most notably Fernand Léger, Robert Delaunay, and Albert Gleizes; and later the Spanish Juan Gris came in and grew to be their most impressive colleague. Matisse, original leader of the *fauves,* stepped aside to follow his own constructive and decorative aims. It was he who provided the name of the school by dismissing a picture of Braque's as ". . . only cubist."

The cubists went on from the mere cubing of physical forms to the almost total disintegration of the object and the freest manipulation, bending, or total displacement of planes. They went on to success, too, as the most talked-of school —or "ism"—internationally among all those that irrupted in Paris.

Their importance may finally be seen in a clarification of theory rather than in a rich and broad contribution of actual paintings. They were so frankly concerned with a new sort of reality that no one could mistake their intention: no one

Picasso: *The Demoiselles of Avignon. Museum of Modern Art, New York*

could believe that the old aims of painting, cherished from the Renaissance to neo-impressionism, had been other than abandoned. They served to demolish the last pretense of the sacredness of "art as imitation." By their arrangement of planes—the planes of the natural object disassembled and rearranged in more affective compositions—they increased knowledge of the ways in which the several painters' means serve to create movement within the canvas. They gave hints of the nature of the internal rhythmic orchestration which had been recognized in Cézanne's work but not explained. Many of the compositions of Braque and of Picasso within the strictest cubist technique give back a refreshing if tenuous pleasure. They are supreme in one small field of abstract expression. In their early period they all but eliminated color.

A versatile and exceptionally gifted painter was André Derain, but he proved himself less a leader and originator than a sensitive follower. Some of his finest work was done when he was, by evidence of the canvases, a Cézannist. He was one of the *fauves*, of the color-mad sort, then was influenced by cubism, veered toward other sorts of abstraction, finally became a comparative independent. He was among the "solid moderns" of French painting from 1910 to the nineteen-fifties; but his talent was slighter, his originality not to be compared with that of the big three: Rouault, Picasso, Matisse. Other members of the School of Paris, similarly of rather lesser rank, were Raoul Dufy, who flirted briefly with cubism, then developed a charming method of painting in which nature is seen in calligraphic, inexact outlines overlaid with appar ently careless washes of gay color; Maurice de Vlaminck, who made a mannerism—a very appealing one—of Cézanne's way of assembling washy-looking planes as a pattern, and thus assured himself a place as master of one kind of landscape; and Marie Laurencin, for a time slightly touched by cubism but in general a feminizing (and less serious) "wild man." More important than these, perhaps, was Fernand Léger, who emerged from the cubist adventure with a personal style of abstract painting which seems the more modern because the forms in his pictures are reminiscent of machine parts—bolts and rods and cylinders and the like. At the opposite extreme within the School was Maurice Utrillo, who never felt the force of the advances toward abstraction, who took only the feeling for plastic manipulation in so far as it could be applied to views. His total work consists of pictures of the streets or vistas of Montmartre in Paris or glimpses of suburban towns. These pictures were painted from memory and from postcards—a circumstance that has not at all prevented their wide popularity and Utrillo's rating as one of the minor masters.

The Big Three

Henri Matisse, leader of the *fauves* in 1905, and successful teacher of young revolutionaries from all countries, shied away from cubism in 1907–1908. In following an independent course he became the first artist of the group to gain acknowledgment as a world master, though he forfeited to Picasso the leadership of the School of Paris. Matisse's experiments in near-abstraction were late and secondary to his main development; though, like all the revolutionaries from Whistler to Degas, he was deeply indebted to the Japanese print—and to Chinese painting and Negro sculpture, and, through Gauguin, to Persian painting. A colorist in the fullest sense, a lover of Oriental art, a follower especially of Gauguin among the original post-impressionists, he gave his life to creating an art decorative and sensuous. It is not rash to say that just before the time of his death in 1955 he was the greatest frankly decorative painter in the Western world.

His paintings are almost unfailingly gay and rhythmical and charming. They are shallow in depth behind the frame, and the objects in them are hardly more than two-dimensional. They invariably retain an anchor in objective reality.

Matisse put in faces and bodies, flowers and furniture, but he had—and asked—no interest in these things. His purpose was to weave shallow color- and line- and texture-harmonies from them in deliciously patterned arabesques. His touch is unmistakable; his canvases are bright and animated; his place as a superb decorator is secure.

Not all Matisse's pictures are as rich and eye-filling as the *Moorish Screen* reproduced here. There are earlier canvases that seem empty by comparison. In them the broad areas of color and the adjustment of the few objective elements make for a formal or rhythmic aspect no less affective. At one time, about 1910, he wholly eliminated background and accessories and got his formal effect by the rhythmic and linear composition of a few figures—as in *The Dance*, at Moscow.

Somewhere between the decorative method of Matisse and the soft, hazy color-harmonizing of the impressionists is the appealing art of Pierre Bonnard. With more than a hint of the sensuous, even voluptuous quality of Renoir, he had his own way of embedding linear or structural design while capitalizing upon the broken-color surface technique. For fully forty years he was one of the most enchanting of colorists among the French moderns.

Of Pablo Picasso history will certainly record this: from about 1908 to a time well after mid-century he was the most talked-of painter in the world. He was also one of the most prolific, one of the most versatile. His successive changes of style or school amazed his supporters and his rivals alike. Here is no single line of development, no single artistic faith, but a hopping from experiment to unrelated experiment. At a half-dozen stopping points Picasso paused long enough to produce pictures that gave him standing as one of the foremost living painters. Then he might be off to an impossibly different pursuit. The only constant was that after 1925 the

Matisse:
The Moorish Screen.
Collection
Robert Treat Paine, 2nd,
Boston

effects of cubism could be seen in every major work down to the nineteen-fifties.

Picasso left his native Spain and settled in Paris in 1903, at the age of twenty-two. He quickly outgrew an ambition to follow in the footsteps of Toulouse-Lautrec. Fortunately he came under the spell of Cézanne's painting method. (The *Salon d'Automne* of 1904 gave a whole room to Cézanne.) Before he helped in 1907 to invent cubism, in an ever more ardent effort to get back to essential form, Picasso had behind him two well-marked "periods" of creation. In both the blue period and the rose period he produced pictures which have seemed to later observers masterpieces. Without radical suppression or distortion of nature, he showed himself to be fully in the current of form-seeking

painting, with a special leaning toward Cézanne-like "realization."

Some appreciators are willing to stop there in considering Picasso as a modern master. When he joined with the *fauves,* and especially when he descended into the inanities of cubism, they feel, he became a conjurer and little more. But most observers, the critical world, and the museums showed less prejudice, and presumed masterpieces from Picasso's hand, from late as well as early periods, appeared on the walls of discriminating collectors.

Certain merits in his work are fundamental. As early as 1904 he showed himself a draftsman almost without peer. His drawings are nearly perfect in the old realistic sense. His picture-sense on the compositional side is unfailing. Anything

Picasso: *The Blue Boy.*
Collection
Edward M. M. Warburg,
New York

he touches comes alive—is obviously a "Picasso." This distinction is evident whether he is moving toward abstraction or making one of his startling about-faces toward facsimile art.

In the sequence of styles in this one man's picturing can be read, more easily than in any other artist's body of work, the changing history of art in the period 1910–55. Matisse's style, or Rouault's, is more single; but Picasso was leader; the methods he did not create, he mastered. Always he added a hallmark of his own.

For ten years, until about 1918, he was ab-

Picasso: *Night Fishing at Antibes. Museum of Modern Art, New York*

sorbed in various phases of cubism: the original sort, depending on displacement of planes and geometrization; the paste-up sort, in which misplaced eyes, noses, breasts, and the like permitted more intense pictorial livingness; etc., etc. But in 1919 he was recapturing interest in the object (which he had never totally abandoned) and was entering upon his so-called classic period. In the classic pictures he filled the frame with massive, carefully drawn figures in compositions perfectly readable to the realist but marked also by a sense for pictorial form not demanded in earlier eras. The massive, amply full figures—with hardly a breath of distortion or deformation—added up to one more unequivocal success.

For the rest, the successes came largely in phases of revived cubism. The immense horror-picture *Guernica,* of 1937, is a socially conscious document in intention, illustrating the terrors of the destruction of a Loyalist town by the Spanish Fascist air force. Certainly, however, it enters the consciousness of most observers rather as a cubist decoration in the familiar paper-flat technique than as social comment. The subject-matter is by-passed unless one wants to study it out labori-

ously. As if to stress the point that the cubist method had for thirty years been used to de-emphasize subject-interest, there hangs nearby on the walls of the Museum of Modern Art, New York, Picasso's *Girl before a Mirror,* of 1932, which *is* frankly and wholly decorative. Not far away is a later canvas, with a little more pictorial depth but equally a landmark in the march of decorative cubism: the *Night Fishing at Antibes.* The subject-matter can be studied out, but even those few observers who know the way of French night-fishing are not likely to register the objective merits of the piece; the decorative values, the sensuous values, the vitality as form, come near being all.

Those who believe that Picasso will survive as a giant through the siftings of history might fairly be asked what it is in these paintings, often termed modern masterpieces, and what it is in Picasso's work as a whole, that warrants ranking him first among France's modernists. The answer might be something like this: there is a sort of pictorial grandeur, a compositional completeness, an unfailing formal aliveness, in all these pictures. Such are the qualities that have

Braque: *Abstraction. Phillips Gallery, Washington*

been of foremost concern to creative painters since Cézanne. The search instituted by Cézanne ended most richly in Picasso's work. All other schools in France, the center of progress until World War II, have been minor as compared to this one.

There *were* other schools—most notably the purists, who carried forward toward an art freed of subject, and the *surréalistes*. But before their story is briefly recorded it is well to describe the work of one other French painter who was never involved in any of the doctrinaire schools: Rouault. Even so great an upheaval as cubism failed to disturb his independence. And a last word should be said of the individual charm of the paintings of Georges Braque, who not only had been at the heart of the cubist advance but stayed within the confines of cubism through all his later life. In retrospect his is an unexciting sort of art, composed quietly and with modest coloring, without any real subject-interest. But as a display of pleasing formal improvising, of flat-pattern composing, of musical-architectural har-

monizing, it is, as a single body of work, unrivaled. As to the possibility that such art is but a novelty, a passing phase, let the observer ponder the fact that Braque practiced cubism for a full half-century.

Georges Rouault had been one of the original *fauves* and perhaps the wildest of all the painters shown in the "cage" in 1905. He went his own independent way, however, untroubled by the cries of fellow artists that cubism constituted the only true revolution. By 1905 many of the idioms of his art had already been fixed: the heavy outlines; the dark, smoky backgrounds; the color reminiscent of stained-glass windows; the general feeling of largeness because the figures fill the canvases to their limits. But most astonishing is his surety of plastic design at the same time that he held, unlike the mass of moderns, to subject-interest. Not only did he refuse to join those who were suppressing subject; he returned to themes bearing messages—he even brought back religious painting in a world increasingly skeptical.

At the time of the early *fauve* exhibitions

Rouault: *The Old Clown.*
Collection Edward G. Robinson,
Beverly Hills, California

Rouault matched his apparently violent technique with a vengeful attack on the worst evils of civilization, especially on prostitution and venal law courts. The prostitutes he depicted are miserable and horrible, obviously emblematic of man's degradation from his once godlike estate; his judges are stupid, bloated, self-interested. But as his own deeply religious convictions matured Rouault no longer belabored sin, so to speak, but took subjects from the circuses, produced portraits, and roamed in practically all the objective fields known to painters.

If he was obsessed now, it was with the idea of suffering. In *The Old King* the king's accouterments are rich, gorgeous, but the face is sick. In *The Old Clown* the professional merrymaker is, as age comes upon him, serious, baffled, morose. It is to be remembered that at the same time— though the observer's mind has got round to these ironies—the two pictures are masterpieces of construction in the modern manner. The aesthetic sense will long since have responded to the formal vitality, the plastic aliveness bound up in Rouault's singularly personal coloring, in the monumental plane-patterning, in the melodious interplay of heavy outlines. A little later came the period of proclaimed religious subject-matter, oftenest the Crucifixion, occasional major pictures from the Passion of Christ, and a masterly smaller series that illustrates varied Bible subjects.

It was not until 1930 that Rouault's fame spread internationally, so that he became a figure to be discussed with Matisse, Picasso, and Braque. But that part of the public which distrusted the cubists because they seemed to draw away from the great tradition of Western art, which felt that Matisse's decorative painting was less serious, if not trivial, in the light of what art had been, turned to Rouault as possibly the greatest living painter. If one held to what might be termed "the rights of the subject," one could hardly come to any other choice.

Rouault thus held fast to objectivism, however distorted his image might seem in the eyes of old-fashioned realists. Picasso and Matisse never pushed on to total elimination of the object. In the heyday of the School of Paris one had to go a considerable distance from the studios of Montmartre and the Latin Quarter to find any flourishing group of abstract painters. Nevertheless the march away from facsimile painting continued. Paris had its minor schools working in the direction of non-objectivism. The most important was that of the purists.

After Cubism

The next logical step after cubism, the purists argued, was to dematerialize the object further and create paintings in which the abstract virtues of order, precision, and clarity transcended all other values. They thought thus to align painting with the industrial design of the period. Pictures must have the clean, precise, and sheer qualities that characterize airplanes and motor cars and mass-produced pots and pans. Subject-matter in a painting introduced elements that were accidental and improvised. These elements must be reduced to no more than intimations and suggestions.

But in achieving purification on the subject side, and compactness and precision on the technical side, the purists permitted their art to become thin and pale. They threw out so much of what is possible to brush and color and to man's emotion that purism is likely to be remembered in history as merely a stage in a revolutionary process. The chief one of the painters involved was Amédée Ozenfant. His associate Charles-Edouard Jeanneret successfully carried the purist principles over into architecture under his better-known name, Le Corbusier. Both men wrote books and affected the modern movement as theorists. Incidentally Ozenfant, who had reduced subject to a shadow, later said pithily that "a fine subject never did anybody any harm."

Of the painters associated—at times—with

Paris, Piet Mondrian, a Hollander, was the only one who in the early years, say before 1920, came to an effective and influential non-objectivism. When he returned to his own country he founded in 1917 with Theo van Doesburg the *de Stijl* group at Leiden. After going back to Paris at the close of World War I he painted in complete non-objectivism. He decreed that the picture rectangle could be divided only geometrically, and that the resulting patches of canvas could be painted only in flat colors. His became an art of precise adjustment of color areas, exquisite and tranquil—but most of the resources and effects of the historic painting art had been sacrificed. Mondrian and a Russian painter who had come to a similar abstract style, Kazimir Malevich, really had a better claim to the name "purist" than had Ozenfant.

The drift toward non-objectivism among the painters of Paris, except in the case of Mondrian, led into an alliance with revolutionaries of other sorts, particularly with the dadaists. The art known as dada need not be taken very seriously in the historical view. Its purpose was frankly the destruction of art and the discrediting of reason. Tired of the war, cynical by habit, perverse, the dadaists wanted chiefly to demolish the pretensions, principles, and reputations of realists, Cézannists, cubists, and other established schools. Some of the most gifted young painters of the time, neglected and disillusioned, joined with the pioneers of dada when that school widened its field and ran up a banner with a new name: *surréalisme*. The surrealists set out on a creative adventure of their own, composing in a realm of "dream reality." They were very intellectual and very Freudian.

Surrealist pictures were supposed to rise from the subconscious self. Some artists insisted on nothing less than complete automatism. A great deal of irresponsibility and perversity persisted from dada, and a great deal of embarrassingly personal data got onto canvas; but an authentic body of somewhat dreamlike painting resulted, too. Giorgio di Chirico painted what seemed like classic landscapes emptied of life, nostalgically remote, lucidly familiar. They are sometimes termed metaphysical landscapes. His most gifted companion was the Spaniard Joan Miró, who got away from the dream or hallucination element and (a little later, in the thirties) showed himself a finely creative near-abstractionist. Working with vaguely suggestive shapes in space, he produced pictures with formal unity, elegance, and visual freshness. Other artists who rose above the cramping conventions of the surrealist school were André Masson, Jean Lurçat, and Yves Tanguy. There were members, of course, who poured out their psychic contents in ways that attracted a wider and perhaps less educated public—most notably Salvador Dali.

Paris continued to draw students from all Europe and the Americas during the decade between the impressionist revolt and the opening of World War II. It was the center of experiment in the Western world, and most of the accomplishment within the expressionist revolution is easily related to the pioneering of Cézanne, van Gogh, Seurat, Gauguin, and the *fauves*. The only other considerable point of study and new departure was Munich. Generally speaking, the studios of Paris provided the routine training for routine-minded artists from all over the world and fed the creative spirit of the inventive ones. Some studied and stayed on in Paris: the Spaniard Picasso, the Italian Modigliani, and the Rumanian sculptor Brancusi. Others of the giants destined to make history partook of the Parisian training and inspiration, then returned to practice in their native lands. Such were Rivera of Mexico and the German sculptor Lehmbruck.

Germany, Italy, Russia, and England

Before World War I Germany came nearest to establishing an independent and creative school of modernism in painting. The subjective expressionists flourished from about 1905 to 1930. Their beginnings may be found in the history of a school called *Die Brücke*—"The Bridge"—in Dresden. It was with this group that Nolde, Schmidt-Rottluff, and Pechstein (already mentioned on page 615) were brought to international notice. Their method of painting was subjective, emotional, plastically strong—some

would say violent and wayward. Others practicing in this earliest expressionist school were Eric Heckel, Ernst Ludwig Kirchner, and Paula Modersohn-Becker. It is worth noting, as indicating the exceptional divergence from Paris, that the Scandinavian pioneer Edvard Munch was their first mentor, and that exotic sculpture had a strong influence upon them. It was less the Latin Cézanne than the Northern-born van Gogh who became their idol among the post-impressionists in France. Another who influenced them was the Belgian James Ensor, who had practiced as the *fauves* did some years before the *fauve* school was named in 1905, who dream-painted long before *surréalisme* was heard of. Oscar Kokoschka later became their greatest fellow-traveler.

The *Brücke* group in Dresden actually brought together its members and mapped its revolutionary program in 1904, before the *fauves* exhibited together in 1905 in Paris. The second notable school of revolutionaries in Germany, the *Blaue Reiter* or "Blue Knights" group in Munich, came to life only in 1911. A preceding organization had long been in touch with the French *fauves* and had exhibited their works. The Blue Knights wanted to go further in insurgency. The most famous members were Vasili Kandinski, Franz Marc, and (little known at first) Paul Klee. This movement, the reader will notice, developed just before the outbreak of World War I. After the war's end members of the *Blaue Reiter* group were to shape art theory at the third of Germany's historic centers of modernism, the Bauhaus, established first in 1918 at Weimar and later moved to Dessau. The Bauhaus constituted far more than a school of painting. It was actually a radical architectural-industrial school. Its influence was felt in industrial design and in architectural design in all countries. Its painter-teachers were world leaders. They brought to the Bauhaus the distinction of being the world's center of experiment in non-objective painting. They were Kandinski, Klee, the German-American Lyonel Feininger, and the Polish Alexei von Javlenski. It was Kandinski who was the pioneer and the total abstractionist among them.

Vasili Kandinski, born in Russia in 1866, was

Kandinski: *Improvisation No. 30. Chicago Art Institute*

in 1900 producing pictures hardly more distinctive than those of any other impressionist, although marked by more than usual coherence. Slowly his style metamorphosed from a realistic phase into a decorative-illustrational phase with peasant-art affinities. Then came an increasing reach for underlying abstract rhythms, until in 1910 he was experimenting in formal organizations with only the vaguest recollective reference to nature. Finally there were long series of "improvisations," "impressions," and "compositions," sometimes wholly abstract, more often with faint hints of subject-matter.

For a time Kandinski worked from the hypothesis of a visual scale corresponding to the scale of sound vibrations, and he used musical terminology freely. There was much studio talk about painting as color-music. But his later theory was based less on the assumption of a correspondence in scale, more on the vision of an art parallel to music in its independence from nature, but equally free in creative expression according to its own slowly unfolding and particular laws.

Kandinski was an avowed mystic and definitely described his paintings as soul-expression. Those who distrust any but "natural" sight and intellectual meaning deny his compositions anything but a sensuous loveliness. But the audience has steadily increased that apprehends in his pictures a profound formal expressiveness, accepting this even as an echo of cosmic order.

Of the *Improvisation No. 30* reproduced here the artist once wrote: "The 'content' of the picture is what the spectator *lives* or *feels* while

Marc: *The Three Horses. Formerly Folkwang Museum, Essen*

under the effect of the form and color combinations." He explained a definite intention for each element of the organization: the cross-like main motives, the plane arrangement, the color areas in relation to two main centers of interest, and the interplay of lines and contours. Regarding the roughly indicated cannon in one corner, he said: "I did not intend to give a representation of war."

Paul Klee was a lesser figure, though perhaps a more widely beloved one. He is known almost exclusively by modestly small pictures, scattered over a great range of territory from absolute abstraction to surrealistic objectivity and grotesques. He was one of those artists who produced pictures which seem at first glance no more consequential than the scratch-drawings of children, but each with a teasing form appeal. Apparently everything he touched, whatever the subject-matter or lack thereof, has a hint of formal magic. For a time Klee was grouped with the *surréalistes* of Paris, although his fragile dream-fantasies antedated the formation of the school by many years.

The Nazi regime in Germany discouraged or effaced the several modernist groups, according to the degree of their radicalism—it actually closed the Bauhaus and suppressed its activities. (The artists there had not found near-abstract art incompatible with democratic-socialistic ideals.) The German museums which had installed the world's finest public displays of post-realistic art were again remade and subordinated the moderns to "more normal" manifestations, and particularly to something considered typical Nordic expression. The expressionists were exiled or curbed, and examples of their work were exposed in Berlin in a "Chamber of Horrors."

Thus the hands that mark the progress of art evolution can be artificially stayed. But two of the less radical of the insurgents later came in for both German and international appreciation: Karl Hofer and Franz Marc (who had been killed in World War I). Marc had been influenced by the cubists, and he practiced for a time in a field close to absolute abstraction. But his later fame has been won through pictures in which the formal rhythms are clearly built around familiar animal forms. Perhaps the favorite is *The Three Horses*, wherein an explicit underlying structure is made manifest in agreeable linear rhythms with elementary tonal counterpoint.

The leading countries of Europe all contributed essentially to the modern movement in its later years. Italy, where the futurists created such excitement about 1910 with a theory and a method which turned out to produce a superficial variation of realistic illustration, sent key men to the international center at Paris—most notably Giorgio di Chirico and Amedeo Modigliani. The latter's figure paintings, which would be stark except for their linear harmonies (hinting of his great admiration for the Italian primitives), are among the least frightening of the products of expressionism. They became immensely popular as soon as the artist had tragically died in 1920.

The Russians, besides contributing the leader Kandinski to the German school, were represented in Paris by Marc Chagall, who committed what the realists considered some of the wildest excesses of expressionism. He is represented also by some of the richest and most decorative of imaginative painting, in the range between naïve primitivism and the dream-fantasies of the *surréalistes*. Hans Arp, an Alsatian who later changed his name to Jean Arp and threw in his lot with the revolutionary schools in Paris, was a pioneer (somewhat under Kandinski's tutelage); he helped especially to develop abstract sculpture—as in his pieces named *Human Concretions*. These are sheer-surfaced, pleasing in contour, and plastically alive. They are suggestive of human forms at some time antecedent to the growth of limbs, features, etc. Arp and Mondrian were founders of a group named the Neo-Plasticists, which held together for a time and then disappeared into the larger development that is abstract expressionism.

In England a long path of progress might be marked, from the cautious insurgency of Walter Sickert and P. Wilson Steer, pioneers in the famous "protest" society organized in 1885, the New English Art Club; to the vigorous selective realism of Sir William Orpen and the borderline intellectualism of Augustus John; through varied phases of frankly reflected French post-impressionism; to the welter of unfocused experiment evident in London just before World War II. The body of British painting of the half-century after 1885 is singularly weak in grasp of those formal values which were at the heart of the achievement in France and Germany; and even the English would be at a loss to suggest a painter out of those fifty years who approached world importance. Most gifted and original, perhaps, was Paul Nash, who markedly wove abstract patterns but within limits set by an intellectual approach and a draftsman's (rather than a colorist's) technique. The national tradition remained strongly realistic or neo-romantic—and the Royal Academy flourished—long after most of Europe and America had moved toward the abstract. In England the sculptor Henry Moore outdistanced every painter (in international estimation), though the canvases of Graham Sutherland and of John Piper were well known by the nineteen-fifties for originality, sensitivity, and mastery of plastic organization. No two painters in the modern idiom could be more unlike. Sutherland's pictures are well within the definition of surrealism, conceived out of the subconscious, dealing with shapes (seldom pleasing at first) in space, extremely distorted if matched against nature. Piper's landscapes, on the other hand, can generally be traced to an outside origin; but the artist's emotion, his intensification of some symbolic feature, his disciplining of surface elements while holding to the structure and bone of the object, bring him safely over into the expressionist field.

Modernism in America

In the United States painting and sculpture in the twentieth century have been more independent, although there has been only one painter of stature comparable to that of Matisse, Picasso, or Kandinski. In the years before the recognition of Cézanne's significance a few painters had pioneered in their own distinctive ways—some of them, notably Eakins and Twachtman, inspired directly by contacts with the life of Paris but inventive enough to touch on

Weber: *The Broken Tree*

markedly original expression; others, particularly Ryder, individualistic and remote. But it was the Armory Show in New York in 1913 that shocked America into awareness of French and German modernism, at the same time bringing about a focus of American effort.

The routine showing—disregarding the academicians and other realists—could be illustrated by groups obviously connected with the successive French schools: a large number of competent Cézannists; a vigorous reflection of fauvism, not without native flavor; a small group of derivative cubists; and finally, and most rich in independent creativeness, a group of adventurers in nonrepresentational or near-abstract fields. It is among these last, painters seeking an art self-contained, owing little to literary and associative values, that one finds the names likely to survive in history.

The group of creative insurgents who, immediately before 1913, were carrying on the main tradition of international radicalism included Marsden Hartley, Max Weber, Walt Kuhn, and Abraham Walkowitz. Hartley, who had lived through the early struggle against the forces of conservatism and had achieved moderate success in several phases of modernism, once said, "I have no interest in the subject-matter of a picture, not the slightest." But during the decade before his death in 1943 he turned back to subjects familiar from his youth in New England; and, without becoming factual, he wove the spirit of scenes and objects into pictures simple, strong, and formally vital. He seemed to become more American because he moved into a line of formal endeavor that came down from the mystic Ryder, and he lifted himself to a place among the top few native painters of his era.

The one highly original and consistent success among the American moderns was that of John Marin. No stranger to the work of the *fauves* and the cubists in his early painting years, he nevertheless became the most individualistic of artists and by 1920 had created a style so per-

Marin: *Wind on Land and Sea*

sonal as to be unmistakable in any gallery. He took from nature what he wanted, but his finest pictures are only a step this side of abstraction. No other artist in his time used the water-color medium quite so electrically. The pictures are fresh, spontaneous, lyric. They are also vigorous and intense, sometimes explosively alive. What is essential in the landscape or seascape is there: its rock structure, its architecture. But it is got down in a calligraphic equivalent and covered over with washes that are musically played with, rhythmically organized. Marin's was the top expressionist achievement in America up to the time of his death in 1953. In his final years his landscapes in oil seemed to many observers as intensely alive and beautiful as his water-colors. The reader will find an illustration of Marin's typically expressive and moving *Lower Manhattan,* an early water-color, among the color plates preceding the Introduction to this book.

If there was anything approaching a "school"

of American modernism in the years 1920–50, its character has eluded description. The United States was the home of individual achievements, of experiment in numberless directions. There was no norm. Among those who clung to subject-matter in a substantial way Yasuo Kuniyoshi, an American born of Japanese parents, was most able, by reason of an accomplished expressionist technique. Maurice Sterne leaned in the same direction. John Carroll retained much that the wilder moderns would have sacrificed in the search for plastic order, but his paintings were endowed with formal rhythm, and he distorted where distortion lent meaning to his subject—or brought increase of mood. Edward Hopper simplified down to the point where his city scenes, not so much distorted as emptied out, afforded the feel of the place, the *genius loci,* as had no one's "views" before him. Henry Mattson found his inspiration in a love of the sea; by some intuitive magic he put into his seascapes a sort

Mattson: *Wings of the Morning. Metropolitan Museum of Art*

of mystic splendor. His *Wings of the Morning* indicates how strong may be the abstract rhythm within types of painting not markedly non-realistic.

In the other direction in those decades, among artists who served notice in their pictures that subject was secondary, outstanding was Georgia O'Keeffe. Her approximations of flower forms and of landscapes have a clean, clear beauty almost geometrical. Added is a feminine exquisiteness of finish. Lyonel Feininger, who had formed his style during a forty-year stay in Europe—most notably at the Bauhaus, 1919–33—returned to America in 1936 and practiced an enchanting art that dealt more with the means to formal expression, especially with tilting and intersecting planes, than with anything out of nature as commonly viewed. He seldom lost touch with the sea and ships as subjects—or, at one time, skyscrapers—but the picture was above all a formal arrangement. Generally it was delicate in color, seemingly fragile in construction. Among younger men in those years Joseph de Martini was notable for the way in which he

worked gradually from the selective realist's view of the object to that of the modern who seeks plastic equivalents.

History in the two decades between 1930 and 1950 was made not only in the marketplace center that is New York but in communities scattered over the United States. Especially productive were groups painting on the West Coast. Of these the groups centered at Portland, Oregon, and Seattle, Washington, were most original. Facing west to the Orient, they seemed to absorb a little of the magic of Chinese and Japanese painting; or perhaps it was only an attitude toward art that was transmitted. At any rate a member of the younger generation, Morris Graves, found a new way of statement—and acceptance beyond the borders of America. Kenneth Callahan, too, lifted his work into a modern formal appeal, while in subject-matter he was constantly aware of what the inner eye rather than the outer reported. An exchange continually recurring might be cited: Darrel Austin went eastward from Portland to New York and practiced a wholly individualistic, sometimes fan-

Graves: *Wounded Gull. Phillips Gallery, Washington*

tastic art, expressionist in technique, vivid and jewel-like in color; and Mark Tobey left New York to settle in Seattle in 1923, to find his Europe-derived manner of painting transformed. He also studied in the Orient. His near-abstractions and their influence, in Europe as well as in America, however, belong to a movement summarized a few pages ahead.

For a time, especially in the nineteen-thirties and -forties, the old quarrel between modernists and realists flared up in the United States and was made to appear a quarrel between foreign art and native art. A group of talented painters became famous as advocates of "The American Scene." The depicters of the actual rural scene joined with certain realistic satirists of city life in what came to be known as the American Scene school. Together they attacked "foreign charlatans and Frenchified art." They argued that the human and social values of native illustrational

art outweighed the nebulous and perhaps non-existent values of what the moderns termed plastic excellence. Of course, the mass media, newspapers and popular magazines, sided with them and gave countless pages to glorifying the regional realism of Grant Wood, John Steuart Curry, Thomas Benton, Reginald Marsh, and a host of lesser topical painters. Nevertheless, modernism continued to gain; the pleasing smooth technique lost ground to expressionist impetuousness; the exact illustrational imaging gave way as the beauties of near-abstract formal composing brought about a lesser valuation of subject. By 1950 the moderns had so far won their objectives that "American Scene" was thereafter hardly heard of. There was enough formal achievement in occasional canvases to make it certain that some products of the school would live on in museums and in popular prints. Grant Wood especially, with a feeling for pictorial architecture combined with (on occasion) a relish for ironic truths about American life—as in a devastating painting entitled *Daughters of the Revolution* and in *American Gothic*—seemed sure of survival. Wood died in 1942, at the age of fifty.

A second flare-up over art occurred in the nineteen-thirties, when "socially conscious" painting became a national issue. The division between those who wanted full liberty for the artist and those who wanted satiric and propagandist art controlled from above was pointed up by the fact that under the government's WPA project in 1933–36 as many as 5200 artists, including most of the creative painters, were being supported publicly. (No other event ever gave American art so great an impulse forward.) A few artists doubtless abused the privilege, thus secured to them, of painting as they wished. A few had Communist leanings; certainly many others were class-conscious and used their art to call attention to social evils, whether in slums, in courtrooms, or in legislative halls. What came out of the activity as permanently valuable was the art of a few painters who had added formal understanding to their high technical equipment. William Gropper, intuitively gifted, scored especially with his paintings and prints of the national Senate in action. Ben Shahn, in a very personal style of painting, commented bitingly on many controversial events, from the Sacco-Vanzetti case to the latest labor crisis, always from the anti-Fascist side.

Modern Mexican Painting

If in these pages there has been a tendency to credit the moderns of 1880–1950 with making their more impressive advance in the mastering of nonrepresentational elements, it is not necessarily to imply that painting with human and social content had come to an end. The outstanding gain had been in the discovery or recovery of deep and musical values in art near abstraction; but the special enjoyments in that range of art are merely different from, not destructive of, the painting that has theme and meaning. In this category Mexico led the modern advance.

It is to the credit of a group of Mexicans that they have, without weakening of the abstract structure, restored art that is socially meaningful, even instructive and thought-provoking. They have widened the boundaries of modern painting, showing how the grasp upon formal organization can be made to serve within mural-art limitations; exhibiting, moreover, the first notable union of regional or social content with organizational mastery.

Diego Rivera and José Clemente Orozco were the outstanding creative figures of the Mexican group. Rivera studied in Spain and in Paris, found in Cézanne's pictures the magic that determined the future course of his art, and returned to Mexico to plunge into the workers' rebellion. His best work was in murals designed for schools and public buildings in Mexico, utilizing native materials and usually flavored strongly with socialistic ideas and propagandist purpose. There are a number of Rivera's representative works on walls in the United States, but with less of the characteristic directness and conviction. Orozco was a more original figure, with a strong mastery of plastic effect, and he was equally devoted to art as a reflection of the workers' world, if not as a weapon to help secure its coming. The finest of his murals were executed in Mexico, but he worked in the United States also, where a characteristic and moving series can be seen at Dartmouth College. Orozco died in 1949 at the age of sixty-five, still an uncompromising "radical," creator of a vigorous, not to say violent style not likely ever to be imitated. Whatever his limitations, he achieved frequently a sort of majestic largeness and power, well illustrated in the detail shown on page 638, from one of the murals at Dartmouth College Library. As in the case of Picasso's *Guernica*, the average observer may well miss the significance of the daring theme of the series and yet be satisfied with the aesthetic experience.

While Rivera and Orozco worked with themes "of a certain magnitude," others of the Mexicans ranged over the whole territory from gay abstractions to monumental story-pictures. Carlos Mérida was on the nonrepresentational side. David Alfaro Siqueiros, on the other hand,

Orozco: Detail from mural series,
Dartmouth College Library, Hanover, New Hampshire

painted some of the heaviest and most powerful propaganda pictures known to modernism—and some of the most savage. Rufino Tamayo had become by 1950 one of the giants of Mexican creative painting. Both he and Siqueiros had proved themselves outstanding muralists in the tradition of Rivera and Orozco.

Other Latin American countries harbored na- tive schools of painting and illustrated the divi- sion between academic-realist art and modern experiment. But no school developed in a way that seemed to concern the rest of the world. In two or three countries the Mexican example was potent, with a consequent trend toward expres- sion of native life in terms of local historical (generally Indian) idiom; but the French influ-

Brooks: *No. 27, 1950. Whitney Museum of American Art, New York*

ence was strong too. A few individuals impressed gallery-goers in international circles—most notably Cândido Portinari of Brazil, the Chilean Matta, and Wilfredo Lam of Cuba. Portinari might be recognized as typically Latin American, but Matta and Lam had their training in Parisian surrealism and later arrived at individual styles still suggestive of dream-reality. Matta especially moved toward abstraction.

Abstract Expressionism

About the year 1955 a truth transcending national accomplishments came clear. Abstract expressionism had become a universal mode of painting and sculpture. Museum directors, critics, and artists were using the term as once they had employed the label "cubism," or "surrealism."

The world of art observers could see abstract expressionism in *avant-garde* museums and galleries, and especially at the great annual and biennial exhibitions of painting and sculpture. Not only had abstract expressionism become the most easily identifiable "style" since cubism; it had apparently capped the progress of revolution as initiated by Cézanne three generations earlier. The spread of creative centers over most of the world, and the waning of France as leader in the nurturing of artists, were pointed up by the appearance of Americans and Germans, Britons and Italians, Chileans and Mexicans and Russians, in the ranks of internationally known practitioners. Paris was not outranked as a world center of art life; but the new work and the impetus toward an international style were coming from elsewhere.

It was widely conceded that there could be

Tobey: *Agate World*. Tempera. *Seattle Art Museum*

no going back to painting as it had been before Cézanne. It was also largely accepted that significant international practice had continued since 1905 in two lines: one leading to an art so nearly nonobjective that only the description "abstract expressionism" could properly label it; the other leading to a more emotional or subjective expressionism, in which the object remained as symbol, signal, or image. This meant that the word "abstraction" was being employed in both its meanings: as implying a totally nonobjective expression; and as labeling those paintings in which an essential emotion or impact was abstracted or drawn out from an object or subject still detectable in the picture.

In any case, for sheer pictorial interest and aesthetic "shock" the abstract expressionists were out ahead of all other groups. In the search for original pictorial forms the young, adventurous, and competently trained painters were scoring in

Winter: *Signs before Green. Kleemann Galleries, New York*

this field that was large enough to encompass the followers of the original French expressionists—be they called *fauves* or not—and the German expressionists in the Kandinski-Marc line, and notably the Americans who had found inspiration in the Far East.

The American artist who had most influence internationally was Mark Tobey of the Seattle group. His "white-line painting" followed directly upon his study with a Chinese painter and calligrapher. What the observer saw was a picture that had its origin in the artist's consciousness of the objective world—*Mountains; The Street; Above the Earth*—but a picture that conveyed an inner vision by means of a spatial composition, fixed, in this phase of his work, more especially by a tracing over with calligraphic white lines. This was but one phase of Tobey's accomplishment, but the one that first caught the attention of European artists. Other Americans who rose to the top group of so-called abstract

expressionists at about the same time were Jackson Pollock, Robert Motherwell, Mark Rothko (born in Russia), Theodoros Stamos (Greek-born), and James Brooks. There had been four painters dating back to pioneer experiment with marked originality in this field: Arthur B. Carles, Stuart Davis, Raymond Jonson, and Karl Knaths. All had been active abstractionists as early as the nineteen-thirties. Hans Hofmann, a German-American, both painter and teacher, had extraordinary influence on young American artists in the field of abstract expressionism.

In Germany, Fritz Winter (who once had studied with Kandinski at the famous Bauhaus) developed one of the most agreeable personal styles, tending toward the purely nonobjective, from about 1949, when he was released after years of almost incredible deprivation in Siberian work-camps. His organizations in space are at once alive and quietly restful, and somehow, subjectless, they seem familiar and meaningful.

In France, Pierre Soulages showed exceptional power and intensity, though his images or symbols from life were so vague that the meaning of the picture was left to be half guessed, half conceived by the observer. In his painting, as in that of certain Americans, there was a hinted awareness of the world-wide interest in outer space, of its exploration, and of the differences between life on earth (even in the machine age) and life in a spatial universe newly comprehended. Other Parisians—Georges Mathieu, Hans Hartung (born German), and Nicolas de Staël (born Russian)—reinforced the impression that a new conception of forms in space had entered into the consciousness of artists. Cubism was very little recollected, and indeed a northern style had prevailed, as against the Latin that had so long dominated internationalism. Certain French writers made the point that the Americans had arrived at their sort of abstract expressionism after study of the Orient and under the influence of Kandinski; and that the French had arrived at practically the same position through an unbroken tradition in which the chief agents, a generation back, had been the surrealists.

Another German, K. R. H. Sonderborg, heir to whatever riches of abstractionism remained from the era of the masters of the Bauhaus and influenced, too, by study of Far Eastern art, served to set in the public mind the advance away from cubism. His paintings especially intimate the new awareness of outer space.

We are, of course, at the very edge of history here, on the border of speculation, in danger of prophecy. What history can say is that in the middle decade of the twentieth century the most vital and creative international group emerged with a fresh understanding of the spatial problems of the painter, and produced an *œuvre* agreeable to a very wide audience, an *œuvre* of which illustrations on pages 639–41 are typical.

In Sculpture a Revolution

Michelangelo had laid down his tools in the mid-sixteenth century. He had in a sense disrupted the history of sculpture: he had been so great that he overshadowed every contemporary sculptor, and after his death his shadow still seemed to reduce in size those who succeeded him, through two centuries or more. There were a few mannerists, as already noted, and then came the adventure of the baroque. In the north the Gothic impetus waned but slowly. The schools of woodcarving in Germany prolonged the production of appealing religious figures, but finally became hardly more than folk-art centers, as at Nuremberg and Oberammergau. In France, where the baroque style had been welcomed at first, its most damaging tendencies were soon restrained. A neoclassicism prevailed; its realism was at first stressed, and culminated in the work of Houdon; its classic calm and chill ended in the art of Canova. In all those years between 1550 and 1900 there was only this secondary activity. After 1550—unless Houdon be excepted—neither Italy nor France nor Germany nor Spain produced a figure worthy to stand in the first rank. In England from the inception of the Renaissance until the twentieth century there was not a sculptor whose name need be recalled. A good case could be made out for the thesis that the Western world bred not a single sculptural genius between Michelangelo and Rodin—some would say between Michelangelo and Lehmbruck; that is, between 1550 and 1910.

Auguste Rodin (1840–1917) is most fairly considered as the final figure in the march of realism. He refined naturalism to the last point in statues so lifelike that he had to prove that he had not actually taken casts from the human body. In other works he accepted the impressionist theories, fixing in clay or stone the momentary attitude or gesture, and playing with the surface for effects of shimmering light; and indeed the stippled or rippled finish affords a pretty vibration unprecedented in earlier work. It was from these beautifully modulated, impressionistic things, including especially statues such as *The Kiss,* shown here, *The Eternal Idol,* and *Pygmalion and Galatea,* that he gained on three continents the reputation of being the greatest modern sculptor. There was a luminous, a soft quality about the figures and groups which workmen turned into stone from his clay models—he

Rodin: *The Kiss*

was not himself a stonecutter—and altogether an aura of caressability. He also was a great portraitist, and there were brutally powerful pieces such as the famous *Thinker,* and pictorially ambitious groups such as *The Burghers of Calais.* In a very few late statues Rodin pushed over into a sort of subjective expressionism, beyond the confines of realism, as in the *Balzac,* page 644 (which Paris officially and spectacularly rejected). Rodin's impressionistic pieces had enormous influence upon young sculptors in the rest of the world at the century's end. His most successful French fol-

lower was Charles Despiau, who became a remarkably sensitive and revealing portraitist. Students flocked to Paris from all the continents, especially from America, and they learned to finish their pieces with Rodinesque sparkle.

The true revolutionary change came about 1900, when an international movement got under way toward the overthrow of impressionism—and all other varieties of sculpture dependent upon transcribed natural effects—and toward the achievement of nonrepresentational values. A few men began to simplify the masses of their work, returning to the natural blockiness of sculpture. They definitely, even self-consciously, worked to restore the stony look of the statue (as against the light, painty aspects that had developed with the lapse into clay modeling). As regards subject-matter, they discounted the surface view and distorted freely for characteristic structure and intensified feeling.

In short, the twentieth-century sculptor became an expressionist. He became careless as to nature in order to express at a higher degree of intensity (1) his own feelings, (2) the characteristic values of the sculptural medium, and (3) the inner as against the surface character of the model.

In France, Aristide Maillol, who lived until 1944, was a pioneer in the process of simplification and return to typical sculptural largeness and reposefulness. He achieved also a certain measure of abstract rhythm, although he seldom ventured into arbitrary distortion of nature's forms. Antoine Bourdelle departed even less from the currently popular impressionistic canons, but he had a sound architectural sense. He produced some compactly designed panels, and two or three of his free-standing groups are among the most popular exhibits within "the new sculpture" by reason of an exceptional aspect of power and animation. The truer revolutionary was Henri Gaudier-Brzeska, a genius who was killed in World War I at the age of twenty-four. His few mature works are instinct with the love of heavy sculptural materials as such, and with a passion for expression in massive, even mountainous terms.

In France after the First World War the leader of the moderns was the Rumanian Constantin Brancusi, who at times cleared sculpture of almost the last trace of representation, achieving forms affective by their exquisite geometrical poise and their intensified sensuous charm. It is doubtful that many of his abstractions will rank as immortal works, but he did more than anyone else to open a new field of extreme formalism to sculptors; and his "statues" possess a distinctive appeal to observers who are not still bound in fealty to the realists. He was perhaps the first to deserve the name "abstract expressionist" in the field of sculpture. His *Bird,* hardly more than a sheer,

Rodin: *Balzac. Rodin Museum, Paris*

subtly tapered shaft suggesting flight—purified of such material parts as head, wings, feet, etc.—is his best-known work (see page 646).

The Germans pioneered in expressionist sculpture and produced, in Wilhelm Lehmbruck, its foremost master. Among the early radicals Franz Metzner had been notable. But the one genius—not only in German but possibly in all twentieth-century sculpture to date—was Lehmbruck, who began work about 1900, spent a decade at Düsseldorf, then two or three years in Paris, returned to Germany, and for a time lived in Switzerland during the war years. He committed suicide in his Berlin studio in 1919, at the age of thirty-eight. His work—"only a torso," as his biographer puts it—has the typical modern directness and strength, but with extreme sensitivity.

Lehmbruck: *Kneeling Figure. Museum of Modern Art, New York*

Certain of the figures and busts are characterized by the heaviness, by the organization of elementary masses, that belongs to the first phase of revolt against naturalistic overelaboration. Later Lehmbruck developed a method of elongation of forms, evidently out of a search for elusive sculptural values similar to Cézanne's search for the "plastic realization" in painting. Most famous of the examples in this technique of distortion by attenuation is the *Kneeling Figure*. One version of the over-lifesize figure is at the Museum of Modern Art in New York, and the room in which it is placed seems to gain dignity, quietude, and splendor from the statue.

Of later sculptors in Germany, Georg Kolbe was most appreciated both at home and abroad. He began as an impressionist, gradually simplified his way of statement and strengthened the abstract structure, emerging in the nineteen-twenties as a world leader of the moderate wing of the radicals. Ernst Barlach also traveled an acceptable middle way.

Similar tempered insurgency is illustrated in the work of the Swedish sculptor Carl Milles (long resident in the United States). He reached a higher degree of expression by surface formalization, in harmony with architectural environment, rather than by the heedless subjective-emotional approach. The Yugoslav Ivan Meštrović became a popular international figure by similar considered and slight deviation from the older formulas. His masterpiece is a series of stylized figures incidental to a memorial chapel at Cavtat near Ragusa.

In modern England sculpture took its place among the creative arts for the first time well after the turn of the century. Eric Gill, with an exceptional "feel for the stone," was the leading native figure, although Frank Dobson showed a more determined reach for the monumental plastic rhythm, along the line of Maillol-like simplification. But the man who fought the fight for modernism in England, setting artistic London by the ears again and again, was the American-born Jacob Epstein.

Epstein went to London at the age of twenty-five, in 1905, and was an individualistic creator in the following fifty years, going forward at first with the "wildest" experimenters and most sensitive innovators, but again lapsing back to an impressionistic technique and aim. His most characteristic work is, perhaps, in the field of psychologic portraiture, with a somewhat exaggerated clay-pellet technique. Closer to the main current of modernism are the monumental figures upon public buildings in London, sculpturally expressive but sufficiently architectural.

As for those who abandoned "reality" in the fullest expressionist sense, in England, Henry Moore had achieved supreme position by the

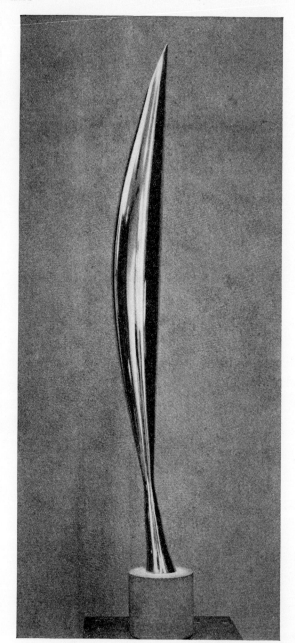

Brancusi: *Bird in Space*. Bronze. *Museum of Modern Art, New York*

mid-nineteen-thirties. He went on to gain an international reputation as the most powerful and one of the most original, if disturbing, of modernists. His phase of full nonobjectivism did not last long. Rather he is known by a long series of

Lachaise: *Head. Collection
Mrs. Q. A. Shaw McKean,
Boston*

figures of men and women in distorted approximations, most often recumbent. These pleased and moved a growing audience that felt an elemental melodic appeal. At the same time they puzzled and distressed many observers who granted a validity even to Brancusi's purified forms or Lehmbruck's attenuated but reposeful figures. No one else provoked quite so much debate as to whether the figures—based obviously upon the beautiful human body—were perversely lumpy and twisted deformations or, on the other hand, approximations cunningly re-formed to evoke a profound sculptural emotion and a sense of elemental earthy humanness. In any case Moore's preoccupation with the stone (or wood) could not do other than return the art toward fundamentals; and his concern with ovoid,

cubical, and spherical forms answered a deep-felt need to experience beginning things, simple, reposeful things. He once said, "There are universal shapes to which everybody is subconsciously conditioned." His art may become eloquent to some who have resisted his "distortions" of the body, when the full significance of that pronouncement is understood. An illustration characteristic of his middle-period work, a very small version in lead of the recumbent-figure theme, is on page 599.

If the United States had lost to England a great creative figure in Epstein, it had gained another in the coming of Gaston Lachaise from France in 1906. At the time of his death in New York in 1935 he was recognized as an elder master among American modernists. He

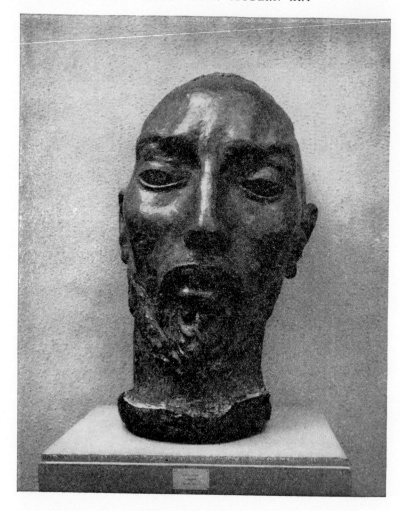

De Creeft: *Himalaya.*
Beaten lead.
*Whitney Museum
of American Art*

left a body of work ranging from sensitive impressionism, through strongly formalized simplifications, to ruthless distortion for plastic intensification. The head (page 647) is typical of his portrait work. Its simple stone-heavy "feel" was revolutionary at a time when portraits all took on the lightness and restlessness of the clay. Among those who added abstract sculptural values to a "natural" statement, in a guarded modernism calculated not to offend the realistic-minded, William Zorach scored notably. In the more radical direction, and known throughout the world as an innovator, was Alexander Archipenko, a Ukrainian who had been a leading figure in Germany before he came to the United States in 1924. He indulged in more radical experimentation in sculptural mediums and methods than has any other modern. His happiest results, many feel, were in a near-abstract sort of composition derived from the human figure, manipulated for mass-relationships, yet with deft capitalization of linear harmonies and of the sensuous surface values of metals or glazed clay.

By 1950 the creation of new techniques and the utilization of materials not before familiar in the halls of sculpture had transformed the look of modernist shows. Yet nothing could change the fact that the early and great post-realistic advance had been in the direction of recovery of the stone feeling and the achievement of ample and massive effects. In England, Gill and Moore particularly had served to restore respect for the stone. In the United States a dozen men served in the same way; in two of them the passion for

Marini: *Horse and Rider.*
Bronze.
Lillie P. Bliss bequest,
Museum of Modern Art,
New York

the basic rock material carried over into the finished work so successfully that they will be remembered as pioneers. John B. Flannagan spoke of "the eternal nature of the stone itself" as first among the virtues revealed in his successful pieces. Polygnotos Vagis, also an intuitive, said that he never began a carving until the block of stone itself suggested the subject, even compelled him to it. He felt, in a sense, that he released the stone, not a "subject." The works of these two men—in the midst of so much sculpture that is airy, or like grille-work, or spiky—seems basic wherever encountered. José de Creeft, if not

quite so given to proclaiming the stone, achieved something like top place in the American galleries, with products equally massive and elemental, during the nineteen-forties. He was able moreover, in a piece such as the *Himalaya,* shown here, to add overtones of spiritual feeling and ancient thought. Somehow de Creeft, more than any of his fellows, touched upon basic sculptural grandeur.

From Europe two additional figures had emerged to claim international attention, both far from abstract expression but incorporating into their works the form values without which modern art would not be modern. The Italian Marino Marini, working sensitively in portraiture but better known for a series of statues of horse-and-rider, claimed the interest of all lovers of the sculptural art. Harking back to antiquity for certain of his surface effects, he no less surely belonged among the moderns in his intuitive (or perhaps cunning) use of distortion and intensification. Regarding the statue on page 649, it should be explained that the intensification of emotion is due somewhat to the fact that Marini had watched observantly the effect upon peasants and horses of bombing planes flying overhead. The second sculptor to claim international attention in the early nineteen-fifties was Alberto Giacometti, a Swiss who finally settled in Paris. His figures, elongated and often carrying a somewhat humorous implication, were strewn about, in small size, in space that somehow became part of a coherent sculptural organization. The single figures seemed unimportant and seldom had personality. But the figure and surroundings had compositional effectiveness, even formal magic. Giacometti, in his somewhat larger single figures, can be seen to have gained something from the attenuated forms cast in bronze by the ancient Etruscans, and his work of this order has influenced a considerable number of younger sculptors.

Abstract expressionism did not occupy the main courses of the sculptural field in mid-century as it had the main courses of painting. The great names were still those of expressionists whose aims were far from nonobjectivism: Moore, Marini, de Creeft, and the others just mentioned. Though the number of exhibiting abstract sculptors increased each year during the early nineteen-fifties, no one artist emerged as having gone beyond the near-abstractions of Brancusi or the "concretions" of Jean (formerly Hans) Arp. One man only made a world reputation, and that with a sort of product that escapes all the historical definitions of sculpture. The American Alexander Calder, who, his friends thought, should have known better because he was the son of the respected traditional sculptor A. Stirling Calder, began by creating figures with bent wire, and then went on to abstractions called mobiles. The

wire figures were like the outlines of sculpture, with the solid sculptural core removed. They were spirited and appealing—often humorous. The mobiles were constructions of wires, rods, and shaped sheets of metal, with occasionally a solid suspended part. They were designed to hang in the air, where any drift of wind turned them slowly. That they had a fascinating grace can hardly be denied, since they enjoyed an international vogue through the decades following 1930. But we are again at the very limits of history. The future alone can tell whether the definition of sculpture will be widened to include these moving constructions. And such is the case as regards stabiles, another invention of Calder's, and as regards many of the newly introduced forms of metal "sculpture." The welded constructions, the wrought-iron "figures," and the wire-cage contraptions, all created with sincere conviction out of personal vision, simply have not arrived at the stature—as arts—that would give them place in a world history.

Modern Architecture

In the period between 1600 and 1900 architecture had in general lapsed into that strange sort of imitation known as eclecticism. Toward the end engineers and builders developed new principles and new materials, and modified the structural core of the building, but the academic architect had the last word and draped over the front one of his stereotyped façades, in Gothic or Greek, Renaissance or Romanesque, Byzantine or Roman.

It seems to the present historian that each of these types had validity in its own time and should be discussed in relation to that time; furthermore, it is unimportant that the builders of the Panthéon in Paris and Grant's Tomb in New York chose a "classic" style, and that some of the best universities chose the Gothic. The structures usually paraded as the masterpieces of eighteenth- and nineteenth-century architecture, the Madeleine and the Brandenburg Gate, Blenheim Palace and the Houses of Parliament, are records of what builders did when there was no

"Falling Waters" House, Bear Run, Pennsylvania. Frank Lloyd Wright, architect

basically creative architecture. It will perhaps seem to future generations a matter of amazement that the authorities in the nineteenth century agreed that all possible styles had been invented, giving architectural students portfolios of historic façades to be adapted as masks, believing that engineering is something to be hidden, not expressed.

The story of architecture is important again in the late nineteenth century. Then the ranks of the eclectics were broken. The first burst of creative insurgency came in America when Louis Sullivan declared war on the imitation of past styles, particularly castigating the pseudo-classicists of the nineties. It was Sullivan who started the battle-cry that has sounded so often in the sixty years since: "Form must follow function." He had added training as an engineer to his education as a decorator, and his first effort was to get back to expression based on engineering. Each building material, each part, Sullivan pointed out, had a structural function determined by the engineer; let it be declared, not hidden behind historical surface forms. It is hardly too much to say that in the machine age each building part functions as a machine part; let the dynamics of it be declared.

Forty years after Sullivan's first efforts, one finds the later American skyscrapers that do express simply and marvelously their materials and their engineering, their soaring and their beehive function; and houses that are space made livable, with a concrete wall here, a glass screen there, no longer subject to the tyranny of the masonry.

It was Frank Lloyd Wright, at first a student and apprentice with Sullivan, then a creator in his own right and with an intenser originality, who fought the fight for expressive building through the first thirty years of the new century, and who was eventually recognized as the foremost modern master of architecture. His early prairie-type houses in the Chicago area, his industrial buildings, his concrete block houses in California, his freer later houses in a dozen states —all these were challenges to his eclectic fellow architects, each building reflecting a new way of approach to the art, each expressive of its site and use, and each touched with the special creative individuality of Wright the artist.

The one example of Wright's designing illustrated (page 651), the house over a waterfall at Bear Run in Pennsylvania, indicates how fully the architect had departed from past precedents, how completely he had made a style of his own out of contemporary materials and methods. The building would be unthinkable in any earlier historic period. His career of more than fifty years of designing was dotted with solutions as original, as attractive. By the early nineteen-fifties, when modern architecture was no longer a cause or an eccentricity, rather the accepted thing, Frank Lloyd Wright had been honored in innumerable countries, even by the academies.

After 1920 modern architecture in America and in Europe, slowly gathering adherents, turned to the task of establishing a standardized basis, of determining a new maximum of expressiveness of functional use and of industrial-age materials and structural methods, with the elimination of every element or detail that might be considered merely ornamental. There came thus the "functionalist" architecture which was particularly popular in Holland and in pre-Nazi Germany, and later in Italy, France, and Czechoslovakia.

There had been pioneers in Europe in the days of Sullivan's and Wright's early insurgency, most notably H. P. Berlage in Holland, and Otto Wagner and Joseph Hoffmann in Vienna. As the machine-age sheerness and functionalist logic gained ground, a new internationalism developed. The later leaders were the French-Swiss Le Corbusier and the German (later in London, then in America) Walter Gropius.

Nearest to creator of a distinctive style in Europe, and therefore nearest a master in the individualistic sense in which Wright was one, was Mies van der Rohe, a German. He most successfully expressed the idea of architecture as space conditioned for living as against the idea of architecture as primarily weight-bearing walls. In the United States the ultra-simple "machine-house" became best known through the work of William Lescaze of New York and Richard J. Neutra in California. Soon there was hardly a country in the Western world that could not claim a start toward this architecture of a new age and a new way of visioning. Russia, after taking to modern architecture as a revolutionary country should, officially and curiously abandoned the new style and reverted, under the Stalin bureaucracy, to a badly conceived sort of academic classicism.

It was not until after World War II that modern architecture took over the several important fields of construction in all progressive countries. The business building, including the skyscraper, became largely a thing of steel stilts, with interior space merely screened with glass and metal (or masonry). Not very much originality was shown in varying the two common types, with horizontal banding or vertical accent. Industrial building likewise lacked variety of expression— perhaps because the style had been born in simplicity and became easy for mere engineers to execute as architect-engineers. But Frank Lloyd Wright again came forward to create a number of memorable industrial buildings. As for houses, there was the widest interpretation of living needs. A hundred architects across America began to practice in the field of what may be called the space-division house (as against the house boxed in with four weight-carrying outer walls); and surprisingly the public came to feel that "modern" was more homelike than had been the "colonial" or "Cape Cod" or "English cottage." Especially a new informality appeared in domestic architecture; no one type of modern design, such as functionalist, prevailed. Rather there was every sort of improvisation with movable walls, large glass areas, and expression of materials as the basis for decoration. Territorially it surprised some observers when the South American countries turned up with an extraordinary

Buildings in Rockefeller Center, New York. Reinhard & Hofmeister,
Corbett, Harrison & MacMurray, and Hood & Fouilhoux, original architects

amount of sensitively designed "modern" architecture during the nineteen-fifties. In all countries the tame virtues of a three-hundred-year-old eclecticism had ended.

There has been extensive and sometimes bitter discussion over the question: Are the fine arts finished? It has seemed to some materialists that a practical, industrialized, intellectually emancipated civilization might have no place for painting, sculpture, and the more delicate crafts. The machine, by standardization in mass production, had debased the ornamental crafts, had apparently crowded out the arts. Science, it was argued, would provide other occupations and appreciations.

It was a view short-sighted and not a little illogical. The profounder certainty is that the machine, taking over the work-burden of mankind, will free men more than ever before to practice and to enjoy in those fields immemorially considered the highest to which the human faculties can be given, the spiritual and the aesthetic. Science, instead of destroying art, is, in a sense, on the verge of giving for the first time in history adequate time for production, and universal leisure to enjoy. Atomic research is taking care of that.

It is doubly interesting, then, to note that science, besides opening an enlarged way to art, imparts a style to most of the objects formerly shaped by hand. The very use of machines as manufacturing tools tends to establish recognizable style-marks, to determine a basic likeness, in everything "manufactured," in a body of mass-produced objects created by "industrial designers."

It is too soon to assert that a characteristic stylistic language has been created. Rather the old crafts of the manual age have been undermined, their style-marks (as in hand-carving or intricate modeling) rendered invalid as an expression of the age, and a way has been opened to a different decorative phraseology. It is not to be overlooked that already the skyscraper and the function-based house and the streamlined train, the automobile and the bathtub and the kitchen cabinet, the powder-compact and the electric lamp and the airplane, all have a like design character, in which long lines are guarded against breaking, surfaces are kept sheer, masses are manipulated for formal rhythms, and the sensuous values of materials are capitalized.

It is thus that styles are born. In this case the machine, symbol of the age, dictates the idioms. The art spirit is again active, is creating in the one place which would have seemed least likely to the materialist—and to the artist—of a generation ago: among the machines.

The oldest existing piece of human writing, it is said, inscribed on a clay tablet in a museum at Istanbul, begins with these words: "Alas, things are not what they used to be!" One-half of mankind perpetually hangs its hopes and judgments —and its enjoyments—upon the past; the best and ultimate things belong to the days gone beyond recall. But there are always a few men, artist-prophets, who look forward, who are inspired by what is and what can be, rather than by what has been. Through them there comes periodically a fresh creative release. Art blossoms in a new form. Because it is unlike the old, the conservative party damns it and exclaims, "Alas, things are not what they used to be!"

The historian is inevitably caught between the two parties. He usually writes as if progress had stopped. He must, nevertheless, if he claims to be of his own time, reassess the work of the ages. The safest point of view is that of thirty years back. In adopting one nearer his own enjoyment he opens the way to judgment by an experience too personal and a perspective too short. If that has happened here, the fault may be in part atoned for by the continual stress upon art as a growing, changing thing. Men now see, as for many centuries they did not, that there are no final rules for either creation or judgment.

We seem today to be on the first courses of a creative slope, after an epochal revolutionary turn. There will be other turns, other slopes. The best knowledge of history would seem to be that which affords greatest pleasure in all that has been created by the hands of artists, up to the moment of recording, without the erection of barriers against further release. Equipped with that knowledge, prizing that open-mindedness, one is prepared to partake freely of a joy that artists have been storing up through all man's time on earth, and will further increase, endlessly.

TABLE OF DATES

ACKNOWLEDGMENTS

DESCRIPTIVE BIBLIOGRAPHY

INDEX AND GLOSSARY

TABLE OF DATES

This is a check list, in chronological order, of a limited number of monuments and events in European art, and of outstanding European artists. It is noticeable that only in the thirteenth century did the name of the artist become of prime importance, and the dates of his birth and death a matter of record.

2000–1450 B.C. Cretan civilization. Palaces at Cnossus

c. 1500 B.C. Civilization of Mycenae and other Peloponnesian city-states

c. 1500 B.C. Stonehenge

c. 1400–1200 B.C. Dorians conquer Greece

c. 1000 B.C. Homer

776 B.C. First Olympiad

c. 750 B.C. Etruscan beginnings. Cycladic marbles

8th century B.C. Geometric style, vases and small sculptures

6th–5th centuries B.C. Etruscan culmination

6th century B.C. Greek archaic "Apollos"

Late 6th century B.C. Master vase-painters; Execias

Early 5th century B.C. Temple of Zeus, Olympia; masters of red-figured vases; Euphronius

Mid-5th century B.C. Parthenon: Age of Pericles, Phidias

Late 5th century B.C. Erechtheum

4th century B.C. Praxiteles

334–331 B.C. Alexander conquers Persia and Egypt; Alexandria founded

323–146 B.C. Hellenistic era

Early 1st century A.D. Ara Pacis, Rome: Augustan Age

1st century A.D. Colosseum, Rome; Pont du Gard

2nd century A.D. Pantheon

328 A.D. Constantinople founded

386 A.D. Basilica of St. Paul outside the Walls, Rome

c. 440 Tomb of Galla Placidia, Ravenna

532–37 Santa Sophia, Constantinople

Mid-6th century Ravenna, churches and mosaics

c. 8th century Celtic arts, Ireland

711 Mohammedans first invade Europe

c. 800 Charlemagne's capital at Aix-la-Chapelle

11th–12th centuries St. Ambrogio, Milan

11th–12th centuries Pisa group

Late 11th and early 12th centuries Romanesque churches of Caen, Bayeux, etc.

c. 1100 St. Mark's, Venice

c. 1100–1125 Romanesque sculpture, Vézelay, Moissac, etc.

12th century Norman architecture in England

12th–13th centuries Chartres cathedral

13th century High Gothic: Amiens, Reims, Paris

1296 Start of Florence Cathedral

13th–14th centuries Alhambra: Moors in Spain

14th–15th centuries English Gothic cathedrals

c. 1220–84 Nicola Pisano

c. 1240–1302 Cimabue

1255–1319 Duccio

c. 1276–1337 Giotto

1285–1344 Simone Martini

1308–68 Orcagna

c. 1366–1426 Hubert van Eyck

c. 1370–1427 Gentile da Fabriano

c. 1370–1440 Jan van Eyck

1377–1446 Brunelleschi

c. 1378–1438 Jacopo della Quercia

1378–1455 Ghiberti

1386–1466 Donatello

1387–1455 Fra Angelico

1395–1455 Pisanello

1397–1475 Uccello

1399–1464 Rogier van der Weyden

c. 1400 Culmination of Russian icon-painting

1400–82 Luca della Robbia

1401–28 Masaccio

1406–69 Filippo Lippi

1416–92 Piero della Francesca

1420–98 Benozzo Gozzoli

1429–1507 Gentile Bellini

c. 1430–94 Memling

1430–1516 Giovanni Bellini

1431–1506 Mantegna

1435–88 Verrocchio

1444–1510 Botticelli

1445–91 Schongauer

1446–1523 Perugino

1449–94 Ghirlandaio

1452–1519 Leonardo da Vinci

c. 1455–1522 Carpaccio

1462–1521 Piero di Cosimo

1471–1528 Dürer

1472–1553 Cranach

1475–1564 Michelangelo

1476–1545 Baldung

1477–1576 Titian

1478–1511 Giorgione

1483–1520 Raphael

1485–1530 Grünewald

1486–1531 Andrea del Sarto

1494–1534 Correggio

1497–1543 Holbein

1500–71 Cellini

1518–94 Tintoretto

1525–69 Brueghel

1525–78 Moroni

1528–88 Veronese

c. 1542–1614 El Greco

c. 1565–1609 Caravaggio

1577–1640 Rubens

1580–1666 Hals

1588–1652 Ribera

1594–1665 Poussin

1598–1680 Bernini

1599–1660 Velázquez

1599–1641 Van Dyck

1600–82 Claude Lorrain

1606–69 Rembrandt

1617–81 Ter Borch

1617–82 Murillo

c. 1628–82 Ruisdael

1629–c. 1677 De Hooch

1632–75 Vermeer

1684–1721 Watteau

1696–1770 Tiepolo

1697–1768 Canaletto

1697–1764 Hogarth

1699–1779 Chardin

1703–70 Boucher

1712–93 Guardi

1723–92 Reynolds

1727–88 Gainsborough

1728–79 Mengs

1732–1806 Fragonard

1741–1828 Houdon

1746–1828 Goya

1748–1825 David

1757–1827 Blake

1768–1821 Crome

1769–1830 Lawrence

1775–1851 Turner

1776–1837 Constable

1780–1867 Ingres

1791–1824 Géricault

ACKNOWLEDGMENTS

One of the pleasures of assembling the materials for a book like this is in collecting the photographs to be used for illustration, and association with the museum officials who are charged with care of the original masterpieces. There is then the actual living with the photographs, each a reminder of an aesthetic experience, each in itself a giver of experience. To those who cooperated in the choice and procurement of the prints one is grateful—and wishes to make suitable acknowledgment.

The thanks of the present writer are overwhelmingly due to the staff of the Metropolitan Museum of Art in New York. The members of the staff, from the Director down, took interest in the original book, and eventually permitted fifty-three paintings and other objects from the Museum's collections to be reproduced. Other aid from the Metropolitan Museum is acknowledged in the Preface, where, I feel, so extraordinary a case of interested cooperation should be acknowledged.

The Museum of Fine Arts, Boston, was generous in permitting twenty objects from its collections to be reproduced, aiding especially in the field of Oriental art. I am grateful to the Freer Gallery of Art, Washington, D.C., for no fewer than seven illustrations in the Oriental field. The William Rockhill Nelson Gallery of Art, Kansas City, provided nine illustrations; the City Art Museum, St. Louis, two. The Chicago Art Institute is represented by six works. The staff not only had one detail photographed especially for this book but provided a photograph of a work outside their collections. The American Museum of Natural History, New York, similarly found for me a photograph of a rare prehistoric work, besides making available four photographs of museum-owned objects. The National Gallery of Art, Washington, is represented by four paintings.

I wish to acknowledge special cooperation from the museums at the great universities. The staff at the Fogg Museum of Art, Harvard University, aided by opening their photograph files to me for study, and the superb collections of the Museum are represented by eight illustrations. Three additional illustrations are from the Dumbarton Oaks Collection, Washington, now administered by the Fogg Museum. A third museum owned by Harvard University, the Peabody Museum, Cambridge, is represented by one illustration. The University Museum, Philadelphia, owned by the University of Pennsylvania, has been notably cooperative and has supplied nine illustrations for the book. There is one painting from the Gallery of Fine Arts, Yale University.

Gratitude is due the Philadelphia Museum for six illustrations—five of them to be credited to the Johnson Collection. Four illustrations are from the Worcester Art Museum; three each from the Toledo Museum of Art, Toledo, Ohio; the Isabella Stewart Gardner Museum, Boston; and the Huntington Library and Art Gallery, San Marino, California. The Frick Art Reference Library, New York, has kindly authorized the use of three photographs, two of paintings in the great Frick Collection, one of a painting owned by Miss Helen Clay Frick. Other American museums that provided photographs are the Cleveland Museum of Art; the Addison Gallery of American Art; Phillips Academy, Andover; the California Palace of the Legion of Honor, San Francisco; the Textile Museum of the District of Columbia; the Seattle Art Museum; and the Whitney Museum of American Art, New York. If I seem to gather these institutions coldly into a list, my thanks are nonetheless warmly felt. With pleasure, too, I thank the Royal Ontario Museum of Archaeology, Toronto, for cooperation and for the two photographs reproduced.

To the Phillips Gallery, Washington, and to Duncan Phillips, its director, I am particularly indebted. From this specialized gallery there are four illustrations in the book. The Museum of Modern Art in New York (as noted in the Preface) has laid me under a debt that is both personal and professional. Their own collections are represented by only four paintings in my pages (the modern section of my book being necessarily so small in relation to all history). But the Museum staff provided ten other photographs, especially in the fields of prehistory, African art, and certain types of modernism, and put me in touch with owners of the objects.

Of organizations designed to help the scholar (or mere

writer), the one in New York known as the Iranian Institute, later the Asia Institute, now closed, was most helpful. It supplied eleven illustrations, mostly in the field of Persian art. I am especially indebted to the Institute's director, Arthur Upham Pope, for advice and because a photograph he personally took appears at page 264. The Oriental Institute of the University of Chicago permitted reproduction of two sculptures in its own collection, and provided four photographs of Persian and Hittite objects *in situ*. I am indebted also to the New York Public Library and to the Hispanic Society of America, New York, for fugitive photographs. There are two illustrations from books in the rich collections of the Pierpont Morgan Library, New York. The officials of Dartmouth College, Hanover, New Hampshire, courteously permitted the reproduction of a detail from a mural painting by Orozco. The officials of Rockefeller Center in New York provided the picture on page 653 (repeated in part on the title page).

When the first edition of this history was in preparation, certain government agencies of European nations offered to obtain and clear for publication the photographs needed from their countries. The Italian Tourist Information Office, acting with the government fine-arts department and the heads of museums, provided fifty-seven photographs, mostly of paintings and sculptures in official galleries, and underwrote the fees for reproduction. For this sort of cooperation one continues to be grateful even after the lapse of the many years between first and latest edition. The German Railroads Information Office similarly provided twenty-six subjects, mostly from museum walls, but including a few architectural and sculptural monuments. The French Information Center provided twenty-two photographs, largely from the *Archives Photographiques*, the subjects almost altogether from the Louvre. The list of state agencies ends with the equally courteous Swedish Travel Information Bureau, which provided the photograph of the Oseberg ship, and the Indian State Railways, which supplied a better photograph of the Taj Mahal than I had been able to find elsewhere. In Europe, aside from the photographs obtained from government agencies, three must be credited to the Musée Guimet, Paris; one to the Musée de l'Homme, Paris; and one to the Rodin Museum, Paris.

In Britain the directors and photograph departments of the museums and galleries cooperated directly. I am grateful to the British Museum for ten subjects; and to the Victoria and Albert Museum for five photographs of objects owned and two photographs of the Borobudor reliefs. To the National Gallery, London, I am grateful for permission to reproduce ten paintings. The book includes also three from the National Portrait Gallery, and two from the National Gallery, Millbank (better known as the Tate Gallery). The National Gallery of Scotland at Edinburgh provided one print (photographer Annan); and one print came from the Corporation Art Gallery, Glasgow. The Seurat picture came from the Samuel Courtauld Collection, now at London University. The portrait by Lawrence in the Windsor Castle collection was reproduced by gracious permission of the late King George VI.

The Royal Museum, Amsterdam, permitted reproduction of four photographs; the Museum at the Hague, two; the Boymans Museum, Rotterdam, and the Frans Hals Museum, Harlem, one each. To the Antwerp Museum I am indebted for three photographs of exhibited pictures, and for one of the celebrated St. Bavon altarpiece in Ghent. The Brussels Museum provided four illustrations of paintings in its own collection, and the Communal Museum in Bruges, in addition to an illustration of a single picture from its walls, courteously supplied the photographs of two of the panel pictures by Memling at the Hospice of St. John in that city.

Among individual collectors whose paintings are illustrated, I wish to thank especially Edward M. M. Warburg, New York; Edward G. Robinson, Beverly Hills, California; Robert Treat Paine, 2nd, Boston; and Adelaide M. de Groot. The late Maitland Griggs provided two illustrations for the first edition, and they are carried on into the present version of the book.

Of collectors in other countries, Dr. Reginald le May has been generous enough to permit reproduction of photographs of three Siamese sculptures in his own collection, and to provide one photograph of a head of Buddha in the National Museum at Bangkok. The museum officials have also given their permission. I am indebted to the Cambridge University Press, publishers of Dr. le May's book, *A Concise History of Buddhist Art in Siam*, for their added authorization to reproduce these photographs. The Earl of Ellesmere courteously permitted reproduction of Poussin's *The Baptism*. One of the African sculptures is illustrated by courtesy of Baron Eduard von der Heydt, Locarno, Switzerland. I have to thank M. Louis Carré of Paris for permission to reproduce two African sculptures.

The following galleries in New York have provided photographs not otherwise available, and I am grateful to them: Duveen Brothers, the Knoedler Galleries, the Willard Gallery, the Curt Valentin Gallery, the Kleemann Galleries, Ton Ying and Company, C. T. Loo and Company, and the Hammer Galleries. Special thanks are due to J. B. Neumann of the New Art Circle for help in obtaining photographs and for data about modern movements in Europe. Among European galleries I have to thank Spink and Sons, London, for the photograph of a Cycladic figure. Paul Cassirer in Berlin helped me to find adequate photographs of Lehmbruck's sculpture and other modern works. Finally I may add, among friendly services, that of the late Arnold Genthe in contributing the photograph of the columns of the Parthenon, and that of Warren Cheney in providing the two photographs on pages 290 and 291.

Every writer on art becomes indebted to certain firms specializing in the sale of photographs. My debt is more especially to three firms in Florence, Italy: Fratelli Alinari, Giacomo Brogi, and Francesco Pineider (who handles the very fine line of Anderson photographs). They all provided photographs for my book, sometimes through the government agencies I have mentioned, sometimes direct. In Paris I obtained for this book four photographs from the veteran M. Giraudon, and one from H. Roget-Viollet; the Tel agency provided three. I am indebted also to the Mansell firm in London, and to the Asuka-en firm at Nara, Japan. Here in America I acquired two illustrations through the Kean Archives, Philadelphia, including the exceptional Stonehenge print, and one from the Hedrich-Blessing firm in Chicago.

The Kunstverlag Wolfrum in Vienna courteously supplied two photographs of paintings in the Kunsthistorische Museum there.

Published books were the sources of twelve illustrations in the original edition, and I am grateful now, as I was when they were first used, to the authors and publishers of those volumes: *Domenico Theotocopuli El Greco*, by August L. Mayer; *Les Médailles d'Antonio Pisano dit le Pisanello*, by Henry Nocq and Léon Marotte; *La Sculpture Irlandaise*, by Françoise Henry; *Late Antique, Coptic and Islamic Textiles of Egypt*, by Volbach and Kuehnel (by courtesy of E. Weyhe); *Les Sculptures Chames au Musée de Tourane*, by H. Parmentier; *Les Temples de la Période Classique Indo-Javanaise*, by M. P.-Verneuil; *Tree and Serpent Worship*, by James Fergusson; *Griechische Vasenmalerei*, by A. Furtwängler and K. Reichhold; *Greek Vase Paintings*, by Gottfried von Lücken; *Découvertes en Chaldée*, by E. de Sarzac; and *La Caverne d'Altamira* by Cartailhac and Breuil.

DESCRIPTIVE BIBLIOGRAPHY

Only books in English are included. Books written for the general reader or the interested student are favored over those designed for the specialist-researcher. In each subdivision a small, selected list of titles appears; these volumes are briefly characterized, and they can be counted upon to lead the student to specialized study in any particularized field.

General Histories of Art

Multiple-volume histories of art (in English) are rare. Two are worthy of shelf room, though they are a quarter-century old. Most important is *History of Art*, by Elie Faure, translated from the French by Walter Pach (5 vols., New York, 1921–30). Not factual, not systematic, it is brilliant, inspirational, and modern. Generously illustrated. *History of Art*, by José Pijoan, translated from the Spanish (3 vols., New York, 1927–28), is of the opposite sort, conventional, full of facts, and weighted with scholarly opinion. Very little Oriental material. Profusely illustrated, 2600 cuts. *The Pelican History of Art*, of which a few volumes appear each season, is planned to cover the art of the world in 48 volumes. It is well printed, in general well written by authorities chosen for scholarship and modern point of view. The illustrations are profuse and well chosen, but in each volume they are banked at the end, thus creating a hindrance for the reader who likes to enjoy picture with text. The monumental Pelican series promises to afford British and American readers their soundest foundation for systematic study of the arts. Of books which, like the present one, attempt condensation of all art history into a single volume, a standard one is *Art Through the Ages,* by Helen Gardner (3rd ed., New York, 1948). Profusely illustrated, almost encyclopedic in coverage, and valuable for reference, it is patchy and hardly satisfactory for straightaway reading or browsing. *History of World Art,* by Everard M. Upjohn, Paul S. Wingert, and Jane Gaston Mahler (New York, 1949), is also a teacher's book, factual and accurate. The Oriental section is very good, and more than usual attention is given to architecture; but the whole lacks something of enthusiasm and feeling, and the separation of text and illustrations results in continual interruption of reading for reference to plates. An unconventional account, devoting special attention to primitive and Oriental works, and to striking or unusual objects, is *History of the World's Art,* by Hermann Leicht, translated from the German (London, 1952). Nearly 500 illustrations. It is the most interesting of recent surveys. Most useful of the histories that exclude Oriental material is *Art in the Western World,* by David M. Robb and J. J. Garrison (3rd ed., New York, 1953). This is a college textbook, well documented, with elaborate chronological tables, glossary, and bibliographies. Accounts of architecture, sculpture, painting, and the minor arts are presented separately, not interrelated. There are 648 illustrations. Many of the same virtues may be found in *A History of Western Art,* by John Ives Sewall (New York, 1953); the illustrations seem to this author better chosen and better reproduced—but are grouped at the chapter beginnings, away from the relevant descriptions. There is a long, exceptionally complete text, not very easily read. Better designed and pleasanter

to handle than any of the previously named books is *The Story of Art,* by E. H. Gombrich (6th ed., revised, New York, 1954). The illustrations are a delight; they are large and are printed with the text on heavy calendered paper. But for these luxuries the author pays in having to cut down his text drastically—there is, for instance, nothing about Indian and Indonesian art. Simply and pleasantly written, especially for teen-agers—but, as the author notes, books for young people should not differ from books for adults. Better than many a larger book. Though it has been called a history of art, *Voices of Silence,* by André Malraux (New York, 1953), is considerably less than a systematic account; but it is considerably more in its brilliant reaches of thought about the changes of man in relation to art of the great epochs. For readers with a taste for philosophy and speculation it is the number-one recent book about art's history.

General Histories of Architecture

Marvelously complete, with over 4000 illustrations, is *A History of Architecture on the Comparative Method,* by Sir Banister Fletcher (16th ed., New York, 1954). It is not for continuous reading but useful for browsing and reference. *The Pelican History of Art* series includes some books confined to the building art, as *Architecture in Britain 1530 to 1830,* by John Summerson (1953). Presumably a complete multiple-volume history of architecture will gradually be set into the Pelican series. A favorite textbook, yet affording interesting reading to others than students, is *Architecture through the Ages,* by Talbot Hamlin (revised ed., New York, 1953). Authoritative world coverage by an architect-writer who is thoroughly modern. Profusely illustrated. By way of contrast in length and size, covering only building in the Western world, is *Architecture: 5000 Years of Building,* by Joseph Watterson (New York, 1950). A smaller book, pleasant to read, discriminatingly illustrated.

Histories of Painting

The outstanding series has been appearing for some years, and is now almost complete, under the title *The Great Centuries of Painting,* directed by Albert Skira. In most volumes the illustrations, all in color, are more notable than the text—they are, indeed, hardly less than luxurious. The subjects range from prehistoric painting to contemporary painting, with coverage of several eras not before summarized in popular editions, such as: *Egyptian Painting,* text by Arpag Mekhitarian (Geneva, Paris, New York, 1954); *Etruscan Painting,* text by Massimo Pallottino (Geneva, 1952); and *Gothic Painting,* text by Jacques Dupont and Cesare Gnudi (Geneva, 1954). Other volumes cover individual centuries—the seventeenth, the eighteenth, etc. The brief texts are generally authoritative and scholarly. A second series is issued by the Skira publishing house under the title *Painting: Colour: History,* and includes *Italian Painting* (3 vols.) and *Spanish Painting* (2 vols.), all illustrated with large color plates. These titles appear in the topical lists that follow. Another series that utilizes exclusively color plates in large size is *The Library of Great Painters,* issued by Abrams in New York. New volumes appear each season. If the reader wishes to see the work of Raphael or El Greco or Rembrandt or Cézanne or Picasso, set out sumptuously in color, with a brief appreciative and annotated text, he can already turn to this series. (There are smaller, inexpensive series, some in pocket size, that may serve as introduction.) Of single-volume histories of painting the most widely circulated is *The Harper History of Painting: The Occidental Tradition,* by David M. Robb (New York, 1951). It is a standard school text, academically written and conventionally arranged. Many illustrations. There is an eighteen-page glossary. An indispensable aid for study is *Encyclopedia of Painting,* edited by Bernard S. Myers with many contributing associates (New York, 1955). The subtitle accurately suggests its scope: "Painters and Painting of the World from Prehistoric Times to the Present Day." It contains capsule biographies and definitions, in general very good. The hundreds of illustrations are better than those in most reference works, excepting the color reproductions.

Histories of Sculpture

There is in print no accurate, readable, and complete history of world sculpture, or even a picture book that covers any large segment of the field. Seekers can be referred hopefully to the Pelican volumes, which will eventually cover all countries and periods. The handsome Phaidon Press books, generally stressing pictures, with brief but useful text, have included notably fine volumes on sculpture—*Etruscan Sculpture, Roman Portraits, The Sculptures of Michelangelo, Donatello,* etc.—but promise no complete coverage of the subject. *A History of Sculpture,* by G. H. Chase and C. R. Post (New York, 1925), was standard in its day: an authoritative, documented review, but anti-modern and negligent of Oriental art, and therefore to be read with caution.

Prehistoric and Primitive Art

The broadest treatment is *Primitive Art,* by Erwin O. Christensen (New York, 1955). It is a factual review, authoritative, heavily illustrated, with classified bibliography. Useful still as an introduction is *Primitive Art,* by Franz Boas (new ed., Irvington-on-Hudson, 1951); it has been a standard work since 1927. Most exciting and most sumptuous is a Skira book, *Prehistoric Painting: Lascaux or the Birth of Art,* with text by Georges Bataille (Switzerland, 1955). Authoritative, beautifully written, superbly illustrated in color. A second fine book about Lascaux is *The Lascaux Cave Paintings,* by Fernand Windels (New York, 1950). It is somewhat less lyric—but a very good book about an extraordinary art "find." See also *Art in the Ice Age: Spanish Levant Art: Arctic Art,* by Johannes Maringer and Hans-Georg Bandi (New York, 1953). In this the caveman's art is set forth scientifically and humanly, with remarkably fine illustrations. *Four Hundred Centuries of Cave Art,* by Abbé T. Breuil (Montignac, 1952), is an encyclopedic summary by a leading authority, with more than 500 illustrations. For guides to four important areas of Late Stone Age art, see: *Indian Art of the United States,* by Frederic H. Douglas and René d'Harnoncourt (New York, 1941); *Twenty Centuries of Mexican Art* (New York and Mexico City, 1940); *Ancient Arts of the Andes,* by Wendell C. Bennett, New York, 1954); and *Arts of the South Seas,* by Ralph Linton and Paul S. Wingert (New York, 1946). These are publications of the Museum of Modern Art and contain maps, bibliographies, and scholarly descriptive essays. They are beautifully illustrated. The Mexican volume covers the complete history of Mexican art but stresses especially the prehistoric phase. The standard artists' book on Mayan and other Amerindian art of Mexico and Central America is *Medieval American Art,* by Pál Kelemen (2 vols., New York, 1943). It is a remarkably complete survey, with a separate volume containing many hundreds of illustrations. Another luxurious book about Amerindian art, especially that found north of the Mexican border, is *The Eagle, the Jaguar, and the Serpent,* by Miguel Covarrubias (New York, 1954). About Negro sculpture, see *African Sculpture Speaks,* by Ladislas Sergy (New York, 1952). This is up-to-date, elementary, and well illustrated. Its bibliography will lead on to many earlier books on the subject. Scholarly and useful is *African Negro Art,* by James J. Sweeney (New York, 1935), a publication of the Museum of Modern Art.

Mesopotamian Art

The fullest and best treatment is a volume of the Pelican series: *The Art and Architecture of the Ancient Orient,* by Henri Frankfort (1954). It is much more than a scientific or academic account—one of the best books of its type. With bibliography. See also *The Development of Sumerian Art,* by C. Leonard Woolley (New York, 1935). The Hittites are treated in Frankfort's book. The latest account, and a very interesting background book, is *The Secret of the Hittites,* by C. W. Ceram (New York, 1956). See also *Hittite Art,* by Maurice Vieyra (London, 1955), a brief but illuminating account, with 122 pictures. Broader in coverage, in that it includes the story of archaeology in Mesopotamia, Egypt, and the Holy Land, is *Light from the Ancient Past: the Archaeological Background of the Hebrew-Christian Religion,* by Jack Finegan (Princeton, 1946). It is a popular treatment by a scholar, readable and packed with quotations; 204 illustrations.

Egyptian Art

Possibly the best general work is *The Art of Ancient Egypt,* with introductory text by Hermann Ranke (Vienna, 1936). A Phaidon book, it is beautifully illustrated, modern, and authoritative. For exceptional pictures, with a minimum of text, see *Egyptian Art,* by Etienne Drioton (New York, 1950). Of the other sort, a scholarly book, flatly factual, is *Egyptian Sculpture,* by Margaret Alice Murray (New York, 1930). It has plentiful small illustrations. *Egyptian Painting,* with text by Arpag Mekhitarian (Geneva, Paris, New York, 1954), is well written and has many and excellent color illustrations (Skira). Not a true factual history, but brilliantly and wittily written—a pleasure to read—is *Pyramid and Temple,* by Julius Meier-Graefe (New York, 1930).

Greek Art

The older books about Greek art are the better ones. A popular, romantic introduction to Greek culture is *The Glory That Was Greece,* by J. C. Stobart (3rd revised ed., New York, 1935). A scholarly and reliable work is *The Art of the Greeks,* by H. B. Walters (revised ed., New York, 1922). *The Sculpture and Sculptors of the Greeks,* by Gisela M. A. Richter (New Haven, 1950), is scholarly, exhaustive, and abundantly illustrated. On vase-painting there is the excellent *Greek Vase Painting,* by Ernst Buschor (New York, 1921). See also *Masterpieces of Greek Drawing and Painting,* by Ernst Pfuhl (New York, 1955). An unusual short introduction is *Approach to Greek Art,* by Charles Seltman (London and New York, 1948), a readable essay with banked plates.

Etruscan and Roman Art

The most thorough treatment of Etruscan art is *An Introduction to Etruscan Art,* by P. J. Riis (New York and Copenhagen, 1954). It is a background book long needed; but it is archaeological rather than appreciative. There are 123 smallish plates. More striking artistically, though with brief text, is *Etruscan Sculpture* (New York, 1941), a Phaidon book featuring large plates. See also *The Art of the Etruscans,* by Massimo Pallottino (New York, 1956), a brief summary with exceptional photographic illustrations. For the older, conventional view of Roman art see *The Grandeur That Was Rome,* by J. C. Stobart (3rd revised ed., London, 1934). It is very readable. *The Art of the Romans,* by H. B. Walters (London, 1911), is still useful. *Art in Ancient Rome,* by Eugénie Strong (2 vols., New York, 1928), is a carefully detailed guide book with nearly 600 thumbnail illustrations. A good recent picture book of Roman monuments is *Marvels of Ancient Rome,* by Margaret R. Scherer (New York, 1955); but this treats only partly of *ancient* Rome, its ruins and relics. *Roman Painting,* text by Amedio Maiuri (Geneva, 1953), thoroughly covers the earliest painting in Italy (excepting Etruscan), in a surprising number of works. The generally later Christian art is excluded. This and the following are Skira de luxe volumes, illustrated in color. *Etruscan Painting,* text by Massimo Pallottino (Geneva, 1952), includes a readable and scholarly essay.

Oriental Art: the Far Orient

To enter into the spirit of Oriental art it is well to begin with such persuasive books as *The Flight of the Dragon,* by Laurence Binyon (London, 1927); *The Spirit of Man in Asian Art,* by Laurence Binyon (Cambridge, Mass., 1936); and *The Vision of Asia: An Interpretation of Chinese Art and Culture,* by L. Cranmer-Byng (New York, 1933). These are all on the philosophical and interpretative side, not factual—as are the earlier books of Herbert A. Giles, Arthur Waley, and Raphael Petrucci. A small but good elementary book is *Introduction to Chinese Art and History,* by Arnold Silcock (enlarged ed., New York, 1948). A larger book with many fine illustrations is *A Short History of Chinese Art,* by Ludwig Bachhofer (New York, 1946). It is scholarly and readable. A simple, appealing introduction, well illustrated, is *Four Thousand Years of China's Art,* by Dagny Carter (revised ed., New York, 1951). It is compact, yet covers all the visual arts. *Chinese Painting,* by William Cohn (revised ed., London, 1951), is one of the beautifully designed Phaidon books, with authoritative text and fine illustrations. *The Art and Architecture of China,* by Laurence Sickman and Alexander Soper (Baltimore, 1956), is a scholarly and thorough book—monumental as compared with the others listed. A *Pelican History,* it provides the sort of complete factual coverage much needed up to this time. A companion volume, equally thorough, is *The Art and Architecture of Japan,* by Robert Treat Paine and Alexander Soper (Baltimore, 1955). An excellent small introductory volume is *The Enduring Art of Japan,* by Langdon Warner (Cambridge, 1952)—authoritative, readable, well illustrated. *Handbook of Japanese Art,* by Noritake Tsuda (Tokyo, 1936), with 345 illustrations, is very useful as a reference work. Scythian art, as an independent style and in relation to Chinese art, is best treated in *The Animal Style in South Russia and China,* by M. Rostovtzeff (Princeton, 1929).

Indian and Indonesian Art

The Art and Architecture of India: Buddhist, Hindu, Jain, by Benjamin Rowland (Baltimore, 1953), in the Pelican series, is authoritative, readable, complete. It treats briefly also Far Indian art. The plates are banked at the end. *The Art of India: Traditions of Indian Sculpture, Painting and Architecture,* by Stella Kramrisch (New York, 1954), is made up mostly of lush photographs of the lusher elements in Indian art, with added color plates of painting. It affords a revelation of the richness of Hindu sculpture. *The Art of Indian Asia,* by Heinrich Zimmer (New York, 1955), is a standard scholarly work in two volumes, one of text, one of plates. A monument in its time, and useful still, is the well written and thoroughgoing *History of Indian and Indonesian Art,* by Ananda K. Coomaraswamy (New York, 1927). An excellent book about the arts of those Eastern countries that derived their style from India is *The Culture of South-East Asia,* by Reginald le May (London, 1954), a running text, without footnotes, about the art of Burma, Siam, Cambodia, and Java; 215 photographs, maps. The same author's *A Concise History of Buddhist Art in Siam* (Cambridge, 1938) treats more exhaustively the art of the one country, with 205 illustrations.

Persian Art

Persian or Iranian art of ancient times is treated in *Iran in the Ancient East,* by Ernest E. Herzfeld (New York, 1941). The whole Persian story is told in summary, primarily in groups of pictures, some in color, with covering text, in *Masterpieces of Persian Art,* by Arthur Upham Pope (New York, 1945). A very good introduction, appreciative, modern. The same scholar-writer edited the monumental *A Survey of Persian Art* (6 vols., New York, 1938–39), which can be found in the greater public and university libraries. See also *Persian Miniature Painting,* by Laurence Binyon, J. V. S. Wilkinson, and Basil Gray (London, 1933). There is no comprehensive popular work on the Islamic arts. The best introduction is *A Handbook of Muhammadan Art,* by M. S. Dimand (revised and enlarged ed., New York, 1947), which is limited in that it describes only the collections in the Metropolitan Museum of Art.

Early Christian, Byzantine, and Medieval Art

Two of the best treatments, by a great scholar, are *Early Christian Art* (Princeton, 1942) and *Mediaeval Art* (New York, 1942), both by Charles Rufus Morey. The former, with 211 banked pictures, covers the evolution of the Christian arts to the eighth century. *Mediaeval Art* is broader in scope and more readable, the number-one book in the field. It covers Early Christian, Byzantine, Romanesque, and Gothic art, and is generously and discriminatingly illustrated. Excellent is *Monuments of Romanesque Art,* by Hanns Swarzenski (Chicago, 1954). There are 557 illustrations, generally large, mostly of small sculptures, illuminations, and enamels; with a scholarly introduction. The "barbarian" strain and Eastern influences are illuminatingly treated in *Early German Art,* by Harold Picton (London, 1939). A standard book, very good, is *Medieval Sculpture in France,* by Arthur Gardner (New York and Cambridge, 1931). Another standard book has long been *Byzantine Art,* by D. Talbot Rice (London, 1935). A revised edition is in the inexpensive Pelican paper-backed series (1954). It is scholarly, tolerant, easy to read. Excellent bibliographical notes. Colorful, sumptuous illustrations are stressed in the Skira book *Byzantine Painting,* text by André Grabar (Geneva, 1952). Mosaics, frescoes, miniatures, and enamels are presented wholly in color plates. The survival of Byzantine icon-painting in Russia is beautifully summarized in *Masterpieces of Russian Painting,* by A. I. Anisimov and others (London, 1930). *Gothic Painting,* text by Jacques Dupont and Cesare Gnudi (Geneva, 1954), includes illuminations, stained glass, and paintings in an account of international developments from the late twelfth century through Sienese and early Florentine, German, and other schools. Color plates.

Flemish and Dutch Art

The Flemish story is told in *The Last Flowering of the Middle Ages,* by Baron Joseph van der Elst (Garden City, 1945). Readable, well illustrated. For reference and a swift survey there is *Art in Flanders,* by Max Rooses (New York, 1931); it is useful still, with its 608 tiny illustrations and running commentary. Another older book still recommended is *The Van Eycks and Their Followers,* by Martin Conway (New York, 1921), the most literary and appreciative treatment. Both Flemish and Dutch painting are included in *The Masters of Past Time,* by Eugène Fromentin (New York, 1948), a

Phaidon book with 100 illustrations. It is an old, old text (1875) revised and fitted with exceptionally fine plates. The most appealing treatise about the Dutch achievement is perhaps *Dutch Painting,* by R. H. Wilenski (2nd ed., London, 1947), with 132 plates.

Italian Art

Four famous essays of about the year 1900 have been reprinted and fitted with modern illustrations in *The Italian Painters of the Renaissance,* by Bernard Berenson (Garden City, 1953). It is the best appreciative treatise, with 16 color plates and a bank of 400 black-and-white plates. *Classic Art: An Introduction to the Italian Renaissance,* by Heinrich Wölfflin (New York, 1952), is another old book that wears well after nearly sixty years in print. It is perhaps the best treatment of the high Renaissance and has 200 illustrations. Both of the preceding are Phaidon books. The Skira series in three more or less independent volumes is a luxurious pictorial showing with good, documented texts, all by the same authors: *Italian Painting: The Creators of the Renaissance,* by Lionel Venturi and Rosabianca Skira-Venturi (Geneva, 1950); *Italian Painting: The Renaissance* (Geneva, Paris, New York, 1951); and *Italian Painting: from Caravaggio to Modigliani* (Geneva, Paris, New York, 1952). Getting back to more modest, less displayful books, one can recommend still *A History of Italian Painting,* by Frank Jewett Mather, Jr. (New York, 1935). *Italian Painting,* by P. G. Konody and R. H. Wilenski (London, n.d.), makes good reading, is thorough, and is well illustrated. There are innumerable histories of Renaissance architecture; for most students and most readers one can recommend *An Outline of European Architecture,* by Nikolaus Pevsner (4th enlarged ed., Baltimore, 1953). An inexpensive paperbound book, it tells interestingly the Renaissance story in its setting between Gothic and baroque. Sufficiently illustrated.

Spanish Art

For foundation one can best read the Spanish chapters in Pijoan's *History of Art.* The best widely circulated works are the Skira publications, *Spanish Painting: from the Catalan Frescos to El Greco,* by Jacques Lassaigne (Geneva, 1952); and *Spanish Painting: from Velasquez to Picasso,* same author (Geneva, 1952). Easily read; generously illustrated in color.

German and Russian Art

The most readable and attractive work on German art for most art-lovers will be *Dürer and His Times,* by Wilhelm Waetzoldt (New York, 1950), a Phaidon book with many plates. For broader coverage see *German Painting: XIV–XVI Centuries,* by Alfred Stange (New York, 1950), with many large plates. There is one very good and recent book about the Russian arts: *The Art and Architecture of Russia,* by George Heard Hamilton (Baltimore, 1954). It covers "from the Christianization of Russia in 988 to the fall of the Empire in 1917" and has 180 illustrations.

French Art

Of introductory works one of the best is *French Painting,* by R. H. Wilenski (revised ed., London, 1949). It is complete, modern, readable, and well illustrated. Most entertaining is *An Account of French Painting,* by Clive Bell (New York, 1932). It is brief, witty, and illuminating. An old guide book is useful still: *Art in France,* by Louis Hourticq (New York, 1924). It has 943 tiny illustrations. The first French volume in the Pelican series augurs well: *Art and Architecture in France 1500 to 1700,* by Anthony Blunt (Baltimore, 1954). A good, straightaway account, carefully annotated, with excellent illustrations, especially for architecture.

English Art

The best popular introduction is perhaps *English Painting,* by R. H. Wilenski (London, 1947). Comprehensive, modern, fully and judiciously illustrated. The first English volume of the Pelican series is *Painting in Britain 1530 to 1790,* by Ellis Waterhouse (Baltimore, 1953); it is a thoroughly academic account, affording the solidest sort of foundation. *Creative Art in Britain from the Earliest Times to the Present,* by William Johnstone (London, 1950), is an unconventional and patchy history but an interesting and convincing account of the creative British heritage. *The Oxford History of English Art,* to be completed in 11 volumes, will be scholarly and in every way dependable. An excellent available volume is *English Art, 871–1100,* by D. Talbot Rice (Oxford, 1952). A very solid, heavily documented work is *English Painting from the Seventh Century to the Present Day,* by Charles Johnson (New York, 1932).

Nineteenth- and Twentieth-Century Art

An older book, but modern in its judgments, is *Landmarks in 19th Century Painting,* by Clive Bell (New York, 1927). For pleasurable reading it still tops the list. For systematic treatment and rich color plates, see Skira's *The Nineteenth Century,* by Maurice Raynal (Geneva, 1954). The present writer's *The Story of Modern Art* (New York, 1955) covers the period from about 1790 to 1940, with 373 illustrations. The American story begins in this period; the best full account, both accurate and modern, is *Art in America: A Complete Survey,* edited by Holger Cahill and Alfred H. Barr, Jr. (revised ed., New York, 1935), with satisfactory illustrations. See also *Art and Life in America,* by Oliver W. Larkin (New York, 1949), which has extensive bibliographies. *Modern Mexican Painters,* by MacKinley Helm (New York, 1941), is a good first-hand account, with 82 illustrations. *Forms and Functions of Twentieth Century Architecture,* edited by Talbot Hamlin (4 vols., New York, 1952), is a remarkably complete symposium regarding every aspect of modern building design; heavily illustrated. For inspiration read the several books of Frank Lloyd Wright. To get his bearings among the many books about contemporary art, the reader will do well to go to the long shelf of volumes issued by the Museum of Modern Art. From *History of Impressionism,* by John Rewald (New York, 1946), to *Masters of Modern Art* (1954), these volumes are certain to be authoritative, attractive in format, and generously illustrated. The smaller volumes, like the larger, include accurate biographic as well as appreciative material, and suggestive reading lists. A luxuriously made book is *Modern Painting,* by Maurice Raynal (Geneva, 1956). It affords a good step-by-step account, along with Skira's usual large color plates. Of the several editions, obtain the latest.

INDEX AND GLOSSARY

Glossary definitions are in parentheses following each word. Where the definition has been given in the text, the word is followed by the letters "def." and the page number, in parentheses. Italic figures, preceded by the letters *ill.,* or *Col. Pl.,* indicate illustrations.

Abstract art and abstract expressionism, xxii, 639–43; sculpture, 644
Abstraction, Braque, *ill.,* 626
Acropolis, Athens, buildings, 120ff. *See also* Erechtheum; Parthenon; Temple of Athene Nike
Adam, Robert (1727–92), 531, 548
Adam and Eve, Cranach, 466, *ill.,* 456
Adoration of the Kings, The, Brueghel, 448, *ill.,* 449
Adoration of the Kings, Lucas van Leiden, *ill.,* 476
Adoration of the Lamb (St. Bavon Altarpiece, Ghent), 436–37, *ill.,* 437
Adoration of the Magi, Gentile da Fabriano, *ill.,* 355
Aegean art, 71–90; geographical extent, 73; King Minos' palace, 76–77; metal-work, 83–86; painting, 80–81; pottery, 76–78, 86; sculpture, 75, 77–80, 87, 89. *See also* Minoan art; Mycenaean art
Aesthetics, *see* Theories of Art
African art, bushmen, 6–11, *ill.,* 3, 7. *See also* Negro art
African Venus, sculpture, *ill.,* 594
Akkad, *see* Babylonian-Assyrian art
Alberti, Leon Battista (1404–72), 337–38
Alexandria, Egypt, 135
Alhambra (palace), Granada, Spain, 267–68; Court of the Lions, *ill.,* 267; Hall of Ambassadors, ornament, *ill.,* 259
Altamira, Spain, cave painting, 2, 13, 15–16
Amenhotep III in His Chariot, ill., 67
America, pre-Columbian art in, Aztec, 598; influence on 20th-century art, 598; Mayan, 598; Mexican, 598. *See also* Primitive art
American art, *see* United States
American Scene art, 636–37
American School of Oriental Research, 24
Amerindian handicrafts: basketry, 5–6; carving, 11; pottery, *ill.,* 8; symbolism in, 11. *See also* tribe names
Amiens cathedral, 301, 302, 304, 305, 310; exterior, *ill.,* 302; interior, *ill.,* 303; vaulting and buttresses, *ill.,* 304
Amphoras, from Dipylon, Athens, *ill.,* 100
Anatomy Lesson, The, Rembrandt, 480, *ill.,* 481
Andrea da Firenze (active 1343–77), 328

Angelico, Fra, *see* Fra Angelico
Angkor Vat, temple, Cambodia, 220–221; frieze, *ill.,* 221
Animal art, *see* Scythian sculpture
Annunciation, Campin, 439, 440, *ill.,* 439
Annunciation, Russian icon, *ill.,* 242
Annunciation, Simone Martini, *ill.,* 320
Annunciation, The, Fra Angelico, *ill.,* 328
Apollo, Temple of Zeus, Olympia, *ill.,* 93
Apollo of Tenea, ill., 107
Appreciation, *see* Theories of Art
Ara Pacis altar, Rome, reliefs, *ill.,* 160
Arabesque (from "Arab," Mohammedan design of decorative scrolls and figures), 260, *ill.,* 258, 259, 264
Arabian art, *see* Mohammedan art
Arahat Entering into Nirvana, Lin Lingkuei, Sung Dynasty, *ill.,* 203
Arcadian Landscape, Magnasco, *ill.,* 514
Arch (in architecture, a construction of wedge-shaped blocks [*voussoirs*] used to span an opening of curved shape), Gothic pointed arch, transition from Romanesque type, 303; Renaissance round arch, 336; Roman, use of, 160–61; Sumerian use, 25
Archipenko, Alexander (1887–   ), 648
Architectural orders, Greek, 118–24, *ill.,* 124
Arena Chapel, Padua, 325; murals, 322, *ill.,* 325
Armory Show, New York (1913), 633
Arp, Hans (1888–   ), 632, 650
Artist's Daughters, The, Gainsborough, *ill.,* 535
Ascension of St. John, Giotto, *ill.,* 313
Ash-Can School (The Eight), American painters, 578
Ashurbanipal (Assyrian king) 29, 33; palace reliefs, *ill.,* 32, 33
Ashurnatsirpal (Assyrian king), palace reliefs, *ill.,* 30, 31
Assumption of the Virgin, The, El Greco, *ill.,* 409
Assyrian art, *see* Babylonian-Assyrian art
Athenian and colonial coins, *ill.,* 137
Attic red-figured hydria (painted jar), *ill.,* 104
Austen, Darrel (1907–   ), 635

Autun Cathedral, sculpture, *ill.,* 271
Avalokitesvara, Ceylon, bronze, *ill.,* 214
Aztec art, 598; *Mask of Xipe, ill.,* 597

Babylonian-Assyrian art, 19–23, 28–37; architecture, 29, 30–31; "hanging gardens," 34; Ishtar Gate, 34, *ill.,* 35; *Lion* from Street of Parades, *ill.,* 34; Nebuchadnezzar's palace, 34; sculpture, 20–21, 31, 32, 35; Sennacherib's palace, 31; "Tower of Babel," 34. *See also* Sumeria and Sumerian art.
Bacchus and Ariadne, Tintoretto, *ill.,* 400
Bacchus and Ariadne, Titian, *ill.,* 389
Baldacchino (in architecture, a canopy-like structure, usually erected over an altar), 506
Baldung, Hans (Hans Grien, 1476–1545), 466, 467, *ill.,* 467
Balzac, Rodin, *ill.,* 644
Baptism, The, Poussin, *ill.,* 500
Barbarian arts, 271–73
Barbizon school of painting, 563–564
Bargagli, Scipione, quoted, 312
Bark of Dante, The, Delacroix, 562, *ill.,* 562
Barlach, Ernst (1870–1938), 646
Barnes, Albert C., xxi
Barnes, Matthew (1880–1951), 618
Baroque art (def., 505–506), 504–522; architecture, 504–508, *ill.,* 384, 505, 507; characteristics of, 504, 507; "oblique line," 509–10; painting, 509 (*see also* Rubens); Santa Maria della Salute, *ill.,* 505; sculpture, 508, 522; Spain, 506–507; Spanish America, 507. *See also* Bernini; Rococo; St. Peter's, Rome
Bartolommeo, Fra (1472–1517), 372, 373
Basilica (oblong public hall of exchange or assembly in ancient Rome, also early Christian church type), 153–54; adoption in Byzantine architecture, 230; Ravenna, 234; St. Paul Outside the Walls, Rome, *ill.,* 154
Basketry, Amerindian, compared with classical forms in art, 6, *ill.,* 5, 6
Baths of Caracalla, Rome, 154–55
Bathers, Cézanne, *ill.,* 603
Battersea Bridge, Whistler, xiv, 609–610, *ill.,* 611

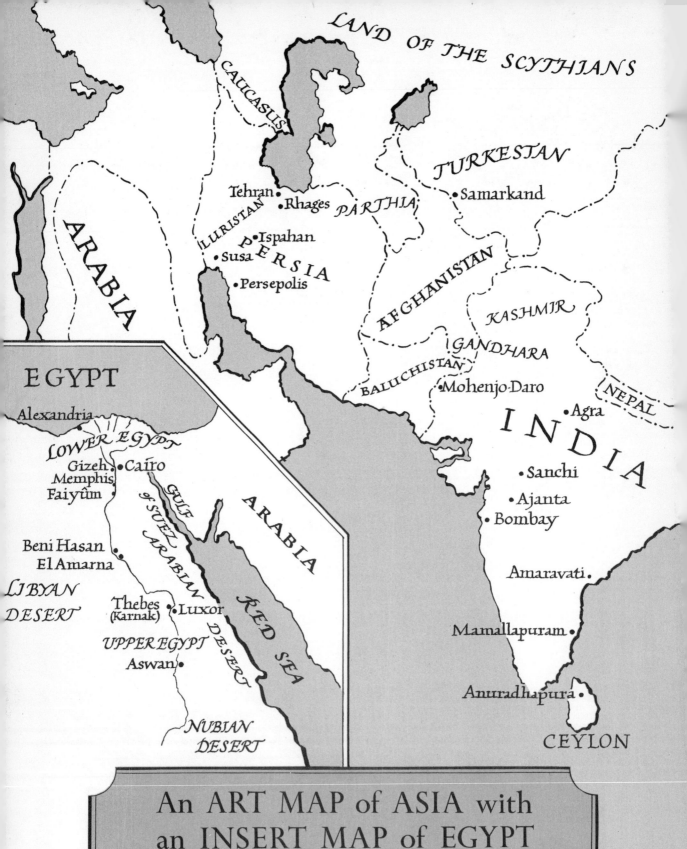

LAND OF THE SCYTHIANS

CAUCASUS

TURKESTAN

ARABIA

ILURISTAN
Tehran •
• Rhages
PARTHIA
• Samarkand

• Ispahan
PERSIA
• Susa
• Persepolis

AFGHANISTAN

KASHMIR

GANDHARA

BALUCHISTAN
Mohenjo-Daro
NEPAL

• Agra

INDIA

EGYPT

Alexandria

LOWER EGYPT

Gizeh • Cairo
Memphis
Faiyûm

GULF OF SUEZ

ARABIA

ARABIAN DESERT

RED SEA

• Sanchi

• Ajanta
• Bombay

Beni Hasan
El Amarna

LIBYAN
DESERT

Thebes
(Karnak) • Luxor

UPPER EGYPT
Aswan •

Amaravati •

Mamallapuram •

NUBIAN
DESERT

Anuradhapura •

CEYLON

An ART MAP of ASIA with
an INSERT MAP of EGYPT

A number of the cities and sites named in the map are important in the history of art only. The
state boundaries of both ancient and modern civilizations are in many cases only approximate.